African Americans: A Concise History

Volume Two: Since 1865

Darlene Clark Hine
Michigan State University

William C. Hine
South Carolina State University

Stanley Harrold
South Carolina State University

Prentice
Hall

UPPER SADDLE RIVER, NEW JERSEY 07458

Library of Congress Cataloging-in-Publication Data

Hine, Darlene Clark.
  African Americans: a concise history / Darlene Clark Hine, William C. Hine, Stanley Harrold.
    p. cm.
  Rev. ed. of: The African-American odyssey.
  Includes bibliographical references and index.
  ISBN 0-13-111441-7 (combined volume)
    1. African Americans—History. I. Hine, William C. II. Harrold, Stanley. III. Hine, Darlene Clark.
African-American odyssey. IV. Title.

E185.H534 2004
973'.0496073—dc21   2002031271

To Carter G. Woodson & Benjamin Quarles

Editorial Director: Charlyce Jones-Owen
Senior Acquisitions Editor: Charles Cavaliere
Associate Editor: Emsal Hasan
Director of Production and Manufacturing: Barbara Kittle
Production Editor: Louise Rothman
Editorial Assistant: Adrienne Paul
Prepress and Manufacturing Manager: Nick Sklitsis
Prepress and Manufacturing Buyer: Sherry Lewis
Marketing Director: Beth Mejia
Marketing Manager: Claire Bitting
Cover Design: Jayne Conte, Art Director and Designer
Cover Art: Archibald Motley, Jr., "Barbeque," 1934. Oil on canvas 36 1/4 x 40 1/8 in.
    The Howard University Gallery of Art, Washington, D.C.
Manager, Production Formatting and Art: Guy Ruggiero
Electronic Art Creation: Mirella Signoretto

This book was set in 10/12 New Baskerville by Lithokraft II and was printed and bound
by RR Donnelley-Crawfordsville. The cover was printed by Phoenix Color Corporation.

© 2004 by Pearson Education, Inc.
Upper Saddle River, New Jersey 07458

Printed in the United States of America

10 9 8 7 6 5 4 3 2 1

0-13-111443-3

Pearson Education Ltd., London
Pearson Education Australia Pty., Limited, Sydney
Pearson Education Singapore, Pte., Ltd.
Pearson Education North Asia Ltd., Hong Kong
Pearson Education Canada, Ltd., Toronto
Pearson Educación de Mexico, S.A. de C.V.
Pearson Education—Japan, Tokyo
Pearson Education Malaysia, Pte., Ltd.
Pearson Education, Upper Saddle River, New Jersey

➤ Contents ⬅

PART IV   SEARCHING FOR SAFE PLACES

CHAPTER 14   White Supremacy Triumphant: African Americans
in the South in the Late Nineteenth Century   233

CHAPTER 23   Modern Black America, 1980 to Present   466

→ PREFACE ←

One ever feels his two-ness,—an American, a Negro; two souls, two thoughts, two unreconciled strivings; two warring ideals in one dark body." So wrote W. E. B. Du Bois in 1897. African-American history, Du Bois maintained, was the history of this double-consciousness. Black people have always been part of the American nation that they helped to build. But they have also been a nation unto themselves, with their own experiences, culture, and aspirations. African-American history cannot be understood except in the broader context of American history. American history cannot be understood without African-American history.

Since Du Bois's time our understanding of both African-American and American history has been complicated and enriched by a growing appreciation of the role of class and gender in shaping human societies. We are also increasingly aware of the complexity of racial experiences in American history. Even in times of great racial polarity some white people have empathized with black people and some black people have identified with white interests.

It is in light of these insights that *African Americans: A Concise History* tells its story. That story begins in Africa, where the people who were to become African Americans began their long, turbulent, and difficult journey, a journey marked by sustained suffering as well as perseverance, bravery, and achievement. It includes the rich culture—at once splendidly distinctive and tightly intertwined with a broader American culture—that African Americans have nurtured throughout their history. And it includes the many-faceted quest for freedom in which African Americans have sought to counter white oppression and racism with the egalitarian spirit of the Declaration of Independence that American society professes to embody.

Nurtured by black historian Carter G. Woodson during the early decades of the twentieth century, African-American history has blossomed as a field of study since the 1950s. Books and articles have appeared on almost every facet of black life. This book, based on *The African-American Odyssey,* is about one-third the length of its parent text, and is designed for one-semester courses or for instructors who want a concise narrative that can be supplemented with more specialized readings. *African Americans* may also serve as a supplementary text in American history survey courses. It has benefitted from constructive criticism provided by instructors across the United States who have adopted *The African-American Odyssey. African Americans* draws on recent research to present black history in a clear and direct manner, within a broad social, cultural, and political framework. It also provides thorough coverage of African-American women as active builders of black culture.

African Americans balances accounts of the actions of African-American leaders with investigations of the lives of the ordinary men and women in black communities. This community focus helps make this a history of a people rather than an account of a few extraordinary individuals. Yet the book does not neglect important political and religious leaders, intellectuals, entrepreneurs, and entertainers. And it provides extensive coverage of African-American art, literature, and music.

African-American history started in Africa, and this narrative begins with an account of life on that continent from earliest times to the sixteenth century and the beginning of the forced migration of millions of Africans to the Americas. Succeeding chapters present the struggle of black people to maintain their humanity during the slave trade and slavery in North America.

The coming of the American Revolution during the 1770s initiated a pattern of black struggle for racial justice in which periods of optimism alternated with times of repression. Several chapters analyze the building of black community institutions, the antislavery movement, the efforts of black people to make the Civil War a war for emancipation, their struggle for equal rights as citizens during Reconstruction, and the strong opposition these efforts faced. There is also substantial coverage of African-American military service, from the War for Independence through American wars of the nineteenth and twentieth centuries.

During the late nineteenth century and much of the twentieth century, racial segregation and racially motivated violence that relegated African Americans to second-class citizenship provoked despair, but also inspired resistance and commitment to change. Chapters on the late nineteenth and early twentieth centuries cover the great migration from the cotton fields of the South to the North and West, black nationalism, and the Harlem Renaissance. Chapters on the 1930s and 1940s—the beginning of a period of revolutionary change for African Americans—tell of the economic devastation and political turmoil caused by the Great Depression, the growing influence of black culture in America, the racial tensions caused by black participation in World War II, and the dawning of the civil rights movement.

The final chapters tell the story of African Americans during the second half of the twentieth century. They relate the successes of the civil rights movement at its peak during the 1950s and 1960s and the efforts of African Americans to build on those successes during the more conservative 1970s and 1980s. Finally, there are portrayals of black life during the concluding decade of the twentieth century and of the continuing impact of African Americans on life in the United States.

In all, *African Americans* tells a compelling story of survival, struggle, and triumph over adversity. It will leave students with an appreciation of the central place of black people and black culture in this country and a better understanding of both African-American and American history.

Special Features

Several special features and pedagogical tools within *African Americans* are designed to reinforce the narrative and help students grasp key issues.

- Brief chronologies throughout the narrative provide students with a snapshot of the temporal relationship among significant events.
- End-of-chapter timelines establish a chronological context for events in African-American history by juxtaposing them with events in American history and in the rest of the world.
- Review questions encourage students to analyze the material they have read and to explore alternative perspectives.
- Recommended reading and additional bibliography lists direct students to more information about the subject of each chapter.
- Maps, charts, and graphs help students visualize the geographical context of events and grasp significant trends.
- Illustrations, tied to the text with informative captions, provide a visual link to the African-American past.
- Color inserts provide a sample of the richness of the folk and fine art African Americans have produced throughout their history.
- The appendix includes documents central to the history of African Americans.

Supplementary Instructional Materials

The supplements that accompany *African Americans* provide instructors and students with resources that combine sound scholarship, engaging content, and a variety of pedagogical tools to enrich the classroom experience and students' understanding of African-American history.

Instructor's Manual with Test-Item File.   The Instructor's Manual with Test-Item File provides summaries, outlines, learning objectives, lecture and discussion topics for each chapter. Test materials include multiple choice, essay, identification and short-answer, chronology, and map questions.

Practice Tests   (Volumes I and II). This free student study aid includes a summary for each chapter, reviews key points and concepts, and provides multiple choice, essay, chronology, and map questions.

Documents Set   (Volumes I and II). The Documents Set supplements the text with additional primary and secondary source material covering the social, cultural, and political aspects of African-American history. Each reading includes a short historical summary and several review questions.

Prentice Hall and Penguin Bundle Program.   Prentice Hall and Penguin are pleased to provide adopters of *African Americans* with an opportunity to receive significant discounts when orders for *African Americans* are bundled together with Penguin titles in American history, such as *The Interesting Narrative* by Olaudah Equiano, *The Narrative of the Life of Frederick Douglass,* and *Why We Can't Wait* by Martin Luther King Jr.

 Prentice Hall's new **Research Navigator**™ helps your students make the most of their research time. From finding the right articles and journals, to citing sources, drafting and writing effective papers, and completing research assignments, **Research Navigator**™ simplifies and streamlines the entire process.

Complete with extensive help on the research process and three exclusive databases full of relevant and reliable source material including EBSCO's ContentSelect Academic Journal Database, *The New York Times* Search by Subject Archive, and *Best of the Web* Link Library, **Research Navigator**™ is the one-stop research solution for your students.

Research Navigator™ is FREE when packaged with *African Americans*. Contact your local sales representative for more details or take a tour on the web at http://www.researchnavigator.com.

History Central.   Prentice Hall is pleased to provide instructors online support resources for their courses in African-American history. Located at www.prenhall.com/history, History Central contains PowerPoint™ slides, lecture notes, maps, documents, and visuals. Contact your local Prentice Hall representative for details.

Acknowledgments

In preparing *African Americans: A Concise History* we have benefitted from the work of many scholars and the help of colleagues, librarians, friends, and family.

Special thanks are due to the following scholars for their substantial contributions to the development of this textbook:

Hilary Mac Austin, *Chicago, Illinois;* Claude A. Clegg, *Indiana University;* Delia Cook, *University of Missouri at Kansas City;* Mary Ellen Curtin, *Southwest Texas State University;* Brian W. Dippie, *University of Victoria;* W. Marvin Dulaney, *College of*

Charleston; Sherry DuPree, *Rosewood Heritage Foundation;* Roy F. Finkenbine, *Wayne State University;* Abiodun Goke-Pariola, *Georgia Southern University;* John H. Haley, *University of North Carolina at Wilmington;* Peter Banner-Haley, *Colgate University;* Robert L. Harris Jr., *Cornell University;* Wanda Hendricks, *University of South Carolina;* Rickey Hill, *DePauw University;* William B. Hixson, *Michigan State University;* Ebeneazer Hunter, *De Anza College;* Barbara Williams Jenkins, *South Carolina State University;* Earnestine Jenkins, *University of Memphis;* Hannibal Johnson, *Tulsa, Oklahoma;* Wilma King; *University of Missouri, Columbia;* Joseph Kinner, *Gallaudet University;* Karen Kossie-Chernyshev, *Texas Southern University;* Frank C. Martin, *South Carolina State University;* Kenneth Mason, *Santa Monica College;* Jacqueline McLeod, *Western Illinois University;* Andrew T. Miller, *Union College;* Freddie Parker, *North Carolina Central University;* Christopher R. Reed, *Roosevelt University;* Linda Reed, *University of Houston;* John David Smith, *North Carolina State University at Raleigh;* Mark Stegmaier, *Cameron University;* Marshall Stevenson, *Ohio State University;* Robert Stewart, *Trinity School, New York;* Matthew Whitaker, *Arizona State University;* Harry Williams, *Carleton College;* Andrew Workman, *Mills College;* Deborah Wright, *Avery Research Center, College of Charleston*

Many librarians provided valuable help tracking down important material. They include Aimee Berry, Ruth Hodges, Doris Johnson, Minnie Johnson, Barbara Keitt, Andrew Penson, and Mary L. Smalls, all of Miller F. Whittaker Library, South Carolina State University; James Brooks and Jo Cottingham of the interlibrary loan department, Cooper Library, University of South Carolina; and Allan Stokes of the South Caroliniana Library at the University of South Carolina. Kathleen Thompson and Marshanda Smith provided important documents and other source material.

Seleta Simpson Byrd of South Carolina State University and Linda Werbish of Michigan State University provided valuable administrative assistance.

Each of us also enjoyed the support of family members, particularly Barbara A. Clark, Robbie D. Clark, Emily Harrold, Judy Harrold, Carol A. Hine, Peter J. Hine, Thomas D. Hine, and Alma J. McIntosh.

Finally, we gratefully acknowledge the essential help of the superb editorial and production team at Prentice Hall: Charlyce Jones-Owen, vice president and editorial director for the humanities, whose vision got this project started and whose unwavering support saw it through to completion; Charles Cavaliere, acquisitions editor for history, who kept us on track; Adrienne Paul, editorial assistant; Rochelle Diogenes, editor-in-chief for development; Gerald Lombardi, who provided valuable organizational, substantive, and stylistic insights; Louise Rothman, production editor, who saw it efficiently through production; Claire Bitting, marketing manager, who provided valuable insight into the history textbook market; and Emsal Hasan, associate editor, who pulled together the book's supplementary material.

➤ About The Authors ⬥

Darlene Clark Hine is John A. Hannah Professor of History at Michigan State University. She is president of the Southern Historical Association (2002–2003). Hine received her B.A. at Roosevelt University in Chicago, and her M.A. and Ph.D. from Kent State University, Kent, Ohio. Hine has taught at South Carolina State University and at Purdue University. In 2000–2001 she was a fellow at the Center for Advanced Study in the Behavioral Sciences at Stanford University. She is the author and/or editor of fifteen books, most recently *The Harvard Guide to African American History* (Cambridge: Harvard University Press, 2000) coedited with Evelyn Brooks Higginbotham and Leon Litwack. She coedited a two-volume set with Earnestine Jenkins, *A Question of Manhood: A Reader in Black Men's History and Masculinity* (Bloomington: Indiana University Press, 1999, 2001); and with Jacqueline McLeod, *Crossing Boundaries: Comparative History of Black People in Diaspora* (Bloomington: Indiana University Press, 2000). With Kathleen Thompson she wrote *A Shining Thread of Hope: The History of Black Women in America* (New York: Broadway Books, 1998), and edited with Barry Gaspar, *More than Chattel: Black Women and Slavery in the Americas* (Bloomington: Indiana University Press, 1996). She won the Dartmouth Medal of the American Library Association for the reference volumes coedited with Elsa Barkley Brown and Rosalyn Terborg-Penn, *Black Women in America: An Historical Encyclopedia* (New York: Carlson Publishing, 1998). She is the author of *Black Women in White: Racial Conflict and Cooperation in the Nursing Profession, 1890–1950* (Bloomington: Indiana University Press, 1989). Her forthcoming book is entitled *Black Professional Class and Race Consciousness: Physicians, Nurses, Lawyers, and the Origins of the Civil Rights Movement, 1890–1955.*

William C. Hine received his undergraduate education at Bowling Green State University, his master's degree at the University of Wyoming, and his Ph.D. at Kent State University. He is a professor of history at South Carolina State University. He has had articles published in several journals, including *Agricultural History, Labor History,* and the *Journal of Southern History.* He is currently writing a history of South Carolina State University.

Stanley Harrold, Professor of History at South Carolina State University, received a B.A. from Allegheny College and an M.A. and Ph.D. from Kent State University. He is coeditor with Randall M. Miller of *Southern Dissent,* a book series published by the University Press of Florida. He received during the 1990s two National Endowment for the Humanities Fellowships to pursue research dealing with the antislavery movement. His books include: *Gamaliel Bailey and Antislavery Union* (Kent, Ohio: Kent State University Press, 1986), *The Abolitionists and the South, 1831–1861* (Lexington: University Press of Kentucky, 1995), *Antislavery Violence: Sectional, Racial, and Cultural Conflict in Antebellum America,* coedited with John R. McKivigan, (Knoxville: University of Tennessee Press, 1999), *American Abolitionists* (Harlow, U.K.: Longman, 2001), and *Subversives: Antislavery Community in Washington, D.C., 1828–1865* (Baton Rouge: Louisiana State University Press, 2003). He has published articles in *Civil War History, Journal of Southern History, Radical History Review,* and *Journal of the Early Republic.* He is completing a book entitled *The Addresses to the Slaves and the Rise of Aggressive Abolitionism in America, 1842–1850.*

→ Chapter 12 ←

The Meaning of Freedom: The Promise of Reconstruction, 1865–1868

The End of Slavery

With the collapse of slavery, many black people were quick to inform white people that whatever loyalty and cooperation they might have shown as slaves had never been a reflection of their inner feelings. Near Opelousas, Louisiana, a Union officer asked a young black man why he did not love his master, and the youth responded sharply. "When my master begins to lub me, den it'll be time enough for me to lub him. What I wants is to get away. I want to take me off from dis plantation, where I can be free."

Emancipation was traumatic for many former masters. A Virginia freedman remembered that "Miss Polly died right after the surrender, she was so hurt that all the negroes was going to be free." Another former slave, Robert Falls, recalled that his master assembled the slaves to inform them that they were free. "I hates to do it, but I must. You all ain't my niggers no more. You is free. Just as free as I am. Here I have raised you all to work for me, and now you are going to leave me. I am an old man, and I can't get along without you. I don't know what I am going to do."

Other slaves bluntly displayed their reaction to years of bondage. Aunt Delia, a cook with a North Carolina family, revealed that for a long time she had secretly gained retribution for the indignity of servitude. "How many times I spit in the biscuits and peed in the coffee just to get back at them mean white folks." In Goodman, Mississippi, a slave named Caddy learned she was free and rushed from the field to find her owner. "Caddy threw down that hoe, she marched herself up to the big house, then, she looked around and found the mistress. She went over to the mistress, she flipped up her dress and told the white woman to do something. She said it mean and ugly. This is what she said: 'Kiss my ass!'"

On the other hand, some slaves, especially elderly ones, were fearful and apprehensive about freedom. On a South Carolina plantation, an older black woman refused to accept emancipation. "I ain' no free nigger! I is got a marster and mistiss! Dee right dar in de great house. Ef you don' b'lieve me, you go dar an' see."

Reuniting Black Families

As slavery ended, the most urgent need for many freed people was finding family members who had been sold away from them. Husbands, wives, and children went to great lengths to reassemble their families after the Civil War. For years after the end of slavery, advertisements appeared in black newspapers appealing for information about missing kinfolk. The following notice was published in the *Colored Tennessean* on August 5, 1865:

> Saml. Dove wishes to know of the whereabouts of his mother, Areno, his sisters Maria, Neziah and Peggy, and his brother Edmond, who were owned by Geo. Dove of Rocking-ham County, Shenandoah Valley, Va. Sold in Richmond, after which Saml. and Edmond were taken to Nashville, Tenn., by Joe Mick; Areno was left at the Eagle Tavern, Rich-mond. Respectfully yours, Saml. Dove, Utica, New York.

In North Carolina a northern journalist met a middle-age black man "plodding along, staff in hand, and apparently very footsore and tired." The nearly exhausted freedman explained that he had walked almost six hundred miles looking for his wife and children who had been sold four years earlier.

There were emotional reunions as family members found each other after years of separation. Ben and Betty Dodson had been apart for twenty years when Ben found her in a refugee camp after the war. "Glory! glory! hallelujah," he shouted as he hugged his wife. "Dis is my Betty, shuah. I foun' you at las'. I's hunted and hunted till I track you up here. I's boun' to hunt till I fin' you if you's alive."

Other searches had more heart-wrenching results. Husbands and wives sometimes learned that their spouses had remarried during the separation. Believing that his wife had died, the husband of Laura Spicer remarried—only to learn after the war that Laura was still alive. Sadly, he wrote to her but refused to meet with her. "I would come and see you but I know I could not bear it. I want to see you and I don't want to see you. I love you just as well as I did the last day I saw you, and it will not do for you and I to meet."

Tormented, he wrote again pledging his love. "Laura I do not think that I have change any at all since I saw you last—I thinks of you and my children every day of my life. Laura I do love you the same. My love to you never have failed. Laura, truly, I have got another wife, and I am very sorry that I am. You feels and seems to me as much like my dear loving wife, as you ever did Laura."

One freedman testified to the close ties that bound many slave families when he replied bitterly to the claim that he had had a kind master who had fed him and never used the whip. "Kind! yes, he gib men corn enough, and he gib me pork enough, and he neber gib me one lick wid de whip, but whar's my wife?—whar's my chill'en? Take away de pork, I say; take away de corn, I can work and raise dese for myself, but gib me back de wife of my bosom, and gib me back my poor chill'en as was sold away."

Land

Former slaves believed that their future as a free people was tied to the possession of land. But just as it had been impossible to abolish slavery without the intervention of the U.S. government, it would not be possible to procure land without federal

Former slaves assembled in a village near Washington, D.C. Black people welcomed emancipation, but without land, education, or employment, they faced an uncertain future.
Library of Congress

assistance. At first, federal authorities seemed determined to make land available to freedmen.

Special Field Order #15

Shortly after his army arrived in Savannah, Union General William T. Sherman announced that freedmen would receive land. On January 16, 1865, he issued Special Field Order #15. This military directive set aside a 30-mile-wide tract of land along the Atlantic coast from Charleston, South Carolina, 245 miles south to Jacksonville, Florida. White owners had abandoned the land, and Sherman reserved it for black families. The head of each family would receive "possessory title" to forty acres of land. Sherman also gave the freedmen the use of army mules, thus giving rise to the slogan, "Forty acres and a mule."

Within six months, 40,000 freed people were working 400,000 acres in the South Carolina and Georgia low country and on the Sea Islands. Former slaves generally avoided the slave crops of cotton and rice and instead planted sweet potatoes and corn. They also worked together as families and kinfolk. Most men preferred that their wives and daughters not work in the fields as slave women had had to do.

The Port Royal Experiment

Meanwhile, hundreds of former slaves had been cultivating land for three years. In late 1861, Union military forces carved out an enclave around Beaufort and Port Royal, South Carolina, that remained under federal authority for the rest of the war.

Under the supervision of U.S. officials and northern reformers, ex-slaves began to work the land in what came to be known as the "Port Royal Experiment." When Treasury agents auctioned off portions of the land for nonpayment of taxes, freedmen purchased some of it. But northern businessmen bought most of the real estate and then hired black people to raise cotton.

White owners sometimes returned to their former lands only to find that black families had taken charge. A group of black farmers told one former owner, "We own this land now, put it out of your head that it will ever be yours again."

The Freedmen's Bureau

As the war ended in early 1865, Congress created the Bureau of Refugees, Freedmen, and Abandoned Lands—commonly called the Freedmen's Bureau. The bureau was placed under the control of the U.S. Army, and General Oliver O. Howard who was eager to aid the freedmen.

The bureau was given enormous responsibilities. It was to help freedmen obtain land; gain an education; negotiate labor contracts with white planters; settle disputes involving black and white people; and provide food, medical care, and transportation for black and white people left destitute by the war. However, Congress never provided sufficient resources to carry out these tasks.

The Freedmen's Bureau never had more than nine hundred agents spread across the South from Virginia to Texas. Mississippi, for example, had twelve agents in 1866. Few of the agents were black because few military officers were black. John Mercer Langston of Virginia was an inspector of schools assigned to the bureau's main office in Washington, D.C., while Colonel Martin R. Delany worked with freedmen on the South Carolina Sea Islands.

The need for assistance was desperate. The bureau established camps for the homeless, fed the hungry, and cared for orphans and the sick as best it could. It distributed more than thirteen million rations—consisting of flour, corn meal, and sugar—by 1866. The bureau provided medical care to one-half million freedmen and thousands of white people who were suffering from smallpox, yellow fever, cholera, and pneumonia. Many more remained untreated.

In July 1865, the bureau took a first step toward distributing land when General Howard issued Circular 13 ordering agents to "set aside" forty-acre plots for freedmen. But the allocation had hardly begun when the order was revoked, and it was announced that land already distributed under General Sherman's Special Field Order #15 was to be returned to its previous white owners.

The reason for this reversal in policy was that President Andrew Johnson, who had become president after Lincoln's assassination in April 1865, began to pardon hundreds and then thousands of former Confederates and restore their lands to them. General Howard was forced to tell black people that they had to relinquish the land they thought they had acquired. In a speech before some two thousand freedmen on South Carolina's Edisto Island in October 1865, Howard pleaded with his audience to "lay aside their bitter feelings, and to become reconciled to their old masters."

A committee rejected Howard's appeal for reconciliation and forgiveness and they insisted that the government provide land.

You ask us to forgive the land owners of our island. You only lost your right arm in war and might forgive them. The man who tied me to a tree and gave me 39 lashes and who stripped and flogged my mother and my sister and who will not let me stay in his empty hut except I will do his planting and be satisfied with his price and who combines with others to keep away land from me well knowing I would not have anything to do with him if I had land of my own—that man I cannot well forgive.

Howard returned to Washington and attempted to persuade Congress to make land available. Congress refused, and President Johnson was determined that white people would get their lands back. It seemed so sensible to most white people. Property that had belonged to white families for generations simply could not be given to freedmen. Freedmen saw matters differently. They deserved land that they and their families had worked without compensation for generations. Freedmen believed it was the only way to make freedom meaningful and to gain independence from white people. As it turned out, most freedmen were forced off land they thought should belong to them.

In early 1866, Congress attempted to provide land for freedmen with the passage of the Southern Homestead Act. More than three million acres of public land were set aside for black people and southern white people who had remained loyal to the Union. Much of this land, however, consisted of swampy wetlands or unfertile pine woods. More than four thousand black families—three-quarters of them in Florida—did claim some of this land, but many of them lacked the financial resources to cultivate it. Eventually southern timber companies acquired much of it.

To make matters worse, by 1866 bureau officials tried to force freedmen to sign labor contracts with white landowners—putting black people once again under white authority. Black men who refused to sign contracts could be arrested. Theoretically, these contracts were legal agreements between two equals: landowner and laborer. But bureau agents pressured freedmen to accept unequal terms.

Occasionally, the landowner would pay wages to the laborer. But because most landowners lacked cash to pay wages, they agreed to provide the laborer with part of the crop. The laborer, often grudgingly, agreed to work under the supervision of the landowner. The contracts required labor for a full year; the laborer could neither quit nor strike.

By the 1870s, the system of sharecropping dominated most of the South. There were no wages. Freedmen worked land as families—not in gangs—and not under direct white supervision. When the landowner provided seed, tools, fertilizer, and work animals, the black family received one-third of the crop. There were many variations on these arrangements, and frequently black families were cheated out of their fair share of the crop.

The Black Church

In the years after slavery, the church became the most important institution among African Americans other than the family. Not only did it fill deep spiritual and inspirational needs, it offered enriching music, provided charity and compassion to those in need, developed community and political leaders, and was free of white supervision.

Before slavery's demise, free black people and slaves often attended white churches where they were encouraged to participate in religious services conducted by white clergymen and where they were treated as second-class Christians.

Once liberated, black men and women organized their own churches with their own ministers. Most black people considered white ministers incapable of delivering a meaningful message. Nancy Williams recalled, "Ole white preachers used to talk wid dey tongues widdout sayin' nothin', but Jesus told us slaves to talk wid our hearts."

Northern white missionaries were sometimes appalled by the unlettered black preachers who nevertheless communicated emotionally with their parishioners. A visiting white clergyman was humbled on hearing a black preacher who lacked education but made up for it with devout faith. "He talked about Christ and his salvation as one who understood what he said. . . . Here was an unlearned man, one who could not read, telling of the love of Christ, of Christian faith and duty in a way which I have not learned."

Other black and white religious leaders anguished over what they considered moral laxity and displaced values among the freed people. They preached about honesty, thrift, temperance, and elimination of sexual promiscuity. They demanded an end to "rum-suckers, bar-room loafers, whiskey dealers and card players among the men, and to those women who dressed finely on ill gotten gain."

Church members struggled to buy land and to build churches. Most former slaves founded Baptist and Methodist churches. These denominations tended to be less subject to outside control. Their doctrine was usually simple and direct without complex theology. The African Methodist Episcopal (AME) church made giant strides in the South after the Civil War.

In Charleston, South Carolina, the AME church was resurrected after an absence of more than forty years. In 1822, during the turmoil over the Denmark Vesey plot, the AME church was forced to disband and its leader had to flee (see Chapter 8). But by the 1870s, three AME congregations were thriving in Charleston. In Wilmington,

This unidentified photograph depicts the quality of housing that most former slaves inhabited in the decades after the Civil War. The black family shown here is attired in their best clothes as they pose for the photographs.
Library of Congress

North Carolina, the 1,600 members of the Front Street Methodist Church decided to join the AME church soon after the war ended. They replaced the white minister with a black man.

White Methodists initially encouraged cooperation with black Methodists and helped establish the Colored (now Christian) Methodist Episcopal church (CME). But the white Methodists lost some of their fervor after they tried but failed to persuade the black Methodists to keep political issues out of the CME church and to dwell sole-ly on spiritual concerns.

The Presbyterian, Congregational, and Episcopal churches appealed to the more prosperous members of the black community. Their services tended to be more for-mal and solemn. Black people who had been free before the Civil War were usually af-filiated with these congregations and remained so after the conflict. Well-to-do free black people in Charleston organized St. Mark's Protestant Episcopal Church when they separated from the white Episcopal church. But they retained their white minis-ter as rector.

The Roman Catholic church made modest inroads among black Southerners. There were all-black parishes in St. Augustine, Savannah, Charleston, and Louisville after the Civil War. For generations prior to the conflict large numbers of well-to-do free people of color in New Orleans had been practicing Catholics, and their descen-dants remained faithful to the church. On Georgia's Skidaway Island Benedictine monks established a school for black youngsters in 1878 that survived for nearly a decade.

Religious differences among black people notwithstanding, the black churches, their parishioners, and clergymen would play a vital role in Reconstruction politics. More than one hundred black ministers were elected to political office after the Civil War.

Education

Freedom and education were inseparable. To remain illiterate after emancipation was to remain enslaved. Almost every freed black person wanted to learn. Elderly people were especially eager to read the Bible. Even before slavery ended, black people began to establish schools. In 1861, Mary Peake, a free black woman, opened a school in Hampton, Virginia. On South Carolina's Sea Islands, a black cabinetmaker began teach-ing openly after having covertly operated a school for years. In 1862 northern mission-aries arrived on the Sea Islands to begin teaching. Laura Towne, a white woman, and Charlotte Forten, a black woman from a prominent Philadelphia family, opened a school on St. Helena's Island as part of the Port Royal Experiment. They enrolled 138 children and fifty-eight adults. By 1863, there were 1,700 students and forty-five teachers at thirty schools in the South Carolina low country.

With the end of the Civil War, northern religious organizations in cooperation with the Freedmen's Bureau organized hundreds of day and night schools. Classes were held in stables, homes, former slave cabins, taverns, churches, and even—in Sa-vannah and New Orleans—in the old slave markets. Former slaves spent hours in the fields and then trudged to a makeshift school to learn the alphabet and arithmetic. In

1865, black ministers created the Savannah Educational Association, raised $1,000, employed fifteen black teachers, and enrolled six hundred students.

In 1866, the Freedmen's Bureau set aside one-half million dollars for education. The bureau furnished the buildings while former slaves hired, housed, and fed the teachers. By 1869, the Freedmen's Bureau was involved with 3,000 schools and 150,000 students. Even more impressive, by 1870 black people had contributed one million dollars to educate their people.

Black Teachers

Freedmen usually preferred black teachers. The Reverend Richard H. Cain, an AME minister who came south from Brooklyn, New York, said that black people needed to learn to control their own futures. "We must take into our own hands the education of our race. . . . Honest, dignified whites may teach ever so well, it has not the effect to exalt the black man's opinion of his own race, because they have always been in the habit of seeing white men in honored positions, and respected."

Black men and women responded to the call to teach. Virginia C. Green, a northern black woman felt compelled to go to Mississippi. "Though I have never known servitude they are . . . my people. Born as far north as the lakes I have felt no freer because so many were less fortunate. . . . I look forward with impatience to the time when my people shall be strong, blest with education, purified and made prosperous by virtue and industry." Hezekiah Hunter, a black teacher from Brooklyn, New York, commented in 1865 on the need for black teachers. "I believe we best can instruct our own people, knowing our own peculiarities—needs—necessities. Further—I believe we that are competent owe it to our people to teach them our speciality." And in Malden, West Virginia, when black residents found that a recently arrived eighteen-year-old black man could read and write, they promptly hired him to teach.

In some areas of the South, the sole person available to teach was a poorly educated former slave equipped primarily with a willingness to teach his or her fellow freedmen. One such teacher explained, "I never had the chance of goen to school for I was a slave until freedom. . . . I am the only teacher because we can not doe better now." Many northern teachers, black and white, provided more than the basics of elementary education. Black life and history were occasionally read about and discussed. Abolitionist Lydia Maria Child wrote *The Freedmen's Book,* which offered short biographies of Benjamin Banneker, Frederick Douglass, and Toussaint L'Ouverture. More often northern teachers, struggled to impart middle-class values by teaching piety, thrift, cleanliness, temperance, and timeliness.

Black Colleges

Northern churches and religious societies established dozens of colleges, universities, academies, and institutes across the South in the late 1860s and the 1870s (see Map 12–1). Most of these institutions provided elementary and secondary education. Few black students were prepared for actual college or university work. The American Missionary Association—an abolitionist and Congregationalist organization—worked

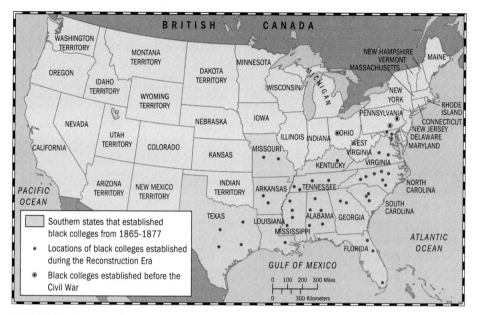

MAP 12–1   The Location of Black Colleges Founded before and during Reconstruction.
Three black colleges were founded before the Civil War. In Pennsylvania, Cheyney University
opened in 1837, and it was followed by the establishment of Lincoln University in 1854. In
1856, Wilberforce University was founded in Ohio. After the Civil War, northern black and
white missionary groups fanned out across the South and—frequently with the assistance of
Freedmen's Bureau officials—founded colleges, institutes, and normal schools in the former
slave states.

with the Freedmen's Bureau to establish Berea in Kentucky, Fisk in Tennessee, Hampton in Virginia, Tougaloo in Alabama, and Avery in South Carolina. The primary purpose of these schools was to educate black students to become teachers, although Howard University, founded in Washington, D.C., in 1867 also had a law school. One of its graduates, Charlotte Ray, became the first African-American woman lawyer in 1872.

In Missouri, the black enlisted men and the white officers of the 62nd and 65th Colored Volunteers raised $6,000 to establish Lincoln Institute in 1866, which would become Lincoln University. The American Baptist Home Mission Society founded Virginia Union, Shaw in North Carolina, Benedict in South Carolina, and Morehouse in Georgia. Northern Methodists helped establish Claflin in South Carolina, Rust in Mississippi, and Bennett in North Carolina. The Episcopalians were responsible for St. Augustine's in North Carolina and St. Paul's in Virginia. These and many other similar institutions formed the foundation for the historically black colleges and universities.

Response of White Southerners

White Southerners considered efforts by black people to learn absurd. For generations, white Americans had looked on people of African descent as inferior. When efforts were made to educate former slaves, white Southerners reacted with hostility.

One white woman told a teacher: "I do assure you, you might as well try to teach your horse or mule to read, as to teach these niggers. They can't learn."

After slavery's end, some white people went out of their way to prevent black people from learning. Countless schools were burned. In Canton, Mississippi, black people collected money to open a school—only to have white residents inform them that the school would be burned and the teacher lynched if it opened. One female teacher at a freedmen's school was killed.

Other white Southerners grudgingly tolerated the desire of black people to acquire an education. One planter conceded in 1870, "Every little negro in the county is now going to school and the public pays for it. This is one hell of [a] fix but we can't help it, and the best policy is to conform as far as possible to circumstances."

Most white people refused to attend school with black people. No integrated schools were established after emancipation. Most black people were more interested in gaining an education than in caring whether white students attended school with them. When black youngsters tried to attend a white school in Raleigh, North Carolina, the white students stopped going to it. In Charleston, South Carolina, black and white children briefly attended the same school, but they were taught in separate classrooms.

Violence

In the days, weeks, and months after the end of the Civil War, an orgy of brutality and violence swept across the South. Embittered white Southerners lashed out at black people. There were beatings, murders, rapes, and riots.

Black people who demanded respect, wore better clothing, refused to step aside for white people, or asked to be addressed as "mister" or "misses" were attacked. In South Carolina, a white clergyman shot and killed a black man who protested when another black man was removed from a church service. In Texas, one black man was killed because he failed to remove his hat in the presence of a white man. A black woman was beaten for "using insolent language," while a black worker in Alabama was killed for speaking sharply to a white overseer. In Virginia, a black veteran was beaten after announcing that he had been proud to serve in the Union Army.

A Freedmen's Bureau agent in North Carolina explained the intense white hostility. "The fact is, it's the first notion with a great many of these people, if a Negro says anything or does anything that they don't like, to take a gun and put a bullet into him, or a charge of shot."

There was also large-scale violence. Near Pine Bluff, Arkansas, in 1866, a white mob burned a black settlement and lynched twenty-four men, women, and children. An estimated two thousand black people were murdered around Shreveport, Louisiana. In Texas white people killed one thousand black people between 1865 and 1868.

In May 1866 in Memphis, white residents went on a brutal rampage after black veterans forced local police to release a black prisoner. The city was already beset with racial tensions caused in part by an influx of rural refugees. White people, led by Irish policemen, invaded the black section of Memphis and destroyed hundreds of homes, churches, and schools. Forty-six black people and two white men died.

On July 30, 1866, in New Orleans, white people—angered that black men were demanding political rights—assaulted black people on the street and in a convention hall. City policemen, who were mostly Confederate veterans, shot down the black delegates as they fled. Thirty-four black people and three of their white allies died. Federal troops eventually stopped the bloodshed. General Philip H. Sheridan characterized the riot as "an absolute massacre."

Little was done to stem the violence. Most Union troops had been withdrawn from the South and demobilized after the war. The Freedmen's Bureau was usually unwilling and unable to protect the black population. Black people were in no position to retaliate. Instead, they sometimes attempted to bring the perpetrators to justice. In Orangeburg, South Carolina, armed black men brought three white men to the local jail who had been wreaking violence in the community. In Holly Springs, Mississippi, a posse of armed black men apprehended a white man who had murdered a freedwoman.

For black people, the system of justice was thoroughly unjust. Southern juries remained all-white and refused to convict white people charged with harming black people. In Texas in 1865 and 1866, five hundred white men were indicted for murdering black people. Not one was convicted.

The Crusade for Political and Civil Rights

In October 1864 in Syracuse, New York, 145 black leaders gathered in a national convention. Some of the century's most prominent black men and women attended, including Henry Highland Garnet, Frances E. W. Harper, William Wells Brown, Francis L. Cardozo, Richard H. Cain, Jonathan J. Wright, and Jonathan C. Gibbs. They embraced the basic tenets of the American political tradition and proclaimed that they expected to participate fully in it.

Anticipating a future free of slavery, Frederick Douglass optimistically declared "that we hereby assert our full confidence in the fundamental principles of this government... the great heart of this nation will ultimately concede us our just claims, accord us our rights, and grant us our full measure of citizenship under the broad shield of the Constitution."

Even before the Syracuse gathering, northern Republicans met in Union-controlled territory around Beaufort, South Carolina, and nominated the state's delegates to the 1864 Republican national convention. Among those selected were Robert Smalls and Prince Rivers, former slaves who had exemplary records with the Union Army. The probability of black participation in postwar politics seemed promising indeed.

But northern and southern white leaders would largely determine whether black Americans would gain political power or acquire the same rights as white people. As the Civil War ended, President Lincoln was more concerned with restoring the seceded states to the Union than in opening political doors for black people. Yet Lincoln suggested that at least some black men deserved to vote. On April 11, 1865, he wrote,

"I would myself prefer that [the vote] were now conferred on the very intelligent, and on those who serve our cause as soldiers." Three days later Lincoln was assassinated.

Presidential Reconstruction under Andrew Johnson

Vice President Andrew Johnson then became president and initially seemed inclined to befriend the freedmen. In 1864, he had told black people, "I will be your Moses, and lead you through the Red Sea of War and Bondage to a fairer future of Liberty and Peace." But Andrew Johnson was no friend of black Americans.

Born poor in eastern Tennessee, Johnson was the only senator from the seceded states to remain loyal to the Union. He had nonetheless acquired five slaves and the conviction that black people were so inferior that white men must forever govern them. In 1867, Johnson argued that black people could not exercise political power and that they had "less capacity for government than any other race of people . . . wherever they have been left to their own devices they have shown a constant tendency to relapse into barbarism."

Johnson began to placate white Southerners. In May 1865, he granted blanket amnesty and pardons to former Confederates willing to swear allegiance to the United States. The main exceptions were high former Confederate officials and those who owned property in excess of $20,000, a large sum at the time. Yet even these leaders could appeal for individual pardons. And appeal they did. By 1866, Johnson had pardoned more than 7,000 high-ranking former Confederates and wealthier Southerners. Moreover, he had restored land to those white people who had lost it to freedmen.

Johnson's actions permitted long-time southern leaders to regain political influence and authority only months after the end of America's bloodiest conflict. As black people and radical Republicans watched in disbelief, Johnson appointed provisional governors in the former Confederate states. Leaders in those states then called constitutional conventions, held elections, and prepared to regain their place in the Union. Johnson merely insisted that each Confederate state formally accept the Thirteenth Amendment (ratified in December 1865, it outlawed slavery) and repudiate Confederate war debts.

The southern constitutional conventions gave no consideration to the inclusion of black people in the political system or to guaranteeing them equal rights. As one Mississippi delegate explained, "'Tis nature's law that the superior race must rule and rule they will."

Black Codes

White legislators gathered in state capitals across the South to determine the status and future of the freedmen. With little debate, the legislatures drafted the so-called black codes. Southern politicians gave no thought to providing black people with the political and legal rights associated with citizenship.

The black codes sought to ensure the availability of a subservient agricultural labor supply controlled by white people. Freedmen had to sign annual labor contracts with white landowners. South Carolina required black people who wanted to establish a business to purchase licenses costing from $10 to $100. The codes permitted black children ages two to twenty-one to be apprenticed to white people and spelled out their obligations in detail. Corporal punishment was legal. Employers were designated "masters" and employees "servants." The black codes also restricted black people from loitering or vagrancy, using alcohol or firearms, hunting, fishing, and grazing livestock. The codes did guarantee rights that slaves had not possessed. Freedmen could marry legally, engage in contracts, purchase property, sue or be sued, and testify in court. But black people could not vote or serve on juries. The black codes conceded—just barely—freedom to black people.

Bearing a remarkable resemblance to a slave auction, this scene in Monticello, Florida, shows a black man auctioned off to the highest bidder shortly after the Civil War. Under the terms of most southern black codes, black people arrested and fined for vagrancy or loitering could be "sold" if they could not pay the fine. Such spectacles infuriated many Northerners and led to demands for more rigid Reconstruction policies.
The Granger Collection

Black Conventions

Alarmed by these threats to their freedom, black people met in conventions across the South in 1865 and 1866 to protest and chart their future. Men who had been free before the war dominated the conventions. Many were ministers, teachers, and artisans. Few had been slaves. Women and children also attended—as spectators, not delegates—but women often offered suggestions and criticism. These meetings were hardly radical affairs. Delegates respectfully insisted that white people live up to the principles embodied in the Declaration of Independence and the Constitution.

At the AME church in Raleigh, North Carolina, delegates asked for equal rights and the right to vote. At Georgia's convention they protested against white violence and appealed for leaders who would enforce the law without regard to color. "We ask not for a Black Man's Governor, nor a White Man's Governor, but for a People's Governor, who shall impartially protect the rights of all, and faithfully sustain the Union."

Delegates at the Norfolk meeting reminded white Virginians that black people were patriotic. "We are Americans. We know no other country. We love the land of our birth." But they protested that Virginia's black code caused "invidious political or legal distinctions, on account of color merely." They requested the right to vote and added that they might boycott the businesses of "those who deny to us our equal rights."

Two conventions were held in Charleston, South Carolina—one before and one after the black code was enacted. At the first, delegates stressed the "respect and affection" they felt toward white Charlestonians. They even proposed that only literate men be granted the right to vote if it were genuinely applied to both races. The second convention denounced the black code and insisted on its repeal. Delegates again asked for the right to vote and the right to testify in court. "These two things we deem necessary to our welfare and elevation." They also appealed for public schools and for "homesteads for ourselves and our children." White authorities ignored these black conventions and their petitions. They were confident that they had relegated the freedmen to a subordinate role.

By late 1865, President Johnson's reconstruction policies had aroused black people. One black Union veteran summed up the situation. "If you call this Freedom, what do you call Slavery?" Republicans in Congress also opposed Johnson's policies toward the freedmen and the former Confederate states.

The Radical Republicans

Radical Republicans, as more militant Republicans were called, were especially disturbed that Johnson seemed to have abandoned the ex-slaves to their former masters. They considered white Southerners disloyal and unrepentant, despite their military defeat. Moreover, radical Republicans were determined to include black people in the political and economic system.

Among the most influential radical Republicans were Charles Sumner, Benjamin Wade, and Henry Wilson in the Senate and Thaddeus Stevens, George W. Julian, and James M. Ashley in the House. These men had fought for the abolition of slavery and were reluctant to compromise. They were honest, tough, and articulate, but also abrasive, self-righteous, and vain. Black people appreciated them. One black veteran wrote Charles Sumner in 1869, "Your name shall live in our hearts forever."

Radical Proposals

Thaddeus Stevens introduced a bill in Congress in late 1865 to confiscate 400 million acres from the wealthiest 10 percent of Southerners and distribute it free to freedmen. The remaining land would be auctioned off in plots no larger than five hundred acres. Few legislators supported the proposal. Even those who wanted fundamental change considered confiscation a gross violation of property rights. Instead, radical Republicans supported voting rights for black men—to protect black people—and to secure the South for the Republican party.

Moderate Republicans, however, found the prospect of black voting almost as objectionable as the confiscation of land. Most white Northerners—Republicans and Democrats—favored denying black men the right to vote in their states. Eight northern states did not permit black men to vote, and after the war, proposals to guarantee the right to vote to black men were defeated in New York, Ohio, Kansas, and the Nebraska Territory.

Yet most white Northerners objected even more strongly to defiant white Southerners. Journalist Charles A. Dana described the attitude of many Northerners. "As for negro suffrage, the mass of Union men in the Northwest do not care a great deal. What scares them is the idea that the rebels are all to be let back . . . and made a power in government again, just as though there had been no rebellion."

In December 1865, Congress created the Joint Committee on Reconstruction to determine whether the southern states should be readmitted to the Union. The committee confirmed reports of widespread mistreatment of black people and white arrogance.

The Freedmen's Bureau Bill
and the Civil Rights Bill

In early 1866, Senator Lyman Trumball, a moderate Republican from Illinois, introduced two major bills. The first was to provide more financial support for the Freedmen's Bureau and extend its authority to defend the rights of black people.

The second proposal was the first civil rights bill in American history. It made any person born in the United States a citizen (except Indians) and entitled them to rights protected by the U.S. government. Black people would possess the same legal rights as white people. The bill was clearly intended to invalidate the black codes.

President Johnson vetoed both measures. He claimed that the bill to continue the Freedmen's Bureau would permit too "vast a number of agents" to exercise arbitrary power over the white population. He insisted that the civil rights bill benefited black people at the expense of white people. "In fact, the distinction of race and color is by the bill made to operate in favor of the colored and against the white race."

The Johnson vetoes drove moderate Republicans into the radical camp and strengthened the Republican party. Congress overrode both vetoes. The Republicans

Federal Reconstruction Legislation, 1865–1867	
1865	Freedmen's Bureau established
1865	Thirteenth Amendment passed and ratified
1866	Freedmen's Bureau Bill and the Civil Rights Act of 1866 passed over Johnson's veto
1866	Fourteenth Amendment passed (ratified 1868)
1867	Reconstruction Acts passed over Johnson's veto

broke with Johnson in 1866, defied him in 1867, and impeached him in 1868 (failing to remove him from office by only one vote in the Senate).

The Fourteenth Amendment

To secure the legal rights of freedmen, Republicans passed the Fourteenth Amendment. Its first section guaranteed citizenship to every person born in the United States. This included virtually every black person. It made each person a citizen of the state in which he or she resided. It defined the specific rights of citizens and then protected those rights against the power of state governments. Citizens had the right to due process (usually a trial) before they could lose their life, liberty, or property.

Eleven years after Chief Justice Roger Taney declared in the *Dred Scott* decision that black people were "a subordinate and inferior class of beings" who had "no rights that white people were bound to respect," the Fourteenth Amendment vested them with the same rights of citizenship other Americans possessed.

The amendment also threatened to deprive states of representation in Congress if they denied black men the vote. The end of slavery had also made obsolete the three-fifths clause in the Constitution, which had counted slaves as only three-fifths (or 60 percent) of a white person in calculating a state's population and determining the number of representatives each state was entitled to in the House of Representatives. Republicans feared that southern states would count black people in their populations without permitting them to vote, thereby gaining more representatives than those states had had before the Civil War. The amendment mandated that the number of representatives each state would be entitled to in Congress (including northern states) would be reduced if that state did not allow adult males to vote.

Democrats opposed the Fourteenth Amendment. Southern states refused to ratify it except for Tennessee. Women's suffragists felt betrayed because the amendment limited suffrage to males. Despite this opposition, the amendment was ratified in 1868.

Radical Reconstruction

By 1867, radical Republicans in Congress had wrested control over Reconstruction from Johnson, and they then imposed policies that brought black men into the political system as voters and office holders. It was a dramatic development, second in importance only to emancipation and the end of slavery.

Republicans swept the 1866 congressional elections despite the belligerent opposition of Johnson and the Democrats. With two-thirds majorities in the House and Senate, Republicans easily overrode presidential vetoes. Two years after the Civil War ended, Republicans dismantled the state governments established in the South under President Johnson's authority. They instituted a new Reconstruction policy.

Republicans passed the First Reconstruction Act over Johnson's veto in March 1867. It divided the South into five military districts, each under the command of a general (see Map 12–2). Military personnel would protect lives and property while new civilian governments were formed. Elected delegates in each state would draft a new constitution and submit it to the voters.

The Reconstruction Act stipulated that all adult males in the states of the former Confederacy were eligible to vote, except for those who had actively supported the Confederacy or were convicted felons. Once each state had formed a new government and approved the Fourteenth Amendment, it would be readmitted to the Union with representation in Congress.

The advent of radical Reconstruction was the culmination of black people's struggle to gain legal and political rights. Since the 1864 black national convention in Syracuse and the meetings and conventions in the South in 1865 and 1866, black leaders had argued that one of the consequences of the Civil War should be the inclusion of black men in the body politic. The achievement of that goal was due to their persistent and persuasive efforts, the determination of radical Republicans, and, ironically, the obstructionism of Andrew Johnson who had played into their hands.

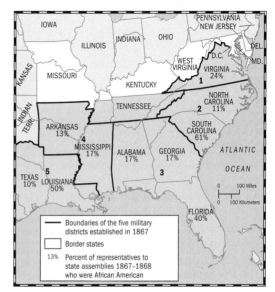

MAP 12–2   Congressional Reconstruction.   Under the terms of the First Reconstruction Act of 1867, the former Confederate states (except Tennessee) were divided into five military districts and placed under the authority of military officers. Commanders in each of the five districts were responsible for supervising the reestablishment of civilian governments in each state.

Full of enthusiasm, black men and women rushed into the political arena in 1867. Although women could not vote, they joined men at the meetings, rallies, parades, and picnics that accompanied political organizing in the South. For many former slaves, politics became as important as the church and religious activities. Black people flocked to the Republican party and the new Union Leagues.

The Union Leagues had been established in the North during the Civil War, but they expanded across the South in the late 1860s. The Leagues were social, fraternal, and patriotic groups in which black people often outnumbered white people. They gave people an opportunity to sharpen leadership skills and gain a political education.

Gaining citizenship, legal rights, and the vote generated more expectations and demands for advancement. For example, black people insisted on equal access to public transportation. After a Republican rally in Charleston, South Carolina, in April 1867, several black men staged a "sit-in" on a nearby horse-drawn streetcar before they were arrested. In Charleston, black people were permitted to ride only on the outside running boards of the cars. They wanted to sit on the seats inside. Within a month, the streetcar company gave in. Similar protests occurred in Richmond and New Orleans.

Black workers also struck across the South in 1867. Black longshoremen in New Orleans, Mobile, Savannah, Charleston, and Richmond walked off the job. Black laborers were usually paid less than white men for the same work, and this led to labor unrest. In 1869, a black Baltimore longshoreman, Isaac Myers, organized the National Colored Labor Union.

White Southerners were outraged that black people could claim the same legal and political rights that they possessed. Such a possibility seemed preposterous to people who had an abiding belief in the absolute inferiority of black people. A statement by Benjamin F. Perry, whom Johnson had appointed provisional governor of South Carolina in 1865, captures the depth of this racist conviction. "The African," Perry declared, "has been in all ages, a savage or a slave. God created him inferior to the white man in form, color and intellect, and no legislation or culture can make him his equal. . . . His hair, his form and features will not compete with the caucasian race, and it is in vain to think of elevating him to the dignity of the white man. God created differences between the two races, and nothing can make him equal."

Some white people, taking solace in their belief in the innate inferiority of black people, concluded they could turn black suffrage to their advantage. White people, they assumed, should easily be able to control and manipulate black voters just as they had controlled black people during slavery. White Southerners who believed this, however, were destined to be disappointed, and their disappointment would turn to fury.

Conclusion

Why were black Southerners able to gain citizenship and access to the political system by 1868? Most white Americans did not suddenly abandon two hundred fifty years of ingrained beliefs that people of African descent were their inferiors. The advances that African Americans achieved fit into a series of complex political developments after the Civil War. Black people themselves had fought and died to preserve the

Union, and they had earned the grudging respect of many white people and the admiration of others. Black leaders insisted that their rights be recognized.

White Northerners—led by the radical Republicans—were convinced that President Andrew Johnson had made an error in permitting white Southerners to retain pre–Civil War leaders while the black codes virtually made freedmen slaves again. Republicans were determined that white Southerners realize their defeat had doomed the prewar status quo. Republicans established a Reconstruction program to disfranchise key southern leaders while providing legal rights to freedmen. The right to vote, they reasoned, would give black people the means to deal with white Southerners while strengthening the Republican party in the South.

The result was to make the mid to late 1860s one of the few high points in African-American history. During this period, not only was slavery abolished, but black Southerners were also able to organize schools and churches, and black people acquired rights that would have been incomprehensible before the war. Yet most freedmen still lacked land and had no realistic hope of obtaining much if any of it. White violence and cruelty continued almost unabated across much of the South. Still, for millions of African Americans, the future looked more promising than it had ever before in American history.

Review Questions

1. What did freedom mean to ex-slaves? How did their priorities differ from those of African Americans who had been free before the Civil War?

2. What did the former slaves and the former slaveholders want after emancipation? Were these desires realistic?

3. Why did African Americans form separate churches, schools, and social organizations after the Civil War? What role did the black church play in the black community?

4. How effective was the Freedmen's Bureau?

5. Why did southern states enact black codes?

6. Why did radical Republicans object to President Andrew Johnson's Reconstruction policies?

7. Why did black men gain the right to vote but not to possess land?

8. Did congressional Reconstruction secure full legal and political equality for African Americans as American citizens?

Recommended Reading

Ira Berlin and Leslie Rowland, eds. *Families and Freedom: A Documentary History of African-American Kinship in the Civil War Era.* New York: Cambridge University Press, 1997. A collection of documents that conveys the aspirations and frustrations of freedmen.

TIMELINE

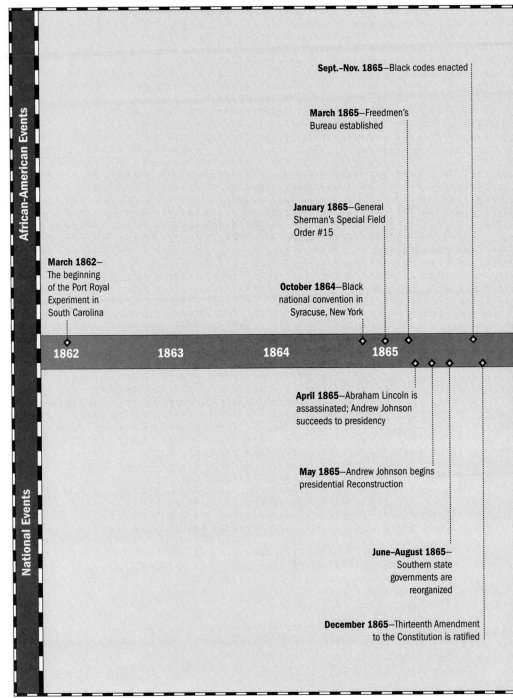

African-American Events

Sept.–Nov. 1865—Black codes enacted

March 1865—Freedmen's Bureau established

January 1865—General Sherman's Special Field Order #15

March 1862— The beginning of the Port Royal Experiment in South Carolina

October 1864—Black national convention in Syracuse, New York

1862   1863   1864   1865

National Events

April 1865—Abraham Lincoln is assassinated; Andrew Johnson succeeds to presidency

May 1865—Andrew Johnson begins presidential Reconstruction

June–August 1865— Southern state governments are reorganized

December 1865—Thirteenth Amendment to the Constitution is ratified

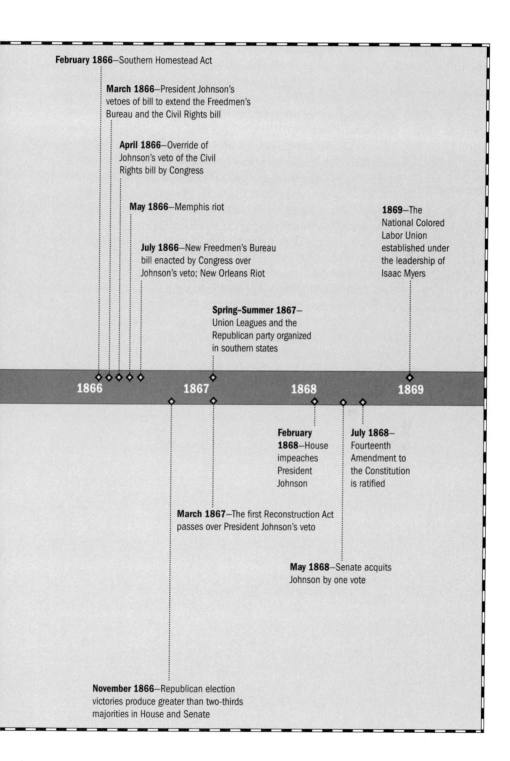

February 1866—Southern Homestead Act

March 1866—President Johnson's vetoes of bill to extend the Freedmen's Bureau and the Civil Rights bill

April 1866—Override of Johnson's veto of the Civil Rights bill by Congress

May 1866—Memphis riot

1869—The National Colored Labor Union established under the leadership of Isaac Myers

July 1866—New Freedmen's Bureau bill enacted by Congress over Johnson's veto; New Orleans Riot

Spring–Summer 1867—Union Leagues and the Republican party organized in southern states

1866   **1867**   **1868**   **1869**

February 1868—House impeaches President Johnson

July 1868—Fourteenth Amendment to the Constitution is ratified

March 1867—The first Reconstruction Act passes over President Johnson's veto

May 1868—Senate acquits Johnson by one vote

November 1866—Republican election victories produce greater than two-thirds majorities in House and Senate

W. E. B. Du Bois. *Black Reconstruction in America: An Essay toward a History of the Part Which Black Folk Played in the Attempt to Reconstruct Democracy in America, 1860–1880.* New York: Russell & Russell, 1935. A classic account of Reconstruction challenging the traditional interpretation that it was a tragic era marked by corrupt and inept black rule of the South.

Eric Foner. *Reconstruction: America's Unfinished Revolution, 1863–1877.* New York: Harper & Row, 1988. The best and most comprehensive account of Reconstruction.

Herbert G. Gutman. *The Black Family in Slavery and Freedom, 1750–1925.* New York: Oxford University Press, 1976. An illustration of how African-American family values and kinship ties forged in slavery endured after emancipation.

Tera W. Hunter. *To 'Joy My Freedom: Southern Black Women's Lives and Labors after the Civil War.* Cambridge, MA: Harvard University Press, 1997. An examination of the interior lives of black women, their work, social welfare, and leisure.

Gerald D. Jaynes. *Branches without Roots: Genesis of the Black Working Class in the American South, 1862–1882.* New York: Pantheon, 1986. The changes in work and labor in the aftermath of slavery.

Leon F. Litwack. *Been in the Storm Too Long: The Aftermath of Slavery.* New York: Alfred A. Knopf, 1979. A rich and detailed account of the transition to freedom largely based on recollections of former slaves.

→ Chapter 13 ←

The Meaning of Freedom:
The Failure of Reconstruction, 1868–1877

Constitutional Conventions

Black men as a group first entered politics as delegates to constitutional conventions in the southern states in 1867 and 1868. Each of the former Confederate states, except Tennessee, which had already been restored to the Union, elected delegates to these conventions. Most southern white men were Democrats and boycotted these elections to protest both Congress's assumption of authority over Reconstruction and the extension of voting privileges to black men. Thus, the delegates were mostly Republicans who represented three constituencies. One consisted of white northern migrants who moved to the South in the wake of the war. They were known as carpetbaggers, because they were said to have arrived in the South with all their possessions in a single carpet bag. A second group consisted of native white Southerners, mostly small farmers in devastated upland regions of the South who hoped for economic relief from Republican governments. This group was called scalawags, or scoundrels, by other southern white people. African Americans made up the third and largest Republican constituency.

Of the 1,000 men elected as delegates to the ten state conventions, 265 were black. Black delegates were a majority only in the South Carolina and Louisiana conventions. In most states, including Alabama, Georgia, Mississippi, Virginia, North Carolina, Arkansas, and Texas, black men made up 10 percent to 20 percent of the delegates. At least 107 of the 265 had been born slaves; about 40 had served in the Union Army. Several were well-educated teachers and ministers. Most went on to hold other political offices.

These delegates produced impressive constitutions that ensured that all adult males could vote. Except in Mississippi and Virginia, they did not disfranchise many former Confederates. They conferred broad guarantees of civil rights. In several states they provided the first statewide systems of public education. These constitutions were progressive, not radical. Black and white Republicans hoped to attract support from white Southerners for the new state governments these documents created by encouraging state support for private businesses, especially railroad construction.

Elections were held in 1868 to ratify the new constitutions and elect officials. In some states, Democrats boycotted the elections. In others, they voted against ratification. In still other states they supported ratification and attempted to elect as many Democrats as possible to office. Congress required only a majority of those voting—not a majority of all registered voters—to ratify the constitutions. In each state a majority of those voting eventually did vote to ratify, and in each state, black men were elected to political offices.

Black Political Leaders

Over the next decade, 1,465 black men held political office in the South. Though black leaders individually and collectively enjoyed significant political leverage, white Republicans dominated politics during Reconstruction. In general the number of black officials in a state reflected the size of that state's African-American population. Black people were a substantial majority of the population in just Mississippi and South Carolina, and most of the black office holders came from those two states and Louisiana, where black people were a bare majority. In most states, such as Arkansas, North Carolina, Tennessee, and Texas where black people made up between 25 percent and 40 percent of the population, far fewer black men were elected to office (see Table 13–1).

Initially, black men chose not to run for the most important political offices because they feared their election would further alienate already angry white Southerners. But after white Republicans swept into office in 1868, black men were elected to many key political positions. No black man was elected governor, but Lieutenant Governor P. B. S. Pinchback served one month (from December 1872 to January 1873) as

---

Table 13–1
African-American Population and Officeholding during Reconstruction in the States Subject to Congressional Reconstruction

	African-American Population in 1870	African Americans as a Percentage of Total Population	Number of African-American Office Holders during Reconstruction
South Carolina	415,814	58.9	314
Mississippi	444,201	53.6	226
Louisiana	364,210	50.1	210
North Carolina	391,650	36.5	180
Alabama	475,510	47.6	167
Georgia	545,142	46.0	108
Virginia	512,841	41.8	85
Florida	91,689	48.7	58
Arkansas	122,169	25.2	46
Texas	253,475	30.9	46
Tennessee	322,331	25.6	20

Source: Eric Foner, *Freedom's Lawmakers: A Directory of Black Officeholders during Reconstruction* (1993), xiv; The Statistics of the Population of the United States, Ninth Census (1873), xvii.

governor in Louisiana after the white governor was removed from office. Blanche K. Bruce and Hiram Revels represented Mississippi in the U.S. Senate. Beginning with Joseph Rainey in 1870 in South Carolina, fourteen black men served in the U.S. House of Representatives during Reconstruction. Six men served as lieutenant governors. In Mississippi and South Carolina, a majority of the representatives in state houses were black men, and each of these states had two black speakers of the house in the 1870s. Jonathan J. Wright served seven years as a state supreme court justice in South Carolina. Four black men served as state superintendents of education, and Francis L. Cardozo served as South Carolina's secretary of state and then treasurer. One hundred twelve black state senators and 683 black representatives were elected during Reconstruction. There were also forty-one black sheriffs, five black mayors, and thirty-one black coroners. Tallahassee, Florida, and Little Rock, Arkansas, had black police chiefs.

Many of these men were well qualified. Of the 1,465 black office holders, at least 378 had been free before the Civil War, and 933 were literate. Sixty-four had attended college or professional school. There were also 237 ministers and 172 teachers. At least 129 had served in the Union Army, and 46 had worked for the Freedmen's Bureau.

Several black politicians were wealthy, and a few were former slave owners. Antoine Dubuclet, who became Louisiana's treasurer, had owned more than one hundred slaves and land valued at more than $100,000 before the Civil War. Former slave Ferdinand Havis became a member of the Arkansas House of Representatives. He owned a saloon, a whiskey business, and two thousand acres near Pine Bluff, where he became known as "the Colored Millionaire."

Although black men did not dominate any state politically, a few did dominate districts with sizable black populations. Before he was elected to the U.S. Senate, Blanche K. Bruce all but controlled Bolivar County, Mississippi, where he served as sheriff, tax collector, and superintendent of education. Former slave and Civil War hero Robert Smalls was the political "kingpin" in Beaufort, South Carolina. He served successively in the South Carolina house and senate, and in the U.S. House of Representatives. He was also a member of the South Carolina constitutional conventions in 1868 and 1895. He was a major figure in the Republican party, and served as customs collector in Beaufort from 1889 to 1913.

The Issues

Many, but not all, black and white Republican leaders favored increasing the authority of state governments to promote the welfare of all the state's citizens. Before the Civil War, most southern states did not provide schools, medical care, assistance for the mentally impaired, or prisons. Such concerns—if attended to at all—were left to local communities or families.

Education and Social Welfare

Black leaders were eager to promote education among black people. Republican politicians created statewide systems of public education throughout the South. It was a difficult and expensive task. Schools had to be built, teachers employed, and text-books provided. To pay for it, taxes were increased in states still reeling from the war.

Some people—black and white—opposed compulsory education laws, preferring to let parents determine whether their children should attend school or work to help the family. Some black leaders favored a poll tax on voting if the funds it brought in were spent on the schools. Thus, while Reconstruction leaders established a strong commitment to public education, the results they achieved were uneven.

Furthermore, white parents refused to send their children to integrated schools. Though no laws required segregation, public schools during and after Reconstruction were invariably segregated. Black parents were usually more concerned that their children should have schools to attend than whether the schools were integrated. New Orleans, however, was an exception; it provided integrated schools.

Reconstruction leaders also supported higher education. In 1872, Mississippi legislators took advantage of the 1862 Federal Morrill Land-Grant Act, which provided states with funds for agricultural and mechanical colleges, to found the first historically black state university: Alcorn A&M College. The South Carolina legislature created a similar college and attached it to the Methodist-sponsored Claflin University.

Black leaders in the state legislature compelled the University of South Carolina, which had been all white, to admit black students and hire black faculty. Many, but not all, of the white students and faculty left.

Despite the costs, Reconstruction leaders also created the first state-supported institutions for the insane, the blind, and the deaf in the South. Some southern states during Reconstruction began to offer medical care and public health programs. Orphanages were established. State prisons were built. Black leaders also eliminated corporal punishment for many crimes and reduced the number of capital crimes.

Civil Rights

Black politicians were often the victims of racial discrimination when they tried to use public transportation and accommodations such as hotels and restaurants. Rather than provide separate arrangements for black customers, white-owned businesses simply excluded black patrons. This was true in the North, as well as the South. Robert Smalls, for example, the Civil War hero who had commandeered a Confederate supply ship to escape from Charleston in 1862 (see Chapter 11), was ejected from a Philadelphia streetcar in 1864. After protests, the company agreed to accept black riders. In Arkansas Mifflin Gibbs and W. Hines Furbish successfully sued a local saloon after they had been denied service. In South Carolina Jonathan J. Wright won $1,200 in a lawsuit against a railroad after he had purchased a first-class ticket but had been forced to ride in the second-class coach.

Black leaders were determined to open public facilities to all people, in the process revealing deep divisions between themselves and white Republicans. In several southern states they introduced bills to prevent proprietors from excluding black people from restaurants, barrooms, hotels, concert halls, and auditoriums, as well as railroad coaches, streetcars, and steamboats. Many white Republicans and virtually every Democrat attacked such proposals as efforts to promote social equality. The white politicians blocked these laws in most states. Only South Carolina—with a black majority in the house and many black members in the senate—enacted such a law, but it was not effectively enforced. In Mississippi, the Republican governor James L. Alcorn vetoed a bill to outlaw racial discrimination by railroads. In Alabama and North Carolina, civil rights bills were defeated, while Georgia and Arkansas enacted measures that encouraged segregation.

Land

Black politicians sought to promote economic development in general and for black people in particular. For example, white landowners sometimes arbitrarily fired black agricultural laborers near the end of the growing season and then did not pay them. To prevent such situations, black politicians secured laws that required laborers to be paid before the crop was sold or at the time when it was sold. Proposals to regulate the wages of laborers invariably failed because most Republicans did not believe that states had the right to regulate wages and prices.

Legislators also protected the property of small farmers against seizure for nonpayment of debts. Black and white farmers who lost land, tools, animals, and other property because they could not pay their debts were unlikely ever to recover financially. "Stay laws" prohibited, or "stayed," authorities from taking property. Besides affording financial protection to poor farmers, Republicans hoped these laws would draw white yeomen away from the Democratic party.

Black leaders were unable to provide land to landless black and white farmers. Many black and white political leaders believed that the state had no right to distribute land. Again, South Carolina was the exception. Its legislature created a state land commission in 1869.

The commission could purchase and distribute land to freedmen. It also gave the freedmen loans on generous terms to pay for the land. Unfortunately, the commission was corrupt, inefficient, and had little fertile land to distribute. However, it did enable more than fourteen thousand black families and a few white families to acquire land in South Carolina.

Though some black leaders were reluctant to use the states' power to distribute land, others had no qualms about raising property taxes so high that large landowners would be forced to sell some of their property to pay their taxes. Abraham Galloway of North Carolina explained, "I want to see the man who owns one or two thousand acres of land, taxed a dollar on the acre, and if they can't pay the taxes, sell their property to the highest bidder. . . and then we negroes shall become the land holders."

Business and Industry

Black and white leaders had an easier time enacting legislation to support business and industry. Like most Americans after the Civil War, Republicans believed that expanding the railroad network would generate prosperity. State governments approved the sale of bonds supported by the authority of the state to finance railroad construction. In Georgia, Alabama, Texas, and Arkansas, the railroad network did expand. But the bonded debt of these states soared and taxes increased to pay for it. Moreover, railroad financing was often corrupt.

So attractive were business profits that some black political leaders formed corporations. They invested modest sums and believed—like so many capitalists—that the rewards outweighed the risks. In Charleston, twenty-eight black leaders (and two white politicians) formed a horse-drawn streetcar line they called the Enterprise Railroad to carry freight between the city wharves and the railroad terminal. Black leaders in South Carolina also created a company to extract the phosphate used for fertilizer from riverbeds and riverbanks in the low country. Neither business lasted long. Black men found it far more difficult than white entrepreneurs to finance their corporations.

Black Politicians and Republican Factionalism

Southern black political leaders did create the foundation for public education, for providing state assistance for the blind, deaf, and insane, and for reforming the criminal justice system. They tried, but mostly failed, to outlaw racial discrimination in public facilities. They encouraged state support for economic revival and expansion.

But black leaders could not create programs that significantly improved the lives of their constituents. Because white Republicans almost always outnumbered them, they could not enact an agenda of their own. Moreover, black leaders often disagreed among themselves about specific issues and programs. Those leaders who had not been slaves and had not been raised in rural isolation were less likely to be concerned with land and agricultural labor. More prosperous black leaders showed more interest in civil rights and encouraging business. Even when they agreed about the need for public education, black leaders often disagreed about how to finance it and whether it should be compulsory.

Disagreements among black leaders paled in comparison to the internal conflicts that divided the Republican party during Reconstruction. The Republican party in the South constantly split into factions as groups fought with each other. Most disagreements were over who should run for and hold political office.

During Reconstruction, hundreds of would-be Republican leaders—black and white—sought public offices. If they lost the Republican nomination in county or state conventions, they often formed a competing slate of candidates. Then Republicans ran against each other and against the Democrats in the general election. It was not a recipe for political success.

These bitter and angry contests were based less on race and issues than on the desperate desire to gain an office that would pay even a modest salary. Most black and white Republicans were not well off; public office assured them a modicum of economic security.

Ironically, these factional disputes led to a high turnover in political leadership and the loss of that very economic security. Few office holders served three or four consecutive terms in the same office during Reconstruction. This made for inexperienced leadership and added to Republican woes.

Opposition

Even if black and Republican leaders had been less prone to internecine conflict and more effective in adopting a political platform, they might still have failed to sustain themselves for long. Most white Southerners led by conservative Democrats remained opposed to letting black men vote or hold office. As a white Floridian put it, "The damned Republican party has put niggers to rule us and we will not suffer it." For most white Southerners, the only acceptable political system was one that excluded black men and the Republican party.

As far as most white people were concerned, the end of slavery and the enfranchisement of black men did not make black people their equals. They did not accept the Fourteenth Amendment. They blamed the Republicans for an epidemic of waste and corruption in state government. But most of all, they considered it outrageous that former slaves could vote and hold office.

James S. Pike spoke for many white people when he ridiculed black leaders in the South Carolina House of Representatives in 1873:

> The body is almost literally a Black Parliament. . . . The Speaker is black, the Clerk is black, the door-keepers are black, the little pages are black, the chairman of the Ways and Means is black, and the chaplain is coal-black. At some of the desks sit colored men whose types it would be hard to find outside of Congo; whose costume, visages, attitudes, and expression, only befit the forecastle of a buccaneer. It must be remembered, also, that these men, with not more than a half a dozen exceptions, have been themselves slaves, and that their ancestors were slaves for generations.

Pike's observations circulated widely in both North and South.

White Southerners were determined to rid themselves of Republicans and the disgrace of having to live with black men who possessed political rights. White Southerners would "redeem" their states by restoring white Democrats to power. This did not simply mean defeating black and white Republicans in elections; it meant removing them from any role in politics. White Southerners believed that any means—fair or foul—were justified in exorcising this evil.

The Ku Klux Klan

This thinking gave rise to militant terrorist organizations, such as the Ku Klux Klan, the Knights of the White Camellia, the White Brotherhood, and the Whitecaps. Threats, intimidation, beatings, rapes, and murder would restore conservative white Democratic rule and force black people back into subordination.

The Ku Klux Klan was founded in Pulaski, Tennessee, in 1866 as a social club for Confederate veterans. One of the key figures in the Klan's rapid growth was former Confederate General Nathan Bedford Forrest, who became its Grand Wizard. The Klan drew its members from all classes of white society, not merely from among the poor. Businessmen, lawyers, physicians, and politicians were active in the Klan as well as farmers and planters.

The Klan and other terrorist organizations functioned mainly where black people were a large minority and where their votes could affect the outcome of elections. Klansmen virtually took over areas of western Alabama, northern Georgia, and Florida's panhandle. The Klan controlled the up country of South Carolina and the area around Mecklenburg County, North Carolina. However, in the Carolina and Georgia low country where there were huge black majorities, the Klan never appeared.

The Klan and similar societies reduced support for the Republican party and helped eliminate its leaders. Often wearing hoods and masks to hide their faces, white terrorists embarked on a campaign of violence rarely matched and never exceeded in American history.

Mobs of marauding terrorists beat and killed hundreds of black people—and many white people. Black churches and schools were burned. Republican leaders were threatened and often killed. The black chairman of the Republican party in South Carolina, Benjamin F. Randolph, was murdered as he stepped off a train in

University of North Carolina Historical Collection

Rutherford B. Hayes Presidential Center

The flowing white robes and cone-shaped headdresses associated with the Ku Klux Klan today are mostly a twentieth-century phenomenon. The Klansmen of the Reconstruction era, like these two men in Alabama in 1868, were well armed, disguised, and prepared to intimidate black and white Republicans. The note is a Klan death threat directed at Louisiana's first Republican governor, Henry C. Warmoth.

1868. Black legislator Lee Nance and white legislator Solomon G. W. Dill were murdered in 1868 in South Carolina. In 1870 black lawmaker Richard Burke was killed in Sumter County, Alabama, because he was considered too influential among "people of his color."

As his wife looked on, Jack Dupree—a local Republican leader—had his throat cut and was eviscerated in Monroe County, Mississippi. In 1870, North Carolina Senator John W. Stephens, a white Republican, was murdered. After Alabama freedman George Moore voted for the Republicans in 1869, Klansmen beat him, raped a girl who was visiting his wife, and attacked a neighbor. An Irish-American teacher and four black men were lynched in Cross Plains, Alabama, in 1870.

White men attacked a Republican campaign rally in Eutaw, Alabama, in 1870 and killed four black men and wounded fifty-four other people. After three black leaders were arrested in 1871 in Meridian, Mississippi, for delivering what many white people considered inflammatory speeches, shooting broke out in the courtroom. The Republican judge and two of the defendants were killed, and in a wave of violence, thirty black people were murdered, including every black leader in the small community. In the same year, a mob of five hundred men broke into the jail in Union County, South Carolina, and lynched eight black prisoners who had been accused of killing a Confederate veteran.

Nowhere was the Klan more violent than in York County, South Carolina. Almost the entire adult white male population joined in threatening and attacking the black population. Hundreds were beaten and at least eleven killed. Terrified families fled into the woods. Appeals for help were sent to Governor Robert K. Scott.

But Scott did not send aid. He had already sent the South Carolina militia into areas of Klan activity, and even more violence had resulted. The militia was made up mostly of black men, and white terrorists killed militia officers. Scott could not send white men to York County because most of them sympathized with the Klan. Thus, Republican governors like Scott responded ineffectually. Republican-controlled legislatures passed anti-Klan measures but enforcement was weak.

A few Republican leaders did deal harshly and effectively with terrorism. Governors in Tennessee, Texas, and Arkansas declared martial law and sent in hundreds of well-armed white and black men to quell the violence. Hundreds of Klansmen were arrested, many fled, and three were executed in Arkansas. But when Governor William W. Holden of North Carolina sent the state militia after the Klan, he succeeded only in provoking an angry reaction. Subsequent Klan violence in ten counties helped Democrats carry the 1870 legislative elections, and the North Carolina legislature then removed Holden from office.

The Fifteenth Amendment
and the Enforcement Acts

The federal government under Republican domination tried to protect black voting rights and defend Republican state governments in the South. In 1869 Congress passed the Fifteenth Amendment, which was ratified in 1870. It stipulated that a person could not be deprived of the right to vote because of race: "The right of citizens of

Federal Reconstruction Legislation: 1868–1877
1869   Fifteenth Amendment passed (ratified 1870)
1870   Enforcement Act passed
1871   Ku Klux Klan Act passed
1875   Civil Rights Act of 1875 passed

the United States to vote shall not be denied or abridged by the United States or by any State on account of race, color, or previous condition of servitude."

Northern black men were the amendment's immediate beneficiaries because, before its adoption, black men could vote in only eight northern states. Yet to the disappointment of many, the amendment said nothing about women voting and did not outlaw poll taxes, literacy tests, and property qualifications that could disfranchise citizens.

In direct response to the terrorism in the South, Congress passed the Enforcement Acts in 1870 and 1871, and the federal government expanded its authority over the states. The 1870 act outlawed disguises and masks and protected the civil rights of citizens. The 1871 act—known as the Ku Klux Klan Act—made it a federal offense to interfere with an individual's right to vote, hold office, serve on a jury, or enjoy equal protection of the law. Those accused of violating the act would be tried in federal court. For extreme violence, the act authorized the president to send in federal troops and suspend the writ of habeas corpus. (Habeas corpus is the right to be brought before a judge and not be arrested and jailed without cause.)

Black congressmen, who had long advocated federal action against the Klan, endorsed the Enforcement Acts. Representative Joseph Rainey of South Carolina wanted to suspend the Constitution to protect citizens. "I desire that so broad and liberal a construction be placed on its provisions, as will insure protection to the humblest citizen. Tell me nothing of a constitution which fails to shelter beneath its rightful power the people of a country."

Armed with this new legislation, the Justice Department moved against the Klan. Hundreds of Klansmen were arrested. Faced with a full-scale rebellion in late 1871 in South Carolina's up country, President Ulysses S. Grant declared martial law in nine counties, suspended the writ of habeas corpus, and sent in the U.S. Army. Mass arrests followed, but the government lacked the resources to bring hundreds of men to court for lengthy trials. Few Klansmen were punished severely, especially considering the enormity of their crimes.

The North Loses Interest

Klan violence did not overthrow any state governments, but it undermined freedmen's confidence in the ability of these governments to protect them. Meanwhile, Radical Republicans in Congress grew frustrated that the South and especially black people continued to demand so much of their time year after year. There was less and less sentiment in the North to continue support for the freedmen.

By the mid-1870s, there was more discussion in Congress of patronage, veterans' pensions, railroads, taxes, tariffs, the economy, and monetary policy than civil rights or the future of the South. Republicans began to question the necessity for more support for African Americans. Others, swayed by white Southerners' views of black people, began to doubt the wisdom of universal manhood suffrage. Many white people who had nominally supported black suffrage began to believe the complaints about corruption among black leaders and the claims that freedmen were incapable of self-government. Some white Northerners began to conclude that Reconstruction had been a mistake.

Economic conditions contributed to changing attitudes. A financial crisis—the Panic of 1873—sent the economy into a slump. Businesses and financial institutions failed, unemployment soared, and prices fell. In 1874, the Democrats recaptured a majority in the House of Representatives for the first time since 1860.

One of the casualties of the financial crisis was the Freedmen's Savings Bank, which failed in 1874. The Freedmen's Savings and Trust Company had been chartered by Congress in 1865 but was not connected to the Freedmen's Bureau. However, the bank's advertising featured pictures of Abraham Lincoln, and many black people assumed that it was a federal agency. Freedmen, black veterans, black churches, fraternal organizations, and benevolent societies opened thousands of accounts in the bank. Most of the deposits totaled under $50, and some amounted to only a few cents.

Though the bank had many black employees, its board of directors consisted of white men. They unwisely invested the bank's funds in risky ventures. With the Panic of 1873, the bank lost large sums in unsecured railroad loans. To restore confidence, its directors asked Frederick Douglass to serve as president and persuaded him to invest $10,000 of his own money to help shore up the bank. Douglass lost his money, and African Americans from across the South lost more than one million dollars when the bank closed in June 1874. Eventually about half the depositors received three-fifths of the value of their accounts.

The End of Reconstruction

Before Reconstruction finally expired, Congress made one final—some said futile—gesture to protect black people from racial discrimination when it passed the Civil Rights Act of 1875. Championed by Senator Charles Sumner of Massachusetts, it was originally intended to open public accommodations including schools, churches, cemeteries, hotels, and transportation to all people regardless of race. It passed in the Republican-controlled Senate in 1874 shortly before Sumner died. But House Democrats held up passage until 1875.

The act stipulated "That all persons . . . shall be entitled to the full and equal enjoyment of the accommodations, advantages, facilities, and privileges of inns, public conveyances on land or water, theaters, and other places of public amusement." After its passage, no attempt was made to enforce these provisions, and in 1883, the U.S. Supreme Court declared the act unconstitutional. Justice Joseph Bradley wrote that

MAP 13–1 Dates of Readmission of Southern States to the Union and Reestablishment of Democratic Party Control. Once conservative, white Democrats regained political control of a state government from black and white Republicans, they considered that state "redeemed." The first states the Democrats "redeemed" were Georgia, Virginia, and North Carolina. Louisiana, Florida, and South Carolina were the last. (Tennessee was not included in the Reconstruction process under the terms of the 1867 Reconstruction Act.)

the Fourteenth Amendment protected black people from discrimination by states but not by private businesses. Black newspapers likened the decision to the *Dred Scott* case a quarter century earlier.

Reconstruction ended as it began—in violence and controversy. By 1875, conservative white Democrats had regained control of all the former Confederate states except Mississippi, Florida, Louisiana, and South Carolina (see Map 13–1). Democrats had learned two valuable lessons. First, few black men could be persuaded to vote for the Democratic party—no matter how much white leaders wanted to believe that former slaves were easy to manipulate. Second, intimidation and violence would win elections in areas where the number of black and white voters was nearly equal. The federal government had stymied Klan violence in 1871, but by the mid-1870s the government had become reluctant to send troops to the South to protect black citizens.

Violent Redemption

In Alabama in 1874, black and white Republican leaders were murdered, and white mobs destroyed crops and homes. On election day in Eufaula, white men killed seven and injured nearly seventy unarmed black voters. Black voters were also driven from the polls in Mobile. Democrats won the election and redeemed Alabama.

White violence accompanied every election in Louisiana from 1868 to 1876. After Republicans and Democrats each claimed victory in the 1872 elections, black people seized the small town of Colfax along the Red River to protect themselves against a Democratic takeover. They held out for three weeks, and then on Easter Sunday in 1873, a well-armed white mob attacked the black defenders, killing 105 in the worst single day of bloodshed during Reconstruction. In 1874 the White League almost redeemed Louisiana in an astonishing wave of violence. Black people were murdered, courts were attacked, and white people refused to pay taxes to the Republican state government. Six white and two black Republicans were murdered at Coushatta. In September, President Grant finally sent federal troops to New Orleans after 3,500 White Leaguers attacked and nearly wiped out the black militia and the Metropolitan Police. But the stage had been set for the 1876 campaign.

In 1874 white Mississippians, no longer fearful that the national government would intervene in force, unleashed a campaign of violence known as the "Shotgun Policy" that was extreme even for Reconstruction. Many Republicans fled and others were murdered. In late 1874, an estimated three hundred black people were hunted down outside Vicksburg after black men armed with inferior weapons had lost a "battle" with white men. In 1875, thirty teachers, church leaders, and Republican officials were killed in Clinton. The white sheriff of Yazoo county, who had married a black woman and supported the education of black children, had to flee the state.

Mississippi Governor Adelbert Ames appealed for federal help, but President Grant refused: "The whole public are tired out with these annual autumnal outbreaks in the South . . . [and] are ready now to condemn any interference on the part of the Government." No federal help arrived, and many black voters went into hiding on election day, afraid for their lives. Democrats redeemed Mississippi and prided themselves that they—a superior race representing the most civilized of all people—were back in control.

In Florida in 1876, white Republicans noted that support for black people in the South was fading. They nominated an all-white Republican slate and even refused to renominate black Congressman Josiah Walls.

South Carolina Democrats were divided between moderate and extreme factions, but they united to nominate former Confederate General Wade Hampton for governor after the Hamburg Massacre. The prelude to this event occurred on July 4, 1876—the nation's centennial—when two white men in a buggy confronted the black militia that was drilling on a street in Hamburg, a small, mostly black town. Hot words were exchanged, and days later, Democrats demanded that the militia be disarmed. White rifle club members from around the state arrived in Hamburg and attacked the armory, where forty black members of the militia defended themselves. The rifle companies brought up a cannon and reinforcements from nearby Georgia. After the militia ran low on ammunition, white men captured the armory. One white man was killed, twenty-nine black men were taken prisoner, and the other eleven fled. Five of

Editorial cartoonist Thomas Nast chronicled the travails of freedmen during the twelve years of Reconstruction in the pages of *Harper's Weekly*. Here Nast deplores the violence and intimidation that accompanied the 1876 election campaign and questions the willingness of white Americans to respect the rights of black Americans
Library of Congress

the black men identified as leaders were shot down in cold blood. The rifle companies invaded and wrecked Hamburg. Seven white men were indicted for murder. All were acquitted.

The Hamburg Massacre incited South Carolina Democrats to imitate Mississippi's "Shotgun Policy." It also forced a reluctant President Grant to send federal troops to South Carolina. In the 1876 election campaign, hundreds of white men in red flannel shirts turned out on mules and horses to support Wade Hampton in his contest against incumbent Republican Governor Daniel Chamberlain and his black and white allies. When Chamberlain and fellow Republicans tried to speak in Edgefield, they were shouted down by six hundred Red Shirts.

Democrats beat and killed black people to prevent them from voting. Democratic leaders instructed their followers to treat black voters with contempt. "In speeches to negroes you must remember that argument has no effect on them. They can only be influenced by their fears, superstition, and cupidity. . . . Treat them so as to show them you are a superior race and that their natural position is that of subordination to the white man."

As the election approached, black people in the up country of South Carolina knew that it would be dangerous if they tried to vote. But in the low country, black people went on the offensive and attacked Democrats. In Charleston, a white man was killed in a racial melee. At Cainhoy, a few miles outside Charleston, armed black men killed five white men.

A few black men supported Wade Hampton. He had a paternalistic view of black people and, although he considered them inferior to white people, promised to respect their rights. Martin Delany believed that Hampton and the Democrats were more trustworthy than unreliable Republicans; Delany campaigned for Hampton and was later rewarded with a minor political post. A few conservative black men during Reconstruction also supported the Democrats and curried their favor. Most black people despised them. When one black man threw his support to the Democrats, his wife threw him out, declaring that she would prefer to "beg her bread" than live with a "Democratic nigger."

The Compromise of 1877

Threats, violence, and bloodshed accompanied the elections of 1876, but the results were contradictory. Both Democrats and Republicans claimed to have won in Florida, Louisiana, and South Carolina, the last three southern states that had not been redeemed. This created a stand-off between the two presidential candidates, the Republican Rutherford B. Hayes and the Democrat Samuel J. Tilden. Hayes had won 167 electoral votes. Tilden had 185. Whoever took the nineteen electoral votes of the three contested states would be the next president.

The controversy precipitated a constitutional crisis in 1877. Eventually, a compromise was arranged. Democrats accepted a Hayes victory, but Hayes promised that he would not support Republican governments in Florida, Louisiana, and South Carolina. Hayes withdrew the last federal troops from the South, and the Republican administrations in those states collapsed.

Redemption was now complete. Each of the former Confederate states was under the authority of white Democrats. Henry Adams, a black leader from Louisiana, explained what had happened. "The whole South—every state in the South had got into the hands of the very men that held us as slaves."

Conclusion

The glorious hopes that emancipation and the Union victory in the Civil War had aroused among African Americans in 1865 appeared forlorn by 1877. To be sure, black people were no longer slave laborers or property. They lived in tightly knit families that white people no longer controlled. They had established hundreds of schools, churches, and benevolent societies. The Constitution now endowed them with freedom, citizenship, and the right to vote. Some black people had even acquired land.

But Reconstruction was mostly a failure. The epidemic of terror and violence made it one of the bloodiest eras in American history. Thousands of black people had been beaten, raped, and murdered since 1865, simply because they had acted as free people. Too many white people were determined that black people would not have the same rights that white people enjoyed. White Southerners would not tolerate either the presence of black men in politics or white Republicans who accepted black

TIMELINE

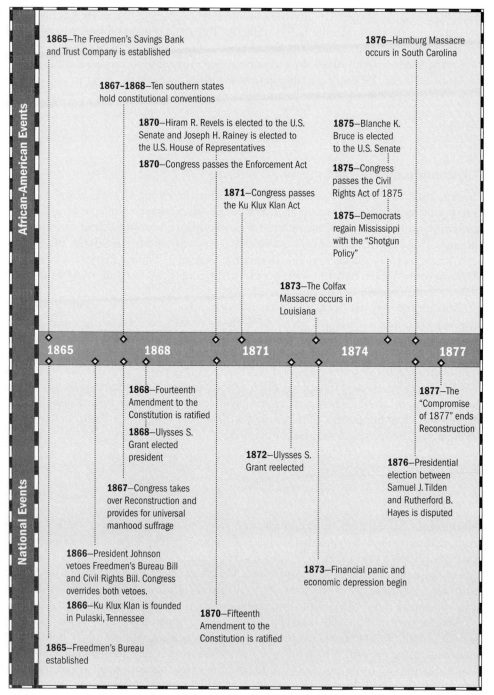

African-American Events

1865—The Freedmen's Savings Bank and Trust Company is established

1876—Hamburg Massacre occurs in South Carolina

1867–1868—Ten southern states hold constitutional conventions

1870—Hiram R. Revels is elected to the U.S. Senate and Joseph H. Rainey is elected to the U.S. House of Representatives

1870—Congress passes the Enforcement Act

1871—Congress passes the Ku Klux Klan Act

1875—Blanche K. Bruce is elected to the U.S. Senate

1875—Congress passes the Civil Rights Act of 1875

1875—Democrats regain Mississippi with the "Shotgun Policy"

1873—The Colfax Massacre occurs in Louisiana

1865   **1868**   **1871**   **1874**   **1877**

National Events

1868—Fourteenth Amendment to the Constitution is ratified

1868—Ulysses S. Grant elected president

1867—Congress takes over Reconstruction and provides for universal manhood suffrage

1866—President Johnson vetoes Freedmen's Bureau Bill and Civil Rights Bill. Congress overrides both vetoes.

1866—Ku Klux Klan is founded in Pulaski, Tennessee

1865—Freedmen's Bureau established

1870—Fifteenth Amendment to the Constitution is ratified

1872—Ulysses S. Grant reelected

1873—Financial panic and economic depression begin

1877—The "Compromise of 1877" ends Reconstruction

1876—Presidential election between Samuel J. Tilden and Rutherford B. Hayes is disputed political involvement. Gradually most white Northerners and even Radical Republicans grew weary of intervening in southern affairs and became convinced again that black men and women were their inferiors. Reconstruction, they concluded, had been a mistake.

Furthermore, black and white Republicans hurt themselves by indulging in fraud and corruption and by engaging in divisive factionalism. But even if Republicans had been honest and united, white southern Democrats would never have accepted black people as worthy to participate in the political system.

Southern Democrats would accept black people in politics only if Democrats could control black voters. But black voters understood this, rejected control by former slave owners, and were loyal to the Republican party—as flawed as it was.

But as grim a turn as life may have taken for black people by 1877, it would get even worse in the decades that followed.

Review Questions

1. What issues most concerned black political leaders during Reconstruction?

2. What did black political leaders accomplish and fail to accomplish during Reconstruction? What contributed to their successes and failures?

3. How would you respond to those who argued that black political leaders were unqualified to hold office so soon after the end of slavery?

4. To what extent did African Americans dominate southern politics during Reconstruction? Should we refer to this era as "Black Reconstruction"?

5. Why was it so difficult for the Republican party to maintain control of southern state governments during Reconstruction?

6. What was "redemption?" What happened when redemption occurred? What factors contributed to redemption?

7. How effective was Reconstruction in assisting black people to make the transition from slavery to freedom? How effective was it in restoring the southern states to the Union?

Recommended Reading

Eric Foner. *Freedom's Lawmakers: A Directory of Black Officeholders during Reconstruction.* New York: Oxford University Press, 1993. Biographical sketches of every known southern black leader during the era.

John Hope Franklin. *Reconstruction after the Civil War.* Chicago: University of Chicago Press, 1961. An excellent summary and interpretation of the post-war years.

William Gillette. *Retreat from Reconstruction, 1869–1879.* Baton Rouge, LA: Louisiana State University Press, 1979. An analysis of how and why the North lost interest in the South.

Thomas Holt. *Black Over White: Negro Political Leadership in South Carolina*. Urbana, IL: University of Illinois Press, 1979. A masterful and sophisticated study of black leaders in the state with the most black politicians.

Michael L. Perman. *Emancipation and Reconstruction, 1862–1879*. Arlington Heights, IL: Harlan Davidson, Inc., 1987. Another excellent survey of the period.

Howard N. Rabinowitz, ed. *Southern Black Leaders of the Reconstruction Era*. Urbana, IL: University of Illinois Press, 1982. A series of biographical essays on black politicians.

Frank A. Rollin. *Life and Public Services of Martin R. Delany*. Boston: Lee and Shepard, 1883. This is the first biography of a black leader by an African American. The author was Frances A. Rollin, but she used a male pseudonym.

→ Chapter 14 ←

White Supremacy Triumphant: African Americans in the South in the Late Nineteenth Century

Black people struggled against a rising tide of white supremacy in the late nineteenth century. White Southerners—and most white Northerners—were convinced that as a race they were superior to black people. They were certain that black people must play only a subservient role in society. During slavery, white Southerners had taken that subservience for granted. With slavery's end, black people allied themselves with Radical Republicans during Reconstruction and challenged white supremacy. The federal government enforced—though unevenly—the rights of all citizens to enjoy equal protection of the law. But the commitment of the Republicans and the federal government had largely collapsed by the mid-1870s.

As memories of the Civil War dimmed and antagonism between white Northerners and Southerners faded, many northern white people became less concerned with the South. Congress, the president, and the Supreme Court abandoned the commitment to protect civil and legal rights of African Americans. Political and judicial leaders embraced a laissez-faire approach to social and economic issues. The government would keep hands off the expanding railroad, steel, and petroleum industries. Neither would government safeguard the rights of black citizens. The Supreme Court interpreted the Fourteenth Amendment to protect corporations from government regulation, but it failed to protect the basic rights of black people.

As a result, the conservative white Democrats who had regained political power in the South were no more than mildly fearful that the U.S. government or Republicans would intrude as white authority expanded over virtually every aspect of the lives of southern African Americans in the last quarter of the nineteenth century. Between 1875 and 1900, black people in the South were gradually excluded from politics. They were segregated in public life and denied equal, even basic, rights. They were forced to behave in a demeaning and deferential manner to white people. Most of them were limited to doing menial agricultural and domestic jobs that left them poor and dependent on white landowners and merchants. They were often raped, lynched, and beaten. The southern system of justice was systematically unjust.

Unwilling and unable to tolerate such conditions, some African Americans left the South for Africa or the American West. However, most black people remained in the

South where many acquired a semblance of education, some managed to purchase land, and a few even prospered.

Politics

In the late nineteenth century, black people remained important in southern politics. Black men served in Congress, state legislatures, and local governments (see Table 14-1). They received federal patronage appointments. But as southern Democrats

Table 14–1
Black Members of the U.S. Congress, 1870–1901

Dates	Name	State	Occupation	Prewar Status
1. 1870–1879	Joseph H. Rainey	South Carolina	Barber	Slave, then freed
2. 1870–1873	Jefferson Long	Georgia	Tailor, storekeeper	Slave
3. 1870–1873	Hiram Revels*	Mississippi	Barber, minister, teacher, college president	Free
4. 1871–1877	Josiah T. Walls	Florida	Editor, planter, teacher, lawyer	Slave
5. 1871–1873	Benjamin Turner	Alabama	Businessman, farmer, merchant	Slave
6. 1871–1873	Robert C. DeLarge	South Carolina	Tailor	Free
7. 1871–1875	Robert B. Elliott	South Carolina	Lawyer	Free
8. 1873–1879	Richard H. Cain	South Carolina	AME minister	Free
9. 1873–1875	Alonzo J. Ransier	South Carolina	Shipping clerk, editor	Free
10. 1873–1875	James T. Rapier	Alabama	Planter, editor, lawyer, teacher	Free
11. 1873–1877, 1882–1883	John R. Lynch	Mississippi	Planter, lawyer, photographer	Slave
12. 1875–1881	Blanche K. Bruce*	Mississippi	Planter, teacher, editor	Slave
13. 1875–1877	Jeremiah Haralson	Alabama	Minister	Slave
14. 1875–1877	John A. Hyman	North Carolina	Storekeeper, farmer	Slave
15. 1875–1877	Charles E. Nash	Louisiana	Mason, cigar maker	Free
16. 1875–1887	Robert Smalls	South Carolina	Ship pilot, editor	Slave
17. 1883–1887	James E. O'Hara	North Carolina	Lawyer	Free
18. 1889–1893	Henry P. Cheatham	North Carolina	Lawyer, teacher	Slave
19. 1889–1891	Thomas E. Miller	South Carolina	Lawyer, college president	Free
20. 1889–1891	John M. Langston	Virginia	Lawyer	Free
21. 1893–1897	George W. Murray	South Carolina	Teacher	Slave
22. 1897–1901	George H. White	North Carolina	Lawyer	Slave

*Revels and Bruce served in the Senate and the twenty remaining black legislators served in the House of Representatives.

disfranchised black voters, the number of black politicians declined until the political system was virtually all white by 1900.

When Reconstruction ended in 1877, black men who held major state offices were forced out. In South Carolina, Lieutenant Governor Richard H. Gleaves resigned in 1877, but not without a protest. "I desire to place on record, in the most public and unqualified manner, my sense of the great wrong which thus forces me practically to abandon rights conferred on me, as I fully believe by a majority of my fellow citizens of this State."

For a time, some conservative white Democrats accepted limited black participation in politics as long as no black leader had power over white people and black participation did not challenge white domination. In turn, some black men supported the Democrats and were elected to state legislatures in the 1880s. Most black voters, however, remained loyal Republicans even though the party had become a hollow shell of what it had been during Reconstruction.

Democrats skillfully created oddly shaped congressional districts to confine much of the black population of a state to one district. A black Republican usually represented these districts while the rest of the state elected white Democrats to Congress. This diluted black voting strength, and it reduced the number of white people represented by a black congressman. Thus, Henry Cheatham of North Carolina, John Mercer Langston of Virginia, Thomas E. Miller of South Carolina, and George H. White of North Carolina were elected to the House of Representatives long after Reconstruction had ended.

But these black men could not persuade their white colleagues to enact significant legislation to benefit their black constituents. They did, however, get Republican presidents to appoint black men and women to federal positions in their districts, and they spoke out about the plight of African Americans. North Carolina's George H. White, for example, rebuked white leaders for their readiness to label black people as inferior while denying them the means to prove otherwise. "It is easy . . . to taunt us with our inferiority, at the same time not mentioning the causes of this inferiority. It is rather hard to be accused of shiftlessness and idleness when the accuser . . . closes the avenues for labor and industrial pursuits to us. It is hardly fair to accuse us of ignorance when it was made a crime under the former order of things to learn enough about letters to even read the Word of God."

Democrats and Farmer Discontent

Black involvement in politics survived Reconstruction, but it did not survive the nineteenth century. Divisions within the Democratic party and the rise of a new political party—the Populists—accompanied successful efforts to remove black people entirely from southern politics.

Militant Democrats stridently opposed the more moderate and paternalistic conservatives who took charge after Reconstruction. In the eyes of the militants, these redeemers seemed too willing to tolerate even limited black participation in politics, while showing little interest in the needs of white yeoman farmers. Dissatisfied independents, "readjusters," and other disaffected white people resented the domination of the Democratic party by former planters, wealthy businessmen, and lawyers who often favored limited government and reduced state support for schools, asylums, orphanages, and prisons while encouraging industry and railroads. Nor did the redeemer and paternalistic Democrats always agree among themselves. Some did favor agricultural education, the establishment of boards of health, and even separate colleges for black students. This lack of redeemer unity permitted insurgent Democrats and even Republicans sometimes to exploit economic and racial issues to undermine Democratic solidarity.

Many farmers felt betrayed as the industrial revolution transformed American society. They fed and clothed America, but large corporations, banks, and railroads dominated economic life. Farmers now depended on banks for loans, were exploited when they bought and sold goods, and found themselves at the mercy of railroads when they shipped their crops. As businessmen got richer, farmers got poorer.

Small independent (yeoman) farmers in the South suffered from a sharp decline in the price of cotton between 1865 and 1890. Many were forced into tenant farming and sharecropping. By 1890 most farmers, both black and white—between 58 percent and 62 percent in each state in the deep South—worked land they did not own.

In response to their economic woes and political weakness, farmers organized. In the 1870s they formed the Patrons of Husbandry, or Grange. The Grange promoted the formation of cooperatives and involvement in politics. Grangers especially favored government regulation of the rates railroads charged to transport crops. By the early 1880s, many hard-pressed small farmers turned to farmers' alliances. These organizations encouraged farmers to buy and sell products cooperatively and to unite politically. They favored railroad regulation, currency inflation (to increase crop prices and ease debt burdens), and support for agricultural education. By 1888 many of them joined in the National Farmers' Alliance.

The Colored Farmers' Alliance

Although the alliances were radical on economic issues, they did not challenge the racial status quo. Black farmers formed their own Colored Farmers' Alliance. It spread across the South in 1888 and 1889 and became one of the largest black organizations in American history. The alliances maintained strict racial distinctions but promised to cooperate to resolve their economic woes.

However, black and white alliance members did not always see their economic difficulties from the same perspective. Some of the white farmers owned the land that the black farmers worked. Black men saw their alliance as a way of getting a political education. In 1891, sixteen black men organized a branch of the Colored Farmers' Alliance in St. Landry Parish in Louisiana. Their purpose was to help their race and their families and to acquire enough information to vote effectively. "This organization is for the purpose of trying to elevate our race, to make us better citizens, better husbands, better fathers and sons, to educate ourselves so that we may be able to vote more intelligently on questions that are of vital importance to our people."

But many white alliance members harbored serious doubts about the right of black men to vote, and they opposed electing black men to office. Paradoxically, they also encouraged black men to vote as long as the black voters supported candidates the alliances backed, and by the late 1880s alliance-backed candidates in the South were elected to state legislatures, to Congress, and to four governorships.

The Populist Party

By 1892, many alliance farmers threw their political support to a new political party— generally known as the Populist party. The Populists hoped to wrestle control of the nation's economy from bankers and industrialists and their allies in the Republican and Democratic parties and to let the "people" shape the country's economic destiny. In 1892 they nominated James B. Weaver of Iowa for president. The Populists urged southern white and black men to unite politically to support the Populists.

The foremost proponent of black and white political unity was Thomas Watson of Georgia. He and other Populist leaders believed that economic and political cooperation could transcend racial differences. During the 1892 campaign, Watson explained that black and white farmers faced the same economic exploitation, but that they failed to cooperate with each other because of race. "The white tenant," he said,

> lives adjoining the colored tenant. Their homes are almost equally destitute of comforts. Their living is confined to bare necessities. They are equally burdened with heavy taxes. They pay the same high rent for gullied and impoverished land. . . .

> Now the Peoples' Party says to these two men, You are kept apart that you may be separately fleeced of your earnings. You are made to hate each other because upon that hatred is rested the keystone of the arch of financial despotism which enslaves you both. You are deceived and blinded that you may not see how this race antagonism perpetuates a monetary system which beggars both.

Despite such remarks, Watson was not calling for improved race relations. He opposed economic exploitation that was disguised by race, but supported segregation.

Watson later became a racial demagogue who thoroughly supported white supremacy. But in 1892, Watson and the Populists desperately wanted black and white voters to support Populist candidates. The Populists lost the national election that year and again in 1896, although they did win congressional and governor's races. Southern Democrats, outraged at the Populist appeal for black votes, resorted again to fraud and terror to prevail. It is not a coincidence that in 1892, when the Democrats carried every southern state, 235 people were lynched in the United States, more than in any other year in U.S. history.

The Populist challenge heightened the fears of southern Democrats that black voters could tip the balance of elections if the white vote split. But years before the alliances and the Populists emerged, southern Democrats had begun to eliminate the black vote.

Disfranchisement

As early as the late 1870s, southern Democrats had found ways to undermine black political power. Violence and intimidation, so effective during Reconstruction, continued in the 1880s and 1890s. Frightened, discouraged, or apathetic, many black men stopped voting. Black sharecroppers and renters could sometimes be intimidated or bribed by their white landlords not to vote, or to vote for candidates the landlord favored.

There was also simple injustice. In 1890, black congressman Thomas E. Miller ran for reelection and won—or so he thought. But he was charged with using illegal ballots and declared the loser. He appealed to the South Carolina Supreme Court, which ruled that while his ballots were printed on the required white paper, it was "white paper of a distinctly yellow tinge." He did not return to Congress.

More militant Democrats in the South were not content to rely on an assortment of unreliable methods to curtail the black vote. Some "legal" means had to be found to prevent black men from voting. However, the Fifteenth Amendment to the Constitution explicitly stated that the right to vote could not be denied on "account of race, color, or previous condition of servitude."

White leaders worried that if they imposed what were then legally acceptable barriers to voting—literacy tests, poll taxes, and property qualifications—they would also disfranchise many white voters. But resourceful Democrats found ways around this problem. In 1882, for example, South Carolina passed the Eight Box Law, which required voters to deposit separate ballots for separate election races in the proper ballot box. Illiterate voters could not identify the boxes unless white election officials assisted them.

Mississippi made the most successful effort to eliminate black voters without openly violating the Fifteenth Amendment. Black men had continued to vote in Mississippi despite hostility and intimidation. In 1889 black leaders from forty Mississippi counties protested the "violent and criminal suppression of the black vote." In response white men called a constitutional convention to do away with the black vote.

With one black delegate and 134 white delegates, the convention adopted complex voting requirements that—without mentioning race—disfranchised black voters. Voting required proof of residency and payment of all taxes, including a two-dollar poll tax. A person who had been convicted of arson, bigamy, or petty theft—crimes the delegates associated with black people—could not vote. People convicted of so-called white crimes—murder, rape, and grand larceny—could vote.

Above all, the new Mississippi constitution required voters to be literate, but with a notable exception. Illiterate men could still qualify to vote by demonstrating that they understood the constitution if the document was read to them. It was taken for granted that white voting registrars would accept almost all white applicants and fail most black applicants seeking to register under this provision.

Black voting had been declining in South Carolina since the end of Reconstruction. In the 1876 election, 91,870 black men voted; in the 1888 election, only 13,740 did. Unhappy that even so few voters might decide an election, U.S. senator Benjamin R. Tillman won approval for a constitutional convention in 1895. The convention followed Mississippi's lead and created an "understanding clause," but not without a vigorous protest from black leaders.

Six black men and 154 white men were elected to the South Carolina convention. The six black men protested black disfranchisement. Thomas E. Miller explained that the basic rights of citizens were at stake. "The Negroes do not want to dominate. They do not and would not have social equality, but they do want to cast a ballot for the men who make their laws and administer the laws. I stand here pleading for justice to a people whose rights are about to be taken away with one fell swoop." It was all for naught. Black voters were disfranchised in South Carolina.

In 1898, Louisiana added a new twist to disfranchisement. Its grandfather clause stipulated that only men who had been eligible to vote before 1867—or whose father or grandfather had been eligible before that year—would be qualified to vote. Since virtually no black men had been eligible to vote before 1867—most had just emerged from slavery—the law immediately disfranchised almost all black voters. In Louisiana in 1896, 130,000 black men voted; in 1904, 1,342 voted.

Except for Kentucky and West Virginia, each southern state had enacted elaborate restrictions on voting by the 1890s. As a result, few black men continued to vote, and no black men were elected to office.

Segregation

When black attorney T. McCants Stewart visited Columbia, South Carolina, in 1885, he told readers of the New York *Age* that he had been pleasantly received and had encountered little discrimination. "I can ride in first class cars on the railroads and in the streets. I can go into saloons and get refreshments even as in New York. I can stop in and drink a glass of soda and be more politely waited upon than in some parts of New

The Spread of Disfranchisement

	State	Strategies
1889	Florida	Poll tax
	Tennessee	Poll tax
1890	Mississippi	Poll tax, literacy test, understanding clause
1891	Arkansas	Poll tax
1893, 1901	Alabama	Poll tax, literacy test, grandfather clause
1894, 1895	South Carolina	Poll tax, literacy test, understanding clause
1894, 1902	Virginia	Poll tax, literacy test, grandfather clause
1897, 1898	Louisiana	Poll tax, literacy test, grandfather clause
1899, 1900	North Carolina	Poll tax, literacy test, grandfather clause
1902	Texas	Poll tax
1908	Georgia	Poll tax, literacy test, understanding clause, grandfather clause

Source: Goldfield et al., *The American Journey* (1991, Prentice Hall).

England." Stewart's visit occurred before most segregation laws requiring separation of the races in public places had been enacted. In fact, the word *segregation* was almost never used before the twentieth century.

Not that black and white people mingled freely in the 1880s and the 1890s. They did not. Since Reconstruction, schools, hospitals, asylums, and cemeteries had been segregated. Many restaurants and hotels did not admit black people, and many black people did not venture where they felt unwelcome or where they were likely to meet hostility. But what came to be known as "Jim Crow" had not yet become legally embedded in the southern way of life.

The term *Jim Crow* originated with a minstrel show routine called "Jump Jim Crow" that a white performer, Thomas "Daddy" Rice, created in the 1830s and 1840s. Rice blackened his face with charcoal and ridiculed black people. How Rice's character came to be synonymous with segregation and discrimination is not clear. What is clear is that by the end of the nineteenth century Jim Crow and segregation were rapidly expanding in the South.

In the decades following slavery's demise, segregation evolved gradually as an arrangement to enforce white control and domination. Many white Southerners resented the presence of black people in public facilities. If black people were—as white Southerners believed—a subordinate race, then their proximity in shops, parks, and on trains suggested an unacceptable equality in public life.

Moreover, many black people acquiesced in some facets of racial separation. During Reconstruction, people of color formed their own churches and social organizations. Black people were more comfortable around people of their own race than they were among white people. Furthermore, black Southerners often accepted separate seating in theaters, concert halls, and other facilities that previously had been closed to them. Segregation was better than exclusion.

Plessy v. Ferguson

The first segregation laws involved passenger trains. Most black passengers found themselves confined to grimy second-class cars crowded with smoking and tobacco-chewing black and white men. Hitched at the head of the train just behind the smoke-belching locomotive, these cars were filthy with soot and cinders.

In 1891, when the Louisiana legislature required segregated trains within the state, black people challenged the law and hoped to demonstrate its absurdity by enlisting the support of a black man who was almost indistinguishable from a white person. In 1892 Homer A. Plessy bought a first-class ticket and attempted to ride on the coach designated for white people. Plessy, who was only one-eighth black, was arrested for violating the new segregation law.

The case—*Plessy v. Ferguson*—wound its way through the judicial system. Plessy's lawyers argued that segregation deprived their client of equal protection of the law guaranteed by the Fourteenth Amendment. But in 1896 the U.S. Supreme Court in an 8 to 1 decision upheld Louisiana's segregation statute. Speaking for the majority, Justice Henry Brown ruled that the law, merely because it required separation of the races, did not deny Plessy his rights, nor did it imply that he was inferior. The lone dissenter from this "separate but equal" doctrine, Justice John Marshall Harlan, whose father had owned slaves, likened the majority opinion to the *Dred Scott* decision. Thus, with the complicity of the Supreme Court, the Fourteenth Amendment no longer afforded black Americans equal treatment under the law. After the *Plessy* decision, southern states and cities passed hundreds of laws that created an American apartheid—an elaborate system of racial separation.

Segregation Proliferates

In the late nineteenth century, before the automobile, the electric streetcar was the primary form of public transportation in American cities and towns. Beginning with Georgia in 1891, states and cities across the South segregated these vehicles. In some communities, the streetcar companies had to operate separate cars for black and white passengers; in other towns they designated separate sections within individual cars. The companies often resisted segregation, citing the expense of duplicating equipment and hiring more employees.

But black people were even more bitterly opposed to Jim Crow streetcars. There were streetcar boycotts in at least twenty-five southern cities between 1891 and 1910. Black people refused to ride segregated cars in Atlanta, Augusta, Jacksonville, Montgomery, Mobile, Little Rock, and Columbia. Initially, the boycotts succeeded in Atlanta and Augusta, where segregation was briefly abandoned. The boycotts seriously hurt the streetcar companies.

Black people also attempted to form alternative transportation companies. In 1905 the black community in Nashville organized a black-owned bus company and committed $25,000 to it. They purchased five buses, but they could not raise enough capital to keep the company going, and it failed after a few months.

Jim Crow proceeded inexorably. "White" and "colored" signs appeared in railroad stations, theaters, auditoriums, and restrooms and over drinking fountains. Southern white people were willing to go to any length to keep black and white people apart. Courtrooms maintained separate Bibles for black and white witnesses "to swear to tell the truth." By 1915, Oklahoma mandated white and colored public telephone booths. New Orleans attempted to segregate customers of black and white prostitutes, but only achieved mixed results.

Although *Plessy v. Ferguson* required "separate but equal" facilities for black and white people, when facilities were made available to black people, they were inferior to those afforded white people. Often no facilities at all were provided for people of color. They were simply excluded. Few hotels, restaurants, libraries, bowling alleys, public parks, amusement parks, swimming pools, golf courses, or tennis courts would admit black people. The only exceptions would be black people who accompanied or assisted white people. For example, a black woman caring for a white child could visit a "white only" public park with the child, but she dare not visit it with her own child.

Racial Etiquette

Since slavery, white people had insisted that black people act in a subservient manner. Such behavior made white dominance clear. After emancipation, white Southerners sought to maintain that dominance through a complex pattern of racial etiquette that determined how black and white people dealt with each other in their day-to-day affairs.

Black and white people did not shake hands. Black people were supposed to stare at the ground when addressing white men and women. Black men removed their hats in the presence of white people. Black people went to the back door, not the front door, of a white house. A black man or boy was never to look at a white woman. A black man in Mississippi observed, "You couldn't smile at a white woman. If you did you'd be hung from a limb." It was a serious offense if a black male touched a white woman, even inadvertently.

White customers were always served first in a store, even if a black customer had been the first to arrive. Black women could not try on clothing in white businesses. White people did not use titles of respect—mister, Mrs., miss—when addressing black adults. They used first names, or "boy" or "girl," or sometimes even "nigger." Older black people were sometimes called "auntie" or "uncle." But black people were expected to use mister, Mrs., and miss when addressing white people, including adolescents. "Boss" or "cap'n" might do for a white man.

Violence

In the late nineteenth century, the South was a violent place. Political and mob violence continued unabated into the 1890s as Democrats used force to drive black and white Republicans out of politics.

In 1886 in Washington County in eastern Texas, Democrats were determined to keep the political control that they had won in 1884 through fraud. Masked Democrats tried to seize ballot boxes in a Republican precinct. But armed black men resisted and, with a shotgun blast, killed one of the white men. Eight black men were arrested. A mob of white men broke into the jail and lynched three of them. The white Democratic sheriff did not investigate the lynching. But the black man charged with firing the shotgun was sentenced to twenty-five years in prison.

In the tiny South Carolina community of Phoenix in 1898, a white Republican candidate for Congress urged black men to fill out an affidavit if they were not permitted to vote. This produced a confrontation with Democrats. Shots were fired, and the Republican candidate was wounded. White men then went on a rampage through rural Greenwood County. Black men were killed—how many is unknown. Others had to humiliate themselves by bowing down and saluting white men.

An even bloodier riot erupted in Wilmington, North Carolina. Black men still held political offices in 1898 in Wilmington, including seats on the city council. White Democrats were determined to drive them from power. During the tense campaign, the young editor of a local black newspaper, Alex Manly, published an editorial condemning white men for the sexual exploitation of black women. Manly also suggested that black men had sexual liaisons with rural white women, which infuriated the white community. "Poor white men are careless in the matter of protecting their women, especially on the farms. . . . Tell your men that it is no worse for a black man to be intimate with a white woman than for a white man to be intimate with a colored woman . . . Don't think ever that your women will remain pure while you are debauching ours."

A white mob that included some of Wilmington's business and professional leaders destroyed the newspaper office. At least a dozen black men were murdered. Some 1,500 black residents of Wilmington fled. White people then bought up black homes and property at bargain rates. Black congressman George H. White, who represented Wilmington and North Carolina's second district, served the remainder of his term and then moved north. He ruefully remarked, "I can no longer live in North Carolina and be a man." White was the last black man to serve in Congress from the South until the election of Andrew Young in Atlanta in 1972.

Another riot occurred in New Orleans in 1900. Robert Charles was a 34-year-old literate laborer who had migrated there from rural Mississippi. On July 23, 1900, Charles and a friend were harassed by white New Orleans police officers. One of the officers attempted to beat Charles with a night stick. Failing to subdue the large black man, the officer then drew a gun. Charles pulled out his own gun, and each man wounded the other. Charles fled but was tracked down to a rooming house where he had secluded himself with a Winchester rifle with which he proceeded to shoot his tormentors. Eventually, a white mob that numbered as many as twenty thousand gathered. In the meantime, Charles—an expert marksmen—shot twenty-seven white people, killing seven, including four policemen. Finally, burned out of the dwelling, Charles was shot and his corpse stomped beyond recognition by enraged white people. Four days of rioting ensued in which at least a dozen black people were killed and many more injured.

Lynching

Lynching had become common in the South by the 1890s. Between 1889 and 1932, 3,745 people were lynched in the United States. Most lynchings happened in the South, and black men were usually the victims. Rarely did a sheriff or police officer protect a potential victim, and even if one did, that protection was often not enough.

The people who carried out the lynchings were never tried or convicted. Prominent community members frequently encouraged and participated in lynch mobs. White political leaders, journalists, and clergymen rarely denounced lynching in public. The Atlanta *Constitution* dismissed lynching as relatively inconsequential. "There are places and occasions when the natural fury of men cannot be restrained by all the laws in Christendom."

Lynchings were savage and hideous. Such mob brutality was another manifestation of white supremacy. Black people were murdered, beaten, burned, and mutilated for trivial reasons—or for no reason. Most white Southerners justified lynching as a response to the raping of white women by black men. But many lynchings involved no alleged rape, and even when they did, the victims often had no connection to the alleged offense.

After a white family was murdered in Statesboro, Georgia, in 1904, Paul Reed and Will Cato were convicted of murder and then seized by a mob that invaded the courtroom. They were burned alive in front of a large crowd. Then the violence spread. Albert Roger and his son were lynched "for being Negroes." A black man named McBride attempted to protect his wife who had had a baby three days earlier. He "was beaten, killed, and shot to death."

Lynchings were common and public events in the South at the turn of the century. Often hundreds of people took part in and witnessed these gruesome spectacles.
Library of Congress

Mobs often attacked black people who had achieved economic success. In Memphis, Thomas Moss with two friends opened the People's Grocery Company in a black neighborhood. The store flourished, but it competed with a white-owned grocery. "[T]hey were succeeding too well," one of Moss's friends observed. After the white grocer had had the three black men indicted for conspiracy, black people organized a protest and violence followed. The three black men were jailed. A white mob attacked the jail, lynched them, and then looted their store. Ida B. Wells, a newspaper editor and a friend of Moss, was heartbroken. "A finer, cleaner man than he never walked the streets of Memphis." She considered his lynching an "excuse to get rid of Negroes who were acquiring wealth and property and thus keep the race terrorized and keep the nigger down." Responding to the incident in her paper, Wells began a lifelong crusade against lynching and became an ardent supporter of black voting rights.

Black women were also lynched. In 1914 in Wagoner County, Oklahoma, seventeen-year-old Marie Scott was lynched because her brother had killed a white man who had raped her. In Valdosta, Georgia, in 1918 after Mary Turner's husband was lynched, she publicly vowed to bring those responsible to justice. Though she was eight months pregnant, a mob seized her, tied her ankles together, and hanged her upside down from a tree. A member of the mob slit her abdomen, and her nearly full-term child fell to the ground. The mob stomped the infant to death. They then set her clothes on fire and shot her.

Rape

Although white people often justified lynching as a response to the presumed threat black men posed to the virtue of white women, white men routinely harassed and abused black women. Like lynching, rape inflicted pain and suffering, and demonstrated the power of white men over black men and women.

Black men tried to keep their wives and daughters away from white men. They refused to permit black women to work as maids and domestics in homes where white men were present. One black man commented in 1912, "I believe nearly all white men take, and expect to take, undue liberties with their colored female servants, not only the fathers, but in many cases the sons also." A black man could not easily protect a black woman. He might be killed trying to do it, as an Alabama clergyman pointed out. "[W]hite men on the high ways and in their stores and on the trains will insult our women and we are powerless to resent it as it would only be an invitation for our lives to be taken."

Many white people believed that black women "invited" white males to take advantage of them. Black women were considered inferior, immoral, and lascivious. White people reasoned that it was impossible to defend the virtue of black women because they had none. Governor Coleman Blease of South Carolina pardoned black and white men found guilty of raping black women. "I am of the opinion," he said in 1913, "as I have always been, and have very serious doubts as to whether the crime of rape can be committed upon a negro."

Migration

In 1900, AME minister Henry M. Turner despaired for black people in America. "Every man that has the sense of an animal must see that there is no future in this country for the Negro. [W]e are taken out and burned, shot, hanged, unjointed and murdered in every way. Our civil rights are taken from us by force, our political rights are a farce."

It is, therefore, not surprising that thousands of African Americans fled poverty, powerlessness, and brutality in the South. What is perhaps surprising is that more did not leave. In 1900, 90 percent of black Americans still lived in the southern states. And of those who left the South, most did not head north along the old underground railroad. The Great Migration to the northern industrial states did not begin until about 1915. Emigrants of the 1870s, 1880s, and 1890s were more likely to strike out for Africa, or move west to Kansas, Oklahoma, and Arkansas, or move from farms to southern towns or cities.

In 1877, black leaders in South Carolina, including AME minister and congressman Richard H. Cain, Probate Judge Harrison N. Bouey, and Martin Delany urged black people to migrate to Liberia. Many black communities and churches caught "Liberia Fever" while black people in upper South Carolina still felt the trauma of the political terror that had ended Reconstruction.

A white journalist described the situation in Chester County: "At some places in this county the desire to shake off the dust of their feet against this Democratic State is so great, that they are talking of selling out their crops and their personal effects, save what they would need in their new home." They were given promising though sometimes inaccurate information about Liberia: One potato in Liberia, they were told, could feed an entire family.

Several black men organized the Liberian Exodus Joint Stock Steamship Company. They raised $6,000 and hired a ship, the *Azor*, for the trip to Africa. The ship left Charleston in April 1878 with 206 migrants aboard and 175 left behind because there was not enough room for them. With inadequate food and fresh water and no competent medical care, twenty-three migrants died at sea. The ship arrived in Liberia on June 3.

Once settled in Liberia, several of the migrants prospered. Sam Hill established a seven hundred-acre coffee plantation, and C. L. Parsons became the chief justice of the Liberian Supreme Court. But others did less well, and some returned to the United States. The Liberian Exodus Company experienced financial difficulties and could not pay for further voyages.

Black people also headed west. Between 1865 and 1880, 40,000 black people known as "Exodusters" moved to Kansas. Several hundred were persuaded to migrate by Benjamin "Pap" Singleton, a charismatic ex-slave from Tennessee. W. R. Hill, a black real estate promoter from Kentucky was instrumental in founding the all-black Kansas town of Nicodemus in 1877. Several all-black towns including Boley, Liberty, and Langston were founded in Indian territory that became Oklahoma. Other black migrants settled in Nebraska, the Dakotas, Colorado and elsewhere on the Great Plains and in the Rocky Mountains.

Many black and white people who moved west after the Civil War took advantage of the 1862 Homestead Act that provided 160 acres of federal land free to those who would settle on it and farm it for at least five years. It was often a bleak and lonely existence where trees were few and rain infrequent. People lived in sod houses and relied on cow (or buffalo) chips for heat and cooking as they struggled to endure.

Railroads encouraged migration by offering reduced fares. Some western farmers and agents were eager to sell land, but some of it was of little value. Some of the white residents of Mississippi and South Carolina, which had large black majorities in their population, were glad to see the black people go. Others were alarmed at the loss of cheap black labor.

Some black leaders opposed migration and urged black people to stay put. In 1879, Frederick Douglass insisted that more opportunities existed for black people in the South than elsewhere. "Not only is the South the best locality for the Negro on the ground of his political powers and possibilities, but it is best for him as a field of labor. He is there, as he is nowhere else, an absolute necessity." Robert Smalls urged black people to come to his home county of Beaufort, South Carolina, "where I hardly think it probable that any prisoner will ever be taken from jail by a mob and lynched."

Many black people left the poverty and isolation of farms and moved to nearby villages and towns in the South. Others went to larger southern cities including Atlanta, Richmond, and Nashville, where they settled in growing black neighborhoods. Urban areas offered more economic opportunities than rural areas. Though black people were usually confined to menial labor, city work paid cash on a fairly regular basis, whereas rural residents received no money until their crops were sold. Towns and cities also afforded more social activities. Black youngsters in towns spent more time in school than rural children, who had to help work the farms.

Black women had a better chance than black men of finding regular work in a town, though it was usually as a domestic or cleaning woman. This economic situation adversely affected the black family. Before the increase in migration, husband and wife headed 90 percent of black families. But with migration, many black men remained in rural areas where they could get farm work while women went to urban communities. Often these women became single heads of households.

Black Farm Families

Most black people remained poverty-stricken sharecroppers and renters on impoverished land white people owned. They were poorly educated. They lacked political power. They were always in debt. Many rural black families remained close to involuntary servitude in the decades after Reconstruction. They lived in drafty, leaky cabins without electricity or running water. Outdoor toilets created health problems. Medical care was often unavailable. Diets were dreary and unbalanced—mostly pork and cornbread—and deficient in vitamins and protein.

Sharecroppers

Most black farm families (and many white families as well) were sharecroppers. Sharecropping had emerged during Reconstruction as landowners allowed the use of their land for a share of the crop. The landlord also usually provided housing, horses or mules, tools, seed, and fertilizer as well as food and clothing. Depending on the agreement or contract, the landowner received from one-half to three-quarters of the crop.

Sharecropping lent itself to exploitation. By law, verbal agreements were considered contracts. In any case, many sharecroppers were illiterate and could not have read written contracts. The landowner informed the sharecropper of the value of the product raised—typically cotton—as well as the value of the goods provided to the sharecropping family. Though many sharecroppers were aware that the proprietor's calculations were wrong, they could do nothing about it. Also, cotton brokers and gin owners routinely paid black farmers less than white farmers per pound for cotton. A forlorn ditty circulating among black people in the South in the late nineteenth century captured this inequity:

> *A naught's a naught, and a figger's a figger—*
> *All fer de white man—none fer de nigger!*

Black men were forced to accept the white man's word. One Mississippi sharecropper explained, "I have been living in this Delta thirty years, and I know that I have

For more than a century—from the early 1800s until the 1920s—cotton was *the* crop across much of the deep South. First as slaves, then as sharecroppers, renters, and landowners, generations of black people toiled in the cotton fields.
CORBIS

been robbed every year; but there is no use jumping out of the frying pan into the fire. If we ask any questions we are cussed, and if we raise up we are shot, and that ends it."

When they could, black farmers preferred renting to sharecropping. As tenants, they paid a flat charge to rent a given number of acres. Payment would be made in either cash or, more typically, in a specified amount of the crop. Tenants usually owned their own animals and tools. As Bessie Jones explained, "You see, a sharecropper don't ever have nothing. Before you know it, the man done took it all. But the renter always have something, and then he go to work when he want to go to work. He ain't got to go to work on the man's time. If he didn't make it, he didn't get it."

In addition to the landowner, many sharecroppers and renters were also indebted to a local merchant for food, clothing, tools, and farm supplies. The merchant advanced the merchandise but took out a lien on the crop. If the sharecropper or renter failed to repay the merchant, the merchant was legally entitled to all or part of the crop once the landowner had received his payment. Merchants tended to charge high prices and high interest rates. They usually insisted that farmers plant cotton before they would agree to a lien. Cotton could be sold quickly for cash.

Many farmers fell deeply into debt to landowners and merchants. They were cheated. Bad weather destroyed crops. Crop prices declined. Farmers who were in debt could not leave the land until the debt was paid. If they tried to depart, the sheriff pursued them. This was called peonage, and it amounted to enslavement, holding thousands of black people across the South in a state of perpetual bondage. Peonage violated federal law, but the law was rarely enforced. When landowners and merchants were prosecuted for keeping black people in peonage, white juries acquitted them.

Black Landowners

Considering the incredible obstacles against them, black farm families acquired land at an astonishing rate after the Civil War. Many white people refused to sell land to black buyers, preferring to keep them dependent. Black people also found it difficult to save enough money to purchase land even when they could find a willing seller. Still, they steadily managed to accumulate land.

Some black families had kept land that had been distributed in the Carolina and Georgia low country under the Port Royal Experiment and Sherman's Special Field Order #15 (see Chapter 11). In 1880, black people on South Carolina's Sea Islands held ten thousand acres of land worth $300,000.

By 1900, more than one hundred thousand black families owned their own land in the eight states of the deep South. Black land ownership increased more than 500 percent between 1870 and 1900. Most black people possessed small farms of about twenty acres. These small plots of land were often subdivided among sons and grandsons, making it more difficult for their families to prosper. But some black farmers had accumulated impressive estates. Prince Johnson had 360 acres of excellent Mississippi Delta land. Freedman Leon Winter was the richest black man in Tennessee, with real estate worth $70,000 in 1889. Florida farmer J. D. McDuffy had an eight hundred-acre farm near Ocala and raised cantaloupes, watermelons, cabbages, and tomatoes. Texas freedman Daniel Webster Wallace had a ten thousand-acre cattle ranch. Most of these landowners had been born into slavery.

Many white Southerners found it difficult to tolerate black economic success and lashed out at those who had achieved it. When automobiles arrived in the early twentieth century, Henry Watson, a well-to-do black farmer in Georgia, drove a new car to town. Enraged white people surrounded the car, forced Watson and his daughter out at gunpoint, and burned the vehicle. Watson was told, "From now on, you niggers walk into town, or use that ole mule if you want to stay in this city."

In 1916, Anthony Crawford, the owner of 427 acres of prime cotton land in Abbeville, South Carolina, secretary of the Chapel AME Church, a married man with sixteen children, was arrested and then released after he quarreled with a local white merchant over the price of cotton seed. But a mob, infuriated that Crawford spoke so bluntly to a white man, went after him. "When a nigger gets impudent we stretch him out and paddle him a bit," exclaimed one white man. But Crawford resisted and crushed the skull of a white attacker. The mob then stabbed and beat Crawford before the sheriff rescued him and put him in jail. Several hours later, a second mob broke into the jail and beat him to death. His body was left hanging at the fairgrounds. After his first beating, Crawford had told a friend, "I thought I was a good citizen." The coroner's jury ruled that his death had occurred at the hands of persons unknown.

Segregated Justice

The southern criminal justice systems yielded only injustice to black people. Southern lawmakers worried incessantly about what they considered the growing black crime problem, and they worked diligently to control the black population. Vagrancy laws made it easy to arrest any idle black man or one who was passing through a community. Contract evasion laws ensnared black people who attempted to escape peonage and perpetual servitude.

The legal system also became increasingly white after Reconstruction. Black police officers were gradually eliminated, and white policemen acquired a deserved reputation for brutality. Juries were all white by 1900. (No women served on southern juries.) Judges and most attorneys were also white. The few black lawyers faced daunting hurdles. Some black defendants believed—correctly—that they would be found guilty and sentenced to a longer term if they retained a black attorney rather than a white one. Court personnel treated black plaintiffs, defendants, and witnesses with contempt, referring to them as "niggers," "boy," and "gal." Black people were rarely "mister" or "misses" in court proceedings.

A black defendant could not get justice. Black men and women were more often charged with crimes than white people. They were almost always convicted, regardless of the strength of the evidence or the credibility of witnesses. In one of the few instances when a black man was found not guilty of killing a white man, the defendant's attorney advised him to leave town because local white people were unlikely to accept the verdict. He fled but returned twenty years later and was castrated by two white men.

Race was always the priority with jurors. Even when black people were the victims of crime, they were punished. In 1897, in Hinds County, Mississippi, a white man beat a black woman with an axe handle. She took him to court only to have the justice of the peace rule that he knew of "no law to punish a white man for beating a negro woman."

Juries rarely found white people guilty of crimes against black people. In a Georgia case in 1911, the evidence against several white people for holding black families in peonage was so overwhelming that the judge virtually ordered the jury to return a guilty verdict. Nonetheless, after five minutes of deliberation, the jury found the defendants not guilty. Many black and white people were, therefore, astonished in 1898 in Shreveport, Louisiana, when a jury actually found a white man guilty of murdering a black man. He was sentenced to five years in prison.

Black people could receive leniency from the judicial system, but it was not justice. They were much less likely to be charged with a crime against another black person, like raping a black woman, than against a white person. Black people often were not charged with crimes such as adultery and bigamy because white people considered such offenses typical of black behavior.

Black defendants who had some personal or economic connection to a prominent white person were less likely to be treated or punished the same way as black people who had no such relationship. In Vicksburg, Mississippi, a black woman watched as the black man who had murdered her husband was acquitted because a white man intervened. Those black people known as "a white man's nigger" had a decided advantage in court.

Black people received longer sentences and larger fines than white people. In Georgia, black convicts served much longer sentences than white convicts for the same offense—five times as long for larceny, for example. An eighty-year-old black preacher went to prison "for what a white man was fined five dollars." In New Orleans, a black man was sentenced to ninety days in jail for petty theft. According to a local black newspaper, it was "three days for stealing and eighty-seven days for being colored."

Conditions in southern prisons were wretched. Black prisoners—many incarcerated for vagrancy, theft, disorderly conduct, and other misdemeanors—spent months and years in oppressive conditions and were subjected to unrelenting abuse. But conditions could and did get worse.

Southern politicians devised the convict lease system in the late nineteenth century. Businesses and planters leased convicts from the state to build railroads, clear swamps, cut timber, tend cotton, and work mines. The company or planter had to feed, clothe, and house the prisoners. Of course, the convicts were not paid. The state and local community was not only freed of the burden of maintaining prisons, but also received revenue. For example, South Carolina was paid three dollars per month per prisoner. Some states found this so remunerative that officials were encouraged to charge even more black men with crimes so they could contribute to this lucrative enterprise.

Leased convicts endured appalling conditions. They were shackled and beaten, overworked and underfed; they slept on vermin-infested straw mattresses and received little or no medical care. They sustained terrible injuries. Diseases proliferated and hundreds died, meaning that they had, in effect, been sentenced to death for petty crimes.

Businessmen and planters found such cheap labor irresistible, and black prisoners found it "nine kinds of hell." It was worse than slavery because these black lives had no value to either the government or the businesses involved in this sordid system. As one employer explained in 1883, "But these convicts; we don't own em. One dies, get another." The inhumanity of convict leasing became such a scandal that states outlawed it by the early twentieth century. Convicts were returned to state-operated penitentiaries.

Conclusion

With the end of the Civil War and slavery in 1865, more than four million Americans of African descent had looked with hope and anticipation to the future. Four decades later, there were more than nine million African Americans, and more than eight million of them lived in the South. The crushing burden of white supremacy increasingly limited their hopes and aspirations. The U.S. government abandoned black people to white Southerners and their state and local governments. The federal government that had assured their rights as citizens during Reconstruction ignored the legal, political, and economic situation that entrapped most black Southerners.

Although the Thirteenth Amendment abolished slavery, thousands of black people were hopelessly trapped in peonage; thousands of others labored as sharecroppers and renters, indebted to white landowners and merchants. Yet, more than 100,000 black families managed to acquire farms of their own by 1900. Many black farmers had

TIMELINE

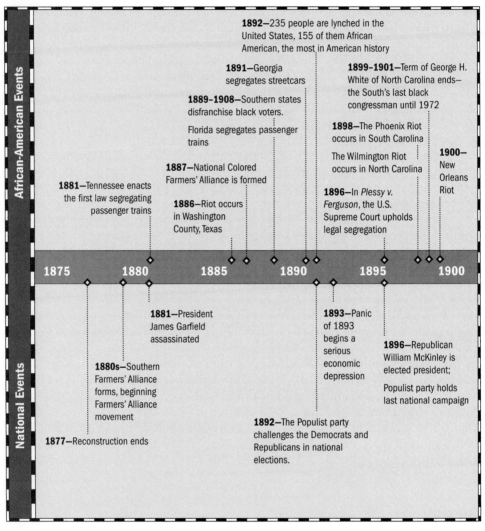

1892—235 people are lynched in the United States, 155 of them African American, the most in American history

1891—Georgia segregates streetcars

1889-1908—Southern states disfranchise black voters.

Florida segregates passenger trains

1887—National Colored Farmers' Alliance is formed

1881—Tennessee enacts the first law segregating passenger trains

1886—Riot occurs in Washington County, Texas

1899-1901—Term of George H. White of North Carolina ends— the South's last black congressman until 1972

1898—The Phoenix Riot occurs in South Carolina

The Wilmington Riot occurs in North Carolina

1896—In *Plessy v. Ferguson*, the U.S. Supreme Court upholds legal segregation

1900— New Orleans Riot

African-American Events

1875 1880 1885 1890 1895 1900

National Events

1881—President James Garfield assassinated

1880s—Southern Farmers' Alliance forms, beginning Farmers' Alliance movement

1877—Reconstruction ends

1893—Panic of 1893 begins a serious economic depression

1892—The Populist party challenges the Democrats and Republicans in national elections.

1896—Republican William McKinley is elected president;

Populist party holds last national campaign

also organized and participated in the Colored Farmers' Alliance and the Populist party, though it brought few tangible benefits.

The Fourteenth Amendment had guaranteed the rights of citizenship that included due process of law. No state could deprive a person of life, liberty, or property without a court proceeding. The amendment also ensured each citizen equal protection of the law. But the Supreme Court had ruled that racial segregation in public places did not infringe on the right to equal protection of the law. And as for the right to life, hundreds of black people had lost their lives at the hands of lynch mobs by the early 1900s.

The Fifteenth Amendment stipulated that race could not be used to deprive a man of the right to vote. Nevertheless, southern states circumvented the amendment with poll taxes, literacy tests, and the grandfather clause. Thus, by 1900, after black men had held political offices across the South for the previous thirty years, no black person served in any elected political position in any southern state.

White people clearly regarded black Americans as an inferior race not entitled to those rights that the Constitution so emphatically set forth. What could black people do about the intolerance, discrimination, violence, and powerlessness that they had to endure? What strategies, ideas, and leadership could they use to overcome the burdens that they were forced to bear? What realistic chances did they have of overcoming white supremacy? How could black people organize to gain fundamental rights that were guaranteed to them?

Review Questions

1. How were black people prevented from voting despite the provisions of the Fifteenth Amendment?

2. What legal and ethical arguments did white Americans use to justify segregation?

3. What accounts for the epidemic of violence and lynching in the South in the late nineteenth century?

4. Why didn't more black people migrate from the South in this period?

Recommended Reading

Edward L. Ayers. *The Promise of the New South: Life after Reconstruction.* New York: Oxford University Press, 1992. An excellent overview of how people lived in the late nineteenth-century South.

Leon Litwack. *Trouble in Mind: Black Southerners in the Age of Jim Crow.* New York: Alfred A. Knopf, 1998. In moving words and testimony, black people describe what life was like in a white supremacist society.

Rayford Logan. *The Negro in American Life and Thought: The Nadir, 1877–1901.* New York: Dial Press, 1954. Explorations of the contours and oppressiveness of racism.

Benjamin E. Mays. *Born to Rebel: An Autobiography.* New York: Charles Scribner, 1971. Eloquent and graphic recollection of what it was like to grow up black in the rural South at the turn of the century.

C. Vann Woodward. *The Strange Career of Jim Crow.* New York: Oxford University Press, 1955. The evolution of legal segregation in the South.

✦ Chapter 15 ✦

Black Southerners Challenge White Supremacy

Living in a society that largely sought to disregard their rights and to exclude them from its institutions and culture, by the late nineteenth century black Americans increasingly relied on each other and the people and institutions in their own communities to sustain themselves. As they had during Reconstruction, they organized and supported churches, schools, and colleges. They established businesses, formed labor unions, and went on strike. They founded their own hospitals. They expressed themselves in music by creating ragtime, jazz, and blues. At times they were allowed to participate with white people in organized sports such as professional boxing, baseball, and college football. More often, they formed their own athletic teams. African Americans refused to allow white supremacy to prevent them from creating a meaningful place for themselves in American society.

Social Darwinism

Pseudoscientific evidence and academic scholarship bolstered the conviction of many Americans that white people, especially those of English and Germanic descent—Anglo-Saxons—were culturally and racially superior to nonwhites and even other Europeans. Sociologists Herbert Spencer and William Graham Sumner drew on Charles Darwin's theory of evolution and concluded that life in modern industrial societies mirrored life in the animal kingdom. This theory, called Social Darwinism, held that through a process of natural selection, the strong would thrive, prosper, and reproduce while the weak would falter, fail, and die. Life was a struggle; only the fittest survived.

Social Darwinism applied to both individuals and "races." It justified great disparities in wealth, suggesting that such men as John D. Rockefeller and Andrew Carnegie were rich because they were "fit," whereas many European immigrants and most African Americans were poor and unlikely to succeed because they were "unfit." The same logic explained the strength and prosperity of the United States, Great Britain, and Germany compared to countries such as Spain and Italy and conveniently explained why African, Asian, and Latin American societies seemed backward and primitive. Americans and Europeans came to believe that they had a responsibility—a duty—to introduce the political, economic, and religious benefits and values of West-ern cultures to the "less advanced" and usually darker peoples of the globe.

Social Darwinism increasingly influenced most Protestant white Americans to be-lieve that people could be ranked from superior to inferior based on their race, na-tionality, and ethnicity. Black people were invariably ranked at the bottom of this hierarchy, and the eastern and southern European immigrants who were flooding the country only slightly above them. Black people were capable, so the reasoning went, of no more than a subordinate role in a complex and advanced society as it rushed into the twentieth century. And if their position was biologically ordained, why should soci-ety pay for their education?

Education and Schools

A black youngster who wanted an education in the late nineteenth century faced for-midable obstacles. Most black people were poor farmers who had few opportunities for an education and even fewer prospects for a career in business or one of the pro-fessions. It is a testimony to their perseverance that so many black people managed to acquire some education and free themselves from illiteracy.

Gaining even a rudimentary education was not easy. Rural schools for black chil-dren rarely operated for more than thirty weeks a year. Because of the demands of field work, most black youngsters could not attend school on a regular basis. Brothers and sisters sometimes alternated work and school with each other on a daily basis.

Schools often lacked plumbing, electricity, books, and teaching materials. Teach-ers were poorly paid and often poorly prepared. Septima Clark remembered her first teaching experience on Johns Island on the South Carolina coast in the early twenti-eth century.

> Here I was, a high-school graduate, eighteen years old, principal in a two-teacher school with 132 pupils ranging from beginners to eighth graders, with no teaching experience, a schoolhouse constructed of boards running up and down, with no slats on the cracks, and a fireplace at one end of the room that cooked the pupils immediately in front of it but al-lowed those in the rear to shiver and freeze on their uncomfortable, hard, back-breaking benches.

Segregated Schools

Though southern states could not afford to support even one first-rate public school system, each of them operated separate schools for black and white children (see Table 15–1). The South had almost no public black high schools. In 1915 in twenty-three southern cities with populations of more than 20,000, including Tampa, New Or-leans, Charleston, and Charlotte, there was not one black public high school. But these twenty-three cities had thirty-six high schools for white youngsters. In 1897 over the vehement protests of the black community, white school officials in Augusta, Geor-gia, transformed Ware High School, the black secondary school, into a black primary

Table 15–1
South Carolina's Black and White Public Schools, 1908–1909

Black Schools		White Schools
2,354	Public Schools	2,712
894	Men Teachers	933
1,802	Women Teachers	3,247
181,095	Total Pupils	153,807
123,481	Average Attendance	107,368
77	Pupils per School	55
63	Pupils per Teacher	35
14.7	Average Number of Weeks of School	25.2
$118.17	Average Yearly Salary for Men Teachers	$479.79
$91.45	Average Yearly Salary for Women Teachers	$249.13
$308,153.16	Total Expenditures	$1,590,732.51

School for most southern black students and teachers was a part-time activity. Because of the demands of agriculture, few rural students, black or white, attended school more than six months a year. Very few teachers were graduates of four-year college programs. The situation was better in urban communities and upper South schools, where the school year lasted longer and education was better financed. But all public schools were segregated in the South.

Source: Department of Education Annual Report, South Carolina, 1908–1909, pp. 935, 961.

school. The U. S. Supreme Court in 1899 in *Cumming v. Richmond County [Georgia] Board of Education* unanimously refused to accept the contention of black parents that the elimination of the black high school violated the "separate but equal" doctrine announced in the *Plessy v. Ferguson* case three years earlier. Augusta was left with two white high schools and none for black people.

Young black people who sought more than a primary education often had to travel to a black college or university that offered a high school program. For example, in 1911, at the age of 16, Benjamin Mays boarded a train and traveled one hundred miles to South Carolina State College and enrolled in the 7th grade. He graduated from high school there in 1916 at the age of 22 and then graduated from Maine's Bates College four years later.

In many communities, black people, with the assistance of churches and northern philanthropists, operated private academies and high schools, such as Georgia's Fort Valley High and Industrial School and Camden, South Carolina's, Mather Academy, to fill the void created by the lack of public schools. Typically those who attended came from the more prosperous families of the black community. In 1890, the number of black youngsters between the ages of fifteen and nineteen attending black public or private high schools in the South was 3,106. By 1910, that number had risen to 26,553.

The Hampton Model

Some black people and many white people regarded education for black youngsters as a pointless exercise. Benjamin Mays's father put little value in education. "My greatest opposition to going away to school was my father. When I knew that I had learned everything that I could in the one-room Brickhouse School and realized how little that was, my father felt that this was sufficient—that it was all I needed. . . . He was convinced that education went to one's head and made him a fool and dishonest." In 1911, South Carolina's governor Coleman Blease was even more blunt: "Instead of making an educated negro, you are ruining a good plow hand and making a half-trained fool."

Many of those who did value schooling were convinced that the most appropriate education for a black child was industrial or domestic training. Black youngsters, these people maintained, should learn skills they could teach others and use to make themselves productive members of the community.

Hampton Normal and Agricultural Institute was founded in 1868 in Virginia and was dominated for decades by Samuel Chapman Armstrong, a white missionary with strong paternalistic inclinations. Hampton trained legions of African Americans and Native Americans to teach skills and to embrace the importance of hard work, diligence, and Christian morality. Armstrong stressed learning trades, such as shoemaking, carpentry, tailoring, and sewing. Hampton placed little emphasis on critical or independent thinking. Students were taught to conform to middle-class values. Armstrong cautioned against black involvement in politics, and he acquiesced in Jim Crow racial practices.

Washington and the Tuskegee Model

Armstrong's prize student and Hampton's foremost graduate was Booker T. Washington, who became the nation's leading apostle of industrial training and one of the most remarkable men in American history. Washington was born a slave in western Virginia in 1856. His father was a white man whose identity is unknown. He was raised by his mother, Jane, in a tidy cabin of split logs on a small farm. As a child, he attended a local school where he learned to read and write.

Intensely ambitious, Washington set off for Hampton Institute in 1872. While there, he was much affected by Armstrong and his curriculum and method of instruction. He worked his way through school and taught for two years at Hampton after graduating. In 1881 he accepted an invitation to found a black college in Alabama—Tuskegee Institute. The result was an institution, which he forged almost single-handedly, that reflected his experience at Hampton and the influence of Armstrong.

From the day he arrived at Tuskegee until his death in 1915, Washington worked tirelessly to persuade black and white people that the surest way for black people to advance was by learning skills and demonstrating a willingness to do manual labor. Washington believed that if black people became prosperous small farmers, artisans, and

Booker T. Washington, looking regal in this portrait, was the most influential black leader in America by 1900. White business and political leaders were reassured by his message that black people themselves were responsible for their economic progress and that people of color should avoid a direct challenge to white supremacy. Although W. E. B. Du Bois appreciated Washington's commitment to the advancement of black people, he believed that more emphasis should be placed on developing an educated elite who would take the lead in solving the race problem. Washington was a Southerner who looked for practical solutions to the problems of everyday life, while Du Bois was a Northerner who stressed the need for intellectual advancement.
The Granger Collection

shopkeepers, they would earn the respect and acceptance of white Americans and eventually eradicate the race problem—all without unseemly protest and agitation.

Washington's message earned accolades and financing from white political leaders and philanthropists, who were more inclined to support the promotion of trades and skills among black people than an academic and liberal education. Disciples of Washington and graduates of Tuskegee fanned out across the South as industrial and agricultural educational training for black youngsters proliferated.

The Morrill Act, which Congress passed in 1862, entitled each state to the proceeds from the sale of federal land (most of it in the West) for establishing land-grant colleges to provide agricultural and mechanical training. However, southern states did not admit black students to their A&M (Agricultural and Mechanical) schools. A second Morrill Act in 1890 permitted states to establish and fund separate black land-grant colleges. By 1915, there were sixteen black land-grant colleges.

Most of the institutions were not actually colleges. Few of their students graduated with bachelor's degrees, and many of them were enrolled in primary and secondary programs. Virtually all the students at the black land-grant schools had to take courses in trades, agriculture, and domestic sciences. Most of the schools required students to do manual labor for which they were paid small sums. Students built and maintained the campuses, and they raised the food served in the school cafeteria. Some of the students were in the "normal" curriculum, which prepared them to teach at a time when most states did not require a college degree for a teaching certificate.

Critics of the Tuskegee Model

Not everyone shared Washington's stress on industrial and agricultural training for young black men and women to the near exclusion of the liberal arts. Washington's program, some critics charged, seemed to be designed to train black people for a subordinate role in American society. Black people, they worried, would continue to labor much as they had in slavery.

W. E. B. Du Bois, a Fisk- and Harvard-trained scholar, and AME Bishop Henry M. Turner believed that education involved intellectual growth and development. According to Du Bois, "The function of the Negro college, then, is clear, it must maintain standards of popular education, it must seek the social regeneration of the Negro, and it must help in the solution of problems of race contact and cooperation. And finally, beyond all this, it must develop men."

Many of the private black colleges resisted the emphasis on agricultural and mechanical training, promoted the liberal arts, and taught Latin, Greek, mathematics, and natural sciences. Henry L. Morehouse of the American Baptist Home Missionary Society explained that the purpose of education was to develop strong minds. He believed that gifted intellectuals—a "talented tenth" as he characterized them in 1896—could lead people forward. Du Bois likewise stressed the need for the best educated 10 percent of the black population to promote progress and to advance the race.

In fairness to Washington, he did not deny the importance of a liberal arts education, but he also believed that industry was the foundation to progress:

> On such a foundation as this will grow habits of thrift, a love of work, economy, ownership of property, bank accounts. Out of it in the future will grow practical education, professional education, and positions of public responsibility. Out of it will grow moral and religious strength. Out of it will grow wealth from which alone can come leisure and the opportunity for the enjoyment of literature and the fine arts.

Ultimately, however, Washington was wrong to believe that education for black people that focused on economic progress would earn the respect of most white Americans. As Du Bois explained, most white people preferred ignorant and unsuccessful black people to educated and prosperous ones:

> If my own city of Atlanta had offered it to-day the choice between 500 Negro college graduates—forceful, busy, ambitious men of property and self-respect—and 500 black cringing vagrants and criminals, the popular vote in favor of the criminals would be simply overwhelming. Why? Because they want Negro crime? No, not that they fear Negro crime less, but that they fear Negro ambition and success more. They can deal with crime by chain-gang and lynch law, or at least they think they can, but the South can conceive neither machinery nor place for the educated, self-reliant, self-assertive black man.

As the next chapter will discuss, what began as a disagreement over the value of practical education would become a passionate debate among Washington, Du Bois, and others over the most effective strategy—accommodation or confrontation—for overcoming Jim Crow and white supremacy.

Church and Religion

In a world in which white people dominated the lives of black people, the church was the most important institution—after the family—that African Americans controlled for themselves. After the Civil War, black people organized their own churches and religious denominations, which thrived as sources of spiritual comfort and centers of social activity. Black clergymen were often the most influential members of the black community.

In 1890 the South had more black Baptists than all other denominations combined. Baptist congregations were more independent and under less supervision by church hierarchy than other denominations. Bishops, for example, in the African Methodist Episcopal Zion church and the African Methodist Episcopal (AME) church exercised considerable authority over congregations as did Methodist and Presbyterian leaders. Many black people (and many southern white people as well) preferred the autonomy of the Baptist churches (Figure 15–1).

But whatever the denomination, the church was integral to the lives of most black people. It fulfilled spiritual needs through sermons and music. It gave black people the opportunity, free from white interference, to plan, organize, and lead. It was especially a sanctuary for black women, who immersed themselves in church activities. Though church members usually had little money to spare, they helped the sick, the bereaved, and people displaced by fires and natural disasters. Black congregations also helped thousands of youngsters attend school and college.

The church service itself was the most important aspect of religious life for most black congregations. Parishioners were expected to participate in the service and not

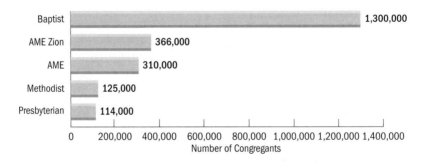

FIGURE 15–1   Church Affiliation among Southern Black People: 1890   The vast majority of black Southerners belonged to Baptist, Methodist, and Presbyterian congregations in the late nineteenth century, though there were about fifteen thousand black Episcopalians and perhaps two hundred thousand Roman Catholics.

Source: Edward L. Ayers, *The Promise of the New South*, pp. 160–161.

merely listen quietly to the sermon. They testified, shouted, laughed and cried, and sometimes fainted. Choirs provided joyful music and solemn songs.

Most congregations did not want scholarly sermons or theologically sound addresses. When Frederick Jones, a well-dressed new black minister in North Carolina, offered a deliberate message brimming with rationality, he was rebuked by a senior member of the congregation. "Dese fellers comes out heah wid dere starched shirts, and dey' beaver hats, and dere kid gloves, but dey don't know nuffin b[o]ut 'ligion."

Many black ministers had little or no education. Benjamin E. Mays's father told him that the clergy did not need an education. "God called men to preach; and when He called them, He would tell them what to say!" Poorly prepared and unqualified clergymen who relied on ungrammatical and rhetorical appeals disturbed some black leaders. In 1890 Booker T. Washington claimed that "three-fourths of the Baptist ministers and two-thirds of the Methodists are unfit, either mentally or morally, or both, to preach the Gospel to any one or to attempt to lead any one." W. E. B. Du Bois wanted black churches free of "the noisy and unclean leaders of the thoughtless mob" and the clergy replaced by thoughtful "apostles of service and sacrifice." But a black Alabama farmer observed that solemn and erudite preachers would not survive: "You let a man preach de true Gospel and he won't git many nickels in his pocket; but if he hollers and jumps he gits all the nickels he can hold and chickens besides."

Black women sometimes led congregations. Nannie Helen Burroughs established Women's Day in Baptist churches. Women delivered sermons and guided the parishioners. But Burroughs complained that Women's Day quickly became more an occasion to raise money than to raise women.

For many black people, the emotional involvement and enthusiastic participation in church services were an escape from their oppressive daily lives. Growing up in rural Greenwood County, South Carolina, Benjamin E. Mays admitted that his Baptist preacher, James F. Marshall, who barely had a fifth-grade education, "emphasized the joys of heaven and the damnation of hell" and that the "trials and tribulations of the world would all be over when one got to heaven." But Mays understood the need for such messages to assuage the impact of white supremacy. "Beaten down at every turn by the white man, as they were, Negroes could perhaps not have survived without this kind of religion."

Black clergymen like Marshall refused to challenge white supremacy. Even veiled comments might invite retaliation or even lynching. When a visiting minister began to criticize white people to Marshall's congregation, Marshall immediately stopped him. Despite the reluctance of many black clergymen to advocate improvement in race relations, many white people still viewed black religious gatherings as a threat. Black churches were burned and black ministers assaulted and killed with tragic regularity in the late-nineteenth-century South.

Black clergymen, like their white counterparts, often stressed middle-class values to their congregations while suggesting that many black people found themselves in shameful situations because of their sinful ways. Black people who had acquired sinful reputations sometimes received funeral sermons that consigned them to eternal damnation in a fiery hell.

Not all black religious leaders avoided discussing white supremacy. Some clergymen insisted that black people demand their rights. AME Bishop Henry M. Turner persistently spoke out on racial matters. In 1883 after the U.S. Supreme Court declared the 1875 Civil Rights Act unconstitutional, Turner called the Constitution "a dirty rag, a cheat, a libel and ought to be spit upon by every Negro in the land."

The Holiness Movement and the Pentecostal Church

Not all black people belonged to mainline denominations. The Holiness movement and the emergence of Pentecostal churches affected Methodist and Baptist congregations. Partly in reaction to the elite domination and stiff authority of white Methodism, the Holiness movement gained a foothold among white people and then spilled over among black Southerners. Holiness churches ordained women such as Neely Terry to lead them. Holiness clergy preached that sanctification allowed a Christian to receive a "second blessing" and to feel the "perfect love of Christ." Believers thus achieved an emotional reaffirmation and a new state of grace.

The Church of God in Christ (COGIC) became the leading black Holiness church. After successful revivals in Mississippi and Memphis, two black former Baptists—Charles Harrison Mason and C. P. Jones—founded COGIC in 1907. However, Mason was expelled after reporting that "a flame touched [his] tongue," and his "language changed." He had spoken in tongues. Mason then organized the Pentecostal General Assembly of the Church of God in Christ, and he assigned several black men to serve as bishops in Mississippi, Arkansas, Texas, Missouri, and California. In 1911 Mason appointed Lizzee Woods Roberson to lead the Woman's Department, which she transformed into a financial powerhouse for COGIC.

In the meantime, Charles Fox Parham, a dynamic white minister, had founded the Pentecostal church in the early twentieth entury in the Houston-Galveston area of Texas. William J. Seymour, who was born a slave in Louisiana, played a key role in the development of the church. After hearing black people speak in tongues in Houston, he went to Los Angeles where he and others also began to speak in tongues. There he founded the highly evangelistic church that became the Pentecostal church. It grew rapidly.

Charles Harrison Mason joined the Pentecostal movement, and under his leadership the Reorganized Church of God in Christ spread across the South. Though there were tensions between black and white believers, the Pentecostal church was the only movement of any significance that crossed the racial divide in early twentieth-century America.

Roman Catholics and Episcopalians

While most African Americans belonged to one of the Baptist or Methodist churches (Booker T. Washington observed that "If a black man is anything but a Baptist or Methodist, someone has been tampering with his religion"), some black people belonged to other denominations.

As many as 200,000 African Americans were Roman Catholic in 1890. They were rarely fully accepted by the church or white Catholics. They were segregated in separate churches with separate parish schools in the South. Augustus Tolton was the first

African-American Roman Catholic priest. Because no American seminary would accept him, he was educated and ordained in 1886 in Rome. For a time, he presided over a parish in Quincy, Illinois, made up mainly of Irish and German Catholics.

Mother Mathilda Beasley came from a prominent free black family in Savannah. Her efforts to establish a community of Franciscan sisters in rural Georgia ultimately failed. In New Orleans, where there were sizable numbers of black Catholics of French and Spanish descent, the Sisters of the Blessed Sacrament established a black high school in 1915 that became Xavier University in 1925.

Fairly or unfairly, most African Americans identified black Episcopalians with wealth and privilege. Many of those Episcopalians traced their heritage to free black families before the Civil War. By 1903 there were approximately 15,000 members of black Episcopal parishes in Richmond, Raleigh, Charleston, and other urban communities in the North and South.

African Americans in the Army and Navy

The Buffalo Soldiers

After the Civil War, the U.S. Army was reduced to fewer than 30,000 troops. Congressional Democrats tried to eliminate black soldiers and their regiments from this reduced force, but Radical Republicans kept the military open to black men. The Army Reorganization Act of 1869 maintained four all-black regiments: the 9th and 10th Cavalry Regiments and the 24th and 25th Infantry Regiments. These four regiments spent most of the next three decades on the western frontier fighting the Plains Indians. Nearly 12,500 black men served during the late nineteenth century in these segregated units commanded—as black troops had been during the Civil War—by white officers, many of whom were Southerners who did not hold black men in high regard.

Military service in the West was wretched for all troops and worse for black soldiers. Too often officers considered black troops lazy, undisciplined, and cowardly. Black regiments were assigned mainly to the New Mexico and Arizona territories and to Texas because the Army thought that black people tolerated heat better than white people.

Black troops faced more than adverse weather. The Army routinely provided them inferior food and inadequate housing. While white soldiers received dried apples and peaches, canned tomatoes, onions, and potatoes, black troops were given foul beef, bad bread, and canned peas unfit for human consumption. In 1867 white troops at Fort Leavenworth in Kansas lived in barracks while black troops were forced to sleep in tents on wet ground. Black regiments were allotted used weapons and equipment. The Army sent its worst horses—often old and lame—to the black cavalry.

Boredom, tedious duty, and loneliness marked army life in the West. Months might pass without combat. Commanders constantly had to deal with desertion and alcoholism. Black soldiers were much less likely to desert or turn to drink than were white troops. For example, in 1877, eighteen men deserted from the all-black 10th Regiment, while 184 white soldiers deserted from the all-white 4th Regiment. Black troops realized that army life compared favorably to the civilian world, which held few opportunities for them. Army food was poor, but the private's pay of $13 per month was regular. Moreover, black troops developed pride in themselves as professional soldiers.

The Plains Indians who resisted U.S. forces were so impressed with their black adversaries that they called them "buffalo soldiers." Indians associated the hair of black men with the shaggy coat of the buffalo—a sacred animal. Black troops considered it a term of respect and began to use it themselves.

It was ironic that white military authorities would employ black men to subdue red people. Most black soldiers, however, had no qualms about fighting Indians, protecting white settlers, or apprehending bandits and cattle rustlers. From the late 1860s to the 1890s, the four black regiments repeatedly engaged hostile Indians. In September 1867, 700 Cheyenne attacked fifty U.S. Army scouts in eastern Colorado. The scouts held out until the 10th Cavalry rescued them. For more than 12 months in 1879 and 1880, the 9th and 10th Cavalry fought the Apaches under Chief Victorio in New Mexico and Texas in a campaign of raid and counterraid before Victorio fled to Mexico where he was killed by the Mexican Army. But the 9th and 10th Cavalry deserve most of the credit for Victorio's defeat with their dogged pursuit of the Apaches over hundreds of miles of rugged terrain.

In late 1890, military units including the 9th Cavalry were sent to the Pine Ridge Reservation in South Dakota where Sioux Indians were holding a religious ceremony known as the Ghost Dance. Some Indians—out of desperation and yearning for the past—believed that the Ghost Dance would bring both their ancestors and the almost extinct buffalo back to the Great Plains. Then white people would vanish, and Indian life would be restored to what it had been decades earlier. But white authorities considered the Ghost Dance a dangerous act of defiance.

On December 29, the 7th Cavalry attempted to disarm a band of Sioux at Wounded Knee on the Pine Ridge Reservation. Shooting erupted, and 146 Indians and twenty-six soldiers were killed. The 9th Cavalry rode 108 miles through a blizzard to come to the aid of the 7th Cavalry.

Civilian Hostility to Black Soldiers

Despite the gallant performance of the buffalo soldiers, civilians frequently treated them with hostility. One of the worst examples of hostility to black troops, the so-called Brownsville Affair, occurred in Texas. In 1906 the 1st Battalion of the 25th Infantry was transferred from Nebraska to Fort Brown in Brownsville, Texas, along the Rio Grande where the black soldiers immediately encountered discrimination from both white people and Mexicans. They were not permitted in public parks, and white businesses refused to serve them. Civilians attacked individual black soldiers.

Shortly after midnight on August 14, shooting erupted in Brownsville. About 150 shots were fired, and a policeman and a resident were injured. Black troops were blamed for the violence when clips and cartridges from the Army's Springfield rifles were found in the street. Two military investigations concluded that black soldiers did the shooting, but no one would confess or name the alleged perpetrators.

With no hearing or trial, President Theodore Roosevelt dismissed three companies of black men—167 soldiers—from the Army. They were barred from rejoining the military and from government employment, and were denied veterans' pensions or benefits. The black community, which had supported Roosevelt, reacted angrily. Booker T. Washington, a Roosevelt supporter, privately wrote, "There is no law, human or divine, which justifies the punishment of an innocent man." Washington added, "I have the strongest faith in the President's honesty of intention, high mindedness of purpose, sincere unselfishness and courage, but I regret for all these reasons all the more that this thing has occurred."

Republican Senator James B. Foraker of Ohio later led a Senate investigation that upheld Roosevelt's dismissals. But Foraker, a strong opponent of Roosevelt, questioned the guilt of the black men. The clips and cartridges that served as evidence were apparently planted. After Roosevelt left office in 1909, the War Department reinstated fourteen of the soldiers. In 1972, the Justice Department posthumously awarded the black soldiers honorable discharges. The only survivor of the Brownsville affair—Dorsie Willis—received $25,000 from Congress and the right to treatment at veteran's facilities.

The Navy

Naval service was even more unappealing than life in the Army. In the late nineteenth century, as the Navy made the transition from timber and sail to steam and steel, approximately one sailor in ten was a black man. Although the Navy's ships were "integrated" in that black and white sailors served on them together, white sailors would not eat or bunk with black sailors or take orders from them. Increasingly, and to enforce a de facto shipboard segregation, black sailors were restricted to stoking boilers in the bowels of naval vessels and to cooking and serving food to white sailors.

Although several black men enrolled as midshipmen at the Naval Academy in the 1870s, they faced social ostracism and none of them graduated. Not until 1949 did a black man graduate from the academy.

Black Cowboys

Black men before, during, and after the Civil War were familiar with horses and mules. As slaves, they tended and cared for animals. Some black men served with the 9th and 10th U.S. Cavalry Regiments and gained experience with horses. It is no wonder that perhaps 5,000 black men rode herd on cattle in the late nineteenth and early twentieth centuries.

Managing cattle was monotonous and dirty work. Yet it required skill as a rider to manage hundreds of ornery and stinking animals. Cowboys had to tolerate weather that ranged from incredibly hot to bitter cold. They had to eat unappetizing food for weeks at a time, sleep on the ground, and go days with little human companionship.

The Spanish-American War

With the western frontier subdued by 1890, many Americans, but by no means all, favored the extension of U.S. political, economic, and military authority to Latin America and the Pacific. European nations had already carved out extensive colonies in

Africa and Asia. In 1893 the U.S. Navy and American businessmen toppled the monarchy in Hawaii, and the United States annexed the islands in 1898.

The same year, the United States went to war to liberate Cuba from Spanish control. As in the Civil War, black men enlisted, fought, and died. Twenty-two black sailors were among the 266 men who died when the battleship U.S.S. *Maine* blew up in Havana harbor, the event that helped trigger the war. Many black Americans were convinced, as they had been in previous wars, that the willingness of black people to support the war against Spain would impress white Americans sufficiently to reduce or even eliminate white hostility. E. E. Cooper, editor of the Washington *Colored American,* declared that the war would bring black people and white people together in "an era of good feeling the country over and cement the races into a more compact brotherhood through perfect unity of purpose and patriotic affinity." The war, he asserted, would help white Americans "unloose themselves from the bondage of race prejudice."

Many Americans, however, questioned the American cause. Some black people saw the war as an effort to extend American racial practices, including Jim Crow, beyond U.S. borders. The Reverend George W. Prioleau, chaplain of the Ninth Cavalry, wondered why black Americans supported what he considered a hypocritical war:

> Talk about fighting and freeing poor Cuba and of Spain's brutality. . . . Is America any better than Spain? Has she not subjects in her very midst who are murdered daily without a trial of judge or jury? Has she not subjects in her own borders whose children are half-fed and half-clothed, because their father's skin is black. . . . Yet the Negro is loyal to his country's flag.

Whether or not they harbored doubts, black men by the thousands served in the Spanish-American War and in the Philippine Insurrection that followed it. Shortly before war was declared, the Army ordered its four black regiments of regular troops transferred from their western posts to Florida to prepare for combat in Cuba. President William McKinley also appealed for volunteers. The War Department designated four of the black volunteer units "immune regiments" because it believed that black men would tolerate the heat and humidity of Cuba better than white troops and that black people were immune or at least less susceptible to yellow fever, which was endemic to Cuba. (Yellow fever was carried by mosquitoes, but this was unknown in 1898. Most people believed that the disease was caused by the tropical Caribbean climate.)

State militia (national guard) units were also called into federal service, and several states, including Alabama, Ohio, Massachusetts, Illinois, Kansas, Virginia, Indiana, and North Carolina, sent all-black militias, as well as white units. But Georgia's governor refused to permit that state's black militia to serve, and New York would not permit black men to enlist in its militia. The states typically followed the federal example and kept black men confined to all-black units commanded by white officers, but there were exceptions.

The buffalo soldiers of the 9th and 10th Cavalry and the 24th and 25th Infantry remained under the leadership of white officers. But the men of several volunteer units insisted that they be led by black officers: "No officers, no fight." So for the first time in American military history, black men commanded all-black units: the 8th Illinois, the

23rd Kansas, and the 3rd North Carolina. Mindful that many people doubted the ability of black men to lead, the colonel of the 8th Illinois cautioned his men, "If we fail, the whole race will have to shoulder the burden." The War Department also permitted black men to serve as lieutenants with other black volunteer units, but all higher ranking officers were white men. Charles Young, a black graduate of West Point who was serving as a military science instructor at Wilberforce University in Ohio, was given command of Ohio's 9th Battalion, and he served with distinction and was promoted from captain to colonel.

As black and white troops assembled in Georgia and Florida before departing for Cuba, black men soon realized that a U.S. uniform did not lessen white racial prejudice. White civilians in Georgia killed four black men of the 3rd North Carolina. All-white juries acquitted those who were charged with the murders. After the white proprietor of a drug store in Lakeland, Florida, refused to serve a black soldier at the soda fountain, a mob of black troops gathered. The proprietor was pistol whipped, and another white man was killed by a stray bullet before the troops were disarmed. In Tampa, where the troops were embarking for Cuba, a bloody riot broke out after drunken white soldiers decided to shoot at a black child for target practice. It is not surprising that when the men of the all-black 3rd Alabama adopted an injured crow as the unit mascot, they named it Jim.

Most of the black units never saw combat. White military authorities considered black men unreliable and inadequately trained for combat. Black volunteer units stayed behind in Florida when white units embarked for Cuba. However, the four regiments of regular black troops, the buffalo soldiers, did go to Cuba, where four black American privates earned the Congressional Medal of Honor.

Black and white troops were best remembered for their role in the assault on San Juan and Kettle Hills overlooking the key Cuban port of Santiago in eastern Cuba. Santiago was the main Spanish naval base in Cuba and its capture would break Spain's hold over the island. In this assault, black soldiers from the 24th Infantry and the 9th and the 10th Cavalry Regiments fought alongside white troops including Theodore Roosevelt's volunteer unit, the Rough Riders. In the fiercest fighting of the war, black and white men were thrown together as they encountered withering Spanish fire. Though for a time the outcome was in doubt, they took the high ground overlooking Santiago harbor. White soldiers praised the performance of the black troops. One commented: "I am not a negro lover. My father fought with Mosby's Rangers [in the Confederate Army] and I was born in the South, but the negroes saved that fight." In his campaign for vice president in 1900, Theodore Roosevelt stated that black men saved his life during the battle. Later, however, Roosevelt reversed himself and accused several black men of cowardice.

As hostilities concluded, men of the 24th Infantry agreed to work in yellow fever hospitals after white regiments refused the duty. About half the black soldiers—some 471 men—contracted yellow fever. Other black troops arrived in Cuba after the war to serve garrison duty. The 8th Illinois and the 23rd Kansas built roads, bridges, schools, and hospitals. The black men were especially pleased at the lack of discrimination and absence of Jim Crow in Cuba. Other black troops from the 6th Massachusetts joined in the invasion of Puerto Rico as the United States took that island from Spain.

The Philippine Insurrection

With the resounding victory in the Spanish-American War, many Americans decided that their nation had an obligation to uplift those less fortunate peoples who had been part of the Spanish Empire. Thus, President William McKinley and American diplomats insisted that the United States acquire Guam, Puerto Rico, and the Philippines from Spain in the treaty that ended the war in December 1898. The Filipinos, however, fully expected the American government to support their independence and were infuriated to learn that the United States intended to annex the Philippines. Under Emilio Aguinaldo, they switched from fighting the Spanish to fighting the occupying U.S. forces.

Many black and white Americans denounced the U.S. effort to take the Philippines. AME Bishop Henry Turner termed it an "unholy war of conquest," and Booker T. Washington believed that the Filipinos "should be given an opportunity to govern themselves."

Nonetheless black men in the military served throughout the campaign in the Pacific islands. Through propaganda, the Filipino rebels attempted to convince black troops to abandon the cause. Posters reminded "The Colored American Soldier" of injustice and lynching in the United States. White troops did not help by calling Filipinos "niggers." Though many black soldiers had reservations about the fighting, they remained loyal. By the time the conflict ended with an American victory in 1902, only five black men had deserted. David Fagen of the 24th Infantry joined Filipino forces and became an officer, fighting American troops for two years before he was killed. Two black men from the 9th Cavalry were executed for desertion, while fifteen white soldiers who deserted had their death sentences commuted.

Though black men had served with distinction as professional soldiers for forty years after the Civil War—on the frontier, in Cuba, and in the Philippines—the Army little valued their achievements and sacrifice, as the Brownsville Affair showed. White leaders persistently relied on passions and prejudices over evidence of achievement. Time and again, these circumstances dashed the hopes of those black civilians and soldiers who believed that the performance of black troops would challenge white supremacy and demonstrate that black citizens had earned the same rights and opportunities as other Americans.

Black Businesspeople and Entrepreneurs

Well-educated black men and women stood no chance of gaining employment with any major business or industrial corporation at the turn of the century. White males not only monopolized management and supervisory positions, but also occupied nearly every job that did not involve manual labor. In 1899 black novelist Sutton E. Griggs described the frustrations that an educated black man encountered:

> He possessed a first class college education, but that was all. He knew no trade nor was he equipped to enter any of the professions. . . . He would have made an excellent drummer,

salesman, clerk, cashier, government official (county, city, state, or national), telegraph operator, conductor, or anything of such a nature. But the color of his skin shut the doors so tight that he could not even peep in. . . . It is true that such positions as street laborer, hod carrier, cart driver, factory hand, railroad hand were open to him; but such menial tasks were uncongenial to a man of his education and polish.

While white supremacy and the proliferation of Jim Crow restricted opportunities for educated black people, those same limitations enabled enterprising black men and women to open and operate businesses that served black clientele. By the early twentieth century, black Americans had established banks, newspapers, insurance companies, retail businesses, barbershops, beauty salons, and funeral parlors. Virtually every black community had its own small businesses and entrepreneurs.

Some black men and women established substantial businesses. In Atlanta, Union Army veteran Alexander Hamilton was a successful building contractor. He supervised construction of the Good Samaritan Building, oversaw the erection of buildings on the Morris Brown College campus, and built many of the impressive houses on Peachtree Street.

Alonzo Herndon was a former slave who also achieved financial success in Atlanta. He operated a fashionable barbershop on Peachtree Street that served well-to-do white men. Herndon expanded and opened two other shops, eventually employing seventy-five men. He also founded the Atlanta Life Insurance Company, the largest black stock company in the world.

In Montgomery, Alabama, H. A. Loveless, a former slave, became a butcher and then diversified by opening an undertaking establishment and operating a hack and dray company. By 1900, Loveless also ran a coal and wood yard and sold real estate.

In Richmond, Virginia, Maggie Lena Walker—the secretary–treasurer of the Independent Order of St. Luke, a mutual benefit society, and a founder of the St. Luke's Penny Savings Bank—became the wealthiest black woman in America. Also in Richmond, former slave John Dabney owned an exclusive catering business that served wealthy white Virginians. He catered two state dinners for President Grover Cleveland. He used his earnings to purchase several houses and to invest in real estate.

Madam C. J. Walker may have been the most successful black entrepreneur of them all. Born Sarah Breedlove in 1867 on a Louisiana cotton plantation, she married at age fourteen and was a widowed single parent by age twenty. In 1905 with $1.50, she developed a formula to nourish and enrich the hair of black women. She insisted that it was not a process to straighten hair.

She sold the product door-to-door in Denver but could not keep up with the demand. The business became a thriving enterprise that employed hundreds of black women. In the meantime, she married Charles Joseph Walker and took his name and the title Madam. As she accumulated wealth, she shared it generously with Bethune Cookman College, Tuskegee Institute, and the NAACP. She was a major contributor to the NAACP's antilynching campaign. When she died of a stroke at age fifty-one in 1919, she was reportedly a millionaire.

Despite such successes, most black people who went into business had difficulty surviving, and many failed. Too often they depended on black customers who were themselves poor. White-owned banks were unlikely to provide credit to aspiring black businesspeople. And even the wealthiest black entrepreneurs did not come close to possessing the wealth the richest white Americans accumulated.

African Americans and Labor

Thousands of black Southerners worked in factories, mills, and mines. Though most textile mills refused to hire black people except for janitorial duties, many black laborers toiled in tobacco and cigarmaking facilities, flour mills, coal mines, sawmills, turpentine camps, and on railroads. Black women worked for white families as cooks, maids, and laundresses. Black workers usually were paid less than white men employed in the same capacity. Conversely, white working people frequently complained that they were not hired because employers retained black workers who worked for less pay. In 1904 in Georgia white railroad firemen went on strike in an unsuccessful attempt to compel railroad operators to dismiss black firemen. Antagonism between black and white laborers was persistent.

Unions

When white workers formed labor unions in the late nineteenth century, they usually excluded black workers. The Knights of Labor, however, founded in 1869, was open to all workers (except whiskey salesmen, lawyers, and bankers), and by the mid-1880s counted 50,000 women and 70,000 black workers among its nearly 750,000 members. But by the 1890s, after unsuccessful strikes and a deadly riot in Chicago, the Knights had lost influence to a new organization, the American Federation of Labor (AFL). Founded in 1886, the AFL was ostensibly open to all skilled workers, but most of its local craft unions barred women and black tradesmen. In contrast, the United Mine Workers (UMW), formed in 1890, encouraged black coal miners to join the union

Though most southern black people worked long hours in cotton fields, there were thousands who toiled in factories, mills, and mines. Here black women stem tobacco in a Virginia factory under the supervision of a white man.

Cook Collection Valentine Museum/Richmond History Center

rather than serve as strikebreakers. By 1900 approximately 20,000 of the 91,000 members of the UMW were black men. The Industrial Workers of the World (IWW), a revolutionary labor organization founded in 1905, brought black and white laborers together in, among other places, the Brotherhood of Timber Workers in the Piney Woods of east Texas.

In 1869 a Baltimore ship caulker, Isaac Myers, organized the National Colored Labor Union, which lasted for seven years. It discouraged strikes and encouraged its members to work hard and be thrifty. It lost whatever effectiveness it had when it was largely taken over by Republican leaders during Reconstruction.

Strikes

During the late nineteenth and early twentieth centuries, most strikes failed because owners could rely on strikebreakers and the police or national guard to bring the strikes to an often violent end. For a time, black shipyard workers in southern ports did achieve some success. Black stevedores who loaded and unloaded ships endured oppressive conditions and long hours for low pay. They periodically went on strike in Charleston, Savannah, and New Orleans. The Longshoremen's Protective Union in Charleston won several strikes in the 1870s. In Nashville in 1871 black dockyard workers went on strike, demanding twenty cents an hour. Steamboat owners broke the strike by hiring state convicts for fifteen cents an hour.

Black and white laborers who toiled in the Louisiana sugarcane fields earned an average of $13 a week in the 1880s. They were paid in scrip—not cash—that was redeemable only in stores the planters owned where prices were exorbitant. Workers lived in 12′ × 15′ cabins that they rented from the planters. In some ways, it was worse than slave labor.

Though the state militia had broken previous strikes, 9,000 black and 1,000 white workers responded to a call for a new strike in 1887 by organizers from the Knights of Labor. They quit the sugar fields in four parishes (as Louisiana counties are called) to demand more pay. The strike was peaceful, but planters convinced the governor to send in the militia. The troops fired into a crowd at Pattersonville and killed four people. The next day local officials killed several strikers who had been taken prisoner. In the town of Thibodaux, "prominent citizens" organized and armed themselves and had martial law declared. More than thirty-five unarmed black people, including women and children, were killed in their homes and churches. Two black strike leaders were lynched. The strike was broken.

Black washerwomen went on strike in Atlanta in 1881. The women, who did laundry for white families, refused to do any more until they were guaranteed $1 per twelve pounds of laundry. The strike was well organized through black churches, and it spread to cooks and domestics. A strike committee used persuasion and intimidation to ensure support. Some three thousand black people joined the strike. White families went two weeks without clean clothes. However, Atlanta's white community broke the strike. Police arrested strike leaders for disorderly conduct. Several black women were fined from $5 to $20. The city council threatened to require each member of the Washer Women's Association of Atlanta to purchase a city business license for $25. Though the strike gradually ended without having achieved its goal, it did demonstrate that poor black women could organize effectively.

Black Professionals

Like business and labor, the medical and legal professions were strictly segregated. Most black physicians, nurses, and lawyers attended all-black professional schools in the late nineteenth century. Black patients were either excluded from white hospitals or confined to all-black wards. Black physicians were denied staff privileges at white hospitals. Thus, black people in many communities formed their own hospitals. Most were small facilities with fifty or fewer beds.

In 1891 Dr. Daniel Hale Williams established Provident Hospital and Training Institute in Chicago, the first black hospital operated solely by African Americans. In 1894 the Freedmen's Hospital was organized in Washington, D.C., and it later affiliated with Howard University. Frederick Douglass Memorial Hospital and Training School was founded in Philadelphia in 1895. Dr. Alonzo McClennan in cooperation with several other black physicians established the Hospital and Training School for Nurses in Charleston, South Carolina, in 1897.

By 1890 there were 909 black (most of whom were male) physicians practicing in the United States. They served a black population of seven and a half million people. Barred from membership in the American Medical Association, black doctors organized the National Medical Association in Atlanta in 1895.

In 1910 in a report issued by the Carnegie Foundation for the Advancement of Teaching, Abraham Flexner recommended improving medical education in the United States by eliminating weaker medical schools. He suggested raising admission standards and expanding laboratory and clinical training in the stronger schools. As a result of the implementation of these recommendations, sixty of 155 white medical schools closed, and among black medical schools, only Howard and Meharry survived. By 1920 there were 3,885 black physicians. Many had completed medical school before the Flexner report was compiled.

The number of black women physicians was actually declining. In 1890 there were ninety black women practicing medicine, and by 1920 there were sixty-five. The number of medical schools had decreased, and most black and white men considered medicine an inappropriate profession for women. But black women also had to contend with the opposition of white women. Isabella Vandervall was a 1915 graduate of New York Medical College and Hospital who was accepted for an internship at the Hospital for Women and Children in Syracuse. When she appeared in person, however, the hospital's female administrator rejected Vandervall, ". . . we can't have you here! You are colored!"

Nursing was another matter. By 1920 there were thirty-six black nurse training schools and 2,150 white nursing schools. White nurses resented the competition from black nurses for positions as private duty nurses. And the black physicians who ran nurse training schools exploited their students by hiring them out, as part of their training, for private duty work but requiring them to relinquish their pay to the schools. Moreover, many people—black and white—regarded black nurses more as domestics than as trained professionals. Unlike white nurses, for example, black nurses were usually addressed by their first names. To confront such obstacles, fifty-two black nurses met in New York City in 1908 and formed the National Association of Colored Graduate Nurses (NACGN). By 1920, the NACGN had five hundred members.

Black physicians and nurses struggled to provide medical care to people who were often desperately ill and sought treatment only as a last resort. Disease and sickness flourished among people who were ill nourished, poorly clad, and inadequately housed. Tuberculosis, pneumonia, pellagra, hookworm, and syphilis afflicted many poor black people—as they also did poor white people. Bessie Hawes, a 1918 graduate of Tuskegee Institute's Nurse Training program, described the kind of situation she faced in rural Alabama:

> A colored family of ten were in bed and dying for the want of attention. No one would come near. I was glad of the opportunity. As I entered the little country cabin, I found the mother in bed. Three children were buried the week before. The father and the remainder of the family were running a temperature of 102–104. Some had influenza, others had pneumonia. No relatives or friends would come near. I saw at a glance I had work to do. I rolled up my sleeves and killed chickens and began to cook. . . . I milked the cow, gave medicine, and did everything I could to help conditions. I worked day and night trying to save them for seven days. I had no place to sleep. In the meantime the oldest daughter had a miscarriage and I delivered her without the aid of any physicians. . . . I only wished that I could have reached them earlier and been able to have done something for the poor mother.

Unlike black physicians and nurses, who were excluded from white hospitals, black lawyers were permitted to practice in what was essentially a white male court system. But white judges and attorneys did not welcome them. Rather than create additional problems for themselves, black defendants and plaintiffs often retained white lawyers in the hope that white legal counsel might improve their chances of receiving justice. As a result, many black attorneys had a hard time making a living from the practice of law.

The American Bar Association (ABA) would not admit black attorneys to membership. Attorney William H. Lewis, a graduate of Amherst College and the Harvard Law School who was appointed an assistant U.S. attorney general by President William Howard Taft in 1911, was expelled by the ABA in 1912 when its leaders discovered he was black. The leaders defended his expulsion by claiming that the association was mainly a social organization. In 1925, black lawyers—led by Howard Law School graduate George H. Woodson—organized the National Bar Association. In 1910 the United States had about 800 black lawyers.

Very few black women were lawyers. Charlotte Ray was the first. In 1900 there were ten black women practicing law. Lutie A. Lytle, who graduated from Central Tennessee Law School in 1879 later returned to that black institution and became the first black woman to be a law professor in the United States.

Music

In the half-century after the Civil War, music created and performed by black people evolved into the uniquely American art forms of ragtime, jazz, and blues. The roots of these extraordinary musical innovations are obscure. Some late-nineteenth-century music can be traced to African musical forms and rhythms. One source is slave work songs; another is the spirituals of the slavery era.

Traveling groups of black men, some of them ex-slaves, put on minstrel shows that featured "coon songs" after the Civil War. Many black Americans resented these popular shows as caricatures of black behavior. At least 600 "coon songs" that attracted a predominantly white audience were published by 1900 including "All Coons Look Alike to Me," "Mammy's Little Pickaninny," and "My Coal Black Lady."

Most black people did not perform in or enjoy the demeaning minstrel shows. They had other forms of musical entertainment. "The Civil Rights Juba" published in 1874, was a precursor to ragtime. In 1871 the Fisk University Jubilee Singers began the first of many fund-raising concert tours that entertained black and white audiences in the United States and Europe for years thereafter with slave songs and spirituals. Other black colleges and universities also sent choirs and singers on similar trips.

Ragtime

Ragtime, which emerged in the 1890s, was composed music, written down for performance on the piano. Ragtime pieces were not accompanied by lyrics and were not meant to be sung. The creative genius of the form, Scott Joplin, was born in Texarkana, Texas, in 1868. He learned to play on a piano his mother bought from her earnings as a maid, and he may have had some training in classical music. Joplin subsequently learned to transfer complex banjo syncopations to the piano as he fused European harmonies and African rhythms. He traveled to Chicago in 1893 and played at the Columbian Exposition. He soon began to write ragtime sheet music that sold well. In 1899 he composed his best-known tune, the "Maple Leaf Rag," named after a social club (brothel) in Sedalia, Missouri. It sold an astonishing one million copies.

Jazz

Jazz gradually replaced ragtime in popularity in the early twentieth century. Unlike ragtime, jazz was mostly improvised, not composed, and it was not confined to the piano. Jazz incorporated African and European musical elements drawn from such diverse sources as plantation bands, minstrel shows, river boat ensembles, and Irish and Scottish folk tunes. The first jazz bands emerged in and around New Orleans where they played at parades, funerals, clubs, and outdoor concerts. Instead of the banjos, pipes, fifes, and violins of earlier black musical groups, these bands relied more on brass, reeds, and drums.

Ferdinand J. La Menthe, regarded as the first prominent jazz musician, was born in 1890 and grew up in a French-speaking family in New Orleans. He was a superb composer and arranger. Later he changed his name to Morton and came to be known as Jelly Roll Morton. He played in the "red light" district of New Orleans known as Storeyville where he was also a pool shark and gambler. He moved to Los Angeles in 1917 and to Chicago in 1922 where he subsequently led and recorded with "Morton's Red Hot Peppers." He died in 1941.

The Blues

In rural, isolated areas of the South, poor black people composed and sang songs about their lives and experiences. W. C. Handy, the father of the blues, later recalled: "Southern Negroes sang about everything. Trains, steamboats, steam whistles, sledge hammers, fast women, mean bosses, stubborn mules." They accompanied themselves on anything from a guitar, to a harmonica, to a washboard. They played in juke joints (rural nightclubs), at picnics, lumber camps, and urban night clubs.

Handy, who was born in Florence, Alabama, in 1873, took up music despite the opposition of his devoutly Christian parents. In the Mississippi Delta in 1903, Handy encountered "primitive," or "boogie," music unlike anything he had heard before. Handy was not initially impressed by the mostly unskilled and itinerant musicians whose lives swirled around cheap whiskey, gambling, prostitution, and violence. "Then I saw the beauty of primitive music. They had the stuff people wanted. It touched the spot. Their music wanted polishing, but it contained the essence. People would pay money for it." Handy went on to compose many tunes including "Memphis Blues" and "St. Louis Blues."

Handy was not the only musician to "discover" the blues. Gertrude Pridget sang in southern minstrel shows. In 1902 she heard a young black woman in a small Missouri town sing forlornly about a lover who had left her. Pridget included the song in her shows. In 1904 she married William "Pa" Rainey and became "Ma" Rainey. Rainey proceeded to create other "blues" songs based on ballads, hymns, and the experiences of black people. As "Mother of the Blues," she recorded extensively in the 1920s and 1930s.

Another legendary blues singer, Bessie Smith was known as the "Empress of the Blues." In the 1920s, she recorded what were known as "race records," produced for black audiences by white companies. Her blues were firmly grounded in African-American musical and oral tradition.

By 1920, two forms of American music were well along in their evolution—jazz and the blues. Both drew on African and American musical elements as well as on European styles. But most of all, jazz and the blues represented the experiences of African Americans and the creativity of the exceptional musicians who developed and performed the music.

Sports

While talented black men and women were making dramatic musical innovations, black athletes found that white athletes and sports entrepreneurs were increasingly opposed to the presence of black men in the boxing ring and on the playing field. In boxing, black men regularly fought white men through the end of the nineteenth century. But many white people, especially Southerners, were offended by the practice. In 1892, George Dixon, a black boxer, won the world featherweight title, and some white men cheered his victory, distressing a Chicago journalist. "It was not pleasant," he complained, "to see white men applaud a negro for knocking another white man out. It was not pleasant to see them crowding around 'Mr.' Dixon to congratulate him on his victory, to seek an introduction with 'the distinguished colored gentleman' while he puffed his cigar and lay back like a prince receiving his subjects." Despite such opinions, there was never any official prohibition of interracial bouts.

Yet the success of another black boxer, heavyweight Jack Johnson, also angered many white Americans. Johnson was born in Galveston, Texas, in 1878 and became a professional boxer in 1897. Between 1902 and 1907 he won fifty-seven bouts against black and white fighters. In 1908 he badly beat the white heavyweight champion, Tommy Burns, in Australia. Many white boxing fans were unwilling to accept Johnson as the champion and looked desperately for "a great white hope" who could defeat him. Jim Jeffries, a former champion, came out of retirement to take on Johnson. In a brutal fight under a scorching sun in Reno, Nevada, in 1910, Johnson knocked Jeffries out in the fifteenth round.

Johnson's personal life, as well as his prowess in the ring, provoked white animosity. Having divorced his black wife, he married a white woman in 1911. Several months later, overwhelmed by social ostracism, she committed suicide. After Johnson married a second white woman, he was convicted of violating the Mann Act, which made it illegal to transport a woman across state lines for immoral purposes. In Johnson's case the "immorality" was his marriage to white women. Sentenced to a year in prison and fined $1,000, Johnson fled to Canada and then to France to avoid punishment. He lost his title to Jesse Willard in 1915 in Havana in the twenty-sixth round in a fight many people believe that Johnson threw. He returned to the United States in 1920 and served ten months in Leavenworth Prison.

Baseball, Basketball, and Other Sports

Baseball was a relatively new sport that became popular after the Civil War. As professional baseball developed in the 1870s and 1880s, both black and white men competed to earn money playing the game. It was not easy. They were the nation's first professional athletes, but professional baseball was unstable. Teams were formed and dissolved with depressing regularity. Players moved from team to team. Some thirty black men played professional baseball in the quarter century after the Civil War.

White players led by Adrian Constantine "Cap" Anson of the Chicago White Stockings tried to get baseball club owners to stop signing black men to contracts. Anson, who was from Iowa, bitterly resented having to play against black men. In 1887, International League officials rescinded a rule that had permitted them to sign black baseball players. One black player, Weldy Wilberforce Walker, protested the exclusion in a letter to *Sporting Life*. He insisted that black men be judged by their skills, not by their color. "There should be some broader cause—such as lack of ability, behavior, and intelligence—for barring a player, rather than his color. It is for these reasons and because I think ability and intelligence should be recognized first and last—at all times and by everyone—I ask the question again, 'Why was the law permitting colored men to sign repealed, etc.?'" There was no intelligent answer to Walker's question. But Jim Crow was now on the baseball diamond. Moses Fleetwood Walker—Weldy's brother—was the last black man to play major league baseball in the nineteenth century as a catcher with Toledo of the American Association. No black men would be allowed to play with white men in major league baseball until Jackie Robinson joined the Brooklyn Dodgers in 1947.

In reaction to their exclusion, black men formed their own teams. By 1900, there were five black professional teams including the Norfolk Red Stockings, the Chicago Unions, and the Cuban X Giants of New York. The Negro Leagues would be an integral (but not integrated) part of sports for the next half century.

James Naismith invented basketball in 1891 in Springfield, Massachusetts. Black youngsters were playing organized basketball by 1906 in YMCAs and later YWCAs in New York City, Philadelphia, and Washington, D.C. By 1910–1911, Howard University and Hampton Institute had basketball teams. In horse racing, black jockeys regularly won major races. Willie Simms won the Kentucky Derby in 1894, 1895, 1896, and 1898. Bicycling and bicycle racing were enormously popular by the 1890s, and in 1900 a black rider, Marshall W. "Major" Taylor, won the U.S. sprint championship.

College Athletics

Most white colleges and universities in the North that admitted black students would not let them participate in intercollegiate sports. (Southern colleges and universities did not admit black students.) There were, however, exceptions. In 1889, W. T. S. Jackson and William Henry Lewis played football for Amherst College. Lewis was the captain of the team in 1890. As a law school student, Lewis played for Harvard and was named to the Walter Camp All-American team in 1892. White institutions with black players often encountered the racism so rampant during the era. In 1907, the University of Alabama baseball team canceled a game with the University of Vermont after learning that the Vermont squad had two black infielders. Moreover, black players were frequently subjected to abuse from opposing teams and their fans.

Intercollegiate athletics emerged at black colleges and universities in the late nineteenth century. White schools occasionally played black institutions. The Yale Law School baseball team, for example, played Howard in 1898. But black college teams were far more likely to play each other. The first football game between two black colleges took place on December 27, 1892, when Biddle University (today Johnson C. Smith University) defeated Livingston College in Salisbury, North Carolina.

Eventually black athletic conferences were formed. The first was Central Intercollegiate Athletic Association (CIAA) organized in 1912 with Hampton, Howard, Virginia Union, and Shaw College in Raleigh, North Carolina, among its early members. The Southeastern Conference was established in 1913 and consisted of Morehouse, Fisk, Florida A&M, and Tuskegee among others. In Texas in 1920, five black colleges founded the Southwestern Athletic Conference: Prairie View A&M, Bishop College, Paul Quinn College, Wiley College, and Sam Houston College.

Conclusion

White supremacy was debilitating, discouraging, and dangerous, but black Americans were sometimes able to turn Jim Crow to their advantage. To lessen the effects of white racism and to improve the economic status of black people, educators like Samuel

TIMELINE

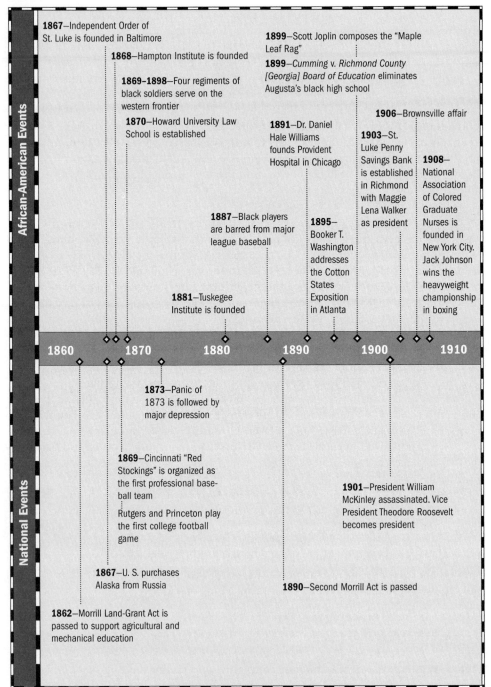

African-American Events

1867—Independent Order of St. Luke is founded in Baltimore

1868—Hampton Institute is founded

1869–1898—Four regiments of black soldiers serve on the western frontier

1870—Howard University Law School is established

1881—Tuskegee Institute is founded

1887—Black players are barred from major league baseball

1891—Dr. Daniel Hale Williams founds Provident Hospital in Chicago

1895—Booker T. Washington addresses the Cotton States Exposition in Atlanta

1899—Scott Joplin composes the "Maple Leaf Rag"

1899—*Cumming* v. *Richmond County [Georgia] Board of Education* eliminates Augusta's black high school

1903—St. Luke Penny Savings Bank is established in Richmond with Maggie Lena Walker as president

1906—Brownsville affair

1908—National Association of Colored Graduate Nurses is founded in New York City. Jack Johnson wins the heavyweight championship in boxing

1860　1870　1880　1890　1900　1910

National Events

1862—Morrill Land-Grant Act is passed to support agricultural and mechanical education

1867—U. S. purchases Alaska from Russia

1869—Cincinnati "Red Stockings" is organized as the first professional baseball team

Rutgers and Princeton play the first college football game

1873—Panic of 1873 is followed by major depression

1890—Second Morrill Act is passed

1901—President William McKinley assassinated. Vice President Theodore Roosevelt becomes president

Chapman Armstrong and Booker T. Washington recommended agricultural and mechanical training for most black Americans. But critics such as W. E. B. Du Bois stressed the need to cultivate the minds as well as the hands of black people to develop leaders.

Black men served with distinction in all-black military units in the Indian wars, the Spanish-American War, and the Philippine Insurrection. But no matter how loyal or how committed black men in uniform were, the white majority never fully trusted them. African Americans could only react with dismay and outrage when President Theodore Roosevelt dismissed 167 black soldiers in 1906 in the Brownsville Affair.

As they tried to shape their own destinies in the late nineteenth century, black Americans developed businesses and facilities to serve their communities in an environment mostly free from white control and interference. Black people relied on their own experiences and imaginations to create new forms of music. They participated in sports with white athletes but more often played separately from them as segregation and white hostility spread.

While black people recognized that their churches, hospitals, schools, and businesses were often inadequately financed and usually less imposing than those of white people, they also knew that at a black school or church, in a black store, or in the care of a black physician or nurse, they would not be abused, mistreated, or ridiculed because of their color.

Review Questions

1. How and why did the agricultural and mechanical training offered by Hampton Institute and Tuskegee Institute gain so much support among black people and white people? Why did black colleges and universities emphasize learning trades and acquiring skills?

2. How compatible was the educational philosophy of the late nineteenth century with the racial ideology of that era?

3. Of what value was an education for a black person in the 1890s or early 1900s? To what use could a black person put an education? What was the benefit of an education?

4. What purpose did the black church serve? What were the strengths and weaknesses of the black church? How would you assess the role of black clergymen in late-nineteenth-century America?

5. How could a black man in the U.S. Army justify participating in wars against Native Americans, the Spanish, and the Filipinos? What motivated black soldiers to serve? How well did they serve?

6. What, if any, benefits did black people derive from the growth and expansion of segregation and Jim Crow?

7. How do you explain the emergence of ragtime, jazz, and the blues in American music? How do you account for their development and popularity?

8. How did segregation affect the development of amateur and professional athletics in the United States?

Recommended Reading

James D. Anderson. *The Education of Blacks in the South, 1860–1931*. Chapel Hill, NC: University of North Carolina Press, 1988. Anderson is highly critical of the education and philosophy promoted and provided by Hampton Institute and Tuskegee Institute.

Edward L. Ayers. *The Promise of the New South: Life after Reconstruction*. New York: Oxford University Press, 1992. This wide-ranging study encompasses almost every aspect of life in the late-nineteenth-century South, including religion, education, sports, and music.

Sutton E. Griggs. *Imperium in Imperio*. New York: Arno Press reprint, 1899. This novel describes the formation of a separate black nation in Texas at the end of the nineteenth century.

Leon Litwack. *Trouble in Mind: Black Southerners in the Age of Jim Crow*. New York: Alfred A. Knopf, 1998. The author lets the words of black people of the time, including lawyers, physicians, and musicians, explain what life was like in an age of intense white supremacy.

Leon Litwack and August Meier, eds. *Black Leaders in the Nineteenth Century*. Urbana, IL: University of Illinois Press, 1988. This volume contains eighteen brief but valuable biographical essays.

Benjamin E. Mays. *Born to Rebel*. New York: Scribner, 1971. Mays's autobiography includes penetrating insights into religion and education among rural black Southerners.

Howard N. Rabinowitz. *Race Relations in the Urban South, 1865–1890*. New York: Oxford University Press, 1978. The author examines black life in Atlanta, Montgomery, Nashville, Raleigh, and Richmond.

➔ Chapter 16 ✦

Conciliation, Agitation, and Migration: African Americans in the Early Twentieth Century

As the twentieth century dawned, black and white Americans had profoundly different views on the future of black people in America. Most white people believed that black Americans were an inferior race. Black people refused to accept the inferiority to which they had been consigned. They devised strategies and organized institutions to enable them to prosper in a hostile society.

However, African Americans and their leaders disagreed about how to secure the constitutional rights and the material comforts that so many white Americans took for granted. Some, following W. E. B. Du Bois, a founder of the Niagara Movement and the National Association for the Advancement of Colored People (NAACP), favored a frontal assault on discrimination, disfranchisement, and Jim Crow. Others, following Booker T. Washington of the Tuskegee Institute, cautioned against the vigorous pursuit of civil rights and political power and insisted that agricultural and industrial training would generate prosperity and self-sufficiency among people of color.

The emergence of the club movement among black women and other self-help organizations enabled more prosperous black people to aid those suffering acutely from poverty and prejudice. Many of the black elite, designated the Talented Tenth, took seriously their responsibilities to aid their brethren.

When the United States entered World War I in 1917, black men responded patriotically, as they had in previous conflicts. They joined a Jim Crow military that was fighting to make the world safe for democracy. But black people in America were not safe, and democracy did not prevail. Riots and racial violence erupted before, during, and after the war.

In the meantime a vast migration of hundreds of thousands of rural black Southerners to northern cities began in earnest after 1910.

Race and the Progressive Movement

By the first decade of the twentieth century, many Americans were concerned and even alarmed about the rapid changes that confronted the United States, including industrialization, the rise of powerful corporations, the explosive growth of cities, and the influx of millions of immigrants. Their apprehensions spawned a disparate collection of efforts at reform known as the progressive movement. In general, progressives believed that America needed a new social awareness to deal with the new problems. But most of the middle- and upper-class white people who formed the core of the movement showed little interest in white racism. Indeed, many were racists themselves. They were primarily concerned with the concentration of wealth in monopolies such as Standard Oil, with pervasive political corruption, and with the plight of urban working-class immigrants. They cared deeply about the debilitating effects of alcohol, tainted food, and prostitution, but little about the grim impact of white supremacy. When Upton Sinclair wrote his muckraking novel *The Jungle* to expose the exploitation of European immigrants in Chicago meatpacking houses, he depicted black people as brute laborers and strikebreakers.

The progressive movement nonetheless offered hope that racial advancement was possible. If efforts were made to improve America, was it not possible that there be some advances achieved in policies and conditions affecting black Americans? But how much militancy or forbearance was necessary to achieve significant racial progress? Should black people demand a meaningful role in a nation that despised them or turn inward and rely mainly on each other rather than plead for white recognition and respect?

Booker T. Washington's Approach

Booker T. Washington was a complex man. Many people found him unassertive, dignified, and patient. Yet he was ambitious, aggressive, and opportunistic as well as shrewd, calculating, and devious. He had an uncanny ability to determine what he might say to other people that would elicit a positive response from them. He became extraordinarily powerful.

His commitment to agricultural and industrial education was the basis for Washington's approach to "the problem of the color line." He was convinced that black men and women who had mastered skills acquired at institutions like Tuskegee and Hampton would be recognized, if not welcomed, as productive contributors to the southern economy. Economic acceptance would lead to political and social acceptance.

The Tuskegee leader outlined his philosophy in the speech he delivered at the opening ceremonies of the Cotton States Exposition in Atlanta in 1895. Black people, he told his segregated audience, would find genuine opportunities in the South. "[W]hen it comes to business, pure and simple, it is in the South that the Negro is given a man's chance in the commercial world." Washington maintained that the lives of black and white Southerners were historically linked and that black people were far more loyal and steadfast than newly arrived immigrants. "[I]n our humble way, we shall stand by you with a devotion that no foreigner can approach, ready to lay down our lives, if need be, in defence of yours, interlacing our industrial, commercial, civil, and religious life with yours in a way that shall make the interests of both races one."

Then in a striking metaphor, he reassured white people that cooperation between the races in the interest of prosperity did not endanger segregation. "In all things that are purely social we can be as separate as the fingers, yet one as the hand in all things essential to mutual progress." Finally, he urged his black listeners to struggle steadily rather than make defiant demands. "The wisest among my race understand that the agitation of questions of social equality is the extremest folly, and that progress in the enjoyment of all the privileges that will come to us must be the result of severe and constant struggle rather than of artificial forcing." Washington was convinced that as African Americans became productive and made economic progress, white people would concede them their rights.

Although the speech was warmly received by many white and black people, not everyone was complimentary. The black editor of the Washington *Bee,* W. Calvin Chase, complained: "He said something that was death to the Afro-American and elevating to white people." Bishop Henry M. Turner of the AME church added that Washington "will have to live a long time to undo the harm he has done our race."

White people regarded Washington's speech as moderate, sensible, and altogether praiseworthy. Almost overnight he was designated the spokesman for African Americans. Washington accepted the recognition and took full advantage of it.

After the Atlanta speech, Washington's influence soared. He received extensive and mostly positive coverage in black newspapers. Some of that popularity stemmed from admiration for his leadership and agreement with his ideas. But Washington also cultivated and flattered editors, paid for advertisements for Tuskegee, and subsidized struggling journalists.

He was especially effective in dealing with prominent white businessmen and philanthropists. They trusted Washington's judgment and consulted him before contributing to black colleges and universities. Washington assured them of the wisdom of investing in the training of black men and women in agricultural and mechanical skills. These students, he repeatedly reminded donors, would be self-sufficient and productive members of southern society.

Washington himself was a political figure to be reckoned with. His connections to white businesspeople and politicians gave him enormous influence. Critics and admirers alike referred to him as "the Wizard of Tuskegee," and the way he wielded his influence as "the Tuskegee Machine." Washington got along superbly with President William McKinley and his successor, Theodore Roosevelt. Washington and Roosevelt regularly consulted each other on political appointments and in 1901 Roosevelt invited Washington to dine at the White House (an invitation that outraged white Southerners).

Most of Washington's political activities were not public. He secretly helped finance unsuccessful court cases against the Louisiana and Alabama grandfather clauses. (The statutes disfranchised those voters—black men—whose grandfathers had not possessed the right to vote; see Chapter 14.) He tried to persuade railroad executives to improve the conditions on segregated coaches and in station waiting rooms. He worked covertly with white attorneys to free a black farm laborer imprisoned under Alabama's peonage law. In many of these secret activities, Washington used code names in correspondence to hide his involvement.

He did not directly or publicly challenge white supremacy. He was willing to accept literacy and property qualifications for voting if they were equitably enforced regardless of race. He also opposed women's suffrage. Washington attacked lynching only occasionally. But he did write an annual letter to white newspapers filled with data on lynchings that had been compiled at Tuskegee. The grim statistics spoke for themselves.

Washington founded the National Negro Business League in 1900 and served as its president until he died in 1915. The League helped to promote black businesses in the black community and brought businessmen together to exchange information. Moreover, its annual meetings allowed Washington to develop support for the Tuskegee Machine from black businessmen who were community leaders from across the nation. Similarly, he worked closely with leaders in black fraternal orders such as the Odd Fellows and Pythians.

Opposition to Washington's conciliatory stance on racial matters steadily intensified. William Monroe Trotter became the most vociferous critic of Booker T. Washington and the Tuskegee Machine. Trotter was the Harvard-educated editor of the Boston *Guardian,* and he attacked Washington as "the Great Traitor," "the Benedict Arnold of the Negro Race," and "Pope Washington." At a 1903 meeting of the National Negro Business League in Boston, Trotter stood on a chair and interrupted a speech by Washington, defiantly asking, "Are the rope and the torch all the race is to get under your leadership?" Washington ignored him, and the police arrested the editor for disorderly conduct.

W. E. B. Du Bois

William Edward Burghardt Du Bois, who was twelve years younger than Booker T. Washington, would eventually eclipse the influence of the Wizard of Tuskegee. Du Bois emerged as the most significant black leader in America during the first half of the twentieth century. While Washington's life had been shaped by slavery, poverty, and the industrial work ethic fostered at Hampton Institute, Du Bois was born and raised in the largely white town of Great Barrington, Massachusetts where he encountered little overt racism and developed a passion for knowledge.

Du Bois graduated from Great Barrington High School at a time when few white and still fewer black youngsters attended more than primary school. He went South to Fisk University in Nashville and graduated at age twenty. He was the first black man to earn a Ph.D. (in history) at Harvard in 1895, and he pursued additional graduate study in Germany.

Du Bois was an intellectual at ease with words and ideas. He wrote sixteen nonfiction books, five novels, and two autobiographies. He was a fearless activist determined to confront Jim Crow and lynching. While Washington solicited the goodwill of powerful white leaders and was comfortable with a gradual approach to the eradication of white supremacy, Du Bois was impatient with white people who accepted or ignored white domination and had little tolerance for black people who were unwilling to demand their rights.

Du Bois was well aware that he and Washington came from dissimilar backgrounds.

I was born free. Washington was born a slave. He felt the lash of an overseer across his back. I was born in Massachusetts, he on a slave plantation in the South. My great-grandfather fought with the Colonial Army in New England in the American Revolution. I had a happy childhood and acceptance in the community. Washington's childhood was hard. I had many more advantages: Fisk University, Harvard, graduate years in Europe. Washington had little formal schooling.

Du Bois was not always critical of Washington. Following Washington's speech at the Cotton States Exposition in 1895, Du Bois wrote to praise him. "Let me heartily congratulate you upon your phenomenal success at Atlanta—it was a word fitly spoken." But in 1903, Du Bois, by then an Atlanta University professor, published *The Souls of Black Folk*. One of the major literary works of the twentieth century, it contained the first formal attack on Washington and his leadership.

Du Bois denounced Washington for failing to stand up for political and civil rights and higher education for black Americans. Du Bois found even more infuriating Washington's willingness to compromise with the white South and Washington's apparent agreement with white Southerners that black people were not their equals. "Mr. Washington represents in Negro thought the old attitude of adjustment and submission . . . and Mr. Washington's programme practically accepts the alleged inferiority of the Negro races."

In concluding, Du Bois stressed that he agreed with Washington on some issues, but disagreed even more about significant ones, and that on these issues it was vital to oppose Washington:

> So far as Mr. Washington preaches Thrift, Patience, and Industrial Training for the masses, we must hold up his hands and strive with him.... But so far as Mr. Washington apologizes for injustice, North or South, does not rightly value the privilege and duty of voting, belittles the emasculating effects of caste distinctions, and opposes higher training and ambition of our brighter minds,—so far as he, the South, or the Nation, does this,—we must unceasingly and firmly oppose them.

Washington worried that the opposition of Trotter, Du Bois, and others would jeopardize the flow of funds from white philanthropists to black colleges and universities. In an effort to reconcile with his opponents, he organized a meeting with them, funded by white philanthropists, at Carnegie Hall in New York City in 1904. But Du Bois and other opponents of Washington came to the gathering determined to adopt a radical agenda. When Washington loyalists monopolized the proceedings, Du Bois quit in disgust.

Du Bois, joined by a small cadre of black intellectuals, then set out to organize an aggressive effort to secure the rights of black citizens. He was convinced that the advancement of black people was the responsibility of the black elite, those he called the Talented Tenth, meaning the upper 10 percent of black Americans. Education, he believed, was the key.

> Work alone will not do it unless inspired by the right ideals and guided by intelligence. Education must not simply teach work—it must teach Life. The Talented Tenth of the Negro race must be made leaders of thought and missionaries of culture among people. No others can do this work, and Negro colleges must train men for it. The Negro race, like all other races, is going to be saved by its exceptional men.

The Niagara Movement

In 1905 Du Bois carried the anti-Washington crusade a step further and invited a select group to meet at Niagara Falls, in Canada. The twenty-nine delegates to this meeting insisted that black people no longer quietly accept the loss of the right to vote. "We believe that [Negro] American citizens should protest emphatically and continually against the curtailment of their political rights." They also demanded an end to segregation, declaring, "All American citizens have the right to equal treatment in places of public entertainment." They appealed for better schools, health care, and housing; protested the discrimination endured by black soldiers; and criticized the racial prejudice of most churches as "wrong, unchristian and disgraceful to the twentieth century civilization." Perhaps most important, the Niagara gathering insisted that white people did not know what was best for black people. "We repudiate the monstrous doctrine that the oppressor should be the sole authority as to the rights of the oppressed."

The Niagara Movement that emerged from this meeting attracted four hundred members and remained active for several years. Du Bois composed annual addresses to the nation designed to arouse black and white support. But the Niagara Movement was no match for the powerful, efficient, and well-financed Tuskegee Machine. Washington used every means at his disposal to undermine the movement. Black newspaper editors like the Washington *Bee's* W. Calvin Chase, who had earlier attacked Washington's Atlanta Compromise address, were paid to attack Du Bois and to praise Washington. Washington dispatched spies to Niagara meetings to report on the organization's activities and let it be known that black federal workers might lose their positions if they joined in the Niagara Movement.

The founders of the Niagara Movement posed in front of a photograph of the falls when they met at Niagara Falls, Ontario, Canada, in 1905. W. E. B. Du Bois is second from the right in the middle row.

Photographs and Prints Division, Shomburg Center for Research in Black Culture, The New York Public Library; Astor, Lenox and Tilden Foundations.

There were also internal problems among Niagara members. Du Bois was an inexperienced leader, and difficulties developed between him and Trotter. In 1908, the Niagara Movement virtually collapsed. Most black and white Americans were not prepared to support an organization that seemed so uncompromising in its demands.

The NAACP and the Urban League

As the Niagara Movement expired, two new organizations: the National Association for the Advancement of Colored People (NAACP) and the National League on Urban Conditions among Negroes, better known as the Urban League, came to life. Both organizations were founded by black and white progressives in New York City. While the Urban League, founded in 1910, was a social welfare organization, dedicated to improving living conditions for urban black people, the NAACP, founded in 1909, was a militant organization dedicated to racial justice. White leaders dominated both organizations, and white contributors largely financed them.

A few white progressives were deeply concerned about the rampant racial prejudice manifested so graphically in lynchings, Jim Crow, black disfranchisement, and a vicious riot in 1908 in Springfield, Illinois—Abraham Lincoln's hometown. After a gathering of leaders in January 1909 in New York City, Oswald Garrison Villard issued

---

The Emergence of National African-American Organizations

1889	Afro-American League organized in Chicago
1892	Colored Women's League of Washington formed
1893	New Era Club founded in Boston
1895	National Federation of Afro-American Women organized in Boston
1896	National Association of Colored Women (NACW) formed in Washington
1897	American Negro Academy founded in Washington
1897	First Phillis Wheatley home established in Detroit
1900	National Negro Business League established in Boston
1905	Niagara Movement organized in Niagara Falls, Ontario, Canada
1909	National Association for the Advancement of Colored People (NAACP) founded in New York City
1910	National League on Urban Conditions among Negroes (Urban League) formed in New York City

a call on February 12—Lincoln's Birthday—to "all believers in democracy to join a national conference to discuss present evils, the voicing of protests, and the renewal of the struggle for civil and political liberty."

Villard was the president and editor of the New York *Evening Post* and the grandson of abolitionist William Lloyd Garrison. Prominent progressives endorsed the call, including social workers Lillian Wald and Jane Addams, literary scholar Joel E. Spingarn, and respected attorneys Clarence Darrow and Moorfield Storey. W. E. B. Du Bois, Ida Wells-Barnett, and Mary Church Terrell were the black leaders most involved in the formation of the NAACP.

The NAACP was determined that black citizens should fully enjoy the civil and political rights the Constitution guaranteed to all citizens. It relied on the judicial and legislative systems in what would be a decades-long effort to secure those rights. The NAACP won its first major legal victory in 1915 when the Supreme Court overturned Oklahoma's grandfather clause in *Guinn v. United States*. But poll taxes and literacy tests continued to disfranchise black citizens.

In 1917 in a case brought by the Louisville NAACP branch and argued before the Supreme Court by Moorfield Storey, the court struck down a local law that enforced residential segregation by prohibiting black people and white people from selling real estate to people of the other race. The NAACP also tried in 1918 to secure a federal law prohibiting lynching. The bill passed in the House of Representatives in 1922 but Senate Democrats blocked it, and it never became law.

W. E. B. Du Bois was easily the most prominent black figure associated with the NAACP during its first quarter century. He became director of publicity and research and edited the NAACP publication, *The Crisis,* while largely leaving leadership and administrative tasks to others.

With *The Crisis,* Du Bois the scholar became Du Bois the propagandist. In the pages of *The Crisis,* he denounced white racism and atrocities and demanded that black people stand up for their rights. "Agitate, then, brother; protest, reveal the truth and refuse to be silenced. . . . A moment's let up, a moment's acquiescence, means a chance for the wolves of prejudice to get at our necks." He would not provoke violence, but he would not tolerate mistreatment either. "I am resolved to be quiet and law abiding, but to refuse to cringe in body or in soul, to resent deliberate insult, and to assert my just rights in the face of wanton aggression." These were not the even-tempered, cautious words of Booker T. Washington to which so many Americans had grown accustomed. *The Crisis* became required reading in many black homes. By 1913 it had thirty thousand subscribers when the membership of the NAACP was only three thousand.

Although Oswald Garrison Villard tried to reassure Washington that the NAACP posed no threat and to gain his support for the new association, many black leaders and members of the NAACP, despised Washington and his ideology. Washington returned the sentiment and worked to subvert the new organization. He looked on Du Bois as little more than the puppet of white people, who dominated the leadership of the NAACP and declined to debate Du Bois. One of Washington's aides commented that "it would be entirely out of place for Dr. Washington to enter into any discussion with a man occupying the place that Dr. Du Bois does, for the reason that Dr. Washington is at the head of a large institution. . . . Dr. Du Bois, on the other hand, is a mere hired man, as it were, in an institution completely controlled by white people."

Washington told an alumnus of Tuskegee that the main aim of the NAACP was to destroy Washington and Tuskegee. "As a matter of straight fact, this organization is for the purpose of tearing down our work wherever possible and I think none of our friends should give it comfort."

He became so obsessed with the NAACP that he was not above manipulating white supremacists to damage those connected with the Association. When he learned that a group of black and white progressives associated with the NAACP were going to gather at the Café Boulevard in New York City in 1911, he allowed an ally to alert the hostile white press, which gleefully described the multiracial dinner in the most inflammatory terms. "Fashionable White Women Sit at Board with Negroes, Japs and Chinamen to Promote 'Cause' of Miscegenation" proclaimed one headline. The New York *Press* added: "White women, evidently of the cultured and wealthier classes, fashionably attired in low-cut gowns, leaned over the tables to chat confidentially with negro men of the true African type."

Ultimately, Washington's efforts to ruin the NAACP and to reduce the influence of its supporters failed. By the time of his death in 1915, the NAACP had grown to over six thousand members and fifty local branches. Its aggressive campaign for civil and political rights replaced Washington's strategy of progress through conciliation and accommodation.

Black Women and the NACW

Years before the Urban League and the NAACP were founded, black women began creating clubs and organizations. The local groups that began forming in the 1870s and 1880s, such as the Bethel Literary and Historical Association in Washington, D.C., were mainly concerned with cultural, religious, and social matters. But many of the mostly middle-class women active in these clubs eventually became involved with community problems. In 1893 black women in Boston founded the New Era Club. They published a monthly magazine, *Woman's Era,* that featured articles on fashion, health, and family life.

In 1895 a New Era Club member, Josephine St. Pierre Ruffin, enraged by white journalist James W. Jack's vilification of black women as "prostitutes, thieves, and liars" who were "altogether without character," issued a call to "Let Us Confer Together" that drew 104 black women to a meeting in Boston. The result was the formation of the National Federation of Afro-American Women, which soon included thirty-six clubs in twelve states. In the meantime, the Colored Women's League of Washington, D.C., which had been founded in 1892, published an appeal in *Woman's Era* for black women to organize a national association at the 1895 meeting of the National Council of Women. At that gathering, representatives from several local black women's clubs organized the National Colored Woman's League.

The two groups—The National Federation of Afro-American Women and the National Colored Woman's League—merged in 1896 to form the National Association of

Colored Women (NACW). The NACW adopted the self-help motto "Lifting as We Climb," and in the reforming spirit of the progressive age, they stressed moral, mental, and material advancement. By 1914 there were fifty thousand members of the NACW in one thousand clubs nationwide.

Two of the most prominent women in the NACW were Mary Church Terrell and Ida Wells-Barnett. Terrell, who became the first president of the NACW, was a graduate of Oberlin College and married a Washington, D.C., municipal judge. She was an active community leader and conscious of her status as a member of the black elite.

Ida Wells-Barnett was born a slave in Mississippi and graduated from Rust College. A fearless opponent of lynching, she married a Chicago newspaper publisher. She was also a strong advocate of women's suffrage in the early twentieth century.

Terrell and Barnett sometimes strongly disagreed over tactics. Terrell considered Barnett too abrasive and uncompromising while Barnett found Terrell too conciliatory. But both women were committed to the causes of racial justice and women's rights.

The clubs sought to confront the problems black people encountered in urban areas as rural Southerners migrated by the thousands in the second and third decades of the twentieth century. Members worked to eradicate poverty, end racial discrimination, and promote education, including the formation of kindergartens and day nurseries. They cared for older people, especially former slaves. They aided orphans; assisted working mothers by providing nurseries, health care, and information on child rearing; and established homes for delinquent and abandoned girls.

Black women also formed Phillis Wheatley clubs and homes across the nation (named in honor of the eighteenth-century African-American poet). The residences offered living accommodations for single, black working women in many cities where they were refused admittance to YWCA facilities. Some Phillis Wheatley clubs also provided nurseries and classes in domestic skills. In Cleveland, nurse Jane Edna Hunter organized a residence for single, black working women who could not find comfortable and affordable housing. In 1911 she formed the Working Girls' Home Association for cleaning women, laundresses, and private duty nurses. With association members contributing five cents a week, Hunter opened a twenty-three-room residence in 1913 that expanded to a seventy-two-room building in 1917.

Anna Julia Cooper
and Black Feminism

"Only the BLACK WOMAN can say 'when and where I enter, in the quiet, undisputed dignity of my womanhood, without violence and without suing or special patronage, then and there the whole Negro race enters with me.'" So wrote Anna Julia Cooper in the late nineteenth century. Not only was Cooper convinced that black women would play a decisive role in shaping the destiny of their people, she labored to dispel the stereotype that black women lacked refinement, grace, and morality.

Cooper was born a slave in Raleigh, North Carolina, in 1858, and graduated from St. Augustine's school. She then earned a bachelor's degree from Oberlin College in 1884 and in 1892 published *A Voice from the South By a Black Woman of the South*. In this collection of essays she stressed the pivotal role that black women would play in the future, and she chastised white women for their lack of support. In 1900 she addressed the Pan African Conference in London.

Cooper was principal of Washington's famed M Street Colored High School (later Paul Laurence Dunbar High School) from 1901 to 1906. She was forced out in 1906 amid allegations that supporters of the powerful Tuskegee Machine resented her emphasis on academic preparation over vocational training. She went on to teach for four years at Missouri's Lincoln University before returning to M Street High as a teacher. Fluent in French, she earned a Ph.D. at the Sorbonne in Paris. She was active with the NACW, the NAACP, and YWCA. She died in 1964 at age 105.

Women's Suffrage

Historically, many black women had supported women's suffrage. Before the Civil War, many abolitionists, including Mary Ann Shadd Cary, Sojourner Truth, and Frederick Douglass, had also backed women's suffrage. Cary and Truth tried unsuccessfully to vote after the war. Black women attended conventions of the mostly white American Woman's Suffrage Association in the 1870s.

Black women were also involved in the long struggle for women's suffrage on the state level. Ida Wells-Barnett was a leader in the Illinois suffrage effort. By 1900 Wyoming, Utah, Colorado, and Idaho permitted women to vote, and by 1918 women in seventeen northern and western states had gained the vote. But as more women won voting rights, women's suffrage became more controversial. The proposed Nineteenth Amendment to the U.S. Constitution drove a wedge between black and white advocates of women's political rights. Many opponents of women's suffrage, especially white Southerners, warned that granting women the right to vote would increase the number of black voters. Some white women advocated strict literacy and educational requirements for voting in an effort to limit the number of black voters, both women and men.

As it turned out, only two southern states—Kentucky and Tennessee—ratified the Nineteenth Amendment before its adoption in 1920. Black suffragists understood that the right to vote meant political power, and political power could be exercised to acquire civil rights and improve education. White Southerners also grasped the importance of voting rights. Thus, despite the Nineteenth Amendment, large numbers of black people in the South—both men and women—remained unable to vote.

The Black Elite

Many of the black leaders described by W. E. B. Du Bois as the Talented Tenth formed protest organizations, joined reform efforts, and organized self-help groups. The leaders were middle- and upper-class black people who were better educated than most Americans—black or white.

In 1897 Episcopal priest Alexander Crummel met with sixteen other black men in Washington, D.C., to form the American Negro Academy. This scholarly organization was made up of "men of African descent" who assembled periodically to discuss and publish works on history, literature, religion, and science. Among those who attended the initial gathering were W. E. B. Du Bois, Paul Laurence Dunbar, Kelly Miller, and Francis Grimke.

Crummel did not hesitate to express his deep convictions on race, religion, and Africa. He had been born in 1818 in New York and spent several years in Liberia in the 1850s and 1860s as an Episcopal missionary. Crummel died in 1898, but the Academy survived as a vibrant intellectual and elitist society.

Carter G. Woodson, Alain Locke, Arthur Schomburg, and James Weldon Johnson subsequently joined its ranks before it disbanded in 1928. It afforded black intellectuals an opportunity to ponder what it meant to be black in America and to develop their racial consciousness, thus nurturing ideas that would mature during the Harlem Renaissance.

Most members of the Academy supported women's rights and women's suffrage. Consequently it was ironic that black women were not invited to become members of the Academy, although black women, like Anna Julia Cooper, Ida Wells Barnett, and Mary Church Terrell, were easily the intellectual equals of the male participants.

By the early twentieth century, there were several hundred wealthy African Americans. These black aristocrats—medical doctors, lawyers, and businessmen—were as sophisticated, refined, and conscious of their status as any group in American society. They distanced themselves from less affluent black and white people, and lived in expensive houses. Many of them possessed fair complexions.

The black elite formed exclusive organizations that jealously limited membership to the small black upper class. In the 1860s the Ugly Fishing Club was transformed into an organization made up of New York City's wealthiest black men. It soon came to be known simply as the Ugly Club, and its membership spread to Newport, Rhode Island, Baltimore, and Philadelphia. In 1904 two wealthy Philadelphia physicians, a dentist, and a pharmacist formed Sigma Pi Beta, better known as Boulé. It was restricted to male college graduates, and it aimed to provide "inspiration, relaxation, intellectual stimulation, and brotherhood." Boulé expanded to seven chapters in cities that included Chicago and Memphis, but its membership totaled a mere 177.

Organizations like the Diamondback Club and the Cosmos Club in Washington, the Loendi Club in Pittsburgh, and the Bachelor-Benedict Club in New York sponsored luxurious banquets, dances, and debutante balls. Several of these groups owned ornate clubhouses. These elite societies and cliques typically competed to demonstrate social exclusivity and preeminence.

Among the black elite were also the African Americans who established the Greek letter black fraternities and sororities. In 1906, seven students at Cornell University formed Alpha Phi Alpha, the first college fraternity for black men. Within a few years, it had chapters at the University of Michigan, Yale, Columbia, and Ohio State. The first black sorority, Alpha Kappa Alpha, was founded in 1908 at Howard University. Several other Greek letter organizations were subsequently launched at Howard: Omega Psi Phi fraternity in 1911, Delta Sigma Theta sorority in 1913, Phi Beta Sigma in 1914, and Zeta Phi Beta sorority in 1920. In addition, in 1911 Kappa Alpha Psi fraternity was founded at Indiana University, and Sigma Gamma Rho sorority was formed in Indianapolis in 1922. Besides providing college students with an opportunity to enjoy each other's company, the black fraternities and sororities stressed scholarship, social graces, and community involvement.

Presidential Politics

Since Reconstruction, black voters had loyally supported the Republican party and its presidential candidates. "The Party of Lincoln" welcomed that support and periodically rewarded black men with federal jobs. Republican presidents Theodore Roosevelt (1901–1909) and William Howard Taft (1909–1913) continued that policy.

But other presidential actions more than offset whatever goodwill these appointments generated. Roosevelt discharged three companies of black soldiers after the Brownsville incident in 1906, and Taft tolerated restrictions on black voters in the South and encouraged the development of a "lily white" Republican party, removing black people from federal jobs in the region.

In 1912 the Republican party split in a bitter feud between President Taft and Theodore Roosevelt, and a third political party—the Progressive party—emerged. The Progressives nominated Roosevelt to run against Taft and the Democratic candidate, Woodrow Wilson. But as the delegates at the Progressive convention in Chicago sang the "Battle Hymn of the Republic," southern black men who had come to the gathering stood outside the hall, denied admission by white Progressives.

It was not a complete shock that militant black leaders like William Monroe Trotter and W. E. B. Du Bois urged black voters to support Woodrow Wilson, the Democrat, in the 1912 presidential election. Wilson was the reform governor of New Jersey, and he had been president of Princeton University. Trotter and Du Bois were impressed with Wilson's academic background and his promise to pursue a progressive policy toward black Americans.

But as president, Wilson proved to be no friend of black people. Born and raised in the South, Wilson had absorbed white southern racial views. Federal agencies and buildings were fully segregated early during Wilson's tenure. In 1914 Trotter and a black delegation met with Wilson to protest segregation in the treasury department and the post office. Wilson defended separation of the races as a means to avoid friction. Trotter vehemently disagreed, and Wilson warned that he would no longer meet with the group if Trotter remained their spokesman.

Black Men and the Military in World War I

In 1915–1916, Wilson faced more than problems with dissatisfied black people. United States–Mexican relations had deteriorated after a revolution and civil war in Mexico. War in Europe threatened to draw the United States into conflict with Germany.

The Punitive Expedition to Mexico

In 1914, U.S. marines landed at Vera Cruz after an attack on American sailors. Then in March 1916, Francisco "Pancho" Villa led a force of Mexican rebels across the border into New Mexico in an effort to provoke war between Mexico and the United States. Fifteen Americans were killed, including seven U.S. soldiers. In response, Wilson dispatched a "punitive expedition" that eventually numbered 15,000 U.S. troops under the command of General John J. "Black Jack" Pershing. Pershing acquired the nickname "Black Jack" after commanding black troops in Cuba during the Spanish–American War.

United States forces, including the black 10th Cavalry (see Chapter 15), spent ten months in Mexico in a futile effort to capture Villa. The 10th Cavalry was, as had been the case with black troops since the Civil War, commanded by white men. But Lieutenant Colonel Charles Young, an 1889 black graduate of the U.S. Military Academy at West Point, helped lead the regiment until the troops were withdrawn from Mexico in 1917 when the United States was about to enter World War I against Germany.

World War I

When World War I erupted in Europe in August 1914, most Americans had no desire to participate. President Wilson issued a proclamation of neutrality. Running for re-election in 1916 on the appealing slogan, "He Kept Us Out of War," Wilson narrowly defeated Republican candidate Charles Evans Hughes. Repeated German submarine attacks on civilian vessels and the loss of American lives, however, infuriated Wilson and many Americans. On April 6, 1917, Congress declared war on Germany. Most African Americans supported the war effort. As in previous conflicts, black people sought to demonstrate their devotion to the country through military service. "If this is our country," declared W. E. B. Du Bois, "then this is our war. We must fight it with every ounce of blood and treasure."

Some white leaders were less enthusiastic about the participation of black men. One southern governor wondered about the wisdom of having the military train and arm thousands of black men at southern camps and posts. General Pershing argued for the use of black troops, but insisted on white leadership. "Under capable white officers and with sufficient training, negro soldiers have always acquitted themselves creditably."

Black Troops and Officers

There were about 10,000 black regulars in the U.S. Army in 1917: The 9th and 10th Cavalry Regiments and the 24th and 25th Infantry Regiments. There were more than 5,000 black men in the Navy, but virtually all of them were waiters, kitchen attendants, and stokers for the ships' boilers. The Marine Corps did not admit black men. During World War I, the newly formed Selective Service system drafted more than 370,000 black men—13 percent of all draftees—though none of the local draft boards had black members. Several all-black state national guard units were also incorporated into federal service.

Though the military remained rigidly segregated, there was political pressure from black newspapers and the NAACP to commission black officers to lead black troops. The War Department created an officer training school at Fort Des Moines, Iowa. Nearly 1,250 black men enrolled—1,000 were civilians and 250 were enlisted men from the regular regiments—and over 1,000 received commissions. However, none of these new black officers were promoted above captain, and the overall command of black units remained in white hands.

Lieutenant Colonel Charles Young was eligible to lead black and white troops in World War I. He had already served in Cuba, the Philippines, Haiti, and Mexico. Several white soldiers complained, however, that they did not want to take orders from a black man, and over Young's protests, military authorities forced him to retire by claiming that he had high blood pressure. Young insisted that he was in good health, and he rode a horse from his home in Xenia, Ohio, to Washington, D.C., to prove it. Young was finally given command of a training unit in Illinois five days before the war ended.

Discrimination and Its Effects

Most white leaders embraced racial stereotypes and expected little from black soldiers. As in earlier American wars, black troops were discriminated against, abused, and neglected. Some had to drill with picks and shovels rather than rifles. At Camp Hill, Virginia, black men lived in tents with no floors, blankets, or bathing facilities through a cold winter. White men failed to salute black officers, and black officers were denied admission to officers' clubs. Morale among black troops was low, and their performance sometimes reflected it.

Military authorities did not expect to use black troops in combat. The Army preferred to employ black troops in labor battalions, as stevedores, in road construction, and as cooks and bakers. Of more than 380,000 black men who served in World War I, only 42,000 went into combat. Black troops represented 3 percent of U.S. combat strength. The Army did not prepare black soldiers adequately for combat, but military leaders complained when black soldiers who did face combat performed poorly in battle.

The 368th Infantry Regiment of the 92nd Division came in for especially harsh criticism. Fighting alongside the French in September 1918, the second and third battalions fell back in disorder. Some black officers and enlisted men ran. The white regimental commander blamed black officers, and thirty of them were relieved of command. Five officers were court-martialed for cowardice; four were sentenced to death and one to life in prison. All were later freed. But black Lieutenant Howard H. Long agreed that the perceptions of white officers caused the poor performance. "Many of the [white] field officers seemed far more concerned with reminding their Negro subordinates that they were Negroes than they were in having an effective unit that would perform well in combat."

Even the white commander of the 92nd Division, General Charles C. Ballou, identified white officers as the main problem. "It was my misfortune to be handicapped by many white officers who were rabidly hostile to the idea of a colored officer, and who continually conveyed misinformation to the staff of the superior units, and generally created much trouble and discontent. Such men will never give the Negro the square deal that is his just due."

While white officials stressed the weaknesses of the 368th Infantry Regiment, they mostly ignored the commendable records of other regiments. The 369th compiled an exemplary combat record. Sent to the front for ninety-one consecutive days, these "Men of Bronze"—as they came to be known—consisted mainly of soldiers from the 15th New York National Guard. They fought alongside the French and were given

French weapons, uniforms, helmets, and food. The 369th never lost a trench nor gave up a prisoner. By June 1918, French commanders were asking for all the black troops the Americans could send.

Most French civilians and troops accepted black soldiers as equals. French authorities awarded the *Croix de Guerre,* one of France's highest military medals, to the men of the 369th, the 371st, and the 372nd Regiments.

Black troops returned to America on segregated ships. The 15th New York National Guard Unit from the 369th Regiment was not permitted to join the farewell parade in New York City. Even when white Americans offered praise, it was riddled with racist stereotypes. The Milwaukee *Sentinel* offered a typical compliment. "Those two colored regiments fought well, and it calls for special recognition. Is there no way of getting a cargo of watermelons over there?"

Du Bois's Disappointment

Black leaders who had supported American entry in the war were embittered at the treatment of black soldiers. During the war in 1918, Du Bois appealed to black people in *The Crisis* to "close ranks" and support the war.

> We of the colored race have no ordinary interest in the outcome. That which the German power represents today spells death to the aspirations of Negroes and all darker races for equality, freedom and democracy. Let us not hesitate. Let us, while this war lasts, forget our special grievances and close ranks with our own white fellow citizens and the allied nations that are fighting for democracy.

Du Bois's unequivocal support may have been connected to his effort to secure an officer's commission in military intelligence. Du Bois did not get his commission. What he did get was criticism for his "close ranks" editorial. His former ally, William Monroe Trotter, said that Du Bois had "finally weakened, compromised, deserted the fight, [and] betrayed the cause of his race." To Trotter, Du Bois was "a rank quitter in the cause for equal rights."

In 1930 Du Bois confessed that he should not have supported U.S. intervention in the war:

> I was swept off my feet during the world war by the emotional response of America to what seemed to be a great call to duty. The thing that I did not understand is how easy and inevitable it is for an appeal to blood and force to smash to utter negation any ideal for which it is used. Instead of a war to end war, or a war to save democracy, we found ourselves during and after the war descending to the meanest and most sordid of selfish actions.

By the end of World War I, Du Bois—who had visited black troops in France—could see that black loyalty and sacrifice had not eroded white racism. He wrote defiantly in *The Crisis* that black people were determined to make America yield to its democratic ideals:

> But by the God of heaven, we are cowards and jackasses if now that the war is over, we do not marshal every ounce of our brain and brawn to fight a sterner, longer, more unbending battle against the forces of hell in our own land.

We return.

We return from fighting.

We return fighting.

Make way for Democracy! We saved it in France, and by the Great Jehovah, we will save it in the United States of America, or know the reason why.

Race Riots

Despite the reformist impulse of the progressive era and the democratic ideals trumpeted as the United States went to war against Germany, most white Americans clung to Social Darwinism and white supremacy. White people reacted with contempt and violence to demands by black people for fairer treatment and equal opportunities in American society. The campaigns of the NAACP, the efforts of the black club women, and the services and sacrifices of black men in the war not only failed to alter white racial perceptions but were sometimes accompanied by a backlash against African Americans. Ten black men still in uniform were lynched in 1919.

The racial violence that had permeated southern life in the late nineteenth century expanded into northern communities as many white Americans responded with hostility to the arrival of black migrants from the South. Black people defended themselves, and casualties among both races escalated (see Map 16–1).

Atlanta 1906

In 1906—eleven years after Booker T. Washington delivered his Cotton States Exposition address there—white mobs attacked black residents in Atlanta. Several factors aggravated white racial apprehensions in the city. In 1902 four black and four white people had been killed in a riot there. Many rural black people, attracted by economic opportunities, had moved to Atlanta. But white residents considered the newcomers more lawless and immoral than the long-time black residents. The Atlanta newspapers ran inflammatory accounts about black crime and black men who brutalized white women. Many of these stories were false or exaggerated. Two white Democrats were engaged in a divisive campaign for a U.S. Senate seat in 1906, and both candidates stirred up racial animosity. There were also determined and ultimately successful efforts underway to disfranchise black voters in Georgia.

On a warm Saturday night, September 22, 1906, a white man on Decatur Street, one of Atlanta's main thoroughfares, waved an Atlanta newspaper emblazoned with the headline: "THIRD ASSAULT," and he hollered, "Are white men going to stand for this?" The crowd roared, "No! Save our women!" "Kill the niggers." A five-day orgy of violence followed.

The mayor, police, and fire departments vainly tried to stop the mob. Thousands of white people roamed the streets in search of black victims who were tortured, beaten, and killed. White men pulled black passengers off streetcars. They destroyed black businesses. As white men armed themselves, the police disarmed black men. Black men and women who surrendered to marauding white mobs in hopes of mercy were

MAP 16–1   Major Race Riots, 1900–1923.   In the years between 1900 and 1923, race conflicts and riots occurred in dozens of American communities as black people migrated in increasing numbers to urban areas. The violence reached a peak in the immediate aftermath of World War I during the Red Summer of 1919. White Americans—in the North and South— were determined to keep black people confined to a subordinate role as menial laborers and restricted to well-defined all-black neighborhoods. African Americans who had made significant economic and military contributions to the war effort and who had congregated in large numbers in American cities insisted on participating on a more equitable basis in American society.

not spared. Black men who fought back only further infuriated the crazed white crowd. Twenty-five black people and one white person died and hundreds were injured.

Du Bois hurried home to Atlanta from a trip to Alabama to defend his wife and child. He waited on his porch with a shotgun for a mob that never came. He later explained, "I would without hesitation have sprayed their guts over the grass." In New York, black editor T. Thomas Fortune demanded retribution: "I cannot believe that the policy of non-resistance in a situation like that of Atlanta can result in anything but contempt and massacre of the race."

Booker T. Washington looked for a silver lining in the awful affair by noting that "while there is disorder in one community there is peace and harmony in thousands of others." He said that black resistance would merely result in more black fatalities. Washington went to Atlanta and appealed for racial reconciliation.

A Committee of Safety of ten black and ten white leaders was formed. Charles T. Hopkins, an influential white Atlantan, warned in strong paternalist terms, "If we let this dependent race be butchered before our eyes, we cannot face God in the judgement day." But little real racial cooperation resulted. No members of the white mob were brought to justice. Black Georgia voters were disfranchised. Atlanta's streetcars were segregated. The city had no public high school for black youngsters. The Carnegie Library did not admit black people, and the Atlanta police force had no black officers.

Springfield 1908

Two years later in August 1908, white citizens of Springfield, Illinois, attacked black residents in an episode that led to the creation of the NAACP in 1909. George Richardson, a black man, was falsely accused of raping a white woman. The sheriff managed to get Richardson out of town. But a mob tore into Springfield's small black population. Six black people were shot and killed, two were lynched, dozens were injured, and damage in the thousands of dollars was inflicted on black homes and businesses. About 2,000 black people were driven out of the community.

There was even more violence in the second decade of the twentieth century as major racial conflicts occurred between 1917 and 1921 in East St. Louis, Illinois; Houston, Texas; Chicago; Elaine, Arkansas; and Tulsa, Oklahoma. Smaller violent confrontations occurred at Washington, D.C.; Charleston, South Carolina; Knoxville, Tennessee; Omaha, Nebraska; and Waco and Longview, Texas. While different incidents sparked each riot, the underlying causes tended to be similar. White residents were concerned that recently arrived black migrants would compete for jobs and housing.

East St. Louis 1917

East St. Louis, Illinois, was a gritty industrial town of nearly sixty thousand across the Mississippi River from St. Louis, Missouri. About 10 percent of the inhabitants were black. The town's schools, public facilities, and neighborhoods were segregated. Racial tensions increased in February 1917 after 470 black workers were hired to replace white members of the American Federation of Labor who had gone on strike against the Aluminum Ore Company. On July 1, several white people drove through a black neighborhood firing guns. Shortly after, two white plainclothes police officers drove into the same neighborhood and were shot and killed by residents who may have believed that the drive-by shooters had returned.

Angry white mobs then sought revenge. Black people were mutilated and killed, and their bodies were thrown into the river. Black homes were burned. Hundreds of black people were left homeless. The police joined the rioters. Thirty-five black people and eight white people died in the violence.

The NAACP sent W. E. B. Du Bois and Martha Gruening to East St. Louis. Their report documented instance after instance of brutality. "Negroes were 'flushed' from the burning houses, and ran for their lives, screaming and begging for mercy. A Negro crawled into a shed and fired on the white men. Guardsmen started after him, but when they saw he was armed, turned to the mob and said: 'He's armed boys. You can have him. A white man's life is worth the lives of a thousand Negroes.'"

The NAACP organized a protest march in New York City and thousands of well-dressed black people marched to muffled drums down Fifth Avenue.

On July 28, 1917, the NAACP organized a silent march in New York City to protest the East St. Louis, Illinois, race riot in which thirty-five black people died as well as to denounce the ongoing epidemic of lynchings. The marchers were accompanied by the beat of muffled drums.
Library of Congress

Houston 1917

A month after the East St. Louis riot, black soldiers in Houston attacked police officers and civilians. The Third Battalion of the 24th Infantry recently had been transferred from Wyoming and California to Camp Logan near Houston where the black troops came face-to-face with Jim Crow. Streetcars and public facilities were segregated. Local white and Hispanic people regularly called the black troops "niggers."

On August 23 a black soldier tried to prevent a police officer, Lee Sparks, from beating a black woman. Sparks clubbed the soldier and hauled him off to jail. Corporal Charles W. Baltimore later attempted to determine what had happened, and he was also beaten and incarcerated. Both soldiers were later released. But a rumor circulated that Baltimore had been slain.

About one hundred armed black soldiers mounted a two-hour assault on the police station. Sixteen white and Hispanic residents, including five policemen, and four black soldiers and two black civilians were killed. The Army charged the sixty-three black soldiers with mutiny. The NAACP retained the son of Texas legend Sam Houston to help defend them, but nineteen black troops were hanged (including Corporal Baltimore) and sixty-seven others sentenced to prison. Officer Lee Sparks remained on the force and killed two black people later that year.

Chicago 1919

Between 1916 and 1919, the black population of Chicago doubled as migrants from the South moved north in search of jobs, political rights, and humane treatment. Many encountered a violent reception. A severe housing shortage strained the boundaries between crowded, segregated black neighborhoods and white residential areas. In the months after World War I ended in November 1918, racial tensions increased as black men were hired to replace striking white workers in several industries in Chicago.

The Chicago riot began on Sunday, July 27, 1919—one day after black troops were welcomed home with a parade down the city's Michigan Avenue. Eugene Williams, a young black man, was swimming in Lake Michigan and inadvertently crossed the invisible boundary that separated the black and white beaches and bathing areas. He was stoned by white people and drowned. Instead of arresting the alleged perpetrators, the police arrested a black man who complained about police inaction.

Williams's death set off a week of violence that left twenty-three black people and fifteen white people dead. More than five hundred were injured, and nearly one thousand were left homeless after fire raged though a Lithuanian neighborhood. The police often joined roaming white mobs as they attacked black pedestrians and streetcar passengers. Black men formed a barrier along State Street to stop the advance of white gangs from the stockyard district. Three regiments of the Illinois National Guard were sent into the streets, but the violence ended only on Saturday, August 1, when heavy rains kept people indoors.

During the riot, the Chicago *Defender,* the city's black newspaper, reported many violent incidents. "In the early [Tuesday] morning a thirteen-year-old lad standing on his porch at 51st and Wabash Avenue was shot to death by a white man who, in an attempt to get away, encountered a mob and his existence became history. A mounted policeman, unknown, fatally wounded a small boy in the block of Dearborn Street and was shot to death by some unknown rioter."

Elaine 1919

In the fall of 1919, black sharecroppers in and around Elaine, Arkansas, attempted to organize a union and withhold their cotton from the market until they received a higher price. Deputy sheriffs tried to break up a union meeting in a black church, and one of the deputies was killed. In retaliation, white people killed dozens of black people. No white people were prosecuted, but twelve black men were convicted of the deputy's murder. They were sentenced to death, and sixty-seven other black men received prison terms of up to twenty years. Many were tortured and beaten while they were held in jail. Ida Wells-Barnett and the Equal Rights League generated enormous publicity about the case. The NAACP appealed the convictions and in 1923 the Supreme Court overturned them.

Tulsa 1921

Violence erupted in Tulsa, Oklahoma, on May 31, 1921, after still another black man was accused of rape. Dick Rowland allegedly assaulted a white woman and rumors circulated that white men intended to lynch him. To protect Rowland, who was later found innocent, black men assembled at the courthouse jail where white men also gathered. Shooting erupted and several black and white men died.

Black men retreated to their neighborhood, known as Greenwood, to protect their families and homes. The governor dispatched the national guard, and the sheriff removed Rowland from the jail. By the morning of June 1, some five hundred white men confronted about one thousand black men across a set of railroad tracks. White men in automobiles were also cruising around the black residential area. Approximately fifty armed black people defended themselves in a black church near the edge of their neighborhood as white men advanced on them. The attackers set fire to the church. As black people fled the burning building, they were shot. More fires were set. About two thousand black residents managed to escape to a convention hall. Forty square blocks and more than 1,000 of Greenwood's homes, churches, schools and businesses went up in flames. White men even used planes to drop incendiary devices on Greenwood. As many as three hundred black people and twenty white people may have perished in what was perhaps the worst episode of violence against civilians in American history until September 11, 2001.

Following a three and a half year investigation in 2001, a commission recommended that the Oklahoma legislature offer a measure of restitution. The legislators appropriated $750,000 to formulate plans for a museum and memorial and created a Greenwood Redevelopment Authority and a scholarship program.

Rosewood 1923

In the first week of January 1923, the small town of Rosewood, Florida, was destroyed and its black residents driven out or killed. Rosewood was a mostly black community located in the pinewoods of west central Florida near the Gulf of Mexico. On New Year's Day, Fannie Taylor, a married white woman in a nearby town, claimed she had been raped and beaten by a black man. Many white people quickly assumed that Jessie Hunter was responsible. Other white people believed that Mrs. Taylor wanted to divert attention from her affair with a white man who was not her husband.

White men sought Hunter and vengeance. Unable to locate him, they beat Aaron Carrier who may have helped Taylor's white lover escape. The mob then killed Samuel Carter after mutilating him. Tensions escalated.

On January 4 a band of angry white men invaded Rosewood. Black people were prepared to defend themselves. Led by Sylvester Carrier and his mother, Sarah, many townspeople had congregated in the Carrier home. The mob fired into the residence killing Sarah Carrier. Two white men who attempted to gain entry into the home were shot and killed. Shooting continued until the mob's supply of ammunition ran out on January 5.

The following day a mob of 250, including Ku Klux Klan members from Gainesville, destroyed Rosewood. The community's black residents fled to the nearby woods, never to return. Rosewood was no more.

More than one hundred black people may have died. In 1994 the Florida legislature appropriated 2.1 million dollars to survivors of Rosewood and to families who lost property in the assault. Ten survivors were still alive and collected $150,000 each. But many black people could not prove that they had been in Rosewood in 1923 or that they were kin to people who had owned property in the town. Much of the money was not disbursed.

The Great Migration

The great migration of African Americans from the rural South to the urban North began as a trickle after the Civil War and became a flood by the second decade of the twentieth century. Between 1910 and 1940, 1,750,000 black people left the South. As a result, the black population outside the South doubled by 1940. Most of the initial wave of migrants were younger people born in the 1880s and 1890s who had no recollection of slavery but who anticipated a better future in the North.

People moved for many reasons. Often they were both pushed from their rural circumstances and pulled toward urban areas. The push resulted from disasters in southern agriculture in the 1910s. The boll weevil destroyed cotton crops across the South and floods devastated Mississippi and Alabama in 1915. The pull resulted from labor shortages created by World War I in northern industry and manufacturing. The war all but ended European immigration to the United States, eliminating a main source of cheap labor. At the same time, European governments and the United States placed huge orders for war material with northern factories. Thousands of jobs became available in industry. Northern businessmen sent labor agents to recruit southern workers.

Many southern white people reacted ambivalently to the loss of black residents. They welcomed the departure of people whom they held in contempt, but they also worried about the loss of tenants and sharecroppers.

Black newspapers encouraged black Southerners to move north. Black railroad porters and dining car employees distributed thousands of copies of the Chicago *Defender* throughout the South. One unnamed black man wrote in the *Defender* that sensible men would leave the poverty, injustice, and violence of the South for the cold weather of the North. "To die from the bite of frost is far more glorious than that of the mob. I beg of you, my brothers, to leave that benighted land. You are free men."

A black resident of one of South Carolina's Sea Islands explained in 1917 that he left to earn more money. "I could work and dig all year on the Island and best I could do would be to make $100 and take a chance of making nothin'. Well, I figured I could make 'roun' thirty or thirty-five dollars every week and at that rate save possibly $100 every two months."

Black people who departed the South escaped the most blatant forms of Jim Crow and the injustice in the judicial system. Black women fled sexual exploitation. Black people in the North could vote. The North offered better public schools. In the early twentieth century the South had almost no public high schools for black youngsters, and the school year in the urban North was not tied to the demands of agriculture.

Some black people migrated to escape the bleak, impoverished life and culture of the rural South. One young woman left South Carolina's St. Helena Island in 1919. "[I] got tired of the Island. Too lonesome. Go to bed at six o'clock. Everything dead. No dances, no moving picture show, no nothing. 'Coz every once in a while they would have a dance, but here you could go to 'em every Saturday night. That's why people move more than anything else."

The decision to migrate could take years of pondering and planning. To depart was to leave family, friends, and familiar surroundings behind for the uncertainty, confusion, and rapid pace of urban communities. Migrants often first moved to southern towns or cities, and then headed for a larger city. Poet and writer Langston Hughes was born in Joplin, Missouri, in 1902 and moved to Lincoln, Illinois. "I had no sooner graduated from grammar school in Lincoln than we moved from Illinois to Cleveland. My stepfather sent for us. He was working in a steel mill during the war, and making lots of money. But it was hard work, and he never looked the same afterwards."

Some people made the decision to move impulsively. After she was fired from her nursing position at Hampton Institute in Virginia in 1905, Jane Edna Hunter decided to go to Florida, but changed her mind:

> En route, I stopped at Richmond, Virginia, to visit with Mr. and Mrs. William Coleman, friends of Uncle Parris. They were at church when I arrived; so I sat on the doorstep to await their return. After these good friends had greeted me, Mrs. Coleman said, 'Our bags are packed to go to Cleveland, Jane. We are going to take you with us.' I was swept off my feet by the cheerful determination of the Colemans. My trunk, not yet removed from the station, was rechecked to Cleveland.

Most migrants remained fond of their southern homes and kinfolk. They returned for holidays, weddings, and funerals. Kelly Miller, who had grown up in South Carolina, spent years as a scholar and teacher at Howard University in Washington, D.C., but he still had "an attachment for the old state that time and distance cannot destroy. After all, we love to be known as a South Carolinian." Thousands of black migrants routinely sent money home to the South.

Though many black Southerners went to Florida, most migrants from the Carolinas and Virginia settled in Washington, Philadelphia, and New York (see Map 16–2). Black people who left Georgia, Alabama, and Mississippi tended to move to Pittsburgh, Cleveland, and Detroit. Migrants from Louisiana, Mississippi, and Arkansas often rode the Illinois Central Railroad to Chicago. Once they experienced a metropolis, many black people then resettled in smaller communities. Migrants to Philadelphia, for example, moved on to Harrisburg or Altoona, Pennsylvania, or to Wilmington, Delaware.

Few black Southerners moved west to California, Oregon, or Washington. California had only twenty-two thousand black residents in 1910. Substantial black migration west did not occur until the 1930s and 1940s. But in 1920 Mallie Robinson made the long trek west. Deserted by her husband, she set out with her five children (including one-year-old Jackie who would become a baseball legend) and eight other relatives. They boarded a train in Cairo, Georgia, traveled to Los Angeles, and settled in nearby Pasadena.

Most black migrants congregated in all-black neighborhoods—Harlem in New York City, Chicago's South Side, Paradise Valley in Detroit, Cleveland's East Side, and the Hill District of Pittsburgh—that later would be called ghettoes. White property owners resisted selling or renting real estate to black people outside the confines of these neighborhoods. And many southern black migrants themselves, wary of white hostility, preferred to live among black people, often friends and family who had preceded them north.

MAP 16–2   The Great Migration and the Distribution of the African-American Population in 1920.   Though several hundred thousand black Southerners migrated north in the second and third decades of the twentieth century, most African Americans remained in the southern states.

Northern Communities

Even before the Civil War, most northern cities had small free black populations. By the late nineteenth century, southern migrants began to gravitate to these urban areas and make their presence felt. Black residents established churches, social organizations, businesses, and medical facilities. They gained representation in community and political affairs.

There was less overt segregation in the North. Most northern states, as well as California, had enacted laws in the late nineteenth century that prohibited racial discrimination in public transportation, hotels, restaurants, theaters, and barbershops. Most of these states also forbade segregated schools. However, many white businesses and communities ignored the statutes and embraced Jim Crow, especially in southern Ohio, Indiana, and Illinois.

Chicago

As early as 1872, Chicago had a black policeman, and in 1876 John W. E. Thomas became the first black man elected to the Illinois Senate. Black physician Daniel Hale Williams established African-American-staffed Provident Hospital on Chicago's South Side in 1891. By 1900, black Chicagoans were the twelfth largest ethnic group in the city.

Chicago's black population surged during the first three decades of the twentieth century as migrants poured into the city. Black institutions flourished. In 1912 an NAACP branch was established. By 1920 black Chicago had eighty Baptist and thirty-six Methodist churches. The Olivet Baptist Church grew from thirty-five hundred members in 1916 to nine thousand by 1922. Because the downtown YMCA barred black men, black people raised $50,000 and Julius Rosenwald of Sears, Roebuck, and Company contributed $25,000 to build the Wabash YMCA for the black community in 1913.

The Chicago *Defender* was the city's leading black newspaper. Its founder, Robert S. Abbott, the son of slaves, began publishing the *Defender* in 1905, and by 1920 it had a nationwide circulation of 230,000. Chicago's first black bank, Jesse Binga's State Bank, was established in 1908, and in 1919 Frank L. Gillespie organized the Liberty Insurance Company.

In 1915 black Chicago's political influence expanded when Oscar DePriest was elected second ward alderman. Two other black men were elected to the city council by 1918. DePriest was elected to the U.S. House of Representatives as a Republican in 1928, becoming the first black congressman since North Carolina's George White left Congress in 1901.

As the number of black people in Chicago swelled, racial tensions exploded in the 1919 race riot. Competition for jobs was a critical issue. White employers, such as the meatpacking companies, regularly replaced white strikers with black workers. Black men took such jobs because most labor unions would not admit them. But a few weeks before the riot in 1919, the Amalgamated Meatcutters Union tried to sponsor a unity parade of black and white stockyard workers. The police prohibited it because, some believed, the meatpacking companies feared that black and white workingmen might unite.

Housing was an even more divisive issue than employment. Chicago's black population was almost entirely confined to an eight-square-mile area on the South Side east of State Street. Prosperous black people who could afford more expensive housing outside the area could not purchase it because of their race. As the black population grew, housing became more congested, and crime and vice increased.

Langston Hughes described the similar housing situation his family experienced in Cleveland:

> Rents were very high for colored people in Cleveland, and the Negro district was extremely crowded, because of the great migration. It was difficult to find a place to live. We always lived, during my high school years, either in an attic or a basement, and paid quite a lot for such inconvenient quarters. White people on the east side of the city were moving out of their frame houses and renting them to Negroes at double and triple the rents they could receive from others. An eight room house with one bath would be cut up into apartments and five or six families crowded into it, each two-room kitchenette apartment renting for what the whole house had rented for before.

Harlem

Harlem was a white community in upper Manhattan that had declined by the latter 1800s. It then enjoyed an incredible building boom that occurred in anticipation of the construction of the subway that would link upper Manhattan to downtown New

York City by the early twentieth century. But real estate speculators overbuilt and were left with empty houses and apartments. Facing foreclosure, many white property owners sold or rented to black people in Harlem. In 1904 Philip A. Payton formed the Afro American Realty company that sold homes and rented apartments to black clients before it failed in 1908.

Harlem's white residents opposed the influx of black people. Some of them formed the Harlem Property Owners' Improvement Corporation in 1910 to block black settlement. However, many white property owners—eager for a profit—preferred to sell to black people than to maintain white unity.

As thousands of black people moved to Harlem, many left the "Tenderloin" and "San Juan Hill" areas of Manhattan's West Side where New York's black residents had lived in the nineteenth century. Black churches took the lead in the "On to Harlem" movement as they occupied churches formerly used by white denominations. Some of the black churches were among the largest property owners in Harlem.

St. Philip's Episcopal Church, the wealthiest black church in the United States, noted for its solemn services and elite parishioners, moved from West 25th Street in the "Tenderloin" in 1910 to Harlem. In 1911, St. Philip's purchased ten apartment houses on West 135th Street between Lenox and Seventh Avenues for $640,000. The Reverend Adam Clayton Powell Sr. and the Abyssinian Baptist Church, St. Mark's Episcopal Church, and the AME Zion Church ("Mother Zion") also moved to Harlem and acquired extensive real estate holdings there. These churches helped make Harlem a black community.

As the black population increased in Harlem, large houses and apartments were often subdivided among working families who could not rent or buy in other areas of New York. They paid higher prices for real estate than white people did. The average Harlem family paid $9.50 a room per month while white working families paid $6.50 for similar accommodations elsewhere in New York.

By 1920, seventy-five thousand black people lived in Harlem. Harlem became the "Negro Capital of the World." Black businesses and institutions, including the Odd Fellows, Masons, Elks, Pythians, the NAACP, and the Urban League moved to Harlem. Black newspapers—the *New York News* and *Amsterdam News*—opened in Harlem to compete with the older *New York Age*. One resident observed, "If my race can make Harlem, good lord, what can't it do?"

Families

Migration placed black families under enormous strains. Relatives frequently moved north separately. Fathers or mothers would leave a spouse and children behind as they sought employment and housing. Children might be left with grandparents for extended periods. Extended family members—cousins, in-laws, brothers and sisters— often shared crowded living space.

Men generally found more opportunities for work in northern industries than did women. There was a huge demand for unskilled labor during and after World War I. In 1915, Henry Ford astounded industrial America when he began to pay employees of the Ford Motor Company in Detroit the unprecedented sum of $5 per day, and that included black men and occasionally black women. However, few black man were pro-moted beyond menial labor. Except for some manufacturing jobs during the war, black women were confined to domestic and janitorial work. Mary Ellen Washington recalled the experience in her family. "In the 1920s my mother and five aunts migrat-ed to Cleveland, Ohio from Indianapolis and, in spite of their many talents, they found every door except the kitchen door closed to them."

Black women employed as domestics lived with white families, worked long hours, and saw more of their white employer's children than they did their own. One maid explained her dreary and unhappy situation:

> I am now past forty years of age and am the mother of three children. My husband died nearly fifteen years ago. . . . For more than thirty years—or since I was ten years old—I have been a servant in one capacity or another in white families.

> I frequently work from fourteen to sixteen hours a day. I am compelled . . . to sleep in the house. I am allowed to go home to my own children, the oldest of whom is a girl of 18 years, only once in two weeks, every other Sunday afternoon—even then I'm not permit-ted to stay all night. . . . I don't know what it is to go to church; I don't know what it is to go to a lecture or entertainment of any kind; I live a treadmill life. . . . You might as well say that I'm on duty all the time—from sunrise to sunrise, every day in the week. I am the slave, body and soul, of this family.

Some vulnerable younger women were lured into prostitution in the intimidating urban environment. Black women's organizations worked to prevent newly arrived mi-grants from falling prey to sexual exploitation. They did not always succeed. Some women made a calculated decision to turn sex to their economic advantage. Sara Brooks caustically commented, "Some women woulda had a man to come and live in the house and had an outside boyfriend too, in order to get the house paid for and the bills. They meet a man and if he promises 'em four or five dollars to go to bed, they's grab it. That's called sellin' your own body, and I wasn't raised like that."

Despite the pressures, black families survived. Most northern black families, though hardly well-to-do, were two-parent households. Fathers were present in seven of ten black families in New York City in 1925. But the great migration transformed southern peasants into an urban proletariat.

Conclusion

In 1900, Booker T. Washington was the nation's most influential black leader. He soothed white people and reassured black Americans as he counseled conciliation, pa-tience, and agricultural and mechanical training as the most effective means to bridge the racial divide. His 1895 speech at the Cotton States Exposition in Atlanta elicited support and praise from both white and black listeners.

The Wizard of Tuskegee had little appreciation for criticism and did not hesitate to attack his opponents, including William Monroe Trotter and W. E. B. Du Bois. He worked to subvert the Niagara Movement and the NAACP. But support for Washing-ton and his conservative strategy diminished. Washington died in 1915. By 1920 the

NAACP assumed the lead in the struggle for civil rights as it fought in the courts and legislatures.

The Talented Tenth of black Americans, distinguished by their educational and economic resources, promoted "self-help" through a variety of organizations—from women's groups to fraternities and sororities—to enhance their own status and to help less affluent black people.

As black men served in World War I and as thousands of black Southerners migrated north, many white Americans became alarmed that African Americans were not as content with their subordinate and isolated status as Booker T. Washington had suggested they were. Some white Americans responded with race riots to prevent black Americans from assuming a more equitable role in American society. By 1920, despite white opposition, black Americans had demonstrated that they would not accept economic subservience and the denial of their rights.

Review Questions

1. Compare and evaluate the strategies promoted by Booker T. Washington with those of W. E. B. Du Bois and the NAACP.

2. On which specific issues did Booker T. Washington and W. E. B. Du Bois agree? On which did they disagree?

3. Assess Booker T. Washington's contributions to the advancement of black people.

4. To what extent did middle-class and prosperous black people contribute to progress for their race? Were their efforts effective?

5. Why did most African Americans support U.S. participation in World War I? Was that support justified?

6. What factors contributed to race riots and violence in the World War I era?

7. Why did many black people leave the South in the 1920s? Why didn't this migration begin earlier or later?

Recommended Reading

W. E. B. Du Bois. *The Souls of Black Folk*. New York: Library of America, 1903. An essential collection of superb essays.

John Hope Franklin and August Meier. *Black Leaders of the Twentieth Century*. Urbana, IL: University of Illinois Press, 1982. A series of "mini biographies" of fifteen people including Washington, Du Bois, T. Thomas Fortune, and Ida Wells-Barnett.

Willard Gatewood. *Aristocrats of Color: The Black Elite, 1880–1920*. Bloomington, IN: Indiana University Press, 1990. An examination of the lives and activities of well-to-do black people.

Lawrence Otis Graham. *One Kind of People: Inside America's Black Upper Class*. New York: HarperCollins, 1999. An informative history and analysis of black America's wealthiest families and organizations.

TIMELINE

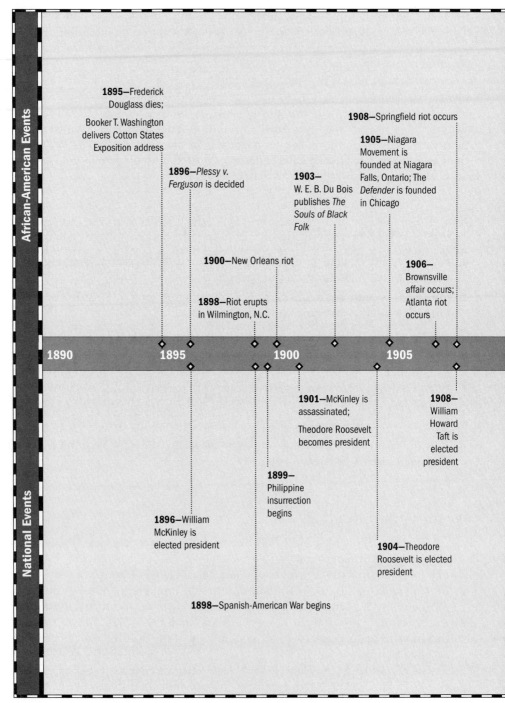

African-American Events

1895—Frederick Douglass dies; Booker T. Washington delivers Cotton States Exposition address

1896—*Plessy v. Ferguson* is decided

1898—Riot erupts in Wilmington, N.C.

1900—New Orleans riot

1903—W. E. B. Du Bois publishes *The Souls of Black Folk*

1905—Niagara Movement is founded at Niagara Falls, Ontario; The *Defender* is founded in Chicago

1906—Brownsville affair occurs; Atlanta riot occurs

1908—Springfield riot occurs

1890   1895   1900   1905

National Events

1896—William McKinley is elected president

1898—Spanish-American War begins

1899—Philippine insurrection begins

1901—McKinley is assassinated; Theodore Roosevelt becomes president

1904—Theodore Roosevelt is elected president

1908—William Howard Taft is elected president

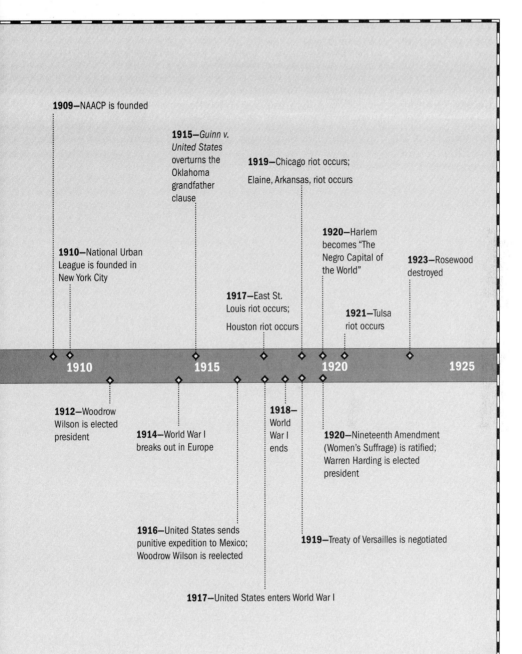

1909—NAACP is founded

1915—*Guinn v. United States* overturns the Oklahoma grandfather clause

1919—Chicago riot occurs; Elaine, Arkansas, riot occurs

1920—Harlem becomes "The Negro Capital of the World"

1923—Rosewood destroyed

1910—National Urban League is founded in New York City

1917—East St. Louis riot occurs; Houston riot occurs

1921—Tulsa riot occurs

1910   1915   1920   1925

1912—Woodrow Wilson is elected president

1918—World War I ends

1914—World War I breaks out in Europe

1920—Nineteenth Amendment (Women's Suffrage) is ratified; Warren Harding is elected president

1916—United States sends punitive expedition to Mexico; Woodrow Wilson is reelected

1919—Treaty of Versailles is negotiated

1917—United States enters World War I

Louis R. Harlan. *Booker T. Washington: The Making of a Black Leader, 1856–1901*. New York: Oxford University Press, 1972 and *Booker T. Washington: The Wizard of Tuskegee, 1901–1915*. New York: Oxford University Press, 1983. The definitive two-volume biography of Washington.

David Levering Lewis. *W. E. B. Du Bois: Biography of a Race, 1868–1919*. New York: Henry Holt and Co., 1993; *W. E. B. Du Bois: The Fight for Equality and the American Century, 1919–1963*. New York: Henry Holt and Co., 2001. A magisterial and exhaustive account of the 95-year life and times of Du Bois.

Deborah Gray White. *Too Heavy a Load: Black Women in Defense of Themselves*. New York: Norton, 1999. An exploration of the contours of black women's history in the twentieth century.

Chapter 17

African Americans and the 1920s

Strikes and the Red Scare

In 1919 and 1920, Americans were bewildered and angered by labor unrest and afraid that the communists (or "Reds") in the new Soviet Union would try to incite a revolution in America. There were 3,600 strikes in 1919 as workers who had deferred demands during the war for pay raises and improved working conditions walked off their jobs. More than 300,000 steel workers in Pittsburgh and Gary, Indiana, struck, including 7,000 unskilled black steel workers in Pittsburgh. In a demonstration of solidarity with striking shipyard workers, most of Seattle's working people shut the city down in a general strike. Americans were even more alarmed when police officers in Boston went on strike.

Political leaders exacerbated these feelings by warning that communists and foreign agents were plotting to overthrow the government. Woodrow Wilson's Attorney General A. Mitchell Palmer ordered 249 aliens deported and some six thousand arrested and imprisoned in gross violation of their rights, but it was an action that many Americans warmly approved. Palmer went too far, however, when he predicted that the Red revolution would begin in the United States on May 1, 1920. There was no revolution, and confidence in Palmer waned.

Prompted in part by the Red Scare, xenophobia (fear of foreigners) swept the nation in the 1920s. Two Sicilian immigrants, Nicola Sacco and Bartolomeo Vanzetti, who were anarchists, were charged in 1920 with a murder that had occurred during a payroll robbery near Boston. They were found guilty and executed in 1927. But their supporters believed that the guilty verdict was due more to their foreign origins and radical beliefs than to conclusive proof that they had committed the murder.

Racism

Many white Americans believed that the United States was under siege as European immigrants and black migrants flooded American cities. Pseudoscholars warned about the peril these "inferior" peoples posed. In 1916 Madison Grant published *The Passing of the Great Race*. Grant warned that America was committing "race suicide," because northern Europeans and their descendants—the Great Race—were being

313

diluted by inferior people from eastern and southern Europe. Lothrop Stoddard's *The Rising Tide of Color* in 1920 argued that people of color would never be equal to white Americans.

These racist claims strengthened the cause of white supremacy in the 1920s and helped "protect" America from the "threat" of immigration. In 1921 and in 1924, Congress imposed quotas that severely restricted immigration from southern and eastern Europe and prohibited it entirely from Asia.

The Birth of a Nation

In 1915 D. W. Griffith released *The Birth of a Nation,* a cinematic masterpiece and historical travesty based on Thomas Dixon's 1905 novel, *The Clansman.* Both the book and the film purported to depict Reconstruction in South Carolina authentically. In this account, immoral and ignorant Negroes joined by shady mulattoes and greedy white Republicans seize control of state government until the heroic Ku Klux Klan saves the state and rescues its white womanhood. The film grossed 18 million dollars (254 million in 2000 dollars) and helped to distort public perceptions about Reconstruction and black Americans.

The NAACP was enraged by *The Birth of a Nation* and fought to halt its presentation. W. E. B. Du Bois complained in *The Crisis* that in the film "the Negro [was] represented either as an ignorant fool, a vicious rapist, a venal or unscrupulous politician or a faithful but doddering idiot." The motion picture unleashed racist violence. After seeing the film in Lafayette, Indiana, an infuriated white man killed a young black man. In Houston, white theatergoers shouted, "Lynch him!" during a scene in which a white actor in blackface pursued the film's star, Lillian Gish. In front of a St. Louis theater, white real-estate agents passed out circulars calling for residential segregation.

Thanks largely to NAACP opposition, the film was banned in Pasadena, California; Wilmington, Delaware; and Boston. In Chicago, Republican Mayor "Big Bill" Thompson appointed AME bishop Archibald Carey to the board of censors, which temporarily banned the film there. Ironically, the NAACP campaign may have provided publicity that attracted more viewers to the film. However, the campaign also helped increase NAACP membership.

The Ku Klux Klan

The Ku Klux Klan, which disappeared after Reconstruction, was resurrected a few months after *The Birth of a Nation* was released. On Thanksgiving night in 1915, William J. Simmons and thirty-four other men gathered at Stone Mountain near Atlanta, and in the flickering shadows of a fiery cross, they brought the Klan back to life.

Klansmen styled themselves as "100 percent Americans" who opposed perceived threats from immigrants, as well as black Americans. The Klan claimed to represent white, Anglo-Saxon, Protestant America. With European immigrants flocking to America, William Simmons announced that the United States was no melting pot. "It is a garbage can! . . . When the hordes of aliens walk to the ballot box and their votes outnumber yours, then that alien horde has got you by the throat."

The Klan found enormous support among apprehensive white middle-class Americans in the North and West. Many of these people believed that the liberal, immoral, and loose lifestyles that they associated with urban life, immigrants, and African Americans threatened their religious beliefs and conservative cultural values. The Klan attacked the theory of evolution, fought for the prohibition of alcoholic beverages, and claimed to uphold the "sanctity" of white womanhood. The KKK opposed Jews, Roman Catholics, and black people. Klansmen burned synagogues and Catholic churches. They beat, branded, and lynched their opponents.

By 1925 the Klan had an estimated five million members, and 40,000 of them marched in Washington, D.C., that year. The Klan attracted small businessmen, shopkeepers, clerks, Protestant clergymen, farmers, and professional people. It was open only to native-born white men, but it also had a Women's Order, a Junior Order for boys, and a Tri K Klub for girls. The Klan was active in Oregon, Colorado, Illinois, and Maine, and it became a potent political force in Indiana, Oklahoma, and Texas where candidates who refused to support or join the Klan stood little chance of election.

The Klan was also an effective money-making machine. Its leaders collected millions of dollars in initiation fees, membership dues, and income from selling Klan paraphernalia. But the Klan declined rapidly in the late 1920s when its leaders fought among themselves. Its claim to uphold the purity of white womanhood was damaged when one of its leaders, D. C. Stephenson, was arrested in Indiana and charged with raping a young woman who subsequently committed suicide. Stephenson was sentenced to life in prison, and the Klan never fully recovered.

Protest, Pride, and Pan-Africanism: Black Organizations in the Twenties

African Americans responded to racism and to larger cultural and economic developments in the 1920s in several ways. The NAACP fought to secure constitutional rights and guarantees by advocacy in the political and judicial systems. Many working-class black people who had migrated to northern cities were attracted to the racial pride promoted by Marcus Garvey and the Universal Negro Improvement Association. There were also attempts to foster racial cooperation among peoples of African descent and to exert diplomatic influence through Pan-African congresses.

The NAACP

During its second decade, the NAACP expanded its influence and increased its membership. In 1916 James Weldon Johnson (who wrote "Lift Every Voice and Sing", the song that was embraced as the Negro National Anthem) joined the NAACP as field secretary. He played a pivotal role in the organization's development and in its growth from 9,000 members in 1916 to 90,000 in 1920. Johnson traveled tirelessly, recruiting members and establishing branches.

Johnson impressed both black and white people. He got along well with W. E. B. Du Bois and was an excellent diplomat. He methodically reported the gruesome details of lynchings, and when some NAACP directors complained in 1921 that these graphic descriptions offended people, Johnson stood his ground. "What we need to do is to root out the thing which makes possible these horrible details. I am of the opinion that this can be done only through the fullest publicity."

In 1918 Johnson hired Walter White to assist him. White was from Atlanta and, like Johnson, a graduate of Atlanta University. White's fair complexion permitted him to move easily among white people to investigate racial discrimination and violence. Though his domineering personality offended some NAACP officials and supporters, White devoted his life to the organization and to racial justice.

Johnson and the NAACP fought hard in Congress to secure passage of the anti-lynching bill in 1921 and 1922 (see Chapter 16). The legislation ultimately failed, but the NAACP succeeded in publicizing the persistence of barbaric behavior by mobs in a nation supposedly devoted to the rule of law. It was the first campaign by a civil rights organization to lobby Congress, and—like the attempt to block *The Birth of a Nation*—it won favorable publicity and goodwill for the NAACP.

Johnson blamed the anti-lynching bill's failure on Republican senators. He charged that the Republican party took black support for granted: "The Republican Party will hold the Negro and do as little for him as possible, and the Democratic Party will have none of him at all." He warned, however, that black voters in the North would abandon the Republicans and pointed out that black voters in Harlem had elected a black Democrat to the state legislature.

The NAACP continued to rely on the judicial system to protect black Americans and enforce their civil rights. By the 1920s, the Democratic party in virtually every southern state barred black people from membership, which excluded them from voting in Democratic primary elections. The result was what were known as "white primaries." Because the Republican party had almost ceased to exist in most of the South, victory in the Democratic primary elections led invariably to victory in the general election. In 1924 the NAACP, in cooperation with its branch in El Paso, filed suit over the exclusion of black voters from the Democratic primary in Texas. In 1927 the Supreme Court ruled in *Nixon v. Herndon* that the Democratic primary was unconstitutional—the first victory in what would become a twenty-year legal struggle to permit black men and women to vote in primary elections across the South.

In Detroit in 1925, black physician Ossian Sweet and his family moved into an all-white neighborhood. For several nights a mob threatened the Sweet family and other people who joined in their defense. One evening, shots were fired from the Sweet home that killed a white man. Twelve occupants of the house were charged with murder. The NAACP retained two of the nation's finest criminal attorneys to defend the Sweets. The Sweets pleaded self-defense, and were acquitted.

Marcus Garvey and the UNIA

With several million enthusiastic followers, Marcus Garvey's Universal Negro Improvement Association (UNIA) became the largest mass movement of black people in American history. The UNIA enabled black people to celebrate one another and their heritage and to anticipate a glorious future. Garvey was a charismatic and flamboyant leader who wove racial pride, Christian faith, and economic cooperation into a black nationalist organization that had spread throughout the United States by the early 1920s.

Garvey was born in 1887 in the British colony of Jamaica, the eleventh child in a rural family. He quit school at age fourteen and became a printer in Kingston, the island's capital; he was promoted to foreman before he was fired in 1907 for prolabor activities during a strike. He traveled to Costa Rica, Panama, Ecuador, and Nicaragua and became increasingly disturbed over the conditions black workers endured in fields, factories, and mines. He returned to Jamaica and set out to educate himself. He spent two years in London where he sharpened his oratorical and debating skills.

He returned to Jamaica and founded the UNIA in 1914. With the slogan: "One God! One Aim! One Destiny!" he stressed the need for black people to organize for their own advancement. Garvey had read Booker T. Washington's *Up from Slavery* and was much impressed with Washington's emphasis on self-help and on progress through education and the acquisition of skills. Garvey also—like Washington—could criticize black people for their lack of progress: "The bulk of our people are in darkness and are really unfit for good society." They had no right to aspire to equality because they had "done nothing to establish the right to equality."

Garvey came to the United States in 1916 just as thousands of African Americans were migrating to cities, and he built the UNIA into a major movement. He urged his listeners to take pride in themselves as they restored their race to its previous greatness. "We must canonize our own saints, create our own martyrs, and elevate to positions of fame and honor black men and women who have made their distinct contributions to our racial history." He reminded people that Africa had a remarkable past. "Africa was peopled with a race of cultured black men, who were masters in art, science and literature; men who were cultured and refined; men, who, it was said, were like the gods. . . Black men, you were once great; you shall be great again." With the formation of the New York division of the UNIA in Harlem in 1917, Garvey exhorted black people to take control of their destiny. Still, he blamed them for their predicament. "That the Negro race became a race of slaves was not the fault of God Almighty. . . it was the fault of the race." Their salvation would result from their own exertion and not from concessions by white people.

Garvey's message and the UNIA spread to black communities large and small. He regularly couched his rhetoric in religious terms, and he came to be known as the Black Moses, a messiah. Garvey dwelled on Christ's betrayal as he identified himself with Jesus. "If Garvey dies, Garvey lives." "Christ died to make men free, I shall die to give courage and inspiration to my race."

Garvey's followers enjoyed the pageantry, ceremonies, and titles that were a part of the UNIA. The African Legionnaires and the Black Cross Nurses, resplendent in their uniforms, assembled in New York's Liberty Hall, and they paraded through Harlem. They prayed from The Universal Negro Catechism and reflected on their connection to Africa: "O Blessed Lord Jesus, redeem Africa from the hands of those who exploit and ravish her."

Garvey and the UNIA also established businesses that employed nearly one thousand black people. The weekly newspaper, *Negro World,* promoted Garvey's ideology. In New York City, the Negro Factories Corporation operated three grocery stores, two restaurants, a printing plant, a steam laundry, and a factory that turned out uniforms, hats, and shirts for UNIA members. The association also owned buildings, vehicles, and facilities in other cities. Garvey proudly declared to white Americans that the

UNIA "employs thousands of black girls and black boys. Girls who could only be washer women in your homes, we made clerks, stenographers. . . . You will see from the start we tried to dignify our race."

Garvey may be best remembered for his proposal to return black people to Africa by way of the Black Star Line, a steamship company he founded in 1919. Garvey sold stock in the company for five dollars a share, and he hoped to establish a fleet with black officers and crew members. In 1920 the company purchased the *Yarmouth,* a dilapidated vessel that became its first ship. Garvey bought two additional ships, the *Kanawha* and the *Booker T. Washington,* but lacked the financial resources to transport anyone to Africa.

He knew that it was unrealistic to expect several million black residents of the Western Hemisphere to join the back-to-Africa enterprise, but he believed that the UNIA could liberate Africa from European colonial rule. The UNIA adopted a red, green, and black flag for the proposed African republic that represented the blood, land, and race of the people of the continent.

The UNIA attempted to establish a settlement in southern Liberia. Garvey also petitioned the League of Nations to permit the UNIA to take possession of the former German colony of Tangaruyka (today's Tanzania) in East Africa. But the major colonial powers in Africa—Britain and France—and the United States thwarted Garvey's plans.

The United States government and several black American leaders also undermined the UNIA and Garvey. J. Edgar Hoover and the Bureau of Investigation (the predecessor of the FBI) considered Garvey a threat to the racial status quo. Hoover

Jamaican-born Marcus Garvey arrived in the United States in 1916 and quickly rose to prominence as the head of the Universal Negro Improvement Association. Garvey appears here in a 1924 parade in Harlem attired in a uniform similar to those worn by British colonial governors in Jamaica, Trinidad, and elsewhere.
New York Daily News

employed black agents to infiltrate the UNIA and compile information that could be used to deport Garvey, who had never become an American citizen.

Garvey had few friends or admirers among African-American leaders because he and they differed fundamentally on strategy and goals. Garvey deplored efforts to gain legal and political rights within the American system. By appealing to the black masses, he rejected Du Bois's notion that the Talented Tenth would lead the race to liberation. He mocked the NAACP as the National Association for the Advancement of Certain People. Not long after he arrived in the United States, Garvey visited the NAACP office in New York, and he commented sourly that it was essentially a white organization. "There was no representation of the race there that any one could recognize. . . . you had to be as near white as possible, otherwise there was no place for you as stenographer, clerk or attendant in the office of the National Association for the Advancement of 'Colored' People."

Garvey called W. E. B. Du Bois a "lazy, dependent mulatto." In return, Du Bois described Garvey as "the most dangerous enemy of the Negro race in America and the world. . . either a lunatic or a traitor." A. Philip Randolph, the black labor leader, called Garvey an "unquestioned fool and ignoramus."

Unlike African-American leaders, Garvey believed that black and white people had separate destinies, and he regarded interracial cooperation as absurd. Thus, Garvey considered a meeting he had with Ku Klux Klan leaders in Atlanta in 1922 consistent with his racial views. He praised the white supremacist organization. "They are better friends to my race, for telling us what they are, and what they mean, thereby giving us a chance to stir for ourselves." He added that "every whiteman is a Klansman. . . and there is no use lying about it."

In 1922 Garvey and three other UNIA leaders were indicted on twelve counts of fraudulent use of the U.S. mail to sell stock in the Black Star Line. Eight African-American leaders wrote to the U.S. Attorney General to condemn Garvey and insist on his prosecution. Though Garvey was guilty of no more than mismanagement and incompetence, he was eventually found guilty and sent to the federal penitentiary in Atlanta in 1925. President Calvin Coolidge commuted his sentence in 1927, and he was deported.

Without Garvey the UNIA barely survived the loss of its inspirational leader, and it declined steadily in the late 1920s and the 1930s. The various UNIA businesses closed, and its property was sold. Garvey was never permitted to return to the United States, and he died in London in 1940. However, his legacy persisted. The Reverend Earl Little, a Baptist minister and the father of Malcolm X, belonged to the UNIA and much admired Garvey. Malcolm X recalled his father's association with Garvey. "I remember hearing that he had black followers not only in the United States but all around the world, and I remember how the meetings always closed with my father saying, several times, and the people chanting after him, 'Up, you mighty race, you can accomplish what you will!'"

Pan-Africanism

As diametrically opposed as Garvey and Du Bois were on most matters, they shared an abiding interest in Africa. Garvey, Du Bois, and other black leaders believed that people of African descent from around the world should come together to share their heritage, discuss their ties to the continent, and to explore ways to moderate—if not eliminate—colonial rule in Africa.

By 1914, European powers had established colonies across almost all of Africa. Only Liberia and Ethiopia (then called Abyssinia) remained independent. Christian missionaries sought to convert Africans, and European companies exploited Africa's human and natural resources. The European powers were convincd that they represented a superior race and culture.

The first Pan-African Congress had convened in London in 1900. Du Bois chaired its Committee on the Address to the Nations of the World. He called for the creation of "a great central Negro state of the world." But Du Bois did not insist on the immediate withdrawal of the European powers from Africa. Instead he recommended that they grant "as soon as practicable the rights of responsible self-government to the black colonies of Africa and the West Indies."

The second Pan-African Congress met in Paris in February 1919, near Versailles, where the peace conference ending World War I was assembled. There were fifty-eight delegates from sixteen nations. Du Bois was among the sixteen African Americans in attendance. (None of them had been to Africa.) Marcus Garvey did not attend. The delegates took seriously the Fourteen Points that U.S. President Woodrow Wilson had proposed to fashion the postwar world. They were especially interested in the fifth point, which called for the interests of colonial peoples to be given "equal weight" in the adjustment of colonial claims after the war. The congress recommended that the League of Nations assume authority over the former German colonies in East Africa. The League later delegated authority to administer those colonies to Britain, France, and Belgium. Two more Pan-African Congresses in the 1920s met in Brussels and London but also failed to influence the policies of the colonial powers.

Labor

The arrival of thousands of black migrants in American cities during and after World War I changed the composition of the industrial workforce and intensified pressure on labor unions to admit black members. By 1916, twelve thousand of the nearly fifty thousand workers in the Chicago stockyards were black people. In Detroit, black laborers made up nearly 14 percent of the workforce in the automobile industry. The Ford Motor Company employed fifty black people in 1916 and 2,500 by 1920.

Yet more than two-thirds of black workers in 1920 were still employed in agriculture and domestic service (see Figure 17–1). Less than 20 percent were engaged in manufacturing. Those who were part of industrial America disproportionately worked in the dreary, dirty, and sometimes dangerous unskilled jobs that paid the least. Still that work paid more than agricultural labor.

Most of the major labor unions would not admit black workers. Since its founding in 1886, the American Federation of Labor (AFL) officially prohibited racial discrimination, but most of its local unions were all white and all male. The AFL was made up of skilled laborers, and less than 20 percent of black workers were skilled. But even those with skills were usually not admitted to the local craft unions that made up the

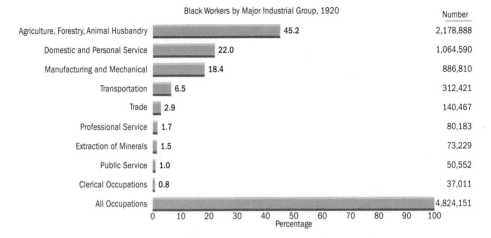

FIGURE 17–1 Black Workers by Major Industrial Group, 1920   By 1920 thousands of African Americans had moved to northern cities and were employed in a variety of mostly unskilled and low-paying industrial jobs that nonetheless paid more than farm labor. Still, agriculture remained the largest single source of employment among black people, and agriculture and domestic service together employed more than two-thirds of African-American men and women. About 5 percent were employed in "white collar" jobs.

Source: Sterling D. Spero and Abram L. Harris, *The Black Worker: The Negro and the Labor Movement* (1928), 81.

AFL. Unions that did admit black workers included those representing cigarmakers, coal miners, garment workers, and longshoremen.

By the World War I years, the NAACP and the Urban League regularly appealed to employers and unions to accept black laborers. The Urban League attempted to convince business owners that black employees would be efficient and reliable. But many employers preferred to divide black and white workers by hiring black men and women as strikebreakers, thereby enraging striking white workers. In 1918 Samuel Gompers, the long-time president of the AFL, agreed to bring more black people into the federation, but there were few tangible results. The Urban League did succeed in persuading the U.S. Department of Labor to establish a Division of Negro Economics to advise the secretary of labor on issues involving black workers.

The Brotherhood of Sleeping Car Porters

By the 1920s, the Pullman company, which owned and operated passenger railroad coaches, was the largest employer of black people in the United States. More than twelve thousand black men worked as porters on Pullman railroad cars. After founding the Pullman Palace Car Company in 1867, George Pullman decided to employ only black men as porters—on the assumption that prosperous white people were accustomed to being waited on by black servants. Furthermore, black employees could be and were paid less than white workers.

Pullman porters toiled for upwards of four hundred hours each month to maintain the coaches and serve the passengers. Porters had to prepare the cars before the train's departure and service them after the train arrived at its destination, though they were paid only for the duration of the trip. They assisted passengers, shined shoes (they had to purchase the polish themselves), and arranged sleeping compartments. To add to the indignity, white travelers invariably called these black men "George," no matter what their actual name was. Porters were paid an average of $67.50 per month—about $810 per year. But with tips, they earned more, occasionally as much as $300 a month. They had to buy their own uniforms during their first ten years of employment.

Though strenuous, Pullman employment was the most satisfactory work many black men could hope to achieve. Barred from business and industry, black men with college degrees worked as sleeping car porters. As poorly paid as they were compared with many white workers, they still earned more than most black schoolteachers. Most of these Pullman employees regarded themselves as solid, respectable members of the middle class.

It seemed unlikely that men as subservient and unobtrusive as the Pullman porters would form a labor union to challenge one of America's most powerful corporations. But they did. The key figure in this effort was A. Philip Randolph. In 1925 a gathering of Pullman porters in Harlem invited Randolph to become their "general organizer" as they formed the Brotherhood of Sleeping Car Porters (BSCP).

A. Philip Randolph

Randolph was a socialist with superb oratorical skills who had earned a reputation as a radical on the streets of Harlem. He was born in 1889 in Crescent City, Florida, and migrated to New York City in 1911 where he attended City College and joined the Socialist party. With Chandler Owen, he founded *The Messenger,* a socialist journal that drew the attention of federal agents. Randolph opposed American involvement in World War I. In 1919 Department of Justice officials arrested Randolph and Owen and held them briefly.

Randolph was handsome, dignified, impeccably dressed, and aloof. But he maintained an unwavering commitment to economic and racial change for more than five decades.

Randolph faced the daunting task of recruiting support for the brotherhood, winning recognition from the Pullman company, and gaining the union's acceptance by the AFL. There was considerable opposition, much of it from within the black community. Many porters were too frightened to join the brotherhood. Black clergymen counseled against union activities. Black newspapers, including the Chicago *Defender,* editorially opposed the BSCP.

But Randolph persevered with the assistance of Milton Webster, who became vice president of the brotherhood after Randolph assumed the presidency. With the slogan "Service not servitude," the two men recruited members, organized the brotherhood, and attempted to negotiate with the Pullman company. Pullman executives ignored Randolph's overtures. They fired porters who joined the union, infiltrated union meetings with company agents, and organized an alternative company union.

Though the NAACP and the Urban League strongly supported the BSCP, progress was slow. In 1928 Randolph threatened to call a strike against the Pullman company but called it off after AFL President William Green promised modest assistance to the as yet unrecognized union. Green's offer saved face for Randolph. It is unlikely that a strike would have succeeded or that most porters would have left the trains. The Great Depression of the 1930s brought layoffs and mass resignations from the brotherhood. The AFL barely responded to repeated charges of discrimination by Randolph, the NAACP, and Urban League. The BSCP nearly collapsed. Not until the passage of legislation during President Franklin D. Roosevelt's New Deal in the mid-1930s did the BSCP make substantial gains.

The Harlem Renaissance

For most of American history, most black and white Americans have shown little interest in serious literature or intellectual developments. The 1920s were no exception. People were far more fascinated by sports, automobiles, the radio, and popular music than they were by poetry, plays, museums, or novels. Still the twenties witnessed a proliferation of creative works by a remarkable group of gifted writers and artists. Among white writers T. S. Eliot, Ezra Pound, Edith Wharton, Ernest Hemingway, Sinclair Lewis, Eugene O'Neill, Willa Cather, and F. Scott Fitzgerald produced literary works that explored a range of themes but were mostly critical of American life and society. Eliot, Pound, Wharton, Fitzgerald, and Hemingway found American culture so unappealing that they exiled themselves in Europe.

Black intellectuals congregated in Manhattan and gave rise to the creative movement known as the Harlem Renaissance. Poets, novelists, and painters probed racial themes and grappled with what it meant to be black in America. There was no precise beginning to this renaissance. As early as 1920, W. E. B. Du Bois wrote in *The Crisis* that the nation was on the verge of a "renaissance of American Negro literature." In 1925 the New York *Herald Tribune* declared that America was "on the edge, if not already in the midst of, what might not improperly be called a Negro renaissance." No matter when it began, the Harlem Renaissance produced a stunning collection of artistic works, especially in creative writing, that continued into the 1930s.

Before Harlem

There had certainly been serious cultural developments among African Americans before the 1920s. From 1897 to 1928 the American Negro Academy functioned as a forum for "the Talented Tenth" as men such as Alain Locke, Kelly Miller and Du Bois reflected on race and color.

At the turn of the century, novelist Charles W. Chestnutt depicted a young black woman's attempt to pass for white in *The House behind the Cedars,* and he wrote about racist violence in the post-Reconstruction South in *The Marrow of Tradition.* Ohio poet Paul Laurence Dunbar wrote evocatively of black life, frequently relying on black dialect, before he died at age thirty-four in 1906. Henry Ossawa Tanner had an illustrious career as a painter.

Carter G. Woodson, the son of Virginia slaves, earned a Ph.D. at Harvard in history and founded the Association for the Study of Negro Life and History in 1915. He stressed the need for the scholarly examination of Negro history and established the *Journal of Negro History* and the *Negro History Bulletin.* He also founded Associated

Publishers to publish books on black history. Woodson wrote several major works, including *The Negro in Our History.* In 1926 he established Negro History Week during February. Not surprisingly, Woodson became known as the "father of Negro history."

During the bloody Red Summer of 1919 when racial violence erupted in Chicago and elsewhere, Claude McKay, a Jamaican who settled—like Marcus Garvey—in New York City wrote a powerful poem, "If We Must Die," in response to the brutal attacks by white people in Chicago on black residents:

> *If we must die, let it not be like hogs*
> *Hunted and penned in an inglorious spot,*
> *While round us bark the mad and hungry dogs,*
> *Making their mock at our accursèd lot.*
> *If we must die, O let us nobly die,*
> *So that our precious blood may not be shed*
> *In vain; then even the monsters we defy*
> *Shall be constrained to honor us though dead!*
> *O kinsmen! We must meet the common foe!*
> *Though far outnumbered let us show us brave,*
> *And for their thousand blows deal one deathblow!*
> *What though before us lies the open grave?*
> *Like men we'll face the murderous, cowardly pack,*
> *Pressed to the wall, dying, but fighting back!*

McKay left the United States for the Soviet Union in 1922, and spent the next twelve years in Europe. In 1928 while in France, he wrote *Home to Harlem,* a novel that depicted life among pimps, prostitutes, loan sharks, and petty criminals. McKay was not on cordial terms with the African-American intellectuals who formed the core of the Harlem Renaissance, and he did not consider himself part of the Talented Tenth.

Writers and Artists

Few white Americans and still fewer black Americans had access to a college education in the early twentieth century. Only slightly more than two thousand African Americans were pursuing college degrees by 1920. Yet the writers and artists who came to be associated with the Harlem Renaissance were the products of some of the nation's finest schools, and with the exception of Zora Neale Hurston, they did not come from isolated, rural southern communities. Hurston was born in Notasulga, Alabama, and raised in the all-black town of Eatonville, Florida, near Orlando. She attended Morgan State University and Howard University, and graduated from Barnard College. Alain Locke was a native of Philadelphia and Phi Beta Kappa graduate of Harvard. He was the first African American to win a Rhodes scholarship to Oxford University, and he also earned a Ph.D. in philosophy from Harvard. Aaron Douglas was born in Kansas and was an art major at the University of Nebraska.

Langston Hughes was born in Joplin, Missouri, and attended Columbia University before he graduated from Pennsylvania's Lincoln University. Jessie Fauset came from a prominent Philadelphia family of color. She was a graduate of Cornell University and

The Harlem Renaissance

1919	Claude Mckay publishes "If We Must Die"
1920	Eugene O'Neill's *The Emperor Jones* opens featuring Charles Gilpin Langston Hughes publishes *The Negro Speaks of Rivers*
1922	*Shuffle Along,* by Noble Sissle and Eubie Blake, opens on Broadway with Florence Mills and Josephine Baker Claude McKay publishes *Harlem Shadows*
1923	Jean Toomer publishes *Cane* The Cotton Club opens *Opportunity: A Journal of Negro Life,* edited by Charles S. Johnson and supported by the National Urban League begins publication
1924	Jessie R. Fauset publishes *There Is Confusion* Walter White publishes *The Fire in the Flint* Paul Robeson stars in Eugene O'Neill's drama *All God's Chillun* *Got Wings*
1925	Countee Cullen publishes his book of poetry, *Color* James Weldon Johnson publishes *The Book of American Negro* *Spirituals* *The New Negro,* edited by Alain Locke, is published
1926	Langston Hughes publishes *The Weary Blues* George Schuyler's "The Negro Art Hokum" appears in *The Nation* The Savoy Ballroom opens Wallace Thurman publishes one issue of *Fire* Florence Mills dies
1927	Langston Hughes publishes *Fine Clothes to the Jew* James Weldon Johnson publishes *God's Trombones: Seven Negro* *Sermons in Verse*
1928	Claude McKay publishes *Home to Harlem* Duke Ellington's band appears at the Cotton Club
1929	Jessie R. Fauset publishes *Plum Bun* Wallace Thurman publishes *The Blacker the Berry . . .* Claude McKay publishes *Banjo* Countee Cullen publishes *The Black Christ* Fats Waller's *Ain't Misbehavin'* opens on Broadway
1930	James Weldon Johnson publishes *Black Manhattan*
1931	Jessie R. Fauset publishes *The Chinaberry Tree*
1933	Jessie R. Fauset publishes her last novel, *Comedy American Style* James Weldon Johnson publishes his autobiography, *Along the Way*
1934	Wallace Thurman dies
1935	Zora Neale Hurston publishes *Mules and Men*
1937	Zora Neale Hurston publishes *Their Eyes Were Watching God*

a member of Phi Beta Kappa; she earned an M.A. from the University of Pennsylvania in romance languages. Jean Toomer was born in Washington, D.C., and was raised largely by his grandparents in a fashionable white neighborhood. Toomer went to the University of Wisconsin and then the Massachusetts College of Agriculture. Wallace Thurman was born in Salt Lake City and attended both the University of Utah and the University of Southern California. Countee Cullen was a native of Lexington, Kentucky, and a Phi Beta Kappa graduate of New York University.

The Renaissance gradually emerged in the early 1920s and then expanded dramatically later in the decade as more creative figures were drawn to Harlem. In 1923 Jean Toomer published *Cane,* a collection of stories and poetry about southern black life. It had a major impact on Jessie Fauset and Walter White. Fauset was the literary editor of *The Crisis,* and in 1924 she finished *There Is Confusion,* the first novel published during the Renaissance. Her novels explored the manners and color consciousness among well-to-do Negroes. Walter White, who was James Weldon Johnson's assistant at the NAACP, published *The Fire in the Flint* in 1924, a novel that dealt with a black physician who confronted white brutality in Georgia.

The Crisis, as well as *Opportunity,* a new publication of the Urban League, published the poetry and short stories of black authors, including Langston Hughes, Countee Cullen, and Zora Neale Hurston. White publishers were also attracted to black literary efforts. In 1925 *Survey Graphic* published a special edition devoted to black life and culture called "Harlem: Mecca of the New Negro." Howard University Professor Alain Locke then edited *The New Negro,* which drew much of its material from *Survey Graphic* as well as *Opportunity* and included silhouette drawings with Egyptian motifs by Aaron

During the summer of 1927, three of the major figures associated with the Harlem Renaissance visited the Booker T. Washington Memorial on the Tuskegee Institute campus in Alabama. One can only wonder what pointed comments about the "Wizard of Tuskegee" were exchanged as (from left to right) Jessie Fauset, Langston Hughes, and Zora Neale Hurston posed to have their photograph taken.

The Beinecke Rare Book and Manuscript Library, Yale University

Douglas. In his opening essay, Locke explained Harlem's literary significance: "Harlem has the same role to play for the new Negro as Dublin has had for the New Ireland or Prague for the New Czechoslovakia."

Sharp disagreements erupted during the Harlem Renaissance over the definition and purpose of black literature. Some, such as Alain Locke, W. E. B. Du Bois, Jessie Fauset, and Benjamin Brawley, wanted black writers to promote positive images of black people in their works. They hoped that inspirational literature could help resolve racial conflict in America, and they believed that black writers should be included in the larger (and mostly white) American literary tradition. Claude McKay, Langston Hughes, and Zora Neale Hurston disagreed. They portrayed the streets and shadows of Harlem and the lives of poor black people. In *The Ways of White Folks,* Hughes ridiculed the notion that writers could promote racial reconciliation.

W. E. B. Du Bois commented caustically after he read Claude McKay's bawdy *Home to Harlem*: "I feel distinctly like taking a bath." Du Bois was less than impressed with Jake, the novel's protagonist, who is intimately involved with the reality of life in Harlem that included opium, alcohol, and sex. Alain Locke dismissed McKay as a mere propagandist, and McKay in turn called Locke "a dyed-in-the-wool pussy-footing professor." Black critic George Schuyler's "The Negro Art Hokum" in *The Nation* ridiculed black writers who contended that black people even had their own expressive culture that was separate from that of white people. "As for the literature, painting, and sculpture of Afroamericans—such as there is—it is identical in kind with the literature, painting, and sculpture of white Americans."

Langston Hughes meanwhile defended the authenticity of black art and literature but insisted that the approval or disapproval of white people and black people was of little consequence:

> We younger Negro artists who create now intend to express our individual dark-skinned selves without fear or shame. If white people are pleased, we are glad. If they are not, it doesn't matter. We know we are beautiful. And ugly too. The tom-tom cries and the tom-tom laughs. If colored people are pleased we are glad. If they are not, their displeasure doesn't matter either. We build our temples for tomorrow, strong as we know how, and we stand on top of the mountain, free within ourselves.

Hughes pursued racial themes in *Fine Clothes to the Jew* (1927), which contained "Red Silk Stockings," a poem that depicted young black women who were tempted by liaisons with white men, a subject that offended some readers.

Even more upsetting to those who wanted to safeguard the reputation of black people was Wallace Thurman, who arrived in New York in 1925. He was a voracious reader with a brilliant mind and an eccentric personality who attracted many loyal admirers. He once wrote, "I cannot bear to associate with the ordinary run of people. I have to surround myself with individuals who for the most part are more than a trifle insane."

In 1926 Thurman published *Fire,* a journal that lasted only one issue but incited enormous controversy. *Fire* included Thurman's short story, "Cordelia the Crude," about a prostitute, and a one-act play by Zora Neale Hurston, "Color Struck." Hurston replicated the speech of rural black Southerners while depicting the jealousy a darker woman feels when a light-skinned rival tries to take her man. Black critic Benjamin Brawley complained that with *Fire* "vulgarity had been mistaken for art."

Thurman, who was a dark black man, antagonized still more people when *The Blacker the Berry.* . . was published in 1929. In it he described the tribulations and sorrows of Emma Lou, a young woman who did not mind being black, "but she did mind being too black." The book made it plain that many black people had absorbed a color prejudice that they inflicted on darker members of their own race.

White People and the Harlem Renaissance

Like many of the writers associated with the Harlem Renaissance, Zora Neale Hurston had a pen that sliced like a scalpel. She called the white people who took an interest in Harlem "Negrotarians," and she labeled her black literary colleagues the "Niggerati." But no matter how they were described, black and white people developed pleasant but often uneasy relationships during the Renaissance.

No white man was more attracted to the cultural developments in Harlem than photographer and writer Carl Van Vechten. In 1926 he caused a furor with his novel, *Nigger Heaven.* Many people were offended by the title, which referred to the balcony where black patrons had to sit in segregated theaters. The novel dealt with the coarser aspects of life in Harlem, which irritated Du Bois, Fauset, and Countee Cullen. But Van Vechten's purpose was in part a call for a more honest depiction of the black experience, and James Weldon Johnson, Walter White, and Langston Hughes approved of the novel.

Most black writers and artists welcomed the encouragement, support, and financial backing they received from white authors, critics, and publishers. White writers, including Eugene O'Neill, Sherwood Anderson, Sinclair Lewis, and Van Wyck Brooks, were fascinated by black people and interested in the works of black authors. Publishers, such as Alfred A. Knopf, brought out the works of Harlem writers. Black and white literary figures gathered for cocktails and music at Carl Van Vechten's apartment.

The attention and support of white people were sometimes accompanied by condescension and disdain. Too many "Negrotarians" considered Harlem and its inhabitants exotic and uncivilized. They found life in Harlem—its clubs, music, and entertainers, as well as its poetry, prose, and painting—lively and sensual compared to white life and culture. Black culture was also—many white people believed—unsophisticated and primitive, which is what made it so fascinating. Black writers like Langston Hughes, Claude McKay, and Countee Cullen wanted to depict black life realistically—from its gangsters to its gamblers. But they resented the notion that black culture was crude and unrefined.

White patrons like Amy Spingarn, whose husband Joel was president of the NAACP Board of Directors, and Charlotte Osgood "Godmother" Mason supported black writers and artists. Spingarn helped finance Langston Hughes's education at Lincoln University. "Godmother" Mason was a wealthy widow who offered substantial amounts of money to black artists. She worked closely with Alain Locke who helped identify Langston Hughes, Zora Neale Hurston, and Aaron Douglas among others who became her "godchildren."

Mason wanted no publicity for herself, but the acceptance of her money had its costs. Mason gave Hughes $150 a month and Hurston $200 a month, as well as an automobile. She also gave Hughes expensive clothing and writing supplies. In return, Mason demanded that the black writers keep her fully informed about their activities, and she did not hesitate to tell them when they were not productive enough. She also tried to influence what they wrote. She preferred that black writers confine themselves to exotic themes. As helpful as Mason's financial assistance and personal encouragement were, she created a system of dependency, and Hughes and Hurston finally broke free from the arrangement.

Harlem's cultural icons sometimes congregated away from the curiosity and paternalism of white admirers. The plush twin town houses of A'Lelia Walker at 108–110 West 136th Street also attracted Harlem's literary figures as well as entertainers. Walker was the daughter of black cosmetics millionaire Madam C. J. Walker. Though she read little herself, A'Lelia Walker enjoyed hosting musicians, writers, and artists. But Harlem artists also gathered in the much less luxurious surroundings of "Niggerati Manor" on 267 West 136th Street, a rooming house where Thurman, Hurston, and Hughes resided in the late 1920s.

The profusion of literary works associated with the Harlem Renaissance did not so much end as fade away. Black writers remained active into the 1930s. Zora Neale Hurston wrote her two most important works then—*Mules and Men* in 1935 and *Their Eyes Were Watching God* in 1937. Claude McKay and Langston Hughes continued to have their work published. But the Great Depression that began in 1929 devastated book and magazine sales. Subscriptions to *The Crisis* and *Opportunity* declined, and both journals published fewer works by creative writers. Many black intellectuals left Harlem.

Harlem and the Jazz Age

As powerful and important as these black literary voices were, they were less popular than the entertainers, musicians, singers, and dancers who were also part of the Harlem Renaissance. Without Harlem, the twenties would not have been the Jazz Age. From wailing trumpets, beating drums, dancing feet, plaintive and mournful songs, Harlem's clubs, cabarets, theaters, and ballrooms echoed with the vibrant and soulful sounds of African Americans. By comparison, white American music seemed sedate and bland.

Black and white people flocked to Harlem to enjoy themselves—and to break the law. In 1919–1920, the Eighteenth Amendment and the Volstead Act prohibited the manufacture, distribution, and sale of alcoholic beverages. But liquor flowed freely in Harlem. Musicians and entertainers, such as Harlem's working-class residents, had migrated there from elsewhere. The blues and their sorrowful tales of troubled and broken relationships arrived from the Mississippi Delta and rural South. Jazz had its origins in New Orleans, but it drew on ragtime and spirituals as it moved to Kansas City and Chicago on its way to Harlem.

The Cotton Club was Harlem's most fashionable nightspot. Opened in 1923 by white gangster Owney Madden, it catered to well-to-do white people who regarded a trip to Harlem as a foreign excursion. The Cotton Club's entertainers and waiters were black, but black patrons were not admitted. The club featured fast-paced revues that included a chorus line of attractive young women—all brown skinned, all under twenty-one years old, and all over 5'6" tall. No dark women appeared. Music was provided by assorted ensembles. Cab Calloway might sing "She's Tall, She's Tan and She's Terrific," or "Cotton Colored Gal of Mine."

In 1928, Edward K. "Duke" Ellington and his orchestra began a twelve-year association with the Cotton Club. Although Ellington had not yet begun to compose his own music in earnest, his band already had an elegant, sophisticated, and recognizable African-American sound. Another club, Connie's Inn, also served a mostly white clientele. Thomas "Fats" Waller played a rambunctious piano at Connie's. Waller's father was the deacon at the Abyssinian Baptist Church in Harlem, and his mother was the organist. The songs and music their son wrote, including "Honeysuckle Rose" and "Ain't Misbehavin'," were hardly sacred, but they were popular. Connie's also put on stunning musical revues, perhaps the best known of which was *Hot Chocolates*. Dancers who performed at Connie's included the legendary Bill "Bojangles" Robinson and Earl "Snakehips" Tucker. Young Louis Armstrong amazed listeners with his virtuoso trumpet and gravelly voice.

Harlem's black residents avoided the Cotton Club or Connie's Inn. They were more likely to step into one of Harlem's less pretentious and less expensive establishments, such as the Sugar Cane. The beer and liquor were cheap. The food was plentiful. The music was good, and there were no elaborate production numbers. Even less impressive clubs and bars remained open after the legal closing hour of 3 A.M. The police looked the other way as the music and alcohol continued through the night. Musicians from "legal" clubs drifted into the after-hours joints and played until dawn.

Another popular—and sometimes necessary—form of entertainment among Harlemites was the rent party. Housing costs in Harlem were extravagant, and white people and real-estate agents refused to rent or sell to black people in most other areas of New York City. To make the steep monthly rent payments, apartment dwellers would push the furniture aside, begin cooking chicken, chitterlings, rice, okra, and sweet potatoes. They would distribute a few flyers and hire a musician or two. The party was usually on a Saturday or a Thursday night. (Most domestic servants had Thursdays off.) Party-goers paid ten cents to fifty cents admission. Food and liquor were sold. With a decent crowd, the month's rent was paid.

Song, Dance, and Stage

Black women became popular as singers and dancers in Harlem and then often appeared in Broadway shows and revues. Florence Mills entranced audiences with her diminutive singing voice in several Broadway productions including *Plantation Review, Dixie to Broadway,* and *Blackbirds* before she died of appendicitis in 1927. Adelaide Hall also appeared in *Blackbirds* and later opened her own nightclubs in London and Paris. Ethel Waters worked her way up from smoky gin joints in Harlem basements where she sang risqué and comic songs to Broadway shows, and then to films. Many years later she toured with the Billy Graham crusade.

White men wrote many of the popular Broadway productions that starred black entertainers. In 1921, however, Eubie Blake and Noble Sissle put on *Shuffle Along*, which became a major hit. Its most memorable tune was "I'm Just Wild about Harry." Sissle and Blake wrote *Chocolate Dandies* in 1924 for a lanky, dark, and funny young lady named Josephine Baker. But in 1925 Baker left New York and moved to Paris where she starred in the *Revue Nègre*, which created a sensation in the French capital. She remained in France for the rest of her life.

White playwright Eugene O'Neill wrote serious drama involving black people. Paul Robeson appeared in O'Neill's *Emperor Jones*. Robeson—who had an illustrious performing career—was a graduate of Rutgers University where he was an All-American football player. He earned a law degree at Columbia University, but abandoned the law for the stage. He appeared in numerous productions, including O'Neill's *All God's Chillun Got Wings*, Shakespeare's *Othello*, Gershwin's *Porgy and Bess*, and Kern and Hammerstein's *Showboat*. He often sang spirituals in his magnificent, rich voice, and later recorded many of them.

Sports

Sports flourished in America in the 1920s. Americans worshiped their athletic heroes. Babe Ruth and Jack Dempsey were as well known as President Calvin Coolidge. Professional athletics, especially baseball and boxing, expanded dramatically. Professional football and basketball emerged later. Black men had been banned from major league baseball in 1887 (see Chapter 15). Nevertheless, in 1901 New York Giants' manager John J. McGraw signed a black man, Charlie Grant, to play second base. McGraw claimed that Grant was "Chief Tokohoma," a full-blooded Cherokee Indian. Chicago White Sox owner Charles Comiskey knew otherwise, and Grant did not play in the major leagues.

Playing among themselves, black baseball players barely made a living as they moved from team to team in an ever-fluctuating and disorganized system that saw teams come and go with monotonous regularity. No leagues functioned effectively for the black players. Black teams crisscrossed the country as they played each other in small towns and large cities for meager amounts of money. It was an insecure and nomadic life.

Rube Foster

Andrew "Rube" Foster was the father of black baseball in twentieth-century America. He was a crafty pitcher from Texas who combined athletic skills with mental dexterity. In 1911 he founded the Chicago American Giants, and he pitched with them regularly until 1915 and then mainly managed after that.

In 1920 he was the catalyst in the formation of the eight-team Negro National League and became its president and secretary. It was the first stable black league, with franchises in Kansas City, St. Louis, Indianapolis, Detroit, Dayton, and two teams in Chicago. The eighth team was the Cuban Stars.

The new league took advantage of the migration of black people to northern cities. The black ball clubs usually played late in the afternoon or in the early evening so that fans could attend after a day's work. (This was before night baseball.) Sunday doubleheaders in Chicago or Kansas City might draw eight to ten thousand people. Players were paid regularly, and athletes on Foster's Giants earned at least $175 a month. The biggest obstacle black teams faced was the lack of their own fields or stadiums. They had to rent from major league clubs, which frequently kept the profits from concessions.

Black baseball thrived in the 1920s thanks mostly to Foster's dedication. He was a tireless worker and strict disciplinarian, but the pressure may have been too much. In 1926 he suffered a mental breakdown and died in 1930. Foster's loss—combined with the impact of the Depression—disrupted the league.

College Sports

Football, baseball, basketball, and track and field were popular at the collegiate level. Amateur sports were not as rigidly segregated as professional baseball. Black men continued to play for white northern universities, although few teams had more than one black player.

Black players on white teams encountered discrimination when the teams traveled. Spectators taunted and threatened them. The Big Ten had an unwritten agreement that basketball coaches would not accept black players. All-white college teams sometimes refused to play against schools with black players.

Sports in black colleges and universities thrived in the 1920s. Baseball and football were the most popular spectator events. With the migration of black people to the North, black colleges began to play football in northern cities. Howard and Lincoln played to a scoreless tie before eighteen thousand people in Philadelphia on Thanksgiving in 1925.

Conclusion

For African Americans who lived through it, the 1920s must have seemed like a depressing continuation of earlier decades. Little appeared to have changed. Racial violence and lynching persisted. *The Birth of a Nation* inflamed racial animosity. "Experts" offered "proof" that people of color were inferior and threatened America's ethnic purity. The Ku Klux Klan became formidable again.

Nevertheless, positive developments in the twenties gave hope for the future. The NAACP became an organization to be reckoned with as it fought for antilynching legislation in Congress and for civil and political rights in the courts. Its membership exceeded one hundred thousand during the twenties. Marcus Garvey offered racial pride and self-respect as he enrolled hundreds of thousands of black people in the UNIA.

Black workers made little progress as they sought concessions from big business and representation within the ranks of organized labor. A. Philip Randolph founded the Brotherhood of Sleeping Car Porters and began a struggle with the Pullman company and the American Federation of Labor that would begin to pay off in the 1930s.

TIMELINE

African-American Events

1919—Pan-African Congress meets in Paris

Black Star Line is founded by Marcus Garvey and the UNIA

1920—Rube Foster organizes the Negro National League in baseball

1921—Tulsa, Oklahoma, race riot occurs

1922—Anti-lynching bill fails in Senate

Marcus Garvey meets with KKK leaders in Atlanta

1923—Rosewood, Florida destroyed

1925—Ossian Sweet case is tried in Detroit

A. Philip Randolph founds the Brotherhood of Sleeping Car Porters

1926—Carter Woodson establishes Negro History Week

1927—U.S. Supreme Court rules against the white primary in *Nixon v. Herndon*

Marcus Garvey is deported from the United States

1919	1921	1923	1925	1927	1929

National Events

1921—Congress establishes quotas to limit immigration

1924—Calvin Coolidge is elected

1927—Charles Lindbergh flies nonstop from New York to Paris

Babe Ruth hits sixty home runs

1929—Stock Market crashes

1920—U.S. Senate rejects the Treaty of Versailles

Eighteenth Amendment (Prohibition) is ratified

Nineteenth Amendment is ratified: women gain the right to vote

Warren Harding is elected president

1925—John T. Scopes "Monkey" trial is heard in Dayton, Tennessee

KKK is at peak of prominence

1928—Herbert Hoover is elected president

1919—Aliens rounded up and deported by A. Mitchell Palmer

Volstead Act is passed

1923—President Harding dies in office

The Harlem Renaissance was a cultural awakening in literature and the arts that was unprecedented in African-American history. The Renaissance allowed thoughtful and creative men and women to grapple with what it meant to be black in a society in which the white majority had defined the black minority as incapable and culturally backward. Hereafter African Americans were less likely to let other people characterize them in demeaning ways.

Black musicians, dancers, singers, entertainers, and athletes made names for themselves and contributed to popular culture in a mostly urban environment. The 1930s would reveal whether the progress of the 1920s would be sustained.

Review Questions

1. To what extent, if any, had the intensity of white supremacy changed by the 1920s?

2. What examples of progress could leaders like W. E. B. Du Bois, James Weldon Johnson, A. Philip Randolph, and Marcus Garvey point to in the twenties?

3. How do you account for Marcus Garvey's lack of acceptance among African-American leaders?

4. Explain how the black nationalism of the Universal Negro Improvement Association differed from the white nationalism of the Ku Klux Klan.

5. What economic opportunities existed for African Americans who had migrated to northern cities?

6. How do you explain the emergence of the literary and artistic movement known as the Harlem Renaissance?

7. How distinctive were black writers, artists, and musicians? Were their creative works essentially a part of American culture or separate from it?

8. Were there any genuine reasons for optimism among African Americans by the late 1920s?

Recommended Reading

William H. Harris. *Keeping the Faith: A. Philip Randolph, Milton P. Webster and the Brotherhood of Sleeping Car Porters, 1925–1937.* Urbana, IL: University of Illinois Press, 1977. This is an excellent account of the struggle of Randolph and the BSCP for recognition.

David Levering Lewis. *When Harlem Was in Vogue.* New York: Alfred A. Knopf, 1981. Lewis captures the life and vitality of Harlem in the twenties.

David Levering Lewis, ed. *The Portable Harlem Renaissance Reader.* New York: Penguin Books, 1994. Essays, poems, and excerpts from the works of virtually every writer associated with the Renaissance are contained in this volume.

Nancy MacLean. *Behind the Mask of Chivalry: The Making of the Second Ku Klux Klan.* New York: Oxford University Press, 1994. This is the most recent study of the revived KKK.

Arnold Rampersad. *The Life of Langston Hughes,* Vol. 1, 1902–1941, *I, Too, Sing America.* New York: Oxford University Press, 1986. Here is a rich study of a complex and extraordinary man and writer.

Judith Stein. *The World of Marcus Garvey: Race and Class in Modern Society.* Baton Rouge, LA: Louisiana State University Press, 1991. This is an effective examination of Garvey and the Universal Negro Improvement Association.

→ Chapter 18 ←

The Great Depression and the New Deal

For African Americans the Great Depression was both an era of suffering made worse by the horrors and burdens of American racism and a time of profound political change that would lay the foundation for future progress. At the beginning of the economic collapse most African Americans were either trapped in the failing southern agricultural system or eking out an existence at the margins of the urban economy. The fall of the economy pushed many black Americans to the edge of starvation. Coming out of the southern-dominated Democratic party, President Franklin Roosevelt's New Deal program for fighting the Depression might have simply reinforced existing racism. Yet the emerging political power of African-American voters in the North, the continuing development of civil rights organizations, and the growth of an anti-racist agenda among radicals and labor unions created the preconditions for a profound change in American politics. Amid economic despair, peonage, lynchings, and labor conflict, black Americans saw glimmers of hope in protests against racial segregation and critiques of capitalist exploitation. The 1930s were, thus, the dark dawn of a new era.

The Cataclysm, 1929–1933

The Great Depression was a cataclysm. National income fell from $81 billion in 1929 to $40 billion in 1932. Americans lost faith in banks, and the resulting panic deepened the despair. Overnight millions lost their savings in bank closings and foreclosures. Individuals responded by buying fewer consumer goods, and in turn businesses cut back production, investment, and payrolls. The result was a downward spiral made worse by increasing numbers of unemployed. According to the American Federation of Labor (AFL), the number of unemployed increased from 3,216,000 in January 1930 to 13,689,000 in March 1933. The standard of living of nearly everyone dropped to a fraction of what it had been before 1929.

Most people blamed the stock market crash and Republican president Herbert Hoover for the hard times, but the explanation is more complicated. The Great Depression was probably caused by a combination of factors, including rampant speculation, corporate capitalism's drive for markets and profits unchecked by federal regulation, the failure of those in the government or private sector to understand the workings of the economy, a weak international trading system, and most important, the great inequality of wealth and income that limited the purchasing power of millions of Americans.

Harder Times for Black America

The economic collapse hit African Americans hard. Most black people remained in the rural South mired in an exploitive agricultural system. As the Depression took hold, prices for cotton, still the mainstay of the southern economy, plunged from eighteen cents a pound in 1929 to six cents in 1933. Families of black sharecroppers and tenant farmers, nearly powerless in the rural South, were reduced to starvation or thrown off the land.

The hard times also struck those one and a half million African Americans who had escaped the South for northern cities. Even during the height of the prosperous 1920s, black Americans witnessed a steady deterioration in their living standards. After 1929 the same forces that impoverished those in the countryside swept those in urban areas further toward the economic margins as waves of refugees from the farms crowded into the cities (see Table 18–1). By 1934, when the federal government noted that 17 percent of white citizens could not support themselves, the figure for black Americans had increased to 38 percent over all. In Chicago, the jobless rate for African-American men was 40 percent, in Pittsburgh 48 percent, in Harlem 50 percent, in Philadelphia 56 percent, and in Detroit 60 percent. The figures were even more dire for black workers in southern cities. In Atlanta, Georgia, 65 percent of black workers needed public assistance, and in Norfolk, Virginia, 80 percent had to apply for welfare.

Table 18–1
Median Income of Black Families Compared to the Median Income of White Families for Selected Cities, 1935–1936

City and Type of Family	Black	White	Black Income as a Percentage of White Income
Husband–Wife Families			
New York	$980	$1,930	51%
Chicago	$726	$1,687	43%
Columbus	$831	$1,622	51%
Atlanta	$632	$1,876	34%
Columbia	$576	$1,876	31%
Mobile	$481	$1,419	34%
Other Families			
Atlanta	$332	$940	35%
Columbia	$254	$1,403	18%
Mobile	$301	$784	38%

Source: Gunnar Myrdal, et al., *An American Dilemma*, Copyright ©1944, 1962 by Harper & Row, Publishers, Inc. Reprinted by permission of Harper Collins Publishers Inc.

African Americans lost jobs in those parts of the economy where they had gained a tenuous foothold. Before 1929, jobs in low-status or demeaning occupations had been regarded as "Negro work" and, hence, were generally immune from white competition. As desperation set in, white Southerners not only competed for these jobs but also used terror and intimidation to compel employers to fire black people. Unions continued to exclude African Americans and pressured manufacturers to hire white people.

Black women workers, overwhelmingly concentrated in domestic service and laundry work, were affected even more than black men. There were fewer jobs because many families could no longer afford domestic help. With many impoverished women coming into the cities, those white people with the money to hire help found that they could pay almost nothing and still employ these desperate women. In 1935 two black women, Marvel Cooke and Ella Baker, published an exposé of the exploitation of these women laborers in *The Crisis*. They entitled the article "The Bronx Slave Market" because the buying and selling of labor reminded them of the old slave marts in the antebellum South. Cooke and Baker described how the black women gathered on particular street corners and waited as well-to-do white women selected them for a day's labor. They received "wages as low as 15 to 25 cents an hour, some working only two or three hours a day." Some black people were hired but never paid.

Many African Americans used the survival strategies developed through centuries of hardship to eke out an existence during the first years of the Great Depression. Survival demanded that black women pool their resources and adhere to a collective spirit. In Chicago, for example, women and their families lived in crowded tenements in which they shared bathrooms and other facilities including hot plates, stoves, and sinks. They bartered and exchanged goods and services because money was so scarce. One woman might dress the hair of a neighbor in return for permission to borrow her dress or use her pots and pans. Another woman might trade bread and sugar for milk, beans, or soap. Grandmothers watched over children as their mothers went to look for a domestic job. They helped each other as best they could.

Rural black women also had to rely on their ingenuity to survive. As one observer in Georgia noted, "In their effort to maintain existence, these people are catching and selling fish, reselling vegetables, sewing in exchange for old clothes, letting out sleeping space, and doing odd jobs. They understand how to help each other. Stoves are used in common, wash boilers go their rounds, and garden crops are exchanged and shared." Nonetheless, the depth and duration of this downturn pressed these mutual aid strategies to the breaking point. By 1933 the clock seemed to have been turned back to 1865 when many African Americans could claim to own little more than their bodies.

Black Businesses in the Depression: Collapse and Survival

Members of the black elite also experienced economic losses. African Americans who had built successful businesses faced the same depression-borne problems as other businesses, but suffered even more because the communities on which they depended

This photograph by Margaret Bourke-White captures the contrast between the American dream of prosperity—for white families—and the harsh realities of life for black Americans during the Depression.
Margaret Bourke-White/LIFE Magazine © TimePix

were poorer. A description of two kinds of business, banking and insurance, illustrates how black enterprises stood or fell during the economic crisis.

The Binga Bank, Chicago's first black-owned-and-operated financial institution had been founded in 1908 by its president Jesse Binga (1865–1950), who had managed the bank so effectively that by 1930 its deposits had grown to more than $1.5 million. The Binga Bank was an important symbol of black capitalism. But the bank's assets were too heavily invested in mortgage loans to black churches and fraternal societies, many of which could not meet their payments after their members lost their jobs. Binga refused to seize the properties of these community institutions, but his restraint, coupled with financial improprieties, led to the bank's failure. On July 31, 1930, Illinois state bank auditors padlocked the institution and filed a federal misuse-of-funds charge against the once proud financier. Sentenced to prison in 1932, Binga was pardoned by President Franklin D. Roosevelt a year later. However, he never rebuilt his bank or his fortune.

Some black businesses did survive the economic cataclysm. Atlanta Life Insurance Company, for example—founded by a former Georgia slave, Alonzo Franklin Herndon in 1905—actually prospered during the Depression. Between 1931 and 1936, the company's assets increased by more than $1 million. This was in part because insurance companies such as Atlanta Life provided an essential service for African Americans, particularly in an era before government provided social security, and could thus depend on a continued flow of premiums. And unlike Binga Bank the officers of the Atlanta Life Insurance Company cut their investment in mortgage loans in the black community.

The Failure of Relief

Before Franklin Roosevelt's New Deal, private charities or, as a last resort, state and local governments were responsible for providing relief from economic hardships. Even in good times these institutions provided too little for all those in need. Moreover, African Americans had a harder time getting aid than white people and were given less when they did get it. The Depression overwhelmed the nation's charitable organizations. In turn, state and local governments could not or would not provide unemployment insurance or increased welfare benefits to ease the pain and suffering of those most vulnerable to the economic disaster.

Despite the economic disaster, President Herbert Hoover hesitated to act. Steeped in the free market orthodoxy of his time, he believed that government should do little to interfere with the workings of the economy. Hoover did try to convince businesses to retain employees and not to cut wages, believing that companies would understand that by doing so they would contribute to the health of the general economy and promote their own long-term interests. The president also approved loans to banks, railroads, and insurance companies by the Reconstruction Finance Corporation, a federal agency set up to rescue large corporations. He hoped that these businesses would reinvigorate production, create new jobs, and restore consumer spending. His faith was misplaced; businesses, seeking to save themselves, took the government loans and still laid off workers.

Hoover was also reluctant to provide direct federal relief. That was the job of local governments and charities. Hoover was trapped in a rigid ideology. He watched with dismay as wandering groups of men, women, and children began settling into what they called "Hoovervilles," sordid clusters of shacks made of tin, cardboard, and burlap. Still, he refused to allow the federal government to directly provide relief.

Hoover's politics were as racist as that of the Democratic party. He wanted to create a white Republican party in the South and cultivated white Southerners by attempting to appoint John Parker, a racist judge, to the U.S. Supreme Court and by displacing black Republican party leaders. Hoover's policy was not new; for decades the national Republican party had treated black voters with contempt and often declined to reward them with patronage appointments. This policy took on a different meaning during the early 1930s against the backdrop of black suffering. As NAACP director Walter White put it, Hoover:

> . . . sat stolidly in the White House, refusing bluntly to receive Negro citizens who wished to lay before him the facts of their steadily worsening plight or to consider any remedial legislation or governmental action. His attitude toward Negroes caused me to coin a phrase which gained considerable currency, particularly in the Negro world, in which I described Hoover as "the man in the lily-White House."

African Americans and the New Deal

In 1932, the third year of the Great Depression, voters overwhelmingly elected New York governor Franklin D. Roosevelt to the presidency. Roosevelt's lopsided victory over Hoover heralded the emergence of a new electoral coalition. The new president appealed to the Democratic party's base of support in the white South, but to this group he added a coalition of western farmers, industrial workers, urban voters from the white ethnic groups in northern cities, and reform-minded intellectuals. But black Americans still clung to the Republican banner. In Chicago, for example, less than 25 percent of black voters cast their ballots for Roosevelt. But this was the last election in which the party of Lincoln could take them for granted. In his first term Roosevelt inaugurated a multitude of programs to counter the Depression—collectively known as the New Deal—which would shift the allegiance of African Americans. Initially his programs continued past patterns of discrimination against African Americans, but by 1935 the New Deal was providing more equal benefits and prompting profound social changes. The result was a new political order that ultimately undermined key portions of the edifice of American racism.

Roosevelt and the First New Deal, 1933–1935

During his first 100 days in office Franklin Roosevelt pressed through Congress a profusion of bold new economic initiatives that came to be known as the first New Deal. To combat the Depression, Roosevelt, unlike Hoover, followed no predetermined plan. Instead he favored experimentation—tempered by political expediency—over ideology as the guide to federal action. With little resistance Congress passed the president's sprawling and complex laws aimed at overhauling the nation's financial, agricultural, and industrial systems. Most hoped, vainly as it turned out, that these changes would bring a return to prosperity. In the meantime Roosevelt moved to counter the immediate suffering of the unemployed with massive federal relief. Many of the first New Deal's programs benefited both white and black people, but the strength of white Southerners in the Democratic party caused much of this early program to be unfairly administered.

The Agricultural Adjustment Act (AAA), designed to protect farmers by giving them subsidies to limit production and thereby stabilize prices, illustrates the key benefits and problems African Americans experienced during the first New Deal. The theory underlying the AAA was that creating scarcity would increase agricultural prices. So farmers would be paid to grow less. The program provided for sharecroppers and tenant farmers to get part of the subsidies and allowed new rural relief agencies to dispense supplementary income to off-season wage workers.

This program pumped billions of dollars into an economic sector on which over 4,500,000 black people relied for their livelihood. The flow of money from the AAA did slow the exodus of black people from farming. During the 1930s, only 4.5 percent of African Americans abandoned farming, compared with 8.6 percent who did so during the 1920s.

But the AAA was often administered unfairly and corruptly. Local control of the AAA resided in the hands of the Extension Service and County Agricultural Conservation Committees, which were supposed to represent all farmers. The county agents, however, were often the planters themselves and the committees mirrored southern politics by excluding black people. During the first two years of the AAA, black farmers complained bitterly that white landlords simply grabbed and pocketed the millions of dollars of benefit checks they were supposed to forward to tenants. To compound the injury, some planters then evicted the sharecroppers and tenants from the land.

The experience of African Americans with the National Industrial Recovery Act (NIRA) mimicked that with the AAA. The NIRA was intended to promote the revival of manufacturing by allowing industries to cooperate in establishing codes of conduct governing prices, wage levels, and employment practices, all of which were to be overseen by a National Recovery Administration (NRA). The NRA oversaw the drafting of the codes but faced resistance from employers and unions in eliminating racial disparities in wage rates and working conditions. Even when African-American advocates did win wage increases for occupations in which black people predominated, the result was often a shift to white labor. Some African-American newspapers and protest organizations claimed that "NRA" really stood for the "Negro Removal Agency" or "Negroes Robbed Again." To the relief of many African Americans the Supreme Court declared the NIRA unconstitutional in spring 1935.

The New Deal's national welfare programs included the Federal Emergency Relief Administration (FERA), the Civilian Conservation Corps (CCC), Public Works Administration (PWA), and Civil Works Administration (CWA). Although inadequate and unfairly administered on local levels, these programs often stood between black people and starvation. FERA provided funds for local and state relief operations. The program pulled millions of people back from the brink of starvation. Because African Americans suffered greater economic devastation, they received benefits at a higher rate than whites. In most cities north and south, 25 to 40 percent of African Americans were on relief rolls that FERA funded wholly or in part. Direct welfare, however, was deemed by many in the Roosevelt administration to be debilitating, so it emphasized hiring the unemployed for public works projects. The Civilian Conservation Corps (CCC) built segregated camps to employ young men and to rescue them from urban poverty and hopelessness. By the time it was abolished in 1945, more than two hundred thousand African-American youth had taken part in the program.

These relief programs helped many African Americans through the worst parts of the Depression. But the programs also tended to be less helpful to black people than they were to whites. For example, the CCC gave only about 5 percent of its slots to black youths during its first year. Likewise, FERA reached few of those in need in the South.

Black Officials in the New Deal

The first New Deal was not completely bleak for African Americans. In addition to the benefits they derived from New Deal relief programs, African Americans also gained new influence and allies within the Roosevelt administration. Their experience reflected both the growing availability of highly trained African Americans for government service and the emerging consciousness among white liberals about the problems—and potential electoral power—of black people.

First Lady Eleanor Roosevelt was revered for her commitment to racial justice. She arranged meetings at the White House for black leaders. She cajoled her husband to consider legislation on behalf of black rights. She defied Jim Crow laws by refusing to sit in a "white only" section while attending a meeting in the South. Moreover, she wrote newspaper columns calling for "fair play and equal opportunity for Negro citizens." She resigned from the Daughters of the American Revolution after it refused to allow a young black opera singer, Marian Anderson, to perform at Constitution Hall in Washington in 1939. (Administration officials arranged for Anderson to perform in front of the Lincoln Memorial on Easter Sunday before a crowd of 75,000.)

Eleanor Roosevelt was joined by other liberals to press the cause of racial justice and to seek the appointment of African Americans throughout the government. The result was that doors to the government began opening in an unprecedented way. For the first time, the government employed professional black architects, lawyers, engineers, economists, statisticians, interviewers, office managers, social workers, and librarians. The Department of Commerce hired Eugene K. Jones, on leave from the National Urban League. The National Youth Administration brought in Mary McLeod Bethune and the Department of Interior employed William H. Hastie and Robert Weaver. Ira De A. Reid joined the Social Security Administration, Lawrence W. Oxley worked for the Department of Labor, and Ambrose Caliver served in the Office of Education.

A core of highly placed African Americans became linked in a network called the Federal Council on Negro Affairs, more loosely known as Roosevelt's "Black Cabinet." Mary McLeod Bethune was the undisputed leader of this body, which consisted primarily of "New Deal race specialists." It numbered twenty-seven men and three women working mostly in temporary emergency agencies such as the Works Progress Administration (WPA) and included such stalwarts as housing administrator Robert Weaver. These advisers pressured the president and the heads of federal agencies to adopt and support color-blind policies and lobbied to advance the status of black Americans.

Black Social Scientists and the New Deal

Many black intellectuals, scholars, and writers believed that the social sciences could be used to adjudicate race relations in the country, and during the New Deal they found greater receptiveness to their work than ever before. Nearly 200 African Americans received Ph.D.s during the 1930s, more than four times the combined total from the first three decades of the century. Several of these young scholars reached the top ranks of the social sciences, studying the problems of black people with a depth of experience and theoretical sophistication lacking in earlier generations of scholars. In sociology E. Franklin Frazier and Charles S. Johnson took the lead. Frazier's pioneering studies of black families placed him at the forefront of debates on social policy. As the editor of *Opportunity*, the journal of the Urban League, throughout the 1930s, Johnson published critiques of American racial policies, as well as the work of black writers. Meanwhile Ralph Bunche became well known in political science, while Abram Harris and Robert Weaver gained renown in economics.

Historians such as Carter G. Woodson, Lorenzo Greene, Benjamin Quarles, and John Hope Franklin advanced the idea that black people had been active agents in the past and not simply the passive objects of white people's actions. Their scholarly emphasis on racial pride, achievement, and autonomy helped to raise black morale.

The increasing importance of black scholars became apparent late in the 1930s when the Carnegie Corporation, a philanthropic foundation, sponsored a study of black life. Although the study was led by Gunnar Myrdal, a Swedish social scientist, nearly half the large staff of scholars were African Americans, and several, particularly Bunche, had a major impact on the work. Published in 1944 as *An American Dilemma*, this massive study profoundly affected public understanding of how racism undermined the progress of African Americans, and it helped to set the agenda for the civil rights movement.

African Americans and the Second New Deal

By late 1935, after two years of slow recovery, much of the first New Deal lay in shambles. The Supreme Court had invalidated much of it and a conservative backlash was emerging. In response Roosevelt pressed for a second burst of legislation marked by the passage of the Social Security Act (SSA), the National Labor Relations Act (NLRA), the creation of the Works Progress Administration (WPA), and other measures more radical than those that had come in 1933. The NLRA, for example, helped unions get established and grow. The SSA provided the rudiments of a social welfare system as well as unemployment and retirement insurance. This new set of laws, known as the second New Deal changed the United States, particularly by strengthening the role of the federal government.

Roosevelt's leftward political shift helped him to win the 1936 presidential election in a landslide. This election cemented a new electoral coalition that yoked the southern wing of the Democratic party with more liberal farmers and working-class voters who were labor union members in the North and West. The Democratic party also began to win the votes of the large African-American populations in the great cities of the North. The great migration had relocated thousands of prospective black voters in northern urban centers, traditional strongholds of Democratic party machines, such as in Chicago. Institutionalized segregation combined with the often conscious choice to live in their own neighborhoods concentrated the black electorate and increased its political power. In 1934, reflecting a shift in partisan allegiance, Chicago's black voters elected Arthur W. Mitchell to Congress, who thus became the first black Democrat ever to win a seat in the House of Representatives.

Mitchell's election was only the beginning of the change in black people's political party identification. The powerful black press fanned the shifting winds, and black urban dwellers began to connect political power with the prospect of improving their economic conditions. By the end of the decade, black urban voters were important in key states such as Illinois, Ohio, Pennsylvania, and New York. This political consciousness led to the election of black state legislators in California, Illinois, Indiana, Kansas, Kentucky, New Jersey, New York, Ohio, Pennsylvania, and West Virginia.

Roosevelt's "Black Cabinet" in a 1938 photograph. Mary McLeod Bethune is in the center
of the front row. The advisors included Robert Weaver, Eugene Kinckle Jones, Ambrose
Caliver, and William H. Hastie among many others.
National Archives and Records/Presidential Library, Scurlock Studios

In another indication of change, some Democrats began supporting antilynching legislation. Congressman Mitchell gave a strong speech in 1935 supporting President Roosevelt as an opponent of lynching. "No President," he declared, "has been more outspoken against the horrible crime of lynching than has Mr. Roosevelt. In speaking of lynching some time ago he characterized it as 'collective murder' and spoke of it as a crime which blackens the record of America." Mitchell told black audiences, "Let me say again, the attitude of the administration at the White House is absolutely fair and without prejudice, insofar as the Negro citizenry is concerned."

There are many complex reasons for the revolutionary transformation in black political allegiance. The shift to the Democratic party did not occur without anxiety. Some black people feared that by joining the party they would open the door for even more white southern Democrats to use national power to thwart black advancement. But by 1936 most African-American voters were willing to take the risk.

The tension between black Democrats and white conservative Democrats erupted at the party's 1936 convention in Philadelphia. The seating of thirty-two black delegates provoked the wrath of southern politicians. The selection of a black Baptist minister to open one session with a prayer outraged South Carolina Senator Ellison D. "Cotton Ed" Smith, who, accompanied by a few other delegates, marched ostentatiously off the floor proclaiming that they refused to support "any political organization that looks upon the Negro and caters to him as a political and social equal." Undaunted, the black minister simply observed that "Brother Smith needs more prayer." The South Carolina delegation adopted a protest resolution denouncing the appearance of black men on the convention's program. The protests of southern white politicians, however, had no effect on the political decisions of black men and women. Heeding the advice of the NAACP, they voted their personal interests.

Despite the rise of black people in the Democratic party, southern congressmen succeeded in excluding many African Americans from key government programs. For example, they insisted on denying the benefits of the National Labor Relations Act and Social Security Act to agricultural laborers and domestic servants. These white

Southerners could not, however, stop the tilt toward fairer administration of programs or the revival of the push for equal rights, which had lain all but dormant since the end of the Reconstruction Era.

An examination of the Works Progress Administration (WPA) illustrates the changes that the second New Deal and the increasing shift of African Americans to the Democratic party wrought. The WPA, with Harry Hopkins (1890–1946) as its head, was created to employ the unemployed. Sustained with $1.39 billion in federal funds, the WPA put thousands of men and women to work building new roads, hospitals, city halls, courthouses, schools, bridges, ports, and local water-supply systems. Larger-scale projects included the Lincoln Tunnel under the Hudson River connecting New York and New Jersey and the Bonneville and Boulder Dams. (Boulder Dam was later renamed the Hoover Dam by a Republican-controlled Congress in 1946.)

The WPA was administered far more fairly than were the first New Deal programs. The national government explicitly rejected racial discrimination and worked to make sure local officials complied. Although far from perfect, by 1939 it provided assistance to one million black families on a far more equitable basis than ever before.

The same pattern prevailed in the WPA's four arts programs—the Federal Art Project, the Federal Music Project, the Federal Theater Project, and the Federal Writers Project—which employed thousands of musicians, intellectuals, writers, and artists. A fifth program, the Historical Records Survey, created in 1937, sent teams of writers, including Zora Neale Hurston, to collect folklore and study various ethnic groups. One team collected the life histories and reminiscences of some two thousand former slaves.

Between 1935 and 1943 the WPA helped artists display their talents and made their work widely available. Among the black artists hired to adorn government buildings, post offices, and public parks were Aaron Douglas, Charles Alston, Richmond Barthe, Sargent Johnson, Archibald Motley, Jr., and Augusta Savage, a sculptor who became the first director of the Harlem Community Art Center in 1937.

The Federal Theater Project established sixteen black theater units. Among their most notable productions was a version of *Macbeth* set in Haiti with an all-black cast. White actor John Houseman and black actress Rose McClendon directed the Harlem Federal Theater Project. This project proved controversial due to the fear of communist influence and the leftist political views of some African-American writers and performers.

Black Protest during the Great Depression

During the 1930s African-American men and women initiated their own agenda and determined to use every resource at their disposal to destroy the obstacles to racial justice and barriers to equal opportunity. The NAACP sponsored a legal campaign against educational discrimination and political disfranchisement led by Charles Houston and Thurgood Marshall, mobilized black communities, and sustained hope in struggle. Black people benefitted from the New Deal, but less than white people did. The disparity between black and white lives was a spur to action. The juxtaposition of black subordination and misery alongside the new forms of federal aid so willingly distributed to white citizens convinced black Americans to intensify their own struggle for their American rights. Many embraced radical critiques of American capitalism, but few ever considered communism a viable alternative to American democracy. Black people would emerge from the Depression more determined than ever to make democracy work for them.

The NAACP and Civil Rights Struggles

During the 1930s the NAACP developed a new effectiveness as an advocate for African-American civil rights. It pressed the government to protect African-American rights and eliminate the racism in government programs. Part of the reason for this new dynamism was the astute leadership of Walter White, who personally investigated forty-two lynchings and eight race riots and was an ardent lobbyist for civil rights legislation and racial justice. Throughout the thirties African Americans of all hues moved into leadership positions in the NAACP and added their names to the membership roles of its many branches.

The new dynamism of the NAACP became apparent in 1930 when Walter White helped defeat Hoover's nomination of Circuit Court Judge John J. Parker of North Carolina to a seat on the United States Supreme Court. Parker had openly embraced white supremacy, stating, for example, that the "participation of the Negro in politics is a source of evil and danger to both races." The NAACP formed a coalition with the American Federation of Labor to derail the Parker nomination. White trumpeted the victory and let it be known that African Americans would not be silent while "the Hoover administration proposed to conciliate southern white sentiment by sacrificing the Negro and his rights."

Du Bois Ignites a Controversy

The NAACP had critics, even within its own ranks. Many younger black people criticized its focus on civil liberties and deplored it for ignoring the economic misery of most African Americans. In 1934 W. E. B. Du Bois, editor of the NAACP's journal *The Crisis*, joined the chorus. Criticizing what he considered the group's overemphasis on integration, Du Bois advocated a program of self-determination so that black people could develop "an economic nation within a nation." Du Bois acknowledged that this internal economy could only meet part of the needs of the African-American community. But he insisted it could be developed and expanded: "This smaller part could be so important and wield so much power that its influence upon the total economy of Negroes and the total industrial organization of the United States would be decisive for the great ends towards which the Negro moves."

Black intellectuals attacked Du Bois for advocating "voluntary segregation." E. Franklin Frazier, for example, called the idea of black businesses succeeding within a segregated economy a black upper-class fantasy. Nevertheless, Du Bois held fast to his position that the NAACP should continue to oppose legal segregation yet combine that opposition with vigorous support to improve segregated institutions as long as discrimination persisted. He was eventually forced from the editorship of *The Crisis*, but his resignation did not end the controversy. By the late 1930s the NAACP had developed more emphasis on economic policy and had stronger ties to the labor movement.

Challenging Racial Discrimination
in the Courts

A dramatic expansion of its legal campaign against racial discrimination enhanced the NAACP's effectiveness. Central to this project was the hiring of Charles Hamilton Houston, a Harvard-trained African-American lawyer and scholar, to lead it. Houston had been vice-dean of Howard University Law School, which he had transformed into a powerful institution for training black attorneys in civil rights law. At the NAACP, Houston laid out a plan for a legal program to challenge inequality in education and the exclusion of black people from voting in the South. Houston used lawsuits both to force state and local governments to live up to the Constitution and to inspire community organization.

Houston sought to force southern states to equalize their facilities. Studies by the NAACP had revealed great disparities in per capita expenditures for white and black students, and huge differences in salaries paid to white and black teachers. In Georgia, for example, the average annual per pupil expenditure for white students was $36.29, compared with $4.59 for black students. White teachers' salaries averaged $97.88 per month, while black teachers received only $49.41. Houston hoped to secure judgments that would so increase the cost of separate institutions that states would be forced to abandon them.

Houston convinced Walter White to hire his former student at the Howard University Law School, Thurgood Marshall, in 1936. Marshall was born in Baltimore in 1908. His father was a dining-car waiter and club steward; his mother was a teacher. During the 1930s Marshall and Houston focused on bringing greater parity between black and white teachers, a project that they hoped would increase NAACP membership among teachers, their students, and parents. The two men, working with a network of African-American attorneys, also attempted to end discrimination against black men and women in professional and graduate schools. Inequalities were obvious here because many southern states offered no graduate facilities of any kind to black students. Like other campaigns, this focus on graduate education was intended to establish precedents that might be used to gain equality in other areas and as an organizing tool for developing strong local NAACP branches. The first significant accomplishment in the NAACP's legal campaign against segregation in graduate and professional education was the Supreme Court's 1938 decision in *Gaines v. Canada*. The Court ordered the state of Missouri to provide black citizens an opportunity to study law in a state-supported institution. Failure to do so, the Court held, would violate the equal protection of the law clause of the Fourteenth Amendment to the United States Constitution. Missouri hastily established a law school for African Americans at the historically black Lincoln University. In the 1940s North Carolina, Texas, Oklahoma, and South Carolina also established law schools for their black citizens.

Thurgood Marshall and the NAACP were encouraged by the *Gaines* decision to challenge the constitutionality of the "separate but equal" doctrine. Ada Lois Sipuel sought admission to the law school of the University of Oklahoma at Norman. In accordance with state statutes she was refused admission but was granted an out-of-state tuition award. In *Sipuel v. Board of Regents of the University of Oklahoma* (1947), Thurgood Marshall argued that this arrangement failed to meet the needs of the state's black citizens. The Supreme Court declared that Oklahoma was obliged under the equal protection clause of the Fourteenth Amendment to provide a legal education for Sipuel. The case established the principle that the state had to provide a separate law school for African-American students in their home states.

Heman Sweatt, a black mail carrier, tested this principle in a suit against the University of Texas Law School. In *Sweatt v. Painter* (1950), the Supreme Court again sided with the NAACP lawyers. In response to Sweatt's initial challenge Texas had created a separate law school that had inadequate library facilities, faculty, and support staff. It was separate but hardly equal. Marshall and local Texas black lawyers argued that the legal education offered Sweatt at the black law school was so inferior that it violated the equal protection clause of the Fourteenth Amendment. Marshall declared, "whether the University of Texas Law School is compared with the original or new law school for Negroes, we cannot find substantial equality in the educational opportunities offered white and Negro law students by the state. In terms of number of the faculty, variety of courses and opportunity for specialization, size of the student body, scope of the library, availability of law review and similar activities, the University of Texas Law School is superior." These early victories laid the legal foundation for the 1954 *Brown v. Topeka Board of Education* decision.

The fight against disfranchisement also helped to mobilize local and state communities and branches. Nowhere was this more apparent than in Texas. In 1923 the Texas legislature enacted the Terrell Law, which declared: "In no event shall a Negro be eligible to participate in a Democratic primary election . . . in . . . Texas." In the one-party South, the primary elections were more important than the general elections, which often merely rubber-stamped the choice made in the primary. Thus, to be denied the right to vote in Democratic party primary elections was to be disfranchised. The NAACP developed a case to test the constitutionality of the Terrell Law and commenced a twenty-year battle through the courts. The Texas branches of the NAACP raised money and coordinated local involvement in the campaign to overthrow the Democratic white primary that disfranchised black Texans.

The Texas white primary fight was the most sustained and intense effort that any NAACP chapter undertook during the interwar period. It won its first victory when the Supreme Court ruled in 1927 in *Nixon v. Herndon* that the Texas Democratic primary was unconstitutional (see Chapter 17). Subsequent decisions further chipped away at the legal basis for the white primary. Finally, in 1944 the Supreme Court issued a ruling in *Smith v. Allwright* that ended the white primary altogether. It was the NAACP's greatest legal victory to that time. Many more would soon follow.

Black Women and Community Organizing

Black women made exceptional contributions to the NAACP during the 1930s through their successful fund-raising efforts and membership drives. Three agitators for racial justice were Daisy Adams Lampkin (c. 1884–1965), Juanita Mitchell (1913–1992), and Ella Baker (1903–1986). These women worked closely with White and the NAACP throughout the Depression and World War II. Lampkin, a native of

Washington, D.C., became in 1915 the president of the Negro Women's Franchise League, a group dedicated to fighting for the vote. In 1930, Walter White enlisted her as regional field secretary of the NAACP, a post she held until she was made national field secretary in 1935. She continued raising funds for the NAACP and remained a leader among black women.

Juanita E. Jackson was raised in Baltimore. She earned a degree in education from the University of Pennsylvania in 1931, then returned to Baltimore, where she helped to found the City-Wide Young People's Forum, which encouraged young people to attack unemployment, segregation, and lynching. From 1935 to 1938 she served as NAACP national youth director. In 1950 she received a law degree from the University of Maryland. As the first black woman admitted to practice law in Maryland, she helped destroy racial segregation on the state's public beaches and in its public schools.

Ella Baker, who became one of the most important women in the civil rights movement of the 1950s and 1960s, began her life's work during the Depression. Born in Norfolk, Virginia, Baker moved to New York City in 1927 and worked as a waitress and as an organizer in radical politics. Within two years after her arrival she had cofounded with George Schuyler the Young Negroes' Cooperative League in Harlem. The group practiced collective decision making and attempted to involve all segments of the community in the cooperatives. As she worked with the young men and women, Baker developed a strong belief in grassroots mobilization. Meanwhile, she also worked with women's and labor groups, such as the Harlem Housewives Cooperative, the Women's Day Workers and Industrial League, and the YWCA. In 1935 she served

The NAACP in the 1930s and 1940s depended on the formidable fund-raising talents of black women like Daisy Lampkin (shown here in a Black Baptist church), Ella Baker, and Juanita Mitchell. These women played a major role in building NAACP membership.

United States Department of the Interior, courtesy Mary McLeod Bethune Council House National Historic Site, Washington, D.C.

as publicity director of the Sponsoring Committee of the National Negro Congress. In 1936 she began work with the WPA. After much persuasion Baker accepted, in 1941, Walter White's offer to become an assistant field secretary of the NAACP. This position enabled her to travel across the country and throughout the South, making friendships that would serve her well in the coming decades. From 1943 to 1946 Baker worked as director of NAACP branches and increased the membership of the organization. After resigning from the NAACP, she joined the staff of the New York Urban League.

Other black women organized outside the NAACP. Black women in Detroit provide a potent illustration of this kind of activity. On June 10, 1930, fifty black women responded to a call issued by Fannie B. Peck, wife of Reverend William H. Peck, pastor of the two-thousand-member Bethel African Methodist Episcopal Church and the president of the Booker T. Washington Trade Association. Out of this initial meeting emerged the Detroit Housewives' League, an organization that combined economic nationalism and black women's self-determination to help black families and businesses survive the Depression. Peck had been inspired by M. A. L. Holsey, secretary of the National Negro Business League. Holsey described the directed spending campaigns that enabled housewives in Harlem to consolidate their economic power to persuade businesses to hire black women and children. Peck became convinced that such an organization would be equally as successful in Detroit. An admirer recalled that Peck effectively "focused the attention of women on the most essential, yet most unfamiliar factor in the building of homes, communities, and nations, namely, 'The Spending Power of Women.'"

By 1934 ten thousand black women belonged to the Detroit organization. The only requirement for membership was a pledge to support black businesses, buy black products, and patronize black professionals, thereby keeping money in the community. The League quickly spread to other cities. Housewives' leagues in Chicago, Baltimore, Washington, Durham (North Carolina), Harlem, and Cleveland used boycotts of merchants who refused to sell black products and employ black children as clerks or stock persons to secure an estimated seventy-five thousand new jobs for black people.

Organized Labor and Black America

The relationship of African Americans to labor unions changed during the 1930s. Before this time most local unions affiliated with the national American Federation of Labor barred black people or restricted them to segregated locals. The New Deal did much to transform the labor movement. The National Labor Relations Act and the militancy of workers provided the opportunity to organize the nation's great mass production industries. Still, leaders of the AFL were unwilling to incorporate into their unions the masses of unskilled workers, many of whom were African American or recent European immigrants. Frustrated by this situation, in 1935 John L. Lewis (1880–1969), head of the United Mine Workers, and his followers formed the Committee for Industrial Organization (CIO) to take on the task.

Unlike the AFL, the CIO was committed to interracial and multiethnic organizing and so enabled more African Americans to participate in the labor movement. Its leaders knew that it was in organized labor's best interest to admit black men and women to membership. As one black union organizer said, "We colored folks can't organize without you and you white folks can't organize without us." But it took a massive change in outlook to achieve this unity. By 1940, the CIO had enlisted approximately 210,000 black members.

A. Philip Randolph's Brotherhood of Sleeping Car Porters (BSCP) remained with the AFL, but it also benefited from New Deal legislation. In 1934 Congress had amended the Railway Labor Act in a way that helped the BSCP to overcome the opposition of the Pullman company. The law required that corporations bargain in good faith with unions if the unions could demonstrate through elections monitored by the National Mediation Board that they represented the corporations' employees. In 1937, long after an election certified the BSCP as the workers' representative, the Pullman company finally recognized the brotherhood. Only then did the AFL grant the BSCP full membership as an international union. After more than twelve years, A. Philip Randolph and thousands of black men won their struggles against a giant corporation and a powerful labor organization.

Although most black people in unions were men, some unions helped improve the lives of black working women. For example, there had been a rigid hierarchy among workers in the tobacco industry since the early nineteenth century, one of the few areas of the economy outside agriculture or domestic service that employed many black women. Jobs were assigned on the basis of race and gender, with black women receiving the most difficult and tedious job, that of "stemmer." In 1939, stemmer Louise "Mama" Harris instigated a series of walkouts at the I. N. Vaughn Company in Richmond. The strikes, which were supported by CIO affiliates, including the white women of the International Ladies Garment Workers Union, led to the formation of the Tobacco Workers Organizing Committee, another CIO affiliate. In 1943, black women union leaders and activists, including Theodosia Simpson and Miranda Smith, were involved in a strike against the R. J. Reynolds tobacco company to force it to the negotiating table. Smith later became southern regional director of the Food, Tobacco, Agricultural, and Allied Workers of America. It was the highest position held by a black woman in the labor movement up to that time.

The Communist Party and African Americans

Throughout the 1930s the Communist party intensified its support of African Americans' efforts to address unemployment and job discrimination and to seek social justice. Some African Americans were attracted to the party because of its militant antiracism and its determination to be interracial. The party expelled members who exhibited racial prejudice and gave black men key leadership positions. James Ford, an African American, ran as the party's vice-presidential candidate in the election of 1932. While few black men and women actually joined the Communist party, some became increasingly sympathetic to left-wing ideas and prescriptions as the Depression wore on.

Many black workers were drawn to the Communist party because it criticized the refusal of organized white labor to include them. The communists maintained that "the low standard of living of Negro workers is made use of by the capitalists to reduce the wages of the white workers." They chided "the mis-leaders of labor, the heads of the reformist and reactionary trade union organizations" for refusing to organize black workers. They insisted "this anti-Negro attitude of the reactionary labor leaders helps to split the ranks of labor, allows the employers to carry out their policy of 'divide and rule,' frustrates the efforts of the working class to emancipate itself from the yoke of capitalism, and dims the class-consciousness of the white workers as well as of the Negro workers." Indeed, much of the push for racial equality within the CIO emanated from those connected with the party.

The International Labor Defense and the "Scottsboro Boys"

The Scottsboro case brought the Communist party to the attention of many African Americans. The case began when nine black youths who had caught a ride on a freight train in Alabama were tried, convicted, and sentenced to death for allegedly raping two white women. Their ordeal began on the night of March 25, 1931, when they were accosted by a group of young white hobos. A fight broke out. The black youths threw the white youths off the train. The losers filed a complaint with the Scottsboro, Alabama, sheriff, charging that black hoodlums had assaulted them. The sheriff ordered his deputies to round up every black person on the train. The sweep netted the nine young black men: Ozie Powell, Clarence Norris, Charlie Weems, Olen Montgomery, Willie Robertson, Haywood Patterson, Eugene Williams, Andy Wright, and Roy Wright. The police also discovered two young white women: nineteen-year-old Victoria Price and seventeen-year-old Ruby Bates.

Afraid of being arrested, and perhaps ashamed of being hobos, Price and Bates falsely claimed that the nine black youths had sexually assaulted them. On the basis of that accusation, the "Scottsboro Boys" (ranging in ages from thirteen to twenty), were given a hasty trial and convicted. Eight received the death sentence. The youngest, a thirteen-year-old, was sentenced to life imprisonment, even though medical examinations of Price and Bates proved that neither had been raped.

While other organizations either dawdled or refused to intervene, the Communist party's International Labor Defense (ILD) appealed the conviction to the United States Supreme Court. The case produced two important decisions that reaffirmed black people's right to the basic protections that all other American citizens enjoyed. In *Powell v. Alabama* (1932), the Court ruled that the nine Scottsboro defendants had not been given adequate legal counsel and that the trial had taken place in a hostile and volatile atmosphere. Asserting that the youths' right to due process as set forth in the Fourteenth Amendment had been violated, the Court ordered a new trial. Alabama did as instructed, but the new trial resulted in another guilty verdict and sentences of death or life imprisonment. The ILD promptly appealed and in *Norris v. Alabama* (1935), the Supreme Court decided that all Americans have the right to a trial by a jury of their peers. The systematic exclusion of African Americans from the Scottsboro juries, the Court held, denied the defendants equal protection under the law, which the Fourteenth Amendment guaranteed. Chief Justice Charles Evans Hughes pointed out that no black citizens had served on juries in the Alabama counties for decades, even though many were qualified to serve. The Court noted that the exclusion was blatant racial discrimination and called for yet another trial.

Despite these defeats, Alabama still pursued the case. Even when Ruby Bates publicly admitted that the rape charge had been a hoax, white Alabamians ignored her. Finally, in 1937, Alabama dropped its charges against five of the nine men, and in the 1940s the state released those still in jail. Altogether, nine innocent black men had collectively served some three-quarters of a century in prison. Clarence Willie Norris, however, escaped and fled to Michigan, returning decades later to receive a pardon from Governor George Wallace.

Debating Communist Leadership

Throughout the Scottsboro case, the NAACP tried to wrest control from the Communist party. Indeed, as the case evolved, tensions between the Communist party and the NAACP for leadership of black America flared into open hostility. The NAACP had hesitated to defend accused rapists, but it moved more decisively after the Communist party had taken the lead.

The contest between the NAACP and the communists reveals the differences between the two groups. The party organized demonstrations and denounced more cautious middle-class organizations. In Harlem, for example, the communists staged a 1931 protest march that attracted over three thousand black men and women and ended with an address by Ada Wright, the mother of two of the defendants, who praised the ILD for its help. The NAACP countered with a carefully orchestrated campaign that questioned the sincerity and effectiveness of the communists and sought to repair its own reputation as an effective advocate for African Americans.

Black public opinion divided in its evaluation of the party. Some black men and women applauded the communists. Journalist Eugene Gordon wrote:

> Negro workers think of the countless times Communists have been beaten insensible for defending . . . Negro workers. . . . They see the ILD . . . supported by the Communist Party, rushing to the defense of the nine Negro youths at Scottsboro before other Negro organizations in the country condescended to glance superciliously in their direction. . . . Seeing and hearing all these things, the Negro worker in the United States would be a fool not to recognize the leadership that he has been waiting for since his freedom.

But other African Americans ridiculed the party. George Schuyler, a columnist for the Pittsburgh *Courier*, objected to the communists' "campaign of vilification . . . against the NAACP:"

> No Ku Kluxer ever denounced the latter organization more vigorously and unfairly. The Communists know they are lying when they assert time and time again that the NAACP wants to see the boys convicted and is betraying the race. They have quite the same sort of grooved mentality as Ku Kluxers, Garveyites and other race fanatics, black and white. The course they tentatively pursue is held the only true one and whoever takes exception is denounced as an enemy of humanity, even though they may have to change that course in a few months.

Although most African Americans applauded the antiracist work that the Communist party supported and performed, there was no chance that they would defect from the traditional American political system as W. E. B. Du Bois wrote in 1931:

> American Negroes do not propose to be the shock troops of the Communist Revolution, driven out in the front to death, cruelty and humiliation in order to win victories for white workers. . . . Negroes know perfectly well that whenever they try to lead revolution in America, the nation will unite as one fist to crush them and them alone.

The National Negro Congress

The infighting between the Communist party and other groups doomed a major attempt to unite all the disparate African-American protest groups into the National Negro Congress (NNC). John P. Davis, a Washington-based economist, organized the NNC, modeling it on his experience as the executive secretary of the Joint Committee on National Recovery (JCNR), a coalition of black groups that pressed for fairness in the early New Deal. The NNC was to be a federation of organizations on a national scale supported by regional councils. Over 800 delegates representing 585 organizations attended its first meeting, held in Chicago in 1936. However, prominent black activists, leaders, and intellectuals were conspicuously absent, notably those associated with the NAACP. A. Philip Randolph was elected president, and Davis became the executive secretary. The group resolved not to be dominated by any one political faction and to build on the strength of all parts of the black community. Although handicapped by lack of funds, the NNC initially worked effectively at the local or community level. With branches in approximately seventy cities, the organization gained for its members increased employment opportunities, better housing, and adequate relief work.The NNC also prodded labor unions, in particular the CIO, to fight for better conditions and higher wages for black workers.

At the NNC's second meeting in Philadelphia in 1937, a skeptical Davis maintained that the Democratic party would never allow black people to benefit fairly from the New Deal. Eventually the increasing importance of communists in the NNC reduced the organization's ability to speak for the majority of black people. By 1940 it was greatly weakened. Randolph was voted out of office, and the once-promising NNC became a front group for the Communist party.

The Tuskegee Study

The 1930s marked the rising prominence of black scholars and intellectuals, but paradoxically, the decade also witnessed the worst manifestation of racism in American science. This shocking episode occurred in Macon County, Alabama. There, in 1932, United States Public Health Service (USPHS) officials initiated a study of syphilis, a sexually transmitted disease that can cause paralysis, insanity, and death. For the subjects of its program—entitled the Tuskegee Study of Untreated Syphilis in the Male Negro—the USPHS recruited 622 black men, all of them poor and the majority illiterate. Of these men, 431 had advanced cases of syphilis; the rest were free of the disease and served as controls for comparison.

The Tuskegee Study was called a treatment program, but it was actually an experiment, designed to chart the progression of a potentially fatal disease. To gain the trust of the men, the government doctors centered their work at Tuskegee Institute and hired a black nurse, Eunice Rivers, who convinced the men that they had "bad blood" and needed special treatment. Although penicillin, which could cure the disease, became available in the 1940s, the men never received it. Instead, they were given placebos, which they were told would cure them.

The men received regular physical examinations, which included a painful lumbar puncture. This insertion of a needle into the spinal cord to obtain fluid for diagnosis often caused the men severe headaches, and in a few cases, resulted in paralysis and even death. For almost forty years, Tuskegee Study doctors observed the men, keeping careful records of their health and performing autopsies on those who died; but they never treated them for syphilis. So little understood was the Tuskegee Study that men not only remained in the program, but believed that they were fortunate to have the physical examination, the hot lunches provided on examination days, and the burial allowance the government guaranteed their families. The medical community knew of the Tuskegee experiment, but the general public learned of it only in 1972 when a reporter broke the story. Black attorney Fred D. Gray of Alabama sued the U.S. government on behalf of the participants and their families, but before the case went to trial, the government made a $9 million settlement to the Tuskegee survivors and the descendants of those who had died.

Conclusion

Notable political changes occurred during the early 1930s: the NAACP came of age, black women found their voice, white left-wing leaders joined with black men and women in interracial alliances, organized labor bridged the race chasm, and black voters switched to the Democratic party. The New Deal had stimulated some economic recovery, and more important, laid the basis for a strong national state and a political coalition that, beginning with World War II, would challenge the nation's racial system.

Review Questions

1. Why did most black Americans switch to the Democratic party? How did President Roosevelt entice black people to abandon their long association with the Republican party?

2. How did black people survive the Great Depression? How did the experiences of black women during the Depression reflect their race, class, and gender status in American society?

3. How did the New Deal agencies and programs affect the lives of African Americans and their communities? How did the New Deal adversely affect black sharecroppers, tenants, and farmers?

TIMELINE

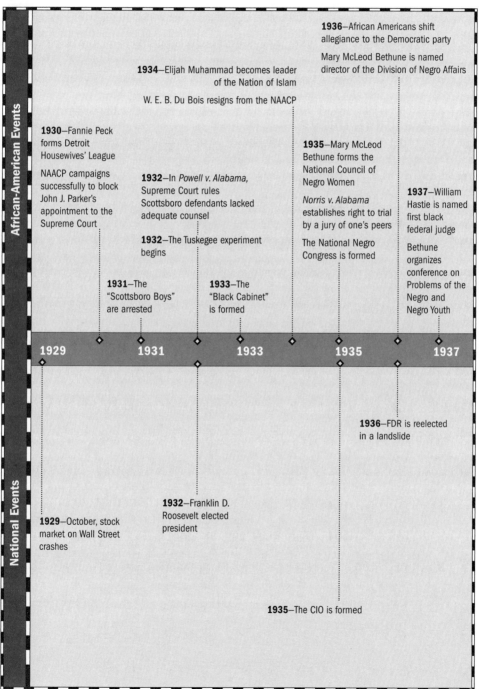

African-American Events

1936—African Americans shift allegiance to the Democratic party

Mary McLeod Bethune is named director of the Division of Negro Affairs

1934—Elijah Muhammad becomes leader of the Nation of Islam

W. E. B. Du Bois resigns from the NAACP

1930—Fannie Peck forms Detroit Housewives' League

NAACP campaigns successfully to block John J. Parker's appointment to the Supreme Court

1932—In *Powell v. Alabama,* Supreme Court rules Scottsboro defendants lacked adequate counsel

1932—The Tuskegee experiment begins

1935—Mary McLeod Bethune forms the National Council of Negro Women

Norris v. Alabama establishes right to trial by a jury of one's peers

The National Negro Congress is formed

1937—William Hastie is named first black federal judge

Bethune organizes conference on Problems of the Negro and Negro Youth

1931—The "Scottsboro Boys" are arrested

1933—The "Black Cabinet" is formed

| 1929 | 1931 | 1933 | 1935 | 1937 |

National Events

1936—FDR is reelected in a landslide

1932—Franklin D. Roosevelt elected president

1929—October, stock market on Wall Street crashes

1935—The CIO is formed

4. Discuss the political, social, and economic repercussions of the large-scale migration of African Americans out of the South during the 1930s.

5. Compare and contrast the Tuskegee experiment with the "Scottsboro Boys" case.

6. Why were W. E. B. Du Bois's *Crisis* editorials "on segregation" so divisive and explosive? Discuss the various responses of black activists and scholars to the idea of voluntary self-segregation.

Recommended Reading

John Egerton. *Speak Now against the Day: The Generation before the Civil Rights Movement in the South.* New York: Knopf, 1994. An excellent survey of the period before the southern civil rights era, with chapters on the Depression in the South and black and white Southerners' reactions to it.

James H. Jones. *Bad Blood: The Tuskegee Syphilis Experiment.* New York: Free Press, 1981. The best and most comprehensive study of the Tuskegee experiment.

Robin D. G. Kelley. *Hammer and Hoe: Alabama Communists during the Great Depression.* Chapel Hill, NC: University of North Carolina Press, 1990. A splendid study of the radicalizing activism of working people in the steel industry and on the farm during the thirties. Kelley does an excellent job of showing why the communists appealed to black workers.

Mark Naison. *Communists in Harlem during the Depression.* Urbana, IL: University of Illinois Press, 1983. A well-researched and clear-sighted study of the Communist party in Harlem and the history of the National Negro Congress.

Susan Reverby. *Tuskegee Truths: Rethinking the Tuskegee Syphillis Study.* Chapel Hill, NC: University of North Carolina Press, 2000.

Harvard Sitkoff. *A New Deal for Blacks: The Emergence of Civil Rights as a National Issue, Vol. I: Depression Decade.* New York: Oxford University Press, 1978. An important work that covers the New Deal era and presents it as a period when the groundwork for the civil rights movement was laid.

Patricia Sullivan. *Days of Hope: Race and Democracy in the New Deal Era.* Chapel Hill, NC: University of North Carolina Press, 1996. An invaluable study showing how the ideas of civil rights and democracy were forged in the New Deal South.

Raymond Wolters. *Negroes and the Great Depression: The Problem of Economic Recovery.* Westport, CT: Greenwood Publisher Group Incorporated, 1974. A solid survey of African Americans in the Depression that covers the impact of the Depression on African Americans, the workings of the Black Cabinet, and the effects of the New Deal agencies on the lives of black Americans.

✦ Chapter 19 ✦

Black Culture and Society
in the 1930s and 1940s

A key theme in black life during the 1930s and 1940s was the strategies African Americans devised to protest segregation, discrimination, and disfranchisement, and to resist the negative racial stereotypes and the appropriation of black culture by white entrepreneurs. At heart this was a quest to shape the representation of black people in American society and create a viable black culture for a rapidly urbanizing people. A central issue in this chapter is the extent to which black culture during the 1930s and 1940s became a source of strength—cultural power—that helped African Americans assert themselves within American society.

Black Culture in a Midwestern City

During the 1930s and 1940s black migrants flocked to St. Louis. Yet because of segregation and discrimination, the black community in St. Louis developed institutions to address their own educational and cultural needs. St. Louis is in the heart of a region often considered remote from the nation's cultural centers. Yet it has produced outstanding jazz musicians, and Chuck Berry virtually invented rock and roll there. However, black people there also supported classical music. A closer look at this support during the 1930s and 1940s reveals the interior diversity of black community life; even though white St. Louisians marginalized or ignored the contributions of black artists in the city.

Schools, churches, labor, and media within the St. Louis black community had to create opportunities for black children to study, appreciate, and perform classical music. The two largest black newspapers, the *St. Louis Argus* and the *St. Louis American,* publicized recitals and concerts. Two all-black institutions supported classical music education: Lincoln University in Jefferson City (founded in 1866) and Sumner High School (founded in 1875 as the first secondary school for black people west of the Mississippi).

By the 1940s Lincoln University had become the premier institution for training St. Louis musicians, and its music instructors were active in the black community's cultural affairs. Sumner High School had orchestras, bands, choirs, and glee clubs. Many of its music teachers had advanced degrees from prestigious music departments. The most influential teacher was Kenneth Billups, an arranger, composer, and founding director of the Legend Singers, a black professional chorus.

The Legend Singers appeared with the St. Louis Symphony and with the Municipal Opera Company (MUNY) in productions of *Showboat,* where they dressed in demeaning slave costumes. Billups's response to criticism of these appearances indirectly addressed the dilemma of black artists in a racially restrictive environment:

> I've seen situations where I felt inwardly . . . I might have had to do some things; for example, let's take this Showboat thing at MUNY Opera. There is the need of a black chorus to go there, and I had the privilege of doing that with my Legend Singers, simply because one of the first requirements was to have a black chorus.

Black churches sponsored religious programs highlighting the works of both black and white composers. Local 197 of the American Federation of Musicians and the St. Louis Music Association, which was the local branch of the National Association of Negro Musicians, promoted black performing organizations and training. These groups sponsored choirs, orchestras, and other musical organizations and devoted part of their members' dues to scholarships and summer choirs for boys and girls.

The Black Culture Industry and American Racism

Black American artists had to confront racism in the culture industry. Individual black creative artists could rarely afford to produce and disseminate their work. This power often resided with record companies, publishers, radio stations, and film studios. Yet black artists in the 1930s and 1940s were shaping a black consciousness that would erupt in the 1950s as the modern civil rights movement.

The political content of black art provoked debate among black artists. Many black Americans expected black artists to use their art to further black freedom from white oppression. The involvement of white people also created tension among black artists. While many white Americans had long appreciated black culture, some had also appropriated it for their own profit.

During the late 1930s and 1940s, corporate America recognized the money that could be made in producing and marketing black culture. But there was a problem: Black artists had to be made "acceptable" if they were to be marketed to affluent white consumers. These artists had to mask their true feelings and expressiveness if they wanted to earn income from their work. Artists who exhibited the right combination of showmanship, charm, and talent could reap financial rewards. The paradox of the black performer—using your art to entertain your oppressor—was most apparent in music.

The Music Culture from Swing to Bebop

Ironically, the very creativity that white Americans valued and often appropriated depended on the artists' ability to preserve some intellectual and emotional autonomy.

Black artists had to balance the need to earn a living with the need to remain true to their art. Black musicians continuously had to refine, expand, and perfect their art not only for themselves and each other but for a white-dominated marketplace. Black music is virtually synonymous with black culture, and segregation often made possible the creation of new cultural expressions. Music encapsulates and reflects the core values and underlying tensions and anxieties in black communities. In black music we witness cultural producers developing strategies of resistance against white domination.

Music was the primary inspiration for the creativity that characterized black cultural movements in America. Avant-garde developments in black music preceded black cultural activity in the visual arts, poetry, drama, dance, literature, film, and sports. Cultural creativity was a potent force for black liberation and occurred simultaneously in different locations in America.

The Great Depression devastated the vibrant black culture industry of the 1920s. Record sales in 1932 were only a sixth of those in 1927. Black musicians like Louis Armstrong had enjoyed a golden age of creativity during the 1920s. The record companies had their separate black music labels and sold thousands of records to southern migrants to the big cities. New bands proliferated. The territorial (traveling) bands took the music to the outposts of black America, while the big bands under Fletcher Henderson, Duke Ellington, Count Basie, and Cab Calloway played in white urban dance halls that admitted black people only as staff or entertainers.

New York was where black musicians felt they had to go to prove themselves. After entertaining affluent white people, or providing backup music for the Apollo Theater in Harlem, black musicians discarded their masks of docility and deference and made a different sound in their own space and on their own time in late-night jam sessions. The small clubs became the most fertile sites for innovation. In them a new kind of jazz was born.

The big band swing style that became popular in the 1930s transformed white American culture. Swing emerged as white bands reduced the music of the more innovative black bandleaders to a broadly appealing formula based on a swinging 4/4 beat, well-blended saxophone sections, and pleasant-sounding vocals. The big swing bands of the 1930s played written-out, completely arranged music. The popularity of swing boosted the careers of black and white bandleaders, but it also disheartened many of the younger black musicians. Tired of swing's predictability, they began improvising in the jazz clubs.

In the 1940s at least seven musicians were among the men most responsible for making a revolution in jazz that became known, scornfully at first, as bebop. These musicians were Charlie Parker, Dizzy Gillespie, Thelonious Monk, Bud Powell, Kenny Clarke, Max Roach, and Ray Brown. Bebop featured complex rhythms and harmonies and highlighted improvisation. Gillespie (1917–1993) said that Kansas City–born Charlie "Yardbird" and then just "Bird" Parker (1920–1955) was "the architect of the style." "Yard and I," Gillespie reminisced, "were so close, so wrapped up in one another, that he would think 'three,' and I would say 'four,' and I would say 'seven,' and he'd say 'eight'. . . . It wasn't difficult for us, really together, sometimes it sounded like one horn playing, and sometimes it was one horn, but sometimes it was both of us sounding like one horn."

White America resisted bebop. The nation was about to enter World War II and was too preoccupied to switch from the big band swing ballroom dancing music to bebop. Moreover, because jazzmen played in small, intimate clubs, not big bands, they had more freedom from the expectations of white society. However, before long, bebop became the principal musical language of jazz musicians around the world.

Bebop was a way of life and had its own attendant styles whose nuances depended on class status and, perhaps, age. Gillespie helped to create one side of bebop style in dress, language, and demeanor. He began to wear dark glasses on stage to reduce the glare from lights after he had cataract surgery. He grew a goatee because shaving every day irritated his bottom lip. He wore pegged pants, jackets with wide lapels, and a beret when men were still wearing hats with brims. Other bebop musicians emulated this attire. Beboppers also created their own slang that mingled colorful and obscene language. They also engaged in a free-wheeling lifestyle that often included love across the color line. But there was a down side to bebop. Some musicians became drug addicts, engaged in parasitical relationships with women, and squandered their money.

Black working-class young men adopted their own style of talking and of hip dressing, reflected in their zoot suits and conked hair. Zoot suits featured high-waisted, baggy, pegged pants and long draped coats. Sixteen-year-old Malcolm Little (later to take the name Malcolm X) purchased a zoot suit when he moved to Boston and plunged into hipster culture. To savor this new identity, he recalled, "I took three of those twenty-five cent sepia-toned, while-you-wait pictures of myself, posed the way 'hipsters' wearing their zoots would 'cool it'—hat dangled, knees drawn close together, feet wide apart, both index fingers jabbed toward the floor." He then took to the floor of the Roseland Ballroom where he shed his life as an unskilled wage worker and became someone freer and more empowered. He recalled the Ballroom's patrons' escape from their dreary urban lives: "They'd jampack that ballroom, the black girls in wayout silk and satin dresses and shoes, their hair done in all kinds of styles, the men sharp in their zoot suits and crazy conks, and everybody grinning and greased and gassed."

Bebop was the dominant black music of the war decade, but after 1945, returning veterans preferred simple love songs and melodies. This contributed to bebop's waning and led to more transformations. All artistic innovation extracts a high price. Bebop was no exception. Many of the most talented musicians, like Billie Holiday, whom we discuss later in this chapter, paid that price in lives decimated by drugs, poverty, sickness, and broken relationships. Few black musicians received the respect, recognition, and financial rewards from white America that their creativity warranted. Ultimately, white Americans wanted the art but not the artists.

Popular Culture for the Masses: Comic Strips, Radio, and Movies

The masses of African Americans participated in more accessible black popular culture. Everyone needed relief from the Depression. Comic strips, radio programs, and movies were affordable and allowed momentary escape. Newspapers passed from hand to hand, and families gathered around the radio for nightly programs of comedy and music. For black city dwellers, the movies offered respite from poverty and want.

The Comics

African Americans knew the difference between the fun that black people made of each other and the mockery white people made of them. During the Depression, comic strips in newspapers and comic books featuring superheroes diverted millions of Americans. Comic strips in black newspapers entertained, but also affirmed, the values of black people. They portrayed humorous situations and tales of intrigue and action.

The Philadelphia *Independent,* a black paper, ran a serial in the thirties called "The Jones Family." This strip, drawn by a cartoonist named Branford, emphasized black people's desire for achievement and respectability. The plot centered around the young Jones boy's search for the "good life" of money, success, love, and a happy marriage. But at every turn, he confronts adversity. Unable to get a job because of the Depression, he becomes an outlaw and narrowly escapes jail. He is constantly "on the run" from oppression. His only consolations are his family and his faithful girlfriend.

"The Jones Family" illuminates the gray areas that most African Americans, regardless of their class, faced when attempting to live coherent lives in the northern cities. While they cherished middle-class values, they often had to live with poverty, crime, and oppression. The black comic strips sought to provide entertaining, nonjudgmental blueprints for middle-class life, but to more alienated black people, they seemed to promote unattainable values and lifestyles.

Radio and Race

With some exceptions, during the Depression black performers in radio and film were marginalized, exploited, or excluded. Commercial radio operated to deliver an audience of white consumers to white advertisers, and it denied black people jobs as announcers, journalists, or technicians. White entertainers schooled in blackface minstrelsy portrayed black radio characters. The major labor unions in the entertainment industry restricted membership to white people. Still—with its vaudeville, big bands, drama, and comedy shows—radio provided relief from the Depression to all Americans, black and white.

The most popular comedy radio program in the early thirties was *The Amos 'n' Andy Show.* The title roles were played by two white performers, Charles Correll and Freeman Gosden, who wrote and performed scripts laced with oxymorons and malapropisms. Skillful showmen, Correll and Gosden ingratiated themselves in Chicago's black community. The Chicago *Defender* endorsed them and they received standing ovations at the Regal Theater in Chicago's black south side. Part of the amusement they generated derived from their mispronounced words, garbled grammar, and their show's minstrel ambience. Each episode highlighted an improbable situation involving the black cab driver (Amos) and his gullible overweight friend (Andy). Other characters included the scheming con artist Kingfish, his overbearing wife Sapphire, and his domineering mother-in-law, Mama. On radio, Gosden and Correll furnished voices for a whole array of other characters. The characters reinforced unflattering racial and gender stereotypes, but the show was not mean spirited. Some of the characters conducted themselves with dignity, modeling such positive values as marital fidelity, strong families, hard work, and economic independence. An *Amos 'n' Andy* movie, *Check and Double Check*—released in 1930 when hard times made black entertainers grateful for any work they could get—featured music by Duke Ellington's orchestra. The movie introduced Ellington to a wider audience of affluent white people and enhanced his reputation.

Black audiences recognized the minstrel stereotyping in *Amos 'n' Andy,* yet many among them still enjoyed the show. A vocal component of the ever more sophisticated and urbanized black population, however, complained that this show, and other radio programs, reinforced negative images—of black women as bossy Sapphires or Mammies and black men as childish clowns. Educator and activist Nannie Helen Burroughs considered the show demeaning. Robert L. Vann, editor of the Pittsburgh *Courier,* argued that it exploited African Americans for white commercial gain. Vann sponsored an unsucceful petition to the Federal Communications Commission to ban the show. In the early 1950s *The Amos 'n' Andy Show* had a brief life as a television series, this time with black actors.

For almost two decades, *Amos 'n' Andy* was the only depiction of black people on the nation's airwaves. Its negative stereotypes of African Americans buttressed white people's notions of their own superiority. The show never demonstrated the psychological or economic costs of racism. It taught white America to laugh at striving black men and women.

The most successful African American on network radio in the late 1930s was Eddie Anderson, who played Jack Benny's sidekick Rochester in NBC's *The Jack Benny Show.* Like the characters in *Amos 'n' Andy,* Anderson's character reinforced negative racial stereotypes. Anderson rationalized his role in a way that suggests discomfort with it:

> I don't see why certain characters are called stereotypes. The Negro characters being presented are not labeling the Negro race any more than "Luigi" is labeling the Italian people as a whole. The same goes for "Beulah," who is not playing the part of thousands of Negroes, but only the part of one person, "Beulah." They're not saying here is the portrait of the Negro, but here is "Beulah."

Race, Representation, and the Movies

In the 1930s and 1940s—after the introduction of sound in motion pictures—black and white producers began to make what were known as race films for African-American audiences. Except for these race films, white film executives had always cast black people in roles designed to reassure and entertain white audiences. Continuing this trend, African Americans in Hollywood movies of the 1930s, were usually cast in servile roles and often portrayed as buffoons. For example, the first black actor to receive major billing in American films, Stepin Fetchit (1902–1985, born Lincoln Theodore Monroe Perry), purportedly earned two million dollars in ten years playing a servile, slow-moving fool.

Black performers appeared as servants in many other box office successes during the Depression era. Among them were Gertrude Howard and Libby Taylor, who played servants to Mae West's characters in *I'm No Angel* (1933) and *Belle of the Nineties* (1934). In *Imitation of Life* (1934), Louise Beavers played a black servant whose light-skinned daughter, played by Fredi Washington, tries to pass for white. The black tap dancer and stage performer Bill "Bojangles" Robinson was featured in four popular films—*The Little Colonel* (1935), *The Littlest Rebel* (1935), *Just around the Corner* (1938), and *Rebecca of Sunnybrook Farm* (1938)—as a servant to white child star Shirley Temple.

The film that most firmly cemented the role of black Americans as servants in the American consciousness was *Gone with the Wind* (1939). Hattie McDaniel and Butterfly McQueen were the black "stars" in this epic adaptation of Margaret Mitchell's romanticized literary salute to the Old South. McDaniel had played servant or "Mammy" roles throughout the 1930s. The image of Mammy, the headscarf-wearing, obese, dutiful black woman who preferred nurturing white families to caring for her own children appealed to white America. But in *Gone with the Wind*, McDaniel gave the performance of a lifetime and in 1940 became the first African American to win an Oscar. Many in the black community criticized her for playing "female Tom" roles. Defensively, McDaniel retorted that she would rather play a maid and earn $700 a week than be one and earn only $7 a week. Some black actors such as McDaniel, dismayed by their relegation to demeaning roles, formed the Fair Play Committee (FPC) to lobby the movie industry for more substantial roles, to get rid of dialect speech, and to ban the term *nigger* from the screen. But in the *Beulah* radio show, which premiered in 1947, McDaniel again played a wise but subservient maid who provides the family that employs her with guidance and direction.

Eventually, during and after World War II, Hollywood developed more sophisticated race-directed movies. Of particular significance was the positive, even romanticized, portrayal of black Americans in a movie financed by the War Department to gain support among African Americans for the U.S. role in WWII. *The Negro Soldier*, directed by Frank Capra in 1944, played to vast audiences of enthusiastic black people. But even before the *The Negro Soldier*, some motion pictures had displayed African Americans positively. Paul Robeson made two movies, *The Emperor Jones* (1933) and *Showboat* (1936), in which he attempted to change how black men and women were represented on screen. He proclaimed in 1934, "In my music, my plays, my films I want to carry always this central idea: to be African. Multitudes of men have died for less worthy ideals; it is even more eminently worth living for." Robeson's films, however, were not box office successes, and he left the United States to pursue his career in Europe. There his commitment to leftist politics made him a target of the anticommunist hysteria that gripped the United States in the late 1940s (see Chapter 20).

To succeed commercially, African-American filmmakers had to disguise their dissent or create art purely for other black people. One of the most enterprising black filmmakers, Oscar Micheaux (1884–1951), made films aimed primarily at the black public, a group that the Hollywood producers of race movies ignored or insulted with stereotypical representations. The black men and women in Micheaux's films were often educated, cultured, and prosperous. Micheaux endowed black Americans with cinematic voice and subjectivity. His films, featured middle-class or identity issues such as "passing for white."

Micheaux produced more than thirty feature films between 1919 and 1948. In 1932, he released *The Exile*, the first sound motion picture to be made by, with, and for black Americans. The following year he produced *Veiled Aristocrats,* about passing for white among Chicago's black professional class. The characters in the film are considered "aristocrats" because they are descended from the white gentry of the Old South and Europe; they are "veiled" because of their color. The plot turns on the revelation that the wealthy "white" heroine is actually "colored," which enables her to marry the talented mulatto hero.

Micheaux tried to transform Hollywood without changing it, much as members of the black bourgeoisie struggled to be included in American society. His films capture the dilemma of black double consciousness. As W. E. B. Du Bois put it, black people always experienced that "peculiar sensation," that "sense of always looking at one's self through the eyes of others, of measuring one's soul by the tape of a world that looks on in amused contempt and pity." Black culture existed within and was shaped by, while simultaneously transforming, American culture. To the degree that black Americans had been assimilated, white American culture was their culture as well.

The white ethnic immigrants who created Hollywood were determined to help marginal and excluded groups like Jews and Italians assimilate into the American mainstream. Hollywood sought to create the illusion that these groups belonged to the power elite. However, these Hollywood entrepreneurs did not do the same for African Americans. Their films during the Depression represented black people as unassimilable. A small cadre of black filmmakers and actors created an alternative cinema for black patrons in which they introduced nuanced and fully human characters.

The Black Chicago Renaissance

Chicago during the 1930s and 1940s was a center of black culture. In contrast to some of the artists of the "Harlem Renaissance," the leading writers in Chicago harbored no illusions that art would solve the problems caused by white supremacy and black subordination. They emphasized the idea that black art had to combine aesthetics and function. It had to serve the cause of black freedom.

Arna Bontemps (1902–1973) was to the Chicago Renaissance what Alain Locke had been to the Harlem Renaissance. "The Depression," Bontemps asserted,

> put an end to the dream world of renaissance Harlem and scattered the band of poets and painters, sculptors, scholars and singers who had in six exciting years made a generation of Americans aware of unnoticed and hitherto unregarded creative talents among Negroes. . . . What they did not dream was that a second awakening, less gaudy but closer to realities, was already in prospect. . . . One way or the other, Harlem got its renaissance in the middle twenties, centering around the *Opportunity* contests and the Fifth Avenue Awards Dinners. . . . Ten years later Chicago reenacted it on WPA [Works Progress Administration] without finger bowls but with increased power.

Born in Louisiana, Bontemps migrated in 1935 to Chicago where he met Richard Wright and joined the South Side Writers Group, which Wright founded in 1936. It offered criticism and moral support to black writers. Bontemps's own writing was influenced by his association with the group. After 1935 his novels and short stories reflected a militant restlessness. In 1936, he published *Black Thunder* about the nineteenth-century slave conspiracy led by Gabriel and in 1939 *Drums at Dusk* about the Haitian Revolution and Toussaint L'Ouverture (1746–1803). Richard Wright's writings also celebrated resistance but with more nuance. He published his master-piece, *Native Son,* in 1940.

Among the artists who launched their careers on WPA funds were Margaret Walker and Willard Motley. Walker attracted widespread attention when her collected poems appeared as the book *For My People* in the Yale Series of Younger Poets. Willard Motley worked with a radio group while writing his powerful novel *Knock on Any Door* (1947), which depicted the transformation of an Italian-American altar boy into a criminal headed for the electric chair.

Before the 1930s, black intellectuals misjudged the potential of Chicago to be-come a vibrant center of black culture. In the late 1920s, black social scientists Charles S. Johnson and E. Franklin Frazier expressed disdain for black Chicago's artistic and intellectual prospects. Frazier proclaimed that "Chicago has no intelligentsia," and in 1923, Johnson asked rhetorically,

> Who can write of lilies and sunsets in the pungent shadows of the stockyards? . . . It is no dark secret why literary societies fail, where there are no Art exhibits or libraries about, why periodicals presuming upon an I.Q. above the age of 12 are not read, why so little lit-erature comes out of the city. No, the kingdom of the second ward [the black neighbor-hood] has no self-sustaining intelligentsia, and a miserably poor acquaintance with that of the world surrounding it.

Johnson did, however, admit that Chicago had "perhaps, the best musical school in the race, as these go."

Johnson and Frazier were too harsh. Just as Chicago's industrial economy nur-tured artists who drew inspiration from and reflected this stratum of moving and striv-ing, strolling and styling black people who wanted to transgress class and geographical lines. These working-class people aspired to enjoy middle-class life. A critical pulse point on Chicago's South Side came to be known as Bronzeville. It measured and re-flected the reality of the lives of ordinary working-class people. As Harlem had its 125th Street, Chicago had 35th and State Street and 47th and South Park (now Martin Luther King Jr. Drive).

Chicago was heir to the Harlem Renaissance. In 1930, Langston Hughes pub-lished *Not without Laughter,* the first major novel about black Chicago. Hughes moved to the city in 1941 and wrote often for the Chicago *Defender.* Chicago epitomized urban industrial America. As the northern terminus of the Illinois Central Railroad, it had long attracted displaced agricultural workers from the southern cotton fields, and by 1930 it had a black population of 233,903. The migrants arrived eager to absorb Chica-go's hard-driving blues and jazz culture.

During the 1920s a discernible class structure among African Americans emerged in Chicago, fueled in part by the new migrants. These men and women expanded the consumer base and gave rise to a cadre of educated professionals and entrepreneurs who appreciated the arts. Chicago's South Side became a black city within a city. Black businesses, such as banks and insurance companies, formed it's financial foundation. Entrepreneur Walter L. Lee started Your Cab Company and each day put on the streets a half dozen chauffeur-uniformed drivers of vehicles. In the late 1940s, John

Johnson would launch a publishing empire with such magazines as *Negro Digest, Jet,* and *Ebony*. These businesses depended on black support. It was in their best interest to support the arts.

Chicago was also a pioneering center for recording and performing music. As black music became a commodity, influential black disk jockeys, like Al Benson, appeared on radio in Chicago. Benson proved to be as skilled a businessman as he was a cultural impresario.

Jazz in Chicago

Within the confines of the South Side of Chicago, black musical giants, such as trumpeter Louis Armstrong (1898–1971) and his wife, Lillian Hardin Armstrong (1898–1971), a respected jazz pianist, nurtured a distinct jazz culture. "Lil" Armstrong was born in Memphis, Tennessee, and received formal music training at Fisk University, the Chicago College of Music, and the New York College of Music. She led her own band and was talented at arranging, composing, and singing. She and Louis Armstrong were married in 1924. Lil Armstrong eventually encouraged her husband to leave King Oliver's Creole Jazz Band and to join Fletcher Henderson in New York. The Armstrongs were divorced in 1938. She continued her recording career with Decca records under the name Lil Hardin.

Duke Ellington in his autobiography, *Music Is My Mistress*, remarked,

> Chicago always sounded like the most glamorous place in the world to me when I heard the guys in Frank Holliday's poolroom talking about their travels. . . . They told very romantic tales about nightlife on the South Side. By the time I got there in 1930, it glittered even more . . . the Loop, the cabarets . . . city life, suburban life, luxurious neighborhoods—and the apparently broken-down neighborhoods where there were more good times than any place in the city.

At this point Ellington was recording some of his best jazz, such as *Mood Indigo* (1930) and *Ko-Ko* (1940).

The seeds that blossomed into full-bodied jazz culture were planted across America at the turn of the century. The most famous musicians, however, all went to or passed through Chicago. As the Chicago Jazz Age came into its own, the beguiling tune *Pretty Baby* became the city's theme song. It was written by Tony Jackson, whom Jelly Roll Morton (the self-proclaimed "inventor of jazz") called "maybe the best entertainer the world has ever seen." The South Side, specifically along State Street between 31st and 35th, was the beating heart of the city's Jazz Age. Chicago was the place aspiring jazz musicians went to prove they had what it took to make a name for themselves.

Gospel in Chicago: Thomas Dorsey

The term *gospel* designates the traditional religious music of the black church. It flourished in Chicago's churches. Gospel music became the backbone of urban and contemporary black religion and is deeply entrenched in worship. The use of

Art and Culture Gallery II

Archibald Motley (1891–1981) was raised in Chicago where his father was a Pullman employee active in the Brotherhood of Sleeping Car Porters. Motley attended the Art Institute of Chicago and graduated in 1918. In works like *Barbecue*, painted in 1934 when he was employed by a New Deal arts program, Motley vividly captured the exuberance and vitality of nightlife in Chicago's Bronzeville.

Archibald Motley, Jr., *Barbecue*, 1934. Oil on canvas, 36 ¼" x 40 ⅛". The Howard University Gallery of Art, Washington, D.C. Photo: Jarvis Grant/Howard University.

Augusta Savage, *Gamin*, 1929. Plaster, 9 ⅛" x 6" x 3 ½". Photo Manu Sassoonian. Schomburg Center for Research in Black Culture, Art & Artifacts Division, The New York Public Library, Astor, Lenox and Tilden Foundations.

As the child of an impoverished preacher near Jacksonville, Florida, Augusta Savage (1892–1962) learned to shape clay figures into farm animals. She eventually moved to New York City and furthered her artistic education at Cooper Union. In 1923 she was rejected for a summer school program in Paris because French officials feared her presence might offend Southern white students. During the New Deal she was an active teacher and administrator with the Works Progress Administration. Only a small number of her works survive. The model for *Gamin* (1929) was a boy from Savage's Harlem neighborhood.

William H. Johnson (1901–1970) was born and raised in Florence, North Carolina. He moved to New York at the age of seventeen and put himself through art school on his earnings as a stevedore. Gaining recognition from his teachers as a young artist of great promise, he moved to Europe in 1926 to pursue his career. Fleeing the growing Nazi menace on the eve of World War II, he returned to New York with his Danish wife in 1938. In his later paintings, including *Lamentation or Descent from the Cross*, (1944), he adopted a flat, deliberately "primitive" style and began documenting African-American life and religion.

Every American is familiar with the work of Selma Burke (1900–1995) without knowing it. She created the profile of President Franklin D. Roosevelt that appears on the Roosevelt dime. Burke's original bronze plaque of the president—which the U.S. mint relied on when it designed the coin—was made for the Recorder of Deeds Building in Washington in 1945. Born in Mooreseville, North Carolina, Burke earned a master of fine arts degree from Columbia University. *Jim*, an undated work, captures the quiet dignity of its subject.

Jacob Lawrence, *The Migration of the Negro Panel No. 1*, 1940-1941. Tempera on masonite 12" x 18". (30.5 x 45.7 cm). Acquired 1942. The Phillips Collection, Washington, D.C.

Though he quit high school and had little artistic training, Jacob Lawrence (born 1917) emerged as one of the most prominent artists of the twentieth century. During the Depression he attended a Works Progress Administration art program in Harlem administered by Augusta Savage. Lawrence was fascinated by black history and enjoyed storytelling. *Migration of the Negro, Panel 1* (1940-1941) is the first of 60 panels documenting the migration of black Southerners to the North.

Romare Bearden, *Watching the Trains Go By*, 1964. Photograph by Sharon Goodman. ©Romare Bearden Foundation/Licensed by VAGA, New York, NY.

Romare Bearden, (1911-1988) a self-taught artist, grew up in Charlotte, North Carolina. In photomontages like *Watching the Trains Go By* (1964), he celebrated rural black folk traditions and rituals. "I use the train," Bearden explained, "as a symbol of the other civilization—the white civilization and its encroachment upon the lives of blacks. The train was always something that could take you away and could also bring you to where you were. And in the little towns it's the black people who live near the trains."

Elizabeth Catlett (born 1919) grew up in Washington, DC. Her father died before she was born, leaving her mother to support three children. Catlett studied art at Howard University. After a brief stint as a high school teacher she attended graduate school at the University of Iowa. *Malcolm X Speaks For Us* (1969), a linoleum block print, is part of her series on African-American heroes.

Steve Prince (born 1968) draws on themes from black history in his work. *Noble Sounds* (1995), addresses the issues of black identity and gender relations within the context of domination and resistance. "The three central characters represent dispossessed populations of the diaspora," Prince explains. "Their mental, physical, and spiritual power is unleashed as they remove the mask that grins and lies" while they dance in front of a white house, symbolic of the master's house on a plantation, with menacing white-hooded figures in the windows.

instruments—tambourines, drums, pianos, horns, guitars, and Hammond organs—characterizes gospel and distinguishes it from the earlier spiritual and black folk music. During the 1930s and 1940s, it developed its own idioms and techniques.

Black "folk churches" encourage free expression, group participation, spontaneous testimonies, prayers, witnessing, and music. Singers and choirs rarely perform the same songs in the same way more than once. The performer must pay attention to the quality of the sound and to the manipulation of timbre, range, and shading. The delivery uses the whole body in synchronized movement. The mechanics of the delivery are designed to intensify the performance, giving it added textual variation and melodic improvisation. Performers expand a melody by a variety of devices, including repetition, shouts, slides, slurs, moans, and grunts. The supporting piano and organ frequently engage in call-and-response interplay.

Thomas Dorsey (1899–1993)—one of Chicago's leading composers of the blues since the mid-twenties—was most responsible for developing black urban gospel. Dorsey's genius lay in his ability to synthesize elements of the blues with religious hymns to create a gospel blues. His gospel pieces, performed with a ragtime-derived, boogie-woogie piano accompaniment, radiated an urban religious spirit. In 1930 Dorsey gained widespread attention when gospel singer Willie Mae Ford Smith (1904–1994) performed his "If You See My Savior, Tell Him That You Saw Me" at the National Baptist Convention meeting in Chicago. In 1932, Dorsey's place in musical history was assured when Theodore Frye, with Dorsey at the piano, performed in the Ebenezer Baptist Church in Chicago "Take My Hand, Precious Lord." The song had a profound impact on gospel performers and their audiences. Dorsey's abundant works provided a foundation for shout worship in the urban Protestant churches formed by transplanted black Southerners in the 1930s and succeeding decades.

One of the greatest gospel singers, Chicago-based Mahalia Jackson (1911–1972), sang and promoted Dorsey's songs all over the country between 1939 and 1944. Jackson once said of the music, "Gospel songs are the songs of hope. When you sing them you are delivered of your burden." During the Depression and World War II, gospel became big business.

Katherine Dunham
and Billie Holiday

The influence of the WPA in Chicago was especially reflected in dance. Dance has always been an integral part of African-American life, and the dances of black people have always been important in the American theater. The first performances by black dancers given within and taken seriously by the concert dance world occurred in the 1930s. The first "Negro Dance Recital in America" was performed in 1931 by the New Negro Art Theater Dance Company, co-founded by Edna Buy and Hemsley Winfield. In that same year, Katherine Dunham (1909–) founded the Negro Dance Group in Chicago, which survived thanks to WPA support. As Dunham later recalled, "Black dancers were not allowed to take classes in studios in the '30s. I started a school because there was no place for blacks to study dance. I was the first to open the way for black dancers and I was the first to form a black dance company."

One of America's premier dance artists, the internationally acclaimed Katherine Dunham (1909–) performed in the Bobli Gardens in Florence, Italy in 1950. A talented choreographer, anthropologist, and writer, Dunham founded one of the first black dance companies. She was an outspoken critic of Jim Crow segregation.
©David Lees/CORBIS

Dunham was unique. Trained in anthropology, she studied African-based ritual dance in the Caribbean. In 1938 her troupe stunned an audience with the sexual vitality of its performance. When the company, now renamed the Katherine Dunham Dance Company, performed in February 1940, audiences and critics were awed. *The New York Times* declared:

> Her performance with her group at the Windsor Theater may very well become a historic occasion, for certainly never before in all efforts of recent years to establish the Negro dance as a serious medium has there been so convincing and authoritative approach. . . . The potential greatness of the Negro dance lies in its discovery of its own roots and the crucial nursing of them into growth and flower. . . . It is because she has showed herself to have both the objective quality of the student and the natural instinct of the artist that she has done such a truly important job.

What kept audiences returning to Dunham dance performances, however, was the dancer's bold sensuality. A reviewer called *Tropical Revue,* for example, "tempestuous and torrid, raffish and revealing." *The New York Sun* marveled, "Shoulders, midsections and posteriors went round and round. Particularly when the cynosure was Miss Dunham, the vista was full of pulchritude."

Dunham explained her motivation:

> I felt a new dance form was needed for black people to be able to appear in any theater in the world and be accepted and exciting. One of the prerequisites of art is uniqueness. Rather than taking years to build a classical ballet company for blacks, I decided to create

a dance with an authentic base for black people. Through my anthropological work, I studied primitive and folk dances and created the Dunham dance from them.

Her success led to film offers. The producers of the all-black musical extravaganza *Cabin in the Sky* hired the dance troupe and gave the feature role of Georgia Brown to Dunham. The role gave Dunham, as the *Times* dance critic wrote, the chance "to sizzle." But it also allowed white audiences to view her as the stereotypical sultry black sexpot.

Nevertheless, the profits from the film funded the dance company and Dunham's research. In 1943 Dunham opened the Katherine Dunham School of Arts and Research in New York which trained artists in dance, theater, literature, and world cultures.

Dunham was not afraid to protest racial segregation, even though it hurt her popularity. In 1944 in Louisville, Kentucky, after a performance, Dunham announced, "This is the last time I shall play Louisville because the management refuses to let people like us sit by people like you. Maybe after the war we shall have democracy and I can return." Dunham was not only a gifted and talented pioneer in dance, but she also underscored the responsibility that a black artist had to the black community to fight racism.

Billie Holiday (1915–1959), another great performer whose career took shape during the Depression, also used her art to challenge the oppression of black people. Holiday, popularly known as "Lady Day," began singing at age fifteen and was discovered three years later by John Hammond, a Chicago jazz producer and promoter. In 1934 she made her debut at the Apollo Theater in Harlem. An incomparable singer known for subtle and artful improvisation, she left a wealth of recordings.

Black Graphic Art

Chicago artists, such as Charles White, Elizabeth Catlett, and Eldzier Cortor, and Harlem's Jacob Lawrence, celebrated working-class black people while implicitly criticizing the racial hierarchy of power and privilege. Their art belonged to the social realism school that flourished in the United States in the 1930s. This art strove to fuse propaganda—both left wing and right wing—to art to make it socially and politically relevant.

As the Depression worsened, black artists used their art to portray the crisis in capitalism. This involved depicting social and racial inequality. Chicago's Charles White wrote that "paint is the only weapon I have with which to fight what I resent. If I could write I would write about it. If I could talk I would talk about it. Since I paint, I must paint about it."

Defense Worker, a painting by Dox Thrash, reflects these concerns. Completed in 1942, just after the United States had entered World War II, it shows an isolated black worker looming over the horizon. The heroic proletarian imagery alludes to the dream of a racially integrated labor force, equal opportunity, and social reform in the wake of the New Deal and the sudden demand for labor triggered by the war.

The Harmon Foundation sponsored five juried exhibitions (1926–31, 1933) of the work of black artists. The William E. Harmon Awards for Distinguished Achievement among Negroes celebrated black artists in the hope that they would serve as role models for others. William E. Harmon, a real-estate investor from Iowa, established the New York–based foundation in 1925. In the 1930s the WPA established art workshops and community art centers in black urban communities, such as Chicago, Cleveland, Detroit and Harlem to teach art to young people and provide work for artists. Sculptor Augusta Savage, as the first director of the Harlem Community Art Center, presided over more than 1,500 students enrolled in day and evening classes. Among the teachers was Selma Burke (1900–1995) who sculpted the relief of Franklin D. Roosevelt that appears on the dime.

The Federal Arts Project, another New Deal agency, sponsored the creation of murals in public buildings, such as post offices and schools, that celebrated American ideals. Murals by black artists celebrated the heritage, contributions to society, and struggles of African Americans. Aaron Douglas, a leading painter of such public art, spoke about his work and that of his colleagues in a 1936 essay, "The Negro in American Culture":

> One of our chief concerns has been to establish and maintain recognition of our essential humanity, in other words, complete social and political equality. This has been a difficult fight as we have been the constant object of attack by all manner of propaganda from nursery rhymes to false scientific racial theories. . . . In this struggle the rest of the proletariat almost invariably has been arrayed against us. . . . But the Negro artist, unlike the white artist, has never known the big house. He is essentially a product of the masses and can never take a position above or beyond their level.

Douglas and other black artists pressed the WPA to appoint more African Americans to its local boards and to hire them for more projects. The Harlem Artists Guild and the Arts and Crafts Guild in Chicago provided forums where black artists could meet and plan strategies to foster the visual arts and support the social and political issues that affected black people's lives.

Black Literature

Black literature, like black art, has been assessed in terms of what it reveals about the social, cultural, and political landscape at a given historical moment. The most distinguishing feature of black literature may be the way that black writers have attempted to create spaces of freedom in their work, to liberate place, a trait that also marks black religious culture and folk cultural practices, such as storytelling. Black literature, like all black cultural production, is valued both for aesthetic reasons on its own and for the way it represents the struggles of black people to attain freedom. Black writers in the 1930s and 1940s felt obliged to address questions of identity and to define and describe urban life to the dispossessed and impoverished black migrants to the cities. They tried to delineate the dimensions of a shared American heritage by portraying the specific contributions that African Americans had made to American society. Black writers also explored the issue of the rights African Americans were entitled to as Americans and the demands they should make on society.

Richard Wright's *Native Son*

In 1940, Richard Wright (1908–1960) published *Native Son,* the first of many important novels by Depression-generation black authors. Its tale of the downfall of the
young Bigger Thomas could be read as a warning about how economic hardship combined with discrimination could lead young black men to violence and rage. Setting
out for an interview for a job as a chauffeur, Bigger meets with his neighborhood
friends who want him to help them rob a grocery store. Bigger's fear of whites prevents
him from going along. Instead, he picks a fight to camouflage his fear and avoid committing the crime. Bigger gets the chauffeur's job, which requires him to drive the
wealthy Dalton family. On his first assignment, he is supposed to drive young Mary
Dalton to a university lecture. But she talks him into picking up her boyfriend, Jan—a
communist—and taking them to a restaurant in the black neighborhood. Jan and
Mary are oblivious to the patronizing way they treat Bigger. After dinner Bigger drives
them around while they make love in the back seat.

When Jan leaves, Bigger takes Mary home. Because she is too drunk to walk, Bigger carries her to her room and is putting her to bed when blind Mrs. Dalton comes to
check on her daughter. Bigger panics. He covers Mary's head with a pillow to keep her
quiet. When Mrs. Dalton leaves, Bigger discovers that he has inadvertently smothered
Mary. He then burns her body in the basement furnace. Not fully grasping what he has
done, Bigger writes a ransom note signed with a phony name to make it seem that
Mary has been kidnapped. When Mary's remains are discovered, Bigger flees. Fearing
that she might betray him, he then murders his girlfriend, Bessie. Bigger is captured
and condemned. The remainder of the novel explores the hysteria and bigotry that
envelop the case, the harsh criminal justice system, the insensitivity of the Communist
party, which seeks to exploit Bigger's plight, and the social ills that plagued Chicago's
African Americans during the Depression.

At the center of the drama is Wright's exploration of how Bigger comes to terms
with his murder of Mary and Bessie. In conversations with Max, his communist lawyer,
he realizes that his irrational fear of white people had caused him to kill the two
women. He also realizes that he was a product of his experiences in the ghetto: "What
I killed for I am."

Wright's novel thrust the impact of urbanization and racism on black men and
women into the consciousness of the American people. One white critic declared,
"Speaking from the black wrath of retribution, Wright insisted that history can be punishment. He told us the one thing even the most liberal whites preferred not to hear:
that Negroes were far from patient or forgiving, that they were scarred by fear, that
they hated every moment of their suppression even when seeming most acquiescent,
and that often enough they hated us the decent and cultivated white men who from
complicity or neglect shared in the responsibility of their plight."

In his closing arguments, the lawyer, Max, warns of the destructive potential of
suppressed black rage:

> The hate and fear which we have inspired in him, woven by our civilization into the very
> structure of his consciousness and into his blood and bones, into the hourly functioning
> of his personality, have become the justification of his existence. . . . Kill him and swell the

tide of pent up lava that will some day break loose, not in a single, blundering crime, but in a wild cataract of emotion that will brook no control.

Native Son was an immediate success. It became a Book-of-the-Month Club selection and has sold millions of copies.

James Baldwin Challenges Wright

Wright showed that success and militancy were not mutually exclusive. A younger generation of black writers, however, especially James Baldwin (1924–1987), took issue with Wright. African Americans, they argued, need not all be portrayed as hapless victims of American racism. In a famous short essay, "Everybody's Protest Novel" in 1949, Baldwin argued that Bigger's tragedy was not that he was black, poor, and scared, but that he had accepted "a theology that denies him life, that he admits the possibility of his being sub-human and feels constrained, therefore, to battle for his humanity according to those brutal criteria bequeathed him at his birth." Baldwin concluded, "The failure of the protest novel lies in its rejection of life, the human being, the denial of his beauty, dread, power, in its insistence that it is his categorization alone which is real and which cannot be transcended." In turn, Wright accused Baldwin of betraying all African-American writers who wrote protest literature. "What do you mean, protest!" Wright demanded. "All literature is protest. You can't name a single novel that isn't protest."

Baldwin answered Wright in a second essay in 1951 entitled, "Many Thousand Gone." "Wright's work," Baldwin declared, "is most clearly committed to the social struggle. . . . [T]hat artist is strangled who is forced to deal with human beings solely in social terms; and who has, moreover, as Wright had, the necessity thrust on him of being the representative of some thirteen million people. It is a false responsibility (since writers are not congressmen) and impossible, by its nature, of fulfillment."

The controversy ended the budding friendship between Wright and Baldwin, and Baldwin, who would inherit the mantle of "best-known black American male writer" (see Chapter 22).

Ralph Ellison and *Invisible Man*

The most intricate novel about the black experience in America written during this era was Ralph Ellison's (1914–1994) *Invisible Man,* which won the National Book Award for fiction in 1952. Partially autobiographical, it traces the life of a young black man from his early years in a southern school (a thinly disguised Tuskegee Institute) through his migration to New York City. The novel explores class tensions within American society and within the black community. It illuminates the interaction between white and black Americans with a balanced incisive perspective.

Ellison argued that the black tradition teaches one "to deflect racial provocation and to master and control pain. . . . It is a tradition which abhors as obscene any trading on one's own anguish for gain or sympathy. . . . It takes fortitude to be a man and no less to be an artist. Perhaps it takes even more if the black man would be an artist."

He concluded, "It would seem to me, therefore, that the question of how the 'sociology of his existence' presses upon the Negro writer's work depends upon how much of his life the individual writer is able to transform into art."

Echoing Du Bois's now classic characterization of the "twoness" of the African-American character, Ellison observed, "[Black people] are an American people who are geared to what is and who yet are driven by a sense of what it is possible for human life to be in this society."

African Americans in Sports

It is in professional sports that black Americans have most demonstrated what human life can achieve when unconstrained by racism. The experiences of black athletes are a microcosm of their lives in American society. The privileges whites enjoyed in sports in this era paralleled the disadvantages and exclusions that were part of black life. In the 1930s two black athletes, Jesse Owens and Joe Louis, captured the world's attention and inspired African Americans.

Jesse Owens and Joe Louis

Jesse Owens (1913–1980) was born on an Alabama sharecropping farm but grew up in Cleveland, Ohio. A talented runner, he studied at Ohio State University and prepared for the 1936 Olympics, which were to be held in Berlin, the capital of Nazi Germany. Many African-American leaders believed that participating in the games would help legitimate the Nazi myth of the superiority of the so-called Aryan race. Owens participated to debunk that myth and became the first Olympian ever to win four gold medals. Hitler left the stadium to avoid congratulating Owens, but African Americans relished Owens's victory over racism.

Joe Louis Barrow (1914–1981), like Owens, was the son of Alabama sharecroppers. His family migrated to Detroit when he was twelve. Although his mother wanted him to be a violinist, young Joe Louis—he dropped the name Barrow—won a string of local boxing victories. In 1935 he faced former heavyweight champion, Primo Carnera in New York before a record crowd of 62,000. The fight had political overtones. Louis was fighting an Italian American at a time when Benito Mussolini, the Fascist dictator of Italy, was about to invade Ethiopia; this was the oldest black independent nation in Africa, whose ruler, Emperor Haile Selassie, many black Americans admired. Louis beat Carnera in the sixth round. Louis held the world heavyweight title from 1937 to 1949.

Breaking the Color Barrier in Baseball

While African Americans were integrated in track and in boxing, professional baseball remained strictly segregated until after World War II. Despite the hardships of the Depression, however, virtually every major black community tried to field its own baseball team. The Negro National League, which had folded in 1932, was revived in 1934, and a second league, the Negro American League, formed in 1937. Many of the players in

African-American Milestones in Sports	
1934	The Negro National League is revived.
1936	Jesse Owens wins four gold medals at Berlin Olympics.
1937	Joe Louis defeats James J. Braddock to win world heavyweight title. The Negro American League is formed.
1938	Joe Louis defeats the German Max Schmeling.
1947	Jackie Robinson signs with the Brooklyn Dodgers to become the first black major league baseball player. Dodgers win the National League Pennant.
1948	Alice Coachman wins a gold medal in the high jump to become the first black woman Olympic champion.
	Larry Doby joins the Cleveland Indians, becoming the first black player in the American League.
	Brooklyn Dodgers hire their second black player, Roy Campanella.
1949	Jackie Robinson wins the National League's Most Valuable Player Award.

the Negro leagues, including such legends as Josh Gibson, Satchel Paige, Leon Day, and Cool Papa Bell, would have equaled or excelled their white counterparts in the major leagues, but, except for Paige, they never had the chance.

In 1947, however, major league baseball, which had been a white man's game since the departure of Fleetwood Walker in 1887, became integrated again when Jackie Robinson (1919–1972) signed to play with the Brooklyn Dodgers. In 1945 Branch Rickey, the general manager of the Dodgers, decided to sign a black ball player to improve the Dodgers' chances of winning the National League pennant and the World Series. After scouting the Negro Leagues, he signed twenty-six-year-old Jackie Robinson.

Robinson was the ideal choice. He was a superb athlete and a man of immense determination. Born in Georgia and raised in southern California, he had been an All-American running back in football at UCLA and then had played baseball for the legendary Kansas City Monarchs of the Negro leagues. Robinson was also committed to racial progress. Robinson played the 1946 season for the Brooklyn Dodgers minor league team in Montreal where he and his wife Rachel were warmly received. But spring training in segregated Florida was difficult.

Robinson broke the color barrier when he opened at first base for the Dodgers in April 1947. Taunted and threatened by some spectators and players, he played spectacular baseball. He was Rookie of the Year in 1947, and the Dodgers won the National League pennant. Robinson retired in 1957 but remained outspoken on racial issues until his death in 1972.

In July 1947 Larry Doby became the first black player in the American League when he joined the Cleveland Indians. As other major league teams also signed black players, the Negro Leagues withered.

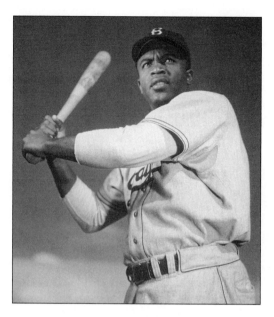

Jackie Robinson (1919–1972) broke baseball's color barrier when he joined the Brooklyn Dodgers in 1947. He silently endured considerable hostility and threats from angry white citizens.
© CORBIS/Bettmann

Black Religious Culture

Just as black religion was the "invisible institution" that helped African Americans to survive slavery, the black church was the visible institution that helped hundreds of thousands of migrants adjust to urban life while affirming an enduring set of core values consisting of freedom, justice, equality, and an African heritage. The term "black church" is a shorthand way of referring to a pluralistic collection of institutions, including seven independent, historic, and black-controlled denominations: the African Methodist Episcopal Church, the African Methodist Episcopal Zion Church; the Christian Methodist Episcopal Church; The National Baptist Convention, Incorporated; the National Baptist Convention of America, Unincorporated; the Progressive National Baptist Convention; and the Church of God in Christ. Together, these denominations account for more than 80 percent of all black Christians.

The black church helped black workers make the transition from being southern peasants to becoming part of a northern urban proletariat. Yet the relationship between black religious tradition and the secular lives of black people was always changing. The blues and jazz performed in nightclubs were transformed into urban gospel music. Many of the nightclub musicians and singers received their training and first performed publicly in their churches. During the Depression, the black church helped black people survive by enabling them to pool their resources and by offering inspiration and spiritual consolation. Here we focus on alternative religious groups that became prominent during the 1930s and 1940s and addressed specific needs growing out of the Depression and the traumatic experience of relocating to alien and often hostile northern cities. Elijah Muhammad's Nation of Islam and Father Divine's Peace Mission Movement combined secular concerns with sacred beliefs. Both strengthened a sense of identity, affirmation, and community among their members.

The Nation of Islam

The Nation of Islam emerged in 1929, the year Timothy Drew died. Drew, who took the name Nobel Drew Ali, was founder of the Moorish Science Temple of America, which flourished in Chicago, Detroit, and other cities in the 1920s. After his death, a modified version of the Moorish Science Temple emerged in 1930 in Detroit. It was led by a mysterious door-to-door peddler of items that supposedly originated in Africa, known variously as Wallace D. Fard, Master Farad Muhammad, or Wali Farad. His teachings that black people were the true Muslims attracted many poor residents in Depression-era Detroit. In addition to the beliefs of Nobel Drew Ali, Fard's Nation of Islam also taught a mixture of Koranic principles, the Christian Bible, his own beliefs, and those of nationalist Marcus Garvey.

In 1934, after establishing a Temple of Islam, Fard disappeared, and one of his disciples, Elijah Poole (1897–1975), renamed Elijah Muhammad by Fard, became leader of the Detroit temple and then of a second temple in Chicago. The Nation attracted the attention of federal authorities during World War II when its members refused to serve in the military. Muhammad was arrested in May 1942 on charges of inciting his followers to resist the draft and was imprisoned in Milan, Michigan, until 1946. After his release he settled in Chicago and began to expand his movement.

The Nation of Islam taught that black people were the Earth's original human inhabitants who had lived, according to Elijah Muhammad, in the Nile Valley. Approximately six thousand years ago, a magician named Yakub produced white people who were banished to Europe where they began to spread evil. Their worst crime was their enslavement of black people. Elijah Muhammad taught that white supremacy was ending and that black people would rediscover their authentic history and culture. To prepare for the coming millennium, he instructed members to adhere to a code of behavior that included abstaining from many traditionally southern black foods, especially pork. Members subscribed to a family-centered culture in which women's role was to produce and rear children. The Nation also demanded part of the South for a black national state.

Father Divine and the Peace Mission Movement

Father Major Jealous Divine (ca. 1877–1965) was born George Baker in Savannah. Little is known about his early life. He captured attention in 1919 when he settled with twenty followers in Sayville, New York, and began what became known in the 1930s as the Peace Mission Movement. Divine secured domestic jobs for many of his followers on the surrounding estates and preached a gospel of hard work, honesty, sobriety, equality, and sexual abstinence. He provided free, or nearly free, meals and shelter for anyone who asked. In 1930, he changed his name to Father Divine. His Peace Movement espoused a racially neutral and economically empowering dogma that offered needy black and white urbanites spiritual guidance and mental and physical healing. Hundreds of people traveled to see Father Divine on weekends, feast at his communal banquet table, and listen to his promises of heaven on earth. The feasts were symbolic of the early Christian Eucharist and became the defining practices of Divine's religion.

In 1931, the police arrested Divine and eighty followers on charges of being a "public nuisance." Three days after a judge sentenced Divine to a year in jail and a $500 fine, the judge died of a heart attack. Divine was quoted as saying, "I hated to do it." The conviction was reversed, and Divine's reputation as a master of cosmic forces soared. Some of his followers now believed that he was God. Aside from the belief in the divinity of Father Divine, members of the Peace Movement were drawn to the mission's strong emphasis on ending racial prejudice and economic inequalities.

In 1933, Divine moved his headquarters to Harlem, where his movement prospered, eventually purchasing key real estate and housing projects called "heavens." His businesses enhanced Divine's ability to provide shelter, jobs, and incomes for his followers. He launched a journal entitled *New Day* in 1937 and used it to disseminate his teachings. Divine also protested social injustice and encouraged his followers to become politically engaged. Between 1936 and 1940, he lobbied strenuously for a federal antilynching law. At the time of Divine's death in 1965, the holdings of the Peace Mission were estimated to be worth $10 million. Father Divine's movement echoed the Protestant ethic: work hard, keep both your mind and body healthy; eat right; dress properly; keep good company; and avoid evil.

Conclusion

The Depression ushered in a period of intense hardship, but as this chapter indicates, it was also a period in which black Americans had an unprecedented impact on American culture. Black people excelled in sports, arts, drama, and music. The Works Progress Administration (WPA) funded a wide spectrum of artists whose cultural productions were accessible, inclusive, and populist.

The Chicago Black Renaissance reflected the impact of the WPA on the lives of hundreds of artists. A new generation of black jazz musicians won worldwide admiration and emulation. Black musicians weaned Americans from swing to bebop, while gospel music became a dynamic genre.

These positive changes were made against a backdrop of entrenched racism. While some African Americans found satisfying jobs in film and radio, many others were excluded or relegated to demeaning, stereotypical roles. This negative typecasting motivated innovative filmmakers to develop alternative films and artistic institutions that showed a more balanced and accurate representation of black life and culture. Such creative ventures seldom produced the profits that white entrepreneurs reaped from marketing black cultural productions to white consumers. The black artists who refused to entertain white America and instead opposed racism and social and economic injustice remained poor and unnoticed by the dominant culture.

Still, black counterculture artists had a tremendous impact on America and reflected a growing determination to resist complete assimilation into white culture. The comic strips, the black press, and the black church preserved black people's dignity. Black culture prepared black people for the next level of struggle against the Jim Crow regime and against all ideologies of white supremacy, both in the United States and abroad.

TIMELINE

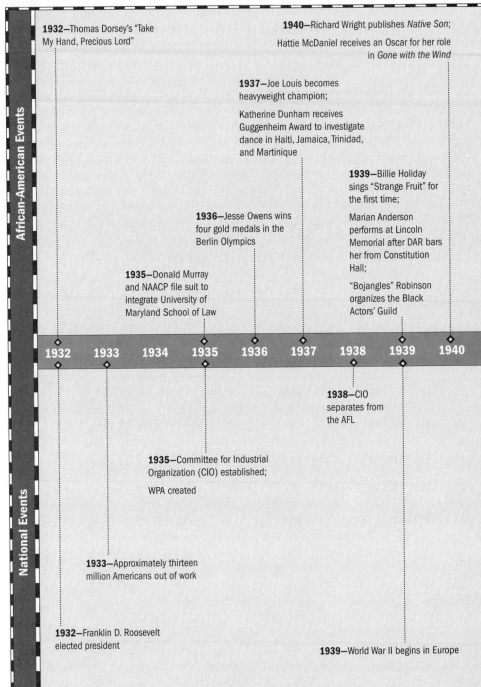

African-American Events

1932—Thomas Dorsey's "Take My Hand, Precious Lord"

1940—Richard Wright publishes *Native Son*; Hattie McDaniel receives an Oscar for her role in *Gone with the Wind*

1937—Joe Louis becomes heavyweight champion;

Katherine Dunham receives Guggenheim Award to investigate dance in Haiti, Jamaica, Trinidad, and Martinique

1939—Billie Holiday sings "Strange Fruit" for the first time;

Marian Anderson performs at Lincoln Memorial after DAR bars her from Constitution Hall;

"Bojangles" Robinson organizes the Black Actors' Guild

1936—Jesse Owens wins four gold medals in the Berlin Olympics

1935—Donald Murray and NAACP file suit to integrate University of Maryland School of Law

1932 1933 1934 1935 1936 1937 1938 1939 1940

National Events

1938—CIO separates from the AFL

1935—Committee for Industrial Organization (CIO) established;

WPA created

1933—Approximately thirteen million Americans out of work

1932—Franklin D. Roosevelt elected president

1939—World War II begins in Europe

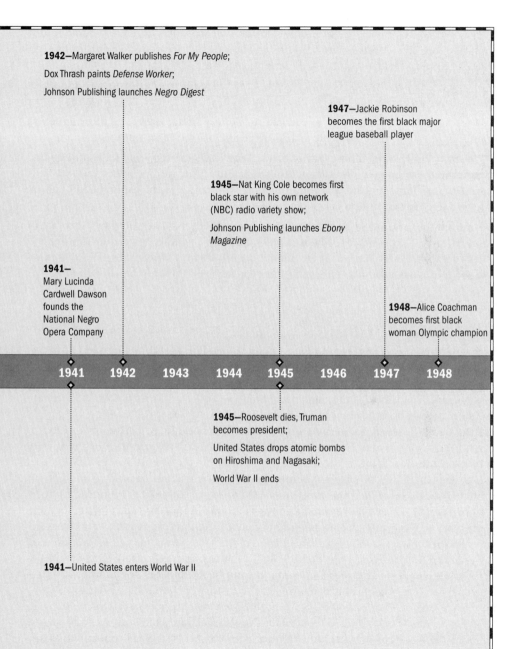

1942—Margaret Walker publishes *For My People*;

Dox Thrash paints *Defense Worker*;

Johnson Publishing launches *Negro Digest*

1947—Jackie Robinson becomes the first black major league baseball player

1945—Nat King Cole becomes first black star with his own network (NBC) radio variety show;

Johnson Publishing launches *Ebony Magazine*

1941— Mary Lucinda Cardwell Dawson founds the National Negro Opera Company

1948—Alice Coachman becomes first black woman Olympic champion

| 1941 | 1942 | 1943 | 1944 | 1945 | 1946 | 1947 | 1948 |

1945—Roosevelt dies, Truman becomes president;

United States drops atomic bombs on Hiroshima and Nagasaki;

World War II ends

1941—United States enters World War II

Review Questions

1. How did the Great Depression affect black culture? How did WPA democratize black expressive culture? How did black religious culture change during this era?
2. How did black artists negotiate the dilemma of dual consciousness? Which parts of black art did white corporate executives find easiest to appropriate for white consumption?
3. How did swing era big band music lead to bebop? What problems did the bebop musicians encounter? How did black music affect American culture?
4. How did Hollywood films portray black Americans during the 1930s and 1940s? How did these images affect white Americans' attitudes and behavior toward black Americans? How did these representations contribute to the emergence of an alternative or independent black cinema?
5. How did the cultural production of the Chicago Renaissance compare with that of the Harlem Renaissance? Why did black athletes become prominent during the 1930s and 1940s? What was their impact on American culture? How did the experiences of black athletes reflect the status of race relations in the United States?

Recommended Reading

William Barlow. *Voice Over: The Making of Black Radio.* Philadelphia: Temple University Press, 1999. A lucidly written, informative cultural history of the evolution of black radio and the personalities who made it a powerful instrument for disseminating black music, culture, language, and politics, and for constructing an African-American public sphere.

Scott DeVeaux. *BeBop: A Social and Musical History.* Berkeley, CA: University of California Press, 1997. A perceptive study of the creative artistry and lives of the pivotal black professional musicians in the jazz world during the 1930s and 1940s and how they made bebop into a commercially successful art movement.

Manthia Diawara, ed. *Black American Cinema.* New York: Routledge, 1993. A collection of provocative essays. Three examine the work of filmmaker Oscar Micheaux. Others provide fresh interpretations of the recent independent cinema movement.

Melvin Patrick Ely. *The Adventures of Amos 'N' Andy: A Social History of an American Phenomenon.* New York: Free Press, 1991. A subtle and penetrating examination of the complexities of racial stereotyping in one of the most influential and controversial radio and television programs in the history of media race relations.

Samuel A. Floyd Jr. *The Power of Black Music: Interpreting Its History from Africa to the United States.* New York: Oxford University Press, 1995. An excellent overview of the history of black music with an insightful comparison of the Harlem and Chicago flowerings.

✦ Chapter 20 ✦

The World War II Era
and the Seeds of a Revolution

On the Eve of War, 1936–1941

As the world economy wallowed in the Great Depression, the international order collapsed in Europe and Asia. Germany under Adolf Hitler (1889–1945) and Italy under Benito Mussolini (1883–1945) created an alliance, known as the Axis. These fascist dictators advocated a political program based on extreme nationalism that suppressed internal opposition and used violence to gain their will abroad. Hitler was driven by a virulent form of racism. Unlike racists in the United States, he blamed Jews for all Germany's social and economic problems. But his Nazi party also despised black people, discriminating against Germans with African ancestors and banning jazz as "nigger" music. Through the late 1930s the Germans and Italians pursued aggressive policies that placed much of Central Europe under their power. In August 1939 Germany signed a pact with the Soviet Union, a prelude to a September 1 attack on Poland by Germany, which the Soviets joined a few weeks later. Britain and France reacted to the invasion by declaring war on Germany, thus beginning World War II.

In Asia during the 1930s, the Empire of Japan sought to extend its power and territory. The Japanese wanted to drive out Britain, France, the Netherlands, and the United States, which had extensive economic interests and colonial possessions in the Far East. Japan also clashed with the Soviet Union in Manchuria and with China, against which the Japanese became involved in a long struggle in the 1930s. The United States supported China and opposed Japan's alliance with Nazi Germany and Fascist Italy. These tensions led to war on December 7, 1941, when the Japanese bombed American warships at Pearl Harbor, Hawaii, and attacked British, Dutch, and American holdings throughout the Pacific.

African Americans
and the Emerging World Crisis

Many African Americans responded to the emerging world crisis with growing activism. When Ethiopia was invaded by Italy in 1935, it was, along with Liberia and Haiti, one of three black-ruled nations in the world, and black communities throughout the

383

United States organized to send it aid. Mass meetings were held in support of the embattled Ethiopians, and reporters from black newspapers brought the horror of this war home to their readers. Despite fierce resistance, the Italians won the war, in part, by using poison gas. The conflict alerted many African Americans to the dangers of fascism and reawakened their interest in Africa.

A war in Spain had a similar effect on leftist African Americans. In 1936 the left-leaning Spanish Republic became embroiled in a civil war against a fascist movement led by General Francisco Franco (1892–1975) whom Germany and Italy supported. About 100 African Americans served in Spain in 1936–1937 with the Abraham Lincoln Battalion, an integrated fighting force of 3,000 American volunteers. Support of the Abraham Lincoln Battalion reflected a commitment by a few African Americans to the communists' vision of internationalism. Mobilization for war, however, would soon bring most black people and their organizations into the fight against fascism abroad and for equality and justice in the United States.

A. Philip Randolph and the March on Washington Movement

In 1939 and 1940 the American government spent so much on arms to prepare for a war that FDR knew was coming that the U.S. economy was finally lifted out of the Depression. But as unemployed white workers streamed into centers of war production, jobless African Americans were left waiting at the gate. Most aircraft manufacturers, for example, would hire black people only in janitorial positions no matter what their skills. Many all-white AFL unions enforced closed-shop agreements that prevented their employers from hiring black workers who were not members of the labor organization. Government-funded training programs rejected black applicants. The United States Employment Service (USES) filled "whites only" requests for defense workers. The military itself made it clear that although it would accept black men in their proportion to the population, about 11 percent at the time, it would put them in segregated units and assign them to service duties. The Navy limited black servicemen to menial positions while the Marine Corps and the Army Air Corps refused to accept them altogether.

When a young African-American man wrote the Pittsburgh *Courier* and suggested a "Double V" campaign—victory over fascism abroad and over racism at home—the newspaper adopted his words as the battle cry for the entire race. This struggle led to the further development of black organizations and transformed the world view of many African-American soldiers and civilians.

Embodying the spirit of the "Double V" campaign, African Americans criticized discrimination in the defense program. Two months before the 1940 presidential election, the NAACP, Urban League, and other groups pressed President Roosevelt to take action. The president listened to their protests, but he responded with little of substance. As a result, during late 1940 the NAACP and other groups staged mass protest rallies. With the election safely won, the president, anxious not to offend white southern politicians he needed to back his war program, refused even to meet with black leaders.

In January 1941, A. Philip Randolph, who was president of the Brotherhood of Sleeping Car Porters, called on black people to direct their protests at the national government. He suggested that ten thousand African Americans march on Washington under the slogan "We loyal Negro-American citizens demand the right to work and fight for our country." Randolph helped to create the March on Washington Movement (MOWM), which soon became the largest mass movement of black Americans since Marcus Garvey's Universal Negro Improvement Association of the 1920s. The MOWM's demands included a presidential order forbidding companies with government contracts from engaging in racial discrimination, eliminating race-based exclusion from defense training courses, and requiring the USES to supply workers on a nonracial basis. Randolph also wanted to abolish segregation in the armed forces and gain the president's support for a law withdrawing the benefits of the National Labor Relations Act from unions that refused to grant membership to black Americans. Departing from the leadership tactics of most other African-American protest groups of the time, Randolph prohibited white participation and encouraged the participation of the black working class.

Randolph's appeal captured the support of many African Americans who had not before taken part in the activities of middle-class dominated groups like the NAACP. Roosevelt, fearing that the protest would undermine America's democratic rhetoric, met with Randolph and other black leaders. The president offered a set of superficial changes but the African Americans stood firm and increased their estimate of the number of black marchers coming to Washington to one hundred thousand. By the end of June 1941, the president capitulated and had his aides draft Executive Order #8802, prompting Randolph to call off the march. It was a grand moment. "To this day," NAACP leader Roy Wilkins wrote in his autobiography, "I don't know if he would have been able to turn out enough marchers to make his point stick . . . but, what a bluff it was. A tall, courtly black man with Shakespearean diction and the stare of an eagle had looked the patrician Roosevelt in the eye—and made him back down."

Executive Order #8802

On the surface at least, the president's order marked a significant change in the government's stance. It stated in part:

> I do hereby affirm the policy of the United States that there shall be no discrimination in the employment of workers in the defense industry or government because of race, creed, color, or national origin.

The order instructed all agencies that trained workers to administer such programs without discrimination. To ensure full cooperation with these guidelines, Roosevelt created the Fair Employment Practices Committee (FEPC) with the power to investigate complaints of discrimination. The order said nothing about desegregation of the military, but private assurances were made that the barriers to entry in key services would be lowered.

Black excitement with the order soon soured as many industries, particularly in the South, engaged in only token hirings. Mere articulation of antidiscrimination principles and the establishment of commissions and committees did not eradicate inequalities. Moreover, the order did not mention union discrimination. Nonetheless, the threat of the march, the issuance of the executive order, and creation of the FEPC marked the formal acknowledgment by the federal government that it bore some responsibility for protecting black and minority rights in employment. Black activists and their allies would have to continue their fight if the order was to have any meaning. Randolph sought to lead them but would find it difficult to do so because of the opposition of key government agencies—notably the military—the political power of southern congressmen, and a belief among white people that winning the war took precedence over racial issues.

Race and the U.S. Armed Forces

The demands of A. Philip Randolph and other black leaders to end segregation in the armed forces met stiffer resistance than their pleas for change in the civilian sector. Black men were expected to serve their country, but most were assigned to segregated service battalions, relegated to noncombat positions, kept out of the more prestigious branches of the service, and faced tremendous obstacles to appointment as commissioned officers.

Much of the armed forces' policy derived from negative attitudes and discriminatory practices common in American society. Reflecting this ingrained racism, a 1925 study by the American War College concluded that African Americans were physically unqualified for combat duty, were by nature mentally inferior, believed themselves to be inferior to white people, were susceptible to crowd psychology, could not control themselves when in danger, and lacked the initiative and resourcefulness of white people.

Based on this and later studies the War Department decided in 1941 that African-American soldiers would be segregated and would serve primarily in noncombat units. These policies ignored evidence of the fighting ability that African Americans had shown in previous wars and that the heroism of Dorie Miller confirmed during the attack on Pearl Harbor. Miller was the son of Texas sharecroppers who had enlisted in the Navy in 1938 and, like all black sailors in the Navy at the time, had been assigned to mess duty as a cook and a waiter. When the Japanese attacked on December 7, 1941, the twenty-two-year-old Miller was below decks on the battleship *Arizona*. When his captain was wounded, Miller braved bullets to help move him to a more protected area of the deck. He then shot down at least two and perhaps six enemy aircraft. Miller had never before fired a machine gun. On May 27, 1942, the Navy cited him for "distinguished devotion to duty, extraordinary courage and disregard for his own personal safety" and awarded him a Navy Cross. The Navy then sent Miller back to mess duty without a promotion.

The Costs of Military Discrimination

Although the War and Navy Departments held to the fiction of "separate but equal" in their segregation program, their policies gave black Americans inferior resources or excluded them entirely. Segregation at Army camps most often meant that black soldiers were placed in the least desirable spots and denied the use of officers' clubs, base

"above and beyond the call of duty"

DORIE MILLER
*Received the Navy Cross
at Pearl Harbor, May 27, 1942*

The War Department did not hesitate to recognize the heroism of Dorie Miller at Pearl Harbor in this recruitment poster, but it neglected to mention that black sailors were routinely relegated to the kitchens and boiler rooms of navy vessels.
Courtesy of the Library of Congress

stores, and recreational areas. Four-fifths of all training camps were located in the South, where black soldiers were harassed and discriminated against off base as well as on. For southern African Americans, even going home in uniform could be dangerous. For example, when Rieves Bell of Starkville, Mississippi, was visiting his family in 1943, three young white men cornered him on a street and attempted to strip off his uniform. Bell fought back and stabbed one of them. The local civilian authorities sentenced Bell to three and a half years in the notorious Parchman state penitentiary for the crime of self-defense.

Perhaps most galling was to see German prisoners of war accorded better treatment than African-American soldiers. Dempsey Travis of Chicago saw "German prisoners free to move around the camp, unlike black soldiers who were restricted. The Germans walked right into the doggone places like any white American. We were wearin' the same uniform, but we were excluded."

Most of the nearly one million African Americans who served during World War II did so in auxiliary units, notably in the transportation and engineering corps. Soldiers in the transportation corps, almost half of whom were black, loaded supplies and drove them to the front lines. As American forces drove toward Germany in 1944 and 1945, African Americans braved enemy fire and delivered the fuel, ammunition, and other goods that made the fight possible. Black engineers built camps, ports, and roads and performed many other tasks to support frontline troops.

Black soldiers performed well in these tasks but were often subject to unfair military discipline. In Europe, black soldiers were executed in vastly greater numbers than whites even though African Americans made up only 10 percent of the total number of soldiers. One of the most glaring examples of unfair treatment was the Navy's handling of a "mutiny" at its Port Chicago base north of San Francisco. On July 17, 1944, in the worst home-front disaster of the war, an explosion at the base killed 320 American sailors, of whom 202 were black ammunition loaders. In the following month 328 of the surviving ammunition loaders were sent to fill another ship. When 258 of them refused to do so, they were arrested. Eventually the Navy convicted fifty men of mutiny and sentenced them to terms of imprisonment ranging from eight to fifteen years.

Black American leaders, including A. Philip Randolph; Walter White of the NAACP; both T. Arnold Hill and Lester Granger of the National Urban League; New York Congressman Adam Clayton Powell Jr.; Robert Vann, editor of the Pittsburgh *Courier*; and Mabel K. Staupers of the National Association of Colored Graduate Nurses, among others, mobilized the black civilian workforce, black women's groups, college students, and an interracial coalition to resist military discrimination. They provoked a public dialogue with government and military officials at a pivotal moment when America's leaders most desired to present a united democratic front to the world.

Examples of black protest abound. In 1942 the NAACP's *Crisis*, and *Opportunity*, the organ of the National Urban League, repeatedly denounced the Army's segregation policy. Walter White inundated the War Department and the president with letters citing examples of improper, hostile, and humiliating treatment of black servicemen by military personnel and in the white communities in which bases were located.

Black Women in the Struggle to Desegregate the Military

The militance of black women contributed to the struggle to desegregate the military. A 1942 editorial in the *Crisis* suggested why:

> [T]he colored woman has been a more potent factor in shaping Negro society than the white woman has been in shaping white society because the sexual caste system has been much more fluid and ill-defined than among whites. Colored women have worked with their men and helped build and maintain every institution we have. Without their economic aid and counsel we would have made little if any progress.

The most prominent example of black women's struggle is found in the history of the National Association of Colored Graduate Nurses (NACGN). Mabel K. Staupers, its executive director, led the fight to eliminate quotas from the U.S. Army Nurse Corps. Although many black nurses volunteered their services during World War II, they were refused admittance into the Navy, and the Army allowed only a few to serve. To draw attention to the unfairness of quotas, Staupers met with Eleanor Roosevelt in November 1944. Staupers described black nurses' troubled relationship with the armed forces. She informed the First Lady that eighty-two black nurses were serving only 150 patients at Fort Huachuca, Arizona, at a time when the Army had a dire nursing shortage and was debating the need to draft nurses. Other black women were caring for German prisoners. Was this to be the special role of the black nurse in the war? "When our women hear of the great need for nurses in the Army and when they enter the service it is with the high hopes that they will be used to nurse sick and wounded soldiers who are fighting our country's enemies and not primarily to take care of these enemies."

Mabel Staupers's efforts bore fruit in early 1945. When the War Department still claimed that there was a shortage of nurses, Staupers mobilized nursing groups of all races to protest the discrimination against black nurses in the Army and Navy Nurse Corps. There was an immediate groundswell of public support to remove quotas. Buried beneath an avalanche of telegrams from an inflamed public, the War Department declared an end to quotas and exclusion. On January 10, 1945, the Army opened its Nurse Corps to all applicants without regard to race, and five days later the Navy followed suit. Within a few weeks, Phyllis Daley became the first black woman inducted into the Navy's Nurse Corps. Over three hundred black nurses were eventually accepted into the Army Nurse Corps.

The Beginning of Military Desegregation

Soldiers and sailors also resisted segregation and discrimination while in the service. Their action included well-organized attempts to desegregate officers' clubs. At Freeman Field, Indiana, for example, one hundred black officers refused to back down

Black women Army nurses, like black male servicemen, served in all-black units in the U.S. military during World War II. The War Department assigned them to care for German prisoners of war but initially prohibited them from caring for sick and wounded white Americans. Under the leadership of Mabel Staupers, black nurses successfully fought against enlistment quotas and other discriminatory treatment.
Library of Congress

when their commanders threatened to arrest them for seeking to use the officers' club. In other bases African-American soldiers responded with violence to violence, intimidation, and threats. Their actions prompted the Army brass to reevaluate their belief in the military efficiency of discrimination.

The War Department began to take on the challenge of reeducating soldiers, albeit in a limited fashion. The Advisory Committee on Negro Troop Policies was charged with coordinating the use of black troops and developing policy on social questions and personnel training. In 1943 the War Department also produced its own propaganda film—*The Negro Soldier*, directed by Frank Capra—to alleviate racial tensions. This patronizing film emphasized the contributions black soldiers had made in the nation's wars since the American Revolution and was designed to appeal to both black and white audiences.

The War Department also attempted to use propaganda to counter black protest groups and the claims of discrimination found in the black press. The key to this effort was fighter Joe Louis, whom the Army believed was "almost a god" to most black Americans. "The possibilities for using him," a secret internal report stated, "are almost unlimited, such as touring the army camps as special instructor on physical training; exhibition bouts, for use in radio or in movies; in a movie appearance a flashback could be shown of Louis knocking out Max Schmeling, the champion of the Germans." The same report also mentioned other prominent black men and women who had "great value in any propaganda programs. Other athletes like Ray Robinson, also track athletes, etc.; name bands like Cab Calloway, [Jimmy] Lunceford; stage, screen and concert stars like Ethel Waters, Bill Robinson, Eddie Anderson, Paul Robeson, etc." This propaganda did little to counter the real incidents of prejudice and discrimination that most black people experienced in their daily lives.

Racism remained strong throughout the war, but the persistent push of protest groups and the military's need for manpower gradually loosened its grip. After the attack on Pearl Harbor, nearly all the services had to relax their restrictions on African Americans. The Navy, previously the most resistant service, began to accept black men as sailors and noncommissioned officers. By 1943 it allowed African Americans into officer training schools. The Marine Corps, exclusively white throughout its history, began taking African Americans in 1942. Black officers were trained in integrated settings in all services except the Army's Air Corps. The War Department even compelled recalcitrant commanding officers to recommend black servicemen for admission to the officer training schools, and soon, over two thousand a year were graduated.

Many African Americans also saw combat, although under white officers. Several African-American artillery, tank destroyer, antiaircraft, and combat engineer battalions fought with distinction in Europe and Asia. Military prejudice seemed to be borne out by the poor showing of the all-black 92nd Combat Division, but investigation revealed that its failure was the result of poor training and leadership by a white officer with no confidence in his men. After the Battle of the Bulge, a massive late-1944 German counterattack, 2,500 black volunteers fought in integrated units. Although the experiment would not be repeated during the war, its success laid the groundwork for later changes. African-American women also found expanded opportunities in the military. Approximately 4,000 black women served in the Women's Army Auxiliary Corps (WAACs).

The Tuskegee Airmen

The most visible group of black soldiers served in the Army Air Force. In January 1941, the War Department announced the formation of an all-black Pursuit Squadron and the creation of a training program at Tuskegee Army Air Field, Alabama, for black pilots.

Unlike all other units in the Army, the 99th Squadron and the 332nd Group, made up of the 100th, 301st, and 302nd Squadrons, had black officers. The 99th went to North Africa in April 1943 and flew its first combat mission on June 2. Later the squadron supported the invasion of Italy and regularly engaged German pilots in aerial combat. General Benjamin O. Davis, Jr. commanded the 332nd Group when it was deployed to Italy in January 1944. In July, the 99th was added to the 332nd and the Group participated in campaigns in Italy, France, Germany, and the Balkans.

The Tuskegee Airmen flew over 15,500 sorties and completed 1,578 missions. During the two hundred missions in which they escorted heavy bombers deep into Germany's Rhineland, not one of the "heavies" was lost to enemy fighter opposition. They destroyed 409 enemy aircraft, sank an enemy destroyer, and knocked out numerous ground installations. They were well regarded and recognized for their heroism. They accumulated 150 Distinguished Flying Crosses, one Legion of Merit, one Silver Star, fourteen Bronze Stars, and 744 Air Medals. Tuskegee pilot Coleman Young (1919–1997, mayor of Detroit 1973–1993) recalled, "once our reputation got out as to our fighting ability, we started getting special requests for our group to escort their group, the bombers. They all wanted us because we were the only fighter group in the entire air force that did not lose a bomber to enemy action. Oh, we were much in demand."

The Transformation of Black Soldiers

Service in World War II gave many African Americans an enhanced sense of themselves and a commitment to the fight for black equality. Unlike the black soldiers in World War I, a greater percentage of those drafted at the outset of World War II were either high school or college graduates. Some black soldiers brought "radical" ideas with them as they were drafted and sent to segregated installations. Many had a strong sense of their own self-worth and dignity. In their study of Chicago, sociologists St. Clair Drake and Horace Cayton noted:

> At least half of the Negro soldiers—and Bronzeville's men fall into this class—were city people who had lived through a Depression in America's Black Ghettoes, and who had been exposed to unions, the Communist movement, and to the moods of racial radicalism that occasionally swept American cities. Even the rural southern Negroes were different this time—for the thirty years between the First and Second World War has seen a great expansion of school facilities in the South and distribution of newspapers and radios.

Serving in the armed forces first exposed many African Americans to a world outside the segregated South. Haywood Stephney of Clarksdale, Mississippi, recalled that when he first encountered segregation in the military he simply thought it was supposed to be that way. He explained, "Because you grow up in this situation you don't see but one side of the coin. Having not tasted the freedom or the liberty of being and doing like other folks then you didn't know what it was like over across the street. So we accepted it." Like many others, his experiences during the war raised fundamental questions about the racial system of the nation.

Douglas Conner, another Mississippi veteran, captured the collective understanding of the social and political meaning of the war shared by the men in his unit, the 31st Quartermaster Battalion stationed in Okinawa: "The air people in Tuskegee, Dorie Miller, and the others gave the blacks a sense that they could succeed and compete in a world that had been saying that 'you're nothing.'" Conner insisted that "because of the world war, I think many people, especially blacks, got the idea that we're going back, but we're not going back to business as usual. Somehow we're going to change this nation so that there's more equality than there is now." The personal transformation that Conner and others experienced helped lay the foundation for a Second Reconstruction in the American South.

Black People on the Home Front

Just as they did in the military, African Americans on the home front fought a dual war against the Axis and discrimination. Black workers and volunteers helped produce goods for the fight while also purchasing war bonds and participating in other defense activities. The changes brought on by the war also created new points of conflict while exacerbating preexisting problems and occasionally igniting full-scale riots. Throughout the war, protest groups and the black press continued to fight employment discrimination and political exclusion.

Black Workers:
From Farm to Factory

The war accelerated the migration of African Americans from rural areas to the cities. Even though the farm economy recovered during the war, high-paying defense jobs and other urban occupations tempted many black farmers to abandon the land. By the 1940s bitter experience had made it clear that there was little future in the cotton fields. Boll weevils, international competition, and mechanization reduced the need for black labor. Indeed, by the end of the war, only 28 percent of black men worked on farms, a decline of 13 percent since 1940. More than three hundred thousand black men left agricultural labor between 1940 and 1944 alone.

The wartime need for workers, backed by pressure from the government, helped break down some of the barriers to employing African Americans in industry. During the war the total number of black workers in nonfarm employment rose from 2,900,000 to 3,800,000. Thousands of African-American workers moved into previously whites-only jobs.

With so many of their men away at war, black women increasingly found work outside the laundry and domestic service that had previously been their lot. Nationally 600,000 black women—400,000 of them former domestic servants—shifted into industrial jobs. As one aircraft worker wryly put it, "Hitler was the one that got us out of the white folks' kitchen." Even those women who stayed in domestic work often saw their wages improve as the supply of competing workers dwindled.

The abundance of industrial jobs helped spur and direct the migration of African Americans during and after World War II. Some 1,500,000 migrants, nearly 15 percent of the population, left the South, swelling the black communities in northern and western cities that had significant war industries. By 1950 the proportion of the nation's black population living in the South had fallen from 77 percent to 68 percent. The most dramatic rise in black population was in southern California. Because of its burgeoning aircraft industry and the success of civil rights groups and the federal government in limiting discrimination, Los Angeles saw its relatively small African-American community increase by more than 340,000 during the war.

Many unions also became more open to African-American workers. Between 1940 and 1945, black union membership rose from two hundred thousand to 1.25 million. Those unions connected to the CIO, particularly the United Automobile Workers, were the most open to black membership, whereas AFL affiliates were the most likely to treat African Americans as second-class members or to exclude them altogether. Some white unionized workers opposed hiring black workers, but their resistance was often deflected by the union leadership, the government, or employers. The growth in black membership did not end racism in unions, but it did provide African Americans with a stronger foundation upon which to protest continuing discrimination in employment.

FEPC during the War

Responding to the ineffectiveness of the Fair Employment Practices Committee (FEPC) during the first years of the war, in May 1943 President Roosevelt issued Executive Order #9346. The order established a new Committee on Fair Employment Practice, increased its budget, and placed its operation directly under the Executive Office of the President. Roosevelt appointed Malcolm Ross, a combative white liberal, to head the committee. Ross initiated nationwide hearings of cases concerning discrimination in the shipbuilding and railroad industries. While these proceedings brought some compliance with FEPC's orders, resistance was more common. In Mobile, Alabama, for example, the white employees of the Alabama Dry Dock and Shipbuilding Company opposed FEPC's efforts to pressure the company to promote twelve of the 7,000 African Americans it employed in menial positions to racially mixed welding crews. The white workers went on a rampage, assaulting fifty African Americans. FEPC thereupon acquiesced in the traditional Jim Crow arrangements for all work assignments. White workers retained their more lucrative positions. As a result of this kind of intransigence, the committee failed to redress most of the grievances of black workers. An effort to continue the committee after the war was defeated.

Anatomy of a Race Riot: Detroit, 1943

One of the bloodiest race riots in the nation's history took place in 1943 in Detroit, Michigan, where black and white workers were competing for jobs and housing. Relations between the two communities had been smoldering for months, with open fighting in the plants and on the streets. White racism, housing segregation, and economic discrimination were part of the problem. The brutality of white police officials was an especially potent factor. Tensions were so palpable that weeks before the riot NAACP leader Walter White had warned that the city could explode.

The immediate trigger for the riot was a squabble on Sunday, June 20, between white and black bathers at the segregated city beaches on the Detroit River. Within hours, two hundred white sailors from a nearby base joined the white mob that attacked individual black men and women. A rumor that white citizens had killed a black woman and thrown her baby over the bridge spread across the city. The riot spread quickly along Woodward Avenue, the city's major thoroughfare, into Paradise Valley where some thirty-five thousand southern black migrants had, in the spring of 1943, joined the city's already crowded black population. By Monday morning downtown Detroit was overrun with white men in search of more victims.

Six thousand federal troops had to be dispatched to Detroit to restore order. When the violence ended, thirty-four people had been killed (twenty-five black and nine white people) and more than 700 injured. Of the twenty-five black people who died, the Detroit police killed seventeen. The police did not kill any of the white men who assaulted African Americans or committed arson. Property damage exceeded two million dollars and one million man hours were lost in war production.

In the aftermath, the city created the Mayor's Interracial Committee, the first permanent municipal body designed to promote civic harmony and fairness. Many white people in Detroit blamed the black press and the NAACP for instigating the riot. They accused the city's black citizens of pushing too hard for economic and political equality under communist influence. One report concluded that black leaders provoked the riot because they had compared "victory over the axis . . . [with] a corresponding overthrow in the country of those forces which . . . prevent true racial equality." In contrast, black leaders, radical trade unionists, and members of other ethnic organizations, especially Jewish groups, blamed, "the KKK, the Christian Front, the Black Dragon Society, the National Workers League, the Knights of the White Camelia, the Southern Voters League, and similar organizations based on a policy of terror and . . . white supremacy."

Old and New Protest Groups

The NAACP grew tremendously during the war. Under the editorial direction of Roy Wilkins, the circulation of the NAACP's *Crisis* expanded from 7,000 to 45,000. The NAACP's membership increased from 50,000 in 1940 to 450,000 at the end of the war. Much of this growth occurred in the South, which had more than 150,000 members by 1945. Supreme Court victories and especially close monitoring of the "Double V" campaign help explain these huge increases.

With success, however, came conflict. Leaders split over the value of integration versus self-segregation and questioned the benefit of relying on legal cases rather than paying more attention to working-class black men and women. Wilkins acknowledged the organization's uncertainty:

> The war was a great watershed for the NAACP. We had become far more powerful, and now the challenge was to keep our momentum. Everyone knew the NAACP stood against discrimination and segregation, but what was our postwar program to be? Beyond discrimination and segregation, where would we stand on veterans, housing, labor-management relations, strikes, the Fair Employment Practices Commission, organizations at state levels,

education? What would we do to advance the fight for the vote in the South? . . . We had a big membership . . . but we didn't know how to use them.

In 1944, southern white liberals joined with African Americans to establish the Southern Regional Council (SRC). This interracial coalition, an important example of the local initiative of private citizens, was devoted to expanding democracy in a region better known for the political and economic oppression and exploitation of its black citizens. The SRC focused attention on the inequalities endemic to black life in the South and challenged the facade of southern white supremacy.

In 1942 a far more strident group called the Congress of Racial Equality (CORE) had been formed in Chicago when an interracial group of Christian pacifists gathered to find ways to make America live up to the ideals of equality and justice on which it based its war program. Activists James Farmer and Bayard Rustin were key in getting the group off the ground. Unlike the NAACP, CORE was a decentralized, intensely democratic organization. CORE dedicated itself to the principles of nonviolent direct action as expounded by Indian leader Mohandas Gandhi. During the war this pacifist organization challenged segregation in the North with sit-ins and other protest tactics that the civil rights movement would later adopt.

African Americans found many ways to fight discrimination. Throughout the 1940s, in countless communities across the South and the Middle West, black women organized women's political councils and other groups to press for integration of public facilities—hospitals, swimming pools, theaters, and restaurants—and for the right to pursue collegiate and professional studies. Others created lasting works in the arts, literature, and popular culture. Women whose names would become virtually synonymous with the modern civil rights movement in the 1950s and 1960s helped to lay its foundation in the World War II era. Ella Baker served as the NAACP field secretary. Rosa Parks began resisting segregation laws on Montgomery, Alabama, buses in the 1940s.

Black college students also began protesting segregation in public accommodations. The spark that ignited the Howard University campus civil rights movement came in January 1943. Three sophomore women, Ruth Powell, Marianne Musgrave, and Juanita Morrow, sat at a lunch counter near the campus and were refused service. They demanded to see the manager and vowed to wait until he came. Instead of the manager, two policemen instructed the waitress to serve them. When the check arrived the trio learned that they had been charged 25 cents each instead of the customary 10 cents. They placed 35 cents on the counter, turned to leave, and were arrested. Ruth Power later reported that "the policemen who arrested us told us we were being taken in for investigation because he had no proof that we weren't 'subversive agents.'" No charges were lodged against the women. They had been arrested to intimidate them, but the incident instead fanned the smoldering embers of resentment in the Howard University student body.

The Cold War

After first Germany and then Japan surrendered in 1945, the United States began the transition to peace. Many of the gains of black men and women were wiped away as the armed forces demobilized and the factories began reinstituting the discriminatory hiring systems in place before the conflict. Nonetheless, in 1945 it was clear that segregation would face a huge challenge in the coming years and that the African-American community was ready to fight.

In early 1945, the United Nations began planning for the peace. However, the opposing interests of the Soviet Union and the United States soon led to a long period of hostility that became known as the Cold War. The overriding goal of the United States and its allies was the "containment" of communism. To this end, the North Atlantic Treaty Organization (NATO) was formed in 1949 to provide a military counterforce to Soviet power in Europe while America helped rebuild Western Europe's economy. The United States forged a similarly close relationship with Japan. Much of the rest of the world, however, became contested terrain.

As the nations of Asia and Africa gained independence from colonial domination over the ensuing decades, the United States struggled to keep them out of the Soviet orbit. It did so through foreign aid, direct military force, and clandestine operations run by the Central Intelligence Agency (CIA). These efforts were matched by a propaganda effort to convince the emerging nations of the world that the United States was a model to be emulated and an ally to be trusted.

The Cold War had an enormous influence on American society precisely when the powerful movement for African-American rights was beginning to emerge. The long conflict resulted in the rise of a permanent military establishment in the United States. Small in scope before World War II, the reorganized American military enlisted millions of men and women by the early 1950s and claimed most of the national budget. The federal government also grew in power during the war and provided a check on the control that white Southerners had so long exercised over race relations in their region. American policy makers also became concerned about the nation's ability to win the allegiance of Africans and other nonwhite people who formed the population of the emerging nations. The Soviet Union could discredit American sincerity by pointing to the deplorable state of race relations within the United States. Hence, during the Cold War, external pressures reinforced efforts to change American racial policy.

African Americans in World Affairs: W. E. B. Du Bois and Ralph Bunche

The Cold War amplified the voices of African Americans in world affairs. Two men, W. E. B. Du Bois and Ralph Bunche, represent alternative strategies for responding to this opportunity. Du Bois was critical of American policy. For half a century he had linked the fate of African Americans with that of Africans and by 1945 was widely hailed as the Father of Pan-Africanism. In that year he directed the Fifth Pan-African Congress, which met in Manchester, England. The Africans who had been radicalized by World War II encouraged the conference to denounce western imperialism. Du Bois considered the United States a protector of the colonial system and opposed its stance in the Cold War. On returning from the Manchester congress, he declared,

> We American Negroes should know . . . until Africa is free, the descendants of Africa the world over cannot escape their chains. . . . The NAACP should therefore put in the forefront of its program the freedom of Africa in work and wage, education and health, and the complete abolition of the colonial system.

In contrast to Du Bois, scholar diplomat Ralph Bunche opted to work within the American system. Bunche held a Harvard doctorate in government and international relations and had spent much of the 1930s studying the problems of African Americans. During World War II Bunche became one of the key American policy makers for Africa, and he was an adviser to the United States delegation at the San Francisco conference that drafted the United Nations (UN) Charter. In 1948 he served as Acting Mediator of the U.N. Special Committee on Palestine, and in 1949 he negotiated an armistice between Egypt and Israel. He received the Spingarn Medal of the NAACP in 1949 and in 1950 he became the first African American to receive the Nobel Peace Prize. Bunche was committed to winning independence for African nations and freedom for his own people. As he wrote,

> Today, for all thinking people, the Negro is the shining symbol of the true significance of democracy. He has demonstrated what can be achieved with democratic liberties even when grudgingly and incompletely bestowed. But the most vital significance of the Negro . . . to American society . . . is the fact that democracy which is not extended to all of the nation's citizens is a democracy that is mortally wounded.

Anticommunism at Home

The rising tensions with the Soviet Union affected all aspects of domestic life in the United States. Conservatives attacked anyone who advocated change. This included people who were, or had been, members of the Communist party, union members, liberals, and people who had fought for African-American rights. The Truman administration (1945–1952) responded to fears of Communist subversion by instituting government loyalty programs. Government employees were dismissed for the merest suspicion of disloyalty. Militant anticommunism in the immediate postwar years led to an explosion of red-baiting hysteria. Wisconsin Republican Senator Joseph McCarthy (1909–1957) and the House Un-American Activities Committee (HUAC) indulged in a relentless pursuit of "communist sympathizers" that ruined many lives. HUAC in particular hounded people in the media and in the entertainment industry. On February 8, 1951, HUAC indicted W. E. B. Du Bois for allegedly serving as an "agent of a foreign principal" in his work with the Peace Information Center. In November a federal judge dismissed all charges against Du Bois. The government had been unable to prove that he was an agent of communism, but fear and personal malice prevented most African-American leaders from defending him.

Paul Robeson was one of the most tragic victims of these anticommunist witch hunts. During the 1930s he worked closely with the Communist party (although he was never a member), becoming one of the most famous defenders of the Soviet Union. Many leftists became disaffected with the USSR after its 1939 pact with Hitler and after its brutal repressiveness became clear. Robeson, however, stuck to his belief in Soviet communism.

In the late 1940s, Robeson's pro-Soviet views and inflammatory statements aroused the ire of the U.S. government and its red hunters. A statement he made at a communist-dominated meeting in 1949 provoked particular outrage. "It is unthinkable," Robeson said, "that American Negroes would go to war on behalf of those [the United States] who have oppressed us for generations against a country [the Soviet

Union] which in one generation has raised our people to full human dignity of mankind." Later in 1949 crowds of rock-throwing locals twice disrupted a Robeson concert in Peekskill, New York.

Throughout the 1940s Robeson consistently linked the struggles of black America with the struggles of people of color, and oppressed workers throughout the Third World. Robeson also refused to sign an affidavit concerning past membership in the Communist party. In response, the U.S. State Department revoked his passport in 1950. The travel ban remained in effect until ruled unconstitutional by the Supreme Court in 1958.

Robeson had combined his art and his politics to attack racial discrimination, segregation, and the ideology of white supremacy and black inferiority as practiced in American society. During the Cold War the state would tolerate no such dissent by even a world-acclaimed black artist. The attacks destroyed Robeson's singing career.

Henry Wallace and the 1948 Presidential Election

Robeson's struggles illustrate how conservative attacks choked off left-wing involvement in the struggle for black equality. The increasing importance of black votes to Democrats, however, meant that key elements of the African-American liberation struggle remained at the center of national politics. Nowhere was this more apparent than in the 1948 presidential election.

President Harry S Truman was expected to lose this election to Thomas Dewey, the popular and well-financed Republican governor of New York. Truman's problems were compounded by a challenge from his former Secretary of Commerce Henry Wallace, who had been Roosevelt's vice president from 1941 to 1945. Wallace ran on the ticket of the communist-backed Progressive party, which sought to take the votes of liberals, leftists, and civil rights advocates disappointed by Truman's moderation. Wallace also supported a peaceful accommodation with the Soviet Union. To undercut Wallace, Truman began to press Congress to pass liberal programs.

Black votes in key northern states were central to Truman's strategy for victory. African Americans in these tightly contested areas could make the difference between victory and defeat, so Truman sought to demonstrate his administration's support of civil rights. In January 1948 he embraced the findings of his biracial Committee on Civil Rights and called for their enactment into law. The committee's report, "To Secure These Rights," recommended passage of federal antilynching legislation, ending discrimination at the ballot box, abolishing the poll tax, desegregating the military, and other measures.

The reaction of white southern politicians caused Truman to pause; but as the election neared, fear of black abandonment at the polls became so great that the Democratic convention passed a strong pro-civil rights plank. Many white Southerners, led by South Carolina's Governor Strom Thurmond, formed their own States' Rights, or "Dixiecrat," party, which carried South Carolina, Alabama, Mississippi, and Louisiana in the election; Wallace carried no state. The failure of the bulwark of white supremacy to prevent the Democratic party from advocating African-American rights, and Truman's ultimate victory despite the defection of hard-line racists, was a turning point in American politics.

Desegregating the Armed Forces

The importance of the black vote, the fight for the allegiance of the emerging nations, and the emerging civil rights movement hastened the desegregation of the military. In February 1948, a communist coup in Czechoslovakia raised the possibility of war between the United States and the Soviet Union and heightened concerns about the willingness of African Americans to serve yet again in a Jim Crow army. When President Truman reinstated the draft in March 1948, A. Philip Randolph, who, in a replay of the March on Washington scenario, had formed the League for Non-Violent Civil Disobedience against Military Segregation in 1947, warned the nation that black men and women would not take a Jim Crow draft lying down. New York Congressman Adam Clayton Powell Jr. declared that there weren't enough jails in America to hold the black men who would refuse to bear arms in a Jim Crow army. On June 24, 1948, the Soviet Union heightened tensions even further when it imposed a blockade on West Berlin. On July 26, Truman issued Executive Order #9981, officially desegregating the armed forces. Executive Order #9981, which mandated "equality of treatment and opportunity for all persons in the armed services without regard to race, color, religion, or national origin," signaled the culmination of a decades-long struggle by black civilians and soldiers to win full integration into the nation's military.

Not until 1950 and the outbreak of the Korean War, however, was Truman's order fully implemented. The war reflected the American Cold War policy of containment, which was intended to stop what American leaders believed to be a worldwide conspiracy orchestrated by Moscow to spread communism. In 1950, after North Korea allied to the Soviets, attacked the American-supported government in South Korea, the United States under UN auspices intervened. Heavy casualties early in the war depleted many combat units. Thus, early in 1951 the Army acted on Truman's executive order and authorized the formal integration of its units in Korea. By 1954 the Army had disbanded its last all-black units and the armed forces became one of the first sectors of American society to abandon segregation.

The Road to *Brown*

In 1954, with the United States Supreme Court's decision in *Brown v. Board of Education of Topeka, Kansas*, progress in the desegregation of American society moved from the military into the civilian realm. Ultimately, the *Brown* decision undermined state-sanctioned segregation in all aspects of American life. The NAACP's legal program of the 1920s and 1930s was largely responsible for this. In 1940 the NAACP set up the Legal Defense and Educational Fund (NAACP-LDEF) to attack the legal foundations of race inequality in American education. Thereafter, NAACP-LDEF fought segregation and discrimination in education, housing, employment, and politics. In the first years of its existence, attorneys for the Fund won stunning victories including a 1944 U.S. Supreme Court decision, *Smith v. Allwright,* declaring white primaries unconstitutional. The career of one NAACP-LDEF lawyer, Constance Baker Motley, symbolizes

The Road to *Brown*	
1938	*Missouri ex rel. Gaines v. Canada*
1948	*Sipuel v. Oklahoma State Board of Regents*
1950	*McLaurin v. Oklahoma*
	Sweatt v. Painter
1954	*Brown v. Board of Education of Topeka*

the struggle to overcome exclusion in American life and the coalescence of disparate forces that carried the seeds of the coming revolution. Motley is our guide on the road to *Brown*.

Constance Baker Motley and Black Lawyers in the South

Constance Baker Motley was born in 1921 to immigrant parents from Nevis, in the British West Indies. She grew up in a tightly knit West Indian community in New Haven, Connecticut. Baker attended integrated schools and developed a strong racial consciousness. She recalled: "[M]y interest in civil rights [was] a very early interest which developed when I was in high school. The fact that I was a Black, a woman, and a member of a large, relatively poor family was also the base of this great ambition [to enter the legal profession]."

The most important event in her early life was a lecture by George Crawford, a 1903 Yale Law School graduate, who worked as an NAACP lawyer in New Haven. The talk concerned the Supreme Court decision in *State of Missouri ex rel. Gaines v. Canada*. Crawford explained that the University of Missouri's law school had denied Gaines admission, but had offered to pay his tuition expenses to an out-of-state school. The NAACP Legal Committee under Charles H. Houston's leadership won a victory when the Supreme Court ruled that the state had violated the clause in the Fourteenth Amendment mandating that state laws provide equal protection regardless of race. After *Gaines*, states were required to furnish within their borders facilities for legal education for black people equal to those offered white citizens.

Baker wanted to go to law school, but her family could not even afford to send her to college. However, Clarence Blakeslee, a local white businessman and philanthropist, offered to finance her education. She attended Fisk University until 1942 and then transferred to New York University, where she earned a bachelor's degree in economics in 1943. She then became the second black woman ever to attend Columbia University Law School. In 1946, shortly after she finished her legal training she married a former New York University law student Joel Motley and went to work with the NAACP's LDEF.

Constance Baker Motley first met Thurgood Marshall in October 1945 when he hired her as a law clerk during her second year in law school. Marshall assigned her to work on the hundreds of Army court martial cases filed after World War II. Motley recalled, "From the first day I knew that this was where I wanted to be. I never bothered interviewing anywhere else." She added, "But for this fortuitous event, I do not think that I would have gotten very far as a lawyer. Women were simply not hired in those days."

In the late 1940s the NAACP-LDEF's attack on inequality in graduate education provided the basis for a full-scale assault on segregation. No longer would the organization be satisfied only to push for fulfillment of the promise of "separate but equal" facilities. In 1948 Ada Lois Sipuel was denied admission to the University of Oklahoma Law School because she was black. The U.S. Supreme Court ordered Oklahoma, in *Sipuel v. Board of Regents of the University of Oklahoma*, to "provide [a legal education] for [Sipuel] in conformity with the equal protection clause of the Fourteenth Amendment and provide it as soon as it does for applicants of any other group." Another case, *Sweatt v. Painter*, which the Supreme Court decided in 1950, began when the University of Texas at Austin attempted to circumvent court orders to admit Heman Sweatt into its law school by creating a separate facility consisting of three basement rooms, a small library, and a few instructors who would lecture to him alone. The court ruled that the University of Texas had deprived Sweatt of intangibles such as "the essential ingredient of a legal education . . . the opportunity for students to discuss the law with their peers and others with whom they would be associated professionally in later life." The Justices also declared illegal the University of Oklahoma's segregation of George W. McLaurin from white students attending the Graduate School of Education. The University of Oklahoma had admitted McLaurin but made him sit in the hallway at the classroom door, study in a private part of the library, and eat in a sequestered part of the lunch room. When he finally gained a seat in the classroom, it was marked "reserved for colored." These cases were important stepping-stones on the road to *Brown*.

A year after the *Sweatt* and *McLaurin* decisions, black parents and their lawyers filed suits in Kansas, South Carolina, Virginia, Delaware, and the District of Columbia asking the courts to apply the qualitative test of the *Sweatt* case to elementary and secondary schools and to declare the "separate-but-equal" doctrine invalid in public education.

Brown and the Coming Revolution

Black lawyers in the South handling civil rights cases were frequently assaulted. On February 27, 1942, for example, NAACP attorney Leon A. Ransom was attacked by a former deputy sheriff in the hall of the Davidson County Courthouse in Nashville, Tennessee. The *Crisis* reported:

> The attack came when Ransom walked out into the hall from the courtroom where he was sitting with Z. Alexander Looby, local NAACP attorney, on a case involving the exclusion of Negroes from a jury. . . . When the scuffle began, Negroes who would have aided Ransom were held back by a former constable (white) named Hill, who drew his gun and shouted: "We are going to teach these northern Negroes not to come down here raising fancy court questions."

At Ransom's death in 1954, Thurgood Marshall eulogized:

> Negro Americans, whether they know it or not, owe a great debt of gratitude to Andy Ransom and men like him who battled in the courts down a span of years to bring us to the

This black student at the University of Oklahoma was not allowed to sit in a classroom with white students. It took two Supreme Court decisions to end such segregation at the University of Oklahoma.
CORBIS

place we now occupy in the enjoyment of our constitutional rights as citizens, in helping to build up the NAACP legal program step by step, in the skill which he gave to individual cases and to the planning of strategy, Dr. Ransom left a legacy to the whole population.

It was no less difficult for a black woman lawyer to venture into the South in search of justice. Black attorney Derrick Bell, who also worked for the LDEF, said of Motley's work,

> Nothing in the Southern lawyers' background could have prepared them for Connie. To them Negro women were either mammies, maids, or mistresses. None of them had ever dealt with a Negro woman on a peer basis, much less on a level of intellectual equality, which in this case quickly became superiority.

Motley was aware of her precarious situation. "Often a southern judge would refer to men attorneys as Mister, but would make a point of calling me 'Connie,' since traditionally Black women in the South were only called by their first name." Housing was another problem. Motley recalled that when in a southern town for a long trial, "I knew that it was going to be impossible to stay in a decent hotel." These lawyers had to depend upon the good graces of local people. Motley explained, "Usually in these situations a Black family would agree to put you up. But there was so much publicity involved with civil rights cases that no Black family dared have us—they were too afraid.

"I wonder how many lawyers have had the experience of preparing for trial in a flophouse. That was the only room I could get."

The black parents of Scott's Branch School in Clarendon County, South Carolina, had approached R. W. Elliott, the chairman of the school board, with a modest request. There were 6,531 black students and only 2,375 white students enrolled in the county's schools. Although the county had thirty buses to convey the white students to their schools, not one bus was available to black school children. Some of the black students had to walk eighteen miles round trip each day. Once they arrived they entered buildings heated by wood stoves and lit by kerosene lamps. For a drink of water or to go to the toilet they had to go outdoors.

With the encouragement of AME pastor and schoolteacher, the Reverend Joseph A. DeLaine, the parents resolved to petition the school board for buses. Elliott's reply was short: "We ain't got no money to buy a bus for your nigger children." In 1949 DeLaine went to the NAACP officials in Columbia, and Thurgood Marshall was there. On December 20, 1950, Harry Briggs, a navy veteran, and twenty-four other Clarendon County residents sued the Summerton School District (Clarendon District 22). The case, *Briggs v. Elliott*, was the first legal challenge to elementary school segregation to originate in the South. Meanwhile, four other cases in different parts of the country were advancing through the federal courts. These would be combined into one case that would decide the fate of the *Plessy* doctrine of "separate but equal."

The years of preparation and hardship paid off. Motley worked with the dream team of black lawyers and academics, an inner circle of advisers that included Louis Redding from Wilmington, Delaware; James Nabrit from Washington, D.C.; Robert Ming from Chicago; psychologist Kenneth Clark from New York; and historian John Hope Franklin to prepare the case, *Brown v. Board of Education of Topeka*, and argue it before the U.S. Supreme Court. Motley, Robert Carter, Jack Greenberg, and Marshall also sought assistance from Spottswood Robinson of Richmond, Virginia, and read papers prepared by historians C. Vann Woodward and Alfred Kelly about the original equalitarian intentions of the post–Civil War amendments and other legislation.

> In his argument, Marshall appealed to the Court to meet the *Plessy* doctrine head on and declare that it is erroneous. It stands mirrored today as a legal aberration, the faulty conception of an era dominated by provincialism, by intense emotionalism in race relations . . . and by the preaching of a doctrine of racial superiority that contradicted the basic concept upon which our society was founded. Twentieth century America, fighting racism at home and abroad, has rejected the race views of *Plessy v. Ferguson* because we have come to the realization that such views obviously tend to preserve not the strength but the weakness of our heritage.

By the time Marshall made this argument, black intellectuals and activists and their white allies had closed ranks in support of integration. To suggest alternatives as the goal for African Americans was to swim against the current.

During late 1953 and early 1954, Chief Justice Earl Warren brought the court to support Marshall's position. On May 17, 1954, the court ruled unanimously that a classification based solely on race violated the Fourteenth Amendment to the U.S. Constitution. Warren declared,

TIMELINE

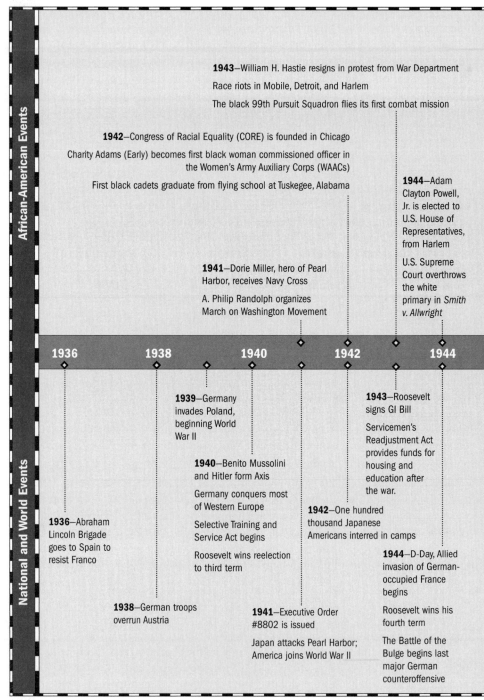

African-American Events

1943—William H. Hastie resigns in protest from War Department

Race riots in Mobile, Detroit, and Harlem

The black 99th Pursuit Squadron flies its first combat mission

1942—Congress of Racial Equality (CORE) is founded in Chicago

Charity Adams (Early) becomes first black woman commissioned officer in the Women's Army Auxiliary Corps (WAACs)

First black cadets graduate from flying school at Tuskegee, Alabama

1944—Adam Clayton Powell, Jr. is elected to U.S. House of Representatives, from Harlem

U.S. Supreme Court overthrows the white primary in *Smith v. Allwright*

1941—Dorie Miller, hero of Pearl Harbor, receives Navy Cross

A. Philip Randolph organizes March on Washington Movement

1936   1938   1940   1942   1944

National and World Events

1939—Germany invades Poland, beginning World War II

1943—Roosevelt signs GI Bill

Servicemen's Readjustment Act provides funds for housing and education after the war.

1940—Benito Mussolini and Hitler form Axis

Germany conquers most of Western Europe

Selective Training and Service Act begins

Roosevelt wins reelection to third term

1942—One hundred thousand Japanese Americans interred in camps

1936—Abraham Lincoln Brigade goes to Spain to resist Franco

1944—D-Day, Allied invasion of German-occupied France begins

Roosevelt wins his fourth term

1938—German troops overrun Austria

1941—Executive Order #8802 is issued

Japan attacks Pearl Harbor; America joins World War II

The Battle of the Bulge begins last major German counteroffensive

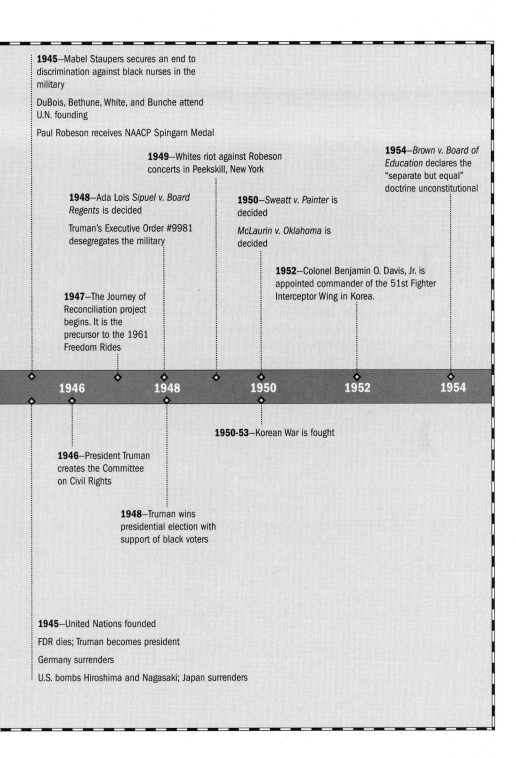

1945—Mabel Staupers secures an end to discrimination against black nurses in the military

DuBois, Bethune, White, and Bunche attend U.N. founding

Paul Robeson receives NAACP Spingarn Medal

1949—Whites riot against Robeson concerts in Peekskill, New York

1954—*Brown v. Board of Education* declares the "separate but equal" doctrine unconstitutional

1948—Ada Lois *Sipuel v. Board Regents* is decided

Truman's Executive Order #9981 desegregates the military

1950—*Sweatt v. Painter* is decided

McLaurin v. Oklahoma is decided

1952—Colonel Benjamin O. Davis, Jr. is appointed commander of the 51st Fighter Interceptor Wing in Korea.

1947—The Journey of Reconciliation project begins. It is the precursor to the 1961 Freedom Rides

1946 **1948** **1950** **1952** **1954**

1950-53—Korean War is fought

1946—President Truman creates the Committee on Civil Rights

1948—Truman wins presidential election with support of black voters

1945—United Nations founded

FDR dies; Truman becomes president

Germany surrenders

U.S. bombs Hiroshima and Nagasaki; Japan surrenders

We come then to the question presented: Does segregation of children in public schools solely on the basis of race, even though the physical facilities and other 'tangible' factors may be equal, deprive the children of the minority group of equal educational opportunities? We believe that it does. . . . To separate them from others of similar age and qualifications solely because of their race generates a feeling of inferiority as to the status in the community that may affect their hearts and minds in a way unlikely ever to be undone. . . . We conclude that in the field of public education the doctrine of "separate but equal" has no place. Separate educational facilities are inherently unequal.

The *Brown* decision would eventually lead to the dismantling of the entire structure of Jim Crow laws that regulated black life in America: movement, work, marriage, education, housing, even death and burial. The *Brown* decision signaled the emerging primacy of equality as a guide to constitutional decisions. This and subsequent decisions helped to advance the rights of other minorities and women. As Motley reflected, "In the *Brown* case and in the decisions that followed, we blazed a trail for others by showing the competence of Black lawyers."

Conclusion

The years between 1940 and 1954 were a dynamic period of black activism and witnessed a rising international consciousness among African Americans. The quest for racial justice became an integral part of the ongoing struggle for economic, political, and social progress. President Roosevelt's Executive Order #8802 was a significant victory for black workers who were able to appeal racial discrimination in defense industries to the Fair Employment Practices Commission. World War II also profoundly transformed black servicemen and servicewomen.

Following the victory in World War II, the Cold War created a climate in America that was both hospitable and hostile to the emerging African-American freedom movement. Radicals such as Paul Robeson and W. E. B. Du Bois found no place in the movement or American society in general. Moderate organizations, such as the NAACP-LDEF, pursuing their goals within the ideological and legal constraints of the nation, would meet with some success. The coming civil rights movement would, however, soon pave the way for a more varied, vibrant, and successful challenge to racism.

Review Questions

1. How did World War II alter the status of African Americans? What were some of the consequences of so many black servicemen fighting in Europe against fascism and Nazism?

2. How did black women participate in the campaign to desegregate the United States military? How did Mabel Staupers win acceptance of black women into the military nurses corps?

3. What were the consequences of the "Double V" campaign? How did African-American civilians support black servicemen? What institutional resources were African Americans able to marshall in their campaign for victory against racism?

4. How did World War II affect the status of black workers in America? What was the significance of A. Philip Randolph's March on Washington Movement, and how did President Roosevelt respond to it?

5. Why did the Cold War originate, and what is its significance for black activism? How did the World War II era promote the rising internationalization of African-American consciousness? Why did the State Department attempt to downplay black dissent in America?

6. Why was 1954 a watershed year in the history of African Americans? Why did President Harry S Truman decide to desegregate the U.S. military? Discuss the decades of preparation by black lawyers that resulted in the victorious *Brown* decision.

Recommended Reading

Richard Kluger. *Simple Justice: The History of "Brown v. Board of Education" and Black America's Struggle for Equality.* New York: Knopf, 1976. An excellent treatment of the historical events leading up to the *Brown* decision and the local individuals and national leaders who played instrumental roles in the legal challenge to Jim Crow segregation in the South.

Genna Rae McNeil. *Groundwork: Charles Hamilton Houston and the Struggle for Civil Rights.* Philadelphia: University of Pennsylvania Press, 1983. An excellent biography of the brilliant Howard University Law School Dean who, as head of the NAACP Legal Council, planned the legal strategy that resulted in the *Brown* decision and transformed American civil rights jurisprudence.

Paula F. Pfeffer. *A. Philip Randolph, Pioneer of the Civil Rights Movement.* Baton Rouge, LA: Louisiana State University Press, 1990. A richly insightful biography of a pioneering labor leader and activist whose March on Washington Movement in 1941 was essential to the formation of the first Fair Employment Practices Committee and the integration of the armed services.

Mark V. Tushnet. *Making Civil Rights Law: Thurgood Marshall and the Supreme Court, 1936–1961.* New York: Oxford University Press, 1994. A fine overview of Charles Houston's protégé and his impressive legal campaign against Jim Crow in numerous cases argued before the United States Supreme Court.

→ Chapter 21 ←

The Freedom Movement, 1954–1965

The 1950s: Prosperity and Prejudice

For most white Americans, the 1950s ushered in an era of unparalleled prosperity. The more affluent fled to the suburbs and by 1960, 52 percent of Americans owned their own homes. The decade is remembered nostalgically as a time of stable nuclear families untroubled by drugs and juvenile delinquency.

For most black Americans, however, the 1950s were less blissful. American society remained rigidly segregated. Jim Crow restrictions and white violence kept millions of African Americans from voting in the deep South.

Nor did most African Americans benefit from the economic boom of the 1950s. Moving into urban centers just as the number of factories and jobs there began to decline, they suffered a higher unemployment rate than any other segment of the population. White workers felt threatened by competition from unemployed black workers. As urban neighborhoods deteriorated, conditions ripened for an explosion.

Brown II

A year after the 1954 *Brown* decision, in May 1955, the Supreme Court issued a second ruling, commonly known as *Brown II*, which addressed the practical process of desegregation. The Court underscored that the states in the suits should begin prompt compliance with the 1954 ruling, and that this should be done with "all deliberate speed." Many black Americans interpreted this to mean "immediately." White Southerners hoped it meant a long time, or never. Ominously, President Eisenhower seemed displeased with the Court's rulings and refused to put the moral authority of his office behind their enforcement.

Nevertheless, in 1955 and early 1956, desegregation proceeded without hindrance in Maryland, Kentucky, Delaware, Oklahoma, and Missouri. Many moderate white southern politicians counseled calm and worked to head off a full-scale conflict between their region and the federal government.

408

Massive White Resistance

White moderates, however, soon found themselves a shrinking minority, as extremists, determined to maintain white supremacy at any cost, prepared for mass resistance to the Court's decisions. The rhetoric of these extremists bordered on hysteria, but found a receptive audience among many white people. A young minister from Virginia named Jerry Falwell, for example, explained that black people were the descendants of Noah's son Ham and destined to be servants because of a curse God had put on him. Falwell also claimed the Supreme Court's decisions were inspired by Moscow. In 1955, leading businessmen, professionals, and clergy began organizing White Citizens' Councils in southern cities, dedicated to preserving the southern way of life and the South's "sacred heritage of freedom." The councils used their power to intimidate black people who challenged segregation. They fired people from their jobs, evicted them from their homes, and refused them credit.

Many white politicians took up the banner of massive resistance. Senator James O. Eastland, from Mississippi, called the *Brown* decision a "monstrous crime." The Virginia legislature closed all public schools in Prince Edward County to thwart integration. Most dramatically, on March 12, 1956, ninety-six southern congressmen led by North Carolina's Senator Sam Ervin Jr. issued "The Southern Manifesto" vowing to preserve segregation and the southern way of life. The Manifesto called the *Brown* decisions an "unwarranted exercise of power by the court, contrary to the Constitution."

The NAACP came under siege after the *Brown* decision as southern states tried to destroy it. By 1957 nine southern states had filed suit to eradicate the organization. Some states, alleging that the NAACP was linked to a worldwide communist conspiracy, made membership illegal. Membership plummeted from 128,716 to 79,677, and the association lost 246 branches in the South.

Under these pressures, desegregation ground to a halt. Massive resistance was challenging the possibility of achieving change through court action alone.

The Lynching of Emmett Till

The violent reaction of white Southerners to the growing assertiveness of black people found expression in the summer of 1955 in the lynching of fourteen-year-old Emmett Till of Chicago, an event that helped galvanize the emerging civil rights movement. Till was visiting relatives in the small town of Money, Mississippi. On a dare from his friends, he entered Bryant's grocery store, bought candy, and said "Bye, baby" to Carolyn Bryant, the wife of the owner, as he left. In the middle of the night a few days after the incident, Bryant's husband and brother-in-law kidnaped Till at gunpoint. His body was later found in the Tallahatchie River. Till had a bullet in his head and had been tortured before his murder. Despite overwhelming evidence and the brave testimony of local black people, an all-white jury acquitted the two men who lynched Till. In early 1956, the murderers sold their confession to *Look* magazine and gloated over their escape from justice.

The Till lynching shaped the consciousness of an entire generation of young African-American activists. Partly this was due to the efforts of Till's mother, Mamie Bradley. She had her son's mangled body displayed in an open casket in Chicago. Thousands of mourners paid their respects, and many vowed to fight the system that made this crime possible. Bradley also traveled around the nation speaking to groups on whom her grief had a profound impact. Myrlie Evers, who would later have a role in the movement, remembered how she felt. "I bled for Emmett Till's mother. I know when she came to Mississippi and appeared at the mass meetings how everyone poured out their hearts to her, went into their pockets when people had only two or three pennies, and gave."

New Forms of Protest: The Montgomery Bus Boycott

Strong local communities formed the core of the civil rights movement and they were often sparked to action by the deeds of brave and committed individuals. The first and one of the most important expressions of this process occurred in Alabama's small capital city of Montgomery (see Map 21–1). This city's African-American community of forty-five thousand was poised to make history.

The Roots of Revolution

The movement in Montgomery was the result of years of organization and planning by protest groups. In addition to its numerous churches, two black colleges, and other social organizations, the Alabama capital had a strong core of protest groups. One, the Women's Political Council (WPC), had been founded in 1946 by Mary Frances Fair Burks, chair of Alabama State College English Department, after the all-white League

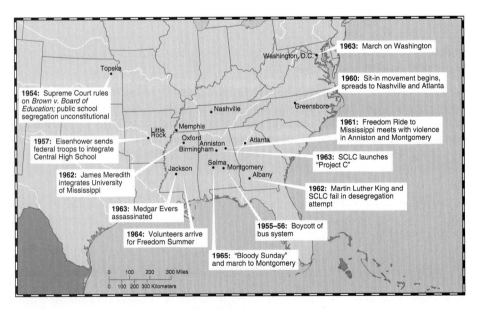

MAP 21–1   Major Events of the Civil Rights Movement   This map shows the location of key events in the struggle for civil rights between 1954 and 1965.

of Women Voters had refused to allow black women to participate in its activities. Although the WPC had only forty members, all middle-class women, its leaders were willing to stand up to powerful white people. The WPC was joined by a chapter of the NAACP led by E. D. Nixon, head of the Alabama chapter of the Brotherhood of Sleeping Car Porters. In 1943, Nixon had founded the Montgomery Voters League to help African Americans navigate Alabama's tortuous voter registration process. In the decade after 1945 these groups searched for a way to mobilize the black community to challenge white power.

Four days after the 1954 *Brown* decision was announced, Jo Ann Robinson, a professor at Alabama State College, wrote a letter to Montgomery's mayor on behalf of the WPC. In it she reiterated the complaints of the black community concerning conditions on the city's buses and ended, "Please consider this plea, for even now plans are being made to ride less, or not at all, on our buses." The mayor ignored the warning and the buses remained as segregated as before. Montgomery's black lawyers and NAACP chapter began laying the groundwork for a test case challenging segregation of the city's bus lines.

On March 2, 1955, a fifteen-year-old girl, Claudette Colvin, was arrested for refusing to give up her seat on a bus to a white person. The WPC was ready to use this incident to initiate the threatened bus boycott, but Nixon felt that Colvin, who was unmarried and pregnant, would not be an appropriate symbol around which to organize. He and other activists resolved to wait for another chance.

Rosa Parks

On Thursday, December 1, 1955, Rosa Parks, a forty-three-year-old department store seamstress and civil rights activist boarded a city bus and moved to the back where African Americans were required to sit. All seats were taken so she sat in one toward the middle of the bus. When a white man boarded the bus, the driver ordered Parks to vacate her seat for him, but Rosa Parks refused to move. She had not planned to resist on that day, but, as she later said, she had "decided that I would have to know once and for all what rights I had as a human being and a citizen. . . . I was so involved with the attempt to bring about freedom from this kind of thing . . . I felt just resigned to give what I could to protest against the way I was being treated, and felt that all of our meetings, trying to negotiate, bring about petitions before the authorities . . . really hadn't done any good at all." With this act of resistance she launched the Montgomery bus boycott movement and inspired the modern civil rights struggle.

The plans of the WPC and NAACP came into play after Parks's arrest for violating Montgomery's transportation laws. She was ordered to appear in court on the following Monday. Meanwhile, E. D. Nixon bailed her out of the city jail and began mobilizing the leadership of the black community behind her. Robinson wrote and circulated a flyer calling for a one-day boycott of the buses followed by a mass meeting of the community to discuss the matter. Robinson took the flyer to the Alabama State College campus and mimeographed thirty thousand copies of it. The WPC had planned distribution routes months earlier, and the next day, Robinson and nearly two hundred volunteers distributed bundles of flyers throughout the black neighborhoods.

Martin Luther King, Jr.

On December 5, 1955, the black community did not ride the buses, and the movement had begun. Nixon and other community leaders decided to form a new organization, the Montgomery Improvement Association (MIA) to coordinate the protest; they also selected a twenty-six-year-old minister, Martin Luther King, Jr., as its president. That evening there was a mass meeting of the black community at the Holt Street Baptist church to decide whether to continue the boycott. King spoke to the crowd and delivered a message that would define the goals of the boycott and the civil rights movement that followed. He connected the core values of America and of the Judeo-Christian tradition to the goals of African Americans nationwide as well as in Montgomery. "We are here this evening," he began,

> for serious business. We are here in a general sense because first and foremost we are American citizens, and we are determined to apply our citizenship to the fullness of its means. . . . You know, my friends, there comes a time when people get tired of being trampled over by the iron feet of oppression. There comes a time, my friends, when people get tired of being flung across the abyss of humiliation, when they experience the bleakness of nagging despair. . . . We are not wrong in what we are doing. If we are wrong, the Supreme Court of this nation is wrong. If we are wrong, the Constitution of the United States is wrong. If we are wrong, God Almighty is wrong. If we are wrong, Jesus of Nazareth was merely a utopian dreamer that never came down to earth. If we are wrong, justice is a lie. Love has no meaning. And we are determined here in Montgomery to work and fight until justice runs down like water, and righteousness like a mighty stream.

King's speech electrified the meeting, which unanimously decided to stay off the city's buses until the MIA's demands were met. The speech also marked the beginning of King's role as a leader of the civil rights movement. King had been raised in a prominent ministerial family with a long history of standing up for African-American rights. King's grandfather had led a protest to force Atlanta to build its first high school for African Americans. King's father spoke out for African-American rights as pastor of Ebenezer Baptist Church. At age fifteen, King had entered Morehouse College but did not embrace the ministry as his profession until he came under the influence of its president, Dr. Benjamin E. Mays. By age twenty-five, King had been awarded a Ph.D. in theology from Boston College. He moved to Alabama with his wife, Coretta Scott King, to become pastor of Dexter Avenue Baptist Church in Montgomery.

King had the ability to inspire moral courage and to teach people how to hold up under pressure. King merged Gandhian nonviolence with black Christian faith and church culture to create a unique ideology well suited for the civil rights struggle. King declared that the boycott would continue with or without its leaders because the conflict was not "between the white and the Negro" but "between justice and injustice." He explained to the boycotting community, "If we are arrested every day, if we are exploited every day, if we are trampled over every day, don't ever let anyone pull you so low as to hate them. . . . We must realize so many people are taught to hate us that they are not totally responsible for their hate." King's faith was severely tested. As the boycott proceeded, his home was bombed. Segregationists also bombed Nixon's home and those of two other black clergymen and MIA leaders, Ralph Abernathy and Fred Shuttlesworth, and inflicted violence on many other boycott participants.

Walking for Freedom

Although men occupied the top leadership positions in the boycott, women were the key to its effectiveness. The boycott lasted 381 days and over its course nearly all the black women previously dependent on the buses to get to work refused to ride them. Some walked twelve miles a day. Others had the support of their white women employers, who provided transportation. And many helped to organize a car pool that proved critical to sustaining the boycott. Mass meetings were held nightly in local churches. Robinson edited the MIA newsletter. Other women supported the boycott in dozens of ways. Some organized bake sales. Others made door-to-door solicitations to raise the $2,000 per week needed to keep the car pools going.

The boycott took 65 percent of the bus company's business, forcing it to cut schedules, lay off drivers, and raise fares. White merchants also suffered. However the city government refused to capitulate. Any white politician who hoped to remain in office had to defend segregation.

Impressive as it was, the boycott by itself could not end segregation on the buses. Black Montgomery also needed the legal backing of the federal government to end Jim Crow. Thus, NAACP lawyers and MIA's lawyer Fred Gray filed a suit in the names of Claudette Colvin, Mary Louise Smith, and three other women.

Friends in the North

The Montgomery movement was not without allies outside the South. Money poured into the MIA's coffers from concerned Americans. Many northern activists who had long been hoping that black Southerners would begin just this kind of resistance also swung into action to help. Two people were particularly important at this juncture: CORE's Bayard Rustin and liberal Jewish lawyer Stanley Levinson. Two and a half months into the boycott, Montgomery officials indicted King and one hundred other leaders on charges of conspiracy to disrupt the bus system. At this juncture Rustin arrived in Montgomery and immediately encouraged the leaders to follow Gandhian practice and submit freely to arrest. In a diary entry, Rustin wrote,

> Many of them did not wait for the police to come but walked to the police station and surrendered. Nixon was the first. He walked into the station and said, "You are looking for me? Here I am." This procedure had a startling effect on both the Negro and the white communities. White community leaders, politicians, and police were dumbfounded. Negroes were thrilled to see their leaders surrender without being hunted down. Soon hundreds of Negroes gathered outside the police station and applauded the leaders as they entered, one by one.

Rustin became one of King's most trusted advisers on nonviolent principles and tactics. Levinson and Ella Baker created a group called In Friendship, which raised money for the boycott.

Levinson was committed to social justice. He had worked with the Communist party, and Rustin had a long history of association with radical groups. Their influence soon attracted the attention of the FBI, which had long been obsessed with black leaders and organizations. King was not a communist, but FBI director J. Edgar Hoover developed an intense hatred of him and other black leaders. At one point Hoover called

King "the most dangerous man in America," and he pressed his subordinates to prove King was a communist and that the civil rights movement was a Moscow-inspired conspiracy. Hoover and his men began tapping King's telephone and hotel rooms and even threatened to expose his extramarital affairs if he did not commit suicide. By the early 1960s the FBI had stopped warning King when it uncovered threats to his life.

Victory

As the bus boycott reached the one-year mark, King and the others grew discouraged, and their hopes seemed to fade in November 1956 when it became clear that the state courts would soon move to declare the car pools illegal. Salvation came from the cases local women and the NAACP had taken to the federal courts. On November 13, 1956, the Supreme Court ordered an end to Montgomery's bus segregation. The *Gayle v. Browder* decision, unlike the *Brown* decision, expressly overturned the 1896 *Plessy v. Ferguson* decision, because like *Plessy* it applied to transportation. The bus company agreed not only to end segregation but to hire African-American drivers and to treat all passengers with equal respect. On the morning of December 21, 1956, black citizens of Montgomery boarded the buses and sat wherever they pleased.

No Easy Road to Freedom: 1957–1960

The victory at Montgomery set an example for future protests. It was the result of a highly organized black community led by committed and capable black leaders. These local efforts were bolstered by the advice and involvement of activists outside the South, the attention of a sympathetic national press, and, crucially, intervention from the federal courts. But local victories could only go so far, particularly as white resistance intensified. In the three years following the boycott, black Southerners and their allies across the nation prepared for a broader movement. At the same time, federal officials outside the judiciary found that they could not ignore the white South's incipient rebellion without grave consequences for the nation and their own power.

The SCLC

By the end of the campaign in Montgomery, Martin Luther King, Jr. had emerged as a moral leader of national stature. On the advice of Levinson, Rustin, and Ella Baker, he helped create a new organization, the Southern Christian Leadership Council (SCLC) to provide an institutional base for continuing the struggle. The SCLC was a federation of civil rights groups, community organizations, and churches that sought to coordinate all the burgeoning local movements. King assumed leadership of the SCLC, crisscrossing the nation in the ensuing years to build support for it. Members of the organization also began training black activists, particularly on college campuses, in the tactics of nonviolent protest. Because the ballot was deemed the critical weapon needed to complete school desegregation and secure equal employment opportunity, adequate housing, and equal access to public accommodations, the SCLC focused on securing voting rights for black people. In the three years after the Montgomery bus boycott, the SCLC also aided black communities in applying the lessons of that struggle to challenge bus segregation in Tallahassee, Florida, and in Atlanta.

The NAACP's leadership doubted the effectiveness of the protest tactics favored by the SCLC. They resented having to divert resources away from work on important court cases to defend people arrested in protests and were troubled by the left-wing connections of King's advisers. While the SCLC and the NAACP worked together, the tensions between them over tactics were never far from the surface.

Civil Rights Act of 1957

Despite President Eisenhower's tepid response to *Brown,* Congress took a modest step toward ending racial discrimination when it enacted the Civil Rights Act of 1957, the first such legislation since the end of Reconstruction. In a departure from the past, liberals in the Senate were able to end a filibuster by Southerners, but the bill they passed was, for all its symbolic import, weak. It created a commission to monitor violations of black civil rights and to propose remedies for infringements on black voting. It upgraded the Civil Rights Section into a division within the Justice Department and gave it the power to initiate proceedings against those states and municipalities that discriminated on the basis of race. This act disappointed black activists because it was not strong enough to counter white reaction and because they felt the Eisenhower administration would not enforce it.

Little Rock, Arkansas

Eisenhower may have had little inclination to support the fight for black rights, but the defiance of Arkansas governor Orville Faubus would soon force him to. At the beginning of the school year in 1957, Faubus posted the Arkansas National Guard outside Little Rock Central High School to prevent nine black youths from entering. Faubus was determined to maintain school segregation. When a federal district court order forced the governor to allow the children into the school, he simply withdrew the state guard and left the children alone to face a hate-filled mob.

To defend the sovereignty of the federal court and the Constitution, Eisenhower had to act. He sent in 1,100 paratroopers from the 101st Airborne to Little Rock and put the state national guard under federal authority. It was the first time since Reconstruction that troops had been sent to the South to protect the rights of African-American citizens. The troops remained in Little Rock Central High School for the rest of the school year. Governor Faubus closed the Little Rock public schools in 1958–1959. Eight of the nine black students withstood the abuse, harassment, and curses of segregationists both inside and outside the facility and eventually desegregated the high school. Other young African Americans throughout the South would show similar courage.

Black Youth Stand Up
by Sitting Down

Beginning in 1960, motivated black college students adapted a strategy that CORE had used in the 1940s—the sit-in—and emerged as the dynamic vanguard of the civil rights movement. Their contributions to the black protest movement accelerated the pace of social change. Before long the movement would inspire even more northern black and white students.

Sit-Ins: Greensboro, Nashville, Atlanta

On February 1, 1960, Ezell Blair, Jr., Joseph McNeil, Franklin McCain, and David Richmond, all freshmen at North Carolina Agricultural and Technical College, decided to desegregate local restaurants by sitting at the lunch counter of Greensboro, North Carolina's Woolworth five-and-dime store where black people were not permitted to dine. At 4:30 in the afternoon the students sat at the counter. They received no service that day, but sat quietly doing their school work until the store closed. This action electrified their fellow students, and the next day many others joined them. Soon black women students from Bennett College and a few white students from the University of North Carolina Women's College joined the protest, and by the fifth day hundreds of young, studious, neatly dressed African Americans crowded the downtown store demanding their rights.

Four students—from the left they are Joseph McNeil, Franklin McCain, Billy Smith, and Clarence Henderson—sit patiently at Woolworth's lunch counter on February 2, 1960, the second day of the sit-in in Greensboro, North Carolina. Although not the first sit-in protest against segregated facilities, the Greensboro action triggered a wave of sit-ins by black high school and college students across the South.
News & Record

Like the black people of Montgomery, the students in Greensboro acted with fore-thought and with the support of their community. They had long debated how they could participate in the desegregation movement. All four of the black students had been members of NAACP college or youth groups. Although they began the sit-in on their own, it quickly gained the support of the black community. Many people in the North and West—both black and white—picketed local stores of the national chains that approved of segregation in the South. After facing the collective power of the black community and their allies for many months, white businessmen and politicians finally gave in to the black community's demands.

The students at Greensboro were not alone in their desire to strike out at discrim-ination. Indeed, at Fisk University in Nashville, Tennessee, Diane Nash, John Lewis, Marion Barry, James Bevel, Curtis Murphy, Gloria Johnson, Bernard Lafayette, and Rodney Powell had begun organizing nonviolent workshops before the Greensboro sit-in. Imbued with youthful idealism, they determined to follow the Reverend James Lawson's teaching on nonviolence and Christian brotherhood. Even better organized than their comrades in North Carolina, twelve days after the first sit-ins began, the Nashville group swung into action. Hundreds were arrested, and those who sat suf-fered insults, violence, arrest, and torture while in jail. Nonetheless, they compelled restaurants to desegregate by May 1960.

Atlanta, Martin Luther King, Jr.'s home base and the site of a large African-American community, spawned an even more dramatic movement. It began after Spelman College freshman Ruby Doris Smith persuaded her friends and classmates to launch sit-ins in the city. On March 15, 1960, at Atlanta University, two students, Julian Bond and Lonnie King, executing a carefully orchestrated plan, deployed two hundred sit-in students to ten different eating places. They targeted government-owned property and public places, including bus and train stations and the state capitol, that should have been willing to serve all customers. At the Federal Building, Bond and his classmates attempted to eat in the municipal cafeteria and were arrest-ed. After hours of incarceration they were released. A jail stint had once been a mark of shame, but these students returned as heroes to the campus. The Atlanta sit-in students broadened their campaign demands to include desegregation of all public facilities, voting rights, and equal access to educational and employment opportuni-ties. On September 27, 1961, the Atlanta elite gave in.

By April 1960 more than two thousand students from black high schools and col-leges had been arrested in seventy-eight southern towns and cities. Local people demonstrated their allegiance to them in numerous ways, but their most effective tac-tic was the economic boycott. When business began to suffer, white leaders proved willing to negotiate the racial status quo. By the summer, more than thirty southern cities had set up community organizations to respond to the complaints of local black citizens.

The SNCC

Recognizing the significance of the regionwide student action and fearing that it would soon melt away, the SCLC's Ella Baker organized a conference for 150 students at her alma mater, Shaw University, in Raleigh, North Carolina. Baker, who managed operations in the SCLC's Atlanta headquarters, chafed under the rigid male leadership of the organization. In contrast, she advocated decentralized leadership and celebrated participatory democracy. Her skepticism about the SCLC struck a chord with the students.

On April 15–17, 1960, delegates representing over fifty colleges and high schools from thirty-seven communities in thirteen states began discussing how to keep the movement going. Baker became the midwife of a new organization named the Student Nonviolent Coordinating Committee (SNCC). The newest addition to the roster of civil rights associations adhered to the ideology of nonviolence, but it also acknowledged the possible need for increased militancy. More accommodating black leaders objected to the students' use of confrontational tactics that disrupted race relations and community peace.

Freedom Rides

The sit-in movement paved the way for the "Freedom Rides" of 1961. CORE's James Farmer and Bayard Rustin resolved that it was time for a reprise of their 1947 mission to ride interstate buses and trains in the upper South. That early effort—a planned bus trip from Washington, D.C., to Kentucky—reached only as far as Chapel Hill, North Carolina. There the group of interracial riders were arrested and sentenced to thirty days on a road gang. This new journey tested the Justice Department's willingness to protect the rights of African Americans to use bus terminal facilities on a nonsegregated basis.

The Freedom Rides showed the world how far some white Southerners would go to preserve segregation. The first ride ran into trouble on May 4, 1961, when John Lewis, one of the seven black riders, tried to enter the white waiting room of the Greyhound bus terminal in Rock Hill, South Carolina, and was beaten by local white people in full view of the police. At Anniston, Alabama, a mob firebombed the bus and beat the riders. A group of local African Americans led by the Reverend Fred Shuttlesworth took many of the shocked and injured riders to Birmingham.

With the police offering no protection, CORE abandoned the Freedom Rides, and most of the original riders left Alabama. But SNCC activists in Nashville refused to let the idea die. At least twenty civil rights workers went to Birmingham where they vowed on May 20 to ride on to Montgomery. Awaiting them in Montgomery was an angry mob of more than 1,000 white people, and not a policeman in sight. This time all the riders had to be hospitalized. Even a presidential aide assigned to monitor the crisis was injured.

News services flashed images of the violence around the world, and the federal government resolved to end the bloodletting. Attorney General Robert Kennedy sent four hundred federal marshals to restore law and order. Martin Luther King, Jr. and Ralph Abernathy joined the conflict on May 21, as 1,200 men, women, and children met at Abernathy's church. Federal marshals surrounded the building. Only then did Governor John Patterson order the National Guard and state troopers to protect the protesters. When the group arrived in Jackson, Mississippi, white authorities arrested them. By summer's end, more than three hundred Freedom Riders had served time in Mississippi's notorious prisons.

The Movement at High Tide

Between 1960 and 1963 the civil rights movement developed the techniques and organization that would finally bring America face to face with the conflict between its democratic ideals and the racism of its politics. Day after day the movement squared off against the die-hard resistance of the white South and created a situation that demanded that the president and Congress take action.

The Kennedy Administration and the Civil Rights Movement

One of the persistent fears of white Southerners was that black Americans, if armed with the ballot, would hold the balance of political power. The presidential election of 1960 proved this to be the case. Initially, many African Americans favored the Republican party's nominee, Richard Nixon, who had advocated strong civil rights legislation. The Democratic nominee, Massachusetts Senator John F. Kennedy, in contrast, had done little to distinguish himself to black Americans in the struggles of the 1950s. As the campaign progressed, however, Kennedy made more sympathetic statements in support of black protests. Meanwhile, Nixon attempted to strengthen his position with white southern voters and remained silent about civil rights issues, even though the Republican party had a strong pro–civil rights record.

Shortly before the election, Martin Luther King was sentenced to four months in prison for leading a nonviolent protest march in Atlanta. Kennedy telephoned King's wife, Coretta Scott King, to offer his support while his brother Robert F. Kennedy used his influence to obtain King's release. These acts impressed African Americans and won their support. African-American voters in key northern cities provided the crucial margin that elected John F. Kennedy. In Illinois, for example, with black voters casting 250,000 ballots for Kennedy, the Democrats carried the state by merely 9,000 votes.

Early in his administration John F. Kennedy grew concerned about the mounting violence occasioned by the civil rights movement. As the Freedom Rides continued across the deep South, the activists provoked crises and confrontations and forced the federal government to intervene in their behalf. Kennedy's primary interest at this point was to prevent disorder and to avoid compromising America's position with the developing nations. But Kennedy had little room to maneuver given the power of white Southerners in Congress.

Despite these limitations, Kennedy did aid the cause of civil rights. He issued Executive Order 11063, which required government agencies to discontinue discriminatory policies in federally supported housing, and he named Vice President Lyndon B. Johnson to chair the newly established Committee on Equal Employment Opportunity. Kennedy also nominated Thurgood Marshall to the Second Circuit Court of Appeals and named journalist Carl Rowan deputy assistant secretary of state. More than forty African Americans took positions in the new administration, including Robert Weaver, director of the Housing and Home Finance Agency; Mercer Cook, ambassador to Norway; and George L. P. Weaver, assistant secretary of labor. Moreover, Kennedy's brother Robert put muscle into the Civil Rights Division of the Justice Department by hiring an impressive team of lawyers.

Like Eisenhower, when President Kennedy felt that intractable southern governors were challenging his authority, he acted decisively. On June 25, 1962, one year after James Meredith had filed a complaint of racial discrimination against the University of Mississippi, the U.S. Circuit Court of Appeals for the Fifth Circuit ruled that the university had to admit him. Mississippi governor Ross Barnett vowed to resist the order but Kennedy sent three hundred federal marshals to uphold it. Thousands of students rioted; two people died, two hundred were arrested, and nearly half the marshals were injured. Kennedy did not back down. He federalized the Mississippi National Guard to ensure Meredith's admission. Although isolated and harassed throughout his time at Ole Miss, Meredith was eventually graduated. Kennedy also compelled Governor George Wallace of Alabama to allow the desegregation of the University of Alabama.

Voter Registration Projects

On June 16, 1961, Robert Kennedy urged student leaders to redirect their energies to voter registration projects and to lessen their concentration on direct-action activities. He and the Justice Department aides persuaded the students that the free exercise of the ballot would result in significant social change. James Foreman, SNCC's executive director, followed Kennedy's lead. By October 1961, SNCC had joined forces with the NAACP, SCLC, and CORE in the voter education project funded by major philanthropic foundations and administered by the Southern Regional Council. SNCC was responsible for Alabama and Mississippi. Drawing heavily on the expertise of Robert Moses and working closely with a cadre of local leaders like Amzie Moore, head of the NAACP in Mississippi's Cleveland county, and Fannie Lou Hamer of Ruleville, SNCC opened a series of voter registration schools. The "graduates" thereupon attempted to register to vote. These attempts unleashed a wave of white violence and murder across Mississippi.

The Albany Movement

In Albany, Georgia, the burgeoning civil rights movement met sophisticated resistance and experienced its most profound defeat up to that time. The movement in Albany began in the summer of 1961 when SNCC members moved into the city to conduct a voter registration project. Soon various local groups decided to form a coalition called the Albany Movement and elected William G. Anderson as its president. The movement's goal expanded to securing the total desegregation of the town.

In Laurie Pritchett, Albany's police chief, the movement faced an uncommonly sophisticated opponent. Pritchett studied the past tactics of SNCC and King and resolved to avoid the violence that brought negative media attention. When students from a black college decided to begin demonstrations by desegregating the bus terminal, Pritchett immediately arrested them after they entered the white waiting room and attempted to eat in the bus terminal dining room. Shrewdly, he charged the students with violating a city ordinance for failing to obey a law enforcement officer. They were not arrested on a federal charge.

The Albany Movement decided to invite King and the SCLC to aid them and to overwhelm the police department by filling the jails with protesters. King answered the call. On December 16, 1961, he and more than 250 demonstrators were arrested, joining the 507 people already in jail. The plan was to stay in jail in order to, as Charles Sherrod explained, "break the system down from within. Our ability to suffer was somehow going to overcome their ability to hurt us." King vowed to remain in jail until the city desegregated. Sheriff Pritchett, however, made arrangements to house almost two thousand people in surrounding jail facilities and trained his deputies to use nonviolent techniques. Thus, Pritchett avoided confrontation, violence, and federal intervention.

On December 18, 1961, two days after King's arrest, the city and the Albany Movement announced a truce. King returned to Atlanta, and the city refused to implement the terms of the agreement. When King and Ralph Abernathy returned to Albany in July 1962 for sentencing on their December arrests, they chose forty-five days in jail rather than admit guilt by paying a fine. The mass marches resumed, but Pritchett had King released from jail to avoid negative publicity. The city's attorney then secured a federal injunction to prevent King and the other leaders from demonstrating. Given his dependence on the federal government, King felt he could not violate the injunction and abandoned the protest. The Albany Movement was King's most glaring defeat.

The Birmingham Confrontation

By early 1963 the movement appeared to be stalled. Black communities in many parts of the South were strong, but their efforts had achieved only modest changes. It was impossible to overcome the power of southern state and local governments without the intervention of the federal government, but national politicians, including President Kennedy, remained reluctant to act unless faced with open defiance by white people or televised violence against peaceful protesters. King and other black leaders knew that if city governments throughout the South followed the model of Sheriff Pritchett in Albany, the civil rights movement might lose momentum. To rejuvenate the movement, the SCLC decided to launch a massive new campaign during 1963, the centennial anniversary of the Emancipation Proclamation.

Birmingham, Alabama, a large, tightly segregated industrial city, was chosen as the site for the action. The city was ripe for such a protest, in part because its black community suffered from police brutality as well as economic, educational, and social discrimination. The Ku Klux Klan terrorized people with impunity. The black community had, however, developed a strong phalanx of protest organizations called the Alabama Christian Movement for Human Rights (ACMHR) led by the Reverend Fred Shuttlesworth. The ACMHR and SCLC planned a campaign of boycotts and demonstrations code-named Project C for Confrontation. Their program would be far more extensive than any before, with demands to integrate public facilities, for guarantees of employment opportunities for black workers in downtown businesses, to desegregate the schools, to improve services in black neighborhoods, and to provide low-income housing. Organizers hoped to provoke the city's public safety commissioner Eugene T. "Bull" Connor, who, unlike Sheriff Pritchett, had a reputation for viciousness. Civil rights leaders believed that Conner's conduct would compel Kennedy to act.

Project C began on April 3 with college students conducting sit-ins. Days later, marches began, and Connor, following the lead of Pritchett, avoided overt violence. When the state courts prohibited further protests, King, Abernathy, and others were arrested on Good Friday, April 12, 1963.

While in jail, King received a letter from eight local clergymen who objected to the "unwise and untimely" protest activities of black citizens. King had smuggled a pen into jail and on scraps of paper, he wrote an eloquent treatise on the use of direct action. His "Letter from Birmingham Jail" was widely published in newspapers and magazines. In it, King dismissed those who called for black people to wait: "I guess it is easy for those who have never felt the stinging darts of segregation to say, 'Wait.'" But, he declared, "freedom is never voluntarily given by the oppressor; it must be demanded by the oppressed." In the letter King also explained, "Nonviolent direct action seeks to create such a crisis and foster such a tension that a community which has constantly refused to negotiate is forced to confront the issue. It seeks so to dramatize the issue that it can no longer be ignored. . . . Any law that degrades human personality is unjust. All segregation statutes are unjust because segregation distorts the soul and damages the personality. It gives the segregator a false sense of superiority and the segregated a false sense of inferiority."

King's letter had a powerful national impact, but the Birmingham movement was beginning to lose momentum because many of the protesters were either in jail or could not risk new arrests. At this juncture James Bevel of the SCLC proposed using schoolchildren to continue the protests. Many observers criticized this idea, as did some of those in the movement. But King and other leaders believed that it was necessary to risk harm to children in order to ensure their freedom. Thus, on May 2 and 3, 1963, thousands of youths, some as young as six, marched. This tactic enraged "Bull" Connor and his officers. The police not only arrested the children but also beat them and set dogs on them. Firefighters aimed their water hoses at the youngsters, ripping the clothes from backs, cutting flesh, and tumbling children down the street. In the ensuing days many of the children and their parents began to fight back, hurling bottles and rocks at their tormentors. As the violence escalated, white businessmen became concerned, and the city came to the bargaining table.

President Kennedy deployed Assistant Attorney General for Civil Rights Burke Marshall to negotiate a settlement. On May 10, 1963, white businessmen agreed to integrate downtown facilities and to hire black men and women. The following night the KKK bombed the A. G. Gaston Motel, where SCLC had its headquarters, and the house that belonged to King's brother, the Reverend A. D. King. Black citizens in turn burned cars and buildings and attacked the police. Only intervention by King and other leaders prevented a riot. White moderates delivered on the promises and the agreement stuck.

Birmingham was a major triumph. The summer of 1963 saw a massive upsurge in protests across the South with nearly eight hundred marches, demonstrations, and sit-ins. Ten civil rights protesters were killed and twenty thousand arrested as the white South sought to stem the tide. In one of the most tragic losses for the movement, white extremist Byron de la Beckwith gunned down Medgar Evers on June 12, 1963, in

Jackson, Mississippi. Evers had been the executive secretary of the NAACP's Mississippi organization and the center of a powerful movement in that city. His cold-blooded murder dramatized the depth of hatred among some white Southerners.

A Hard Victory

The sacrifices in Birmingham and the intensification of the movement throughout the South set the stage for Congress to pass legislation for a Second Reconstruction that would at last fulfill the promise of the first.

The March on Washington

The lingering image of Birmingham and the growing number of demonstrations throughout the South compelled action from President Kennedy. On June 11, 1963, he declared, "We face . . . a moral crisis as a country and a people. It cannot be met by repressive police action. It cannot be left to increased demonstrations in the streets. It cannot be quieted by token moves or talk. It is a time to act in the Congress, in your state and local legislative body, and above all, in all our daily lives. A great change is at hand, and our task, our obligation, is to make that revolution . . . peaceful and constructive for all." Kennedy proposed the strongest civil rights bill the country had yet seen, but despite the public's heightened awareness of discrimination, he could not muster sufficient support in Congress to counter the powerful southern bloc within his own party.

To demonstrate their support for Kennedy's civil rights legislation, SCLC, NAACP, CORE, SNCC, the National Urban League and their leaders resurrected the idea of organizing a march on Washington that A. Philip Randolph had first proposed in 1941. In 1962 Randolph and Bayard Rustin had proposed a march to protest black unemployment. Their call received a tepid response, but after Birmingham many of the major civil rights organizations reconsidered. Reflecting renewed hope, Randolph christened it a march for "Jobs and Freedom."

In August 1963, nearly 250,000 marchers gathered before the Lincoln Memorial to support the civil rights bill and the movement at large. They sang freedom songs and listened to speeches from civil rights leaders. Finally, late in the afternoon, Martin Luther King, Jr. spoke of his vision of the future:

> I say to you today, my friends, that in spite of the difficulties and frustrations of the moment I still have a dream. It is a dream deeply rooted in the American dream. I have a dream that one day this nation will rise up and live out the true meaning of its creed: "We hold these truths to be self-evident; that all men are created equal." I have a dream that one day on the red hills of Georgia the sons of former slaves and the sons of former slaveowners will be able to sit down together at the table of brotherhood. I have a dream that one day even the state of Mississippi, a desert state sweltering with the heat of injustice and oppression, will be transformed into an oasis of freedom and justice. I have a dream that my four children will one day live in a nation where they will not be judged by the color of their skin but by the content of their character. I have a dream today. I have a dream that one day the state of Alabama, whose governor's lips are presently dripping

with the words of interposition and nullification, will be transformed into a situation where little black boys and black girls will be able to join hands with little white boys and white girls and walk together as sisters and brothers. I have a dream today . . .

King's words did not still the angry opposition of some white Southerners. On September 15, 1963, only days after the march on Washington, white racists bombed the 16th St. Baptist Church in Birmingham and killed four little girls attending Sunday school. Chris McNair, the father of the youngest victim, pleaded for calm, "We must not let this change us into something different than who we are. We must be human." In a similar vein, Martin Luther King sadly intoned, "The innocent blood of these little girls may well serve as the redemptive force that will bring new light to this dark city. . . . Indeed, this tragic event may cause the white South to come to terms with its conscience." The event shook the nation, and combined with the reaction to the assassination of John F. Kennedy in November 1963, set the stage for real change.

The Civil Rights Act of 1964

Kennedy's successor Lyndon B. Johnson lobbied hard to secure passage of the landmark Civil Rights Act. Many in the civil rights movement feared that Johnson, a Southerner, would back his region's defiance. Nonetheless, only four days after taking the oath of office, Johnson told the nation that he planned to support the civil rights bill

At the height of his moral authority, Martin Luther King, Jr. (1929–1968) delivers the memorable "I Have a Dream" speech at the 1963 March on Washington. He conveyed a vision of a future America free of the evil of racism where all God's children would be judged by the content of their character, not the color of their skin. King received the Nobel Peace Prize in 1964, and since 1986 the nation honors him with a holiday in his name.

AP/Wide World Photos

as a memorial for the slain president. A master politician, Johnson pushed the bill through Congress despite a marathon filibuster by its opponents.

The Civil Rights Act of 1964 was the culmination of the civil rights movement to that time. The act banned discrimination in places of public accommodation, including restaurants, hotels, gas stations, and entertainment facilities, as well as schools, parks, playgrounds, libraries, and swimming pools. The desegregation of public accommodations irrevocably changed American society. Legally mandated racial separation was now dead. The act also banned discrimination by employers, of labor unions on the basis of race, color, religion, national origin, and sex in regard to hiring, promoting, dismissing, or making job referrals. The act had strong provisions for enforcement. Most important, it allowed government agencies to withhold federal money from any program permitting or practicing discrimination. This provision had particular import for the desegregation of schools and colleges across the country. The act also gave the U.S. attorney general the power to initiate proceedings against segregated facilities and schools on behalf of people who could not do so on their own. Finally it created the Equal Employment Opportunity Commission to monitor discrimination in employment.

Mississippi Freedom Summer

While Congress considered the Civil Rights Act, movement activists renewed their focus on voter registration in the deep South. In the fall of 1963, many CORE and SNCC workers saw segregation crumbling, but they knew that without the ballot, African Americans could never drive racist politicians from office, gain a fair hearing in court, reduce police and mob violence, or get equal services from state and local governments. CORE took responsibility for running registration campaigns in Louisiana, South Carolina, and Florida while SNCC took on the two most repressive states, Alabama and Mississippi. Mississippi was the symbolic center of American racism and white violence. By the summer of 1964 national attention had shifted from Alabama to Mississippi, the site of a massive project known as "Freedom Summer."

The voter registration campaign in Mississippi began in late 1963 when Robert "Bob" Moses mobilized the Council of Federated Organizations (COFO), which had been established in 1961 to aid imprisoned freedom riders. Moses convinced the members of COFO (CORE, SNCC, SCLC, and the NAACP) to sponsor a mock Freedom Election in Mississippi. On election day 80,000 disfranchised black people cast ballots for COFO candidates. Impressed with the turnout, Moses and other COFO members believed that a massive effort to register voters during the summer of 1964 might break the white monopoly on the ballot box.

COFO invited northern white students to participate in the Mississippi project. These students, about one thousand in all, were to be drawn primarily from the nation's most prestigious universities. This move contradicted the movement's emphasis on black empowerment, but COFO leaders calculated that the elite white students would attract media attention and pressure the federal government to provide protection.

Shortly after the project began, three volunteers, two white New Yorkers—twenty-four-year-old Michael Schwerner and twenty-one-year-old Andrew Goodman—and a black Mississippian, twenty-one-year-old James Chaney, disappeared. Cecil Price, deputy sheriff of Philadelphia, Mississippi, had arrested the three on a trumped-up speeding charge and then dumped them on a deserted road where three carloads of Klansmen waited. Schwerner and Goodman were shot to death. Chaney was beaten with chains and then shot.

These events were not publicly known until Klan informers, enticed by a $30,000 reward, led investigators to the spot where the young men had been buried. The disappearance of the three nonetheless focused national attention on white terrorism. During the summer, approximately thirty homes and thirty-seven churches were bombed, thirty-five civil rights workers were shot at, eighty people were beaten, six were murdered, and more than one thousand were arrested. In the face of this terror, many SNCC activists rejected Martin Luther King's commitment to nonviolence, the inclusion of white activists in the movement, and the wisdom of integration. Divisions over these issues increased tensions among the groups that made up the movement.

Despite the problems it encountered, the Freedom Summer organized dozens of Freedom Schools and community centers throughout Mississippi. Its efforts mobilized

Violence and the Civil Rights Movement

May 7, 1955	The Reverend George Lee killed for leading voter registration drive, Belzoni, MS
August 13, 1955	Lamar Smith murdered for organizing black voters, Brookhaven, MS
August 28, 1955	Emmett Louis Till murdered for speaking to white woman, Money, MS
October 22, 1955	John Earl Reese slain by nightriders opposed to black school improvements, Mayflower, TX
January 23, 1957	Willie Edwards, Jr. killed by Klan, Montgomery, AL
September 24, 1957	President Eisenhower orders federal troops to enforce school desegregation, Little Rock, AR
April 27, 1959	Mack Charles Parker taken from jail and lynched, Popularville, MS
May 14, 1961	Freedom Riders attacked in Alabama while testing compliance with bus desegration, Little Rock, AR
September 25, 1961	Voter registration worker Herbert Lee killed by a white legislator, Liberty, MS
April 1, 1962	Civil rights groups join forces to launch voter registration drive
April 9, 1962	Roman Ducksworth, Jr. taken from bus and killed by police, Taylorsville, MS
September 30, 1962	Riots erupt when James Meredith, a black student, enrolls at the University of Mississippi. Paul Guihard, European reporter, killed
April 23, 1963	William Lewis Moore slain during one-man march against segregation, Attalla, AL
May 3, 1963	Birmingham police attack marching children with dogs and fire hoses
June 12, 1963	Medgar Evers, civil rights leader, assassinated, Jackson, MS
September 15, 1963	Schoolgirls Addie Mae Collins, Denise McNair, Carole Robertson, and Cynthia Wesley die in the bombing of the 16th St. Baptist Church, Birmingham, AL
September 15, 1963	Virgin Lamar Ware killed during racist violence, Birmingham, AL
January 31, 1964	Louis Allen, witness to the murder of a civil rights worker, assassinated, Liberty, MS

Violence and the Civil Rights Movement (continued)

April 7, 1964	The Reverend Bruce Klunder killed protesting construction of segregated school, Cleveland, OH
May 2, 1964	Henry Hezekiah Dee amd Charles Eddie Moore killed by Klan, Meadville, MS
June 21, 1964	Civil rights workers James Chaney, Andrew Goodman, and Michael Schwerner abducted and slain by Klan, Philadelphia, MS
July 11, 1964	Lt. Col. Lemuel Penn killed by Klan while driving north, Colbert, GA
February 26, 1965	Jimmie Lee Jackson, civil rights marcher killed by state trooper, Marion, AL
March 11, 1965	Selma to Montgomery march volunteer, the Reverend James Reeb, beaten to death, Selma, AL
March 25, 1965	Viola Gregg Liuzzo killed by Klan while transporting marchers, Selma Highway, AL
June 2, 1965	Oneal Moore, black deputy, killed by nightriders, Varndo, LA
July 18, 1965	Willie Wallace Brewster killed by nightriders, Anniston, AL
August 20, 1965	Jonathan Daniels, seminary student, killed by deputy, Hayneville, AL
January 3, 1966	Samuel Younge Jr., student civil rights activist, killed in dispute over whites-only restroom, Tuskegee, AL
January 10, 1966	Vernon Dahmer, black community leader, killed in Klan bombing, Hattiesburg, MS
June 10, 1966	Ben Chester White killed by Klan, Natchez, MS
July 30, 1966	Clarence Triggs slain by nightriders, Bogalusa, LA
February 2, 1967	Wharlest Jackson, civil rights leader, killed when police fired on protesters, Jackson, MS
February 8, 1968	Students Samuel Hammond Jr., Delano Middleton, and Henry Smith killed when highway patrolmen fire on protestors, Orangeburg, SC
April 4, 1968	Dr. Martin Luther King, Jr. assassinated, Memphis, TN

the state's black people to an extent not seen since the first Reconstruction. Many communities began to develop the rudiments of a political movement, one that would grow in coming years.

The Mississippi Freedom Democratic Party

Freedom Summer intersected with national politics at the Democratic party's national convention in August 1964 in Atlantic City, New Jersey. White Mississippians routinely excluded African Americans from the political process, and Robert Moses encouraged COFO to set up the Mississippi Freedom Democratic Party (MFDP) to challenge the state's regular Democratic delegation at the convention. Under the leadership of veteran activists Fannie Lou Hamer, Victoria Gray, Annie Divine, and Aaron Henry, the MFDP held its first state convention on August 6. Approximately 80,000 citizens put their names on the rolls. The convention elected sixty-four delegates who traveled to the national convention to present their credentials.

The MFDP challenge caused considerable difficulty for the Democratic party. Many liberals wanted to seat the civil rights delegation, but President Lyndon Johnson, who was running for reelection, did not want to alienate white Southerners, fearing that they would vote for Barry Goldwater, his Republican opponent. Liberal Democratic senator Hubert H. Humphrey from Minnesota worked out a compromise calling for Mississippi regulars to be seated if they swore loyalty to the national party and agreed to cast their forty-four votes accordingly. The compromise also provided for the creation of two "at large" seats to be filled by MFDP members, Aaron Henry and Ed King. The rest of the Freedom Democrats could attend the convention as nonvoting guests.

Martin Luther King, Jr., Bayard Rustin, and other black leaders counseled acceptance of this compromise. Johnson and the Democrats, they argued, had achieved much of the legislative program favored by the movement, and if the party were returned to power they could do much more. But most of the MFDP delegation rejected the compromise. Many members of SNCC, bitter and angry, turned their backs on cooperation with white people of any political persuasion.

Selma and the Voting Rights Act of 1965

The Civil Rights Act of 1964 contained provisions for helping black voters to register, but white resistance in the deep South had rendered them ineffective. In Alabama, for example, at least 77 percent of black citizens were unable to vote. Their cause was taken up by Amelia P. Boynton, owner of an employment and insurance agency in Selma, along with her husband and a high school teacher, the Reverend Frederick Reese, who also led the Dallas County Voters League. These three, with others, fought for black enfranchisement and an end to discriminatory treatment. Their struggle would help to pass the Voting Rights Act of 1965, which ended the exclusion of African Americans from southern politics.

Selma's sheriff James G. Clark worked to block voter registration activity. By 1964 fewer than four hundred of the fifteen thousand eligible African Americans had registered to vote in Dallas County. President Johnson refused to deploy federal marshals to the county to protect voter registration workers. Seeking reinforcements, the workers sent a call to Martin Luther King, Jr. and the SCLC. King came and was arrested. In February 1965, during a night march in neighboring Perry County, twenty-six-year-old Jimmie Lee Jackson was shot in the stomach as he tried to shield his mother from a beating by a state trooper. His death and the thrashing of several reporters attracted the national media.

The SCLC announced plans for a mass march from Selma to Montgomery, the state capital, to begin on Sunday, March 7, 1965. At the forefront of six hundred protesters were King; one of his aides, Hosea Williams; and the chairman of SNCC, John Lewis. As the marchers approached the Edmund Pettus Bridge, state troopers and Sheriff Clark's police, teargassed and beat the retreating marchers while their horses trampled the fallen. Captured in graphic detail by television cameras, this battle became known as "Bloody Sunday." Seizing the moment, King and the activists rescheduled a pilgrimage for March 9. But King soon found himself in a dilemma. A federal judge had issued an injunction against the march, and President Johnson and other key officials urged King not to go through with it. King was reluctant to violate a federal injunction, and he knew that he needed Johnson's support to win strong voting rights legislation. But the people of Selma and the hundreds of young SNCC workers would probably march even if King did not.

When the day of the march came, 1,500 protesters marched to the bridge singing freedom songs. To their surprise, King crossed the Pettus Bridge, prayed briefly, and turned around. He had made a face-saving compromise with the federal authorities. SNCC workers felt betrayed, and King's leadership suffered. That evening a white Unitarian minister from Boston, James Reeb, was clubbed to death by local white people. His martyrdom created a national outcry and prompted Johnson to act. On March 15, the president in a televised address to Congress, announced that he would submit voter registration legislation. He electrified civil rights activists when he invoked the movement's slogan to declare, in his Texas drawl, "We shall overcome."

The protests at Selma and the massive white resistance spurred Congress to pass the Voting Rights Act of 1965, which President Johnson signed on August 6. The act outlawed educational requirements for voting in states or counties where less than half the voting age population had been registered on November 1, 1964, or had voted in the 1964 presidential election. It also empowered the attorney general to have the Civil Rights Commission assign federal registrars to enroll voters. The attorney general, Nicholas Katzenbach, immediately deployed federal registrars in nine southern counties. Within months, they had registered approximately 80,000 new voters. In Mississippi, black registrants soared from 28,500 in 1964 to 251,000 in 1968. The era when white supremacy lay at the core of southern politics was over.

Conclusion

The success of the civil rights movement depended on many factors. The federal government intervened at crucial moments to enact civil rights legislation, issue judgments on behalf of the civil rights protesters, and protect the rule of law. Black leaders deliberately provoked confrontations that would ensure intervention by the federal government and garner media coverage. For more than a decade, the freedom fighters of the civil rights movement stormed the legal barricades of segregation. The uncompromising struggle of African Americans, their organizations, and their white allies pressured federal officials in the legislative, executive, and judicial branches of government to enact major civil rights legislation, issue executive orders, and deliver judicial decisions that dismantled segregation in the South.

The victories of this era were far reaching, but as they were achieved, new issues arose that would fracture the movement. The civil rights movement had largely been focused on the South. Black Northerners already had many of the rights granted by the federal legislation of the era; nonetheless, they still suffered from discrimination. Addressing their problems required different techniques and new ways of thinking that would emerge over the coming decade.

TIMELINE

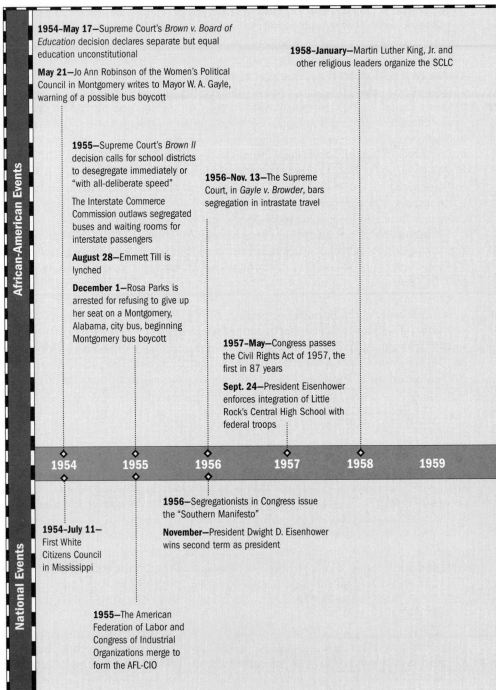

1954–May 17—Supreme Court's *Brown v. Board of Education* decision declares separate but equal education unconstitutional

May 21—Jo Ann Robinson of the Women's Political Council in Montgomery writes to Mayor W. A. Gayle, warning of a possible bus boycott

1958–January—Martin Luther King, Jr. and other religious leaders organize the SCLC

African-American Events

1955—Supreme Court's *Brown II* decision calls for school districts to desegregate immediately or "with all-deliberate speed"

The Interstate Commerce Commission outlaws segregated buses and waiting rooms for interstate passengers

August 28—Emmett Till is lynched

December 1—Rosa Parks is arrested for refusing to give up her seat on a Montgomery, Alabama, city bus, beginning Montgomery bus boycott

1956–Nov. 13—The Supreme Court, in *Gayle v. Browder*, bars segregation in intrastate travel

1957–May—Congress passes the Civil Rights Act of 1957, the first in 87 years

Sept. 24—President Eisenhower enforces integration of Little Rock's Central High School with federal troops

1954   **1955**   **1956**   **1957**   **1958**   **1959**

1956—Segregationists in Congress issue the "Southern Manifesto"

November—President Dwight D. Eisenhower wins second term as president

1954–July 11—First White Citizens Council in Mississippi

National Events

1955—The American Federation of Labor and Congress of Industrial Organizations merge to form the AFL-CIO

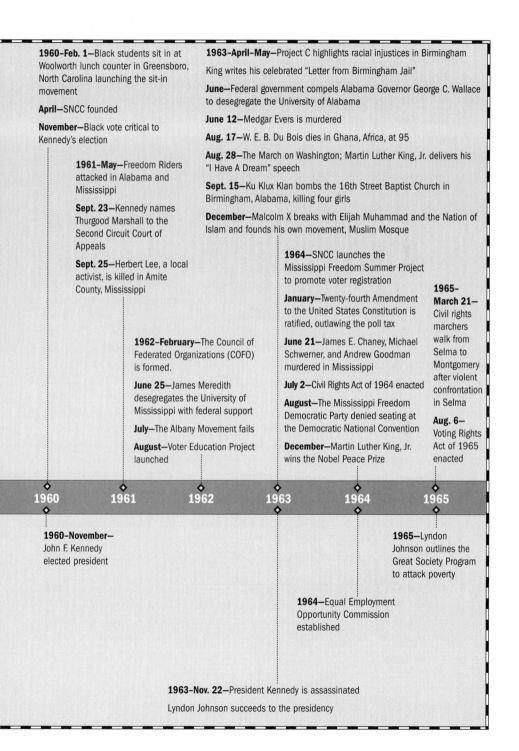

1960-Feb. 1—Black students sit in at Woolworth lunch counter in Greensboro, North Carolina launching the sit-in movement

April—SNCC founded

November—Black vote critical to Kennedy's election

1961-May—Freedom Riders attacked in Alabama and Mississippi

Sept. 23—Kennedy names Thurgood Marshall to the Second Circuit Court of Appeals

Sept. 25—Herbert Lee, a local activist, is killed in Amite County, Mississippi

1962-February—The Council of Federated Organizations (COFO) is formed.

June 25—James Meredith desegregates the University of Mississippi with federal support

July—The Albany Movement fails

August—Voter Education Project launched

1963-April–May—Project C highlights racial injustices in Birmingham

King writes his celebrated "Letter from Birmingham Jail"

June—Federal government compels Alabama Governor George C. Wallace to desegregate the University of Alabama

June 12—Medgar Evers is murdered

Aug. 17—W. E. B. Du Bois dies in Ghana, Africa, at 95

Aug. 28—The March on Washington; Martin Luther King, Jr. delivers his "I Have A Dream" speech

Sept. 15—Ku Klux Klan bombs the 16th Street Baptist Church in Birmingham, Alabama, killing four girls

December—Malcolm X breaks with Elijah Muhammad and the Nation of Islam and founds his own movement, Muslim Mosque

1964—SNCC launches the Mississippi Freedom Summer Project to promote voter registration

January—Twenty-fourth Amendment to the United States Constitution is ratified, outlawing the poll tax

June 21—James E. Chaney, Michael Schwerner, and Andrew Goodman murdered in Mississippi

July 2—Civil Rights Act of 1964 enacted

August—The Mississippi Freedom Democratic Party denied seating at the Democratic National Convention

December—Martin Luther King, Jr. wins the Nobel Peace Prize

1965-March 21—Civil rights marchers walk from Selma to Montgomery after violent confrontation in Selma

Aug. 6—Voting Rights Act of 1965 enacted

1960   1961   1962   1963   1964   1965

1960-November—John F. Kennedy elected president

1965—Lyndon Johnson outlines the Great Society Program to attack poverty

1964—Equal Employment Opportunity Commission established

1963-Nov. 22—President Kennedy is assassinated

Lyndon Johnson succeeds to the presidency

Review Questions

1. What role did "ordinary" or local people play in the civil rights movement? What did children contribute to the overall struggle for social change

2. What key issues and events provoked intervention by the federal government into the civil rights movement? How did legislation dismantle legalized segregation?

3. What were the ideologies, objectives, and tactics of the major civil rights organizations and their leaders?

4. What were the human costs of the civil rights movement?

5. What were the major successes and failures of the freedom movement? What were some of the intergenerational tensions that plagued the movement? In what way did the movement transform American politics and society?

Recommended Reading

Taylor Branch. *Parting the Waters: America in the King Years, 1954–63.* New York: Simon & Schuster, 1988. Richly researched, lively study that places King at the center of American politics during a critically transformative decade.

Clayborne Carson. *In Struggle: SNCC and the Black Awakening of the 1960s.* Cambridge, MA: Harvard University Press, 1981. One of the best historical studies of SNCC and the contributions students made to galvanize the civil rights movement.

Vickie Crawford, Jacqueline Rouse, and Barbara Woods, eds. *Women in the Civil Rights Movement: Trailblazers and Torchbearers.* Brooklyn, NY: Carlson Publishing, 1990. An anthology of essays presented at a symposium. The meeting was designed to draw attention to the women whose contributions to the freedom struggle of the 1950s and 1960s are often overlooked or neglected.

Henry Hampton and Steve Fayer, eds. *The Voices of Freedom: An Oral History of the Civil Rights Movement from the 1950s through the 1980s.* New York: Bantam Books, 1990. A remarkable and indispensable oral history of all the participants in the civil rights movement, from the least well known to the internationally celebrated.

Steven F. Lawson. *Running for Freedom: Civil Rights and Black Politics in America since 1941.* Philadelphia: Temple University Press, 1991. A succinct analysis of the politics, legislative measures, and individuals that figured in the successes and failures of the civil rights movement.

Aldon D. Morris. *The Origins of the Modern Civil Rights Movement: Black Communities Organizing for Change.* New York: Free Press; London: Collier Macmillan, 1984. An important and insightful analysis of the mobilization and organizing strategies pursued by diverse communities for social change that paved the way for the modern civil rights movement.

→ Chapter 22 ←

The Struggle Continues, 1965–1980

The Fading Dream of Racial Integration: White Backlash and Black Nationalism

Even though President Johnson easily defeated Republican Barry Goldwater, the 1964 election was hardly a mandate for civil rights. When, in 1966, Johnson asked Congress for legislation to ban discrimination in housing, his bill died in the Senate. In elections that year, white opposition to civil rights helped elect Republicans, including former movie actor Ronald Reagan as governor of California. Meanwhile, Alabama governor George Wallace, an outspoken opponent of racial integration and civil rights legislation, was emerging as a national political figure.

With many white Americans reluctant to support the goals of the civil rights movement, many black Americans began searching for new approaches to their problems. The reign of terror experienced by COFO (Council of Federated Organizations) workers in Mississippi had undermined the commitment to integration and nonviolence of the civil rights movement and would help radicalize a new, younger generation of activists. Men like Floyd McKissick of the Congress of Racial Equality (CORE) and Stokely Carmichael of the Student Nonviolent Coordinating Committee (SNCC) rejected King's moderation, nonviolence, and universalism. In 1965, after the Selma-to-Montgomery march, Carmichael helped found the Lowndes County (Mississippi) Freedom Organization (LCFO). It became the first political organization in the civil rights movement to adopt the symbol of the black panther.

Black residents of northern and western cities also lost patience with the slow pace of change. Many young black churchmen castigated mainstream white religious groups for their complicity with racism, demanded reparations, and agitated for more power within the National Council of Churches. Out of this tension emerged a Black Theology that critiques racism within white religious groups. It was followed by a Black Feminist Theology that was equally critical of sexism within the black church. Leaders in the development of Black Theology and the expression of a black nationalist Christianity were theologians James H. Cone and the Reverend Albert Cleage Jr. of Detroit who was pastor of the Shrine of the Black Madonna. Black Christian nationalism argued for black symbols of religious faith and asserted the importance of conjoining religion with political activism and social change. Young African Americans, along with diverse black religious leaders, dismayed by the great political and economic disparities between themselves and white Americans, became catalysts for an increasingly radical turn in the civil rights movement.

Malcolm X

After 1965, the year in which he died, no one had more influence on young black activists and the residents of America's ghettoized inner cities than Malcolm X. The son of a Baptist preacher, he was born Malcolm Little in Omaha, Nebraska, and grew up in Lansing, Michigan. His family's home was burned by Klan terrorists, and his father was murdered two years later. His mother was committed to a mental institution, and welfare agencies separated the children. Malcolm quit school after the eighth grade and moved to Boston to live with his sister. There he became involved in the street life of gambling, drugs, and burglary. He was sentenced to a ten-year prison term in 1942. During the six and a half years he spent in prison, he embraced the teachings of Elijah Muhammad of the Nation of Islam and renounced what he considered his "slave name" to become Malcolm X. In 1954 he became minister of Harlem's Temple Number 7. Articulate and charismatic, Malcolm did not believe in nonviolence or advocate integration. In *The Autobiography of Malcolm X*, published in 1965 by the writer Alex Haley of *Roots* fame, Malcolm declared:

> Few white people realize that many black people today dislike and avoid spending any more time than they must around white people. This "integration" image, as it is popularly interpreted, has millions of vain, self-exalted white people convinced that black people want to sleep in bed with them—and that's a lie! Oh you can't tell the average white man that the Negro man's prime desire isn't to have a white woman—another lie! Like a black brother recently observed to me, "Look, you ever smell one of them wet?"

Malcolm's dismissal of the goal of racial integration and King's message of redemption through brotherly love resonated with many younger civil rights workers disillusioned by white violence. "The day of nonviolent resistance is over," Malcolm insisted. And in 1964, he declared, "Revolutions are never based upon love-your-enemy, and pray-for-those-who-despitefully-use-you. And revolutions are never waged by singing 'We Shall Overcome.' Revolutions are based on bloodshed."

Malcolm X's popularity created tensions between himself and the leadership of the Nation of Islam. He grew disillusioned with Elijah Muhammad's aversion to political activism, and Elijah Muhammad grew jealous of Malcolm's success. When Malcolm described the Kennedy assassination as a case of "the chickens coming home to roost" (meaning Kennedy was a victim of the same kind of violence that afflicted black people), Elijah Muhammad suspended him. In 1964, Malcolm broke with the Nation of Islam and founded his own organization, the Muslim Mosque, Inc. That same year he went on a pilgrimage to Mecca that profoundly influenced him. He changed his name to El-Hajj Malik El-Shabazz, founded the Organization for Afro-American Unity (after the Organization of African Unity), repudiated the Nation of Islam doctrine that all white people are evil, and began lecturing on the connection between the civil rights struggle in the South and the struggle against colonialism in Africa. On February 14,

1965, assassins associated with the Nation of Islam killed Malcolm X as he addressed an audience in Harlem.

Malcolm's militant advocacy of self-defense, of "overturning systems" that deprive African Americans of basic human rights, helped to radicalize other black leaders of the civil rights movement.

Stokely Carmichael
and Black Power

In 1966 Stokely Carmichael, a native of Trinidad who had been raised in New York City and educated at Howard University, became chairman of SNCC. He was determined to move SNCC toward black nationalism and dismissed its few white staffers.

About this time, James Meredith began a one-man "march against fear" from Tennessee to Jackson, Mississippi, to encourage black Southerners to register and vote. On this march, he was shot and wounded by white gunmen. In June 1966, after this incident, SNCC and Carmichael joined with other organizations to complete the march. It was at this time that Carmichael popularized the slogan "Black Power" that was to become SNCC's rallying cry. "We been saying freedom for six years and we ain't got nothin'. What we gonna start saying is Black Power." Carmichael explained what black power meant to black Southerners:

> In Lowndes County [Mississippi], for example, black power will mean that if a Negro is elected sheriff, he can end police brutality. If a black man is elected tax assessor, he can collect and channel funds for the building of better roads and schools serving black people—thus advancing the move from political power into the economic arena. . . . Politically, black power means what it has always meant to SNCC: the coming-together of black people to elect representatives and to force those representatives to speak to their needs. It does not mean merely putting black faces into office.

Critics accused advocates of black power of reverse racism, but Carmichael argued that they were promoting racial pride and the development of independent power. However, there was a more disruptive side to the black freedom movement. Its organizations suffered internal problems concerning gender roles, relations between white women and black men, and separatism versus integration. In 1968, CORE followed SNCC's example and ejected its white members with a resulting loss of financial resources. Both organizations began to decline, and by the end of the 1960s, SNCC had virtually disappeared.

Martin Luther King had mixed feelings about the ideology of black power. He welcomed its promotion of black political and economic strength, psychological assertiveness, and cultural pride. But when black power degenerated into a mantra of taunts against white people, King denounced it as "a nihilistic philosophy born out of the conviction that the Negro can't win." King also objected to black power's "implicit and often explicit belief in black separatism."

In May 1967 Hubert G. Brown followed Carmichael as head of SNCC. "H. Rap" Brown, as he became known, heightened the militancy of the black power movement's rhetoric, calling white people "honkies" and the police "pigs." "Violence," he said, was "as American as apple pie." In August 1967 Brown told enthusiastic listeners in the black neighborhood of Cambridge, Maryland, that "black folks built America, and if America don't come around, we're going to burn America down." When a few hours later, a fire erupted in the heart of the city's black community, white firemen refused to fight it. Police charged Brown with inciting a riot and committing arson, but he posted bail and fled. Later he was arrested on other charges.

The National Council of Churches

Black and white leaders of mainstream religious organizations were transformed by black power. In 1946, the Federal Council of Churches, composed of Protestants, Catholics, and Jews, pledged to work for "a non-segregated church and a non-segregated society." Between 1963 and 1965, the National Council of Churches (NCC), contributed financial and moral support to the Civil Rights Movement. In 1963 the NCC founded its Commission on Religion and Race to support the black freedom movement. Although a white controlled and managed operation, three of the eight staff members of the commission were African American: Anna Hedgeman, J. Oscar Lee, and James Breeden. The NCC supported events such as the March on Washington and lobbied for passage of the Civil Rights Act of 1964 and the Voting Rights Act of 1965.

In 1965, the NCC appointed Benjamin Payton as director of the Commission on Religion and Race. Payton, a native of Orangeburg, South Carolina had been educated at Harvard Divinity School and had earned a Ph.D. at Yale. He had taught at Howard University and was a member of the National Baptist Convention, U.S.A., the largest African-American denomination. Under his stewardship the Commission on Religion and Race was incorporated into the Division of Christian Life and Mission, and later became part of the NCC's Department of Social Justice that included five other special task forces. Payton viewed the economic development of black people as the critical prerequisite to improving national racial relations. In 1966 he formed the National Commission of Black Churchmen (NCBC), which became a key mainstream ecumenical church group advocating black power concepts and strategies throughout the rest of the 1960s.

The black power movement spurred the creation of black caucuses within the predominantly white churches. By the early 1970s there were nine such caucuses, including the Black Methodists for Church Renewal, the Black Presbyterians United, and the Episcopal Union of Black Clergy and Laity. Black Roman Catholics insisted that their Church demonstrate more respect for African-American patterns of worship. Black and other minority groups wanted to share real power within the white-dominated churches. Thus, the stage was set for James Forman's Black Manifesto.

In April 1969, James Forman, former Chicago school teacher renowned for his work with SNCC, addressed the National Black Economic Development Conference in Detroit, sponsored by the Interreligious Foundation for Community Organizations (which was supported by predominantly white churches). Forman demanded that white churches pay $500 million in reparations for their participation in and benefit from slavery and racial exploitation. His secular critique of American religion precipitated the withdrawal of mainstream white religious groups from active participation in the civil rights movement. These white groups were offended by Forman's black power rhetoric and revolutionary Marxist ideology. Relations between Blacks and Jews also deteriorated as countercharges circulated of "Jewish racism" and "Black anti-Semitism."

The Black Panther Party

The most institutionalized expression of the new black militancy was the Black Panther Party for Self-Defense created by Huey P. Newton and Bobby Seale in Oakland, California, in October 1966. The Black Panthers combined black nationalist ideology with Marxist-Leninist doctrines. Working with white radicals, they hoped to fashion the party into a revolutionary vanguard dedicated to overthrowing capitalist society and ending police brutality. Eldridge Cleaver, the Panther's minister of education, helped formulate the party's ideology. Cleaver was a convicted rapist who had spent most of his youth in prison, where he became a follower of Malcolm X and began writing the autobiographical essays that would be published as *Soul on Ice* in 1968, the year the party dropped "Self-Defense" from its name. Black people, Cleaver maintained, were victims of colonization, not just disfranchised American citizens. Thus, integrationism could not meet their needs. They needed, instead, like other colonized peoples, to be liberated. "To achieve these ends," he wrote, "we believe that political and military machinery that does not exist now and has never existed must be created. We need functional machinery that is able to deal with these two interrelated sets of political dynamics which, strictly speaking, make up the total political situation on the North American continent." Cleaver and other top Panther leaders were arrested after a shoot-out with Oakland police in 1968. Cleaver escaped and fled into exile. While abroad, he abandoned his radicalism, and became involved with the Republican party and fundamentalist Christianity after his return to the United States in 1975.

Police Repression and the FBI's COINTELPRO

The Panthers alarmed white Americans when they took up arms for self-defense and patrolled their neighborhoods to monitor the police. A series of bloody confrontations and shoot-outs in Oakland distracted attention from the Panthers' community service projects. In Oakland and Chicago, the Panthers arranged free breakfast and health care programs, worked to instill racial pride, lectured and wrote about black history, and launched drug education programs. These activities were captured in the slogan, "Power to the People."

FBI director J. Edgar Hoover was determined to destroy all nationalist groups and their leaders. The FBI cooperated with local law enforcement officials to discredit leaders and to undermine and weaken the Black Panther party. In August 1967 Hoover distributed an explanatory memorandum that detailed the FBI's Counterintelligence Program directed toward black nationalist groups. The purpose, according to the memo, of this new "counterintelligence (COINTELPRO) endeavor is to expose, disrupt, misdirect, discredit, or otherwise neutralize the activities of black nationalist, hate-type organizations and groupings, their leadership, spokesmen, membership, and supporters, and to counter their propensity for violence and civil disorder." Undercover agents infiltrated the Panthers and provoked violence and criminal acts. Not that the Panthers were saints. Huey P. Newton, for example, had a long criminal record. He was imprisoned for murder in 1968 but was acquitted and released only to be charged with murder and assault again in 1974. After fleeing to Cuba, he returned in 1977 and was again acquitted. He was eventually killed at age forty-two in a drug dispute in Oakland in 1989. Still, the FBI and its counterintelligence agents may have provoked much of the violence that became associated with the Black Panther party. Certainly, COINTELPRO helped to shape negative public opinion of black nationalist ideology.

Police killed an estimated twenty-eight Panthers and imprisoned 750 others. In perhaps the most egregious incident, police in Chicago killed Fred Hampton and Mark Clark in their sleep in a predawn raid on the Illinois Black Panther Headquarters on December 4, 1969. The police fired hundreds of rounds; only two shots were fired from within the apartment.

Prisoners' Rights

Despite such repression, black militancy survived in many forms, including the prisoners' rights movement. One of the Black Panthers' social programs had focused on the conditions of black prisoners. By 1970, more than half the inmates in United States prisons were African American. Black activists argued that many African Americans were in jail for political reasons and suffered from unfair sentences and deplorable conditions.

Angela Davis, an assistant professor of philosophy at the University of California at Los Angeles, became the first black woman to be listed on the FBI's Ten Most Wanted list because of her involvement in prisoners' rights. During the late 1960s, she had worked on behalf of the Soledad Brothers, three prisoners—George Jackson, John Clutchette, and Fleeta Drumgo—accused of murdering a white guard at Soledad Prison. On August 7, 1970, George Jackson's younger brother, seventeen-year-old Jonathan Jackson, staged a one-man raid on the San Rafael courthouse in Marin County, California, to try to seize hostages to trade for the Soledad Brothers. In the ensuing shoot-out, Jonathan Jackson, two prisoners, and a judge were killed. Angela Davis, accused of supplying the weapons for the raid, was charged with murder, kidnaping, and conspiracy. After a long ordeal and a national "Free Angela" campaign, a jury acquitted Davis. On August 21, 1971, George Jackson was shot and killed at San Quentin Prison by guards who claimed he was trying to escape.

Across the country, prisoners at Attica, a maximum security prison in northern New York State, began a fast in memory of George Jackson that erupted into a full-scale rebellion. On September 9, 1971, 1,200 inmates seized control of half of Attica and took hostages. Four days later, state police and prison guards suppressed the uprising. Tom Wicker, a columnist for *The New York Times,* filed this report:

> A task force consisting of 211 state troopers and corrections officers retook Attica using tear gas, rifles, and shotguns. After the shooting was over, ten hostages and twenty-nine inmates lay dead or dying. At least 450 rounds of ammunition had been discharged. Four hostages and eighty-five inmates suffered gunshot wounds that they survived. After initial

reports that several hostages had died at the hands of knife-wielding inmates, patholo-gists' reports revealed that hostages and inmates all died from gunshot wounds. No guns were found in the possession of inmates.

The Inner-City Rebellions

The militant nationalism of Malcolm X and Stokely Carmichael and the radicalism of the Panthers reflected growing anger in America's impoverished inner cities. In 1965, 29.1 percent of black households, compared with only 7.8 percent of white households, lived below the poverty line. Almost 50 percent of nonwhite families lived in substandard housing compared with 18 percent of white families. Despite a drop in the number of Americans living in poverty from 38.0 million in 1959 to 32.7 million in 1965, the percentage of poor black people increased from 27.5 percent to 31 percent. In 1965 the black unemployment rate was 8.5 percent, almost twice the white unemployment rate of 4.3. For black teenagers the unemployment rate was 23 percent compared with 10.8 percent for white teenagers. As psychologist Kenneth Clark declared in 1967, "The masses of Negroes are now starkly aware of the fact that recent civil rights victories benefitted a very small percentage of middle-class Negroes while their predicament remained the same or worsened."

The passage of civil rights legislation did not resolve these disparities or diminish inner-city alienation. As jobs moved increasingly to suburbs to which inner-city resi-dents could neither travel nor relocate, inner-city neighborhoods sank deeper into poverty. School dropout rates reached epidemic proportions, crime and drug use in-creased, and fragile family structures weakened. It was these conditions that led mili-tants to liken their neighborhoods to exploited colonies kept in poverty by repressive white institutions. Few white Americans understood the depths of the black despair that flared into violence each summer between 1965 and 1969, beginning with the Watts rebellion of 1965.

Watts

In the summer of 1965, a section of Los Angeles called Watts exploded. Watts was 98 percent black. Its residents suffered from overcrowding, unemployment, inaccessible health care facilities, inadequate public transportation, and crime and drug addiction. Almost 30 percent of the black male population was unemployed. The poverty, com-bined with anger at the often brutal behavior of the Los Angeles police force, proved to be an incendiary combination. On August 11, 1965, a policeman pulled over a young black man for drunk driving. The man was arrested but not before a crowd gathered. When reinforcements arrived, the crowd pelted them with debris. Within hours, Watts was in a total riot.

Governor Pat Brown, a Democrat, sent in the National Guard to restore order, but by the sixth day of the conflagration, Watts had been reduced to rubble and ashes. Thirty-four people had been killed; more than 900 injured; and 4,000 arrested. Total property damage was more than $35 million, equivalent to hundreds of millions of dollars today. The Watts rebellion was the beginning of four summers of uprisings that

The first major urban uprising of the 1960s was in the Watts neighborhood of East Los Angeles in August 1965. It lasted nearly a week and left thirty-four people dead.
AP/Wide World Photos

would engulf cities in the North and Midwest. There were riots in the summer of 1966, but even worse ones erupted in Newark and Detroit in 1967.

Newark, New Jersey

By 1967 white flight to the suburbs had made Newark a majority black city, but one that operated under white political control. The city lacked the means to meet its inhabitants' social needs. The school system deteriorated as unemployment increased. In 1967, Newark had the highest unemployment rate among black men in the nation. As tensions flared and police brutality escalated, white officials ignored black people's complaints. On July 12, after a black cab driver in police custody was beaten, protesters gathered at a police station. When a firebomb hit the wall of the station house, the police charged, clubbing the crowd. This triggered one of the most destructive civic rebellions of the period. During four days of rioting, the police and National Guard killed twenty-five black people—most of them innocent bystanders, including two children; a white policeman and fireman were also killed. Looting and arson caused millions of dollars in property damage.

Detroit

When Detroit erupted a few days after Newark, it caught everyone by surprise except the residents of its inner-city neighborhoods. On the surface Detroit seemed like a model of prosperity and interracial accord. Some of the country's most dynamic popular music flowed from Detroit's Motown recording company. Owned by the astute Berry Gordy, Motown was a classic up-by-the-bootstraps success story that had produced such stars as Diana Ross and Mary Wells. "Before Motown," said Wells, "there were three careers available to a black girl in Detroit—babies, the factories or daywork."

But success like Gordy's was rare among the black migrants and their children, who poured into Detroit during and after World War II. The parents held their disappointment in check, but the children, particularly young men aged between seventeen and thirty-five, sought an outlet for their anger and alienation. Some joined the Nation of Islam; others embraced the Panthers or formed even more radical organizations calling for an all-black nation.

On the night of Saturday, July 23, a police raid on an after-hours drinking establishment in the center of the black community triggered five days of rioting. Congressman John Conyers, the black U.S. representative for Michigan's First District, knew many of the people in the area and tried to get them to disperse, but they refused. Later Conyers said, "People were letting feelings out that had never been let out before, that had been bottled up. It really wasn't that they were that mad about an after-hours place being raided and some people being beat up as a result of the closing down of that place. It was the whole desperate situation of being black in Detroit."

Of the fifty-nine urban rebellions that occurred in 1967, Detroit's was the deadliest. Forty-three black people died, most of them shot by members of the National Guard, which had been sent in by Republican governor George Romney. But even the National Guard, combined with 200 state police and 600 Detroit police, could not restore order. A reluctant President Johnson had to order 4,700 troops of the elite 82nd and 101st Airborne units to Detroit.

The Kerner Commission

On July 29, 1967, in the wake of the Newark and Detroit riots, Johnson established the National Advisory Commission on Civil Disorders, headed by Illinois governor Otto Kerner. The commission included two black members, Republican senator Edward W. Brooke of Massachusetts (elected in 1966 the first black senator since Reconstruction) and Roy Wilkins, executive director of the NAACP. In a speech explaining why he had set up the commission, Johnson declared:

> The only genuine, long-range solution for what has happened lies in an attack—mounted at every level—upon the conditions that breed despair and violence. All of us know what those conditions are: ignorance, discrimination, slums, poverty, disease, not enough jobs. We should attack these conditions—not because we are frightened by conflict, but because we are fired by conscience. We should attack them because there is simply no other way to achieve a decent and orderly society in America.

In its final report, released in 1968, the Kerner Commission indicted white racism as the underlying cause of the riots and warned that America was "moving towards two societies, one white, one black—separate and unequal." The commission emphasized that "Negroes firmly believe that police brutality and harassment occur repeatedly in Negro neighborhoods. This belief is unquestionably one of the major reasons for intense Negro resentment against the police." The report called for massive government aid to the cities, including funds for public housing, better and more integrated schools, two million new jobs, and funding for a "national system of income supplementation." None of its major proposals was enacted.

The Great Society and Vietnam

The urban riots of the late 1960s undercut support for the broadest attack the federal government had yet waged on the problems of poor Americans, what President Johnson called "the Great Society." Much of the legislation Johnson pushed through Congress in 1964 and 1965—the Medicare program, for example, which provided medical care for the elderly and disabled under the Social Security system, or federal aid to education remained popular. But the most ambitious Great Society programs—what Johnson called "an unconditional war on poverty"—were more controversial.

Lyndon Johnson was a savvy politician. He had to be to rise from Stonewall, Texas, to the pinnacle of power. But he never lost sympathy for the disadvantaged and the powerless. As a congressman, he had been an enthusiastic New Dealer. Elected to the Senate in 1948, he had refused to sign the Southern Manifesto (see Chapter 21) and, as majority leader, had overcome southern filibusters to win passage of the 1957 and 1960 Civil Rights Acts. As president, he pushed the 1964 Civil Rights Act and the 1965 Voting Rights Act through Congress.

Johnson's concern for the disadvantaged showed itself in the cornerstone of his War on Poverty, the Economic Opportunity Act of 1964. This act created an Office of Economic Opportunity that administered several programs: Head Start to help disadvantaged preschoolers, Upward Bound to prepare impoverished teenagers for college, and Volunteers in Service to America (or VISTA) to serve as a domestic peace corps to help the poor and undereducated. These programs included community governing boards on which black men and women learned essential political skills.

The War on Poverty was the first government-sponsored effort to involve poor African Americans directly in designing and implementing programs to serve low-income communities. For example, in the New Careers program, residents of poor neighborhoods found jobs as community organizers, day care workers, and teacher aides. The program provided meaningful work, access to education, and critical material resources to poor people, so that they would become leaders in their own communities and run for office. The Community Action Programs (CAPs) insisted on "maximum feasible participation" by the poor. The Education Act increased federal funding to colleges and universities and provided low-interest student loans. This initiative put higher education within the reach of many more Americans than before.

Johnson faced considerable opposition to these programs. Local politicians were especially threatened by programs that empowered the disfranchised and dispossessed. Others, reflecting persistent white stereotypes of African Americans, complained that Johnson was rewarding lawlessness and laziness with handouts to the undeserving poor. The black residents of America's inner cities, for their part, had their expectations raised by the promises of the Great Society only to be frustrated by white backlash and minimal gains. They felt as betrayed by its programs as Johnson's white critics felt robbed by them.

No one will ever know whether Lyndon Johnson could have won his War on Poverty had he been given the resources to do so. Instead, the nation's resources increasingly went into his other war, the war in Vietnam. Statistics tell the story. Under Johnson appropriations for the War on Poverty came to only $10 billion. The war in Vietnam, in contrast, consumed $140 billion.

Johnson and Vietnam

Vietnam was a French colony from the 1860s until the Japanese seized it during World War II. After the war the Vietnamese communists, led by Ho Chi Minh, declared independence, but the French, with massive U.S. financial aid, fought to reassert their control from 1945 until they were finally defeated in 1954. When the French pulled out, the Americans arranged a temporary division of the country into a communist-controlled North Vietnam and a U.S.-supported South Vietnam (which, however, contained many communist guerrillas, called by the Americans "Viet Cong"). As guarantor of South Vietnam, the United States replaced the French as the target for those Vietnamese who were determined to end white colonial rule and unify their country.

For nine years, under Presidents Eisenhower and Kennedy, American aid and advisers propped up the corrupt South Vietnamese government in Saigon. By the time Johnson became president, only massive American involvement—the bombing of North Vietnam and an American Army in South Vietnam—could keep the South Vietnamese government in power. Johnson himself doubted the advisability of a wholesale American commitment and did not want a foreign war to take away resources from the Great Society programs about which he cared so much. "I knew from the start," Johnson claimed later,

> that I was bound to be crucified either way I moved. If I left the woman I really loved—the Great Society—in order to get involved with that bitch of a war on the other side of the world, then I would lose everything at home. All my programs. All my hopes to feed the hungry and shelter the homeless. All my dreams to provide education and medical care to the browns and the blacks and the lame and the poor. But if I left that war and let the Communists take over South Vietnam, then I would be seen as a coward and my nation would be seen as an appeaser and we would both find it impossible to accomplish anything for anybody anywhere on the entire globe.

And so, aware that he was entering a quagmire but determined to slug through it, Johnson intervened in Vietnam—gradually, massively, and inexorably.

After an alleged North Vietnamese attack on U.S. Navy destroyers in the Gulf of Tonkin in August 1964, Johnson pushed a resolution through Congress that gave him authority to escalate American involvement in Vietnam. In the spring of 1965 he authorized the bombing of North Vietnamese targets, but it failed to stop the North Vietnamese from reinforcing their forces in the south. American strength in South Vietnam then grew rapidly. By the end of 1966 there were more than 385,000 U.S. troops there, and by 1968 more than 500,000.

Black Americans
and the Vietnam War

In the mid-1960s, black Americans made up 10 percent of the armed forces. This percentage increased during America's involvement in the Vietnam War. Black overrepresentation among the U.S. troops in Vietnam resulted, in large part, from draft deferments for students who were predominantly white and middle class (such as

George W. Bush). Black men and women entered the military for many reasons, in addition to the draft. One was patriotism. Another was that the military offered educational opportunities that the children of the working black poor could not otherwise obtain. Still another was Project 100,000.

In 1966 the United States Defense Department launched Project 100,000 to reduce the high rejection rate of African Americans by the military. The project enabled recruitment officers to accept applicants whom they otherwise would have rejected because of criminal records or lack of skills. The project supplied more than 340,000 new recruits for Vietnam, 136,000 of whom were African Americans. These recruits saw more combat duty than regular recruits.

Vietnam Destroys
the Great Society

By the end of 1967, the nation seemed to be heading toward total racial polarization. In their rage against economic exploitation and police brutality, some inner-city black people had destroyed many of their own neighborhoods. Frightened white people, unable to comprehend black anger, rallied behind those who promised to restore order. The two men who had seemed the most effective advocates of racial reconciliation—Lyndon Johnson and Martin Luther King, Jr.—were both trying to regain the initiative. Each ended by alienating himself from the other.

By 1967 Johnson's situation was untenable. He had escalated the war in Vietnam without convincing many Americans that it was worth fighting. Johnson hoped that, with more bombing and more troops, the Vietnamese communists would give up, but he knew that if Congress had to choose between spending on the war and spending on domestic programs, it would choose the war. After Johnson asked for a tax increase, his Great Society programs met increasing resistance.

A dramatic example of the ugly mood on Capitol Hill was the House of Representatives' expulsion in 1967 of the most prominent African-American politician in the United States, Adam Clayton Powell, Jr. (1908–1972). Pastor of the Abyssinian Baptist Church in Harlem and a long-time civic activist, Powell had first been elected to represent his Harlem district in 1944 and became the foremost champion of civil rights in the House. As chairman of the Education and Labor Committee, he had been instrumental in passing Johnson's education and antipoverty legislation.

Powell gave ammunition to his enemies. He mismanaged the committee's budget, took trips abroad at government expense, and was threatened with arrest in New York because of his refusal to pay a slander judgment against him. Yet the sentiment behind his ouster owed much to the dislike he inspired as a champion of minorities and the poor and as a flamboyant black man. The Supreme Court, overruling the House, upheld his right to his seat, and Harlem voters kept him in office until his death.

Johnson did not give up on the Great Society. He could initiate no major programs while the Vietnam war lasted, but he pushed a variety of measures, including a law to prohibit discrimination in housing. He also named the NAACP's Thurgood Marshall to the Supreme Court in 1967.

Vietnam trapped Johnson. As the hundreds of thousands who demonstrated against the war reminded him, Vietnam was incontestably "Lyndon Johnson's war." It was not, he would have replied, the war he had wanted to fight—that was the war against poverty and discrimination—but he was committed to seeing it through. He believed that his and the nation's honor were at stake. Optimistic reports in 1967 convinced the president that he might yet prevail.

Then, on January 30, 1968, at the start of the Vietnamese new year (called Tet), communist insurgents attacked across South Vietnam including its capital, Saigon, where they penetrated the grounds of the American embassy. Although American and South Vietnamese forces quickly recaptured all the territory that was lost and inflicted massive casualties on the enemy, the Tet Offensive was a major psychological blow for the American public.

On March 31, 1968, President Johnson told the nation that he would halt the bombing of North Vietnam to encourage the start of peace negotiations, which began in Paris in May. Then, he added that he would not seek renomination as president. Worn out by Vietnam, frustrated in his efforts to achieve the Great Society, the target of bitter criticism, and dispirited by a poor showing in the New Hampshire primary, Lyndon Johnson ended his public career.

King: Searching for a New Strategy

Like President Johnson, Martin Luther King was attacked on many fronts. Many white people considered him a dangerous radical, while black militants considered him an ineffectual moderate. His first response to the urban rebellions in 1965 and 1966 had been to move his campaign to the North to demonstrate the national range of the civil rights movement. In 1966, King and the SCLC set up operations in Chicago at the invitation of the Chicago Freedom Movement. King was confident that he would receive the support of the city's white liberals and the entire black community. His optimism proved unwarranted.

Chicago's mayor Richard Daley viewed King suspiciously but treated him with respect and cautioned the police not to use violence against King's civil rights demonstrators. Because King's movement depended on provoking confrontation, not much happened until King attempted to march into the white ethnic enclave of Marquette Park and the all-white suburb of Cicero.

The ensuing violence attracted the nation's television cameras. Chicago's white liberals joined with King and Daley in negotiating the Summit Agreement on housing, which amounted to a hasty retreat by King in the face of white rage and black militancy. The Chicago strategy was a failure.

But Chicago reinforced two important lessons for King about racial discrimination. It was more than a southern problem and it was inextricably intertwined with the country's economic structure. And so he began to think more critically about the need not only to eradicate poverty but to end systemic economic inequality. "What good is it to be allowed to eat in a restaurant," he remarked, "if you can't afford a hamburger?" In the fall of 1967, he announced plans for his most ambitious and militant project, an integrated, nonviolent "Poor People's Campaign" the following spring. According to the plan, tens of thousands of the nation's dispossessed would descend on Washington to focus attention on the disadvantaged members of American society. Among other things, King and his aides wanted a federally guaranteed income policy.

King on the Vietnam War

While planning the Poor People's Campaign, King began to attack the war in Vietnam. King rejected what he considered the hypocrisy of the federal government's determination to send black and white men to Vietnam "to slaughter, men, women, and children," while failing to protect black American civil rights protesters in places like Albany, Birmingham, and Selma. His statements that the president was more concerned about winning in Vietnam than winning the "war against poverty" in America turned Johnson against him and alienated the more traditional civil rights leaders who supported the war in Vietnam. Nor did the young militants in SNCC, who had already condemned the war, rush to embrace him. But King persisted and became one of the war's most trenchant critics.

King's Murder

His search for a new strategy led King to a closer involvement with labor issues. In February 1968, attempting to gain union recognition for municipal workers in Memphis, 1,300 members of a virtually all-black sanitation workers local went on strike and together with the local black community boycotted downtown merchants. But Memphis mayor Henry Loeb refused to negotiate. On March 18, 1968 King went to Memphis to address the striking sanitation workers.

The occasion was marked by violence. Nevertheless, King returned to Memphis on April 3 and delivered his last and perhaps most prophetic speech:

> I would like to live a long life. Longevity has its place. But I'm not concerned about that now. I just want to do God's will. And He's allowed me to go up to the mountaintop, and I've looked over. And I've seen the promised land. I may not get there with you. But I want you to know tonight that we as a people will get to the promised land. So I'm happy tonight. I'm not worried about anything. I'm not fearing any man. "Mine eyes have seen the glory of the coming of the Lord."

The next day King was murdered by James Earl Ray as he stood on the balcony of the Lorraine Motel in Memphis. His assassination unleashed a torrent of rage in black communities. More than 125 cities experienced uprisings. By April 11, forty-six people were dead, 35,000 were injured, and more than 20,000 had been arrested.

Within days of King's assassination, Congress passed the Civil Rights Act of 1968. Proposed by Johnson two years before, the act outlawed discrimination in the sale and rental of housing and gave the Justice Department authority to bring suits against it.

King's assassination also boosted support for the Poor People's Campaign, which began in May when more than 2,000 demonstrators settled into a shantytown they called Resurrection City in Washington, D.C. For more than a month, they marched daily to various federal offices and took part in a mass demonstration on June 19. On June 24, police evicted them, and the campaign ended, leaving an uncertain legacy.

The Black Arts Movement
and Black Consciousness

The years between 1967 and 1975 witnessed some of the most intense political and cultural discussions in the history of the black freedom struggle. Black power stimulated debate about both the future of black politics in the post-civil rights era and the role of black art and artists in the quest for black liberation. Creative people revisited the long-standing issue of whether black art is political or aesthetic. For a decade, discussion about black culture and identity focused on the relationship between art and the artist, and the political movement within the black community. This period became known as the black arts movement. Among the outstanding poets who helped to shape the revolutionary movement, introducing new forms of black writing and delivering outspoken attacks on "the white aesthetic" while stressing black beauty and pride were Sonia Sanchez, Nikki Giovanni, and Don L. Lee (Haki Madhubuti). One of the best examples of Giovanni's militant poems is "The True Import of Present Dialogue, Black vs. Negro," which appeared in her first collection entitled *Black Feeling, Black Talk*(1967). In a shocking opening line she asked, "nigger/Can you kill/Can you kill/Can a nigger kill/Can a nigger kill a honkie." The poem continues, "Can you kill the nigger/in you/Can you kill your nigger mind/And free your Black hands to/strangle." Sanchez also captured the turbulence of the era. In 1970 she published a collection of poetry entitled, *We a BadddDDD People.*

The formal beginning of the movement was the founding in 1965 of the Black Arts Repertory Theater by writer LeRoi Jones, who changed his name to Imamu Amari Baraka in 1967. Jones was the bridge that linked the political and cultural aspects of black power. He had been associated with the white avant-garde poets in New York in the 1950s but began to change in 1965 from an integrationist to a black cultural nationalist.

The guiding ethos of the black arts movement was the determination of black artists to produce black art for black people and thereby to accomplish black liberation. Baraka declared, "The Black man must seek a Black politics, an ordering of the world that is beneficial to his culture, to his interiorization and judgment of the world. The Black Artist. . . is desperately needed to change the images his people identify with, by asserting Black feeling, Black mind, Black judgment." In 1968 he coedited with Larry Neal the anthology *Black Fire,* which revealed the extent to which black writers and thinkers had rejected the premises of integration in favor of a new black consciousness and nationalist political engagement. As Larry Neal put it:

> The Black Arts Movement is radically opposed to any concept of the artist that alienates him from his community. Black Art is the aesthetic and spiritual sister of the Black Power concept. As such, it envisions an art that speaks directly to the needs and aspirations of Black Americans. In order to perform this task, the Black Arts Movement proposes a radical reordering of the western cultural aesthetic. It proposes a separate symbolism, mythology, critique, and iconography. The Black Arts and the Black Power concept both relate broadly to the Afro-American's desire for self-determination and nationhood. Both concepts are nationalistic. One is concerned with the relationship between art and politics; the other with the art of politics.

The black arts movement was criticized because of its celebration of black maleness, its racial exclusivity, and its homophobia. It was never a unified movement. Other black artists had competing visions of freedom. In 1970 Maya Angelou published an autobiographical novel, *I Know Why the Caged Bird Sings,* that unveiled her experience with sexual abuse and the silencing of black women within black communities. Other black women writers would follow suit and in the 1970s create a black women's literary renaissance. Still, prominent integrationist writers agreed with some of the black arts movement's fundamental tenets.

The works of Langston Hughes, Lorraine Hansberry, Gwendolyn Brooks, and James Baldwin linked the black cultural renaissances of the 1930s, 1940s, and 1950s to the black arts movement. Brooks, for example, stressed the commitment of artist to community and the importance of the relationship between the artist and her audience. She had consistently supported community-based arts programs, and it seemed natural that she should "convert" to a black nationalist perspective during the sixties and join forces with younger artists.

But the most popular black writer of the era, especially among white audiences, was James Baldwin. Baldwin was an integrationist. He resisted the simple inversion of racial hierarchies that characterized some parts of the black power and black arts movements. He wrote: "I think all theories are suspect, that the finest principles may have to be modified, or may even be pulverized by the demands of life, and that one must find therefore, and move through the world hoping that center will guide one aright." Yet Baldwin was as alienated and angry as some of the artists identified with black arts.

In *The Fire Next Time* (1963), he concluded with a phrase that echoed through discussions of the rebellions in Watts, Newark, and Detroit. "If we do not now dare everything, the fulfillment of that prophecy, recreated from the bible in song by a slave, is upon us: 'God gave Noah the rainbow sign, No more water, the fire next time!'"

Baldwin was also an unflinching commentator on white racism who told his white readers, "There appears to be a vast amount of confusion on this point, but I do not know many Negroes who are eager to be 'accepted' by white people, still less to be loved by them; they, the blacks, simply don't wish to be beaten over the head by the whites every instant of our brief passage on this planet." And in *No Name in the Street,* Baldwin declared: "I agree with the Black Panther position concerning black prisoners: not one of them has ever had a fair trial, for not one of them has ever been tried by a jury of his peers." He explained: "White middle-class America is always the jury, and they know absolutely nothing about the lives of the people on whom they sit in judgment: and this fact is not altered, on the contrary it is rendered more implacable by the presence of one or two black faces in the jury box."

Poetry and Theater

The black arts movement had its greatest and most significant impact in poetry and theater. The movement had three geographical centers: Harlem, Chicago and Detroit, and San Francisco.

The Chicago-based *Negro Digest/Black World,* edited by Hoyt Fuller and published by John Johnson, promoted many of the works of the new generation of creative artists. Fuller, a well-connected intellectual with an exhaustive command of black literature, became editor of the monthly magazine in 1961. In 1970 he changed the name of the magazine to *Black World*. The name change identified African Americans with both the African diaspora and Africa itself.

In Detroit, Naomi Long Madgett's Lotus Press and Dudley Randall's Broadside Press republished the previous generation of black poets, notably Gwendolyn Brooks, Margaret Walker, and Sterling Brown. In Chicago, poet and literary critic, Don L. Lee, who changed his name to Haki Madhubuti, launched Third World Press, which published many of the black arts poets and writers.

The Chicago-Detroit publishing nexus promoted new poets like Nikki Giovanni, Etheridge Knight, and Sonia Sanchez. These poets produced some of the most accomplished and experimental work of the black arts movement. It resonated with the sounds of the African-American vernacular, combining the rhythmic cadences of sermons with popular music and black "street speech" into a spirited new form of poetry that was free, conversational, and militantly cool.

Theater was another prominent genre of the black arts movement. Playwright Ed Bullins edited a special issue of the journal *Drama Review* in the summer of 1968 that featured essays and plays by most of the major activists in black arts, including Sonia Sanchez, Ron Milner, and Woodie King, Jr. This volume became the textbook of black arts. In his plays Bullins, who was greatly influenced by Baraka, portrayed ordinary black life and explored the inner forces that prevented black people from realizing their own liberation and full potential. He showed how racism had deformed the black experience and consciousness. Across the country local black communities formed their own theater groups, including Val Gray Ward's Kuumba Workshop in Chicago and Baraka's Spirit House Theater in New Jersey. These groups hosted seminars, guest appearances, fashion shows, art exhibits, dance recitals, parades, and mass media parties.

On the West Coast, in 1969, Robert Chrisman and Nathan Hare launched *The Black Scholar*, the first serious journal to promote black studies. Chrisman compared the black arts movement with the renaissance in Harlem during the 1920s: "More so than the Harlem Renaissance, in which Black artists were always on the leash of white patrons and publishing houses, the Black Arts movement did it for itself. Black people going out nationally, in mass, saying we are an independent Black people and this is what we produce."

Music

The cultural nationalists in the black arts movement made modern jazz musicians icons of the quest for black freedom. Baraka argued that jazz and other black music were the language that black people developed to give uncensored accounts of their experiences. He and other cultural nationalists believed that music could promote black identity and encourage the pride that was vital for political struggle. The music of the jazzmen challenged western conceptions of harmony, rhythm, melody, and tone. In jazz you have to improvise, to create your own form of expression by using whatever information inspires you. The emphasis is not on the original, but on individual articulation.

Poet Nikki Giovanni, a graduate of Fisk University, was one of the major figures in the Black Arts Movement of the 1970s. She once declared "Writing is not who I am, it's what I do." In 1971 she published, *Gemini: An Extended Autobiographical Statement on My First Twenty-Five Years at Being a Black Poet.* It was nominated for a National Book Award.
Prentice Hall

Cultural nationalists perceived jazz to be a self-consciously engaged, economically independent, politically useful art form. Novelist Ralph Ellison put it most succinctly:

> True jazz is an art of individual assertion within and against the group. Each true jazz moment (as distinct from the uninspired commercial performance) springs from a contest in which each artist challenges all the rest; each solo flight, or improvisation, represents (like the successive canvases of a painter) a definition of his identity: as individual, as member of the collectivity and as a link in the chain of tradition.

This outlook explains why Miles Davis's legendary album *Kind of Blue* (1959), one of the most progressive jazz albums ever produced, also became one of the most popular. Davis showed that art could be accessible without sacrificing excellence and rigor. Davis, in the words of one admirer, was able to "dance underwater and not get wet." For black cultural nationalists, Davis projected an image of uncompromising and uncompromised black identity.

Among other intensely celebrated jazzmen were Charlie Parker, Archie Shepp, Ornette Coleman, Pharoah Sanders, Eric Dophy, Thelonious Monk, and John Coltrane. Playwright Ronald Milner described Coltrane as "a man who through his saxophone before your eyes and ears completely annihilates every single western influence."

Jazz, however, tended to appeal to intellectuals. Most black people preferred rhythm and blues, gospel, and soul. During the height of the black consciousness movement, black popular musicians gave performances and concerts to raise funds and to assert racial pride. Aretha Franklin and Ray Charles, for example, allowed SNCC workers to attend their concerts free. Just as the freedom songs had done, the soul music of the black power era helped unify black people.

No history of the era would be complete without mentioning the performances of the "Godfather of Soul," James Brown, the "Queen of Soul," Aretha Franklin's powerful rendition of the song "R.E.S.P.E.C.T.," and the financial contributions of Berry Gordy of Motown. James Brown's "Say It Loud, I'm Black and I'm Proud" became an anthem for the era. Brown was "totally committed to black power, the kind that is achieved not through the muzzle of a rifle but through education and economic leverage."

Berry Gordy contributed to black freedom struggles both artistically and financially. To support King's Chicago movement, Gordy arranged for Stevie Wonder to give a benefit concert at Soldier Field in Chicago. He made cash contributions to black candidates, to the NAACP and its Legal Defense and Educational Fund, and to the Urban League.

With Gordy's encouragement, his performers flirted just enough with black radicalism to gain a patina of militancy. During the late 1960s and early 1970s the musical and lyrical innovations of the Temptations, Stevie Wonder, and Marvin Gaye reflected Motown's politicization. In an address to one of the sessions launching Jesse Jackson's People United to Save Humanity (PUSH) in 1971, Gordy declared, "I have been fortunate to be able to provide opportunities for young people. . . . Opportunities are supposed to knock once in a lifetime, but too often we have to knock for an opportunity. The first obligation we (as black businessmen) have is to ourselves and our own employees, the second is to create opportunities for others." The musician Curtis Mayfield, on the other hand, simply explained, "Our purpose is to educate as well as to entertain. Painless preaching is as good a term as any for what we do."

The Second Phase of the Black Student Movement

The most dramatic expression of militant assertiveness after 1968 occurred among black college students. The black power generation of students was committed to transforming society, although those on predominantly white campuses often seemed to be more reformist than revolutionary. Some observers describe the period of activism between 1968 and 1975 as the "second phase" of the black students movement. The first phase had been launched in the early 1960s by students at southern black colleges.

The Orangeburg Massacre

By 1968 many of the student organizations that had grown out of the civil rights movement, notably SNCC, were in decline. The massacre of black students at South Carolina State College in Orangeburg on February 8, 1968, marks the end of the first phase and the beginning of the second. Students attending the historically black institution had protested a local bowling alley's whites-only admission policy. When the tension and protests escalated, state officials deployed the highway patrol and National Guard. On the evening of February 8, the students assembled at the front of the campus and taunted the officers; some threw rocks, bricks, and bottles. One officer was hit by a piece of lumber. Later, without warning, nine highway patrolmen opened fire on the students with shotguns. The officers killed three young men and wounded twenty-seven. Most of them were shot in the back. All the officers involved were later acquitted, but a young black activist and SNCC leader, Cleveland Sellers, was convicted of rioting, and served nearly a year in prison. He was pardoned in 1993. On February 8, 2001 South Carolina Governor James Hodges apologized to a group of survivors who had assembled in Orangeburg.

Black Studies

The second phase owed much of its inspiration to the black power and black arts movements. It began when many black students began to enroll in predominantly white institutions. These black students demanded courses in black history, culture, literature, and art as alternatives to the "Eurocentric" bias of the average university curriculum. Many black students also formed all-black organizations.

Black students understood that education was essential to empowerment. In 1967 black students accounted for only 2 percent of the total enrollment at predominantly white colleges and universities. This meant that only 95,000 African Americans were among the approximately five million full-time undergraduates at these schools. Rutgers University in New Jersey provides a case study. Out of twenty-four thousand baccalaureate degrees it awarded between 1952 and 1967, only about two hundred went to African Americans. Federal legislation—especially the Civil Rights Act of 1964 and the Higher Education Act of 1965—spurred colleges and universities to take affirmative action to recruit black students. Where there had been about one hundred black undergraduates at Rutgers in 1965, there were more than four hundred by 1968, accounting for nearly 3 percent of the undergraduate enrollment.

On the national level, the overall status of black people in education reflected the accomplishments of the classic phase of the civil rights movement, but the black power generation was determined to make its own mark on the struggle. In 1960, only 227,000 black Americans attended the nation's colleges (including those at predominantly black institutions). By 1977, 1.1 million black students attended America's universities. These students had the sense of being strangers in a white-controlled environment. They resolved to change this situation.

At San Francisco State College, Nathan Hare, formerly a professor at Howard University, and black students demanded not only curriculum changes but also the structural transformation of the college. In the 1966–1967 academic year the Black Student Union (BSU) orchestrated a strike that involved thousands of students of diverse ethnic and racial backgrounds. Among their demands were the creation of an autonomous degree-granting black studies department and the admission of more black students. The college created the first black studies department in 1968, with Hare as its head.

Black students also took over administration buildings at other institutions, demanding not only that the schools offer more black studies courses and programs and hire more black faculty, but often that classrooms and facilities also be made available to local black communities. The upheavals that shut down Columbia University in 1968, for example, began when black student members of the Students Afro-American Society and Students for a Democratic Society demonstrated to block plans to construct a university gymnasium in nearby Morningside Park. The demonstrators argued that the gym was being built despite strenuous objections from the Harlem community.

In 1968, Yale University's Black Student Alliance sponsored a symposium to discuss the need, status, and function of Afro-American Studies. Conference organizer Armstead Robinson saw it as the first attempt to create a viable program of Afro-American Studies. In December 1968 the faculty voted to make Yale one of the first major universities in the country to institute a degree-granting African-American Studies program. In 1969 Harvard University created an Afro-American Studies Department, and other schools soon followed. In 1969, the Institute of the Black World in Atlanta conducted a project to define the methods and purpose of black studies and then sponsored a black studies director's seminar. Ron Karenga wrote what remains a major textbook for the new field, *Introduction to Black Studies.* By 1973 some two hundred black studies programs existed in the United States. By the late 1980s, several of the programs, such as those at Cornell, Yale, and UCLA offered master's degrees in African-American studies. In 1988 Temple University, under the leadership of Molefi Kete Asante, became the first university to offer a Ph.D. in African-American Studies.

Still, there was no universally accepted definition of black studies. James E. Turner, founder of Africana Studies at Cornell, viewed it as a collective, interdisciplinary scholarly approach to the experiences of people of African descent throughout the world. History, in black studies, constituted the foundation for the analysis of common patterns of life that reflected the social conditions of black people. Africana studies or black studies theoreticians have generally agreed on four goals for this new scholarly field. (1) It should develop solutions to the problems facing black people in the African diaspora. (2) It should provide analysis of black culture and life that challenge and replace preexisting Eurocentric models. (3) It should promote social change and educational reform throughout the academy. And (4) it should institutionalize the study of black people as a field with its own theories, methods, ideologies, symbols, language, and culture. In short, the first generation of advocates envisioned black studies as being a revolutionary, historically grounded educational reform movement that sought to make the study of African descendants—their culture, problems, worldviews, and spirituality—a serious scholarly endeavor with practical implications for improving black peoples' lives.

The Election of 1968

In the presidential campaign of 1968, the Democrats provided the excitement but lost the election. In late 1967, Senator Eugene McCarthy of Minnesota entered the race as the antiwar alternative to Lyndon Johnson, but few politicians took him seriously. Robert Kennedy, U.S. senator from New York, was taken seriously, even though by the time he entered the race in mid-March, most of the convention delegates were already pledged to Johnson, and, after Johnson's withdrawal, quickly transferred their allegiance to Vice President Hubert Humphrey. Whether Kennedy could have gained the nomination will never be known because—in the second traumatic assassination of 1968—he was murdered in June. Grief over his death, bitterness over the war, and personal rivalries produced the most tumultuous political convention in modern American history, with Chicago policemen clubbing and gassing antiwar demonstrators.

In November, Republican Richard Nixon narrowly defeated Humphrey. George Wallace, the segregationist ex-governor of Alabama, won 13.5 percent of the popular vote and forty-six electoral votes. Wallace denounced civil rights legislation and court-ordered desegregation, endorsed the repression of demonstrators and rioters, and promised to defeat communism in Southeast Asia.

The Nixon Presidency

Of all modern presidents, Richard Nixon is probably the hardest to pin down with neat ideological labels. By the standards of the early twentieth-first century, much of his record seems progressive: He created the Environmental Protection Agency, endorsed an equal rights amendment to the Constitution that would have prohibited gender discrimination, and signed more regulatory legislation than any other president. His willingness to innovate in policy affecting African Americans can be illustrated by his naming of Daniel Patrick Moynihan, one of Johnson's experts on social policy, to be his domestic policy adviser. But Nixon also pursued a "Southern Strategy" that realigned the Republican party with the white southern backlash to civil rights and weakened the New Deal coalition.

The "Moynihan Report" and FAP

Moynihan first attracted national attention as assistant secretary of labor in the Johnson administration when a confidential memorandum he wrote was leaked to the press. It would later be published as "The Negro Family: The Case for National Action" and is popularly known as the "Moynihan Report." Moynihan's guiding assumption was that civil rights legislation, necessary as it was, would not address the problems of the inner city. There, he argued, the breakdown of the "lower-class" black family had led to the "pathology" of juvenile delinquency, illegitimacy, drug addiction, and poor performance in school. He attributed the vulnerability of the black family to "three centuries of almost unimaginable treatment" by white society, exploitation under slavery, the strain of urbanization, and persistent unemployment.

These forces, he argued, weakened the role of black men and resulted in a disproportionate number of dysfunctional, female-headed families. In the most-often repeated passage in the report, Moynihan declared that the black community had been forced into "a matriarchal structure, [which] because it is so out of line with the rest of American society, seriously retards the progress of the group as a whole, and imposes a crushing burden on the Negro male. . . . Obviously, not every instance of social pathology afflicting the Negro community can be traced to the weakness of family structure. . . [but] once or twice removed, it will be found to be the principal source of most of the aberrant, inadequate, or anti-social behavior that did not establish, but now serves to perpetuate the cycle of poverty and deprivation."

Though based on the work of earlier black scholars, such as E. Franklin Frazier, Moynihan's condemnation of "matriarchy" drew fire. Black social scientists countered that the structure of the black family reflected a functional adaptation that black people had made to survive in a racist American society. Historians Herbert Gutman and John Blassingame argued that Moynihan underestimated the prevalence of two-parent black families in the past. While many of the criticisms of the report were deserved, they diverted attention from its positive thrust. Moynihan wanted to eliminate poverty and unemployment in the black community and he recommended vigorous enforcement of the civil rights laws to achieve equality of opportunity. Moynihan was also one of the first to appreciate how white resentment of the Community Action Program (CAP) and the expansion of the welfare rolls would make both programs politically unfeasible.

Intrigued with Moynihan's independence, Nixon told him to develop a plan to assist poor families. Under the Family Assistance Plan (FAP) that Nixon unveiled in 1969, each family of four with no wage earner would receive an annual payment of $1,600 plus $800 of food stamps. With its across-the-board guarantee of income, the plan eliminated an oppressive welfare bureaucracy and reduced the invidious comparison between "welfare recipients" and everyone else.

Had it passed, FAP would have promoted two-parent families by removing the prohibition against assistance to dependent children whose fathers were alive, well, and living at home. It would also have encouraged work by requiring able-bodied recipients to accept jobs or vocational training and by providing benefits to those accepting low-paying jobs. But the Senate, under pressure both from conservatives who objected to any government programs for the poor and from welfare-rights advocates who complained that the payments were too low, killed it.

Busing

Nixon was acutely aware that he moved in a changed political environment and particularly in a far more conservative Republican party than he had when he lost to John F. Kennedy in 1960. Then, as a presidential candidate, he had had to appease eastern, pro–civil rights liberals. But in 1968, Nixon chose to appease southern segregationists whom Barry Goldwater had attracted to the Republican party in 1964. They demanded that Nixon slow down court-ordered school desegregation in the South. Finally, Nixon could hardly ignore George Wallace, with his racist appeals. In another three-way race in 1972, Wallace might ensure Nixon's defeat.

As a result of these pressures, the Nixon administration perfected its Southern Strategy and embarked upon a collision course with civil rights organizations, such as the NAACP, which supported busing to achieve school integration. Thus, the major battle over civil rights in the early 1970s was over the federal courts' willingness to implement desegregation goals by busing students across district lines. Nixon used the busing controversy to lure Wallace voters. In 1971 he had advised federal officials to stop pressing to desegregate schools through "forced busing." He argued that such efforts were ultimately "counterproductive, and not in the interest of better race relations."

Educational segregation in the North reflected residential segregation. In Boston, site of some of the most acrimonious busing protests, schools in black neighborhoods received less funding than their white counterparts. Buildings were derelict, classes overcrowded and deficient in supplies and equipment, even desks. In 1974 U.S. district judge W. Arthur Garrity found the Boston School Committee guilty of violating the equal protection clause of the Fourteenth Amendment. To achieve racial balance in the Boston schools, the judge ordered the busing of several thousand students between mostly white South Boston, Hyde Park, and Dorchester, and mostly black Roxbury.

White people who opposed busing organized demonstrations and boycotts to prevent their children from being bused into black communities and black children from being bused into white schools. Violence and hostilities persisted for two years.

Nixon and the War

Meanwhile, the war in Vietnam seemed to drag on endlessly. Nixon realized that what most Americans disliked about the war was that it was killing their sons and husbands. So in 1969, he began to phase out direct U.S. involvement. This "Vietnamization," he claimed, was made possible by the growing ability of the South Vietnamese to fight for themselves. What Nixon did not say was that another reason for troop withdrawals was that the morale of American soldiers was plunging rapidly. Drug abuse among troops was widespread, soldiers had killed their officers, and some of those incidents had racial overtones. Nixon's promise to "wind down the war" assured his reelection. In 1972 he defeated South Dakota senator George McGovern in a landslide.

Few in the Nixon administration, however, took South Vietnamese military capability seriously, and Nixon was unwilling to "lose" Vietnam. But opposition to the war also grew. Antiwar demonstrations kept Nixon off balance and may have deterred him from further escalation.

The most dramatic response to Nixon's escalation in the Vietnam war came after the invasion of Cambodia in April 1970. The invasion triggered antiwar protests on many campuses. In one such protest, on May 4, Ohio National Guardsmen shot and killed four white students at Kent State University. The response of students across the country was electric: the first nationwide student strike in American history. Ten days later in Mississippi, the shooting and killing of two black students at Jackson State University attracted much less attention from either white students or the media. Three years later, at the beginning of 1973, the United States and North Vietnam signed a peace agreement. Congress then prohibited the reintroduction of American troops and the resumption of bombing, and in 1974 began cutting off military aid to the South Vietnamese government. The result was predictable: in 1975 South Vietnam collapsed.

Nixon's Downfall

If Nixon assumed the presidency in 1969 with any popular mandate, it was to restore law and order. The disorder that irritated the American public included the inner-city riots, the antiwar demonstrations, and the rise in crime. Nixon pushed legislation through Congress that expanded local law enforcement officials' power to use wire-taps and enter premises without warning.

But Nixon's paranoia and ruthlessness pushed him beyond what the public would tolerate, and even beyond the law itself. He confused criminals with principled protesters and his political opponents, and decided to punish them all. One method was to create a gang of burglars, operating out of the White House to gather incriminating information. In June 1972 they were discovered breaking into Democratic National Committee headquarters in the Watergate apartment complex in Washington. Full details emerged in a Senate investigation in 1973–1974, and on August 9, 1974, threatened with impeachment, Nixon resigned. His downfall, however, left no one of his stature or with his flexible attitude toward public policy to resist the takeover of the Republican party by more dogmatic conservatives. One sign of this was the difficulty Nixon's successor, Gerald Ford, had in securing the 1976 Republican presidential nomination against the right's new hero, Ronald Reagan.

The Rise of Black Elected Officials

Just as King searched for a new strategy after the early victories of the civil rights movement, other black leaders mobilized the newly enfranchised black electorate to win political office. After the adoption of the Voting Rights Act of 1965, Vernon Jordan, director of the Voter Education Project, coordinated registration drives and workshops across the South. As he explained, "Too many of these people have been alienated from the political process for too long. . . and so we have to. . . teach them what a local government is, how it operates, and try to relate their votes to the things they want."

By 1974 there were 1,593 black elected officials outside the South, and by 1980 the number had risen to 2,455. Although black people in northern cities had been able to vote for a century and had been slowly developing political muscle, they had not been able to elect big-city mayors. The rise of black power and the inspiration of the Voting Rights Act, however, signaled a new departure. People now eagerly engaged in the electoral process to achieve a political influence to which their numbers entitled them. In 1967 in Cleveland, where the black population had skyrocketed after World War II, Carl Stokes became the first black mayor of a major American city, winning election with the support of white business leaders and the solid backing of the black community. In the same year prosecutor Richard G. Hatcher became mayor of Gary, Indiana, where the black population had also increased greatly after the war. Hatcher won by a mere 1,389 votes, garnering 96 percent of the black vote and 14 percent of the white vote.

The Gary Convention
and the Black Political Agenda

These victories led to the Gary convention of 1972. The three co-chairs of the convention were Detroit Congressman Charles Diggs, Hatcher, and writer Amiri Baraka of Newark, New Jersey. Political scientist Ronald Walters, who helped plan the convention, recalled that various ideological factions had to be placated to make the convention work: "The most important thing about 1972 was the fact that it was an election year, so it provided the environment for the politics taking place. So you had two groups of people who saw this as an opportunity to make some very important statements. One of these, of course, was the black nationalist movement led by Amiri Baraka, Maulana Karenga, and others at that time." The nationalists interpreted "black power" to mean that black people should control their own communities and create separate cultural institutions from those of white society. These views clashed with the ideas espoused by the black elected officials represented by Stokes and Hatcher. According to Walters, "It was this body of people who really were contending for the national leadership of the black community in the early seventies. And in the seventies this new group of black elected officials joined the civil rights leaders and became a new leadership class, but there was sort of a conflict in outlook between them and the more indigenous, social, grass roots-oriented nationalist movement."

Approximately eight thousand people gathered to develop an agenda for black empowerment. The discussions inspired scores of individual African Americans to run for local office. However, no unified black consensus emerged.

The discussions revealed deep-seated internal divisions that provoked even more impassioned disagreement. Coleman Young and other Michigan delegates walked out to protest a proposal calling for African Americans to reject "discriminatory" unions and form their own. Others walked out over a resolution condemning Israel for its "expansionist policy" toward the Palestinians. Others argued that "forced racial integration of schools" through busing insulted black students and would cost black teachers their jobs.

The Gary convention signaled a shift in the political focus of the black community toward electoral politics and away from mass demonstrations and protest measures. Unity continued to elude subsequent conventions, however, and delegates attending the last National Black Convention at Little Rock, Arkansas, in 1974 abandoned the idea of a black political party. Ideological differences and institutional cleavages precluded cooperation between black nationalists and the rising numbers of black elected officials. These same differences prevented some nationalists and officials from taking seriously the 1972 Democratic party presidential bid of New York congresswoman Shirley Chisholm.

Black People Gain Local Offices

Despite the demise of the National Black Convention movement, African Americans continued to win elections. A few statistics indicate the success of black politicians. When the leaders first convened the Gary convention, there were thirteen African-American members of Congress; by 1997 there were forty. In 1972 there were 2,427 black elected officials; by 1993 there were 8,106. An amendment to the Voting Rights Act in 1975 enabled minorities to mount court challenges to at-large voting practices that diluted the impact of bloc voting; this helped increase the number of black elected officials. Districts were redrawn with a majority or plurality of black voters. In 1985, L. Douglas Wilder was elected lieutenant governor of Virginia, making him the first African-American lieutenant governor in a southern state since Reconstruction. In 1989 he was elected governor, making him the first black governor of any state since Reconstruction.

The National Black Convention Movement of the Black Power Era

1965	Maulana Karenga founds the US (as opposed to them) Organization in Los Angeles, California. Advocates cultural nationalism.
1966	Amiri Baraka founds Spirit House Movers and Players in Newark, New Jersey. Advocates cultural nationalism.
1966	Huey P. Newton and Bobby Seale found the Black Panther party
1966	Stokely Carmichael coins the term "black power."
1966	Representative Adam Clayton Powell, Jr. hosts the first Black Power Conference
1967	Second Black Power Conference, held in Newark, New Jersey, calls for partitioning the United States into separate black and white nations.
1968	Third Black Power Conference is held in Philadelphia, Pennsylvania.
1969	National Black Economic Development Conference held in Detroit, Michigan.
1969	Last Black Power Conference, held in Bermuda, ends in disarray.
1970	Congress of Afrikan Peoples, led by Amiri Baraka, is organized in Atlanta, Georgia. Adopts the slogan, "It's nation time."
1971	The Reverend Jesse Jackson founds People United to Save Humanity (PUSH) in Chicago, Illinois.
1972	National Black Political Convention is held in Gary, Indiana.
1973	National Black Feminist Organization is founded by Eleanor Holmes Norton and Margaret Sloan.
1974	Last National Black Political Convention is held in Little Rock, Arkansas.

Between 1971 and 1975, the number of African-American mayors rose from 8 to 135, and the National Conference of Black Mayors was founded in 1974. In 1973, Coleman Young in Detroit and Thomas Bradley in Los Angeles became the first African-American mayors of cities of more than a million citizens. Bradley won in Los Angeles even though black people made up only 15 percent of the city's electorate. Ten years later, in 1983, Chicago swore in its first black mayor, Harold Washington. The era of the black elected official had arrived.

Economic Downturn

The 1970s were a decade of economic instability. Many black people experienced this economic downturn as a depression. Poor black people were losing ground. In 1969, approximately 10 percent of white men and 25 percent of black men earned less than

$10,000 (in 1984 constant dollars). In 1984 about 40 percent of black men between twenty-five and fifty-five earned less than $10,000 compared with 20 percent of comparable white men. Put a different way, between 1970 and 1986, the proportion of black families with incomes of less than $10,000 grew from 26.8 to 30.2 percent. Still, there were improvements. The black middle class grew. In 1970, 4.7 percent of black families had incomes of more than $50,000; by 1986 the number had almost doubled to 8.8 percent. But in general, the relative economic status of black workers did not improve.

Black Americans and the Carter Presidency

In 1976 the United States celebrated its bicentennial. For African Americans, it was also an important year for another reason. For the first time since 1964, the man most of them voted for was elected president—Jimmy Carter, a former governor of Georgia. Ninety percent of African-American voters favored the soft-spoken, religious Georgia Democrat over incumbent president Gerald Ford. Without their votes, Carter could not have even carried his native South.

Black Appointees

Carter acknowledged his debt to the black electorate by appointing African Americans to highly visible posts. He named Patricia Harris secretary of Housing and Urban Development, making her the first black woman to serve in the Cabinet. Carter appointed Andrew Young, former congressman from Georgia and a long-time political ally, ambassador to the United Nations. (Young was forced to resign in 1979.) Clifford Alexander, Jr. became the secretary of the Army. Eleanor Holmes Norton became the first woman to chair the Equal Employment Opportunity Commission (EEOC). Ernest Green, who had been one of the nine students to desegregate Little Rock's Central High School, was appointed assistant secretary of the Department of Labor. Wade McCree was appointed solicitor general in the Justice Department. Drew Days III became assistant attorney general for civil rights. Historian and former University of Colorado chancellor Mary Frances Berry was appointed assistant secretary for education. Carter also named Louis Martin his special assistant, making him the first African American in a position of influence on the White House staff.

Carter's Domestic Policies

There are many ways to judge the significance of the Carter presidency to African Americans. Carter's black appointments were important. Never had so many black men and women occupied positions that had direct and immediate impact on the day-to-day operations of the federal government. Carter also helped to cement gains for civil rights. He vetoed legislation to stop busing for school children as a means of integrating the schools. He strengthened the enforcement powers of the EEOC. His Justice Department chose cases to prosecute under the Fair Housing Act that involved widespread discrimination, to make the greatest possible impact.

Yet Carter's overall record proved unsatisfactory to most African Americans. Despite a Public Works Employment Act that directed 10 percent of public works funds to minority contractors and helped spur the creation of 585,000 jobs, Carter failed to help Democrats in Congress pass either full-employment or universal health care bills. To balance the budget he also cut social welfare programs, including school lunch programs and financial aid to black students.

Although the sluggish economy undermined Carter's popularity, the event that proved his undoing was the Iran hostage crisis that began in the fall of 1979. For many black people, however, Carter had become a disappointment long before that. They believed that he had done little to help them achieve social justice and economic advancement. Still the nomination of the conservative Ronald Reagan by the Republicans left black voters no alternative. In the election of 1980, 90 percent of black voters again supported Carter, but this time they could not save him. Carter pulled down scores of Democrats with him, and the Republicans regained the Senate for the first time since 1954.

Conclusion

The civil rights movement's victories changed both African-American life and American culture. The black power and black arts movements continued the struggle for freedom in northern and western urban areas where segregation, unemployment, and police brutality sparked rebellions that resulted in deaths and destruction in Watts, Newark, Detroit, and other cities. The black political convention movement did not create a black third party. But one of the most enduring legacies of the era was the rise of black elected officials. Black student militancy persisted despite the destruction of the Black Panther party. Throughout the late 1960s and 1970s, black students fought to create and institutionalize black studies as a new academic field. The black arts and black consciousness movement opened up new avenues for the expression of black unity and identity. A new generation of black poets, dramatists, visual artists and musicians found receptive audiences.

The legislative successes of the early phase of the civil rights movement illuminated how much more needed to be done to achieve a truly egalitarian society. Poor people, black and white, needed jobs, housing, medical care, and education. To varying degrees, Presidents Johnson, Nixon, and Carter attempted to address these needs. Their efforts produced mixed results in the face of a disastrous war in Vietnam and a massive white backlash. In the 1980s Republicans would reap the benefit of the Democratic party's disarray, and the plight of the poor would deteriorate.

Still, some black intellectuals chose a long view in their assessment of the significance of the post–World War II decades of struggle. Historian and theologian Vincent Harding put it most eloquently:

> It may be that the greatest discovery . . . was the fact that there is no last word in the
> human struggle for freedom, justice, and democracy. Only the continuing word, lived out
> by men, women, and children who dance and rest, who wrestle with alligators and stand
> firm before tanks, and presidents, and drug lords and deep, deep, fears. We learn again
> that the continuing word remains embedded in those who determined not to be moved,

TIMELINE

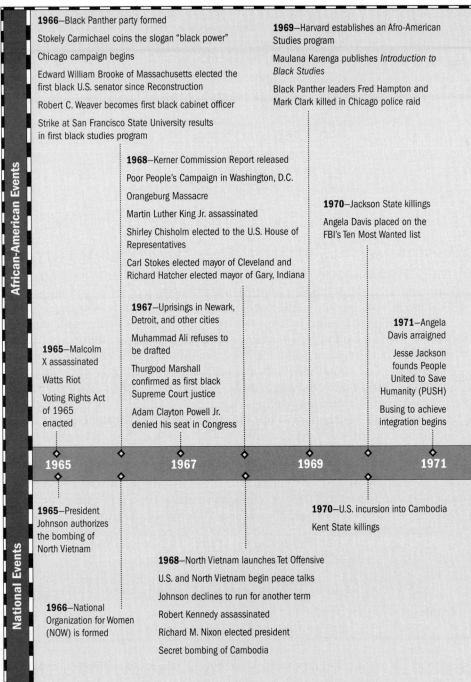

African-American Events

1966—Black Panther party formed

Stokely Carmichael coins the slogan "black power"

Chicago campaign begins

Edward William Brooke of Massachusetts elected the first black U.S. senator since Reconstruction

Robert C. Weaver becomes first black cabinet officer

Strike at San Francisco State University results in first black studies program

1969—Harvard establishes an Afro-American Studies program

Maulana Karenga publishes *Introduction to Black Studies*

Black Panther leaders Fred Hampton and Mark Clark killed in Chicago police raid

1968—Kerner Commission Report released

Poor People's Campaign in Washington, D.C.

Orangeburg Massacre

Martin Luther King Jr. assassinated

Shirley Chisholm elected to the U.S. House of Representatives

Carl Stokes elected mayor of Cleveland and Richard Hatcher elected mayor of Gary, Indiana

1970—Jackson State killings

Angela Davis placed on the FBI's Ten Most Wanted list

1967—Uprisings in Newark, Detroit, and other cities

Muhammad Ali refuses to be drafted

Thurgood Marshall confirmed as first black Supreme Court justice

Adam Clayton Powell Jr. denied his seat in Congress

1965—Malcolm X assassinated

Watts Riot

Voting Rights Act of 1965 enacted

1971—Angela Davis arraigned

Jesse Jackson founds People United to Save Humanity (PUSH)

Busing to achieve integration begins

1965   **1967**   **1969**   **1971**

National Events

1965—President Johnson authorizes the bombing of North Vietnam

1966—National Organization for Women (NOW) is formed

1968—North Vietnam launches Tet Offensive

U.S. and North Vietnam begin peace talks

Johnson declines to run for another term

Robert Kennedy assassinated

Richard M. Nixon elected president

Secret bombing of Cambodia

1970—U.S. incursion into Cambodia

Kent State killings

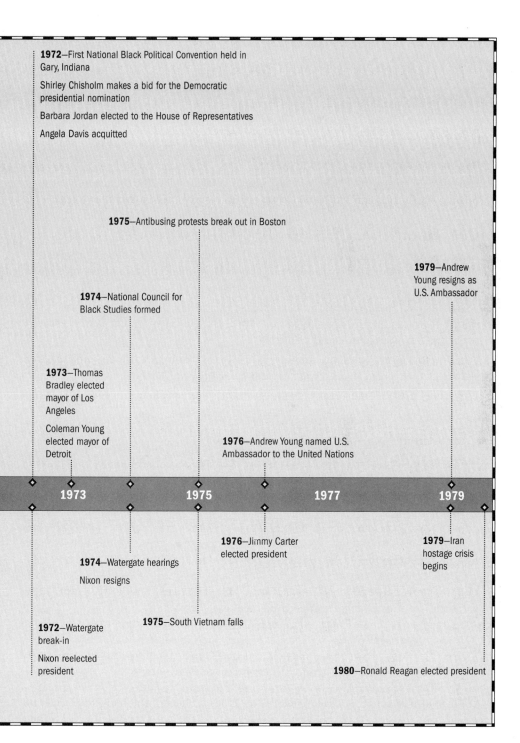

1972—First National Black Political Convention held in Gary, Indiana

Shirley Chisholm makes a bid for the Democratic presidential nomination

Barbara Jordan elected to the House of Representatives

Angela Davis acquitted

1975—Antibusing protests break out in Boston

1979—Andrew Young resigns as U.S. Ambassador

1974—National Council for Black Studies formed

1973—Thomas Bradley elected mayor of Los Angeles

Coleman Young elected mayor of Detroit

1976—Andrew Young named U.S. Ambassador to the United Nations

1973   1975   1977   1979

1976—Jimmy Carter elected president

1979—Iran hostage crisis begins

1974—Watergate hearings

Nixon resigns

1975—South Vietnam falls

1972—Watergate break-in

Nixon reelected president

1980—Ronald Reagan elected president

who know, against all odds, that they will overcome, will continue to create a more perfect union, a more compassionate world. The world remains with those who discover, in the midst of unremitting struggle, deep amazing powers within their own lives, power from, power for, the planet.

Review Questions

1. Why did African-American residents of Watts, Newark, and Detroit rebel in 1965–1966? What did these rebellions suggest about the value of the civil rights movement victories?

2. How did the visions and ideals, successes and failures of Martin Luther King, Jr. compare with those of Lyndon B. Johnson? Why were these men at odds with each other?

3. What role did African Americans play in the Vietnam War?

4. In what ways can the presidency of Richard Nixon be considered progressive? Which reforms initiated by President Lyndon B. Johnson did Nixon advance once he took office?

5. What were the major ideological concerns of the artists of the black arts movement? To what extent did Baldwin and Amiri Baraka have similar views about art, consciousness, aesthetics, and politics?

6. What factors prevented African Americans from forming a third political party? What was the significance of the rise of black elected officials?

7. Why were African Americans disappointed with the presidency of Jimmy Carter?

Recommended Reading

Stokely Carmichael and Charles V. Hamilton. *Black Power: The Politics of Liberation in America.* New York: Vintage Books, 1967. One of the most important books of the era of black power, by Carmichael, who popularized the slogan, and political scientist Hamilton.

Theodore Cross. *The Black Power Imperative: Racial Inequality and the Politics of Nonviolence.* New York: Faulkner Books, 1984. Provides a useful critique of the black power movement and explores the persistence of racial inequality.

Robert Dalleck. *Flawed Giant: Lyndon B. Johnson and His Times 1961–1973.* New York: Oxford University Press, 1998. A definitive biography of President Lyndon Johnson with fresh insights, grounded in exhaustive research.

Henry Hampton and Steve Fayer, eds. *Voices of Freedom: An Oral History of the Civil Rights Movement from the 1950s through the 1980s.* New York: Bantam Books, 1990. Contains the recollections of all the key participants in the critical battles and movements of the three decades that transformed race relations in America.

Robert C. Smith. *We Have No Leaders: African Americans in the Post–Civil Rights Era.* New York: State University of New York Press, 1996. A thoughtful critique of the successes and failures of black politics beginning with the National Black Political Convention in Gary, Indiana, in 1972.

Wallace Terry. *Bloods: An Oral History of the Vietnam War by Black Veterans.* New York: Ballantine Books, 1984. One of the best sources for firsthand accounts of the Vietnam War as experienced by black soldiers.

Brian Ward. *Just My Soul Responding: Rhythm and Blues, Black Consciousness, and Race Relations.* Berkeley, CA: University of California Press, 1998. An excellent study of black popular culture during the civil rights and black power movement era.

Craig Hansen Werner. *Playing the Changes: From Afro-Modernism to the Jazz Impulse.* Urbana, IL: University of Illinois Press, 1994. An insightful study of the gospel, blues, and jazz impulse in the writings of key black writers, including James Baldwin and Leon Forrest, during the post-civil rights movement era.

## Chapter 23

Modern Black America, 1980 to Present

Progress and Poverty

The years after 1970 witnessed the consolidation of black economic, civic, and political progress. In part, this was exemplified by the rising prominence of such visible African Americans as entertainer Oprah Winfrey, Secretary of Commerce Ronald Brown, General and later Secretary of State Colin Powell, and basketball star Michael Jordan. These people, joined by many others, countered notions of white supremacy by rising to the top of their fields.

The very rich remained rare in the black community, but their numbers did grow. Oprah Winfrey, Bill Cosby, Michael Jackson, and Michael Jordan acquired immense fortunes in the entertainment industry. Others, such as Reginald Lewis, made enormous sums in business.

The achievements of the most successful African Americans are impressive, but more significant is the growth of the black middle class. In 1940 only 5.2 percent of black men and 6.4 percent of black women worked in white-collar occupations. By 1990 those figures had risen to 32 percent for black men and 58.9 percent for black women. Although still, on average, below that of white families, black family income has also increased dramatically. In 1940 only 1 percent of black families, compared with 12 percent of white families, had income at least twice as high as the government's poverty line; by 1995 almost 49 percent of black families did, compared with 75 percent of white families. Income in relation to white families also improved. In 1960, for example, two-parent black families earned 61 percent as much as two-parent similar white families, but by 1995 they earned 87 percent as much. This figure is even

Table 23–1 Median Income of Black and White Households, 1992 and 1997				
	1992	1997	Change	Percent Change
White	$36,846	$38,972	$2,126	5.8
Black	$21,455	$25,050	$3,595	16.8

Source: U.S. Census Bureau Study of Income Data, 1997.

more impressive when one considers that a larger proportion of black people live in the low-wage South than do white people.

The economic boom of the Clinton years (1993–2000) was particularly beneficial for black people. Although the median income of black families remains substantially below that of white families, it has risen at a greater rate (see Table 23–1). Black women now make 94 percent of what white women earn. In 1992, 39.1 percent of black households earned less than $15,000 annually; by 1997, the percentage had declined to 31 percent. The overall black poverty rate in 1997 was 26.5 percent, the lowest on record. In real terms, approximately 1.7 million black Americans went off the poverty rolls between 1992 and 1998.

The increasing affluence of many black people rested not only on the removal of racial barriers to their employment and the implementation of affirmative action programs, but also on increased educational attainment. Many more black youths graduate from high school than ever before. In 1960, only 37.7 percent of African Americans between the ages of twenty-five and twenty-nine had completed high school, but by 1995, 86.5 percent had, almost exactly the same proportion (87.4 percent) as for white Americans. Black enrollment in college also rose from a mere 136,000 in 1960 to nearly 1,300,000 in 1990.

Nonetheless, many African Americans remain mired in poverty. The 26.5 percent of African Americans living below the poverty line in 1997 translates into more than nine million people. Most poor black people are trapped in devastated inner-city neighborhoods and are cut off from meaningful participation in the social and economic life of the nation.

The high rate of poverty in the black community disproportionately affects children. More than half of all African Americans under the age of eighteen live in families with only one parent, almost always the mother. Partly for this reason, the poverty rate for black children in 1997 was much higher—39 percent—than the overall black poverty rate. Female-headed single-parent families suffer from limited earning capacity, meager public assistance, poor housing, and inferior education. These conditions help to perpetuate poverty.

Ronald Reagan and the Conservative Reaction

Beginning in the late 1970s American politics took a hard turn to the right. This shift profoundly affected African Americans. With the election of Ronald Reagan to the presidency in 1980, the executive branch ceased to support expanded civil rights. It also sought to reduce welfare programs and staffed agencies and the federal judiciary with opponents of affirmative action. The now overwhelmingly white Republican party became entrenched in the South, ending the Democratic party's dominance in that region.

Reagan's victory marked the emergence of the New Right as the dominant force in American politics. Over the previous decade, many groups unhappy with the changes of the 1960s had developed powerful political organizations that found a home in the Republican party. These groups included those opposed to equal rights for women, to abortion rights, to the Supreme Court's decisions protecting the rights of the accused and banning compulsory prayer from the public schools, and other issues. White Southerners opposed to the civil rights movement and white Northerners angry at school busing, affirmative action, and the tax burden they associated with welfare were a key part of this coalition.

Dismantling the Great Society

One of the New Right's key goals was to reverse the growth of social welfare programs created during and after the New Deal. To this end, from 1981 to 1993 Reagan and his Republican successor George Bush cut federal grants to cities in half and terminated programs crucial to the stability of many black families. As a result, inner-city neighborhoods, where 56 percent of poor residents were African American, became more unstable.

Reagan advanced a "trickle-down" theory of economics. He believed that if the financial position of the wealthiest Americans improved, their increased prosperity would percolate through the middle and working classes to the poor. Unemployment statistics soon challenged this theory. By December 1982, the unemployment rate had risen to 10.8, and the rate for African Americans was twice that of white Americans. The real income of the highest paid 1 percent of the nation, meanwhile, increased from $312,206 to $548,970 during the 1980s.

Black Conservatives

Reagan and Bush often cloaked their intent to undermine rights-oriented policies by appointing black conservatives to key administrative positions. Reagan chose William Bell, for example, to replace the effective Carter appointee Eleanor Holmes Norton as chair of the Equal Employment Opportunity Commission (EEOC). Because Bell was a conservative with few qualifications for the post, civil rights leaders and organizations immediately protested his appointment. Reagan simply replaced Bell the following year with yet another black conservative, Clarence Thomas, who strongly opposed affirmative action. Thomas reduced the commission's staff and allowed the backlog of affirmative action cases to grow to 46,000 and processing time to increase to ten months.

Reagan similarly tried to change the direction of the U.S. Commission on Civil Rights (CCR), but in this case he met with resistance. Since its creation in 1957 the commission had served as a civil rights watchdog, with no real enforcement powers, but with considerable influence on public opinion. Soon after Reagan took office, the CCR began to issue reports critical of his civil rights policies. Reagan responded by trying to load the commission with members sympathetic to his perspective. He replaced the commission's chair, Arthur S. Flemming, who was white, with a black Republican, Clarence Pendleton, former executive director of the San Diego Urban League. The vice chair, however, was Mary Frances Berry, a well-respected, long-time civil rights activist and historian who had been appointed by Carter and who frequently clashed with the new president. In 1984, Reagan tried to remove Berry from the Commission on Civil Rights, but she resisted, suing in court to retain her position. When her suit was successful, she became known as "the woman the president could not fire." Even with Berry, however, the Commission on Civil Rights declined to virtual insignificance under Pendleton during the Reagan years.

Men like Bell, Thomas, and Pendleton were part of a vocal cadre of black, middle-class, conservatives. To augment their influence in the Republican party, these conservatives cultivated a small articulate group of black intellectuals such as Thomas Sowell, Walter Williams, Shelby Steele, Armstrong Williams, Ward Connerly, and, until he broke with the others in the late 1990s, Glenn Loury. However, unlike black politicians in the Democratic camp, black Republican politicians rarely exercised meaningful power within the party. They were expected to embrace the values and goals of the white party leaders. In contrast, elite black Democratic politicians could, and often did, make their influence felt. Moreover, they represented a large and essential constituency within the party.

The Thomas–Hill Controversy

The role of black conservatives acquired its greatest visibility when, in 1991, President George Bush nominated Clarence Thomas to the United States Supreme Court. Thomas was born in 1948 in rural Georgia. He graduated from Holy Cross College and Yale Law School. The symbolism of Thomas, who opposed the expansion of civil rights, replacing Thurgood Marshall, the greatest civil rights lawyer of the twentieth century, could not have been more dramatic.

Thomas's nomination precipitated a public exposure of gender conflict within the black community in history. Marshall had been one of the Court's great liberals and a staunch defender of civil rights. Thomas was a black conservative whose record on civil rights was meager. His credentials for the position were also open to question: He had served only fifteen months as an appellate court judge. However, he was a black man, and the black community was loath publicly to contest his nomination or to challenge the cynical tokenism of the Bush administration. Still, civil rights organizations expressed grave reservations about the Thomas nomination. The Urban League declared, "We welcome the appointment of an African-American jurist to fill the vacant seat left by Justice [Thurgood] Marshall. Obviously, Judge Thomas is no Justice Marshall. But if he were, this administration would not have appointed him. We are hopeful that Judge Thomas' background of poverty and minority status will lead him to greater identification with those in America who today are victimized by poverty and discrimination. And [we] expect the Senate, in the confirmation hearings, to explore whether he is indeed likely to do so."

But the anticipated easy confirmation process derailed when black law professor Anita Hill appeared before the Senate Judiciary Committee, which heard testimony on Thomas's confirmation, to accuse Thomas of sexually harassing her when she worked for him at the EEOC.

Some senators questioned her own character and integrity. Thomas countered her charges with charges of his own. He declared that he was a victim of a "high-tech lynching" in the media and that Hill's accusations were false. Although many in the black community supported Thomas, progressive feminists, white liberals, and some black people supported Hill. Activist black women were especially incensed by the treatment that Hill received from the Senate. Despite the opposition, Clarence Thomas won confirmation to the United States Supreme Court by a narrow 52–48 majority. On the Court, Thomas has proved to be an arch-conservative.

Affirmative Action

The Reagan and Bush administrations distinguished between what might be called the "old civil rights law," which they claimed to support, and the "new civil rights law," which they opposed. Developed in the decade between the *Brown* decision and the Voting Rights Act of 1965, the old civil rights law prohibited intentional discrimination, be it legal segregation in the schools, informal discrimination in the workplace, or racial restrictions on voting. The new civil rights law is concerned with discriminatory outcomes, as measured by statistical disparities, rather than with discriminatory intent. If, for example, black children overall are disproportionately in all-black schools, or if the workforce in a given firm, compared with the community in which it is located, is disproportionately white (or male), or if elected officials in a multiracial state or municipality are disproportionately white, then discrimination is assumed.

The remedies for such historic discrimination, collectively labeled "affirmative action," tend to be statistical in nature. They include increasing the number of minority pupils, minority employees, or (by redrawing the districts from which they were elected) minority elected officials to correspond to the percentage of the relevant minority population. In employment (and in admissions to colleges), the methods used in reaching these goals became known as affirmative action "guidelines." Sometimes guidelines were imposed by court order; more often they were the result of voluntary efforts by legislatures, government agencies, business firms, and universities to comply with civil rights laws and court rulings.

Few civil rights policies in the twentieth century have proved more controversial than affirmative action. Many white Americans argue that it runs contrary to the concept of achievement founded on objective merit and amounts to reverse racial or sexual discrimination. Ironically, because gender discrimination in employment was made illegal in the 1964 Civil Rights Act, prompting federal agencies to scrutinize the percentage of women in a given workforce, white women have been among the major beneficiaries of affirmative action. But the major advocates of affirmative action have been African Americans, most of whom see it as a remedy for centuries of discrimination. The debate over affirmative action has thus, inevitably, led to racial polarization, and it even divided the black community.

The Backlash

Though it has produced more litigation, the issue of affirmative action in employment has been less controversial than that of affirmative action in college admissions. State higher education institutions have been at the center of the controversy both because they are narrowly bound by the Fourteenth Amendment's prohibitions on racial discrimination and because they represent the gateways to upward mobility for millions of Americans, white and black. As the 1970s progressed, in the interest both of aiding disadvantaged minorities and of increasing diversity on campus, admissions offices began using different criteria for white and minority admissions.

Supreme Court Cases on Affirmative Action in Employment

1979	*United Steelworkers v. Weber* upholds preferential treatment in hiring and training by private firms
1980	*Fullilove v. Klutznick* upholds government programs that reserve places for minorities
1984	*Memphis Firefighters v. Stotts* rejects a judicial order for retaining less-senior black employees over white employees during layoffs
1986	*Wygant v. Jackson Board of Education* rejects school board's plan for laying off white teachers while retaining less senior black teachers, but also rejects Reagan administration position that affirmative action be limited to actual victims of discrimination, thus broadly upholding affirmative action
1986	*Local 93 of International Association of Firefighters v. City of Cleveland* upholds promotion of minorities ahead of white applicants with higher test scores and greater seniority
1986	*Local 28 of Sheet Metal Workers v. EEOC* upholds order that union meet minority quota for membership
1987	*U.S. v. Paradise* upholds judicial order imposing racial quotas in hiring and promotions of Alabama state troopers
1987	*Johnson v. Transportation Agency of Santa Clara County* upholds plan that promoted women over men
1987	*American Tobacco Co. v. Patterson* upholds seniority plans in place before 1964 unless discriminatory intent can be shown
1989	*Martin v. Wilks* rules that employees may challenge affirmative action plan after it has gone into effect. This decision is overruled by Congress in the Civil Rights Act of 1991
1989	*Richmond v. J. Croson and Co.* rules that Fourteenth Amendment prohibits set-asides for minority contractors, thus going against spirit of *Weber* and against the letter of *Fullilove v. Klutznick* and implying that all such plans face "strict scrutiny"
1990	*Metro Broadcasting v. FCC* upholds affirmative action plan increasing minority broadcasting owners, returning to *Fullilove*
1995	*Adarand Constructors v. Pena* strikes down a congressional statute requiring 10 percent of federal highway money to go to minority contractors and broadly asserts that any such programs using racial classifications are constitutionally suspect

In the late 1970s reaction to affirmative action set in. The case of *Regents of the University of California v. Bakke* was a key part of this backlash. The medical school at the University of California, as a form of affirmative action, had set aside sixteen of its one hundred places in each entering class for disadvantaged and minority students who were considered for admission in a separate system. White male student Alan Bakke sued the university for discrimination after it rejected his application for admission. The U.S. Supreme Court ruled in Bakke's favor in 1978. However, other legal issues were involved, and the court split without a majority on nearly every one of them. Only one justice declared that affirmative action cases should be judged on the same strict level of scrutiny that was applied to "invidious" discrimination. All the other justices stated that race-conscious remedies could be used in some circumstances to correct past discrimination.

California remains the center of the affirmative action storm because of its multiracial population. In 1995 Republican Governor Pete Wilson ended affirmative action in state employment. In 1996 California voters approved Proposition 209, which banned state agencies from implementing affirmative action programs. The campaign for the proposition was led by Ward Connerly, a conservative black entrepreneur who had received over $140,000 from state contracts set aside for minority businesses. Nonetheless, Connerly maintained that affirmative action had exacerbated the negative stereotyping of African Americans and had failed to address problems of poverty, unemployment, and inadequate education that beset the truly disadvantaged. Instead, it had merely elevated to higher status those least in need of assistance, especially middle-class white women. Finally, Connerly accepted the broader argument that affirmative action violated the concept of individual merit and core American values of equality and opportunity. Since the proposition was upheld by the U.S. Supreme Court, the number of African Americans and other protected minorities admitted to the whole University of California system dropped and the numbers at Berkeley, U.C.'s most prestigious campus, fell precipitously.

Black Political Activism in the Age of Conservative Reaction

Presidents Reagan and Bush did not completely reverse the advancement of the civil rights agenda. The increased participation of black men and women in the upper echelons of the Democratic party reflected the extent to which they had overcome political exclusion. In 1964 there were only 103 black elected officials in the nation; by 1994 there were nearly 8,500. Forty-one African Americans were serving in Congress by 1996. By the mid-1990s black men and women held the mayor's office in four hundred towns and cities. The days of black political powerlessness have ended.

During the Reagan–Bush era, one house of Congress—and often both—was in the hands of the Democratic party. Reflecting the importance of African-American voters to the party, that house used its power to pass many equal rights laws. The Civil Rights Restoration Act of 1988 authorized the withholding of federal funds from an entire institution if any program within it discriminated against women, racial minorities, the aged, or the handicapped. The Fair Housing Act of 1988 provided that either an individual or the Department of Housing and Urban Development (HUD) could bring a complaint of housing discrimination and authorize administrative judges to investigate housing complaints, issue injunctions and fines, and award punitive damages. These laws and the Civil Rights Act of 1991, which protected many of the defenses of civil rights, were a response to Supreme Court decisions that had narrowed the scope of earlier civil rights legislation.

Many African Americans invested symbolic importance in an effort to make Martin Luther King, Jr.'s birthday a national holiday. At first Reagan resisted the effort, but he eventually gave in to pressure from African Americans and their white allies. On November 2, 1983, Reagan signed a law designating the third Monday in January to honor King. On January 20, 1985, the United States officially observed Martin Luther King, Jr. Day for the first time.

Black activism also persisted on the international front. Much of this effort focused on ending the oppressive conditions of apartheid—the complete, social, political, and economic isolation of black people—in South Africa. In 1977 activist Randall Robinson founded TransAfrica to lobby for black political prisoners in South Africa, chief among them Nelson Mandela.

The antiapartheid movement became a major priority for African-American activists. They were able to enlist the sympathy and help of white Americans on college campuses and to pressure many universities and corporations into divesting their investments in South Africa. In 1986 the Black Congressional Caucus persuaded their colleagues to enact a U.S. trade embargo against South Africa and sustain it over President Reagan's veto.

In 1990, bowing to international pressure and a souring domestic economy, South African President F.W. deKlerk ended the twenty-eight-year prison term of its leader, Nelson Mandela. Soon thereafter, South Africa was transformed into a multiracial democracy, and Mandela was elected its president.

Jesse Jackson and the Rainbow Coalition

As Reagan's first term ended, Jesse Jackson announced that he would campaign for the presidency. Jackson's preparation for political battle was not the traditional climb from one elective office to another. Rather, he came up through the ranks of the civil rights movement, working alongside Martin Luther King, Jr., in the Southern Christian Leadership Conference (SCLC) and heading Operation Breadbasket, an organization that attempted to mobilize Chicago's black poor. After King's death, Jackson founded People United to Save (later Serve) Humanity (PUSH), which induced major corporations with large markets in the black community to adopt affirmative action programs. PUSH—EXCEL, which focused on education, was given a large grant by the Carter administration.

In 1983, angered by the effects of Reagan's policies, Jackson and PUSH began a successful drive to register black voters. Jackson's charismatic style engendered enthusiasm, especially as the Democratic party searched for a presidential candidate who could challenge Reagan's popularity.

Jackson had a highly effective style of grassroots mobilization. He began by appealing to what he would call a "rainbow coalition" of people who felt politically marginalized and underrepresented. The Rainbow Coalition was composed of diverse groups, including black people, white workers, liberals, Latinos, feminists, students, and environmentalists. Jackson developed a comprehensive economic policy focusing on tax reform, deficit reduction, industrial policy, and employment. The centerpiece of his plan was "Rebuilding America," a program to coordinate government, business, and labor in a national industrial policy. The Jackson platform, while within the tradition of American liberal reform, was far more progressive than anything his competitors proposed.

Jackson eventually garnered almost one-fourth of the votes in the Democratic primaries and caucuses and one-eighth of the delegates to the convention. His speech to

In 1988, the Reverend Jesse Jackson (1941–)
addressed the Democratic National Convention. He
made two unsuccessful bids for the White House (1984,
1988) but remained a powerful force in the Democratic
party because of his zeal in registering voters and
building coalitions.
PhotoEdit

the convention cemented his position as a voice for progressive change and a spiritual heir to both Martin Luther King, Jr., and Robert Kennedy. Walter Mondale, Jimmy Carter's vice president, who won the nomination, broke new ground when he made Geraldine Ferraro his running mate and the first woman on a major party's presidential ticket. But many Jackson supporters had hoped that Mondale would pick Jackson.

In November 1984, black voters again overwhelmingly favored the Democratic ticket, but Reagan won by a landslide with 59 percent of the popular vote. Clearly, most white Americans backed Reagan's conservative policies. Undeterred by defeat, Jackson worked to build his Rainbow Coalition, reaching out to the unemployed, militant trade unionists, small farmers, and gay people. He criticized the Democratic party's timid opposition to Reagan. Perhaps most important, he inspired the registration of enough new voters to affect several races in the 1986 midterm elections when Democrats held onto control of the House and regained a majority in the Senate.

By the time Jackson announced that he would again run for president in October 1987, he had become a serious contender. He won fifteen presidential primaries and caucuses and garnered seven million votes, one-third of all those cast. His Rainbow Coalition, however, never materialized. His victories in the primaries were based on mobilizing his black supporters; almost all his white support tended to come from college towns and the highly educated. Michael Dukakis, governor of Massachusetts, won the 1988 Democratic nomination.

Despite Jesse Jackson's voter registration drive and the hopes of the black community, Reagan's vice president, George Bush, triumphed in the 1988 election. The most memorable feature of Bush's campaign was a polarizing ad that featured Willie Horton, a black convict who had raped a white woman while on furlough from a Massachusetts prison as part of a program approved by Dukakis and his Republican predecessor as governor. Black leaders criticized the ad as a blatant appeal to white racism, but Bush would not renounce it.

Policing the Black Community

In March 1991, Los Angeles police pulled Rodney Glen King from his car after a high-speed chase and beat him with nightsticks. A bystander captured the incident on videotape, which television newscasts broadcast repeatedly, increasing long-simmering anger over police brutality among African Americans in Los Angeles. When a jury of eleven white Americans and one Hispanic American acquitted the four police officers involved in the incident of all but one of the charges brought against them, south-central Los Angeles erupted. The verdict highlighted the gulf between the perceptions of white and black Americans about the criminal justice system. Where the mostly white jury had seen the police imposing justice and maintaining law and order, black Americans saw proof of police repression and racism. Fifty-two people were killed in the outbreak that followed the verdict. Arsonists and looters devastated much of the community. Thousands of people were injured, four thousand were arrested, and an estimated one-half billion dollars worth of property was damaged or destroyed. The four officers were later retried in federal court on charges of violating King's civil rights. This time juries found two of them guilty and acquitted the other two. Meanwhile, a jury in King's civil suit ordered Los Angeles to pay him $3.8 million in damages.

The Rodney King episode resonated with many black men across the country. Writer Earl Ofari Hutchinson suggested why:

> Black professionals or business owners still tell harrowing tales of being spread-eagle over the hoods of their expensive BMW's or Porsches while the police ran makes on them and tore their cars apart searching for drugs. In polls taken after the Rodney King beating, blacks were virtually unanimous in saying that they believed any black person could have been on the ground that night being pulverized by the police. These were eternal reminders to the "new" black bourgeoisie that they could escape the hood, but many Americans still considered them hoods.

Three such high-profile cases in New York in the late 1990s focused public attention on the relation of black communities to white police authorities. In 1997 a Haitian immigrant, Abner Louima, was beaten and sodomized while in custody at a Brooklyn police station. In 1999, police shot Amadou Diallo, a West African immigrant, forty-one times when they mistook his reaching for a wallet for going for a gun. A jury in Albany acquitted the four police officials charged in the Diallo killing. Later the same year, Patric Dorismond (a Haitian immigrant) was shot and killed after he refused to purchase drugs from, and got into an argument with, undercover police officers. In each case an enraged black community protested the police profiling as one more instance of biases toward black men and one that targeted other minorities for illegal detention.

In October 1998, the human rights group Amnesty International, known for its condemnation of human rights abuse in countries with repressive governments, published a report on police brutality in the United States. The report covered the actions of local and state police, the FBI, the Immigration and Naturalization Service, and the prison system. Its contents came as no surprise to most black Americans or, indeed, to anyone who lived in America's poor, urban neighborhoods. The report detailed violations of the United Nations Code of Conduct for Law Enforcement Officials and the United Nations Basic Principles on the Use of Force and Firearms. Among the violations reported were the following:

- the shooting of unarmed suspects fleeing a minor crime scene
- excessive force used on mentally ill or disturbed people
- multiple shootings of a suspect, sometimes after the suspect was apprehended or disabled
- the beating of unresisting suspects
- the misuse of batons, chemical sprays, and electroshock weapons

These violations all involved the misuse of force during arrests, traffic stops, searches, and so forth. The report also cited sexual abuse of prisoners and the denial of food and water to them. One of the most important points in the Amnesty International report was that most victims of American law enforcement abuse were members of racial and ethnic minorities, while most police officers were white.

It is too easy to interpret these findings as showing that American police officers, as a group, are racists who oppress people they don't like. In fact, the issue of police brutality is less simple. Police officers are under tremendous pressure and live dangerous lives, in part because of the wide availability of guns in American society. No one can be expected to have perfect judgment about using force, and years of dealing with violence can destroy a person's sense of perspective and moral equilibrium.

Neither is the problem of crime by black Americans a simple one. The level of crime in black communities is high. The murder rate, for example, for African Americans in 1997 was seven times that of whites, and black victims accounted for 49 percent of all those murdered, even though African Americans make up only 12 percent of the population. Over 90 percent of those who murder, rape, and assault black people are black people themselves. The murder rate for young black men between the ages of fourteen and seventeen tripled between 1976 and 1993. Although this rate, like the rate of violent crime in the country in general, fell in the 1990s, the security of many African Americans remains imperiled.

Crime has devastated black neighborhoods. High crime rates raise the costs of business, driving jobs and investment dollars out of those areas most in need of them. Fear of violence leads many in the inner cities to barricade themselves inside their homes. Once vibrant neighborhoods have become virtual ghost towns where the silence of the streets is punctuated only by the sound of gunfire. Filmmaker Spike Lee was shocked when he returned to the Brooklyn neighborhood in which he had grown up to shoot his film *Crooklyn*. He found that the streets had become so unsafe that the local children he used as extras had to be taught how to play the games he had played growing up in the 1970s because they had never been allowed to play outside. "Nowa-days," Lee reflected after completing the film in 1994, "these kids, they'll shoot you dead in a second and not even think about it. The two big problems are crack and how accessible guns are. And also, you're talking about what Reagan did during his eight years. If I was a parent, I'd be terrified anytime my children left my sight." Even Rosa Parks, heroine of the civil rights movement, has not been immune to the urban crime wave. In 1994 she was beaten and robbed in her Detroit home by a twenty-eight-year-old unemployed black man. Her assailant recognized Parks but assaulted her anyway.

Being disproportionately the victims of crime, most African Americans have looked to the nation's police departments for aid. Because of their growing political power they have sought, not always successfully, to make the police both responsive to crime and fair in enforcing the laws. One key device for changing the behavior of law enforcement officials has been the appointment of black police chiefs. More than 130 American cities had black police chiefs in the 1990s.

The Clinton Presidency

During his first campaign for the presidency, the personable Democratic party candi-date, Arkansas governor Bill Clinton, was welcomed by black Americans into their churches, schools, and homes. His opponent George Bush had done little to win their loyalty, nominating conservatives to the federal courts and attacking civil rights legisla-tion. White Americans, too, were dissatisfied with Bush whom they blamed for doing little to alleviate an economic downturn.

Politically, Clinton was a centrist. Undeterred by charges of womanizing, draft eva-sion, and marijuana smoking, he sharply attacked Bush's record and promised to make government more responsive. Clinton won in November 1992 with just 43 per-cent of the popular vote to Bush's 38 percent and third-party candidate H. Ross Perot's 19 percent. However, Clinton garnered 78 percent of the black vote in key states in-cluding New Jersey, Michigan, New York, Illinois, and California. The election did not present the Democrats with a clear mandate. While maintaining control of Congress, they lost seats in the House. Republicans would use the ambiguous outcome to oppose most of Clinton's economic programs.

During his tumultuous presidency, most black people considered Clinton, despite major disappointments, the best president on race issues since Lyndon Johnson. In Clinton, black Americans had a friend. Writer Toni Morrison called Clinton the first black president, and in some circles he was called the first woman president because of his support for equal rights for all women, both black and white. He created a cabinet that mirrored the diversity of the American population—in some cases, such as Hazel O'Leary as Secretary of the Department of Energy and Ron Brown as Secretary of Commerce, appointing black people to posts that had nothing to do with race. He also appointed many African-American judges, and he was the first American president to visit black Africa.

In 1996 Clinton became the first Democratic president to win a second term since Franklin Roosevelt. Throughout his two terms in office, Clinton focused attention on the economy, a strategy that won grudging support from moderate Republicans. His objectives were to strengthen the economy and to make more opportunities available for black Americans and other previously excluded groups. Toward these ends, in a significant departure from the policies of his predecessors, he supported a new tax bill that increased the taxes of higher-income Americans. He also advocated expansion of the earned income tax credit to help improve the lives of poor Americans. His college student-aid program made available increased federal loan benefits. The economy boomed during the Clinton presidency, and when he left office in 2001, the country had the lowest poverty rate in 20 years. The Congressional Black Caucus (CBC) provided critical support for his economic programs. In 1993, CBC chairman Representative Kweisi Mfume of Maryland and the highest-ranking black congressman, Representative John Lewis, delivered the caucus vote that saved Clinton's $500 billion economic budget in both the House and Senate. In return, black congressmen gained financial support for inner city neighborhood development, poor families, children, and the elderly. Representative Mfume credited the CBC, for example, for saving the $2.5 billion allocation for food stamps that the Senate phased out and $3.5 billion for empowerment zones in cities and rural areas.

Unemployment plummeted from 7.2 percent when Clinton took office to 5.5 percent in 1995 and continued to decline in ensuing years. American businesses created 10 million new jobs, and many black people found jobs, some for the first time. Reduced federal spending and the 1993 tax increase helped to cut the annual federal deficit in half. As interest rates fell and the stock market soared, optimistic Americans increased their consumer spending.

Many black women had done particularly well. The 2000 census reported that women owned 38 percent of African American-owned businesses, a larger percentage than that of any other minority group and more than the nation's business community as a whole, of which women owned only 26 percent. Still, the census reveals that minority firms account for only 15 percent of all businesses in the nation.

Shortly before his reelection, in August 1996, Clinton signed the Personal Responsibility and Work Opportunity Reconciliation Act, a welfare reform bill. This disappointed many African Americans and political progressives in general. The legislation combined Clinton's own ideas with others espoused in the Republicans' "Contract with America" blueprint for conservative changes. The Republicans had used this platform to win control of both houses of Congress in 1994. The main target of the Personal Responsibility Act was Aid to Families of Dependent Children (AFDC), a program created in 1935 as part of the Social Security Act to prevent children from suffering because of the poverty of their parents. Critics claimed that AFDC stipends discouraged poor mothers from finding work, that it was responsible for the breakdown of the family among the nation's poor, and that it did little to reduce poverty. Proponents of the welfare reform bill also insisted that the states did not have enough flexibility in administering welfare. The conservative welfare "reform" measure ended guarantees of federal aid to poor children, turning control of such programs over to the states along with allocations of block grants. The act denied benefits to legal immigrants, reduced food stamp appropriations, and limited families to five years of benefits. It also required most adult welfare recipients to find employment within two years.

There were good reasons to believe that the welfare reform bill would not accomplish its sponsors' purposes. Most of the people who would be "encouraged to find work" by having their benefits reduced or cut entirely were among the least employable people in the labor force. A study of people terminated from general assistance in Michigan, for example, revealed that as many as two-thirds remained unemployed. As for the bill's effect on families, it is true that most women on welfare had their first children when they were unmarried teenagers, but there is little evidence that cutting welfare will prevent teenage pregnancies, and there is evidence that reforms targeted at improving the collection of child support payments for divorced mothers would reduce welfare costs far more effectively and humanely.

Clinton's support of the welfare act was consistent with his centrist ideology, and it was politically astute. His stance on the Welfare Reform Act immunized him from Republican attacks on the issue and had little impact on his support among African Americans. The president easily defeated his Republican opponent, Senator Robert Dole of Kansas, in the election of 1996.

The preliminary results of the new welfare reform strictures indicated that within a couple of years half of those who had taken jobs had returned to lives of unemployment, poverty, and quiet desperation. As the economy took a downturn in the closing months of Clinton's second term, conditions of poor mothers and children deteriorated steadily. The debate over welfare policy receded to the back burner during the 2000 election campaign and disappeared completely after George W. Bush took office, superseded by the emphasis on tax cuts for the wealthy.

African-American Cultural and Intellectual Movements at the End of the Millennium

The most positive developments for black Americans during the 1980s and 1990s came in the realm of culture. A cultural renaissance emerged in every American community with a substantial African-American presence. Black consciousness institutions flourished. They included black history and culture museums, festivals, expositions, publishing houses, bookstores and boutiques, concerts, theaters, and dance troupes. In 1996, *Publishers Weekly* reported that bookstores specializing in African-American books had increased from a dozen a few years earlier to more than two hundred. By 1994, there were seventy-five African-American publishing companies. In 1998 the National Literary Hall of Fame for Writers of African Descent opened at Chicago State University.

Black painters used outdoor murals to celebrate positive images of the black experience. Playwrights such as August Wilson, Charles Fuller, and George C. Wolfe helped revitalize American theater, and the musician Prince's film *Purple Rain* (1984) broke new ground in African-American rock cinematography. Wilson won two Pulitzer prizes for his plays—*Fences* in 1987 and *The Piano Lesson* in 1990. In 1987 PBS aired Henry Hampton's "Eyes on the Prize," a six-part documentary on the civil rights movement. Spike Lee changed the status of black filmmakers in Hollywood with films such as *Do the Right Thing* and *Malcolm X*. Wynton Marsalis became a leading figure in

American jazz. The Rodney King case inspired two important works: a symphony entitled *56 Blows,* by Alvin Singleton, and a one-woman docudrama entitled "Twilight: Los Angeles, 1992," by Anna Deavere Smith.

The new cultural renaissance differed from the black arts movement of the 1960s and 1970s. The contemporary fluorescence was more inclusive and more appreciative of women artists. It also included the work of openly gay and lesbian artists, such as documentary filmmaker Marlon Riggs, dance choreographer Bill T. Jones, and novelist E. Lynn Harris. Whereas poets and dramatists dominated the earlier movement, novelists—particularly women—hold sway in the new cultural renaissance. And much of the new work appeals to white as much as to black audiences, providing new insights into the lives of people of African heritage in a predominantly European society.

There were signs of this new trend as early as 1977, when Toni Morrison's *Song of Solomon* became a Book-of-the-Month Club selection, the first by a black author since Richard Wright's *Native Son* in 1940. Then Barbara Chase-Riboud made waves with *Sally Hemings* (1979), a fictional treatment of a woman who was both slave to and mistress of President Thomas Jefferson. In 1980, Toni Cade Bambara won the American Book Award for *The Salt Eaters.* At least as significant as these individual books was the founding in 1981 of a new publishing house, Kitchen Table: Women of Color Press. Then, in 1982, Alice Walker won the Pulitzer prize and the American Book Award for *The Color Purple,* which was later made into a movie with Whoopi Goldberg in the starring role. In 1987, Rita Dove won the Pulitzer prize for poetry. In 1993 she became America's poet laureate, and in the same year Toni Morrison became the first African American to win the Nobel prize for literature. President Bill Clinton invited Maya Angelou to read one of her poems at his inauguration ceremony in 1993.

Critics were not the only ones to take an interest in these works. In 1992 novels by three African-American women—Morrison, Walker, and Terry McMillan—made the *New York Times* best-seller list at the same time. This literary flowering reflected a new point of view that Alice Walker labeled "womanism" and others called black feminism. In 2001 the works of four African Americans made the *Times* best-seller list and revealed the expanding readership and growing appreciation of black literature across the racial spectrum.

Black Feminism

The woman's rights movement first blossomed in the 1970s in the wake of the civil rights struggles and the antiwar protests of the 1960s. The National Organization for Women (NOW), founded in 1966, spearheaded efforts to end job discrimination against women, to legalize abortion, and to secure federal and state support for child care. One of the movement's early successes was Title IX of the Educational Amendments Act of 1972, which required colleges and universities to take affirmative action to ensure equal opportunity for women. Another was the Supreme Court's decision in *Roe v. Wade* legalizing abortion.

While modern feminism at first seemed to hold little appeal for most black women, it affected them nonetheless. But later in the 1970s, many black women writers and activists, disillusioned with the attitudes of their male counterparts in the civil rights, black power, and black arts movements, sought to make the struggle against

Prolific writer, accomplished actress, and renowned poet, Maya Angelou (1928–) read an original poem, "On the Pulse of the Morning" at President Clinton's first inauguration in 1993. In 1970 she published her now classic autobiography, *I Know Why the Caged Bird Sings,* that describes her childhood in Stamps, Arkansas. She is the Reynolds Professor of American Studies at Wake Forest University in Winston-Salem, North Carolina.
AP/Wide World Photos

sexism as important as the struggle against racism. Between 1973 and 1975 the National Black Feminist Organization articulated many of the concerns specific to black women, from anger with black men for dating and marrying white women, to internal conflict over skin color, hair texture, and facial features, to the differences between the mobility of white and black women. Black feminists also attacked the myth of the black matriarchy and stereotypical portrayals of black women in popular culture, like the television show *That's My Mama,* featuring an overweight black woman as a domineering mother. Although the organization was short lived, it did break the silence imposed on black women by black liberation movements and on misogyny within black communities. Black feminists helped others to talk openly about domestic violence, rape, and sexual harassment in employment.

Black feminists started journals such as *SAGE* and organizations such as the Association of Black Women Historians, founded by Rosalyn Terborg-Penn and Eleanor Smith. Gradually, their works found readers in the general public and a place in women's studies curricula. The work of visual artists like Faith Ringgold appeared in museums and community centers. As more black women enrolled in college, courses with titles like "Black Women Writers" and "Black Women's History" became part of college black studies curricula. By the early 1990s there were more black women in higher education, graduate, and professional degree programs than there were black men.

The field of black women's history has grown rapidly: scholarly monographs, reference works, anthologies, conferences, and exhibitions have been devoted to the contribution black women have made to the political struggles and artistic accomplishments of African Americans. These historians have explored the role of race, class, and gender in the oppression of marginalized people in American society.

Black Intellectuals

An important part of the recent black cultural renaissance has been the rise to national prominence of black public intellectuals. These individuals go beyond their roles as scholars to participate in public debate and discourse about major issues.

In the past, most public intellectuals were white males. Among the few exceptions were the formidable W. E. B. Du Bois and novelists Richard Wright, James Baldwin, and Ralph Ellison. Within the past two decades, however, many of the most prominent public intellectuals to emerge have been African Americans. Among them are Cornel West, Henry Louis Gates, Jr., William Julius Wilson, Michele Wallace, Ishmael Reed, Stanley Crouch, Charles Johnson, Patricia Williams, John Edgar Wideman, Manning Marable, Robin D. G. Kelley, Michael Eric Dyson, Nell Irvin Painter, and Bell Hooks. Their views range from Marxist to extreme conservative, but they all desire to redefine black identity in this country and to explore how race is involved in its social and political workings. Historian Kelley put it well when he declared, "Culture and questions of identity have been at the heart of some of the most intense battles facing African Americans at the end of the century. . . . Not only has globalization continued to transform black culture, but it has also dramatically changed the nature of work, employment opportunities, class structure, public space, the cultural marketplace, the criminal justice system, political strategies, [and] even intellectual work." The emergence of these figures and the acclaim accorded them mark the end of America's long refusal to acknowledge the intellectual accomplishments of African Americans.

Afrocentricity

In the 1980s and 1990s a philosophy of culture referred to as "Afrocentricity" or "Afrocentrism" captured widespread media and academic attention. Although the philosophy and practice of Afrocentricity had been a prominent feature of black studies courses for more than a decade, Temple University professor Molefi Kete Asante gave it a presence and a personality. In 1980 Asante published *Afrocentricity*, in which he argued that an African-centered perspective was needed to challenge the dominance of Eurocentric values in education. Other leading Afrocentrists include Asa Hillard and John Henrik Clarke.

Many black educators enthusiastically embraced Afrocentricity as a way to celebrate and reclaim a positive African identity and to find unity with other peoples of the

African diaspora. Afrocentrists rejected the idea of America as a melting pot. Assimilation, they argued, meant a rejection of their African cultural heritage. At the heart of this position is a strong indictment of American ideals and institutions for their complicity in the long oppression of black people.

Afrocentrists vigorously defended their perspective. Asante explained to his critics, "Afrocentricity is a terribly maligned concept. Afrocentricity is the idea that African people and interests must be viewed as actors and agents in human history, rather than as marginal to the European historical experience—which has been institutionalized as universal." Similarly, Tsehloane Keto declared that black scholars had to challenge the Eurocentric paradigm that "interpret[ed] the roles of African Americans through the invisible person model, the Ghetto model, the spook who sat by the door model, and the Sambo model." Black historians and social scientists, Afrocentrists argued, had to place Africa and its descendants at the center of their studies to increase appreciation of the contributions of black people in world history.

Many black people, however, insisted that Afrocentricity was regressive and would foster self-segregation. Writer Earl Ofari Hutchinson conceded that Asante's idea merited attention while expressing skepticism about the claims of some Afrocentrist academics: "In their zeal to counter the heavy handed 'Eurocentric' imbalance of history, some have crossed the line between historic fact and fantasy. They've constructed groundless theories in which Europeans are 'Ice People,' suffer 'genetic defects,' or are obsessed with 'color phobias.' They've replaced the shallow European 'great man' theory of history with a feel good interpretation of history." White writers, notably historian Arthur Schlesinger, Jr., in *The Disuniting of America,* weighed in with blistering attacks. White and black critics alike cautioned that the Afrocentrist desire to fabricate "a glorious past" for black people did a disservice to the truth. Harvard University philosophy professor Cornel West assessed both the positive and negative value of Afrocentrism in 1993:

> Afrocentrism, a contemporary species of black nationalism, is a gallant yet misguided attempt to define an African identity in a white society perceived to be hostile. It is gallant because it puts black doings and sufferings, not white anxieties and fears, at the center of discussion. It is misguided because—out of fear of cultural hybridization and through silence on the issue of class, retrograde views on black women, gay men, and lesbians, and a reluctance to link race to the common good—it reinforces the narrow discussions about race.

Louis Farrakhan and the Nation of Islam

Beginning in the 1980s, the Nation of Islam's Minister Louis Farrakhan became a potent source of racial division in the nation. Farrakhan was the son of immigrant parents from the West Indies. He became known as Minister Louis X when he assumed leadership of the Boston Temple of the Nation of Islam. As a young man, Farrakhan attended a black teachers' college in North Carolina but dropped out to become a Calypso singer. In 1955, while performing in Chicago, he heard Elijah Muhammad preach at the Nation of Islam's mosque. This marked a turning point in his life. Farrakhan joined the Nation and quickly ascended within its hierarchy to become minister of the Harlem Mosque No. 7 and Muhammad's national representative. When Elijah Muhammad died in 1975, he designated his son, Wallace Deen Muhammad, or Warith, as he renamed himself, to be his successor. Warith sought to distance the Nation of Islam from the more far-fetched teachings of his father and to bring it more in line with actual Islamic teachings.

Farrakhan opposed Warith's decisions and within three years of Elijah Muhammad's death established himself as the leader of the Nation of Islam. Under Farrakhan's direction, and with $5 million in start-up capital from the Libyan dictator Colonel Muammar Qaddafi and subsequent federal government contracts, the Nation developed a number of economic enterprises, including media ventures, restaurants, clothing stores, and companies to provide security for apartment buildings, distribute soap and cosmetics, and manufacture pharmaceuticals. Farrakhan recruited among poor and marginalized urban African Americans and within the black prison population. The conservatism of the Reagan era complemented the reconstituted Nation's conservative social ideals, which harked back to those advanced by Booker T. Washington at the turn of the century. Farrakhan downplayed the struggle for civic and political rights. In 1985 he declared:

> God wants us to build a new world order: A new world order based on peace, justice and equality. Where do we start? . . . Physical separation is greatly feared [by whites], and it is not now desired by the masses of black people, but America is not willing to give us eight or ten states, or even one state. Let's be reasonable. . . . What we propose tonight is a solution that is in between two extremes. If we cannot go back to Africa, and America will not give us a separate territory, then what can we do here and now to redress our own grievances? . . . We propose that we use the blessings that we have received from our sojourn in America to do for ourselves what we have been asking the whites in this nation to do for us.

Until 1984, most Americans were barely aware of Farrakhan's existence. In that year, however, he broke the Nation of Islam's long-standing tradition of abstaining from politics to support Jesse Jackson's bid for the Democratic presidential nomination and soon ignited a firestorm of controversy. When some Jews took offense at Jackson's off-the-record reference to New York as "Hymietown" during a conversation with two African-American reporters, Farrakhan, whose Fruit of Islam provided security for Jackson's campaign, made matters worse. On the February 24, 1984, "CBS Evening News," Farrakhan warned, "I say to the Jewish people, who may not like our brother: It is not Jesse Jackson you are attacking. . . . When you attack him, you are attacking the millions who are lining up with him. You're attacking all of us. . . . Why dislike us? Why attack our champion? Why hurl stones at him? It's our champion. If you harm this brother, what do you think we should do about it?"

In 1984, as in the past, Farrakhan's verbal assaults against Jews, whom he called a principal enemy of African Americans, attracted support from ultra-right-wing, anti-Semitic forces and condemnation from Jewish Americans. Dredging up anti-Semitic shibboleths reminiscent of Hitler's Germany, Farrakhan blamed Jews for many of the ills plaguing African Americans. Jewish Americans, many of whom had been among the principal allies of African Americans during the civil rights movement, called on African-American organizations and leaders to repudiate Farrakhan and his rhetoric.

The Million Man
and Million Woman Marches

A major event during Farrakhan's tenure at the helm of the Nation of Islam was the Million Man March in Washington, D.C., on October 16, 1995. Farrakhan called this a "Holy Day of Atonement and Reconciliation," to "reconcile our spiritual inner beings and to redirect our focus to developing our communities, strengthening our families, working to uphold and protect our civil and human rights, and empowering ourselves through the Spirit of God, more effective use of our dollars, and through the power of the vote."

While the Million Man March had its detractors, and the actual number of men who attended it was in dispute, it was a symbolic success and generated positive coverage even in the mainstream media. It inspired many black men to become more engaged with their communities and to speak out more forcefully against oppression. On this occasion, the Nation's conservative philosophy of religion, self-respect, family values, community responsibility, and "bootstrap capitalism" found a responsive audience.

Yet the goodwill dissipated when, three months after the march, Farrakhan embarked on a World Friendship Tour to some twenty countries in Africa and the Middle East. To the consternation of many, he met with the leader of the brutally repressive military regime in Nigeria, General Sani Abacha. At home, Farrakhan's intemperate rhetoric continued to attract attention. In the wake of the Million Man March, he failed to forge a coherent strategy to resolve African America's continuing social problems.

Several black intellectuals have made known their objection to or displeasure with Farrakhan, none more effectively than political scientist Adolph Reed. According to Reed, Farrakhan "weds a radical oppositional style to a program that proposes private and individual responses to social problems; he endorses moral repressiveness; he asserts racial essentialism; he affirms male authority; and he lauds bootstrap capitalism. . . . His focus on self-help and moral revitalization is profoundly reactionary and meshes perfectly with the victim-blaming orthodoxy of the Reagan/Bush era."

The success of the Million Man March inspired black women, and later black youths, to organize similar demonstrations. Initiated by two Philadelphia women— Phile Chionesu and Asia Coney—on October 25, 1997, well over half a million black women gathered in Philadelphia. The march was a celebration, a call to unity, and a forum for black women to speak out against domestic violence, inadequate access to quality health care and educational opportunities, and the proliferation of drugs and violence in their communities. The march did not garner nearly as much media attention as had the Million Man March, perhaps because its organizers were relatively unknown. The march nonetheless symbolized the ongoing struggle of black women to be seen and heard in American society and to counter negative stereotypes and derogatory images of black womanhood.

Black Christianity
on the Front Lines

By the 1990s, black Baptists constituted the fourth-largest U.S. religious group, with 8.7 million members. The numbers of black Roman Catholics grew to 9 percent of that denomination. Likewise, the large numbers of Caribbean immigrants increased the numbers of black Episcopalians to 10 percent of that church's 2.4 million members. Throughout the closing decade of the twentieth century, black people made significant strides in many denominations. George A. Stallings was consecrated a bishop of the American Roman Catholic church in 1991, and two years later Pope John Paul II apologized for the Catholic church's support of slavery. In 1990, in an address at the Riverside Church in New York City, Nelson Mandela thanked American churches for their support during South Africa's struggle against apartheid.

In the 214-year history of the African Methodist Episcopal church, no woman had ever been appointed a bishop. But in July 2000, Vashti Murphy McKenzie broke the barrier when she was named bishop of the 18th Episcopal District in Southeast Africa (composed of approximately 200 churches and 10,000 members in Lesotho, Botswana, Swaziland, and Mozambique). Her four-year appointment followed a successful ten-year stint as a pastor of Baltimore, Maryland's Payne Memorial Church, during which time she increased the membership from 300 to more than 1,700. She pledged to concentrate on programs for grassroot economic development, construction of schools, and health care.

With the support of the Delta Sigma sorority, family, and the Baltimore, Maryland, church community, Vashti Murphy McKenzie broke through "the stained-glass ceiling" (her words) to become the first woman to be appointed a bishop in the history of the A.M.E. church. She is a graduate of the University of Maryland and earned a Master of Divinity from Harvard University's Divinity School and a doctorate in ministry at the United Theological Seminary in Dayton, Ohio.
AP/Wide World Photos

Faced with the problems of the black community in the United States and with a changing population, African-American Christians in both traditional and nontraditional religious institutions developed outreach programs to create supportive communities for the embattled and vulnerable. An example of a modern religious reformer is the Reverend Eugene Rivers, founder, along with like-minded former students at Harvard University of the small Azusa Christian Community in a crime-plagued neighborhood in Boston. An evangelical Christian, Rivers believes that "the church is the last best hope that black people have." He turned a former crack house into a Christian settlement named Ella J. Baker House. Its primary goal, Rivers says, is to keep children from killing one another. He and fellow black clergy formed the 10-Point Coalition and entered into a partnership with the police. The collaboration helped eliminate juvenile murders for two-and-a-half years. Rivers advocates a pragmatic black nationalism aimed at developing a rich, viable black civil society centered on the church.

The Hip-Hop Nation

Just as black feminists used the novel and black arts nationalists used poetry, a younger generation of African Americans, collectively known as the hip-hop nation, uses rap music to express its concerns. Rap is a form of rhythmic speaking in rhyme; "hip-hop" refers to the backup music for rap, which is often composed of a collage of excerpts, or "samples," from other songs. "Hip-hop" also refers to the culture of rap.

The first rap hit, "Rapper's Delight" by the Sugar Hill Gang, came out in 1979; it popularized the term "hip-hop." Rap's first superstars were Grandmaster Flash and the Furious Five. In the group's album, "The Adventures of Grandmaster Flash on the Wheels of Steel" (1981), Flash used the disk jockey technique of "scratching"—moving a record back and forth underneath a needle to produce a rhythmic, jarring sound. Flash is also credited with an innovative technique that involved hooking two turntables to the same set of speakers and manipulating different records on the turntables, switching quickly from one to the other to create a third, original composition.

N.W.A., a California group, created "gangsta rap" with their 1989 release of "Straight Outta Compton." In 1991, rapper Ice-T costarred in a box-office smash film, *New Jack City*. This film, along with *Boyz N the Hood* and *Menace II Society*, ushered in a new genre of black urban films that depicted the violence and alienation of many inner-city youths.

Rap draws inspiration from earlier black musical forms—rhythm and blues, soul, jazz, and gospel. Its rhythmic commentary on life in America's black communities draws on earlier black poets and messages of past and present political activists such as Martin Luther King, Jr., Malcolm X, and Louis Farrakhan. Rap lyrics call attention to the dangers of drug use, AIDS, teenage pregnancy, and dropping out of school. As Grandmaster Flash and the Furious Five's lead vocalist Melle Mel rapped, "It's like a jungle sometimes, it makes me wonder, how I keep from going under."

When it first appeared, critics called rap music a fad. They were wrong: After two decades, in February 1999, *Time* magazine signaled the coming of age of this genre of black music with an eleven-page cover story featuring the most celebrated rap performers and producers of the past twenty years. Hip-hop performer Lauryn Hill, twenty-three years old and nominated for an unprecedented ten Grammy Awards in 1999 (she won five), graced the cover of the issue.

Rap lyrics, the rap lifestyle, and rap artists have all aroused the consternation of older African Americans. The post–civil rights, black power, and black feminist elders have criticized rappers for their offensive, misogynist language, gang warfare, and violence against women. In 1995, for example, Black Women for Political Action pressured Time Warner to sell its rap label. The white media pilloried Ice-T for his antipolice lyrics.

2000 and Beyond

The election of 2000 revealed fault lines of culture, geography, race, class, and gender. A gender gap of about 11 percent reflected the fact that men strongly supported Republican, and women favored Democratic, candidates. The middle of the country and the South voted for Republican Texas Governor George W. Bush, while Democratic candidate Vice President Albert Gore, Jr. carried the states of the upper Midwest (Iowa, Minnesota, Wisconsin, Illinois, and Michigan), the Northeast, and the Pacific Coast. Gays and Lesbians voted 70 percent for Gore, while those who identified themselves as conservative Christians voted 80 percent for Bush. The campaign focused largely on economic issues—Social Security, taxes, health care (HMO reform and a prescription-drug benefit for seniors), and education.

Black community leaders and organizations worked hard to register voters and to increase turnout for the 2000 election. The NAACP, for example, spent 9 million dollars on Operation Big Vote. Its organizers even registered more than 11,000 prisoners in county jails in the South.

Although Gore did not effectively address the many concerns of black voters, especially those concerns connected to the criminal justice system, racial profiling by police, and the great disparities in sentencing for drug-related offenses, African Americans gave him ninety percent of their votes. Their support was not enough to ensure victory, however. In a hotly contested election, the outcome finally hung on one state: Florida. In the end, the U.S. Supreme Court, in a 5-to-4 ruling [*Bush v. Gore,* 121 S.Ct. 525 (2000)] decided the issue by halting the recount of ballots in Florida. The Court's majority based its ruling on the Fourteenth Amendment's prohibition of states denying citizens equal protection of the law. The Court insisted that the recount had to be stopped because the Florida Supreme Court, which had authorized it, had failed to provide uniform standards for determining the intent of the voters.

African Americans reported serious discrimination and interference with their voting in Florida. A group of political leaders in Jacksonville, Florida, filed a lawsuit claiming that many of their votes were thrown out as "undervotes" or "overvotes," especially in four city council districts with the highest concentration of African Americans in the state. According to the lawsuit, 26,000 ballots were not counted in Duval County, and more than 9,000 of those were cast in largely African-American precincts where Gore had captured more than 90 percent of the vote. Indeed, the U.S. Civil Rights Commission found that tens of thousands of African Americans were disfranchised in Florida. In a draft report, it declared, "African American voting districts were disproportionately hindered by antiquated and error-prone equipment like the punch card ballot system." This meant that more black and low-income voters, who tended to vote Democratic, had their ballots invalidated.

The Chair of the Commission, Mary Frances Berry, wrote in an essay in *The Journal of American History* (Vol. 88, no. 2, September 2001), "The United States Supreme Court helped undermine the pursuit of equal opportunity by African Americans for most of our history. . . . *Bush v. Gore* was so striking, in part, because the 5–4 majority has been assiduous about deference to state courts and states' rights in general. What the Court has done is to remind us that judges have social and political views that are reflected in their decisions. Each side has used the equal protection clause of the Fourteenth Amendment to convey its policy preferences. But, unlike the majority, in cases involving African American voting and the outcome of the 2000 election, the justices in dissent have remained consistent."

The 2000 Census
and Black America

The 2000 United States census counted 281,421,906 Americans, a 13.2 percent increase from 1990. The numbers recorded the greatest diversity in the nation's history within the population. The census data revealed that the populations of southern and western states had grown significantly. Texas surpassed New York to become the second-most-populous state, following California. One of the most important changes in the 2000 census form was the listing of six racial categories instead of the usual two. Each citizen could, thus, choose any combination of two or more races, a mind-numbing selection of sixty-three possible racial classifications. Approximately 6.8 million people, 2.4 percent of the total population of the United States, identified themselves as belonging to more than one race. For the first time in U.S. history, African Americans were no longer the largest minority group: According to the 2000 census the nation's population consists of 35.3 million Hispanics, 34.7 million African Americans, and 1.8 million Americans who consider themselves to be a mixture of black and some other race, such as American Indian, Asian, Pacific Islander, or white.

Reparations

In 1969 James Foreman, in his "Black Manifesto," called on America's churches and synagogues to collect $500 million as "a beginning of the reparations due us as a people who have been exploited and degraded, brutalized, killed, and persecuted." While Foreman's call was widely publicized, churches made no serious effort to respond to his demand. Four years later, Boris Bittker, a Yale Law School professor, argued in *The Case for Black Reparations* that slavery and the persistence of government-sanctioned racial discrimination justified the creation of a program to compensate black Americans. Since 1993, John Conyers, a black Democratic congressman from Detroit, has introduced a bill in every session of Congress—not to pay reparations, but to establish a federal commission to investigate slavery and the legacy of racial discrimination. The bill has never come to the floor of the House for a vote.

In 2000, the issue of reparations for slavery finally received widespread attention when Randall Robinson, founder and president of TransAfrica, published *The Debt:*

What America Owes to Blacks. Robinson reasoned that since Jews and Japanese Americans have been compensated for the indignities and horrors that they experienced in World War II, African Americans were also due financial indemnification for slavery, for "246 years of an enterprise murderous both of a people and their culture." Robinson maintained that many African Americans still bear the scars of slavery in terms of poor housing, inadequate health care, and insufficient educational opportunities. He insists that reparations would remedy the effect of such inequalities.

Some black writers and journalists adamantly reject these arguments. Two black journalists, William Raspberry and Juan Williams, object to the very idea of reparations. Instead, Raspberry favors a greater investment in education for African Americans, "not because of debts owed to or incurred by our ancestors, but because America needs its citizens to be educated and productive." Williams declared that "The suffering of long-dead ancestors is not a claim check for a bag full of cash. I don't want any money that belongs to any slave. That is obscene. The struggle of African-Americans for civil rights is not about selling out for a check."

September 11, 2001

Americans of virtually every racial, religious, and ethnic background were stunned and saddened on a Tuesday morning in September 2001, when four commercial airliners were commandeered by terrorists and crashed into New York's World Trade Center, the Pentagon in Washington, and rural Pennsylvania. Several hundred African Americans perished among the 3,000 people who died that day.

Leonard Pitts, Jr., a black syndicated columnist for the *Miami Herald,* captured the feelings of many Americans when he wrote a rousing defense of the United States and its people against an unknown adversary. "Did you want to tear us apart?" he asked. "You just brought us together. Let me tell you about my people. We are a vast and quarrelsome family, a family rent by racial, cultural, political and class division, but a family nonetheless. We're frivolous, yes, capable of expending tremendous emotional energy on pop cultural minutiae, a singer's revealing dress, a ball team's misfortune, a cartoon mouse. . . . Some people—you, perhaps—think that any or all of this makes us weak. You're mistaken. We are not weak. Indeed, we are strong in ways that cannot be measured by arsenals."

If the debate over reparations dramatized the separate pasts that black and white Americans have experienced, then the tragedy of September 11, 2001, served to remind Americans of every background of the bond and the history that we all share.

Conclusion

New forms of music, art, literature, dance, and film reflect the divisions and the strengths of contemporary black America. Without a unifying movement, various black constituencies developed their own strategies to secure the resources to advance their interests. Black women organized feminist groups, welfare mothers joined welfare rights organizations, black professionals created caucuses and networked, students fought for the institutionalization of black studies programs at colleges and universities, and artists founded museums and publishing concerns and launched aesthetic movements. Meanwhile, politicians forged national caucuses and local associations. Writers produced trenchant commentaries about black life in America and penned memoirs and autobiographies that placed their private pains in the collective consciousness of the nation. Black gays and lesbians focused attention on their struggle to eradicate homophobia.

Jesse Jackson, whose Rainbow Coalition of the 1980s reflected this creative fragmentation, a quest for unity amidst diversity, asked at the 1988 Democratic convention, "Shall we expand, be inclusive, find unity and power; or suffer division and impotence?" His question remains unanswered as the black odyssey toward freedom and the transformation of American society continues into the next millennium.

Review Questions

1. To what extent and in what key areas did the Reagan and Bush presidencies nullify or dismantle much of the Great Society legislation? How did African Americans respond to the era of Republican conservative reform?

2. What was the significance of Jesse Jackson's campaigns for the Democratic presidential nomination? What explains the chasm between black and white America over Minister Louis Farrakhan?

3. What factors contributed to the gulf between black middle-class Americans and poor African Americans in the inner city?

4. Why do so many Americans associate welfare with black people?

5. Why did affirmative action become one of the most contested issues of the 1990s? What are the differences between the old civil rights and the new civil rights? How did affirmative action in the workplace differ from affirmative action in education?

6. How did the Rodney King case illuminate the different perceptions black and white Americans have of the police and the justice system?

7. What were some of the major issues or concerns of black women in the 1990s? What factors gave rise to black feminism? What is the black women's literary renaissance?

8. Why have black intellectuals devoted increased attention to identity and culture issues?

Recommended Reading

Cathy J. Cohen. *The Boundaries of Blackness: AIDS and the Breakdown of Black Politics.* Chicago: University of Chicago Press, 1999. A black political scientist provides a sophisticated and provocative exploration into the social, political, and cultural impact of the AIDS epidemic on the African-American community.

Patricia Hill Collins. *Black Feminist Thought: Knowledge, Consciousness, and the Politics of Empowerment.* Boston: Unwin Hyman, 1990. A classic text in the study of black feminist theory and practice at the intersection of race, class, and gender by one of black studies' foremost sociologists.

TIMELINE

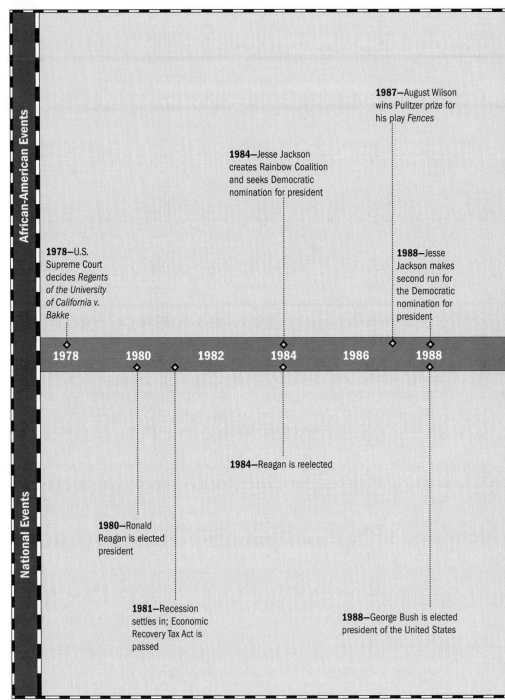

African-American Events

1987—August Wilson wins Pulitzer prize for his play *Fences*

1984—Jesse Jackson creates Rainbow Coalition and seeks Democratic nomination for president

1978—U.S. Supreme Court decides *Regents of the University of California v. Bakke*

1988—Jesse Jackson makes second run for the Democratic nomination for president

1978   1980   1982   1984   1986   1988

1984—Reagan is reelected

1980—Ronald Reagan is elected president

National Events

1981—Recession settles in; Economic Recovery Tax Act is passed

1988—George Bush is elected president of the United States

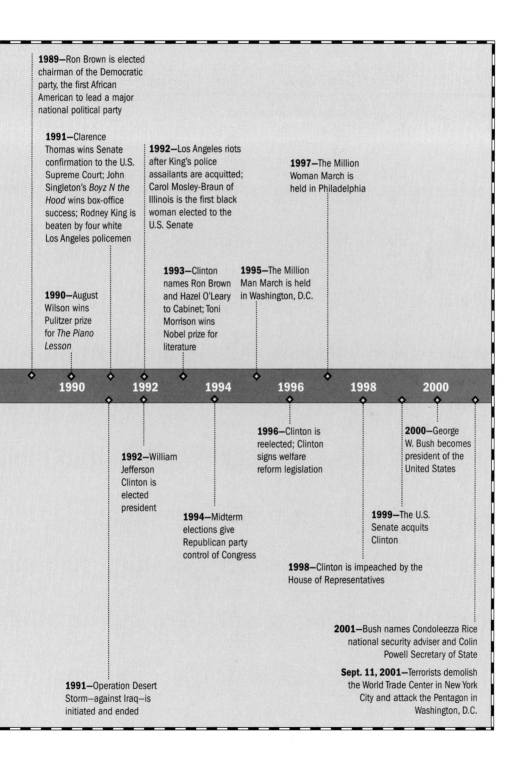

1989—Ron Brown is elected chairman of the Democratic party, the first African American to lead a major national political party

1991—Clarence Thomas wins Senate confirmation to the U.S. Supreme Court; John Singleton's *Boyz N the Hood* wins box-office success; Rodney King is beaten by four white Los Angeles policemen

1992—Los Angeles riots after King's police assailants are acquitted; Carol Mosley-Braun of Illinois is the first black woman elected to the U.S. Senate

1997—The Million Woman March is held in Philadelphia

1993—Clinton names Ron Brown and Hazel O'Leary to Cabinet; Toni Morrison wins Nobel prize for literature

1995—The Million Man March is held in Washington, D.C.

1990—August Wilson wins Pulitzer prize for *The Piano Lesson*

1990   **1992**   **1994**   **1996**   **1998**   **2000**

1996—Clinton is reelected; Clinton signs welfare reform legislation

2000—George W. Bush becomes president of the United States

1992—William Jefferson Clinton is elected president

1994—Midterm elections give Republican party control of Congress

1999—The U.S. Senate acquits Clinton

1998—Clinton is impeached by the House of Representatives

2001—Bush names Condoleezza Rice national security adviser and Colin Powell Secretary of State

Sept. 11, 2001—Terrorists demolish the World Trade Center in New York City and attack the Pentagon in Washington, D.C.

1991—Operation Desert Storm—against Iraq—is initiated and ended

Robin D. G. Kelley. *Yo' Mama Is DysFunkshional!* Boston: Beacon Press, 1998. Insightful essays about America's culture wars and an excellent critique of social science scholarship about black working-class culture and aesthetics by one of this generation's finest historians.

Ismael Reed. *Airing Dirty Laundry.* Reading, MA: Addison-Wesley Publishing Company, 1993. A collection of provocative, iconoclastic, and entertaining essays written by one of America's most insightful cultural critics.

Deborah Gray White. *Too Heavy a Load: Black Women in Defense of Themselves, 1894–1994.* New York: W. W. Norton, 1998. A brilliant study by a black woman historian of black women and the organizations they founded to fight for the ballot, against segregation, and against the sexism and misogyny of black nationalism in the contemporary era.

→ Epilogue ←

"A Nation Within a Nation"

Since the first Africans were brought to these shores in the seventeenth century, black people have been a constant and distinct presence in America. During the prolonged course of the Atlantic slave trade, approximately 600,000 Africans were sold into servitude in what became the United States. By the outbreak of the Civil War in 1861 there were nearly four million African Americans in this country. Today black people number over 30 million and make up slightly over 10 percent of the nation's population.

Initially regarded merely as an enslaved labor force to produce cash crops and not as a people who would or could enjoy an equal role in the political and social affairs of American society, African Americans constituted a separate ethnic, racial, and cultural group. For more than two centuries they remained outcasts.

People of African descent developed decidedly ambivalent relationships with the white majority in America. Never fully accepted and never fully rejected, black people relied on their own resources as they created their own institutions and communities. In 1852 Martin Delany declared, "We are a nation within a nation." A half century later W. E. B. Du Bois observed that the black man wanted to retain his African identity and to be an American as well. "He would not Africanize America, for America has too much to teach the world and Africa. He would not bleach his Negro soul in a flood of white Americanism, for he knows that Negro blood has a message for the world. He simply wishes to make it possible for a man to be both a Negro and an American, without being cursed and spit upon by his fellows, without having the doors of Opportunity closed roughly in his face."

Sometimes in desperation or disgust, some black people have been willing to abandon America or reject assimilation. The slaves who engaged in South Carolina's 1739 Stono rebellion attempted to reach Spanish Florida. As early as 1773, slaves in Massachusetts pledged to go to Africa after emancipation. From the 1790s to the start of the Civil War, visions of nationhood in Africa attracted a minority of African Americans. During the 1920s, Marcus Garvey and the Universal Negro Improvement Association glorified Africa while seeking black autonomy in the United States. By the 1950s, Elijah Muhammad, Malcolm X, and the Nation of Islam attracted black people by emphasizing a separate black destiny.

Yet in spite of the horrors of slavery, the indignity and cruelty of Jim Crow, and the unrelenting violence and discrimination inflicted on people of color, most African Americans have not rejected America but worked and struggled to participate fully in the American way of life. African slaves accepted elements of Christianity, and their descendants found solace in their spiritual beliefs. Black Americans have embraced American principles of brotherhood, justice, fairness, and equality before the law that are embedded in the Declaration of Independence and the Constitution. Again and again, African Americans have insisted that America be America, that the American majority live up to its professed ideals and values.

The nation within a nation has never been homogeneous. There have been persistent class, gender, and color divisions. There have been tensions and ideological conflicts among black leaders and organizations as they sought strategies to overcome racial inequities and white supremacy. Some leaders, such as Booker T. Washington, have emphasized self-reliance and economic advancement while others, including W. E. B. Du Bois and leaders of the NAACP, have advocated full inclusion in the nation's political, economic, and social fabric.

Furthermore, African Americans have been far more than victims, than an exploited labor force, than the subjects of segregation and stereotypes. They have contributed enormously to the development and character of American society and culture. As slaves, they provided billions of hours of unrequited labor to the American economy. Black people established churches, schools, and colleges that continue to thrive. Black people demonstrated a willingness to fight and die for a country that did not fully accept or appreciate their sacrifices. African Americans have made remarkable and innovative contributions to art, music, folklore, science, politics, and athletics that have shaped and enriched American society.

America is no longer what it was in 1700, 1800, or 1900. Chattel slavery ended in 1865. White supremacy is no longer fashionable or openly acceptable. Legal segregation was prohibited a generation ago. The capacity and willingness of Americans of diverse backgrounds and origins to live together in harmony has vastly improved in recent decades. Though we are now in the twenty-first century, the long odyssey of people of African descent has not ended nor will it end in the immediate future. Black people will continue to help mold and define this society, and they will continue to be "a nation within a nation."

➤ Appendix ⬿

Selected Articles and Amendments
from The Constitution of the United States

The following selections from the Constitution are clauses and amendments that pertain specifically to the stature of African Americans within the United States.

The Preamble

We the people of the United States, in order to form a more perfect union, establish justice, insure domestic tranquility, provide for the common defense, promote the general welfare, and secure the blessings of liberty to ourselves and our posterity, do ordain and establish this Constitution for the United States of America. . . .

Article I

SECTION 2

3. Representatives and direct taxes shall be apportioned among the several States which may be included within this Union, according to their respective numbers, which shall be determined by adding to the whole number of free persons, including those bound to service for a term of years, and excluding Indians not taxed, three fifths of all other persons. The actual enumeration shall be made within three years after the first meeting of the Congress of the United States, and within every subsequent term of ten years, in such manner as they shall by law direct.

SECTION 9

1. The migration or importation of such persons as any of the States now existing shall think proper to admit, shall not be prohibited by the Congress prior to the year one thousand eight hundred and eight, but a tax or duty may be imposed on such importation, not exceeding ten dollars for each person.

Amendment XIII [Ratified December 6, 1865]

SECTION 1.   Neither slavery nor involuntary servitude, except as punishment for crime whereof the party shall have been duly convicted, shall exist within the United States, or any place subject to their jurisdiction.

SECTION 2.   Congress shall have power to enforce this article by appropriate legislation.

Amendment XIV [Ratified July 9, 1868]

SECTION 1.   All persons born or naturalized in the United States, and subject to the jurisdiction thereof, are citizens of the United States and of the State wherein they reside. No State shall make or enforce any law which shall abridge the privileges or immunities of citizens of the United States; nor shall any State deprive any person of life, liberty, or property, without due process of law; nor deny to any person within its jurisdiction the equal protection of the laws.

SECTION 2.   Representatives shall be apportioned among the several States according to their respective numbers, counting the whole number of persons in each State, excluding Indians not taxed. But when the right to vote at any election for the choice of electors for President and Vice President of the United States, representatives in Congress, the executive and judicial officers of a State, or the members of the legislature thereof, is denied to any of the male inhabitants of such State, being twenty-one years of age, and citizens of the United States, or in any way abridged, except for participating in rebellion, or other crime, the basis of representation there shall be reduced in the proportion which the number of such male citizens shall bear to the whole number of male citizens twenty-one years of age in such State.

SECTION 3.   No person shall be a senator or representative in Congress, or elector of President and Vice President, or hold any office, civil or military, under the United States, or under any State, who having previously taken an oath, as a member of Congress, or as an officer of the United States, or as a member of any State legislature, or as an executive or judicial officer of any State, to support the Constitution of the United States, shall have engaged in insurrection or rebellion against the same, or given aid or comfort to the enemies thereof. But Congress may by a vote of two thirds of each House, remove such disability.

SECTION 4.   The validity of the public debt of the United States, authorized by law, including debts incurred for payment of pensions and bounties for services in suppressing insurrection or rebellion; shall not be questioned. But neither the United States nor any State shall assume or pay any debt or obligation incurred in aid of insurrection or rebellion against the United States, or any claim for the loss or emancipation of any slave; but all such debts, obligations, and claims shall be held illegal and void.

SECTION 5.   The Congress shall have the power to enforce, by appropriate legislation, the provisions of this article.

Amendment XV [Ratified February 3, 1870]

SECTION 1. The right of citizens of the United States to vote shall not be denied or abridged by the United States or by any State on account of race, color, or previous condition of servitude.

SECTION 2. The Congress shall have power to enforce this article by appropriate legislation.

Amendment XXIV [Ratified January 23, 1964]

SECTION 1. The right of citizens of the United States to vote in any primary or other election for President or Vice President, for electors for President or Vice President, or for Senator or Representative in Congress, shall not be denied or abridged by the United States or any State by reason of failure to pay any poll tax or other tax.

SECTION 2. The Congress shall have power to enforce this article by appropriate legislation.

The Emancipation Proclamation

By the President of the United States of America:

Whereas, on the twenty-second day of September, in the year of our Lord one thousand eight hundred and sixty-two, a proclamation was issued by the President of the United States, containing, among other things, the following, to wit:

> That on the first day of January, in the year of our Lord one thousand eight hundred and sixty-three, all persons held as slaves within any State or designated part of a State, the people whereof shall then be in rebellion against the United States, shall be then, thenceforward, and forever free; and the Executive Government of the United States, including the military and naval authority thereof, will recognize and maintain the freedom of such persons, and will do no act or acts to repress such persons, or any of them, in any efforts they may make for their actual freedom.

> That the Executive will, on the first day of January aforesaid, by proclamation, designate the States and parts of States, if any, in which the people thereof, respectively, shall then be in rebellion against the United States; and the fact that any State, or the people thereof, shall on that day be, in good faith, represented in the Congress of the United States by members chosen thereto at elections wherein a majority of the qualified voters of such State shall have participated, shall, in the absence of strong countervailing testimony, be deemed conclusive evidence that such State, and the people thereof, are not then in rebellion against the United States.

Now, therefore I, Abraham Lincoln, President of the United States, by virtue of the power in me vested as Commander-in-Chief, of the Army and Navy of the United States in time of actual armed rebellion against the authority and government of the United States, and as a fit and necessary war measure for suppressing said rebellion, do, on this first day of January, in the year of our Lord one thousand eight hundred and sixty-three, and in accordance with my purpose so to do publicly proclaimed for the full period of one hundred days, from the day first above mentioned, order and designate as the States and parts of States wherein the people thereof respectively, are this day in rebellion against the United States, the following, to wit:

Arkansas, Texas, Louisiana, (except the Parishes of St. Bernard, Plaquemines, Jefferson, St. John, St. Charles, St. James Ascension, Assumption, Terrebonne, Lafourche, St. Mary, St. Martin, and Orleans, including the City of New Orleans), Mississippi, Alabama, Florida, Georgia, South Carolina, North Carolina, and Virginia, (except the forty-eight counties designated as West Virginia, and also the counties of Berkley, Accomac, Northampton, Elizabeth City, York, Princess Ann, and Norfolk, including the cities of Norfolk and Portsmouth), and which excepted parts, are for the present, left precisely as if this proclamation were not issued.

And by virtue of the power, and for the purpose aforesaid, I do order and declare that all persons held as slaves within said designated States, and parts of States, are, and henceforward shall be free; and that the Executive government of the United States, including the military and naval authorities thereof, will recognize and maintain the freedom of said persons.

And I hereby enjoin upon the people so declared to be free to abstain from all violence, unless in necessary self-defense; and I recommend to them that, in all cases when allowed, they labor faithfully for reasonable wages.

And I further declare and make known, that such persons of suitable condition, will be received into the armed service of the United States to garrison forts, positions, stations, and other places, and to man vessels of all sorts in said service.

And upon this act, sincerely believed to be an act of justice, warranted by the Constitution, upon military necessity, I invoke the considerate judgment of mankind, and the gracious favor of Almighty God.

In witness whereof, I have hereunto set my hand and caused the seal of the United States to be affixed. Done at the City of Washington, this first day of January, in the year of our Lord one thousand eight hundred and sixty-three, and of the Independence of the United States of America the eighty-seventh.

By the President: Abraham Lincoln

William H. Seward, Secretary of State.

Key Provisions of the Civil Rights Act of 1964

An Act

To enforce the constitutional right to vote, to confer jurisdiction upon the district courts of the United States to provide injunctive relief against discrimination in public accommodations, to authorize the Attorney General to institute suits to protect constitutional rights in public facilities and public education, to extend the Commission on Civil Rights, to prevent discrimination in federally assisted programs, to establish a Commission on Equal Employment Opportunity, and for other purposes.

Title I—Voting Rights

SECTION 101 . . .(2) No person acting under color of law shall—

(A) In determining whether any individual is qualified under State law or laws to vote in any Federal election, apply any standard, practice, or procedure different from the standards, practices, or procedures applied under such law or laws to other individuals within the same county, parish, or similar political subdivision who have been found by State officials to be qualified to vote;

(B) deny the right of any individual to vote in any Federal election because of an error or omission on any record or paper relating to any application, registration, or other act requisite to voting, if such error or omission is not material in determining whether such individual is qualified under State law to vote in such election;

(C) employ any literacy test as a qualification for voting in any Federal election unless (i) such test is administered to each individual and is conducted wholly in writing, and (ii) a certified copy of the test and of the answers given by the individual is furnished to him within twenty-five days of the submission of his request made within the period of time during which records and papers are required to be retained and preserved . . .

Title II—Injunctive Relief Against Discrimination in Places of Public Accommodation

SECTION 201.   (a) All persons shall be entitled to the full and equal enjoyment of the goods, services, facilities, and privileges, advantages and accommodations of any place of public accommodation, as defined in this section, without discrimination or segregation on the ground of race, color, religion, or national origin. (b) Each of the following establishments which serves the public is a place of public accommodation within the meaning of this title if its operations effect commerce, or if discrimination or segregation by it is supported by State action:

(1) any inn, hotel, motel, or other establishment which provides lodging to transient guests, other than an establishment located within a building which contains not more than five rooms for rent or hire and which is actually occupied by the proprietor of such establishment as his residence;

(2) any restaurant, cafeteria, lunchroom, lunch counter, soda fountain, or other facility principally engaged in selling food for consumption on the premises, including, but not limited to, any such facility located on the premises of any retail establishment; or any gasoline station;

(3) any motion picture house, theater, concert hall, sports arena, stadium or other place of exhibition or entertainment;

(4) any establishment (A)(i) which is physically located within the premises of any establishment otherwise covered by this subsection, or (ii) within the premises of which is physically located any such covered establishment, and (B) which holds itself out as serving patrons of such covered establishment. . . .

(d) Discrimination or segregation by an establishment is supported by State action within the meaning of this title if such discrimination or segregation

(1) is carried on under color of any law, statute, ordinance, or regulation; or

(2) is carried on under color of any custom or usage required or enforced by officials of the State or political subdivision thereof; or

(3) is required by action of the State or political subdivision thereof. . . .

SECTION 202.   All persons shall be entitled to be free, at any establishment or place, from discrimination or segregation of any kind on the ground of race, color, religion, or national origin, if such discrimination or segregation is or purports to be required by any law, statute, ordinance, regulation, rule, or order of a State or any agency or political subdivision thereof.

SECTION 203.   No person shall (a) withhold, deny, or attempt to withhold or deny, or deprive or attempt to deprive, any person of any right or privilege secured by section 201 or 202, or (b) intimidate, threaten, or coerce, or attempt to intimidate, threaten, or coerce any person with the purpose of interfering with any right or privilege secured by section 201 or 202, or (c) punish or attempt to punish any person for exercising or attempting to exercise any right or privilege secured by section 201 or 202.

Title III—Desegregation of Public Facilities

SECTION 301.(a)   Whenever the Attorney General receives a complaint in writing signed by an individual to the effect that he is being deprived of or threatened with the loss of his right to the equal protection of the laws, on account of his race, color, religion, or national origin, by being denied equal utilization of any public facility which is owned, operated, or managed by or on behalf of any State or subdivision thereof, other than a public school or public college as defined in section 401 of title IV hereof, and the Attorney General believes the complaint is meritorious and certifies that the signer or signers of such complaint are unable, in his judgment, to initiate and maintain appropriate legal proceedings for relief and that the institution of an action will materially further the orderly progress of desegregation in public facilities, the Attorney General is authorized to institute for or in the name of the United States a civil action in any appropriate district court of the United States against such parties and for such relief as may be appropriate. And such court shall have and shall exercise jurisdiction of proceedings instituted pursuant to this section. The Attorney General may implead as defendants such additional parties as are or become necessary to the grant of effective relief hereunder. . . .

Title VI—Nondiscrimination in Federally Assisted Programs

SECTION 601.   No person in the United States shall, on the ground of race, color, or national origin, be excluded from participation in, be denied the benefits of, or be subjected to discrimination under any program or activity receiving Federal financial assistance.

SECTION 602.   Each Federal department and agency which is empowered to extend Federal financial assistance to any program or activity, by way of grant, loan, or contract other than a contract of insurance or guaranty, is authorized and directed to effectuate the provisions of section 601 with respect to such program or activity by issuing rules, regulations, or orders of general applicability which shall be consistent with achievement of the objectives of the statute authorizing the financial assistance in connection with which the action is taken. No such rule, regulation, or order shall become effective unless and until approved by the President. Compliance with any requirement adopted pursuant to this section may be effected

> (1) by the termination of or refusal to grant or to continue assistance under such program or activity to any recipient as to whom there has been an express finding on the record, after opportunity for hearing, of a failure to comply with such requirement, but such termination or refusal shall be limited to the particular political entity, or part thereof, or other recipient as to whom such a finding has been made and, shall be limited in its effect to the particular program, or part thereof, in which such non-compliance has been so found . . .

Title VII—Equal Employment Opportunity . . .

Discrimination Because of Race, Color, Religion, Sex, or National Origin

SECTION 703.   (a) it shall be an unlawful employment practice for an employer—

(1) to fail or refuse to hire or to discharge any individual, or otherwise to discriminate against any individual with respect to his compensation, terms, conditions, or privileges of employment, because of such individual's race, color, religion, sex, or national origin; or

(2) to limit, segregate, or classify his employees in any way which would deprive or tend to deprive any individual of employment opportunities or otherwise adversely affect his status as an employee, because of such individual's race, color, religion, sex, or national origin.

(b) it shall be an unlawful employment practice for an employment agency to fail or refuse to refer for employment, or otherwise to discriminate against, any individual because of his race, color, religion, sex, or national origin, or to classify or refer for employment any individual on the basis of his race, color, religion, sex, or national origin.

(c) it shall be an unlawful employment practice for a labor organization—

(1) to exclude or to expel from its membership, or otherwise to discriminate against, any individual because of his race, color, religion, sex, or national origin;

(2) to limit, segregate, or classify its membership, or to classify or fail or refuse to refer for employment any individual, in any way which would deprive or tend to deprive any individual of employment opportunities, or would limit such employment opportunities or otherwise adversely affect his status as an employee or as an applicant for employment, because of such individual's race, color, religion, sex, or national origin; or

(3) to cause or attempt to cause an employer to discriminate against an individual in violation of this section.

(d) It shall be an unlawful employment practice for any employer, labor organization, or joint labor-management committee controlling apprenticeship or other training or retraining, including on-the-job training programs to discriminate against any individual because of his race, color, religion, sex, or national origin in admission to, or employment in, any program established to provide apprenticeship or other training. . . .

Other Unlawful Employment Practices

SECTION 704.   (a) It shall be an unlawful employment practice for an employer to discriminate against any of his employees or applicants for employment, for an employment agency to discriminate against any individual, or for a labor organization to discriminate against any member thereof or applicant for membership, because he has opposed any practice made an unlawful employment practice by this title, or because he has made a charge, testified, assisted, or participated in any manner in an investigation, proceeding, or hearing under this title.

(b) It shall be an unlawful employment practice for an employer, labor organization, or employment agency to print or publish or cause to be printed or published any notice or advertisement relating to employment by such an employer or membership in or any classification or referral for employment by such a labor organization, or relating to any classification or referral for employment by such an employment agency, indicating any preference, limitation, specification, or discrimination, based on race, color, religion, sex, or national origin, except that such a notice or advertisement may indicate a preference, limitation, specification, or discrimination based on religion, sex, or national origin when religion, sex, or national origin is a bona fide occupational qualification for employment.

Equal Employment Opportunity Commission

SECTION 705.   (a) There is hereby created a Commission to be known as the Equal Employment Opportunity Commission, which shall be composed of five members, not more than three of whom shall be members of the same political party, who shall be appointed by the President by and with the advice and consent of the Senate. One of the original members shall be appointed for a term of one year, one for a term of two years, one for a term of three years, one for a term of four years, and one for a term of five years, beginning from the date of enactment of this title, but their successors shall be appointed for terms of five years each, except that any individual chosen to fill a vacancy shall be appointed only for the unexpired term of the member whom he shall succeed. The President shall designate one member to serve as Chairman of the Commission, and one member to serve as Vice Chairman. The Chairman shall be responsible on behalf of the Commission for the administrative operations of the Commission, and shall appoint, in accordance with the civil service laws, such officers, agents, attorneys, and employees as it deems necessary to assist it in the performance of its functions and to fix their compensation in accordance with Classification Act of 1949, as amended. . . .

Key Provisions of the Voting Rights Act of 1965

An Act

To enforce the fifteenth amendment to the Constitution of the United States, and for other purposes.

Be it enacted by the Senate and House of Representatives of the United States of America in Congress assembled, That this Act shall be known as the "Voting Rights Act of 1965."

SECTION 2.   No voting qualification or prerequisite to voting, or standard, practice, or procedure shall be imposed or applied by any State or political subdivision to deny or abridge the right of any citizen of the United States to vote on account of race or color.

SECTION 4.   (a) To assure that the right of citizens of the United States to vote is not denied or abridged on account of race or color, no citizen shall be denied the right to vote in any Federal, State, or local election because of his failure to comply with any test or device in any State with respect to which the determinations have been made under subsection (b). . . (1) demonstrate the ability to read, write, understand, or interpret any matter, (2) demonstrate any educational achievement or his knowledge of any particular subject, (3) possess good moral character, or (4) prove his qualifications by the voucher of registered voters or members of any other class. . . .

SECTION 10.   (a) The Congress finds that the requirement of the payment of a poll tax as a precondition to voting (i) precludes persons of limited means from voting or imposes unreasonable financial hardship upon such persons as a precondition to their exercise of the franchise, (ii) does not bear a reasonable relationship to any legitimate State interest in the conduct of elections, and (iii) in some areas has the purpose or effect of denying persons the right to vote because of race or color. Upon the basis of these findings, Congress declares that the constitutional right of citizens to vote is denied or abridged in some areas by the requirement of the payment of a poll tax as a precondition to voting.

SECTION 11.   (a) No person acting under color of law shall fail or refuse to permit any person to vote who is entitled to vote under any provision of this Act or is otherwise qualified to vote, or willfully fail or refuse to tabulate, count, and report such person's vote.

(b) No person, whether acting under color of law or otherwise, shall intimidate, threaten, or coerce, or attempt to intimidate, threaten, or coerce any person for voting or attempting to vote, or intimidate, threaten, or coerce, or attempt to intimidate, threaten, or coerce any person for urging or aiding any person to vote or attempt to vote, or intimidate, threaten, or coerce any person for exercising any powers or duties under section 3 (a), 6, 8, 9, 10, or 12 (e).

✦ ADDITIONAL BIBLIOGRAPHY ✦

Chapter 1   Africa

Prehistory, Egypt, and Kush

William Y. Adams. *Nubia—Corridor to Africa*. Princeton, NJ: Princeton University Press, 1984.

Martin Bernal. *Black Athena: The Afroasiatic Roots of Classical Civilization*. New Brunswick, NJ: Rutgers University, 1987.

Nicholas C. Grimal. *A History of Ancient Egypt*. Oxford, England: Blackwell, 1993.

Donald Johanson, Lenora Johanson, and Blake Edgar. *Ancestors: In Search of Human Origins*. New York: Villard Books, 1994.

Susan Kent. *Gender in African Prehistory*. Walnut Creek, CA: Altamira, 1998.

Mary R. Lefkowitz and Guy MacLean Rogers, eds. *Black Athena Revisited*. Chapel Hill, NC: University of North Carolina Press, 1996.

Michael Rice. *Egypt's Making: The Origins of Ancient Egypt, 5000–2000 B.C.* New York: Routledge, 1990.

Derek A. Welsby. *The Kingdom of Kush: The Napatan and Merotic Empires*. Princeton, NJ: Markus Wiener, 1998.

Western Sudanese Empires

Nehemiah Levtzion. *Ancient Ghana and Mali*. London: Methuen, 1973.

Nehemiah Levtzion and J. F. Hopkins, eds. *Corpus of Early Arabic Sources for West African History*. New York: Cambridge University Press, 1981.

Roland Oliver and Brian M. Fagan. *Africa in the Iron Age*. New York: Cambridge University Press, 1975.

Roland Oliver and Caroline Oliver, eds. *Africa in the Days of Exploration*. Englewood Cliffs, NJ: Prentice Hall, 1965.

J. Spencer Trimington. *A History of Islam in West Africa*. New York: Oxford University Press, 1962.

The Forest Region of the Guinea Coast

I. A. Akinjogbin. *Dahomey and Its Neighbors, 1708–1818*. New York: Cambridge University Press, 1967.

Daryll Forde, ed. *African Worlds*. New York: Oxford University Press, 1954.

Samuel Johnson. *History of the Yorubas*. Lagos: C.M.S., 1921.

Robert W. July. *Precolonial Africa*. New York: Scribner's, 1975.

Robin Law. *The Oyo Empire, c. 1600–c.1836*. Oxford: Clarendon, 1977.

R. S. Rattray. *Ashanti*. Oxford: Clarendon, 1969.

Walter Rodney. *A History of the Upper Guinea Coast, 1545–1800*. Oxford: Clarendon, 1970.

Culture

Harold Courlander, ed. *A Treasury of African Folklore*. New York: Marlowe, 1996.

Susan Denyer. *African Traditional Architecture: An Historical and Geographical Perspective*. London: Heinemann, 1978.

Ruth Finnegan. *Oral Literature in Africa.* 1970; reprint, Nairobi: Oxford University Press, 1976.

Werner Gillon. *A Short History of African Art.* New York: Viking, 1984.

Paulin J. Hountondji. *African Philosophy: Myth and Reality.* Bloomington, IN: University of Indiana Press, 1984.

John S. Mbiti. *An Introduction to African Religion.* London: Heinemann, 1975.

J. H. Kwabena Nketia. *The Music of Africa.* New York: Norton, 1974.

Chapter 2   Middle Passage

The Slave Trade in Africa

Bernard Lewis. *Race and Slavery in the Middle East: An Historical Enquiry.* New York: Oxford University Press, 1990.

Suzanne Miers and Igor Kopytoff, eds. *Slavery in Africa.* Madison, WI: University of Wisconsin Press, 1977.

Suzanne Miers and Richard Roberts. *The End of Slavery in Africa.* Madison, WI: University of Wisconsin Press, 1988.

Claire C. Robertson and Martin A. Klein, eds. *Slavery in Africa.* Madison, WI: University of Wisconsin Press, 1983.

John K. Thornton. *The Kingdom of Kongo: Civil War and Transition, 1641–1718.* Madison, WI: University of Wisconsin Press, 1983.

The Atlantic Slave Trade

Paul Edwards, ed. *Equiano's Travels.* London: Heinemann, 1967.

Herbert S. Klein. *The Middle Passage: Comparative Studies in the Atlantic Slave Trade.* Princeton, NJ: Princeton University Press, 1978.

Paul E. Lovejoy. *Africans in Bondage: Studies in Slavery and the Slave Trade.* Madison, WI: University of Wisconsin Press, 1986.

Daniel P. Mannix and Malcom Cawley. *Black Cargoes: A History of the Atlantic Slave Trade, 1518–1865.* New York: Viking, 1962.

Rosemarie Robotham, ed. *Spirits of the Passage: The Transatlantic Slave Trade in the Seventeenth Century.* New York: Simon & Schuster, 1997.

Lief Svalesen. *The Slave Ship Fredensborg.* Bloomington, IN: Indiana University Press, 2000.

Hugh Thomas. *The Slave Trade: The Story of the Atlantic Slave Trade, 1440–1870.* New York: Simon and Schuster, 1997.

Vincent Bakpetu Thompson. *The Making of the African Diaspora in the Americas, 1441–1900.* New York: Longman, 1987.

John Vogt. *Portuguese Rule on the Gold Coast, 1469–1682.* Athens, GA: University of Georgia Press, 1979.

The West Indies

Edward Brathwaite. *The Development of Creole Society in Jamaica, 1770–1820.* New York: Oxford University Press, 1971.

William Claypole and John Robottom. *Caribbean Story: Foundations.* Kingston: Longman, 1980.

Melville J. Herskovits. *The Myth of the Negro Past.* Boston: Beacon, 1941.

Keith Albert Sandiford. *The Cultural Politics of Sugar: Caribbean Slavery and Narratives of Colonialism.* New York: Cambridge University Press, 2000. The Granger Collection, New York.

Chapter 3   Black People in Colonial North America, 1526–1763

Colonial Society

Wesley Frank Craven. *The Southern Colonies in the Seventeenth Century, 1607–1689.* Baton Rouge, LA: Louisiana State University Press, 1949.

John J. McCusker and Russell R. Menard. *The Economy of British America, 1607–1789.* Chapel Hill, NC: University of North Carolina Press, 1985.

Gary B. Nash. *Red, White, and Black: The Peoples of Early America,* 3d edition. Englewood Cliffs, NJ: Prentice Hall, 1992.

Origins of Slavery and Racism in the Western Hemisphere

David Brion Davis. *The Problem of Slavery in Western Culture.* Ithaca, NY: Cornell University Press, 1966.

Ronald Sanders. *Lost Tribes and Promised Lands: The Origins of American Racism.* Boston: Little, Brown, 1978.

Frank Tannenbaum. *Slave and Citizen: The Negro in the Americas.* New York: Knopf, 1946.

Betty Wood. *The Origins of American Slavery: Freedom and Bondage in the English Colonies.* New York: Hill and Wang, 1997.

The Chesapeake

Allan Kulikoff. *Tobacco and Slaves: The Development of Southern Cultures in the Chesapeake, 1680–1800.* Chapel Hill, NC: University of North Carolina Press, 1986.

Gloria L. Main. *Tobacco Colony: Life in Early Maryland, 1650–1720.* Princeton, NJ: Princeton University Press, 1982.

Edmund S. Morgan. *American Slavery, American Freedom: The Ordeal of Colonial Virginia.* New York: Norton, 1975.

Mechal Sobel. *The World They Made Together: Black and White Values in Eighteenth-Century Virginia.* Princeton, NJ: Princeton University Press, 1987.

The Carolina and Georgia Low Country

Judith Ann Carney. *Black Rice: The African Origins of Rice Cultivation in the Americas.* Cambridge, MA: Harvard University Press, 2001.

Daniel C. Littlefield. *Rice and Slaves: Ethnicity and the Slave Trade in Colonial South Carolina.* Baton Rouge, LA: Louisiana State University Press, 1985.

Julia Floyd Smith. *Slavery and Rice Culture in Low Country Georgia, 1750–1860.* Knoxville, TN: University of Tennessee Press, 1985.

Betty Wood. *Slavery in Colonial Georgia, 1730–1775.* Athens, GA: University of Georgia Press, 1984.

The Northern Colonies

Lorenzo J. Greene. *The Negro in Colonial New England, 1620–1776.* 1942; reprint, New York: Atheneum, 1968.

Edgar J. McManus. *Black Bondage in the North.* Syracuse, NY: Syracuse University Press, 1973.

William D. Piersen. *Black Yankees: The Development of an Afro-American Subculture in Eighteenth-Century New England.* Amherst, MA: University of Massachusetts Press, 1988.

African-American Culture

John B. Boles. *Black Southerners, 1619–1869.* Lexington, KY: University Press of Kentucky, 1983.

Margaret W. Creel. *A Peculiar People: Slave Religion and Community Culture among the Gullahs.* New York: New York University Press, 1988.

Michael Gomez. *Exchanging Our Country Marks: The Transformation of African Identities in the Colonial and Antebellum South.* Chapel Hill, NC: University of North Carolina Press, 1998.

Herbert Gutman. *The Black Family in Slavery and Freedom.* New York: Pantheon, 1976.

Melville J. Herskovits. *The Myth of the Negro Past.* 1941; reprint, Boston: Beacon, 1990.

Joseph E. Holloway, ed. *Africanisms in American Culture.* Bloomington, IN: Indiana University Press, 1990.

Henry Mitchell. *Black Belief: Folk Beliefs of Blacks in America and West Africa.* New York: Harper & Row, 1975.

Joel Williamson. *New People: Miscegenation and Mulattoes in the United States.* New York: Free Press, 1980.

Black Women in Colonial America

Joan Rezner Gunderson, "The Double Bonds of Race and Sex: Black and White Women in a Colonial Virginia Parish," in Darlene Clark Hine, Wilma King, and Linda Reed, eds. *We Specialize in the Wholly Impossible: A Reader in Black Women's History.* Brooklyn, NY: Carlson, 1995.

Darlene Clark Hine and Kathleen Thompson. *A Shining Thread of Hope: The History of Black Women in America.* New York: Broadway, 1998, Chapter 1.

Jane Kamensky. *The Colonial Mosaic: American Women, 1600–1760: Rising Expectations from the Colonial Period to the American Revolution.* New York: Oxford University Press, 1995.

Resistance and Revolt

Herbert Aptheker. *American Negro Slave Revolts.* 1943; reprint, New York: International Publishers, 1974.

Thomas J. Davis. *A Rumor of Revolt: The "Great Negro Plot" in Colonial New York.* New York: Free Press, 1985.

Merton L. Dillon. *Slavery Attacked: Southern Slaves and Their Allies, 1619–1865.* Baton Rouge, LA: Louisiana State University Press, 1990.

Eugene D. Genovese. *From Rebellion to Revolution: Afro-American Slave Revolts in the Making of the Modern World.* Baton Rouge, LA: Louisiana State University Press, 1979.

Gerald W. Mullin. *Flight and Rebellion: Slave Resistance in Eighteenth-Century Virginia.* New York: Oxford University Press, 1972.

Chapter 4   Rising Expectations: African Americans and the Struggle for Independence, 1763–1783

The Crisis of the British Empire

Stephen Conway. *The British Isles and the War of American Independence.* New York: Oxford University Press, 2000.

Edward Countryman. *The American Revolution.* New York: Hill and Wang, 1975.

Douglas E. Leach. *Roots of Conflict: British Armed Forces and Colonial Americans, 1677–1763.* Chapel Hill, NC: University of North Carolina Press, 1986.

Pauline Maier. *From Resistance to Revolution: Colonial Radicals and the Development of American Opposition to Britain, 1765–1776.* New York: Knopf, 1972.

Peter David Garner Thomas. *Revolution in America: Britain and the Colonies, 1765–1776.* Cardiff, U.K.: University of Wales, 1992.

The Impact of the Enlightenment

Bernard Bailyn. *The Ideological Origins of the American Revolution.* Cambridge, MA: Harvard University Press, 1967.

Henry Steele Commager. *The Empire of Reason: How Europe Imagined and America Realized the Enlightenment.* Garden City, NY: Anchor, 1977.

Paul Finkelman. *Slavery and the Founders: Race and Liberty in the Age of Jefferson.* London: M.E. Sharpe, 1996.

J.G.A. Pocock. *The Machiavellian Moment: Florentine Political Thought and the Atlantic Republican Tradition.* Princeton, NJ: Princeton University Press, 1975.

Frank Shuffelton, ed. *The American Enlightenment.* Rochester, NY: University of Rochester Press, 1993.

African Americans and the American Revolution

Lerone Bennett, Jr. *Before the Mayflower: A History of Black America.* 6th ed., Chicago: Johnson, 1987, Chapter 3.

Ira Berlin. "The Revolution in Black Life," in Alfred F. Young, ed., *The American Revolution: Explorations in the History of American Radicalism.* DeKalb, IL: Northern Illinois University Press, 1976, 349–82.

Jeffrey J. Crow. *The Black Experience in Revolutionary North Carolina.* Raleigh, NC: North Carolina Department of Cultural Resources, 1977.

Merton L. Dillon. *Slavery Attacked: Southern Slaves and Their Allies, 1619–1865.* Baton Rouge, LA: Louisiana State University Press, 1990, Chapter 2.

Sylvia R. Frey. "Between Slavery and Freedom: Virginia Blacks in the American Revolution." *Journal of Southern History,* 69 (August 1983): 375–98.

Jack P. Greene. *All Men Are Created Equal: Some Reflections on the Character of the American Revolution.* Oxford: Clarendon, 1976.

Sidney Kaplan and Emma Nogrady Kaplan. *The Black Presence in the Era of the American Revolution.* Amherst, MA: University of Massachusetts Press, 1989.

Peter Kolchin. *American Slavery, 1619–1877.* New York: Hill and Wang, 1993, Chapter 3.

Duncan McLeod. *Slavery, Race, and the American Revolution.* New York: Cambridge University Press, 1974.

Gary B. Nash. *Forging Freedom: The Formation of Philadelphia's Black Community, 1720–1840.* Cambridge, MA: Harvard University Press, 1988.

Peter H. Wood. "'The Dream Deferred': Black Freedom Struggles on the Eve of White Independence," in Gary Y. Okihiro, ed. *In Resistance: Studies in African, Caribbean, and Afro-American History.* Amherst, MA: University of Massachusetts Press, 1986, 166–87.

Antislavery and Emancipation in the North

Robin Blackburn. *The Overthrow of Colonial Slavery, 1776–1848.* New York: Verso, 1988, Chapter 3.

Merton L. Dillon. *The Abolitionists: The Growth of a Dissenting Minority.* New York: Norton, 1974, Chapter 1.

Dwight L. Dumond. *Antislavery: The Crusade for Freedom in America*. 1961; reprint, New York: Norton, 1966.

Joanne Pope Melish. *Disowning Slavery: Gradual Emancipation and "Race" in New England, 1780–1860*. Ithaca, NY: Cornell University Press, 1998.

Gary B. Nash. *Freedom by Degrees: Emancipation in Pennsylvania and Its Aftermath*. New York: Oxford University Press, 1991.

_____. *Race and Revolution*. Madison, WI: Madison House, 1990.

James Brewer Stewart. *Holy Warriors: The Abolitionists and American Slavery*. Revised ed., New York: Hill and Wang, 1997, Chapter 1.

Biography

Silvio A. Bedini. *The Life of Benjamin Banneker*. New York: Scribner, 1972.

William Henry Robinson. *Phillis Wheatley and Her Writings*. New York: Garland, 1984.

Chapter 5   African Americans in the New Nation, 1783–1820

Emancipation in the North

James D. Essig. *The Bonds of Wickedness: American Evangelicals Against Slavery, 1770–1808*. Philadelphia: Temple University Press, 1982.

Joanne Pope Melish. *Disowning Slavery: Gradual Emancipation and "Race" in New England, 1780–1860*. Ithaca, NY: Cornell University Press, 1998.

Gary B. Nash and Jean R. Soderlund. *Freedom by Degrees: Emancipation in Pennsylvania and Its Aftermath*. New York: Oxford University Press, 1991.

Shane White. *Somewhat More Independent: The End of Slavery in New York City, 1770–1810*. Athens, GA: University of Georgia Press, 1991.

Arthur Zilversmit. *The First Emancipation: The Abolition of Slavery in the North*. Chicago: University of Chicago Press, 1967.

Proslavery Forces

Paul Finkelman. *Slavery and the Founders: Race and Liberty in the Age of Jefferson*. Armonk, NY: M. E. Sharpe, 1996.

Duncan J. MacLeod. *Slavery, Race, and the American Revolution*. New York: Cambridge University Press, 1974.

Donald G. Nieman. *Promises to Keep: African Americans and the Constitutional Order, 1776 to the Present*. New York: Oxford University Press, 1991.

Donald L. Robinson. *Slavery in the Structure of American Politics, 1765–1820*. New York: Harcourt Brace Jovanovich, 1971.

Larry E. Tise. *Proslavery: A History of the Defense of Slavery in America, 1701–1840*. Athens: University of Georgia Press, 1987.

Free Black Institutions and Migration Movements

Carol V. R. George. *Segregated Sabbaths: Richard Allen and the Emergence of Independent Black Churches, 1760–1840*. New York: Oxford University Press, 1973.

Eddie S. Glaude. *Exodus! Religion, Race, and Nation in Early Nineteenth-Century Black America*. Chicago: University of Chicago Press, 2000.

Sheldon H. Harris. *Paul Cuffe: Black America and the Africa Return.* New York: Simon & Schuster, 1972.

Leon Litwack. *North of Slavery: The Negro in the Free States.* Chicago: University of Chicago Press, 1961.

William A Muraskin. *Middle-Class Blacks in a White Society: Prince Hall Freemasonry in America.* Berkeley, CA: University of California Press, 1975.

Julie Winch. *Philadelphia's Black Elite: Activism, Accommodation, and the Struggle for Autonomy, 1787–1848.* Philadelphia: Temple University Press, 1988.

Carter G. Woodson. *The Education of the Negro Prior to 1861.* 1915; reprint, Brooklyn, NY: A&B Books, 1998.

The South

John Hope Franklin. *The Free Negro in North Carolina, 1790–1860.* 1943; reprint, New York: Russell and Russell, 1969.

Peter Kolchin. *American Slavery, 1619–1877.* New York: Hill and Wang, 1993.

John Chester Miller. *The Wolf by the Ears: Thomas Jefferson and Slavery.* 1977; reprint, Charlottesville, VA: University Press of Virginia, 1991.

T. Stephen Whitman. *The Price of Freedom: Slavery and Manumission in Baltimore and Early National Maryland.* Lexington, KY: University of Kentucky Press, 1997.

Slave Revolts, Resistance, and Escapes

Herbert Aptheker. *American Negro Slave Revolts.* 1943; reprint, New York: International, 1983.

Merton L. Dillon. *Slavery Attacked: Southern Slaves and Their Allies, 1619–1865.* Baton Rouge, LA: Louisiana State University Press, 1990.

Eugene D. Genovese. *From Rebellion to Revolution: Afro-American Slave Revolts in the Making of the Modern World.* Baton Rouge, LA: Louisiana State University Press, 1979.

John R. McKivigan and Stanley Harrold, eds. *Antislavery Violence: Sectional, Racial, and Cultural Conflict in Antebellum America.* Knoxville, TN: University of Tennessee Press, 1999.

Gerald W. Mullin. *Flight and Rebellion: Slave Resistance in Eighteenth-Century Virginia.* New York: Oxford University Press, 1972.

James Sidbury. *Ploughshares into Swords: Race, Rebellion, and Identity in Gabriel's Virginia, 1730–1810.* New York: Cambridge University Press, 1998. The Library Company of Philadelphia.

Chapter 6   Life in the Cotton Kingdom

Slavery and Its Expansion

Stanley M. Elkins. *Slavery: A Problem in American Institutional and Intellectual Life.* 3d ed. Chicago: University of Chicago Press, 1976.

Eugene D. Genovese. *The Political Economy of Slavery: Studies in the Economy and Society of the Slave South.* 1961; reprint, New York: Random House, 1967.

Lewis C. Gray. *History of Agriculture in the Southern United States to 1860.* 1933; reprint, Clifton, NJ: A. M. Kelley, 1973.

Larry Koger. *Black Slaveowners: Free Black Slave Masters in South Carolina, 1790–1860.* 1985; reprint, Columbia, SC: University of South Carolina Press, 1994.

Donald P. McNeilly. *The Old South Frontier: Cotton Plantations and the Formation of Arkansas Society, 1819–1861.* Fayetteville, AR: University of Arkansas Press, 2000.

Larry Eugene Rivers. *Slavery in Florida: Territorial Days to Emancipation.* Gainsville, FL: University Press of Florida, 2000.

Kenneth M. Stampp. *The Peculiar Institution: Slavery in the Antebellum South.* 1956; reprint, New York: Vintage Books, 1989.

Urban and Industrial Slavery

Ronald L. Lewis. *Coal, Iron, and Slaves: Industrial Slavery in Maryland and Virginia, 1715–1865.* Westport, CT: Greenwood, 1979.

Robert S. Starobin. *Industrial Slavery in the Old South.* New York: Oxford University Press, 1970.

Midori Takagi. *Rearing Wolves to Our Own Destruction: Slavery in Richmond, Virginia, 1782–1865.* Charlottesville, VA: University Press of Virginia, 1999.

Richard C. Wade. *Slavery in the Cities: The South 1820–1860.* 1964; reprint, New York: Oxford University Press, 1967.

The Domestic Slave Trade

Frederic Bancroft. *Slave Trading in the Old South.* 1931; reprint, Columbia, SC: University of South Carolina Press, 1996.

Walter Johnson. *Soul by Soul: Life Inside the Antebellum Slave Market.* Cambridge, MA: Harvard University Press, 1999.

Michael Tadman. *Speculators and Slaves: Masters, Traders, and Slaves in the Old South.* 1989; reprint, Madison, WI: University of Wisconsin Press, 1996.

The Slave Community

John W. Blassingame. *The Slave Community: Plantation Life in the Antebellum South.* 2d ed. New York: Oxford University Press, 1979.

Eugene D. Genovese. *Roll, Jordan, Roll: The World the Slave Made.* 1974; reprint, Vintage Books, 1976.

Herbert Gutman. *The Black Family in Slavery and Freedom.* 1976; reprint, Vintage Books, 1977.

Charles Joyner. *Down by the Riverside: A South Carolina Community.* Urbana, IL: University of Illinois Press, 1984.

Leslie Howard Owens. *This Species of Property: Slave Life and Culture in the Old South.* 1976; reprint, New York: Oxford University Press, 1977.

Todd L. Savitt. *Medicine and Slavery: The Diseases and Health Care of Blacks in Antebellum Virginia.* Urbana, IL: University of Illinois Press, 1978.

Maria Jenkins Schwartz. *Born in Bondage: Growing Up Enslaved in the Antebellum South.* Cambridge, MA: Harvard University Press, 2000.

Enslaved Women

David Barry Gaspar and Darlene Clark Hine, eds. *More Than Chattel: Black Women and Slavery in the Americas.* Bloomington, IN: University of Indiana Press, 1996.

Darlene Clark Hine, Wilma King, and Linda Reed, eds. *"We Specialize in the Wholly Impossible": A Reader in Black Women's History.* Brooklyn, NY: Carlson, 1996.

Patricia Morton, ed. *Discovering the Women in Slavery: Emancipating Perspectives on the American Past.* Athens, GA: University of Georgia Press, 1996.

Deborah Gray White. *Ar'n't I a Woman? Female Slaves in the Plantation South.* New York: Norton, 1985.

Slave Culture and Religion

John B. Boles, ed. *Masters and Slaves in the House of the Lord: Race and Religion in the American South, 1740–1870.* Lexington, KY: University Press of Kentucky, 1988.

____.*When I Can Read My Title Clear: Literacy, Slavery, and Religion in the Antebellum South.* Columbia, SC: University of South Carolina Press, 1991.

Janet Duitsman Cornelius. *Slave Missions and the Black Church in the Antebellum South.* Columbia, SC: University of South Carolina Press, 1999.

Lawrence W. Levine. *Black Culture and Black Consciousness: Afro-American Folk Thought from Slavery to Freedom.* New York: Oxford University Press, 1977.

Albert J. Raboteau. *Slave Religion: The "Invisible Institution" in the Antebellum South.* New York: Oxford University Press, 1978.

Chapter 7   Free Black People in Antebellum America

Community Studies

Tommy L. Bogger. *Free Blacks in Norfolk, Virginia, 1790–1860: The Darker Side of Freedom.* Charlottesville, VA: University Press of Virginia, 1997.

Letitia Woods Brown. *Free Negroes in the District of Columbia, 1790–1846.* New York: Oxford University Press, 1972.

Graham Russell Hodges. *Slavery and Freedom in the Rural North: African Americans in Monmouth County, New Jersey, 1665–1865.* Madison, WI: Madison House, 1995.

James Oliver Horton. *Free People of Color: Inside the African-American Community.* Washington: Smithsonian Institution Press, 1993.

James Oliver Horton and Lois E. Horton. *Black Bostonians: Family Life and Community Struggle in the Antebellum North.* New York: Holmes and Meier, 1979.

Gary B. Nash. *Forging Freedom: The Formation of Philadelphia's Black Community, 1720–1840.* Cambridge, MA: Harvard University Press, 1988.

Christopher Phillips. *Freedom's Port: The African-American Community of Baltimore, 1790–1860.* Urbana, IL: University of Illinois Press, 1997.

Bernard E. Powers, Jr. *Black Charlestonians: A Social History, 1822–1885.* Fayetteville, AR: University of Arkansas Press, 1994.

Harry Reed. *Platform for Change: The Foundations of the Northern Free Black Community, 1775–1865.* East Lansing, MI: Michigan State University Press, 1994.

Julie Winch. *Philadelphia's Black Elite: Activism, Accommodation, and the Struggle for Autonomy, 1787–1848.* Philadelphia: Temple University Press, 1988.

State-Level Studies

Barbara Jeanne Fields. *Slavery and Freedom on the Middle Ground: Maryland During the Nineteenth Century.* New Haven, CT: Yale University Press, 1985.

John Hope Franklin. *The Free Negro in North Carolina, 1790–1860.* Chapel Hill, NC: University of North Carolina Press, 1943.

John H. Russell. *The Free Negro in Virginia, 1619–1865.* 1913; reprint, New York: Negro Universities Press, 1969.

H. E. Sterkx. *The Free Negro in Antebellum Louisiana.* Rutherford, NJ: Fairleigh Dickinson University Press, 1972.

Marina Wilkramangrake. *A World in Shadow—The Free Black in Antebellum South Carolina.* Columbia, SC: University of South Carolina Press, 1973.

Race Relations

Eugene H. Berwanger. *The Frontier Against Slavery: Western Anti-Negro Prejudice and the Slavery Expansion Controversy.* Urbana, IL: University of Illinois Press, 1967.

Phyllis F. Field. *The Politics of Race in New York: The Struggle for Black Suffrage in the Civil War Era.* Ithaca, NY: Cornell University Press, 1982.

Noel Ignatiev. *How the Irish Became White.* New York: Routledge, 1995.

David Roediger. *The Wages of Whiteness: Race and the Making of the American Working Class.* New York: Verso, 1991.

Joel Williamson. *New People: Miscegenation and Mulattoes in the United States.* New York: Free Press, 1980.

Carol Wilson. *Freedom at Risk: The Kidnapping of Free Blacks in America, 1780–1865.* Lexington, KY: University Press of Kentucky, 1994.

Women and Family

Herbert G. Gutman. *The Black Family in Slavery and Freedom, 1750–1925.* New York: Pantheon Books, 1977.

Jacqueline Jones. *Labor of Love, Labor of Sorrow: Black Women, Work and the Family from Slavery to the Present.* New York: Basic Books, 1985.

Suzanne Lebsock. *The Free Women of Petersburg: Status and Culture in a Southern Town, 1784–1860.* New York: Norton, 1984.

Bert James Loewenberg and Ruth Bogin, eds. *Black Women in Nineteenth-Century American Life.* University Park, PA: Pennsylvania State University Press, 1976.

T.O. Madden, Jr., with Ann L. Miller. *We Were Always Free: The Maddens of Culpeper County, Virginia, a 200 Year Family History.* New York: Norton, 1992.

Dorothy Sterling, ed. *We Are Your Sisters: Black Women in the Nineteenth Century.* New York: Norton, 1984.

Institutions and the Black Elite

Vincent P. Franklin. *The Education of Black Philadelphia.* Philadelphia: University of Pennsylvania Press, 1979.

Carlton Mabee. *Black Education in New York State.* Syracuse, NY: Syracuse University Press, 1979.

Eileen Southern. *The Music of Black America.* 2d ed. New York: Norton, 1983.

Loretta J. Williams. *Black Freemasonry and Middle-Class Realities.* Columbia, MO: University of Missouri Press, 1980.

Chapter 8   Opposition to Slavery, 1800–1833

The Relationship among Evangelicalism, Reform, and Abolitionism

Robert H. Abzug. *Cosmos Crumbling: American Reform and the Religious Imagination.* New York: Oxford University Press, 1994.

Gilbert H. Barnes. *The Antislavery Impulse, 1830–1844.* 1933; reprint, Gloucester, MA: Peter Smith, 1973.

Ronald G. Walters. *American Reformers, 1815–1860.* Baltimore: Johns Hopkins University Press, 1978.

American Abolitionism Before 1831

David Brion Davis. *The Problem of Slavery in the Age of Revolution.* Ithaca, NY: Cornell University Press, 1975.
_____. *The Problem of Slavery in Western Culture.* Ithaca, NY: Cornell University Press, 1966.
_____. *Slavery and Human Progress.* Ithaca, NY: Cornell University Press, 1987.
Merton L. Dillon. *The Abolitionists: The Growth of a Dissenting Minority.* New York: Norton, 1974.
_____. *Benjamin Lundy and the Struggle for Negro Freedom.* Urbana, IL: University of Illinois Press, 1966.
Sean Wilentz, ed., *David Walker's Appeal.* 1829; reprint, New York: Hill and Wang, 1995.

Slave Revolts and Conspiracies

Herbert Aptheker. *American Negro Slave Revolts.* 1943; new ed., New York: International Publishers, 1974.
Douglas R. Egerton. *Gabriel's Rebellion: The Virginia Slave Conspiracies of 1800 & 1802.* Chapel Hill, NC: University of North Carolina Press, 1993.
_____. *He Shall Go Out Free: The Lives of Denmark Vesey.* Madison, WI: Madison House, 1999.
Alfred N. Hunt. *Haiti's Influence on Antebellum America: Slumbering Volcano in the Caribbean.* Baton Rouge, LA: Louisiana State University Press, 1988.
John Lofton. *Denmark Vesey's Revolt: The Slave Plot That Lit a Fuse to Fort Sumter.* Kent, OH: Kent State University Press, 1983.
Stephen B. Oates. *The Fires of the Jubilee: Nat Turner's Fierce Rebellion.* New York: Harper & Row, 1975.

Black Abolitionism and Black Nationalism

Leroy Graham. *Baltimore: Nineteenth-Century Black Capital.* Washington, DC: University Press of America, 1982.
Vincent Harding. *There Is a River: The Black Struggle for Freedom in America.* New York: Harcourt, Brace, Jovanovich, 1981.
Floyd J. Miller. *The Search for Black Nationality: Black Colonization and Emigration, 1787–1863.* Urbana, IL: University of Illinois Press, 1975.
Marilyn Richardson. *Maria W. Stewart: America's First Black Woman Political Writer.* Bloomington, IN: Indiana University Press, 1987.
Sterling Stuckey. *Slave Culture: Nationalist Theory and the Foundations of Black America.* New York: Oxford University Press, 1987.
Lamont D. Thomas. *Rise to Be a People: A Biography of Paul Cuffe.* Urbana, IL: University of Illinois Press, 1986.
Julie Winch. *Philadelphia's Black Elite: Activism, Accommodation, and Struggle for Autonomy, 1787–1840.* Philadelphia: Temple University Press, 1988.

Chapter 9   Let Your Motto Be Resistance, 1833–1850

General Studies of the Antislavery Movement

Herbert Aptheker. *Abolitionism: A Revolutionary Movement.* Boston: Twayne, 1989.
Merton L. Dillon. *The Abolitionists: The Growth of a Dissenting Minority.* New York: Norton, 1974.
Lawrence J. Friedman. *Gregarious Saints: Self and Community in American Abolitionism, 1830–1870.* New York: Cambridge University Press, 1982.

Stanley Harrold. *American Abolitionists.* Harlow, United Kingdom: Longman, 2001.

James Brewer Stewart. *Holy Warriors: The Abolitionists and American Slavery.* 2d ed., New York: Hill and Wang, 1997.

The Black Community

John Brown Childs. *The Political Black Minister: A Study in Afro-American Politics and Religion.* Boston: G.K. Hall, 1980.

Leonard P. Curry. *The Free Black in Urban America, 1800–1850: The Shadow of a Dream.* Chicago: University of Chicago Press, 1981.

Martin E. Dann. *The Black Press, 1827–1890.* New York: Capricorn, 1971.

James Oliver Horton and Lois E. Horton. *In Hope of Liberty: Culture, Community, and Protest among Northern Free Blacks, 1700–1860.* New York: Oxford University Press, 1997.

David E. Swift. *Black Prophets of Justice: Activist Clergy before the Civil War.* Baton Rouge, LA: Louisiana State University Press, 1989.

Black Abolitionists

Howard Holman Bell. *A Survey of the Negro Convention Movement, 1830–1861.* New York: Arno, 1969.

_____, ed. *Minutes of the Proceedings of the National Negro Conventions, 1830–1864.* New York: Arno, 1969.

R. J. M. Blackett. *Building an Antislavery Wall: Blacks in the Atlantic Abolitionist Movement, 1830–1860.* Baton Rouge, LA: Louisiana State University Press, 1983.

Women

Blanch Glassman-Hersh. *Slavery of Sex: Feminist-Abolitionists in Nineteenth-Century America.* Urbana, IL: University of Illinois Press, 1978.

Darlene Clark Hine, ed. *Black Women in American History: From Colonial Times through the Nineteenth Century.* 4 vols. New York: Carlson, 1990.

Julie Roy Jeffrey. *The Great Silent Army of Abolitionism: Ordinary Women in the Antislavery Movement.* Chapel Hill, NC: University of North Carolina Press, 1998.

Jean Fagan Yellin. *Women and Sisters: Antislavery Feminists in American Culture.* New Haven, CT: Yale University Press, 1990.

Biography

William S. McFeely. *Frederick Douglass.* New York: Simon & Schuster, 1991.

Nell Irvin Painter. *Sojourner Truth: A Life, A Symbol.* New York: Norton, 1996.

Joel Schor. *Henry Highland Garnet: A Voice of Black Radicalism in the Nineteenth Century.* Westport, CT: Greenwood, 1977.

Dorothy Sterling. *Freedom Train: The Story of Harriet Tubman.* Garden City, NY: Doubleday, 1954.

James Brewer Stewart. *William Lloyd Garrison and the Challenge of Emancipation.* Arlington Heights, IL: Harlan Davidson, 1992.

Victor Ullman. *Martin R. Delany: The Beginnings of Black Nationalism.* Boston: Beacon, 1971.

Underground Railroad

Larry Gara. *The Liberty Line: The Legend of the Underground Railroad.* Lexington, KY: University of Kentucky Press, 1961.

Wilbur H. Siebert. *The Underground Railroad from Slavery to Freedom.* 1898; reprint, New York: Arno, 1968.

William Still. *The Underground Railroad.* 1871; reprint, Chicago: Johnson Publishing, 1970.

Black Nationalism

Rodney Carlisle. *The Roots of Black Nationalism.* Port Washington, NY: Kennikat, 1975.

Floyd J. Miller. *The Search for Black Nationality: Black Emigration and Colonization, 1787–1863.* Urbana, IL: University of Illinois Press, 1975.

Chapter 10   "And Black People Were at the Heart of It"; The United States Disunites over Slavery

California and the Compromise of 1850

Eugene H. Berwanger. *The Frontier against Slavery: Western Anti-Negro Prejudice and the Slave Extension Controversy.* Urbana, IL: University of Illinois Press, 1967.

Holman Hamilton. *Prologue to Conflict: The Crisis and Compromise of 1850.* Lexington, KY: University of Kentucky Press, 1964.

Rudolph M. Lapp. *Blacks in the Gold Rush California.* New Haven, CT: Yale University Press, 1977.

The Fugitive Slave Law and Its Victims

Stanley W. Campbell. *The Slave Catchers: Enforcement of the Fugitive Slave Law, 1850–1860.* Chapel Hill, NC: University of North Carolina Press, 1968.

Gary Collison. *Shadrach Minkins.* Cambridge, MA: Harvard University Press, 1998.

Albert J. von Frank. *The Trials of Anthony Burns.* Cambridge, MA: Harvard University Press, 1998.

Jonathan Katz. *Resistance at Christiana: The Fugitive Slave Rebellion at Christiana, Pennsylvania, September 11, 1851: A Documentary Account.* New York: Crowell, 1974.

Thomas P. Slaughter. *Bloody Dawn: The Christiana Riot and Violence in the Antebellum North.* New York: Oxford University Press, 1991.

The Late 1850s

Walter Ehrlich. *They Have No Rights: Dred Scott's Struggle for Freedom.* Westport, CT: Greenwood Press, 1979.

Don E. Fehrenbacher. *The Dred Scott Case: Its Significance in American Law and Politics.* New York: Oxford University Press, 1978.

Robert W. Johannsen. *Stephen A. Douglas.* New York: Oxford University Press, 1973.

Kenneth M. Stampp. *America in 1857: A Nation on the Brink.* New York: Oxford University Press, 1990.

John Brown and the Raid on Harpers Ferry

Paul Finkelman. *And His Soul Goes Marching On: Responses to John Brown and the Harpers Ferry Raid.* Charlottesville, VA: University of Virginia Press, 1995.

Truman Nelson. *The Old Man John Brown at Harpers Ferry.* New York: Holt, Rinehart, and Winston, 1973.

Stephen Oates. *To Purge This Land with Blood: A Biography of John Brown.* New York: Harper & Row, 1970.

Benjamin Quarles. *Blacks on John Brown.* Urbana, IL: University of Illinois Press, 1972.

Secession

William L. Barney. *The Road to Secession.* New York: Praeger, 1972.

Steven A. Channing. *Crisis of Fear: Secession in South Carolina.* New York: Simon & Schuster, 1970.

Kenneth M. Stampp. *And the War Came: The North and the Secession Crisis, 1860–1861.* Baton Rouge, LA: Louisiana State University Press, 1950.

Abraham Lincoln

Gabor Boritt, ed. *The Lincoln Enigma.* New York: Oxford University Press, 2001.

David Herbert Donald. *Lincoln.* New York: Simon & Schuster, 1995.

Stephen B. Oates. *With Malice toward None: A Life of Abraham Lincoln.* New York: Harper & Row, 1977.

Benjamin Thomas. *Abraham Lincoln: A Biography.* New York: Alfred A. Knopf, 1952.

Novels

Martin R. Delany. *Blake or the Huts of America.* Boston: Beacon Press, 1970.

Harriet Beecher Stowe. *Uncle Tom's Cabin, or Life among the Lowly.* New York: Modern Library, 1985.

Chapter 11   Liberation: African Americans and the Civil War

Military

Joseph T. Glatthaar. *Forged in Battle: The Civil War Alliance of Black Soldiers and White Officers.* New York: The Free Press, 1990.

———. *The March to the Sea and Beyond: Sherman's Troops in the Savannah and Carolina Campaign.* New York: New York University Press, 1985.

Herman Hattaway and Archer Jones. *How the North Won: A Military History of the Civil War.* Urbana, IL: University of Illinois Press, 1983.

Geoffrey Ward and Ken Burns. *The Civil War.* New York: Alfred A. Knopf, 1990.

Stephen R. Wise. *Gate of Hell: Campaign for Charleston Harbor, 1863.* Columbia, SC: University of South Carolina Press, 1994.

African Americans and the War

Peter Burchard. *One Gallant Rush: Robert Gould Shaw and His Brave Black Regiment.* New York: St. Martin's Press, 1965.

Leon Litwack. *Been in the Storm So Long: The Aftermath of Slavery.* New York: Alfred A. Knopf, 1979.

Edward A. Miller. *Gullah Statesman: Robert Smalls from Slavery to Congress, 1839–1915*. Columbia, SC: University of South Carolina Press, 1995.

Benjamin Quarles. *The Negro in the Civil War.* Boston: Little, Brown, 1953.

Willie Lee Rose. *Rehearsal for Reconstruction: The Port Royal Experiment.* Indianapolis, IN: Bobbs Merrill, 1964.

Noah A. Trudeau. *Like Men of War: Black Troops in the Civil War, 1862–1865.* Boston: Little Brown, 1998.

Bell I. Wiley. *Southern Negroes, 1861–1865.* New Haven, CT: Yale University Press, 1938.

Documents, Letters, and Other Sources

Virginia M. Adams, ed. *On the Altar of Freedom: A Black Soldier's Civil War Letters from the Front.* [Corporal James Henry Gooding]. Amherst, MA: University of Massachusetts, 1991.

Ira Berlin, et al., eds. "Freedom: A Documentary History of Emancipation, 1861–1867," Series 1, Volume I, *The Destruction of Slavery.* New York: Cambridge University Press, 1985.

Robert F. Durden. *The Gray and the Black: The Confederate Debate on Emancipation.* Baton Rouge, LA: Louisiana State University Press, 1972.

"Freedom: A Documentary History of Emancipation, 1861–1867," Series 1, Volume III, *The Wartime Genesis of Free Labor: The Lower South.* New York: Cambridge University Press, 1990.

Michael P. Johnson and James L. Roark, eds. *No Chariot Letdown: Charleston's Free People of Color on the Eve of the Civil War.* Chapel Hill, NC: University of North Carolina Press, 1984.

James McPherson. *The Negro's Civil War: How American Negroes Felt and Acted during the War for the Union.* New York: Pantheon, 1965.

Edwin S. Redkey, ed. *A Grand Army of Black Men: Letters from African American Soldiers in the Union Army, 1861–1865.* New York: Cambridge University Press, 1992.

Reminiscences

Thomas Wentworth Higginson. *Army Life in a Black Regiment.* Boston: Beacon Press, 1962.

Elizabeth Keckley. *Behind the Scenes: Or Thirty Years a Slave and Four Years in the White House.* New York: Oxford University Press, 1968.

Susie King Taylor. *Reminiscences of My Life in Camp.* Boston: Taylor, 1902.

Chapter 12   The Meaning of Freedom: The Promise of Reconstruction, 1865–1868

Education

James D. Anderson. *The Education of Blacks in the South, 1860–1935.* Chapel Hill, NC: University of North Carolina Press, 1988.

Ronald E. Butchart. *Northern Schools, Southern Blacks, and Reconstruction: Freedmen's Education, 1862–1875.* Westport, CT: Greenwood Press, 1981.

Edmund L. Drago. *Initiative, Paternalism, and Race Relations: Charleston's Avery Normal Institute.* Athens, GA: University of Georgia Press, 1990.

Robert C. Morris. *Reading, 'Riting, and Reconstruction: The Education of the Freedmen in the South, 1861–1890.* Chicago: University of Chicago Press, 1981.

Joe M. Richardson. *Christian Reconstruction: The American Missionary Association and Southern Blacks, 1861–1890.* Athens, GA: University of Georgia Press, 1986.

Willie Lee Rose. *Rehearsal for Reconstruction: The Port Royal Experiment.* Indianapolis, IN: Bobbs Merrill, 1964.

Brenda Stevenson, ed. *The Journals of Charlotte Forten Grimke.* New York: Oxford University Press, 1988.

Land and Labor

Barbara J. Fields. *Slavery and Freedom on the Middle Ground: Maryland during the Nineteenth Century.* New Haven, CT: Yale University Press, 1985.

Jacqueline Jones. *Labor of Love, Labor of Sorrow: Black Women, Work and Family, from Slavery to the Present.* New York: Basic Books, 1985.

Edward Magdol. *A Right to the Land: Essays on the Freedmen's Community.* Westport, CT: Greenwood Press, 1977.

Claude F. Oubre. *Forty Acres and a Mule: The Freedmen's Bureau and Black Landownership.* Baton Rouge, LA: Louisiana State University Press, 1978.

Roger L. Ransom and Richard Sutch. *One Kind of Freedom: The Economic Consequences of Emancipation.* New York: Cambridge University Press, 1977.

Julie Saville. *The Work of Reconstruction: From Slave to Wage Labor in South Carolina, 1860–1870.* New York: Cambridge University Press, 1994.

James D. Schmidt. *Free to Work: Labor, Law, Emancipation, and Reconstruction, 1815–1880.* Athens, GA: University of Georgia Press, 1998.

Leslie A. Schwalm. *A Hard Fight for We: Women's Transition from Slavery to Freedom in South Carolina.* Urbana, IL: University of Illinois Press, 1997.

Black Communities

John W. Blassingame. *Black New Orleans, 1860–1880.* Chicago: University of Chicago Press, 1973.

Cyprian Davis. *The History of Black Catholics in the United States.* New York: Crossroad, 1990.

Robert F. Engs. *Freedom's First Generation: Black Hampton, Virginia, 1861–1890.* Philadelphia: University of Pennsylvania Press, 1979.

William E. Montgomery. *Under Their Own Vine and Fig Tree, The African American Church in the South 1865–1900.* Baton Rouge, LA: Louisiana State University Press, 1993.

Bernard E. Powers, Jr. *Black Charlestonians: A Social History, 1822–1885.* Fayetteville, AR: University of Arkansas Press, 1994.

Clarence E. Walker. *A Rock in a Weary Land: The African Methodist Episcopal Church during the Civil War and Reconstruction.* Baton Rouge, LA: Louisiana State University Press, 1982.

James M. Washington. *Frustrated Fellowship: The Black Baptist Quest for Social Power.* Macon, GA: Mercer University Press, 1986.

Chapter 13   The Meaning of Freedom: The Failure of Reconstruction

Reconstruction in Specific States

Edmund L. Drago. *Black Politicians and Reconstruction in Georgia.* Athens, GA: University of Georgia Press, 1982.

———. *Hurrah for Hampton: Black Red Shirts in South Carolina during Reconstruction.* Fayetteville, AR: University of Arkansas Press, 1998.

Luther P. Jackson. *Negro Officeholders in Virginia, 1865– 1895*. Norfolk, VA: Guide Quality Press, 1945.

Peter Kolchin. *First Freedom: The Responses of Alabama's Blacks to Emancipation and Reconstruction*. Westport, CT: Greenwood Publishing, 1972.

Merline Pitre. *Through Many Dangers, Toils, and Snares: The Black Leadership of Texas, 1868–1900*. Austin, TX: Eakin Press, 1985.

Joe M. Richardson. *The Negro in the Reconstruction of Florida, 1865–1877*. Tallahassee, FL: Florida State University Press, 1965.

Buford Stacher. *Blacks in Mississippi Politics, 1865–1900*. Washington, DC: University Press of America, 1978.

Ted Tunnell. *Crucible of Reconstruction: War, Radicalism and Race in Louisiana, 1862–1877*. Baton Rouge, LA: Louisiana State University Press, 1984.

Charles Vincent. *Black Legislators in Louisiana During Reconstruction*. Baton Rouge, LA: Louisiana State University Press, 1976.

Joel Williamson. *After Slavery: The Negro in South Carolina: 1861–1877*. Chapel Hill, NC: University of North Carolina Press, 1965.

National Politics: Andrew Johnson and the Radical Republicans

Michael Les Benedict. *A Compromise of Principle: Congressional Republicans and Reconstruction*. New York: Norton, 1974.

Eric L. McKitrick. *Andrew Johnson and Reconstruction, 1865–1867*. Chicago: University of Chicago Press, 1960.

James M. McPherson. *The Struggle for Equality: Abolitionists and the Negro in the Civil War and Reconstruction*. Princeton, NJ: Princeton University Press, 1964.

Hans L. Trefousse. *The Radical Republicans: Lincoln's Vanguard for Racial Justice*. Baton Rouge, LA: Louisiana State University Press, 1969.

Economic Issues: Land, Labor, and the Freedmen's Bank

Elizabeth Bethel. *Promiseland: A Century of Life in a Negro Community*. Philadelphia: Temple University Press, 1981.

Carol R. Bleser. *The Promised Land: The History of the South Carolina Land Commission, 1869–1890*. Columbia, SC: University of South Carolina Press, 1969.

Donald G. Nieman. *To Set the Law in Motion: The Freedmen's Bureau and Legal Rights for Blacks, 1865–1869*. Millwood, NY: KTO, 1979.

Carl R. Osthaus. *Freedmen, Philanthropy and Fraud: A History of the Freedman's Savings Bank*. Urbana, IL: University of Illinois Press, 1976.

Violence and the Ku Klux Klan

George C. Rable. *But There Was No Peace: The Role of Violence in the Politics of Reconstruction*. Athens, GA: University of Georgia Press, 1984.

Allen W. Trelease. *White Terror: The Ku Klux Klan Conspiracy and Southern Reconstruction*. New York: Harper & Row, 1973.

Lou Falkner Williams. *The Great South Carolina Ku Klux Klan Trials, 1871–1872*. Athens, GA: University of Georgia Press, 1996.

Autobiography and Biography

Mifflin Wistar Gibbs. *Shadow & Light: An Autobiography*. Lincoln, NE: University of Nebraska Press, 1995.

Peter D. Klingman. *Josiah Walls*. Gainesville, FL: University Presses of Florida, 1976.

Peggy Lamson, *The Glorious Failure: Black Congressman Robert Brown Elliott and Reconstruction in South Carolina*. New York: Norton, 1973.

Edward A. Miller. *Gullah Statesman: Robert Smalls: From Slavery to Congress, 1839–1915*. Columbia, SC: University of South Carolina Press, 1995.

Loren Schweninger. *James T. Rapier and Reconstruction*. Chicago: University of Chicago Press, 1978.

Okon E. Uya. *From Slavery to Public Service: Robert Smalls, 1839–1915*. New York: Oxford University Press, 1971.

Chapter 14   White Supremacy Triumphant: African Americans in the South in the Late Nineteenth Century

State and Local Studies

Eric Anderson. *Race and Politics in North Carolina, 1872–1901: The Black Second*. Baton Rouge, LA: Louisiana State University Press, 1981.

Helen G. Edmonds. *The Negro and Fusion Politics in North Carolina, 1894–1901*. Chapel Hill, NC: University of North Carolina Press, 1951.

William Ivy Hair. *Carnival of Fury: Robert Charles and the New Orleans Riot of 1900*. Baton Rouge, LA: Louisiana State University Press, 1976.

Neil R. McMillen. *Dark Journey: Black Mississippians in the Age of Jim Crow*. Urbana, IL: University of Illinois Press, 1989.

David M. Oshinsky. *"Worse than Slavery": Parchman Farm and the Ordeal of Jim Crow Justice*. New York: The Free Press, 1999.

George B. Tindall. *South Carolina Negroes, 1877–1900*. Columbia, SC: University of South Carolina Press, 1952.

Vernon Wharton. *The Negro in Mississippi, 1865–1890*. Chapel Hill, NC: University of North Carolina Press, 1947.

Biographies and Autobiographies

Albert S. Broussard. *African-American Odyssey: The Stewarts, 1853–1963*. Lawrence, KS: University Press of Kansas, 1998.

Alfreda Duster, ed. *Crusade for Justice: The Autobiography of Ida B. Wells*. Chicago: University of Chicago Press, 1972.

Henry O. Flipper. *The Colored Cadet at West Point*. New York: Arno Press, 1969.

John F. Marszalek, Jr. *Court Martial: The Army vs. Johnson Whittaker*. New York: Scribner, 1972.

Linda McMurry. *To Keep the Waters Troubled: The Life of Ida B. Wells*. New York: Oxford University Press, 1998.

Patricia A. Schechter. *Ida B. Wells-Barnett and American Reform, 1882–1930*. Chapel Hill, NC: University of North Carolina Press, 2001.

Politics and Segregation

Grace Hale. *Making Whiteness: The Culture of Segregation in the South, 1890–1940*. New York: Pantheon Books, 1998.

J. Morgan Kousser. *The Shaping of Southern Politics: Suffrage Restriction and the Establishment of the One-Party South, 1880–1910*. New Haven, CT: Yale University Press, 1974.

Michael Perman. *Struggle for Mastery: Disfranchisement in the South, 1888–1908*. Chapel Hill, NC: University of North Carolina Press, 2001.

Lynching

James Allen, Hinton Als, John Lewis, and Leon F. Litwack. *Without Sanctuary: Lynching Photography in America*. Santa Fe, NM: Twin Palms Books, 2000.

W. Fitzhugh Brundage. *Lynching in the New South: Georgia and Virginia, 1880–1930*. Urbana, IL: University of Illinois Press, 1993.

_____. ed. *Under Sentence of Death: Lynching in the South*. Chapel Hill, NC: University of North Carolina Press, 1997.

Sandra Gunning. *Race, Rape, and Lynching: The Red Record of American Literature, 1890–1912*. New York: Oxford University Press, 1996.

National Association for the Advancement of Colored People. *Thirty Years of Lynching in the United States, 1889–1918*. New York: NAACP, 1919.

Migration, Mobility, and Land Ownership

William Cohen. *At Freedom's Edge: Black Mobility and the Southern White Quest for Racial Control, 1861–1915*. Baton Rouge, LA: Louisiana State University Press, 1991.

Pete Daniel. *The Shadow of Slavery: Peonage in the South, 1901–1969*. Urbana, IL: University of Illinois Press, 1972.

Nell Painter. *Exodusters: Black Migration to Kansas after Reconstruction*. New York: Alfred A. Knopf, 1977.

Loren Schweninger. *Black Property Owners in the South, 1790–1915*. Urbana, IL: University of Illinois Press, 1990.

Chapter 15   Black Southerners Challenge White Supremacy

Education

Eric Anderson and Alfred A. Moss, Jr. *Dangerous Donations: Northern Philanthropy and Southern Black Education, 1902–1930*. Columbia, MO: University of Missouri Press, 1999.

James D. Anderson and V. P. Franklin, eds. *New Perspectives on Black Education*. Boston: G. K. Hall, 1978.

Henry A. Bullock. *A History of Negro Education in the South from 1619 to the Present*. Cambridge, MA: Harvard University Press, 1967.

Religion

Cyprian Davis. *The History of Black Catholics in the United States*. New York: Crossroad, 1990.

Harold T. Lewis. *Yet With a Steady Beat: The African American Struggle for Recognition in the Episcopal Church*. Valley Forge, PA: Trinity Press International, 1996.

Iain MacRobert. *The Black Roots and White Racism of Early Pentecostalism in the USA.* Basingstoke, United Kingdom: Macmillan, 1988.

Edwin S. Redkey, ed. *The Writings and Speeches of Henry McNeal Turner.* New York: Arno Press, 1971.

Clarence E. Walker. *A Rock in a Weary Land: The African Methodist Episcopal Church during the Civil War and Reconstruction.* Baton Rouge, LA: Louisiana State University Press, 1982.

The Military and the West

John M. Carroll, ed. *The Black Military Experience in the American West.* New York: Liveright, 1973.

Willard B. Gatewood, ed. *Smoked Yankees and the Struggle for Empire: Letters from Negro Soldiers, 1898–1902.* Urbana, IL: University of Illinois Press, 1971.

William Loren Katz. *The Black West.* New York: Touchstone Books, 1996.

William H. Leckie. *The Buffalo Soldiers: A Narrative of the Negro Cavalry in the West.* Norman, OK: University of Oklahoma Press, 1967.

John D. Weaver. *The Brownsville Raid.* New York: Norton, 1971.

Labor

Tera W. Hunter. *To 'Joy My Freedom: Southern Black Women's Lives and Labors after the Civil War.* Cambridge, MA: Harvard University Press, 1997.

Gerald D. Jaynes. *Branches without Roots: Genesis of the Black Working Class in the American South, 1862–1882.* New York: Oxford University Press, 1986.

The Professions

V. N. Gamble. *The Black Community Hospital: Contemporary Dilemmas in Historical Perspective.* New York: Garland, 1989.

Darlene Clark Hine. *Speak Truth to Power: Black Professional Class in United States History.* Brooklyn, NY: Carlson Publishing Co., 1996.

J. Clay Smith, Jr. *Emancipation: The Making of the Black Lawyer, 1844–1944.* Philadelphia: University of Pennsylvania Press, 1993.

_____. ed. *Rebels in Law: Voices in History of Black Women Lawyers.* Ann Arbor, MI: University of Michigan Press, 1998.

Music

W. C. Handy. *Father of the Blues: An Autobiography.* New York: Macmillan, 1941.

John Edward Hasse, ed. *Ragtime, Its History, Composers, and Music.* London: Macmillan, 1985.

Alan Lomax. *Mr. Jelly Roll: The Fortunes of Jelly Roll Morton, New Orleans Creole and "Inventor of Jazz."* New York: Grove Press, 1950.

Gunther Schuller. *Early Jazz: Its Roots and Musical Development.* New York: Oxford University Press, 1968.

Sports

Ocania Chalk. *Black College Sport.* New York: Dodd, Mead and Co., 1976.

Robert W. Peterson. *Only the Ball Was White: Negro Baseball: A History of Legendary Black Players and All-Black Professional Teams before Black Men Played in the Major Leagues.* New York: Prentice-Hall, 1970.

Andrew Ritchie. *Major Taylor: The Extraordinary Career of a Championship Bicycle Racer.* San Francisco: Bicycle Books, 1988.

Randy Roberts. *Papa Jack: Jack Johnson and the Era of White Hopes.* New York: The Free Press, 1983.

Chapter 16   Conciliation, Agitation, and Migration: African Americans in the Early Twentieth Century

Leadership Conflicts and the Emergence of African-American Organizations

Charles F. Kellogg. *NAACP: A History of the National Association for the Advancement of Colored People.* Baltimore: Johns Hopkins University Press, 1967.

August Meier. *Negro Thought in America, 1880–1915.* Ann Arbor, MI: University of Michigan Press, 1967.

Alfred A. Moss, Jr. *American Negro Academy: Voice of the Talented Tenth.* Baton Rouge, LA: Louisiana State University Press, 1981.

B. Joyce Ross. *J. E. Spingarn and the Rise of the N.A.A.C.P.* New York: Atheneum, 1972.

Lawrence C. Ross, Jr. *The Divine Nine: The History of African-American Fraternities and Sororities.* New York: Kensington Books, 2000.

Elliott Rudwick. *W. E. B. Du Bois.* New York: Atheneum, 1968.

Nancy Weiss. *The National Urban League, 1910–1940.* New York: Oxford University Press, 1974.

Shamoon Zamir. *Dark Voices: W. E. B. Du Bois and American Thought, 1888–1903.* Chicago: University of Chicago Press, 1995.

African-American Women in the Early Twentieth Century

Anna Julia Cooper. *A Voice from the South.* New York: Oxford University Press, 1988.

Elizabeth Clark-Lewis. *Living In, Living Out: African American Domestics in Washington, D.C., 1910–1940.* Washington: Smithsonian Institution Press, 1994.

Cynthia Neverdon-Morton. *Afro-American Women of the South and the Advancement of the Race, 1895– 1925.* Knoxville, TN: University of Tennessee Press, 1998.

Jacqueline A. Rouse. *Lugina Burns Hope: A Black Southern Reformer.* Athens, GA: University of Georgia Press, 1989.

Stephanie J. Shaw. *What a Woman Ought to Be and to Do: Black Professional Women Workers during the Jim Crow Era.* Chicago: University of Chicago Press, 1996.

Rosalyn Terborg-Penn. *African American Women in the Struggle for the Vote, 1850–1920.* Bloomington, IN: Indiana University Press, 1998.

African Americans in the Military in the World War I Era

Arthur E. Barbeau and Florette Henri. *Black American Troops in World War I.* Philadelphia: Temple University Press, 1974.

Edward M. Coffman. *The War to End All Wars: The American Military Experience in World War I.* Madison, WI: University of Wisconsin Press, 1986.

Arthur W. Little. *From Harlem to the Rhine: The Story of New York's Colored Volunteers.* New York: Covici, Friede, 1936.

Bernard C. Nalty. *Strength for the Fight: A History of Black Americans in the Military.* New York: The Free Press, 1986.

Cities and Racial Conflict

Michael D'Orso. *Rosewood.* New York: Boulevard Press, 1996.

St. Clair Drake and Horace R. Clayton. *Black Metropolis: A Study of Negro Life in a Northern City.* 2 vols. Chicago: Harcourt, Brace and Co., 1945.

Sherry Sherrod Dupree. *The Rosewood Massacre at a Glance.* Gainesville, FL: Rosewood Forum, 1998.

Scott Ellsworth. *Death in a Promised Land: The Tulsa Race Riot of 1921.* Baton Rouge, LA: Louisiana State University Press, 1982.

Robert V. Haynes. *A Night of Violence: The Houston Riot of 1917.* Baton Rouge, LA: Louisiana State University Press, 1976.

Hannibal Johnson. *Black Wall Street, From Riot to Renaissance in Tulsa's Historic Greenwood District.* Austin, TX: Eakin Press, 1998.

David M. Katzman. *Before the Ghetto: Black Detroit in the Nineteenth Century.* Urbana, IL: University of Illinois Press, 1973.

Kenneth L. Kusmer. *A Ghetto Takes Shape: Black Cleveland, 1870–1930.* Urbana, IL: University of Illinois Press, 1976.

Gilbert Osofsky. *Harlem: The Making of a Ghetto, 1890–1930.* New York: Harper & Row, 1966.

Christopher Reed. *The Chicago NAACP and the Rise of Black Professional Leadership, 1910–1966.* Bloomington, IN: Indiana University Press, 1997.

Elliott M. Rudwick. *Race Riot at East St. Louis, July 2, 1917.* Cleveland: World Publishing, 1966.

Roberta Senechal. *The Sociogenesis of a Race Riot: Springfield, Illinois, in 1908.* Urbana, IL: University of Illinois Press, 1990.

Allan H. Spear. *Black Chicago: The Making of a Negro Ghetto, 1890–1920.* Chicago: University of Chicago Press, 1967.

Joe William Trotter, Jr. *Black Milwaukee: The Making of an Industrial Proletariat, 1915–1945.* Urbana, IL: University of Illinois Press, 1985.

William Tuttle. *Chicago in the Red Summer of 1919.* New York: Atheneum, 1970.

Lee E. Williams. *Anatomy of Four Race Riots: Racial Conflict in Knoxville, Elaine (Arkansas), Tulsa, and Chicago, 1919–1921.* Hattiesburg, MS: University and College Press of Mississippi, 1972.

The Great Migration

Peter Gottlieb. *Making Their Own Way: Southern Blacks' Migration to Pittsburgh, 1916–1930.* Urbana, IL: University of Illinois Press, 1987.

James R. Grossman. *Land of Hope: Chicago, Black Southerners, and the Great Migration.* Chicago: University of Chicago Press, 1989.

Florette Henri. *Black Migration, 1900–1920.* Garden City, NY: Anchor Press, 1975.

Carole Marks. *Farewell—We're Good and Gone: The Great Black Migration.* Bloomington, IN: Indiana University Press, 1989.

Milton C. Sernett. *Bound for the Promised Land: African American Religion and the Great Migration.* Durham, NC: Duke University Press, 1997.

Joe William Trotter, Jr., ed. *The Great Migration in Historical Perspective.* Bloomington, IN: Indiana University Press, 1991.

Autobiography and Biography

W. E. B. Du Bois. *Dusk of Dawn.* New York: Harcourt, Brace & Co., 1940.

———. *The Autobiography: A Soliloquy on Viewing My Life from the Last Decade of Its First Century.* New York: International Publishers, 1968.

Stephen R. Fox. *The Guardian of Boston: William Monroe Trotter.* New York: Atheneum, 1970.

Kenneth R. Manning. *Black Apollo of Science: The Life of Ernest Everett Just.* New York: Oxford University Press, 1983.

Linda O. McMurry. *George Washington Carver: Scientist and Symbol.* New York: Oxford University Press, 1981.

Arnold Rampersad. *The Art and Imagination of W. E. B. Du Bois.* Cambridge, MA: Harvard University Press, 1976.

Mary Church Terrell. *A Colored Woman in a White World.* New York: Arno Press reprint, 1940.

Emma Lou Thornbrough. *T. Thomas Fortune.* Chicago: University of Chicago Press, 1970.

Booker T. Washington. *Up from Slavery.* New York: Doubleday, 1901.

Chapter 17   African Americans and the 1920s

The Ku Klux Klan

David M. Chalmers. *Hooded Americanism: A History of the Ku Klux Klan.* New York: Franklin Watts, 1965.

Kenneth T. Jackson. *The Ku Klux Klan in the City.* New York: Oxford University Press, 1967.

The NAACP

Charles F. Kellogg. *NAACP: A History of the National Association for the Advancement of Colored People.* Baltimore: Johns Hopkins University Press, 1967.

Robert L. Zangrando. *The NAACP Campaign against Lynching, 1909–1950.* Philadelphia: Temple University Press, 1980.

Black Workers, A. Philip Randolph, and the Brotherhood of Sleeping Car Porters

Jervis B. Anderson. *A. Philip Randolph: A Biographical Portrait.* New York: Harcourt, Brace, Jovanovich, 1973.

David E. Bernstein. *Only One Place of Redress: African Americans, Labor Regulations and the Courts from Reconstruction to the New Deal.* Durham, NC: Duke University Press, 2001.

Jack Santino. *Miles of Smiles, Years of Struggle: Stories of Black Pullman Porters.* Urbana, IL: University of Illinois Press, 1989.

Marcus Garvey and the Universal Negro Improvement Association

Randall K. Burkett. *Garveyism as a Religious Movement: The Institutionalization of a Black Civil Religion.* Metuchen, NJ: Scarecrow Press, 1978.

E. David Cronon. *Black Moses: The Story of Marcus Garvey and the Universal Negro Improvement Association.* Madison, WI: University of Wisconsin Press, 1955.

Marcus Garvey. *Philosophy and Opinions of Marcus Garvey.* New York: Atheneum, 1969.

Theodore Kornweibel, Jr. *Seeing Red: Federal Campaigns against Black Militancy, 1919–1925.* Bloomington, IN: Indiana University Press, 1998.

The Harlem Renaissance

Arna W. Bontemps, ed. *The Harlem Renaissance Remembered.* New York: Dodd, Mead, 1972.

Nathan Huggins. *Harlem Renaissance.* New York: Oxford University Press, 1971.

Bruce Kellner, ed. *The Harlem Renaissance: A Historical Dictionary of the Era.* Westport, CT: Greenwood Press, 1984.

Steven Watson. *The Harlem Renaissance: Hub of African American Culture, 1920–1930.* New York: Pantheon, 1995.

Biographies and Autobiographies

Pamela Bordelon, ed. *Go Gator and Muddy the Water: Writings by Zora Neale Hurston from the Federal Writers Project.* New York: Norton, 1999.

Wayne F. Cooper. *Claude McKay, Rebel Sojourner in the Harlem Renaissance: A Biography.* Baton Rouge, LA: Louisiana State University Press, 1987.

Thadious M. Davis. *Nella Larsen: Novelist of the Harlem Renaissance.* Baton Rouge, LA: Louisiana State University Press, 1994.

Robert Hemenway. *Zora Neale Hurston: A Literary Biography.* Urbana, IL: University of Illinois Press, 1977.

Gloria T. Hull. *Color, Sex, and Poetry: Three Women Writers of the Harlem Renaissance.* Bloomington, IN: Indiana University Press, 1987.

James Weldon Johnson. *Along the Way.* New York: Viking Press, 1933.

Cynthia E. Kerman. *The Lives of Jean Toomer: A Hunger for Wholeness.* Baton Rouge, LA: Louisiana State University Press, 1987.

Eugene Levy. *James Weldon Johnson: Black Leader, Black Voice.* Chicago: University of Chicago Press, 1973.

Chapter 18   The Great Depression and the New Deal

Politics

Adam Fairclough. *Better Day Coming: Blacks and Equality, 1890–2000.* New York: Viking, 2001.

Kenneth W. Goings. *"The NAACP Comes of Age": The Defeat of Judge John J. Parker.* Bloomington, IN: Indiana University Press, 1990.

Charles V. Hamilton. *Adam Clayton Powell, Jr., the Political Biography of an American Dilemma.* New York: Atheneum, 1991.

Darlene Clark Hine. *Black Victory: The Rise and Fall of the White Primary in Texas.* Millwood, NY: KTO Press, 1979.

Charles F. Kellogg. *NAACP: A History of the National Association for the Advancement of Colored People.* Baltimore: Johns Hopkins University Press, 1967.

John B. Kirby. *Black Americans in the Roosevelt Era: Liberalism and Race.* Knoxville, TN: University of Tennessee Press, 1980.

Christopher R. Reed. *The Chicago NAACP and the Rise of Black Professional Leadership, 1910–1966.* Bloomington, IN: Indiana University Press, 1997.

Bernard Sternsher, ed. *The Negro in Depression and War: Prelude to Revolution, 1930–1945.* Chicago: Quadrangle Books, 1969.

Mark V. Tushnet. *The NAACP's Legal Strategy against Segregated Education, 1925–1950.* Chapel Hill, NC: University of North Carolina Press, 1987.

Nancy J. Weiss. *Farewell to the Party of Lincoln: Black Politics in the Age of Lincoln.* Princeton, NJ: Princeton University Press, 1983.

Labor

Lizabeth Cohen. *Making a New Deal: Industrial Workers in Chicago, 1919–1939.* New York: Cambridge University Press, 1990.

Dennis C. Dickerson. *Out of the Crucible: Black Steelworkers in Western Pennsylvania, 1875–1980.* Albany, NY: SUNY Press, 1986.

William H. Harris. *The Harder We Run: Black Workers since the Civil War.* New York: Oxford University Press, 1982.

August Meier and Elliott Rudwick. *Black Detroit and the Rise of the UAW.* New York: Oxford University Press, 1979.

Education

James D. Anderson. *The Education of Blacks in the South, 1860–1935.* Chapel Hill, NC: University of North Carolina Press, 1988.

Horace M. Bond. *The Education of the Negro in the American Social Order.* New York: Octagon Books, 1934, rev. 1966.

Richard Kluger. *Simple Justice: The History of Brown v. Board of Education and Black America's Struggle for Equality,* 1976.

Mark V. Tushnet. *Making Civil Rights Law: Thurgood Marshall and the Supreme Court, 1935–1961,* 1994.

Doxey Wilkerson. *Special Problems in Negro Education.* Washington, DC: U.S. Government Printing Office, 1939.

Black Radicalism

Dan Carter. *Scottsboro: A Tragedy of the American South.* Baton Rouge, LA: Louisiana State University Press, 1969.

Kenneth W. Goings. *Mammy and Uncle Mose: Black Collectibles and American Stereotyping.* Bloomington, IN: Indiana University Press, 1994.

Michael K. Honey. *Southern Labor and Black Civil Rights: Organizing Memphis Workers.* Urbana, IL: University of Illinois Press, 1993.

Jacqueline Jones. *Labor of Love, Labor of Sorrow: Black Women, Work, and the Family from Slavery to the Present.* New York: Basic Books, 1985.

Nicholas Natanson. *The Black Image in the New Deal: The Politics of FSA Photography.* Knoxville, TN: University of Tennessee Press, 1992.

Richard H. Pells. *Radical Visions and American Dreams: Culture and Social Thought in the Depression Years.* New York: Harper & Row, 1973.

Daryl Michael Scott. *Contempt and Pity: Social Policy and the Image of the Damaged Black Psyche, 1880–1996.* Chapel Hill, NC: University of North Carolina Press, 1997.

Mark Solomon. *The Cry Was Unity: Communists and African Americans, 1917–1936.* Jackson, MS: University Press of Mississippi, 1998.

Richard W. Thomas. *Life for Us Is What We Make It: Building Black Community in Detroit, 1915–1945.* Bloomington, IN: Indiana University Press, 1992.

Economics

Charles T. Banner-Haley. *To Do Good and to Do Well: Middle Class Blacks and the Depression, Philadelphia, 1929–1941.* New York: Garland, 1993.

Abram L. Harris. *The Negro as Capitalist: A Study of Banking and Business among American Negroes.* Originally published by the American Academy of Political and Social Sciences, 1936; Reprint, Chicago: Urban Research Press, 1992.

Alexa Benson Henderson. *Atlanta Life Insurance Company: Guardian of Black Economic Dignity*. Tuscaloosa, AL: University of Alabama Press, 1990.

Robert E. Weems, Jr. *Black Business in the Black Metropolis: The Chicago Metropolitan Assurance Company, 1924–1985*. Bloomington, IN: Indiana University Press, 1996.

Biography and Autobiography

Andrew Buni. *Robert L. Vann of the Pittsburgh Courier*. Pittsburgh: University of Pittsburgh Press, 1974.

Joanne Grant. *Ella Baker: Freedom Bound*. New York: John Wiley, 1998.

Wil Haywood. *King of the Cats: The Life and Times of Adam Clayton Powell, Jr.* Boston: Houghton Mifflin, 1993.

Spencie Love. *One Blood: The Death and Resurrection of Charles R. Drew*. Chapel Hill, NC: University of North Carolina Press, 1996.

Genna Rae McNeil. *Groundwork: Charles Hamilton Houston and the Struggle for Civil Rights*. Philadelphia: University of Pennsylvania Press, 1983.

Nell Irvin Painter. *The Narrative of Hosea Hudson: His Life as a Negro Communist in the South*. Cambridge, MA: Harvard University Press, 1979.

Paula F. Pfeffer. *A. Philip Randolph, Pioneer of the Civil Rights Movement*. Baton Rouge, LA: Louisiana State University Press, 1990.

George S. Schuyler. *Black and Conservative: The Autobiography of George S. Schuyler*. New Rochelle, NY: Arlington House, 1966.

Gilbert Ware. *William Hastie: Grace under Pressure*. New York: Oxford University Press, 1984.

Roy Wilkins with Tom Mathews. *Standing Fast: The Autobiography of Roy Wilkins*. New York: Da Capo Press, 1994.

Chapter 19   Black Culture and Society in the 1930s and 1940s

Art

Sharon F. Patton. *African-American Art*. New York: Oxford University Press, 1998.

Richard J. Powell. *Black Art and Culture in the 20th Century*. New York: Thames and Judson, 1997.

William E. Taylor and Harriet G. Warkel. *A Shared Heritage: Art by Four African Americans*. Bloomington, IN: Indiana University Press, 1996.

Black Chicago Renaissance

Robert Bone. "Richard Wright and the Chicago Renaissance." *Callaloo* 9, no. 3 (1986):446–468.

Craig Werner. "Leon Forrest, the AACM and the Legacy of the Chicago Renaissance." *The Black Scholar* 23, no. 3/4 (1993): 10–23.

Culture

St. Clair Drake and Horace R. Cayton. *Black Metropolis: A Study of Negro Life in a Northern City*. New York: Harper & Row, 1962.

Gerald Early, ed. *"Ain't But a Place": An Anthology of African American Writing about St. Louis*. St. Louis: Missouri Historical Society Press, 1998.

Geneviève Fabre and Robert O'Meally, eds. *History and Memory in African-American Culture*. New York: Oxford University Press, 1994.

Kenneth W. Goings. *Mammy and Uncle Mose: Black Collectibles and American Stereotyping.* Bloomington, IN: Indiana University Press, 1994.

Robin D. G. Kelley. *Race Rebels: Culture, Politics, and the Black Working Class.* New York: Free Press, 1994.

Lawrence Levine. *Black Culture and Black Consciousness: Afro-American Folk Thought from Slavery to Freedom.* New York: Oxford University Press, 1977.

Tommy L. Lott. *The Invention of Race: Black Culture and the Politics of Representation.* Malden, MA: Blackwell Publishers, 1999.

Daryl Scott. *Contempt and Pity: Social Policy and Image of the Damaged Black Psyche, 1880–1996.* Chapel Hill, NC: University of North Carolina Press, 1997.

Mel Watkins. *On the Real Side: Laughing, Lying, and Signifying.* New York: Simon & Schuster, 1994.

Robert E. Weems Jr. *Desegregating the Dollar: African American Consumerism in the Twentieth Century.* New York: New York University Press, 1998.

Dance

Katherine Dunham. *A Touch of Innocence.* London: Cassell, 1959.

Terry Harnan. *African Rhythm–American Dance.* New York: Knopf, 1974.

Films

Donald Bogle. *Brown Sugar: Eighty Years of America's Black Female Superstars.* New York: Crown Publishers, 1980.

Thomas Cripps. *Making Movies Black: The Hollywood Message Movie from World War II to the Civil Rights Era.* New York: Oxford University Press, 1993.

Literature

Ralph Ellison. "The World and the Jug." In Joseph F. Trimmer, ed. *A Casebook on Ralph Ellison's Invisible Man* (pp. 172–200). New York: T. Y. Crowell, 1972.

Michael Fabre. *The Unfinished Quest of Richard Wright.* Iowa City: University of Iowa Press, 1973.

Henry Louis Gates and Nellie Y. McKay, eds. *Norton Anthology of African American Literature.* New York: W. W. Norton, 1997.

Joyce Ann Joyce. *Richard Wright's Art of Tragedy.* New York: Warner Books, 1986.

Robert G. O'Meally. *The Craft of Ralph Ellison.* Cambridge, MA: Harvard University Press, 1980.

Arnold Rampersad. *The Life of Langston Hughes.* New York: Oxford University Press, 1986.

Margaret Walker. *Richard Wright, Daemonic Genius: A Portrait of the Man, a Critical Look at His Work.* New York: Morrow, 1988.

Music and Radio

William Barlow. *Looking Up at Down: The Emergence of Blues Culture.* Philadelphia: Temple University Press, 1989.

Thomas Brothers, ed. *Louis Armstrong: In His Own Words.* New York: Oxford University Press, 1999.

Jack Chalmers. *Milestones I: The Music and Times of Miles Davis to 1960.* Toronto, Canada: University of Toronto Press, 1983.

John Chilton. *The Song of the Hawk: The Life and Recordings of Coleman Hawkins.* Ann Arbor, MI: University of Michigan Press, 1990.

Donald Clarke. *Wishing on the Moon: The Life and Times of Billie Holiday.* New York: Viking Penguin, 1994.

Linda Dahl. *Morning Glory: A Biography of Mary Lou Williams.* New York: Pantheon Books, 2000.

Miles Davis and Quincy Troupe. *Miles: The Autobiography.* New York: Simon & Schuster, 1989.

Duke Ellington. *Music Is My Mistress.* New York: Da Capo Press, 1973.

John Birks Gillespie and Wilmot Alfred Fraser. *To Be or Not . . . to Bop: Memoirs/Dizzy Gillespie with Al Fraser.* New York: Doubleday, 1979.

Michael Harris. *The Rise of Gospel Blues: The Music of Thomas Andrew Dorsey in the Urban Church.* New York: Oxford University Press, 1992.

Allan Keiler. *Marian Anderson: A Singer's Journey.* New York: Scribner, 2000.

Robert G. O'Meally. *Lady Day: The Many Faces of Billie Holiday.* New York: Arcade Publishers, 1991.

Thomas Owens. *Bebop: The Music and Its Players.* New York: Oxford University Press, 1955.

Barbara Dianne Savage. *Broadcasting Freedom: Radio, War, and the Politics of Race, 1938–1948.* Chapel Hill, NC: University of North Carolina Press, 1999.

Jules Schwerin. *Got to Tell It: Mahalia Jackson, Queen of Gospel.* New York: Oxford University Press, 1992.

Alyn Shipton. *Groovin' High: The Life of Dizzy Gillespie.* New York: Oxford University Press, 1999.

Eileen Southern. *The Music of Black Americans: A History,* 2d ed. New York: W. W. Norton, 1983.

J. C. Thomas. *Chasin' the Trane: The Music and Mystique of John Coltrane.* Garden City, NY: Doubleday, 1975.

Dempsey J. Travis. *Autobiography of Black Jazz.* Chicago: Urban Research Press, 1983.

Sports

Arthur Ashe, with the assistance of Kip Branch, Ocania Chalk, and Francis Harris. *A Hard Road to Glory: A History of the African-American Athlete.* New York: Warner Books, Inc., 1988.

Richard Bak. *Joe Louis: The Great Black Hope.* New York: Da Capo Press, 1998.

Robert Peterson. *Only the Ball Was White: A History of Legendary Black Players and All-Black Professional Teams.* New York: McGraw Hill, 1984.

Arnold Rampersad. *Jackie Robinson: A Biography.* New York: Knopf, 1997.

Jackie Robinson. *I Never Had It Made.* New York: G. P. Putnam's Son, 1972.

Jeffrey T. Sammons. *Beyond the Ring: The Role of Boxing in American Society.* Urbana, IL: University of Illinois Press, 1988.

Religion

Claude Andrew Clegg III. *An Original Man: The Life and Times of Elijah Muhammad.* New York: St. Martin's Griffin, 1997.

C. Eric Lincoln and Lawrence H. Mamiya. *The Black Church in the African American Experience.* Durham, NC: Duke University Press, 1990.

Elijah Muhammad. *The True History of Elijah Muhammad: Autobiographically Authoritative.* Atlanta: Secretrius Publications, 1997.

Jill Watts. *God, Harlem USA: The Father Divine Story.* Berkeley, CA: University of California Press, 1992.

Robert Weisbrot. *Father Divine and the Struggle for Racial Equality*. Urbana, IL: University of Illinois Press, 1983.

Chapter 20   The World War II Era and Seeds of a Revolution

African Americans and the Military

Robert Allen. *Port Chicago Mutiny: The Story of the Largest Mass Mutiny in U.S. Naval History*. New York: Warner Books-Amistad Books, 1989.

Richard Dalfiume. *Desegregation of the U.S. Armed Forces: Fighting on Two Fronts 1939–1953*. Columbia, MO: University of Missouri Press, 1969.

Charles W. Dryden. *A-Train: Memoirs of a Tuskegee Airman*. Tuscaloosa, AL: University of Alabama Press, 1997.

Charity Adams Earley. *One Woman's Army: A Black Officer Remembers the WAC*. College Station, TX: Texas A & M University Press, 1989.

Darlene Clark Hine. *Black Women in White: Racial Conflict and Cooperation in the Nursing Profession, 1890–1950*. Bloomington, IN: Indiana University Press, 1989.

Ulysses Lee. *The Employment of Negro Troops*. Washington, DC: Center of Military History, 1990.

Neil McMillen, ed. *Remaking Dixie: The Impact of World War II on the American South*. Jackson, MS: University Press of Mississippi, 1997.

Mary Penick Motley. *The Invisible Soldier: The Experience of the Black Soldier, World War Two*. Detroit: Wayne State University Press, 1975.

Alan M. Osur. *Blacks in the Army Air Forces during World War II: The Problem of Race Relations*. Washington, DC: Office of Air Force History, 1977.

Lou Potter. *Liberators: Fighting on Two Fronts in World War II*. New York: Harcourt Brace Jovanovich, 1992.

Stanley Sandler. *Segregated Skies: All-Black Combat Squadrons of WWII*. Washington, DC: Smithsonian Institution Press, 1992.

Howard Sitkoff. "Racial Militancy and Interracial Violence in the Second World War," *Journal of American History* 58, no. 3 (1971): 663–83.

Paul Stillwell, ed. *The Golden Thirteen: Recollections of the First Black Naval Officers*. Annapolis, MD: Naval Institute Press, 1993.

Black Urban Studies

Albert Broussard. *Black San Francisco: The Struggle for Racial Equality in the West, 1900–1954*. Lawrence, KS: University of Kansas Press, 1993.

Dominic Capeci. *The Harlem Riot of 1943*. Philadephia: Temple University Press, 1977.

Black Americans, Domestic Radicalism, and International Affairs

William C. Berman. *The Politics of Civil Rights in the Truman Administration*. Columbus, OH: Ohio State University Press, 1970.

John Morton Blum. *V Was for Victory: Politics and American Culture during World War II*. New York: Harcourt Brace Jovanovich, 1996.

Mary L. Dudziak. *Cold War Civil Rights: Race and the Image of American Democracy*. Princeton, NJ: Princeton University Press, 2000.

Richard M. Freeland. *The Truman Doctrine and the Origins of McCarthyism.* New York: New York University Press, 1985.

Herbert Garfinkel. *When Negroes March: The March on Washington Movement in the Organizational Politics for FEPC.* New York: Atheneum, 1973.

Joseph Harris. *African American Reactions to War in Ethiopia, 1936–1941.* Baton Rouge, LA: Louisiana State University Press, 1994.

Gerald Horne. *Black and Red: W. E. B. Du Bois and the Afro-American Response to the Cold War.* Albany, NY: State University of New York Press, 1986.

Sudarshan Kapur. *Raising Up a Prophet: The Afro-American Encounter with Gandhi.* Boston: Orbis, 1992.

Andrew Edmund Kersten. *Race and War: The FEPC in the Midwest, 1941–46.* Urbana, IL: University of Illinois Press, 2000.

George Lipsitz. *Rainbow at Midnight: Labor and Culture in the 1940s.* Urbana, IL: University of Illinois Press, 1994.

August Meier and Elliott Rudwick. *CORE: A Study in the Civil Rights Movement, 1942–1968.* Urbana, IL: University of Illinois Press, 1975.

Gail Williams O'Brien. *The Color of the Law: Race, Violence and Justice in the Post-World War II South.* Chapel Hill, NC: University of North Carolina Press, 1999.

James T. Patterson. *Brown v. Board of Education: A Civil Rights Milestone and Its Troubled Legacy.* New York: Oxford University Press, 2000.

Brenda Gayle Plummer. *Rising Wind: Black Americans and U.S. Foreign Affairs, 1935–1960.* Chapel Hill, NC: University of North Carolina Press, 1996.

Linda Reed. *Simple Decency and Common Sense: The Southern Conference Movement, 1938–1963.* Bloomington, IN: Indiana University Press, 1991.

William R. Scott. *The Sons of Sheba's Race: African-Americans and the Italo-Ethiopian War, 1935–1941.* Bloomington, IN: Indiana University Press, 1993.

Patricia Scott Washburn. *A Question of Sedition: The Federal Government's Investigation of the Black Press during World War II.* New York: Oxford University Press, 1986.

Autobiography and Biography

Andrew Buni. *Robert Vann of the Pittsburgh Courier.* Pittsburgh: University of Pittsburgh Press, 1974.

Martin Bauml Duberman. *Paul Robeson: A Biography.* New York: Ballantine Press, 1989.

Shirley Graham DuBois. *His Day Is Marching On: A Memoir of W. E. B. DuBois.* New York: Lippincott, 1971.

Kenneth R. Janken. *Rayford W. Logan and the Dilemma of the African-American Intellectual.* Amherst, MA: University of Massachusetts Press, 1993.

Spencie Love. *One Blood: The Death and Resurrection of Charles Drew.* Chapel Hill, NC: University of North Carolina Press, 1996.

Manning Marable. *W. E. B. DuBois: Black Radical Democrat.* Boston: Twayne, 1986.

Constance Baker Motley. *Equal Justice under Law: An Autobiography.* New York: Farrar, Straus and Giroux, 1998.

Pauli Murray. *Song in a Weary Throat: An American Pilgrimage.* New York: Harper and Row, 1987.

Bayard Rustin. *Troubles I've Seen.* New York: HarperCollins, 1996.

Studs Terkel, ed. *The Good War.* New York: Pantheon, 1984.

Brian Urquhart. *Ralph Bunche: An American Life.* New York: W. W. Norton, 1993.

Gilbert Ware. *William Hastie: Grace under Pressure.* New York: Oxford University Press, 1984.

Roy Wilkins with Tom Mathews. *Standing Fast: The Autobiography of Roy Wilkins.* New York: Da Capo Press, 1994.

Juan Williams. *Thurgood Marshall: American Revolutionary.* New York: Times Books, 1998.

Chapter 21   The Freedom Movement, 1954–1965

General Overviews of Civil Rights Movement and Organizations

Robert Fredrick Burk. *The Eisenhower Administration and Black Civil Rights.* Knoxville, TN: University of Tennessee Press, 1984.

Stewart Burns. *Daybreak of Freedom: The Montgomery Bus Boycott.* Chapel Hill, NC: University of North Carolina Press, 1997.

John Dittmer. *Local People: The Struggle for Civil Rights in Mississippi.* Urbana, IL: University of Illinois Press, 1994.

Adam Fairclough. *To Redeem the Soul of America: The Southern Christian Leadership Conference and Martin Luther King, Jr.* Athens, GA: University of Georgia Press, 1987.

David R. Goldfield. *Black, White and Southern: Race Relations and the Southern Culture, 1940 to the Present.* Baton Rouge, LA: Louisiana State University Press, 1991.

Martin Luther King, Jr. *Stride Towards Freedom: The Montgomery Story.* New York: Harper, 1958.

Steven F. Lawson. *Black Ballots: Voting Rights in the South, 1944–1969.* New York: Columbia University Press, 1976.

Manning Marable. *Race, Reform, and Rebellion: The Second Reconstruction in Black America, 1945–1982.* Jackson, MS: University Press of Mississippi, 1984.

August Meier and Elliot Rudwick. *CORE: A Study of the Civil Rights Movement, 1942–1968.* New York: Oxford University Press, 1973.

Anne Moody. *Coming of Age in Mississippi.* New York: Dial Press, 1968.

Donald G. Nieman. *Promises to Keep: African-Americans and the Constitutional Order, 1776 to the Present.* New York: Oxford University Press, 1991.

Robert J. Norrell. *Reaping the Whirlwind: The Civil Rights Movement in Tuskegee.* New York: Knopf, 1985.

Charles M. Payne. *I've Got the Light of Freedom: The Organizing Tradition and the Mississippi Freedom Struggle.* Berkeley, CA: University of California Press, 1995.

Fred Powledge. *Free at Last? The Civil Rights Movement and the People Who Made It.* Boston: Little, Brown, 1991.

Howell Raines. *My Soul Is Rested: Movement Days in the Deep South Remembered.* New York: Putnam, 1977.

Belinda Robnett. *How Long? How Long? African-American Women in the Struggle for Civil Rights.* New York: Oxford University Press, 1997.

Juan Williams. *Eyes on the Prize: America's Civil Rights Years, 1954–1965.* New York: Viking, 1987.

Black Politics/White Resistance

Numan V. Bartley. *The Rise of Massive Resistance: Race and Politics in the South during the 1950's.* Baton Rouge, LA: Louisiana State University Press, 1969.

Elizabeth Jacoway and David R. Colburn. *Southern Businessmen and Desegregation.* Baton Rouge, LA: Louisiana State University Press, 1982.

Doug McAdam. *Freedom Summer.* New York: Oxford University Press, 1988.

Neil R. McMillen. *The Citizen's Council: A History of Organized Resistance to the Second Reconstruction.* Urbana, IL: University of Illinois Press, 1971.

Frank R. Parker. *Black Votes Count: Political Empowerment in Mississippi after 1965.* Chapel Hill, NC: University of North Carolina Press, 1990.

Autobiography and Biography

Daisy Bates. *The Long Shadow of Little Rock: Memoir.* New York: David McKay Co., 1962.

Taylor Branch. *Pillar of Fire: America in the King Years, 1963–65.* New York: Simon & Schuster, 1998.

Eric R. Burner. *And Gently He Shall Lead Them: Robert Parris Moses and Civil Rights in Mississippi.* New York: New York University Press, 1994.

Septima Clark. *Ready from Within: Septima Clark and the Civil Rights Movement.* Navarro, CA: Wild Tree Press, 1986.

Robert S. Dallek. *Flawed Giant: Lyndon Johnson and His Times, 1961–1973.* New York: Oxford University Press, 1998.

Dennis C. Dickerson. *Militant Mediator: Whitney M. Young, Jr., 1921–1971.* Lexington, KY: University Press of Kentucky, 1998.

James Farmer. *Lay Bare the Heart: An Autobiography of the Civil Rights Movement.* New York: Arbor House, 1985.

Cynthia Griggs Fleming. *Soon We Will Not Cry: The Liberation of Ruby Doris Smith Robinson.* Lanham, MD: Rowman & Littlefield, 1998.

David J. Garrow. *Bearing the Cross: Martin Luther King, Jr., and the Southern Christian Leadership Conference.* New York: William Morrow & Company, 1986.

_____. *The FBI and Martin Luther King, Jr.* New York: Penguin Books, 1981.

Chana Kai Lee. *For Freedom's Sake: The Life of Fannie Lou Hamer.* Urbana, IL: University of Illinois Press, 1999.

David Levering Lewis. *King: A Critical Biography.* New York: Praeger, 1970.

Jo Ann Gibson Robinson, with David Garrow. *The Montgomery Bus Boycott and the Women Who Started It.* Knoxville, TN: University of Tennessee Press, 1987.

Timothy B. Tyson. *Radio Free Dixie: Robert F. Williams and the Roots of Black Power.* Chapel Hill, NC: University of North Carolina Press, 1999.

Reference Works

Charles Eagles, ed. *The Civil Rights Movement in America.* Jackson, MS: University Press of Mississippi, 1986.

Charles S. Lowery and John F. Marszalek, eds. *Encyclopedia of African-American Civil Rights: From Emancipation to the Present.* New York: Greenwood Press, 1992.

Chapter 22   The Struggle Continues, 1965–1980

Black Panthers

Philip S. Foner, ed. *The Black Panther Speaks.* Philadelphia: Lippincott, 1970.

Toni Morrison, ed. *To Die for the People: The Writings of Huey P. Newton.* New York: Writers and Readers Publishing, 1995.

Kenneth O'Reilly. *Racial Matters: The FBI's Secret File on Black America, 1960–1972.* New York: Free Press, 1989.

Robert Scheer, ed. *Eldridge Cleaver: Post-Prison Writings and Speeches.* New York: Random House, 1969.

Black Power and Politics

Robert L. Allen. *Black Awakening in Capitalist America*. Trenton, NJ: Africa World Press, Inc., 1990.

Elaine Brown. *A Taste of Power: A Black Woman's Story*. New York: Pantheon, 1992.

James H. Cone. *Martin & Malcolm & America: A Dream or a Nightmare*. Maryknoll, NY: Orbis, 1991.

Sidney Fine. *Violence in the Model City: The Cavanagh Administration, Race Relations and the Detroit Riot of 1967*. Ann Arbor, MI: University of Michigan Press, 1989.

James F. Finley, Jr. *Church People in the Struggle: The National Council of Churches and the Black Freedom Movement, 1950–1970*. New York: Oxford University Press, 1993.

Frye Gaillard. *The Dream Long Deferred*. Chapel Hill, NC: University of North Carolina Press, 1988.

B. I. Kaufman. *The Presidency of James E. Carter, Jr.* Lawrence, KS: University of Kansas Press, 1993.

Steven Lawson. *In Pursuit of Power: Southern Blacks and Electoral Politics, 1965–1982*. New York: Columbia University Press, 1985.

C. Eric Lincoln, *The Black Muslims in America*. Boston: Beacon Press, 1961.

J. Anthony Lukas. *Common Ground*. New York: Knopf, 1985.

John T. McCartney. *Black Power Ideologies: An Essay in African-American Thought*. Philadelphia, PA: Temple University Press, 1992.

William B. McClain. *Black People in the Methodist Church*. Cambridge: Schenkman, 1984.

Larry G. Murphy. *Down by the Riverside: Readings in African American Religion*. New York: New York University Press, 2000.

William E. Nelson, Jr. and Philip J. Meranto. *Electing Black Mayors: Political Action in the Black Community*. Columbus, OH: Ohio State University Press, 1977.

Gary Orfield. *Must We Bus? Segregated Schools and National Policy*. Washington, DC: Brookings Institution, 1978.

Robert A. Pratt. *The Color of Their Skin: Education and Race in Richmond, Virginia, 1954–89*. Charlottesville, VA: University Press of Virginia, 1992.

James R. Ralph Jr. *Northern Protest: Martin Luther King, Jr., Chicago, and the Civil Rights Movement*. Cambridge, MA: Harvard University Press, 1993.

Diane Ravitch. *The Great School Wars*. New York: Basic Books, 1974.

Wilbur C. Rich. *Coleman Young and Detroit Politics*. Detroit, MI: Wayne State University Press, 1989.

Bobby Seale. *Seize the Time*. New York: Random House, 1970.

James Melvin Washington. *Frustrated Fellowship: The Black Baptist Quest for Social Power*. Macon, GA: Mercer University Press, 1986.

Delores S. Williams. *Sisters in the Wilderness: The Challenge of Womanist God-Talk*. Maryknoll, NY: Orbis, 1993.

Gayraud S. Wilmore. *Black Religion and Black Radicalism*. New York: Anchor Press, 1973.

Black Studies and Black Students

Talmadge Anderson, ed. *Black Studies: Theory, Method, and Cultural Perspectives*. Pullman, WA: Washington State University Press, 1990.

Jack Bass and Jack Nelson. *The Orangeburg Massacre*. Cleveland, OH: Word Publishing, 1970.

William H. Exum. *Paradoxes of Protest: Black Student Activism in a White University*. Philadelphia, PA: Temple University Press, 1985.

Richard P. McCormick. *The Black Student Protest Movement at Rutgers*. New Brunswick, NJ: Rutgers University Press, 1990.

Cleveland Sellers, with Robert Terrell. *The River of No Return: The Autobiography of a Black Militant and the Life and Death of SNCC.* New York: William Morrow, 1987.

Class and Race

Jack M. Bloom. *Class, Race, and the Civil Rights Movement.* Bloomington, IN: Indiana University Press, 1987.

Martin Gilens. *Why Americans Hate Welfare: Race, Media, and the Politics of Antipoverty Policy.* Chicago: University of Chicago Press, 1999.

Michael Katz. *The Undeserving Poor: From the War on Poverty to the War on Welfare.* New York: Pantheon Books, 1989.

Bart Landry. *The New Black Middle Class.* Berkeley, CA: University of California Press, 1987.

William Julius Wilson. *The Truly Disadvantaged: The Inner City, the Underclass, and Public Policy.* Chicago: University of Chicago Press, 1987.

Black Arts and Black Consciousness Movements

William L. Andrews, Frances Smith Foster, and Trudier Harris, eds. *The Oxford Companion to African American Literature.* New York: Oxford University Press, 1997.

James Baldwin. *Notes of a Native Son.* New York: Dial Press, 1955.

_____. *Nobody Knows My Name.* New York: Dial Press, 1961.

_____. *The Fire Next Time.* New York: Dial Press, 1963.

_____. *No Name in the Street.* New York: Dial Press, 1972.

Imamu Amiri Baraka. *Dutchman and the Slave, Two Plays by LeRoi Jones.* New York: William Morrow, 1964.

Samuel A. Hay. *African American Theater: An Historical and Critical Analysis.* Cambridge, MA: Cambridge University Press, 1994.

LeRoi Jones. *Blues People: Negro Music in White America.* New York: William Morrow, 1963.

LeRoi Jones and Larry Neal, eds. *Black Fire: An Anthology of Afro-American Writing.* New York: William Morrow, 1968.

Frank Kofsky. *Black Nationalism and the Revolution in Music.* New York: Pathfinder Press, 1970.

Larry Neal. *Visions of a Liberated Future: Black Arts Movement Writings.* New York: Thunder's Mouth Press, 1989.

Leslie Catherine Sanders. *The Development of Black Theater in America: From Shadow to Selves.* Baton Rouge, LA: Louisiana State University Press, 1988.

Suzanne E. Smith. *Dancing in the Streets: Motown and the Cultural Politics of Detroit.* Cambridge, MA: Harvard University Press, 2000.

Autobiography and Biography

Imamu Amiri Baraka. *The Autobiography of LeRoi Jones.* New York: Freundlich Books, 1984.

Dennis C. Dickerson. *Militant Mediator: Whitney M. Young, Jr.* Lexington, KY: University Press of Kentucky, 1998.

James Farmer. *Lay Bare the Heart: An Autobiography of the Civil Rights Movement.* New York: Arbor House, 1985.

Jimmie Lewis Franklin. *Back to Birmingham: Richard Arrington, Jr., and His Times.* Tuscaloosa, AL: University of Alabama Press, 1989.

Elliott J. Gorn, ed. *Muhammad Ali: The People's Champ.* Urbana, IL: University of Illinois Press, 1995.

Charles V. Hamilton. *Adam Clayton Powell, Jr.: The Political Biography of an American Dilemma.* New York: Atheneum, 1991.

Hil Haygood. *King of the Cats: The Life and Times of Adam Clayton Powell, Jr.* Boston: Houghton Mifflin Co., 1993.

David Remnick. *King of the World: Muhammad Ali and the Rise of an American Hero.* New York: Random House, 1998.

Mary Beth Rogers. *Barbara Jordan: American Hero.* New York: Bantam Books, 1998.

Kathleen Rout. *Eldridge Cleaver.* Boston, MA: Twayne Publishers, 1991.

Bobby Seale. *Seize the Time.* New York: Random House, 1970.

Nancy J. Weiss. *Whitney M. Young, Jr., and the Struggle for Civil Rights.* Princeton, NJ: Princeton University Press, 1989.

Chapter 23   Modern Black America, 1980 to Present

Black Culture Studies

Brian Cross. *It's Not about a Salary . . . Rap, Race and Resistance in Los Angeles.* London: Verso, 1993.

Michael Eric Dyson. *Between God and Gangsta Rap: Bearing Witness to Black Culture.* New York: Oxford University Press, 1996.

Patricia Liggins Hill, general ed. *Call and Response: The Riverside Anthology of the African American Literary Tradition.* New York: Houghton Mifflin, 1999.

bell hooks. *Outlaw Culture: Resisting Representations.* New York: Routledge, 1994.

Robin D. G. Kelley. *Race Rebels: Culture, Politics, and the Black Working Class.* New York: Free Press, 1994.

Terry McMillan. *Five for Five: The Films of Spike Lee.* New York: Stewart, Tabori & Chang, 1991.

Joan Morgan. *When Chickenheads Come Home to Roost: My Life as a Hip-Hop Feminist.* New York: Simon & Schuster, 1999.

Tricia Rose. *Black Noise: Rap Music and Black Culture in Contemporary America.* Hanover, NH: Wesleyan University Press, 1994.

Greg Tate. *Flyboy in the Buttermilk.* New York: Fire-side, 1992.

Deborah Willis, *Reflections in Black: A History of Black Photographers, 1840 to the Present.* New York: W.W. Norton, 2000.

Black Politics and Economics

Andrew Billingsley. *Climbing Jacob's Ladder: The Enduring Legacy of African-American Families.* New York: Simon & Schuster, 1993.

Barry Bluestone and Bennett Harrison. *The Deindustrialization of America: Plant Closings, Community Abandonment, and the Dismantling of Basic Industry.* New York: Basic Books, 1982.

Martin Carnoy. *Faded Dreams: The Politics and Economics of Race in America.* Cambridge, U.K.: Cambridge University Press, 1994.

Robert Dallek. *Ronald Reagan: The Politics of Symbolism.* Cambridge, MA: Harvard University Press, 1984.

W. Avon Drake and Robert D. Holsworth. *Affirmative Action and the Stalled Quest for Black Progress.* Urbana, IL: University of Illinois Press, 1996.

Robert Gooding-Williams, ed. *Reading Rodney King: Reading Urban Uprising.* New York: Routledge, 1993.

Lani Guinier. *Tyranny of the Majority: Fundamental Fairness and Representative Democracy.* New York: Free Press, 1995.

Andrew Hacker. *Two Nations: Black and White, Separate, Hostile, Unequal.* New York: Ballantine Books, rev., 1995.

Charles P. Henry. *Jesse Jackson: The Search for Common Ground.* Oakland, CA: Black Scholar Press, 1991.

Anita Faye Hill and Emma Coleman Jordan, eds. *Race, Gender, and Power in America: The Legacy of the Hill–Thomas Hearings.* New York: Oxford University Press, 1995.

Douglas S. Massey and Nancy A. Denton. *American Apartheid: Segregation and the Making of the Underclass.* Cambridge, MA: Harvard University Press, 1993.

Adolph Reed, Jr. *The Jesse Jackson Phenomenon: The Crisis in Afro-American Politics.* New Haven, CT: Yale University Press, 1986.

Andrea Y. Simpson. *The Tie That Binds: Identity and Political Attitudes in the Post–Civil Rights Generation.* New York: New York University Press, 1998.

William Julius Wilson. *The Bridge over the Racial Divide: Rising Inequality and Coalition Politics.* Berkeley, CA: University of California Press, 1999.

Identity Studies

Molefi Kete Asante. *The Afrocentric Idea.* Philadelphia: Temple University Press, 1987.

Martin Bernal. *Black Athena: The Afroasiatic Roots of Classical Civilization: The Fabrication of Ancient Greece, 1785–1985.* New Brunswick, NJ: Rutgers University Press, 1987.

F. James Davis. *Who Is Black? One Nation's Definition.* University Park, PA: Pennsylvania State University Press, 1991.

Tsehloane Keto. *Vision, Identity and Time: The Afrocentric Paradigm and the Study of the Past.* Dubuque, IA: Kendall/Hunt Publishing Co., 1995.

Wilson Jeremiah Moses. *Afrotopia: The Roots of African American Popular History.* Cambridge, MA: Cambridge University Press, 1998.

Arthur M. Schlesinger, Jr. *The Disuniting of America.* New York: W. W. Norton, 1992.

Clarence Walker. *You Can't Go Home Again.* New York: Oxford University Press, 2001.

Cornel West. *Race Matters.* Boston: Beacon Press, 1993.

Liberation Studies

Derrick Bell. *Faces at the Bottom of the Well: The Permanence of Racism.* New York: Basic Books, 1992.

Michael C. Dawson. *Behind the Mule: Race and Class in African-American Politics.* Princeton, NJ: Princeton University Press, 1994.

W. Marvin Dulaney. *Black Police in America.* Bloomington, IN: Indiana University Press, 1996.

Henry Hampton and Steve Fayer. *Voices of Freedom: An Oral History of the Civil Rights Movement from the 1950s through the 1980s.* New York: Bantam Books, 1990.

Randall Robinson. *The Debt: What America Owes to Blacks.* New York: Plume, 2000.

Race, Gender, and Class

Michael Awkward. *Negotiating Difference: Race, Gender, and the Politics of Positionality.* Chicago: University of Chicago Press, 1995.

Paul M. Barrett. *The Good Black: A True Story of Race in America.* New York: Dutton, 1999.

Lois Benjamin. *The Black Elite: Facing the Color Line in the Twilight of the Twentieth Century.* Chicago: Nelson-Hall Publishers, 1991.

Ellis Cose. *The Rage of the Privileged Class.* New York: HarperCollins, 1993.

Douglas G. Glasgow. *The Black Underclass: Poverty, Unemployment, and Entrapment of Ghetto Youth.* New York: Random House, 1981.

Lawrence Otis Graham. *Our Kind of People: Inside America's Black Urban Class.* New York: HarperCollins, 1999.

Stanlie M. James and Abena P. A. Busia, eds. *Theorizing Black Feminisms: The Visionary Pragmatism of Black Women.* New York: Routledge, 1993.

Christopher Jencks. *Rethinking Social Policy: Race, Poverty, and the Underclass.* Cambridge, MA: Harvard University Press, 1992.

Jonathan Kozel. *Savage Inequalities: Children in America's Schools.* New York: Crown, 1991.

Haki R. Madhubuti. *Black Men—Obsolete, Single, Dangerous? Afrikan American Families in Transition: Essays in Discovery, Solution, and Hope.* Chicago: Third World Press, 1990.

Leith Mullings. *On Our Own Terms: Race, Class, and Gender in the Lives of African American Women.* New York: Routledge, 1997.

Jill Nelson. *Voluntary Slavery: My Authentic Negro Experience.* Chicago: Noble Press, 1993.

Black Conservatives

Thomas Sowell. *Preferential Policies: An International Perspective.* New York: William Morrow, 1990.

Shelby Steele. *A Dream Deferred: The Second Betrayal of Black Freedom in America.* New York: HarperCollins, 1998.

Shelby Steele/CCC. *The Content of Our Character: A New Vision of Race in America.* New York: St. Martin's Press, 1990.

Autobiography and Biography

Amy Alexander, ed. *The Farrakhan Factor: African-American Writers on Leadership, Nationhood and Minister Louis Farrakhan.* New York: Grove Press, 1998.

Marshall Frady. *Jesse: The Life and Pilgrimage of Jesse Jackson.* New York: Random House, 1996.

Randall Robinson. *Defending the Spirit: A Black Life in America.* New York: NAL/Dutton, 1998.

➤ INDEX ➤

W9-BMQ-483

Hello Raspberry Pi!

Python programming for kids and other beginners

Ryan Heitz

NPL F
Nashville Public Library | FOUNDATION

In honor of
Phyllis Baker Vandewater
and
Emily Robinson Vandewater

M
ANNING
HELTER ISLAND

NPLF.ORG

For online information and ordering of this and other Manning books, please visit
www.manning.com. The publisher offers discounts on this book when ordered in
quantity. For more information, please contact:

Special Sales Department
Manning Publications Co.
20 Baldwin Road
PO Box 761
Shelter Island, NY 11964
Email: orders@manning.com

Manning Publications Co.
20 Baldwin Road
PO Box 761
Shelter Island, NY 11964

Development editor: Dan Maharry
Copyeditor: Tiffany Taylor
Proofreader: Alyson Brener
Technical proofreader: Romin Irani
Typesetter: Marija Tudor
Cover designer: Leslie Haimes

ISBN: 9781617292453

Printed in the United States of America
1 2 3 4 5 6 7 8 9 10 – MAL – 18 17 16

To Juliana, Daniel, and John

Brief contents

Contents

Preface

In 2013, a parent and friend of mine asked if I would teach a Python course to middle school students at a local school. My friend gently asked if I could somehow use the Raspberry Pi computer in the course. I love learning new things and I had been reading a lot about the Raspberry Pi. So as you can imagine, I was tremendously excited at the opportunity of using it and emphatically said "Yes!" That event began my journey of developing a course for kids on programming in Python and using the Raspberry Pi and later, this book.

Quickly, as I worked with the Raspberry Pi, I became a disciple of the Raspberry Pi inventors: the best way for kids to learn programming is by giving them an affordable, ready-to-program computer. It was the perfect platform to learn how to program.

As a teacher of computer science, I grew to deeply appreciate Python. I became convinced that it was not only a great programming language, but its focus on readability and simplicity made it perfect for kids to learn as their first programming language.

Fast forward in time—after teaching Python using the Raspberry Pi to many classes of kids, I had developed a set of engaging and funny projects that the kids enjoyed. Just as important, the students learned! The feedback from the kids and the parents was fantastic! Imagine kids rushing to take part in a programming class. It was wonderful!

A few months after developing my course, Nicole Butterfield and Robin de Jongh of Manning Publications contacted me about turning it into a book. I was thrilled at the prospect of bringing the activities and projects from the computer lab into the hands of kids everywhere. What is more, this book would fill an important gap. What I had found when I originally started teaching my course was that there were no books on the Raspberry Pi and programming in Python that were designed for kids. Since the main reason for inventing the Raspberry Pi was to get more kids programming, I was enthusiastic to work on this project.

Nearly two years later, and several versions of the Raspberry Pi later, I'm proud to present this book to the kids and other beginners who want to learn to program. I hope you enjoy using this book and it starts you on your own journey in computer science!

Acknowledgments

Thank you to my wife, Juliana, and our two children, Daniel and John, for their endless support and patience through the long days, nights, and weekends I needed to write this book.

I'd also like to thank Manning Publications for having the vision to pursue this project. In particular, thanks to Robin de Jongh and Nicole Butterfield who kicked off this project by finding and encouraging me; to publisher Marjan Bace for his commitment to me and to this book; to Ozren Harlovic for orchestrating the book review process; to Kevin Sullivan and Mary Piergies for overseeing production; to Chuck Larson for the wonderful work on the graphics; to Tiffany Taylor for her outstanding copyediting; to Alyson Brener for her thorough proofreading; to Candace Gillhoolley and Ana Romac for promoting the book; to technical development editors Donald Bailey, Joel Kotarski, Jeanne Boyarsky, and John Hyaduck; and to Romin Irani, technical proofreader.

This book was significantly improved by my editor at Manning, Dan Maharry, who helped to develop and edit the book from concept to finished product. I'd like to thank Dan for his excellent insights, support, encouragement, and guidance throughout the process.

A big thank you to all the technical reviewers who read the manuscript at various stages of its development and contributed invaluable feedback: Adam Hinden, Antonio Mas Rodriguez, Betsy Hoofnagle, Catherine Freytag, Dr. Christian Mennerich, Dan Kacenjar, David Kerns, Ema Battista, Fanick Atchia, Grace Kacenjar, Henry Freytag, Jaqueline Currie, John Pentakalos, Keenan Hom, Kevin Adjaho Atchia, Matthew

xv

Giblin, Nathan Sperry, Odysseas Pentakalos, Sam Kerns, Richard Freytag, Savannah Wilson, and Scott M. King.

Thank you also to all the readers who bought and read the MEAP (Manning Early Access Program) versions of the chapters and who took the time to post comments in the Author Online forum. You helped make this a better book!

The Raspberry Pi Foundation, original inventors, and community deserve a special mention. Thank you for designing something that is helping children to learn computer science. I'd also like to thank Guido van Rossum, the inventor of Python; the Python Software Foundation; and the Python user community, for creating and maintaining a simple and useful programming language for everyone.

About this book

The Raspberry Pi is a small, low-cost computer invented in the U.K. by the Raspberry Pi Foundation. It provides an easy-to-use tool for learning to program in Python. The Raspberry Pi, with its companion memory card, is preloaded with all the software you need to jump into programming in Python. The Raspberry Pi is made for you to learn to code by playing with it. It includes many input and output ports to give you flexibility in how you connect it. Much like a desktop computer, you need to connect a keyboard, mouse, monitor, and power cable to get started.

This book will teach you how to set up your Raspberry Pi, to write programs in Python, and to use your Raspberry Pi and Python to complete some projects. We'll cover the basics of Python: displaying text, gathering input, repeating commands, creating logic, as well as using the input and output pins of your Raspberry Pi for projects.

This book does not cover advanced Python topics, nor act as a comprehensive reference for Python. Since it is a book for beginners, these topics have been left out for clarity and brevity. If you'd like to learn more Python, there are links to online resources throughout the book.

This book is for kids and other beginners who would like to learn to program. It's also for kids who have a Raspberry Pi and want to learn what they can do with it. We'll introduce you to your Raspberry Pi and teach you Python in a natural, playful way, introducing topics and giving you activities to do using your Raspberry Pi. You don't need to have any prior programming experience. As long as you know how to use a mouse and open up programs by clicking on icons or menu items, you'll do great.

This book requires a Raspberry Pi, cables, and some other parts to complete the projects and activities. These items are needed throughout the book:

- Raspberry Pi 2 Model B
- 8 GB SD memory card, preloaded with the Raspberry Pi Foundation's NOOBS (New Out of the Box Software)
- USB power supply with micro USB cable (must deliver 1.2 A @ 5 V)
- USB keyboard
- USB mouse
- TV or monitor
- Cable to connect to TV or monitor (specific cables for your TV or
- monitor are discussed in chapter 1)

To complete the projects in part 3, you'll also need these parts:

- Solderless breadboard
- GPIO ribbon cable for the Raspberry Pi 2 Model B (40 pin)
- GPIO breakout board
- 1 dozen jumper wires, male-to-male
- 1 red LED (light-emitting diode)
- 1 green LED
- 1 blue LED
- 1 red, green, blue (RGB) LED
- 3 push buttons
- 3 resistors, 10K ohm
- 3 resistors, 180 ohm (or between 100 and 300 ohms)
- Headphones or powered computer speakers

You can typically find all these items in a Raspberry Pi starter kit or available individually through online retailers and stores that sell the Raspberry Pi, such as CanaKit, Sparkfun, or Adafruit.

Roadmap

This book is divided into three parts.

Part 1 introduces you to the Rasperry Pi, shows you how to set it up, and provides an introduction to the Python programming language:

- Chapter 1 provides an overview of the Raspberry Pi and how to set it up for the first time.
- Chapter 2 shows you how to write your first Python programs and introduces you to doing math and displaying text with Python.

Part 2 shows you how to build different text-based games while learning how to gather input, display information, make decisions, and repeat instructions in Python:

- Chapter 3 teaches you how to create your first interactive Python game, the Silly Sentence Generator 3000, by asking users to type in something and then displaying funny messages to the screen.
- Chapter 4 explores how to give your programs logic and use repeating loops as you create a Norwegian Blue Guessing Game.
- Chapter 5 demonstrates how to build a Cave Adventure Game, give users multiple choices, check input from users, and create your own Python functions.

Part 3 involves making your Raspberry Pi interact with the world around it:

- Chapter 6 explains setting up your Pi with an electronics breadboard, building a simple circuit, and controlling an LED (light) using your Raspberry Pi and Python.
- Chapter 7 dives into creating an interactive guessing game that uses lights to respond to a player's input, letting them know with different colors whether their answer is right or wrong.
- Chapter 8 teaches you how to listen to your Pi's input pins by making a project that combines light and sound to make your own DJ Raspi sound mixer.

Code conventions and downloads

All source code in this book is in a `fixed-width font like this`, which sets it apart from the surrounding text. In many listings, the code is annotated to point out key concepts. I have tried to format the code so that it fits within the available page space in the book by adding line breaks and using indentation carefully.

The code accompanying this book is hosted at the GitHub repository: https://github.com/rheitz/hello-raspberry-pi. It is also available for download as a zip file from the publisher's website at www.manning .com/books/hello-raspberry-pi.

Author Online

Purchase of *Hello Raspberry Pi!* includes free access to a private web forum run by Manning Publications where you can make comments about the book, ask technical questions, and receive help from the author and other users. To access the forum and subscribe to it, point your web browser to www.manning.com/books/hello-raspberry-pi. This Author Online (AO) page provides information on how to get on the forum once you're registered, what kind of help is available, and the rules of conduct on the forum.

Manning's commitment to our readers is to provide a venue where a meaningful dialog among individual readers and between readers and the author can take place. It's not a commitment to any specific amount of participation on the part of the author, whose contribution to the AO remains voluntary (and unpaid). We suggest you try asking the author some challenging questions, lest his interest stray!

The AO forum and the archives of previous discussions will be accessible from the publisher's website as long as the book is in print.

About the author

Ryan Heitz is a teacher, programmer, maker, father, and big kid. He is the cofounder of Ideaventions, a Science Center for kids, and Ideaventions Academy for Mathematics and Science, a private school focused on science and technology. He specializes in teaching kids how to experience computer science in a fun and engaging way. As a programmer, Ryan has developed software for everything from NASA data collection systems to web mapping applications.

Getting started

Get ready to explore Python using your Raspberry Pi! You'll need a Raspberry Pi and a few other parts and cables for part 1. Here's your shopping list:

- Raspberry Pi 2 Model B
- 8 GB SD memory card, preloaded with the Raspberry Pi Foundation's NOOBS (New Out Of the Box Software)
- USB power supply with micro USB cable (must deliver 1.2 A @ 5 V)
- USB keyboard
- USB mouse
- TV or monitor
- Cable to connect to TV or monitor (specific cables for your TV or monitor are discussed in chapter 1)

Optional item:

- Raspberry Pi case

Part 1 will get you on your way to using your Raspberry Pi and launch you into programming it with Python. In chapter 1, you'll set up your Raspberry Pi, learn how to start (or boot) it up, and then look around inside the Pi's desktop. Chapter 2 is where you'll start exploring the Python language. You'll create your first programs and learn to give instructions to your Raspberry Pi using Python.

By the end of part 1, you'll know how to get a Raspberry Pi up and running. You'll be able to write a Python program and interact with your Pi to make it do things like figure out the cost of a cheeseburger meal and display silly messages on the screen.

Meet Raspberry Pi

In this chapter, you'll learn how to

- *Set up your Raspberry Pi*
- *Install an operating system—Raspbian—on your Pi*
- *Find and open applications*
- *Write your first bit of code in Python*

What kinds of things do you think you can do with a Raspberry Pi?

1 Play games.

2 Watch videos.

3 Create a video game.

4 Listen to music.

5 Make a sound mixer for a dance party.

6 Build a robot.

Believe it or not, these are all projects you can do yourself, and if you learn to program in Python, the sky is the limit. You can achieve quite a lot on your Pi, as long as you can write a program to do it. But before we talk about that, let's take a look at a Raspberry Pi and discover what makes it tick.

What is the Raspberry Pi?

The *Raspberry Pi*, sometimes referred to as the *Pi*, is a small, low-cost computer invented in the U.K. by the Raspberry Pi Foundation. It provides an easy-to-use tool to help you learn to code in Python (the *Pi* part of its name came from the focus on using it to code in Python).

About the size of a deck of cards, it isn't as powerful as a laptop or desktop computer; its computing power is more similar to that of a smart phone. But what it lacks in processing power, it makes up for in its many features:

- Its readiness for programming in Python
- The many ways you can use it
- Its small size and cost

The Pi, with its companion memory card, is preloaded with all the software you need to jump into programming in Python. Type in commands, and see what happens. Enter a program you find on the internet or in a magazine, run it, and see how it works. The Pi is made for you to learn to code by playing with it, using it, and interacting with it.

Once you learn to program in Python, you can use your Pi as a base for all sorts of projects—with your imagination, the possibilities are endless! The Pi's small size makes it easy to carry around and include in projects. Hide it on a shelf or mount it on a wall with a camera to make a security system; power it with a rechargeable battery pack if you need it to be portable; or even attach it to a remote-controlled car or helicopter. And if you happen to mess something up, it's simple to recover. Even if you manage to break the Pi, it's pretty cheap to replace.

At its core, the Raspberry Pi is a circuit board that has all the components found in many computers. The next section checks out the components of the Pi and explores what they do. Let's go!

Exploring your Raspberry Pi's parts: hardware

Ever look closely at an insect under a magnifying glass, or take apart a toy? Humans are naturally curious about what makes things work. What are the different parts, and what do they do? What parts are unique? Let's treat the Raspberry Pi the same way, explore its parts, and learn how to set it up.

Luckily, you don't have to break it open to see its parts. You can see the Raspberry Pi's components displayed before you on the green circuit board in your hand (see figure 1.1). Let's walk through the parts of the Raspberry Pi and see what they do. We'll be focusing on the Raspberry Pi 2 Model B; if you have a Raspberry Pi 1 Model B+ or B, see appendix B for more information.

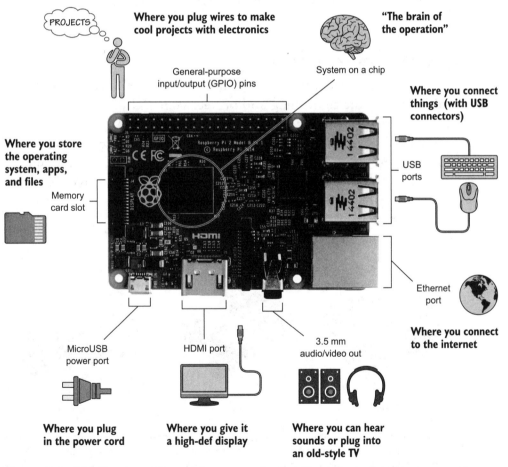

Figure 1.1 The Raspberry Pi provides an excellent platform for learning to program in Python. It includes many input and output ports to give you flexibility in how you connect it. As you would with a desktop computer, you need to connect a keyboard, mouse, monitor, and power cable before you can start using your Pi.

Defining some tech terms

Input and *output* are terms used for communication to and from a computer.

USB refers to a common connector found on computers. It's used to plug in a keyboard, a mouse, flash drives, and many other computer peripherals.

HDMI is a standard way to connect devices to high-definition TVs or monitors. We'll talk about this more later, when we discuss connecting a TV or monitor to your Raspberry Pi.

Ethernet is a technology used to connect computers together into a network. This port provides a way to plug in and connect to the internet or your home network if a wireless connection isn't available.

Giving your Pi a cozy home: Pi cases

We all like to be warm and cozy in our homes. A Raspberry Pi is no different. Do the right thing and protect your Pi by putting it in a case (see figure 1.2). If your Pi didn't come with a case, you have a lot of options. You can buy one or make your own. My favorite approach is to make my own case from wood, cardboard, a plastic container, or even LEGOs. The key is making sure your Pi is protected from accidental drops and, ideally, spills. But before you close up your Pi in a case, let's take a closer look at some of its features.

Paper   Plastic   Aluminum

Figure 1.2 A case protects your Raspberry Pi from damage while making it easy to access the ports. Some people use a case to give their Pi a unique personality. You can purchase a case or, better yet, make your own. Plastic cases are the most common, but these pictures show examples of cases made from paper, plastic, and aluminum. You could even try using LEGOs to make one.

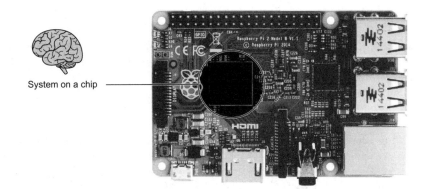

System on a chip

Figure 1.3 The Raspberry Pi's system on a chip (SoC) contains its computing and graphics processing power and working memory. The Pi uses the ARM11 microprocessor as its CPU and the VideoCore IV for its GPU. The ARM11 microprocessor is found in handheld electronics such as smart phones and gaming systems. The SoC in the Raspberry Pi 2 Model B comes with 1 GB of RAM.

The brain of your Pi: system on a chip

Meet the brain of your Raspberry Pi. The *system on a chip (SoC)* is the black square in the middle of the Pi circuit board in figure 1.3. This incredible chip is a package of many parts: the central processing unit (CPU), the graphics processing unit (GPU), the digital signal processor, and the Pi's working memory. The chip provides the computing power, graphics power, and memory to run apps and play videos.

The Pi's CPU handles running applications and executing instructions. The same processor is also found in smart phones and e-readers. Think of it as the part of your brain that allows you to follow instructions and calculate the answer to math problems.

The GPU is like the visual part of your brain that allows you to visualize a 3D object in your mind or track a ball thrown to you. It handles the Pi's multimedia tasks, like processing digital images, drawing graphics, and playing videos. The GPU gives your Pi surprisingly good high-definition video-playback capabilities. Both the central processor and the graphics processor share the Pi's working memory, or RAM, which is part of the SoC.

Working memory: RAM

Question: Can you remember the following grocery store list? *Bananas, milk, peanut butter, jam, bread.* Read the list once more, and then look away from the book and try to recite the list from memory.

To remember it, you need to hold the names of the items in your memory. You only have to store them for a short time. Once you go to the store and buy the items, you can forget them.

When a computer is working, it does much the same thing. It may have to re-member and process millions of instructions and bits of information each sec-ond, but it can often forget them once it's done processing them. The computer does this using working memory or *random access memory (RAM)*. It's packed in the SoC, and it gives your Raspberry Pi the ability to process instructions quickly by remembering pieces of information as it's working and forgetting them when they're no longer needed—much like how the neurons in your brain work together to remember a grocery list. Later, we'll talk about storing infor-mation for the long term and where that happens.

Connecting a keyboard and mouse: USB ports

Meet the *USB* ports on your Raspberry Pi. The two metal, rectangular boxes each contain two USB ports, shown in figure 1.4. USB stands for *Universal Serial Bus.*[1] The Pi provides USB ports to allow you to con-nect a keyboard, a mouse, flash drives, and other USB peripherals.

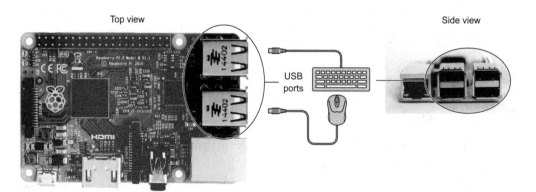

Figure 1.4   The Raspberry Pi 2 Model B has four USB ports. They're on the board in two sets of two, side by side. The USB ports are useful for connecting a keyboard and mouse to your Pi. A USB hub can also be plugged in to allow for even more peripherals.

---

[1] The *U* for *Universal* is because it provides computer makers and computer equipment makers with a stan-dard way to connect things to computers. Things connected to a computer are often called *peripherals*.

Why are they called ports?

Back in ancient times, when Romans walked around and spoke Latin to each other, the word for a gate or door was *porta*. Although computers don't have doors or gates, they have places where you plug things in, called *ports*.

Ports allow electrical signals to go in and out of your computer. Without ports, you wouldn't be able to view your computer's screen, download web pages, or move a mouse.

Let's pretend you could shrink and that you had special glasses so you could see these electrical signals. What would you see when I pressed the E key on the keyboard? You'd see an electrical signal flying from the keyboard through the keyboard's wire, through the port on the computer, and into the computer. The port acts like a gate, allowing signals to go into or out of your computer.

Get your keyboard and mouse. Let's plug them into your Pi.

CONNECTING A KEYBOARD

You'll need a keyboard that plugs into a USB port. Figure 1.5 shows an example of a keyboard with a USB connector.[2]

To attach your keyboard to your Pi, plug the wire from your keyboard into your Raspberry Pi's USB port. There are four USB ports on your Pi. It doesn't matter which one you choose.

Figure 1.5 You need a USB keyboard to type and enter commands on your Raspberry Pi. The keyboard plugs into one of the four available USB ports on the Raspberry Pi 2 Model B.

---

[2] If you don't have a keyboard with a USB connector, have no fear. You can find one for under $15 online or at your local computer or electronics store.

> **TIP**   If the keyboard's USB connector doesn't fit into the Raspberry Pi's USB connector, flip over the connector and try again. USB connectors only fit in one way.

Fantastic! Your keyboard is connected to your Pi. It's time to move on to adding a mouse.

CONNECTING A MOUSE

For this step, you need a mouse that plugs into a USB port. The keyboard is using one of your Raspberry Pi's four USB ports. Plug your mouse into one of the other ports.

ANOTHER OPTION: WIRELESS KEYBOARD AND MOUSE COMBINATION

If you own a wireless keyboard and mouse combination, instead of using wires, you can plug the USB dongle into one of the USB ports on the Pi. This frees up one of your USB ports, which can be handy should you decide to attach multiple USB devices such as a USB Wi-Fi adapter or USB flash drives, or if you want fewer wires on your desk.

Excellent! Giving your Pi the ability to store and retrieve information is your next task.

Storing memories: your Pi gets a memory card

We all like to remember things that are important to us. Birthdays, vacations, and holidays are wonderful times, and we've invented ways to help us recall them. You might use a scrapbook or a photo album to store memories. Even after many years, you can open these books and remember these past events.

In addition to working memory (RAM), computers also need a way to remember things, even if they're turned off for long periods of time. The Raspberry Pi, like all computers, has this capability for memory storage, letting it save and retrieve data, files, and applications. Much like a photo album lets you recall holidays, the Pi's memory storage allows you to store important applications and information. You'll use this capability when you learn how to save sets of Python instructions or programs.

SD MEMORY CARD

A Raspberry Pi is different from most computers because its memory storage is contained on an SD memory card, whereas most laptops and desktops use a hard drive. Files, applications, and even the Pi's operating system are all stored on the SD memory card, whether it's a Python game you're creating or a new music player app for your Pi. If you purchase a Raspberry Pi kit, it will come with an SD card (see figure 1.6).[3]

Top view of Raspberry Pi

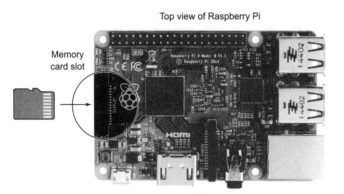

Top view of Raspberry Pi
with SD memory card inserted

Bottom view of Raspberry Pi

Figure 1.6 An SD memory card provides the storage memory used by the Raspberry Pi to hold all the software and files, including the operating system. Raspberry Pi kits come with an SD memory card preloaded with the software needed to start up your Pi. The two left images show the location of the SD memory card slot on the underside of the Pi board. The right image shows an SD memory card inserted into the SD card slot.

---

[3] See http://elinux.org/RPi_SD_cards for more information on compatible cards.

SD cards come in various sizes

SD cards come in three sizes: the full-size SD card (largest), the miniSD, and the microSD (smallest). The Raspberry Pi 2 Model B uses a microSD card.

You can add more storage to your Pi by attaching USB peripherals such as a USB flash drive or a USB hard drive.

NOOBS

Your Raspberry Pi kit comes with an SD card preloaded with NOOBS. Developed by the Raspberry Pi Foundation, *New Out of the Box Software (NOOBS)* is a set of files that helps you set up your Pi for the first time. If you lose yours or need a NOOBS SD memory card, you can buy new ones online. Alternatively, if you have an SD card and want to install NOOBS on it, go to the Raspberry Pi Foundation website (www.raspberrypi.org/downloads) to learn how.

SD MEMORY CARD SLOT

Figure 1.6 shows the location of the SD memory card slot. This thin, metal slot is on the underside of the Raspberry Pi. For your Pi to work when you plug it in, it must have some initial knowledge to start up and display something on the screen. In addition to this startup information, it must also have a place to store any new information.

INSERTING THE SD CARD IN THE SLOT

Hold the card so that the end with the metal contacts is facing up and toward the Pi. Insert the card along the underside of the board into the slot. You'll hear a small click as the card is pushed into the slot. The card is held in place by a small spring mechanism. The card will only fit in one way, so if it doesn't fit, flip it over. If you need to remove the card, push it in again (you'll hear a click); then you can pull it out.

REPLACING A LOST OR BROKEN SD CARD

If you lose your SD card, you lose the information, applications, and operating system that are stored on the card. It's as if you lost your hard drive on a home computer. You can easily replace the card, but you'll be starting over fresh. Here are the two options for replacing the card:

- Purchase an SD card at the store, and set it up anew. It's recommended that you get an SD memory card with at least 8 GB of storage space. You can download and install the startup software from the Raspberry Pi Foundation at www.raspberrypi.org/downloads. See appendix A for instructions on how to make a new SD card for your Raspberry Pi.

- Buy an SD memory card preinstalled with the Raspberry Pi startup software. You can find cards for sale on the Raspberry Pi Foundation website and at online retailers.

SD CARDS MAKE YOUR PI'S MEMORY PORTABLE

If your Raspberry Pi ever breaks, you can remove the SD memory card and insert it into a new Pi. All your files and software will be there. It's like taking your photo album with you to a new house. The memories are safe in the photo album, ready for you to enjoy.

> TIP   You can set up multiple SD cards for your Raspberry Pi and switch them whenever you want to give your Pi a whole different personality. Maybe set up an SD card for the Pi as a media center, complete with games, music, and videos. Set up another for your Pi robot project. Each memory card can be set up uniquely, with different operating systems, applications, and files. Swap out the SD card and reboot your Pi, and you instantly have a Pi with different traits to meet your needs.

Connecting a TV or monitor: HDMI port

The *HDMI* port, shown in figure 1.7, is for connecting your Raspberry Pi to a TV or monitor. HDMI stands for *high-definition multimedia interface*. The output provides a combined audio and video signal—meaning both sound and picture come out of this port and go to your TV or monitor. If you want a crisp, clear display and you already own a high-definition TV or monitor, then you'll want to connect your Raspberry Pi to it using the HDMI output port. Because the HDMI output contains audio and video signals, if your TV or monitor has built-in

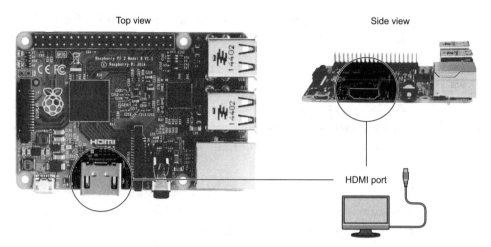

Figure 1.7 The HDMI port on the Raspberry Pi provides a high-definition audio and video signal that can be connected to a TV or monitor. Use an HDMI cable to connect your Pi to your TV or monitor. Depending on the connectors available on the TV or monitor, you may need an adapter.

speakers, the sound from your Raspberry Pi can be set to come out of the speakers rather than through the 3.5 mm audio output.

Now that you know about the HDMI port, let's see how you can connect your Pi to a TV or monitor.

CONNECTING YOUR PI TO A TV OR MONITOR

Once you decide on the TV or monitor you plan to use, you'll need to look for the available video input ports on the TV or monitor (look on the back or sides to find them). What kinds of ports do you see? Unfortunately, manufacturers often provide a variety of different ports. Think of it like a matching game. Your goal is to match the connectors on your TV to the connectors on the Pi. If they don't match, you'll need to use one of the adapters discussed in a minute. Either way, you're sure to get it solved.

IDENTIFYING PORTS AND MAKING THE CONNECTION

Take time to study the connections on your TV or monitor. Try to identify the video ports, comparing them to the pictures of connectors in figure 1.8.

This section provides instructions on how you can connect your Pi to a TV or monitor with either an HDMI or a DVI port. If your TV or monitor has different video input ports, check appendix B for tips on connecting to them.

HDMI

The HDMI port is a metal, mostly rectangular port that is labeled *HDMI*. Connect an HDMI cable from the screen's HDMI port to your Raspberry

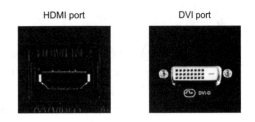

Figure 1.8 HDMI and DVI are common types of video input ports found on modern TVs and monitors. It's easiest to connect a Raspberry Pi to a TV or monitor with an HDMI port. HDMI provides a high-definition picture and doesn't require any adapters or converters—only an HDMI cable, which is included in many Pi kits. The DVI port requires a special adapter to connect with a Pi.

Pi's HDMI port (see figure 1.9). If you've connected your HDMI cable, you can now skip ahead to the discussion of other ports on the Pi.

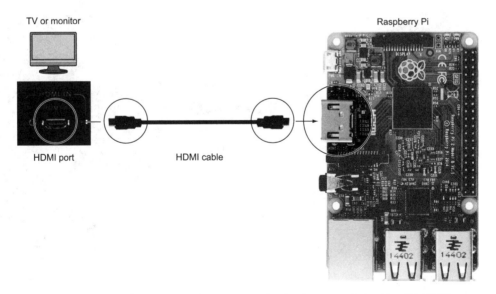

Figure 1.9 A Raspberry Pi can be connected to a TV or monitor using an HDMI cable. Connect the cable from the Pi's HDMI port to the TV's or monitor's HDMI input. In addition to video, the HDMI cable also contains the Pi's audio output, which can be played through the TV's or monitor's speakers.

DVI

DVI ports on TVs and monitors come in several different forms. They're all rectangular ports with three rows of eight square pinholes and a horizontal hole or set of holes next to them. If you already have an HDMI cable, the solution is to purchase an HDMI-to-DVI adapter. You can find these online or in a computer store. Plug the adapter into the computer screen's DVI port, and then plug your HDMI cable into the back of the adapter and the other end into the HDMI port on your Raspberry Pi (see figure 1.10).

Another solution, rather than to use an adapter, is to purchase a DVI-to-HDMI cable. These can be found online or at a computer store. Plug the DVI connector on the cable into your computer screen, and plug the HDMI connector into your Pi's HDMI port.

Great! You've completed an important step by connecting your Pi to a TV or monitor.

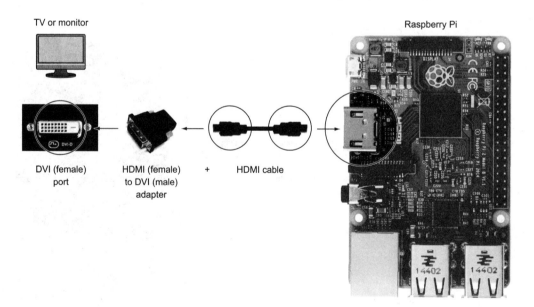

Figure 1.10 The Raspberry Pi can be connected to a TV or monitor with a DVI port using an HDMI-to-DVI adapter and an HDMI cable. One end of the HDMI cable plugs into the Pi's HDMI port. The other is connected to the adapter, and the adapter is connected to the TV or monitor. Adapters are available through online retailers or local computer stores.

Other ports and connections

You'll find other ports on your Raspberry Pi. We'll cover those in later chapters, or you can reference appendix B for more information on specific ports and connections. Some of these include the following:

- *GPIO pins*—The two long rows of pins on the Raspberry Pi are used to send and receive electrical signals. Part 3 of this book will cover how to program those pins and build projects.

- *Internet*—You can connect your Raspberry Pi to the internet or your home network by plugging in an Ethernet cable. But you may find that the easiest way to get online is to use the USB Wi-Fi adapter that is provided in many Raspberry Pi kits. Appendix B has information on the Ethernet port and using USB Wi-Fi adapters.

- *3.5 mm audio/video out*—The small round connector is for plugging in headphones or powered speakers. Chapter 8 will show you how to play sounds as you turn your Raspberry Pi into a music player.

Let's see how you can get power to your Pi.

Powering your Pi: microUSB power port

Power for your Raspberry Pi is supplied through the microUSB power port located near a corner of the board (see figure 1.11). This port is where you connect a power supply to your Pi; it's the same as the port found on many mobile phones. Raspberry Pi kits come with a microUSB power supply.

Figure 1.11 The Raspberry Pi requires a microUSB power supply that provides at least 1.2 A of electric current. If you plan to use all the USB ports on your Pi, you may want one that provides 2 A or more of electric current. The recommended voltage is 5 volts (V), but the Pi can operate at voltages ranging from 4.8 to 5.2 V. If you have a power supply you want to use with your Pi, check its output voltage and current, which are listed on the charger in small print. In this example, the charger has an output of 5.1 V and 2.5 A of current, making it a suitable power supply for a Pi. Using the incorrect voltage or insufficient current can damage or destroy your Pi, so check carefully.

NOTE   Only certain mobile phone chargers can be used to power your Raspberry Pi. The charger must produce sufficient electrical current to power it. If you want to go this route, then you should read the fine print on the charger. The charger must produce 1.2 amp (A) or more for the Pi.

It's alive! Plugging in the Pi

Before plugging your Raspberry Pi into the power supply, go through this quick checklist:

1 Are you sure your keyboard, mouse, and monitor are connected to the Pi?

2 Have you turned on your TV or monitor and set it to the correct input source? For example, if you plugged your Raspberry Pi into the TV's HDMI port, make sure the TV is set to HDMI input.

3 Have you inserted your SD card with NOOBS into your Pi?

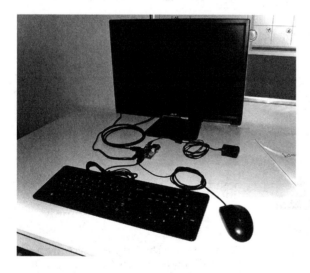

An example setup is shown in figure 1.12.

Figure 1.12 Example setup of a Raspberry Pi with peripherals connected and SD card inserted. A keyboard and mouse are connected to the Pi's two available USB ports. A microUSB power supply is plugged into the Pi; the other end is lying on the desk, ready to be plugged into the wall. An HDMI cable is connected from the Pi's HDMI port to the back of the monitor. The Ethernet port has an Ethernet cable plugged into it from a router (not shown).

TIP   TVs and monitors often allow you to connect multiple video sources. Maybe your TV has a Wii, a DVD player, and a digital video recorder. These TVs and monitors have the option to select which input is displayed to the screen. Use your TV's or monitor's input selector to set the correct input.

All right, if you have all three steps checked off, it's time to power up your Raspberry Pi. Plug your power supply into a wall outlet, and plug the microUSB connector into your Pi. Your Pi's lights will begin to flash. Enjoy the beautiful glow from the lights—this is a sign that your Raspberry Pi is starting up. It's also referred to as *booting*; this is when the computer detects the devices you have connected to it and starts up the computer's operating system (OS). Some believe the term *boot* originated from kicking a horse to get it to start moving. You can imagine that you're giving your Pi a bit of a boot to get it started.

Getting your Pi running: software

You've got your Pi plugged in and ready to rock. It's time to get it running and doing something useful—and for that, you need some software.

An OS is a common set of instructions, or software, that helps manage the computer. Common OSs you've most likely encountered are Microsoft Windows, Apple's OS X, and Linux. All of these OSs control the connection of your keyboard, mouse, monitor, and other peripherals. Most important, the OS serves as a foundation for you to put applications on your computer and use them.

The SD memory card that comes with your Pi kit already contains the files for installing several different OSs on your Pi. We'll step through installing the Raspbian OS—the default for the Pi—and configuring it.

Installing the Raspbian operating system

The first time you boot a Raspberry Pi, you'll need to install an OS on it and then configure it to work nicely for you. Let's walk through the first task: installing an OS. You'll configure it in the next section. Once you plug in your Pi, you'll see the NOOBS menu for selecting an OS, as shown in figure 1.13.

The Raspberry Pi has a variety of OSs that can be installed on it. The Raspberry Pi Foundation recommends the Raspbian OS, and it's what we'll use for this book. Let's go over how to install it on your Pi.

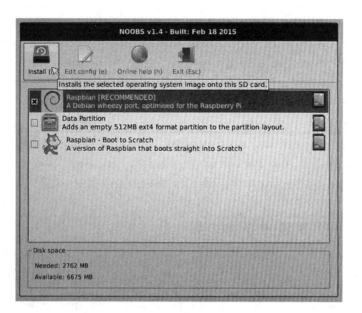

Figure 1.13   The NOOBS selection menu allows you to choose the OS you want to install on your SD card and use with your Raspberry Pi. This menu appears the first time you start up your Pi.

What if you don't see the NOOBS software screen?

If you don't see the NOOBS software screen after your Pi boots up for the first time, then there are a few things to check.

If you don't see lights flashing on your Pi when you plug it in, make sure the electrical outlet you're using has power. Many a Pi owner has accidentally plugged a Pi into a power strip and forgotten to switch on the power strip. Sounds silly, but even the best programmers make mistakes.

If your Pi's lights blink when you plug in the power supply but the screen of your monitor doesn't show anything, make sure the monitor is plugged into an electrical outlet, the HDMI cable is connected from the monitor to the Pi, and you've turned on the monitor.

Finally, if your Pi starts booting up and you see lots of messages displaying on a black screen, but you never see the NOOBS selection menu, it's likely that your SD card has an error. See appendix A for ways to fix an SD card.

Sometimes you'll run into issues with your Pi. If you do, use the troubleshooting steps in appendix A, and search the Raspberry Pi Foundation website[a] to find solutions.

---

[a] The Raspberry Pi Foundation website is www.raspberrypi.org.

On the NOOBS selection menu (see figure 1.13), follow these steps:

1 Select Raspbian (make sure there is an X in the box next to Raspbian; if not, click the box to select it).

2 Click the Install button at the top of the menu.

3 A message appears, warning you that the process will install the OS and that all existing data on your SD card will be overwritten.[4] Select Yes to continue with the installation.

4 Wait for the installation to complete. It will take 5 to 10 minutes, so get a drink or grab a snack while you're waiting.

5 When the installation is done, a box pops up, letting you know the OS was installed successfully. Click OK, and your Raspberry Pi will start loading Raspbian.

6 When it's finished loading Raspbian, your Raspberry Pi reboots itself. A black screen appears, followed by many, many, many messages. Don't worry; the messages are the Pi performing its startup tasks, such as detecting the keyboard, mouse, and TV or monitor.

Kudos to you! You've installed your Raspberry Pi's OS, Raspbian. Now you'll want to configure how it works to suit you.

Configuring the operating system: making it yours

You've finished installing the Raspbian OS on your SD memory card and gotten it running for the first time. The next thing you'll see is the Raspberry Pi configuration screen, shown in figure 1.14.

> TIP   You can't use your mouse with this menu! Use the arrow keys (up, down, left, and right) and Tab key to move around the menu instead. Press Enter to select the highlighted menu item.

Let's walk through some of the basic configuration settings you may want to change.

---

[4] When you're warned that all data will be overwritten, this doesn't include NOOBS, which is retained on the SD card so that you can reinstall the OS if you ever need to.

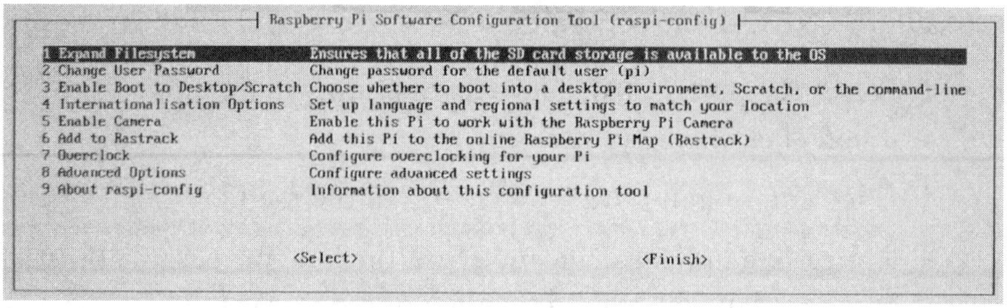

```
┤ Raspberry Pi Software Configuration Tool (raspi-config) ├

1 Expand Filesystem          Ensures that all of the SD card storage is available to the OS
2 Change User Password       Change password for the default user (pi)
3 Enable Boot to Desktop/Scratch  Choose whether to boot into a desktop environment, Scratch, or the command-line
4 Internationalisation Options  Set up language and regional settings to match your location
5 Enable Camera              Enable this Pi to work with the Raspberry Pi Camera
6 Add to Rastrack            Add this Pi to the online Raspberry Pi Map (Rastrack)
7 Overclock                 Configure overclocking for your Pi
8 Advanced Options          Configure advanced settings
9 About raspi-config        Information about this configuration tool



              <Select>                              <Finish>
```

Figure 1.14   When your Pi boots up for the first time, you'll see the Raspberry Pi configuration menu. This menu makes it easier to set up your Pi by allowing you to change settings such as the time zone and keyboard layout. The menu also has the option to set your Pi to always boot to the Raspbian desktop environment.

CHANGING THE KEYBOARD SETTINGS

The Raspberry Pi is made in the U.K., so it's preset to a U.K. keyboard. If you live in other parts of the world, the keyboard may make unexpected characters appear on the screen. For example, you might type a # symbol (Shift-3), and your Pi displays the symbol for a British pound. Weird, right?

You can use the configuration tool to change your Pi's keyboard layout by following these steps:

1 On the Raspberry Pi configuration menu, select option 4—Internationalisation Options—and press Enter.

2 Select Change Keyboard Layout, and press Enter.

3 Select your keyboard model—for example, Dell—and press Enter.

4 You see options for the keyboard layout's country of origin. Select the appropriate country, and press Enter.

5 A list of keyboard layouts appears. Select the one for your location, and press Enter.

6 On the next series of screens, you can set shortcut keys. Set them to match your personal preferences. If you aren't sure, accept the defaults (press Enter until you're back to the configuration menu).

You can always return to the configuration tool if needed. You'll learn how in a later section when you're introduced to the command-line mode for Raspbian.

CHOOSING HOW YOUR RASPBERRY PI STARTS UP

Raspbian, like most OSs, allows you to use it in two different ways (see figure 1.15):

- *Command-line mode*—You type in commands to the OS. This can be tough for novices, because you need to know the commands and type them in exactly. Because this mode is more difficult to use, you'll only use it in this book when you need to run commands that require administrative or super-user permissions. For example, you'll need the command line when you make Python programs that use the GPIO pins or you want to alter your Pi's configuration.

- *Graphical-user-interface (GUI) mode*—Everything appears in windows, icons, and menus that are point and click. Just like on Windows and Mac computers, this will be your main way to interact with your Pi and program in Python. It represents the most natural way to access applications, files, and folders.

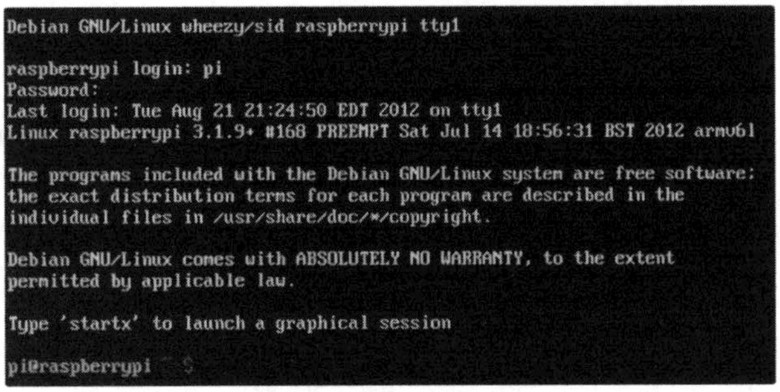

```
Debian GNU/Linux wheezy/sid raspberrypi tty1

raspberrypi login: pi
Password:
Last login: Tue Aug 21 21:24:50 EDT 2012 on tty1
Linux raspberrypi 3.1.9+ #168 PREEMPT Sat Jul 14 18:56:31 BST 2012 armv6l

The programs included with the Debian GNU/Linux system are free software;
the exact distribution terms for each program are described in the
individual files in /usr/share/doc/*/copyright.

Debian GNU/Linux comes with ABSOLUTELY NO WARRANTY, to the extent
permitted by applicable law.

Type 'startx' to launch a graphical session

pi@raspberrypi   $
```

Raspbian command-line mode

Figure 1.15 Example screen images of a command-line mode (top) and a GUI mode (bottom) for a Raspberry Pi running the Raspbian OS. The command-line mode is text-based: you enter instructions at the prompt. The GUI is pretty much the same as a Windows or Mac interface, with windows, icons, and menus that you interact with using a mouse pointer.

Raspbian graphical-user-interface (GUI) mode

Question: Which option do you prefer?

- Your Raspberry Pi booting up to a screen with a blinking cursor, waiting for you to type in commands
- Your Raspberry Pi booting up and showing you a desktop with application icons arranged on the screen, waiting for you to point to and click them with your mouse

If you chose the second option, you can set Raspbian to always boot to the desktop with the following steps:

1 On the Raspberry Pi configuration menu, select option 3—Enable Boot to Desktop/Scratch—and press Enter.

2 Select the second option—"Desktop Log in as user 'pi' at the graphical desktop"—and press Enter.

Fantastic! Next time your Raspberry Pi boots up, you'll be taken to the Raspbian desktop.

> **TIP**   If you decide you prefer to boot the Raspberry Pi to the command line, you can always launch the Raspbian desktop by entering startx at the command line.

> **TIP**   Sometimes you may find yourself using the Raspbian GUI, but you want to use the command line. There is an easy way to change. You can open the command-line mode in a window by clicking the Menu Button, then selecting the Accessories category and clicking the Terminal[5] icon.

MAKING OTHER CHANGES

The Raspberry Pi configuration menu includes other options such as setting up a camera and over-clocking. These are available if you ever want to use them. Check the Raspberry Pi forums for more information on these options.

Saving your configuration and rebooting

If you're happy with the changes made to your Raspberry Pi, follow these steps to exit the Raspberry Pi configuration tool and reboot your Pi:

---

[5] Terminal is short for LXTerminal or Linux terminal. Raspbian is a Linux-based OS, and *terminal* refers to the command-line mode where you can enter commands.

1 On the Raspberry Pi configuration menu, use the arrow keys to select Finish, and press Enter.

2 You're prompted with this message: "Do you want to reboot now?" Select Yes, and press Enter.

Figure 1.16 A view of the Raspbian desktop after your Raspberry Pi boots up. The desktop is similar to the desktop in Microsoft Windows or Apple Mac OS X. Don't worry if your desktop is different from this one. Depending on when you bought your Pi, you may have received an SD card with an older or newer version of Raspbian.

Your Raspberry Pi will display lots of lines of text as it boots up. (Yes, it does that again! Don't worry, it will seem normal to you soon.) This is your Pi's startup sequence when it connects peripherals and starts up the OS. Next, a white screen with a Raspberry Pi will appear, along with a set of icons—this is your Raspbian desktop (see figure 1.16). Congratulations! Your Raspberry Pi is ready to go.

A BIT OF PI IN YOUR FACE: TROUBLESHOOTING

If you don't see the view shown in figure 1.16, don't be discouraged. It's likely that you didn't select the option to boot to desktop. If your screen shows the command-line mode for Raspbian (figure 1.17), you can log in and launch the Raspbian GUI.

```
[ ok ] Setting up ALSA...done.
[info] Setting console screen modes.
[info] Skipping font and keymap setup (handled by console-setup).
[ ok ] Setting up console font and keymap...done.
[ ok ] Setting up X socket directories... /tmp/.X11-unix /tmp/.ICE-unix.
INIT: Entering runlevel: 2
[info] Using makefile-style concurrent boot in runlevel 2.
[ ok ] Network Interface Plugging Daemon...skip eth0...done.
[ ok ] Starting enhanced syslogd: rsyslogd.
[ ok ] Starting periodic command scheduler: cron.
[ ok ] Starting system message bus: dbus.
Starting dphys-swapfile swapfile setup ...
want /var/swap=100MByte, checking existing: keeping it
done.
[ ok ] Starting NTP server: ntpd.
[ ok ] Starting OpenBSD Secure Shell server: sshd.

Debian GNU/Linux 7 raspberrypi tty1

raspberrypi login:
```

Figure 1.17 If you didn't set up your Pi to boot to the Raspbian desktop, the command-line mode will be displayed when your Raspberry Pi boots up. It will ask you for your login name and password.

At the command line, you'll be prompted to enter your login and password. The default login is pi, and the password is raspberry. After entering that information, launch the Raspbian Desktop from the command line using the following steps:

1 Type startx.
2 Press Enter.

Once you execute the command, the Pi will start up the Raspbian GUI mode and display your Raspberry Pi's desktop. If you happen to have a different problem, head to appendix A for troubleshooting ideas.

Getting around: learning Raspbian

Take a cruise around your Raspberry Pi, and look at some of the applications that come already installed with the Raspbian OS.

Finding and opening applications on your Raspberry Pi

There are many applications on your Raspberry Pi. You can access them by clicking the Menu button in the top-left corner of the desktop (see figure 1.18). Enjoy exploring what comes installed on your Pi.

Your files and folders

Similar to Windows Explorer or Mac Finder, Raspbian has some built-in tools to make it easier to navigate the folders and files on your

Figure 1.18 The Raspbian application menu opens when you click the Menu button in the top-left corner of the desktop. You can open an application by moving your mouse over the categories listed on the menu and then clicking the application.

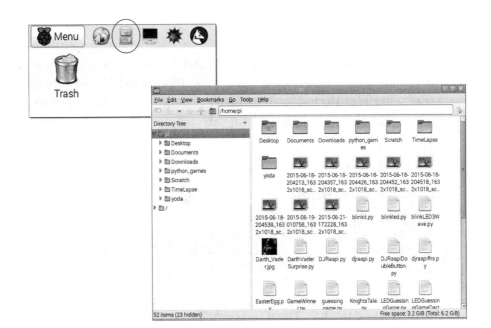

Figure 1.19 File Manager in Raspbian allows you to manage files as you do in Windows Explorer or Mac Finder. You access File Manager using the folder icon in the upper-left corner of the desktop. This is a view of a Pi with a lot of files stored in the /home/pi folder.

Raspberry Pi. In Raspbian, the application for managing files is called *File Manager*, and it's accessed by clicking the folder icon located in the top-left corner of the Raspbian desktop. Figure 1.19 shows the icon and the File Manager application. Just as in Windows Explorer, you can

- Navigate into folders by double-clicking them.
- Drag files to move them to another folder.
- Copy and paste files using the right-click menu on files and folders.
- Rename files.
- Open files by double-clicking them.

The Pi was built for coding. Let's see how you can write code on your Pi.

Writing code

You're going to learn to write code in the Python programming language. Meet a new program, IDLE. IDLE is a tool that'll help you write programs in Python. IDLE stands for Integrated DeveLopment Environment. The Python language was named after Monty Python, and the IDLE acronym is a nod to Eric Idle, one of the founding Monty Python members.

Follow these steps:

Click the Menu button on your desktop.

Select Programming > Python 3.

After a second or two, IDLE opens the Python Shell, as shown in figure 1.20.

> **NOTE** Previous Raspberry Pi models have desktop icons for Python: IDLE and IDLE 3. *You'll use Python 3 (or IDLE 3) for the exercises in this book.* On older Pi models, the IDLE 3 icon opens the Python Shell for Python 3. You may have guessed that the IDLE (without the 3) icon opens IDLE for Python 2.

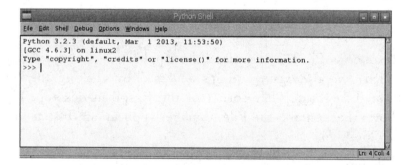

Figure 1.20 IDLE is a development environment that makes it easier to write Python programs. This is the IDLE Python Shell that you can use to enter Python commands or instructions one at a time.

> **NOTE** To start the Python Shell from the Raspbian command line, type python3 and press Enter. You'll see a >>> prompt and may interactively enter Python commands. When you're finished using the Python Shell, type exit() and press Enter to end your Python session.

The Python Shell shown in figure 1.20 allows you to enter Python commands and press Enter to execute them. The command prompt lets you type in commands after the triple greater-than symbols (>>>).

Do the following:

1 Enter 3 + 4.

2 Press Enter.

The screen displays the answer: 7. Try some subtraction:

1 Enter 17 - 9.

2 Press Enter.

The screen displays the answer: 8. Now let's make Python talk to you by printing a message to the screen:

1 Enter print("I am alive!").

2 Press Enter.

Your screen should display "I am alive!"

Outstanding work! You wrote three lines of code. When you pressed Enter after each one, the Raspberry Pi's processor executed those commands and did what you asked. That is powerful!

Fruit Picker Extra: shopping at the Pi Store

Your Raspberry Pi can do many things. We've included special sections throughout the book called *Fruit Picker Extras* to teach you some different things your Pi can do. This Fruit Picker Extra is about shopping at the Pi Store.

The Pi Store is an online app store that provides access to games, apps, and resources for your Pi (see figure 1.21). You can browse the Pi Store from any device, such as a mobile phone or laptop. To access it from your Raspberry Pi, double-click the Pi Store icon on your desktop. If you want to download content to your Pi, you need to have your Pi connected to the internet, and you'll also need to create an IndieCity account with an email address and password.

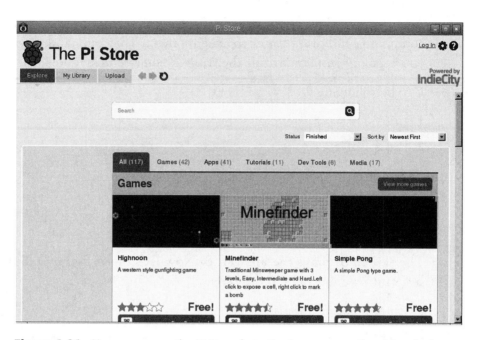

Figure 1.21 You can access the Pi Store from the icon on your Raspbian desktop. The store allows you to browse and download apps and content including games, tutorials, and digital magazines. You'll find free and fee-based content, organized into five categories: Games, Apps, Tutorials, Dev Tools, and Media.

Some apps are free; others require you to pay a fee. You'll find great resources, such as free issues of *MagPi*, the Raspberry Pi community magazine, a digital magazine full of tips, projects, and programming tutorials (look for these in the Pi Store's Media category). Have fun downloading free games and tutorials onto your Pi!

Challenge

Each chapter will have challenges at the end for you to try. If you can't figure them out, check the back of the book (see appendix C) for hints and answers.

Scavenger hunt

Time to explore your Raspberry Pi with a scavenger hunt. The goal is to learn more about the Pi by looking around, opening applications, and playing with them. Try to complete this list of scavenger-hunt items:

1 Find a game where squirrels eat other squirrels. Can you achieve the title of Omega Squirrel? Hint: Double-click the Python Games desktop icon to look for it.

2 Find a calculator application on your Raspberry Pi. Calculate the answer to a math problem: 87×34. Hint: The calculator is found under Menu > Accessories.

3 Without unplugging your Raspberry Pi, can you figure out how to shut down or restart it?

4 Turn your desktop's background black.

5 Bonus: Open Scratch, and try to make a cat dance.

Consider yourself an official Raspberry Pi explorer. If you want, take some more time to click some icons and see what they do. You've accomplished a lot!

Summary

The Raspberry Pi is like other computers in a lot of ways, but with several important differences. The similarities with other computers include these:

- A Pi requires a keyboard, mouse, and monitor, much like other desktop computers. The ports for plugging these in are part of the Pi.

- The Pi can be set up with a desktop OS, Raspbian. It's similar to Microsoft Windows or Apple OS X.

- Although its computing power is limited (similar to a smart phone), the Pi can still allow you to do many things you do on a desktop or laptop, such as browsing websites, playing games, and listening to music.

The Raspberry Pi has qualities and capabilities that make it special and unique. These key differences from other computers include the following:

- The Pi's cost and size are much smaller, making it a great candidate for projects.
- The Pi was designed for programming in Python and comes preloaded with the Python development environment so you can get coding right away.
- The Pi uses an SD memory card to store all files and software, including the OS.
- It has GPIO pins that can send and receive electrical signals. In part 3 of this book, you'll learn how you can use these to create projects that interact with the world around you.

2

Exploring Python

In this chapter, you'll learn how to interact with your Raspberry Pi by using Python to

- *Do math calculations quickly and easily*
- *Store information using variables*
- *Get messages to display on the screen*
- *Create and run your first program in Python*

An exciting part of programming is getting the computer to interact with you. It's the first step toward having the computer feel artificially intelligent.

Playing with Python

One of the best ways to learn to program is by exploring and playing. When you play, you try things and see what happens. You learn by experiencing the act of programming and seeing results. In this approach, you'll try entering different commands and see what happens.

Open IDLE for Python 3 by clicking the Menu button and selecting Programming > Python 3 on your Raspberry Pi's desktop (see figure 2.1). After you click it, you'll need to wait a few seconds while IDLE opens.

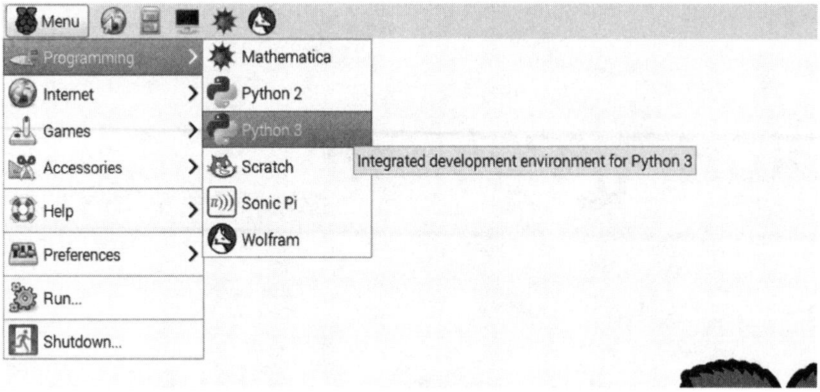

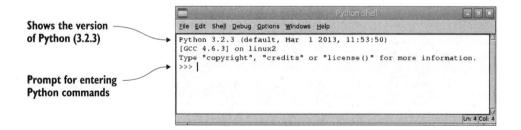

Figure 2.1   The Python 3 icon on your Raspberry Pi opens an interactive programming shell for Python 3.x.

NOTE   There are both Python 3 and Python 2 icons under Menu > Programming on your desktop. Make sure you click Python 3 and not Python 2.

The Python 3 icon opens IDLE.[1] You'll see a prompt, ready for your commands—this is the Python Shell (see figure 2.2). With the Python Shell open, let's see how you can start talking to your Raspberry Pi using Python.

Shows the version of Python (3.2.3)

Prompt for entering Python commands

```
Python 3.2.3 (default, Mar  1 2013, 11:53:50)
[GCC 4.6.3] on linux2
Type "copyright", "credits" or "license()" for more information.
>>>
```

Figure 2.2   The Python 3 application under Menu > Programming on the Raspberry Pi desktop opens IDLE to the Python Shell for Python 3.x.

---

[1]   The specific version of Python preinstalled on your Raspberry Pi may vary depending on when you purchased it. As of this writing, most Raspberry Pis come with Python version 3.2.3.

Discovering Python's mathematical operators

One of the core capabilities of a programming language is its ability to do math, or, in programmer-speak, to perform mathematical operations. Let's try different mathematical operations to see what works and what doesn't.

Adding and subtracting

Suppose you go to your favorite restaurant and order a burger, fries, and an orange soda. You want to know how much you owe. The menu (see figure 2.3) says the burger is $5.49, fries are $1.99, and the orange soda costs $1.49.

Menu
Burger $5.49
Fries $1.99
Soda $1.49

Figure 2.3   The menu at your favorite burger restaurant

Use Python to figure out the total. In the IDLE Python Shell, enter

```
>>> 5.49 + 1.99 + 1.49
```

Press Enter to see Python calculate the result: 8.97, or $8.97 (see figure 2.4).

Great news: you remember you have a coupon for $3.00 off, so let's calculate the total again. In the IDLE Python Shell, enter

```
>>> 8.97 - 3.00
```

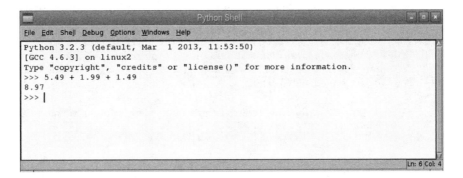

Figure 2.4   Use the + symbol to add numbers in Python.

The result is 5.970000000000001. Whoa! Why isn't it exactly 5.97? Well, it has to do with how computers store numbers as 1s and 0s. We aren't going to go over it here, but the footnote[2] has a web link where you can learn more. For now, the number is close enough for your calculations.

As you can see, Python is pretty good at doing math and uses familiar operators for addition and subtraction:

- The addition operator (+) calculates the sum of two numbers:

  ```
  >>> 4 + 5
  ```

  The result is 9.

- The subtraction operator (–) calculates the difference between two numbers:

  ```
  >>> 8 – 5
  ```

  The result is 3.

Python style: spacing of operators and numbers

Try entering 24 plus 32 without any spaces between the plus sign (+) and the numbers:

```
>>> 24+32
```

Then try it with lots of spaces:

```
>>> 24     +        32
```

Both result in the same answer: 56. When you're doing math, the number of spaces between the numbers and the operator doesn't matter. Python ignores the extra spaces and calculates the sum.

What's the best way? Well, Pythonistas (the name given to those who program in Python) believe that your code should be easy to read. The Python Style Guide[a] recommends using spaces before and after a mathematical operator. You don't have to, but it's easier to read!

---

[a] The Python Style Guide is referred to as PEP 8 and is found online here: www .python.org/dev/peps/pep-0008.

---

[2] Read more about decimal math (also called *floating-point math*) here: https://docs.python.org/3.4/tutorial/floatingpoint.html.

Let's see what other math you can do in Python.

> TIP   When typing in large numbers, don't enter commas to separate groups of three digits. So 1,000 should be entered as 1000. Python can't interpret the comma separators in numbers, so you'll get some odd results if you add them. Python will interpret the commas as if you're typing in a list of numbers. For example, 12,231 is interpreted to be a list of two numbers: 12 and 231. You'll learn more about lists in part 2 of this book.

Multiplying and dividing

After scarfing down your burger, you find yourself hungry for two scoops of ice cream and a slice of raspberry pie for dessert. Ice cream is $1.79 per scoop, and pie is $3.50 per slice, so what is your total?

Use Python to figure it out. Try Python's multiplication operator (*):

```
>>> (2 * 1.79) + 3.50
```

You total bill is $7.08. You also see that you can use parentheses to group things.

Three of your friends join you at the restaurant, and each orders dessert. After more ice cream and pie, the total bill ends up being $33.36. They all agree to split the bill evenly. Use Python's division operator (/) to calculate the price they each should pay:

```
>>> 33.36 / 3
```

The result is $11.12 each. That's a lot of dessert!

With your belly full, you observe how you've seen Python perform multiplication and division and how you can use parentheses for grouping:

- The multiplication operator (*) gives you the product of two numbers:

  ```
  >>> 7 * 3.14
  ```

  The result is 21.98.

- The division operator (/) can divide two numbers:

  ```
  >>> 40 / 8
  ```

The result is 5.

- Parentheses can be used to group numbers so they're evaluated first:

```
>>> (3 + 7) * 10
```

Python answers 100.

What do you think this will result in?

```
>>> 3 + (7 * 10)
```

If you guessed 73, you're right. If you change the location of the parentheses, you'll get a different answer. We'll talk about this more when we examine the order of operations.

Figuring out whole numbers and remainders

Your friend mentions to you that there are 19,272 minutes of school remaining this year. How can you figure out how many hours and minutes? First you divide 19,272 by 60, because there are 60 minutes in an hour. You find that is 321 hours with a remainder of 12 minutes. In Python, you have two operators to give you the whole number and the remainder of a division sum:

- // (floor division) gives you the whole number:

```
>>> 19272 // 60
```

The result is 321.

- % (modulo) gives you the remainder:

```
>>> 19272 % 60
```

The result is 12.

You divided some large numbers, but let's look at how Python can handle even larger ones.

Exponents

An interesting fact you might've learned in Astronomy is that the Earth's distance to the Sun is approximately 1.496×10^8 km. Let's use Python to express this as a number. In Python you use the exponentiation operator (**) as follows:

```
>>> 1.496 * 10**8
```

Python answers 149600000.0 km.

Exponentiation lets you take two numbers (*a, b*) and raise one number to the power of the other(a^b). Python uses the exponentiation operator (**) between the two numbers (*a**b*) to do this. For example, if you wanted to raise 2 to the third power, you'd enter

```
>>> 2 ** 3
```

The result is 8 (2 * 2 * 2 = 8).

Try another:

```
>>> 122 ** 5
```

The result is 27,027,081,632 (122 * 122 * 122 * 122 * 122 = 27027081632).

> **NOTE**   On older versions of Python, you may see 122**5 show the result 27027081632L. This is because previously Python added the letter L to denote really long integers.

Exponentiation can be useful if you're solving problems like these:

- Estimating astronomical distances
- Calculating bank account balances based on a given interest rate
- Predicting a population size for animal colonies based on a given growth rate

Square roots

You can figure out square roots by using an exponent of 1/2, or 0.5. This is the same as taking a square root:

```
>>> 14400**0.5
```

The result is 120.0.

Challenge: stacking Pis!

How many Raspberry Pis would need to be stacked end to end to reach the Sun? You can measure your Pi, and you'll find that a Raspberry Pi measures 85.6 millimeters or 0.0856 meters. First, you need to convert the Pi's measurements to kilometers by dividing 0.0856 by

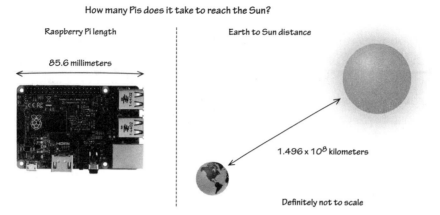

Figure 2.5 The distance from the Earth to the Sun is approximately 149,600,000 km. The Raspberry Pi is 85.6 mm in length.

1,000; then you divide the distance from the Earth to the Sun by the Pi's length in kilometers (see figure 2.5). This should give you the distance to the Sun, expressed as a number of Pis.

Enter the equation into Python:

```
>>> 1.496 * 10**8 / (0.0856 / 1000)
```

Python answers 1747663551401.8694. That is more than 1.7 trillion Raspberry Pis stacked end to end. It's kind of fun to think about that many Pis!

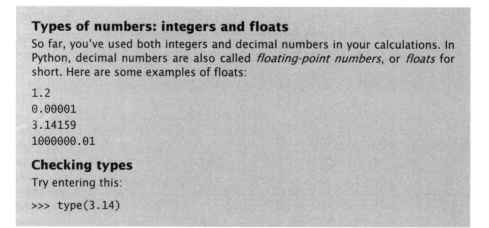

Types of numbers: integers and floats

So far, you've used both integers and decimal numbers in your calculations. In Python, decimal numbers are also called *floating-point numbers*, or *floats* for short. Here are some examples of floats:

```
1.2
0.00001
3.14159
1000000.01
```

Checking types

Try entering this:

```
>>> type(3.14)
```

Python will answer you: <class 'float'>. You've just used Python's built-in tool for checking the type of something. These built-in tools are called *functions*. You'll see more of these later. Let's see what this does:

```
>>> type(10001)
```

Did you guess it? This returns <class 'int'>, where int stands for *integer*.

So far, you've typed in numbers and performed calculations. But if you want to change one number, you have to type all the information again. You also have no way of saving information—you have to look up and type the number each time. Good news! There is a better way.

Storing information using variables

There are times in programming when it's easier to store information than to type it in over and over again. *Variables* provide that special capability. Variables give you a way to store information and retrieve it anytime. Let's look at an example.

Imagine that you own a pizza restaurant, and your prices are shown in figure 2.6.

Menu

Cheese pizza $14.00
Orange soda $1.50
Chicken wings............$8.00

Figure 2.6
The menu at your
pizza restaurant

The first customer, Daniel orders a meal of pizza and orange soda:

```
>>> 14 + 1.5
```

Daniel's meal costs $15.50.

A second customer, Erin orders pizza, orange soda, and wings:

```
>>> 14 + 1.5 + 8
```

Erin's meal costs $23.50.

Each time you want to calculate a meal's cost, you must remember or look up the price of each item and type it in. Imagine if you had a menu of 15 items and 100 customers. It would take forever to look up the items and add their prices together! You'd also be prone to making mistakes. Let's have the computer do this work for you.

Creating variables and assigning values

This is a perfect place to use variables in a program. Variables store information to make your life easier. (We're programmers, and we like to be lazy. At least we're always trying to find a more efficient way to do things.) Let's do this again but create variables for each of the food items. The first step is to define your first variable and set its value:

```
>>> cheese_pizza = 14
```

Let's take a close look at how this code works in figure 2.7.

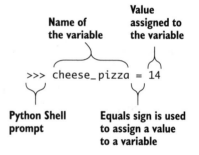

Figure 2.7 A variable stores information and can be created and assigned a value. The equals sign is used as an operator (also known as the *assignment operator*) between the name of the variable on the left and the value assigned to it on the right.

Next, let's create the other two variables for orange soda and wings:

```
>>> orange_soda = 1.5
>>> wings = 8.00
```

Nothing is displayed on the screen after you enter each line, but Python stores the variables and their values in the memory of your Raspberry Pi.

Displaying variable values

How can you check what's stored in a variable? Like the type function earlier, you use another built-in function in Python called print, like this:

```
>>> print(cheese_pizza)
    14
```

Print doesn't mean to print something with paper and ink. In Python, printing means to display something on the screen.

> NOTE   When you're working in the Shell, Python displays the result of expressions. But if you assign a sum to a variable, the Shell doesn't show the value unless you use `print`.

Using `print`, you've seen that `cheese_pizza` has the value 14 stored in it. You should feel confident that your variables are holding the information you put in them.

Let's see if you can use variables to figure out a meal cost (without having to look up numbers):

```
>>> meal_cost = cheese_pizza + orange_soda
```

Print `meal_cost` to see its value:

```
>>> print(meal_cost)
15.5
```

Python displays 15.5. Now, let's calculate the cost of the other meal:

```
>>> meal_cost = cheese_pizza + orange_soda + wings
>>> print(meal_cost)
23.5
```

Python answers 23.5. The more calculations you need to repeat, the more you'll appreciate how variables can save you time and effort. Congratulations—you're using variables to store information!

> DEFINITION   The process of putting a value into a variable is called *assignment*.

Before you start creating a lot of variables, let's learn the guidelines for naming them.

NAMING VARIABLES

Everyone has had the problem of not being able to read someone else's handwriting. The writer might know what they wrote, but you're unable to decipher it. You want to avoid this same confusion with variables. In order to do that, there is a set of guidelines for creating clear variable names—names that make sense to you and to someone else reading your code:

- Don't use any spaces. Instead, use an underscore (_).
- The Python Style Guide recommends using lowercase and underscores between words to make your code easy to read.
- Don't start with a number.
- Don't use any of Python's reserved words for your variable name (see the sidebar "Watch out for reserved words").

Here are some examples of variable names:

```
>>> shoe_size = 10
>>> age = 16
>>> favorite_color = 'blue'
>>> first_name = "John"
>>> pizza_slices_eaten = 4
```

Do your best to use meaningful variable names.

Watch out for reserved words

Certain words in Python are *reserved* because they're part of the Python language. You can't use these words as names for variables:

False	class	finally	is	return
None	continue	for	lambda	try
True	def	from	nonlocal	while
and	del	global	not	with
as	elif	if	or	yield
assert	else	import	pass	
break	except	in	raise	

Python 3.x reserved words are used by Python for special purposes and may not be used for variable names.

ASSIGNING VALUES: THE LEFT SIDE AND RIGHT SIDE

When you're creating a variable and assigning it a value, put the name of your variable on the left side of an equals sign. Put the value you want to set it to on the right side of the equals sign. Let's create a variable name and set it to "King Arthur":

```
>>> name = "King Arthur"
```

In this line, the left side creates a variable called `name`, and the set of characters "King Arthur" is stored in it. Let's learn more about storing text in variables.

Storing strings in variables

Life isn't only about numbers. You may want to create programs that display absurd messages or tell a story on the screen. These messages are a type of data called *strings*. A string is a group of characters.

STRINGS

Python gives you the ability to store a group of characters (or strings) in variables. You've already used strings in the example with "King Arthur".

Here are some things you should know about strings:

- They always must start and end with quotation marks.
- You may use either single quotes ('Hi') or double quotes ("Hi"), but you can't mix them ("Hi'):

  ```
  >>> message = "Greetings Earthlings"
  ```

  Or, in single quotes:

  ```
  >>> message = 'Greetings Earthlings'
  ```

- When a number is placed inside quotation marks, it's a string.
- Strings can be short (zero or only a few characters) or many characters long.
- Strings can even be empty. These are called *zero-length strings*:

  ```
  my_string = ""
  ```

EXAMPLES OF STRINGS

Some examples of strings will give you an idea of what's possible:

```
"Y"
"No"
"Spam"
"Yeah, remarkable bird the Norwegian Blue"
```

```
"There he is!"
"No, no sir, it's not dead. It's resting."
"17"
"RUNAWAY, RUNAWAY, RUNAWAY!"
"Tuesday"
```

MEASURING THE LENGTH OF A STRING

You can use the `len` function to have Python tell you the length of a string. We'll talk more about string functions in chapter 3, but here is an example of using `len`:

```
>>> your_nickname = "Pi Master"
>>> len(your_nickname)
9
```

Or try a longer one:

```
>>> quote = "To be, or not to be, that is the question."
>>> len(quote)
42
```

Even the spaces are counted when determining the length of a string. This is a great point to talk about spaces.

SPACES COUNT

Although spaces may seem like nothing, they're considered characters. You can create strings that are a single space or set of spaces, such as

```
short_set_of_spaces = " "
long_set_of_spaces = "     "
```

You now know about variables and about strings, a type of data that can be stored in them. Let's see how you can vary your variables.

Changing the value of variables

As you may have guessed already, the value stored in a variable can be changed or updated. Try it. You're making up a password for your computer. Create a variable `password`, and set it to `bunny`:

```
>>> password = "bunny"
```

Now let's change the password to `dragon`:

```
>>> password = "dragon"
```

What value do you think is stored in `password`: "bunny" or "dragon"? Let's check the value using the `print` function:

```
>>> print(password)
dragon
```

The value `dragon` is displayed. Notice how Python replaces the value stored in the variable when you assign it a new value.

VISUALIZING VARIABLES AS BOXES

A way to visualize this is to imagine that creating a variable is like making a box—a box for storing information. When you create the box, you give it a name and store a value in it. Figure 2.8 is a graphical depiction of creating a variable and reassigning a value to it.

Changing the value of a variable is easy to do in Python. Let's look at another example.

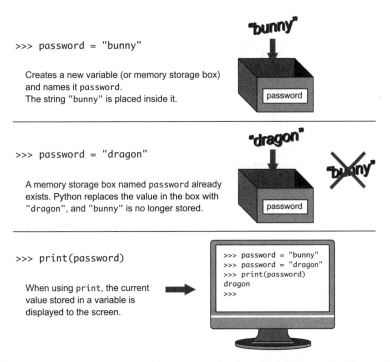

```
>>> password = "bunny"
```

Creates a new variable (or memory storage box) and names it `password`.
The string "bunny" is placed inside it.

```
>>> password = "dragon"
```

A memory storage box named `password` already exists. Python replaces the value in the box with "dragon", and "bunny" is no longer stored.

```
>>> print(password)
```

When using `print`, the current value stored in a variable is displayed to the screen.

```
>>> password = "bunny"
>>> password = "dragon"
>>> print(password)
dragon
>>>
```

Figure 2.8 When a variable is created, it's stored in your Raspberry Pi's memory. You can change the value of a variable at any time. Using the print function, you can display the variable's value on the screen.

VARIABLE REASSIGNMENT

Let's see how Python evaluates these statements:

```
>>> x = 10
```

This sets x equal to the value 10. Next, you do a calculation with x and store the result of the calculation in x:

```
>>> x =  x * 10 + 32
```

When Python evaluates this line, it first tackles the right side of the equals sign:

1 Python evaluates the right side of the equation: x * 10 + 32.
2 Python retrieves the current value of x, 10, and calculates 10 * 10.
3 Python adds 32 to this amount. The right side of the equals sign is 132.
4 It does the left side of the equals sign last. The result, 132, is stored into the variable on the left side of the equals sign: x.

You've seen how Python can store and retrieve information using variables. Variables save you time because they hold the value they're given, meaning you don't have to remember values or look them up. Variables can take the form of numbers or strings, and you can check the value stored in a variable using the print function.

Excellent! You've seen how the order for variable assignment is important. Check out how the order of math operations matters.

ORDER OF OPERATIONS

What do you think Python will return if you enter the following?

```
>>> (3 * 2) * 5**3 / 25 + 10
```

If you guessed 40, you're correct. Python follows the order of operations that you learned in math class.

> TIP   You may recall BOMDAS or PEMDAS from school. This pattern of letters is useful for remembering the order you should evaluate operations in a math equation. Python follows this same order of operations: Brackets (or Parentheses), Orders (or Exponents), Multiplication and Division, and then Addition and Subtraction.

First it evaluates anything grouped in parentheses or brackets. 3 * 2 is equal to 6. Let's replace the 3 * 2 with 6 and go to the next step:

```
>>> 6 * 5**3 / 25 + 10
```

The exponents (or orders) are analyzed next. 5**3 is 125 (the same as 5 * 5 * 5):

```
>>> 6 * 125 / 25 + 10
```

Multiplication and division come next, and you work from the left to the right. 6 * 125 is 750. 750 / 25 is 30:

```
>>> 30 + 10
```

The final step is addition and subtraction. 30 + 10 is 40. Graphically, figure 2.9 shows the order in which the example equation is solved in math and how Python does it.

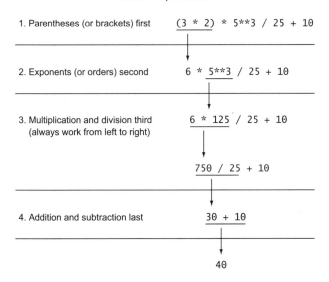

Order of operations

1. Parentheses (or brackets) first   (3 * 2) * 5**3 / 25 + 10

2. Exponents (or orders) second   6 * 5**3 / 25 + 10

3. Multiplication and division third   6 * 125 / 25 + 10
   (always work from left to right)

   750 / 25 + 10

4. Addition and subtraction last   30 + 10

40

Figure 2.9 Python follows the order of operations used in mathematics. You may know it as BOMDAS or PEMDAS: Brackets (or Parentheses), Orders (or Exponents), Multiplication and Division, and finally Addition and Subtraction.

You're pretty good at doing math in Python. You're ready to learn more about using Python to communicate and display text on the screen.

Displaying text on a screen

It's fun to interact with technology and have it respond. This can take the form of playful responses by a computer, making it feel more human. Or computer responses can be more practical, displaying personal data on a website form. In either case, you want your computer to communicate with you.

Displaying text on the screen, also referred to as *printing* in Python, is a direct way for a computer to communicate with you. You can use printing to have your Raspberry Pi do things like this:

- Show random, silly messages.
- Describe spooky scenes as part of an adventure game.
- Spit out the answers to complex math problems.

Printing to the screen is a key way to output all kinds of information.

Using the print function

Earlier in this chapter, you used the print function to display the value of variables. Let's go over more about using the print function. Try printing the message "Hello World!" to the screen like this:

```
>>> print("Hello World!")
Hello World!
```

Take a closer look at how you can use the print function in figure 2.10. Python prints "Hello World!" to the Python Shell.

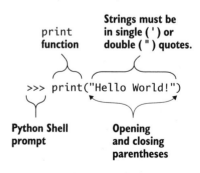

Figure 2.10 The print function in Python displays text on the screen. The string inside the parentheses must be enclosed in single or double quotation marks.

REPEATING TEXT

Let's try something a bit different. Type in

```
>>> message = "Hello, I am your Raspberry Pi!"
>>> print(message)
```

This prints the message on the screen once. You can use the multiplication operator with a string to print it many times:

```
>>> print(message * 100)
```

The message cascades across and down the screen 100 times (see figure 2.11).

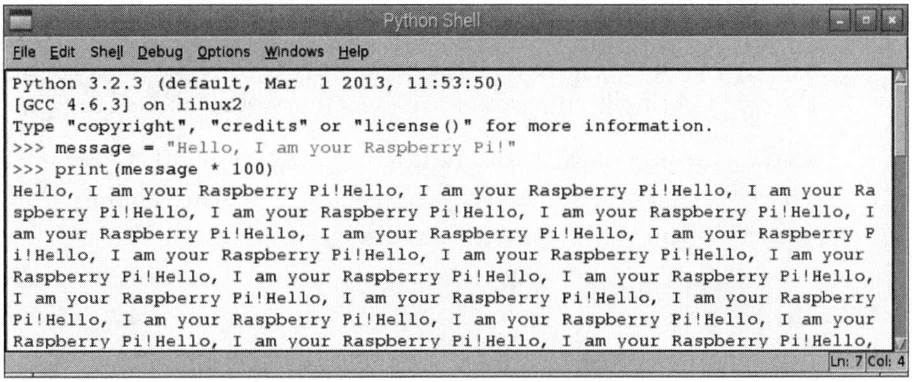

Figure 2.11   The Python print function can display text on the screen repeatedly if you use it with a string and the multiplication operator (*).

Have fun with this. Try some bigger numbers and different messages to see what you get.

Troubleshooting

We're all human, so things can go wrong when we're pressing keys and typing in code. A common error you might make when creating a variable that is storing a string is forgetting to close your quotation marks:

```
>>> message = "Hello, I am your Raspberry Pi!
```

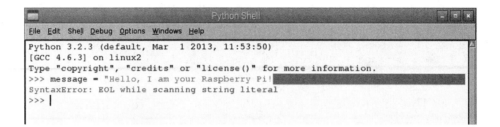

Figure 2.12 Remember to place quotation marks at the beginning and end of your strings. If you forget to close your quotation mark, Python will display an error.

Notice that the quotation mark after the exclamation point is missing. It may sound goofy, but think of quotation marks as hugs. When you hug someone, you wrap your arms around them. One quotation mark must go on either side of a string to complete it. If you ran this code in the Python Shell, you would receive an error, as shown in figure 2.12.

Python displays an error message (`SyntaxError: EOL while scanning string literal`). You can fix it by typing the string again with both the opening and closing quotation marks around it.

Creating programs

Imagine again that you own a pizza shop and you want to use Python to calculate the cost of a meal, including tax. A customer orders a meal of two slices of pizza and orange soda. Let's start by creating two variables with the menu prices:

```
>>> pizza_slice = 3.5
>>> orange_soda = 1.50
```

Create two variables to keep track of the number of slices and number of drinks:

```
>>> num_slices = 2
>>> num_drinks = 1
```

Next let's calculate the cost of the meal without tax:

```
>>> meal_no_tax = (num_slices * pizza_slice) + (num_drinks *
    orange_soda)
```

Define the tax rate of 5%, and figure out the tax:

```
>>> tax = 0.05
>>> meal_cost = meal_no_tax + (meal_no_tax * tax)
>>> print(meal_cost)
8.925
```

Now imagine if one or more of the numbers changed. Let's say pizza slices are now $4.75 and orange soda is $1.75. You'd have to enter all the information again. That takes way too long.

A better way is to put the eight statements into a text file. Then you can tell Python to read the file and execute the instructions.

> **DEFINITION**   A *program* is a set of instructions. Python programs can be created in a text file. The programs can be run (or executed) over and over again.

Now you can run the program again and again, making updates whenever needed. If the cost of menu items changes or a customer wants a different number of slices, you can update the program and run it again. That is a big time-saver!

A computer program is a set of instructions. So far, you've used the Python Shell to type in commands one at a time. Programs allow you to create, save, and run more complex sets of instructions. You can easily edit your programs and run them again. Your programs might be as short as a few lines, or thousands of lines long.

Writing Python programs with IDLE

To write a program, you need a way to input the instructions. IDLE will be your program of choice for this. IDLE is an application that makes it easier to develop programs.

A SPELL CHECKER FOR PYTHON

If you've ever used Microsoft Word or Gmail, you're familiar with the spell-checker feature. It's saved thousands of homework assignments from receiving low grades and stopped misspelled emails from being sent. Each program highlights words you misspell, so you can easily find them and make corrections.

When you write programs, you want something to help catch your mistakes. IDLE does that for you. IDLE automatically color-codes your Python statements to let you know you're using the correct spelling. By using color-coding, IDLE can help alert you if you enter a command incorrectly and highlight errors or bugs. In later chapters, I'll introduce you to some of the features of IDLE.

INTEGRATED DEVELOPMENT ENVIRONMENTS

Other programming languages have software applications similar to IDLE that make the process of programming more enjoyable, help prevent errors, and even suggest fixes. As a group, these software applications are called *integrated development environments (IDEs)*. IDLE is one of the most popular ones for Python.

USING TEXT EDITORS

In addition to IDLE, you can write and save Python programs in any text editor you like. For example, you could use Leafpad or Nano, which are other simple text editors that come with Raspbian. A word of caution: they allow you to write, but they don't help you avoid errors or find mistakes in your code, making IDLE a better choice.

Starting a new program

Let's create our first program. While using the IDLE Python Shell, select File > New Window. You'll see a blank new window appear, with the title Untitled at the top (see figure 2.13). This is the IDLE text editor.

> **TIP** The keyboard shortcut to open a new IDLE text editor window is Ctrl-N.

Let's write a program in the IDLE text editor. Enter the following lines of text:

```
message = "And now for something completely different."
print(message)
```

> **TIP** The text editor automatically highlights keywords in the Python language. In this example, you'll notice print appears in purple text, signifying it's a Python keyword. Strings are color-coded green.

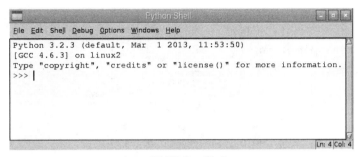

IDLE Python Shell

IDLE text editor

Figure 2.13   The top window is the IDLE Python Shell. The bottom window is the IDLE text editor that can be used to create and edit Python programs. You can open the IDLE text editor using Ctrl-N or by selecting File > New Window from the IDLE Python Shell.

This is a classic line from *Monty Python's Flying Circus*. The show begins with this quote. Figure 2.14 shows the program in the IDLE text editor.

Figure 2.14   IDLE provides a text editor that helps you write Python programs. The editor highlights words to help you compose your programs and identify errors. This program prints a message to the screen.

Now that you've written a program, you'll want to save it so you can open it, run it, and edit it later.

Saving programs

To save the program, choose File > Save. A Save dialog appears. Name the file First-Program, and click Save (see figure 2.15). By default, the file will be saved to your /home/pi folder. If you want, you can create a folder for your Python programs.

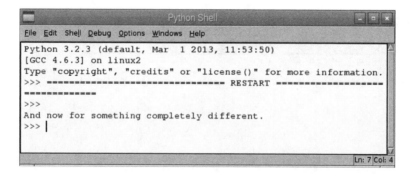

Figure 2.15   Save programs in IDLE using the File > Save menu selection or by pressing Ctrl-S. The default save location is /home/pi. When the file is saved, it has .py appended to the end of its name, signifying that it's a Python program.

TIP   The keyboard shortcut to save a program is Ctrl-S.

NOTE   When you click Save, the program is saved to your /home/pi folder with the extension .py. You can use File Manager to open your /home/pi folder and see the file you've saved: FirstProgram.py.

While using the Python text editor, you can run the program by clicking Run > Run Module, or you can press F5. When you do this, the IDLE Python Shell becomes the active window, and you'll see the message printed to the Shell (see figure 2.16).

```
Python 3.2.3 (default, Mar  1 2013, 11:53:50)
[GCC 4.6.3] on linux2
Type "copyright", "credits" or "license()" for more information.
>>> ===================== RESTART =====================
==============
>>>
And now for something completely different.
>>> |
```

Figure 2.16   You can run programs from the IDLE text editor. Running a program in IDLE displays the results of the program in the Python Shell. This shows the output of your first program by displaying a message.

Python interpreting the program

When you run your program, Python opens the file and interprets each line of text. The first line creates a variable message with the stored value "And now for something completely different." The second line of your program calls Python's print function and passes it the variable message to output to the screen. Excellent—you'll continue to build more programs in the next part of the book.

Fruit Picker Extra: creating documents

This special section is about teaching you new and different things your Pi can do. This extra is about creating documents.

Writing silly things and saving them

Let's start by creating a simple text file and saving it. Using a Raspberry Pi to do homework can be a lot of fun. Maybe you'll write a document describing your latest idea for a game or create a collection of short stories. Rather than use your parent's computer or a pen and paper, use your Raspberry Pi.

Luckily, Raspbian comes with an application called Leafpad. It's a lightweight software program for creating documents with text.

CREATING A TEXT FILE IN LEAFPAD

Here are the simple steps for creating a document in Leafpad:

1 Click the Menu button in the upper-left corner of the desktop.

2 Hover over Accessories.

3 Find Text Editor, and click it. This opens Leafpad.

4 Type in the Leafpad window: I'm a lumberjack and I'm okay! (see figure 2.17).

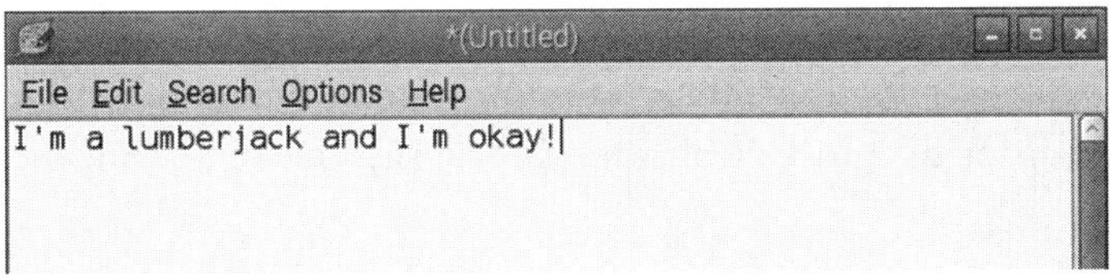

Figure 2.17 Leafpad is a text editor that comes with Raspbian. You can access Leafpad from the Accessories menu.

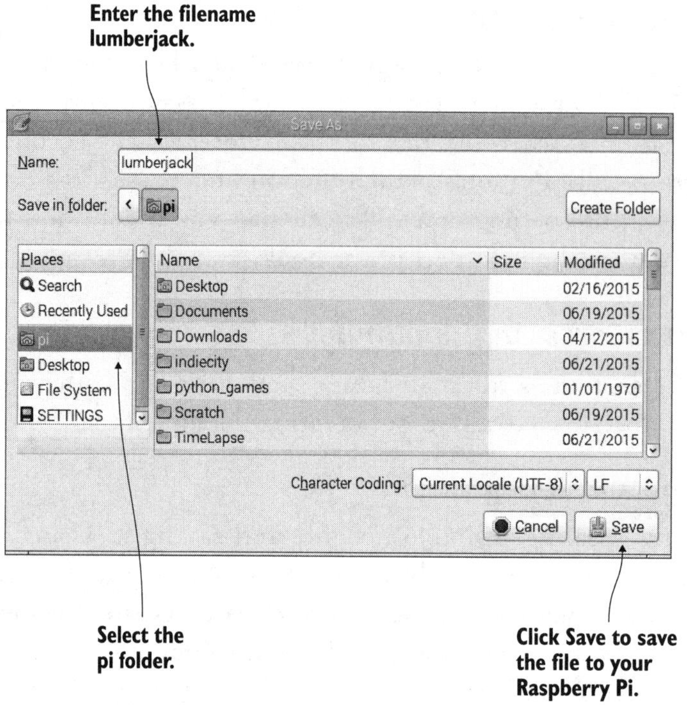

**Enter the filename
lumberjack.**

**Select the
pi folder.**

**Click Save to save
the file to your
Raspberry Pi.**

Figure 2.18 Saving a file in Leafpad lets you choose the folder to save to and enter a filename. The Save window works similarly to how you might save a file in Microsoft Word.

Now that you've created your file, let's save it (see figure 2.18):

1 Select File > Save, or use the keyboard shortcut Ctrl-S.

2 A window appears that you can use to save your file. You need to pick the folder you want to save your file in. Click the folder labeled pi. This is your personal folder where you can save your files.

3 In the Name box, enter lumberjack for the filename.

4 Click the Save button.

Congratulations! You saved the lumberjack file to your Raspberry Pi's memory card in the folder located here: \home\pi (this means the file is saved in the home folder and in a subfolder called pi). The file contains

Nano: a command-line text editor

Leafpad uses windows and is therefore only available from the Raspbian GUI. But if you decide you prefer to use the Raspbian command line, there is a handy text editor called nano that you can use. Type nano in the command line and press Enter to open nano. Nano uses keyboard controls to open, save, and close files. Here is an example of the nano text editor:

You must use the keyboard, not the mouse, to make selections and perform actions in nano. For example, Ctrl-X exits nano. Once you get used to using the command keys to get around, nano is useful if you decide you prefer using Raspbian in command-line mode.

the sentence you typed: "I'm a lumberjack and I'm okay!". Go ahead and close Leafpad.

FINDING A SAVED FILE

You saved the file. Now let's see if you can use File Manager to find it and open it again:

1 Open File Manager.

2 Click the folder icon on the left, labeled pi.

**Displays the current
folder location.**

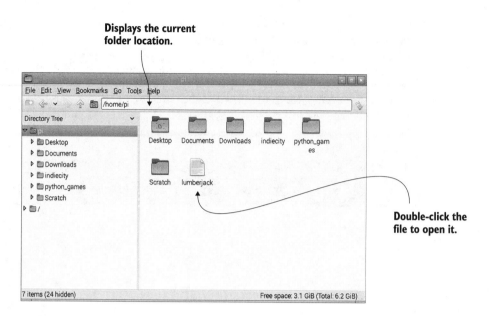

**Double-click the
file to open it.**

Figure 2.19 Viewing the contents of folders using File Manager

3 Look at the folders and files listed in the window. Notice at the top that the pi folder is located at \home\pi. This means the pi folder is located in the folder home on your Raspberry Pi's SD card.

4 Find the lumberjack file in the list of files, and double-click it (see figure 2.19).

Leafpad will open, and you'll see the message you typed. Now let's close Leafpad and learn how to enter some code.

Have fun making documents and exploring other things your Pi can do!

Challenges

Try these challenges, which will test your use of mathematical operators, printing, and variables.

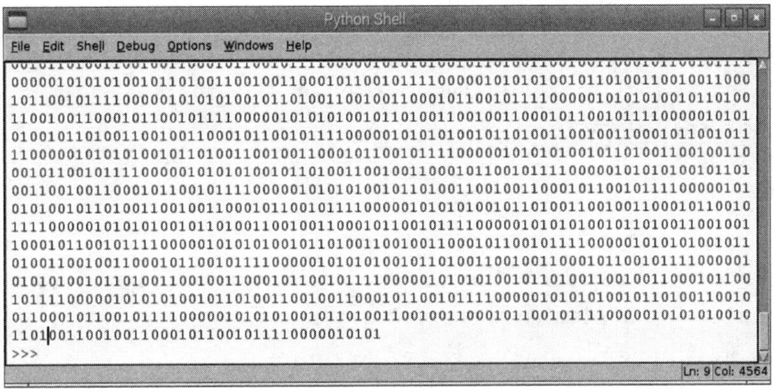

Figure 2.20 Try using the print function and strings to make a screen full of 1s and 0s.

The matrix

Using the print function, create a cascading screen of 1s and 0s as seen in popular computer graphics. Hint: remember how you used print(message * 100) to display a message 100 times on the screen. Figure 2.20 shows an example of what this might look like.

The matrix challenge is about creating a full screen of digits. Experiment with other numbers and characters.

Building a brick wall

For this challenge, create a variable named brick and store a string in it that, when printed over and over again, will make your screen turn into a brick wall (see figure 2.21).

Figure 2.21 This challenge uses the print function and a string named brick to create a brick wall pattern on the screen.

Your goal is to figure out what string should be stored in the variable named brick to make this display. Good luck! Bonus: can you make your bricks look more like raspberries or have them contain the initials RPi for Raspberry Pi?

Pi electrons

For this advanced challenge, let's examine the electrical current flowing into your Raspberry Pi from the power supply. Then, let's see if you can express that electrical current in terms of the equivalent number of electrons flowing into your Pi per second.

> **TIP** You may have learned that electrical current is a measure of charge flowing past a point. One *amp* (or ampere) of current is equal to one *coulomb* of charge flowing each second.

The amount of current your Pi uses depends on how many USB ports you're using, but let's assume your Pi is using one amp. One amp is equivalent to the flow of 1 coulomb of electrical charge flowing per second. A single electron has the charge of 1.60×10^{-19} coulombs (or 0.000000000000000000160 coulombs). How many electrons per second does it take to equal 1 amp flowing into your Raspberry Pi? Hint: You can represent the charge of an electron as 1.60 * 10**-19.

For hints and solutions to the challenges, see appendix C.

Summary

Programming is about being able to interact and communicate with a computer. Your Raspberry Pi comes with IDLE, a development environment for programming in Python. Python provides two different ways you can program:

- Interactively, by entering commands one at a time using the Python Shell. The Shell is useful for quick calculations or testing a command.

- By creating programs, or sets of commands, saved in a file. Programs allow you to write, edit, and run your code over and over again.

One of the first conversations you can have with your Raspberry Pi is to use Python to talk math. Python provides a full set of mathematical operators you can use. Mathematical operators are handy when you need to perform calculations in your programs, such as keeping track of a player's position on the screen. Another way to interact is to use Python's built-in `print` function to display text to your Pi's screen. This lets you create programs that communicate between the computer and you.

An important idea in programming is using variables to store information—they save you time and can be used again and again. In Python, variables can store different types of data, including integers, floats (decimals), and strings. Using variables, you can store information and retrieve it any time. This is a key advantage, because it means you don't have to remember values; Python does it for you. You can also change a variable's value, which is a useful feature when you want to run the same instructions with different inputs.

## Part 2

Playing with Python

Minecraft, Pac-Man, and Super Mario Brothers are great games, and they were all created by programmers like you. You'll have to gain more skills to make games like those, but you can create some basic games pretty quickly. All these games have the game player interact with the computer. The computer is programmed with *logic*: instructions that control how the game reacts to the player's choices. The game is constantly responding to input from the user, whether it is a button press or a key press.

Games are a good way to learn programming because they combine creativity, fun, and logical thinking into one project. Games are also interactive, requiring the user to make choices and the computer to respond to those choices. The goal is to make the game entertaining, so you'll use your creativity and imagination to add magic to your games. You decide how you want to program your game and how it responds!

In part 2, you'll build your own interactive games using Python and your Raspberry Pi. You'll start in chapter 3 by making a program that creates ridiculous sentences. You'll learn to use Python to ask users to enter information, store the information in variables, and make your Pi respond. Chapter 4 dives into how you can create a guessing game that makes your Pi more intelligent: it will make simple decisions based on the player's choices. You'll also see how to use Python to make your Raspberry Pi repeat some instructions over and over again. In chapter

5, you'll don a helmet and headlamp and descend into an underground cave. You'll create a text-based game where the player can choose where to go; based on their choices, they may find riches or face an untimely demise.

3

Silly Sentence Generator 3000: creating interactive programs

In this chapter, you'll see how you can use Python to

- *Create a welcome message for a game*
- *Add notes to your code*
- *Ask users to input (or type in) information and save it using variables*
- *Join strings*
- *Display information back to the user based on that information*

Visit a website, start up a game system, or open a mobile application, and it will probably ask you to enter a name and email address and create a password. These are all computer programs, and once you're logged in, they may display special messages at the top of the screen saying things like "Welcome, Aaron" (or whatever your name is). Some programs are very sophisticated, remembering the games you've played, the badges you've earned, the balance in your account, or the products you've viewed.

iTunes, Netflix, Facebook, and Gmail are all sites that use computer programs that ask you for information, save information, and interact with you based on that information. In this chapter, you'll see how to do this with Python by creating a ridiculously fun word game called Silly Sentence Generator 3000.

Creating a welcome message

In Silly Sentence Generator 3000, the game player (that'll be you) is asked to enter words such as nouns, verbs, adjectives, and so on. You'll store the words as variables and then use them to create ridiculous, nonsensical sentences.[1] Figure 3.1 shows an example of what the finished program looks like.

Think about the program like a machine that takes a set of inputs and then creates an output. You're going to put together the machine by creating the instructions that drive it. Conceptually, this "machine"

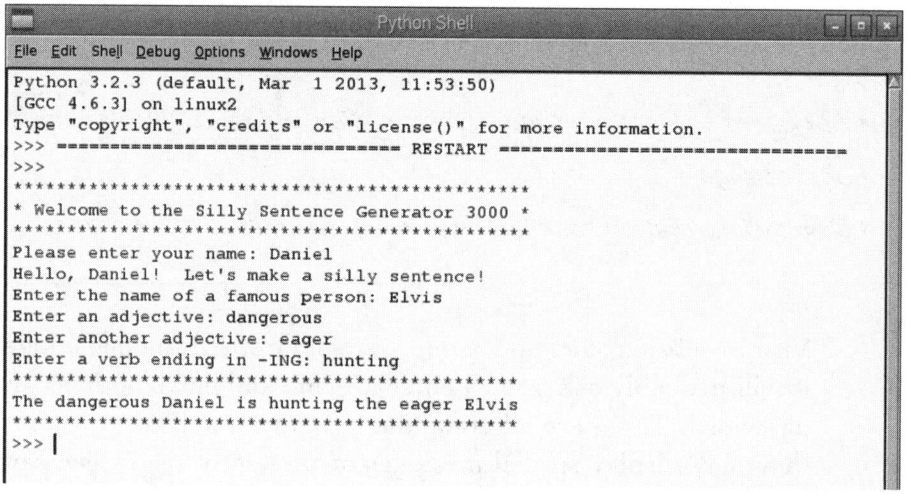

```
                          Python Shell
File  Edit  Shell  Debug  Options  Windows  Help
Python 3.2.3 (default, Mar  1 2013, 11:53:50)
[GCC 4.6.3] on linux2
Type "copyright", "credits" or "license()" for more information.
>>> =============================== RESTART ===============================
>>>
*****************************************************
* Welcome to the Silly Sentence Generator 3000 *
*****************************************************
Please enter your name: Daniel
Hello, Daniel!  Let's make a silly sentence!
Enter the name of a famous person: Elvis
Enter an adjective: dangerous
Enter another adjective: eager
Enter a verb ending in -ING: hunting
*****************************************************
The dangerous Daniel is hunting the eager Elvis
*****************************************************
>>> |
```

Figure 3.1 Silly Sentence Generator 3000 asks the user to enter their name and some words, and then it creates a silly sentence from those words.

---

[1] This is similar to the game Mad Libs, if you've ever played it.

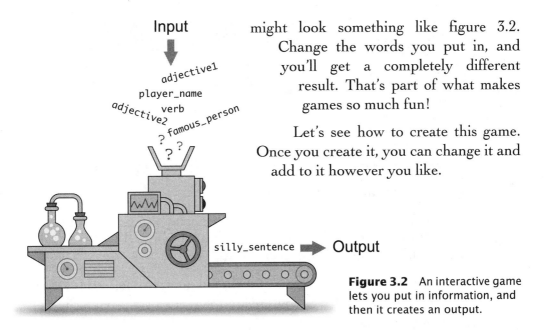

Input

adjective1
player_name
adjective2 verb
? famous_person
? ?

silly_sentence ➡ Output

might look something like figure 3.2. Change the words you put in, and you'll get a completely different result. That's part of what makes games so much fun!

Let's see how to create this game. Once you create it, you can change it and add to it however you like.

Figure 3.2 An interactive game lets you put in information, and then it creates an output.

Starting a new program

If you open a game, one of the first things you see is a main menu or title screen. Let's use what you know about displaying text on the screen to make your program display a title for your game. You start by opening IDLE and creating a new program. Open IDLE for Python 3 by clicking the Menu button and selecting Programming > Python 3 on your Raspberry Pi's desktop (see figure 3.3).

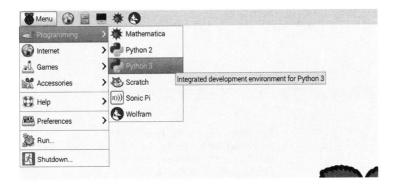

Figure 3.3 Select Menu-->Programming-->Python 3 to open the Python Shell on your Raspberry Pi.

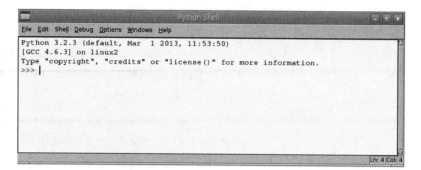

Figure 3.4 The Python Shell

Give your Raspberry Pi a few seconds to open IDLE. After IDLE opens, you'll see the Python Shell (see figure 3.4).

Press Ctrl-N or choose File > New Window to open the IDLE text editor. You'll see a blank window, ready for you to start typing in your program (see figure 3.5).

The Run menu appears in the IDLE text editor. Select Run>Run Program to test your programs.

The new window is labeled Untitled until you have saved the file.

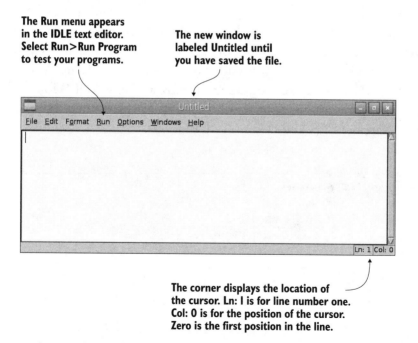

The corner displays the location of the cursor. Ln: I is for line number one. Col: 0 is for the position of the cursor. Zero is the first position in the line.

Figure 3.5 The IDLE text editor is where you can type in your Python program. You can also edit, save, and run programs using the menu options.

Using the print function you learned about in chapter 2, let's make a title screen:

```
print("*" * 48)
print("* Welcome to the Silly Sentence Generator 3000 *")
print("*" * 48)
```

Excellent. Feel free to elaborate on the welcome message and the artwork with different characters. Before you go much further, you should save the program.

Saving the program

Save the program by selecting File > Save or pressing Ctrl-S. This will open a window asking where you want to save the program and what to name it. Let's name it Silly-Sentence (see figure 3.6). By default, IDLE saves your file to your /home/pi folder. Let's use that folder.

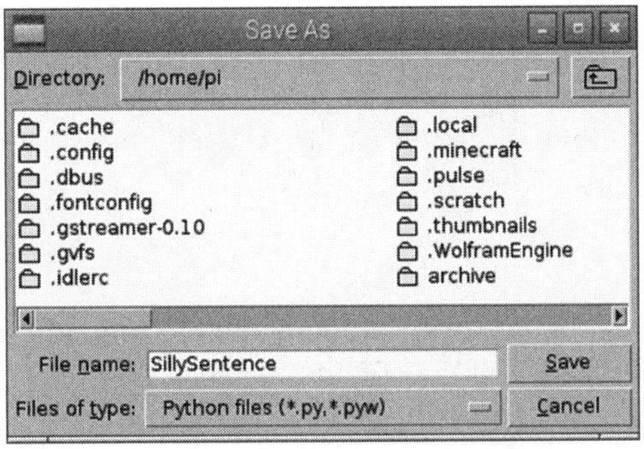

Click Save, and the file will be saved as SillySentence.py (the .py file extension is automatically appended by IDLE). After you save the file, the title at the top of the text editor window will show the filename and file location, as you can see in figure 3.7.

Figure 3.6 Save your file as SillySentence. This stores the file on your Raspberry Pi in your /home/pi folder so you can run the program and make changes to it.

The window title updates after you save. The title changes from Untitled to SillySentence.py.

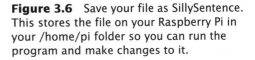

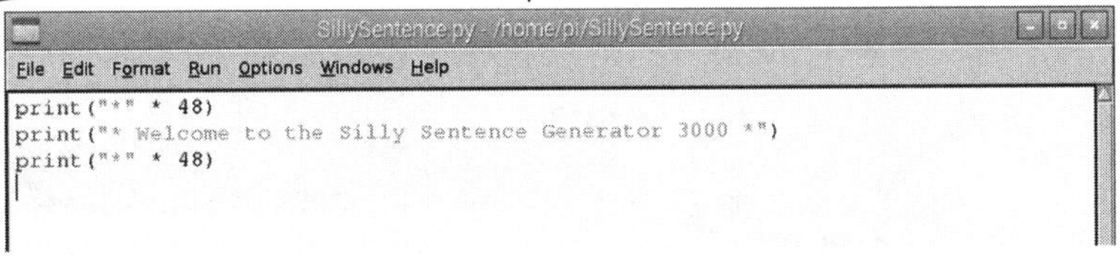

Figure 3.7 The first three lines of your program use the print function to create a welcome message for the Silly Sentence Generator 3000 program.

Guess the output. What do you think you'll get when you run the program?

Let's try it. Click Run > Run Module (or press the keyboard shortcut F5). Python will read each line of your program and execute the commands. The commands print a line of * characters, the welcome message, and another line of * characters to the screen (see figure 3.8).

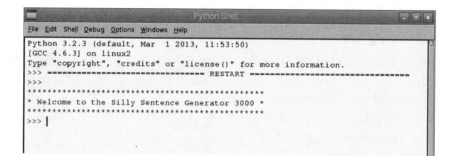

Figure 3.8   Running the program SillySentence.py displays a welcome message on the screen.

Excellent! Now you have a proper welcome message for your game. The next thing you need to do is gather some input from your game player. Some games use button presses, but you'll use the keyboard for this game.

Running programs from the command line

Another way to run a program is from the Raspbian command line. You can access the command line using the Terminal application found under Menu-->Accessories. A window will open with this prompt:

`pi@raspberrypi ~ $`

The terminal shows a prompt, ready for your commands.

To run the Silly Sentence program at the command line, enter

```
pi@raspberrypi ~ $ python3 SillySentence.py
```

The next figure shows this command and the result. Notice that you get the same output at the command line.

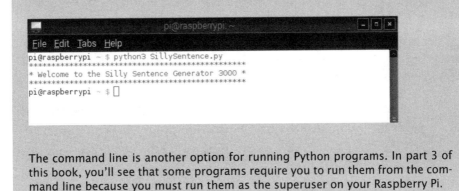

The command line is another option for running Python programs. In part 3 of this book, you'll see that some programs require you to run them from the command line because you must run them as the superuser on your Raspberry Pi.

Adding notes in your code

Imagine a comic book without words. You'd have a hard time understanding what was happening from just the pictures. Maybe you could figure it out if you studied the comic long enough, but words are important for understanding a story. Lines of code can be like a comic book without words: you know something is happening, but you might not be able to tell what without guessing.

That's why programmers invented the idea of adding comments. *Comments* are notes in the code that explain what's happening. They're as much for you as for other people who may read your code. You can use comments to explain why you wrote the program and how parts of the program work.

Using hashtags for comments

You add a comment by starting the line with a hashtag (#) and a space and then typing in your comment text. Let's add comments to the beginning of Silly Sentence Generator 3000 to explain the program's title, its purpose, and who wrote it.

Listing 3.1   *Adding notes to your program*

```
# Title: The Silly Sentence Generator 3000
# Author: Ryan Heitz
# This is an interactive game that creates funny sentences
# based on input from the user
```

Lines beginning with hashtags are comments and are ignored by Python.

```
# Display a welcome message
print("*" * 48)
print("* Welcome to the Silly Sentence Generator 3000 *")
print("*" * 48)
```

Displays a welcome message

Comments are helpful to the humans reading the code. But Python ignores comments when it runs your program. You can check this by saving your program and running it again; you'll see that you get the same result as before.

Easter egg: the Zen of Python

Python has a hidden surprise regarding Python style. In computer programs, these surprises are sometimes called *Easter eggs*. You can find the egg by typing import this in the Python Shell and pressing Enter. A beautiful poem called "The Zen of Python" will appear on your screen.

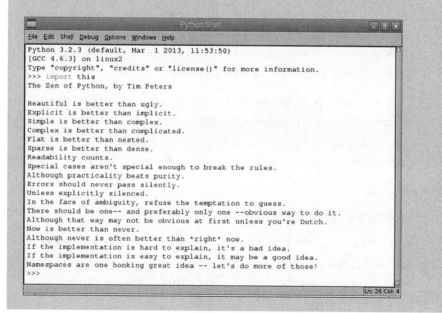

```
Python Shell

File Edit Shell Debug Options Windows Help

Python 3.2.3 (default, Mar  1 2013, 11:53:50)
[GCC 4.6.3] on linux2
Type "copyright", "credits" or "license()" for more information.
>>> import this
The Zen of Python, by Tim Peters

Beautiful is better than ugly.
Explicit is better than implicit.
Simple is better than complex.
Complex is better than complicated.
Flat is better than nested.
Sparse is better than dense.
Readability counts.
Special cases aren't special enough to break the rules.
Although practicality beats purity.
Errors should never pass silently.
Unless explicitly silenced.
In the face of ambiguity, refuse the temptation to guess.
There should be one-- and preferably only one --obvious way to do it.
Although that way may not be obvious at first unless you're Dutch.
Now is better than never.
Although never is often better than *right* now.
If the implementation is hard to explain, it's a bad idea.
If the implementation is easy to explain, it may be a good idea.
Namespaces are one honking great idea -- let's do more of those!
>>>
                                                          Ln: 26 Col: 4
```

The poem emphasizes the philosophy of Python. Some of it talks about advanced topics, but many lines discuss a way of coding that is meant for anyone who uses Python. The seventh line captures a great idea in Python: "Readability counts." It's better to write programs using simple instructions that are easy to read than to try to mash together steps in complicated, long lines of code. Try taking some deep meditational Python breaths before getting back to your project.

Python's creator, Guido van Rossum, said that code is read more often than it's written.[2] Readability is an extremely important part of programming and is a guiding principle in the style of Python programs. Comments are an important way to keep your code easy to read and understand.

Comments are your new friend, and they will make your code easy to read. You'll keep using them to add notes to your code as you collect information from your game player (or user) and create a silly sentence.

Getting and storing information

To gather input from users, you can use the input function. Let's add a line of code in your program that will ask the user for their information and store that information in a variable.

Listing 3.2   *Gathering input from the player*

```
# Title: The Silly Sentence Generator 3000
# Author: Ryan Heitz
# This is an interactive game that creates funny sentences
# based on input from the user

# Display a welcome message
print("*" * 48)
print("* Welcome to the Silly Sentence Generator 3000 *")
print("*" * 48)

# Get the user's name and say hi
player_name = input("Please enter your name: ")
```

Gathers input from the user

---

[2] Check out the resource *PEP 8—the Style Guide for Python*, written by Python's creators: http://legacy.python.org/dev/peps/pep-0008. A wonderful section called "A Foolish Consistency Is the Hobgoblin of Little Minds" talks about the importance of readable code.

When you use the input function, it displays a prompt and awaits the user's reply. After the user enters something and presses Enter, the information is stored in the variable on the left side of the equals sign.

In the IDLE editor, input shows up in purple highlighting, indicating that it's the name of a function in Python. Let's look closely at the input function to see how it works (see figure 3.9).

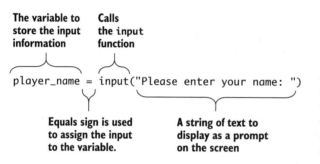

Figure 3.9 The input function displays a prompt to the user. The prompt "Please enter your name: " tells the user what you want them to type in or enter. In this case, you're asking for their name.

On the right side of the equals sign, the input function is called, and you open a set of parentheses. You can give the input function a string that acts as the prompt. This is the message that is displayed on the screen and that says to the user, "Hey you, please type something in"— only more nicely! Make sure your string starts and ends with quotation marks ("").

Run the program by pressing F5 or selecting Run > Run Module. The program displays the welcome message and then an input prompt with a blinking cursor. Python is waiting for your input: it needs you to type something in and press Enter.

On the left side of the equals sign is the name of a variable in which the information will be stored. When you type something in and press Enter, the value of what you typed is stored in the variable player_name as a string.

> **PYTHON 2.X** The input function was previously raw_input in Python 2.X.

Joining strings

As in other apps and websites, you want the user to feel welcome, so let's use their name and give them a proper greeting. A nice message to display on the screen might be

```
"Hello, Ryan! Let's make a silly sentence!"
```

To create a personal feel, you'll create just such a message that joins the user's name with some words welcoming them. You use the plus (+) symbol to join strings:

```
message =  "Hello, " + player_name + "!  Let's make a silly sentence!"
```

If `player_name` equals "Melissa", the message is equal to

```
"Hello, Melissa!  Let's make a silly sentence!"
```

Add this to your program, and display the message to the screen using print.

Listing 3.3   Using + to join strings

```
# Title: The Silly Sentence Generator 3000
# Author: Ryan Heitz
# This is an interactive game that creates funny sentences
# based on input from the user

# Display a welcome message
print("*" * 48)
print("* Welcome to the Silly Sentence Generator 3000 *")
print("*" * 48)

# Get the user's name and say hi
player_name = input("Please enter your name: ")
message = "Hello, " + player_name + "!  Let's make a silly sentence!"
print(message)
```

Joins strings → (annotation pointing to message line)

Displays the message (annotation pointing to print line)

The program has the user input their name, which is stored in the variable `player_name`. On the next line, a message is made by joining strings. The message is displayed on the screen to create a personalized start for the game.

More tools for strings: string methods

To make life easier, Python includes some built-in tools for working with strings. These tools are similar to the functions you saw earlier, but they're called *methods*. Here is an example of a method that capitalizes the first letter of a string:

```
"jOHn".capitalize()
```

The `capitalize` method converts "jOHn" to "John".

Python has a whole set of built-in methods. One method for strings is the `lower` method, which converts a string to all lowercase:

```
"RABBIT".lower()
```

This makes "RABBIT" turn into "rabbit".

Another method, upper, makes all the letters uppercase:

```
"king Arthur".upper()
```

The upper method is great for shouting things. It makes "king Arthur" into "KING ARTHUR".

These methods can save you time[a] and make it easier for you to get things done.

Methods vs. functions

Methods are a type of function, but they use *dot notation*. This means you put a period (.) after the item and then the name of the method. If your item was "John Cleese" and the method you wanted to use was `lower`, you'd write

```
"John Cleese".lower()
```

Parentheses go after the method name. You put in the parentheses any inputs required by the method. You can check the Python documentation online to see what is required.

Some methods don't require any inputs, like the string methods `capitalize`, upper, and lower. But some methods, like count, require inputs. Imagine that you had a set of test answers with T for true and F for false, and you wanted to count the number of true answers. You could use count:

```
>>> TestAnswers = "TTTFFFTTTFTFFFFTTTFFTT"
>>> TestAnswers.count("T")
12
```

There were 12 true answers on the test.

---

[a] You can learn more about the available string methods in the online Python documentation: http://mng.bz/9z49.

Let's go further and add more inputs.

Using more than one input

You have a wonderful start to your game. Now you need to gather multiple inputs from the player. Let's start by asking the player for a noun—the name of a famous person:

```
famous_person = input("Enter the name of a famous person: ")
```

Next, you should get a few more words:

```
adjective1 = input("Enter an adjective: ")
adjective2 = input("Enter another adjective: ")
verb = input("Enter a verb ending in -ING: ")
```

With these multiple inputs, your code should now look like the following listing.

Listing 3.4   Collecting multiple items from the player

```
# Title: The Silly Sentence Generator 3000
# Author: Ryan Heitz
# This is an interactive game that creates funny sentences
# based on input from the user

# Display a welcome message
print("*" * 48)
print("* Welcome to the Silly Sentence Generator 3000 *")
print("*" * 48)

# Get the user's name and say hi
player_name = input("Please enter your name: ")
message = "Hello, " + player_name + "!  Let's make a silly sentence!"
print(message)

# Gather words from the player for our sentences
famous_person = input("Enter the name of a famous person: ")
adjective1 = input("Enter an adjective: ")
adjective2 = input("Enter another adjective: ")
verb = input("Enter a verb ending in -ING: ")
```

Gather words from the player.

You use the input function multiple times to collect a set of words from the user. Each word is stored in a variable on the left side of the equals sign. Try to use names for variables that make sense; it'll be easier to remember what you stored in them later.

Building the sentence

Now let's create the sentence for your Silly Sentence Generator 3000 by joining the words using +:

```
silly_sentence = ("The " + adjective1 + " " + player_name + " is " +
                  verb + " the " + adjective2 + " " + famous_person)
```

Let's take a closer look at this line of code in figure 3.10 to see what's happening.

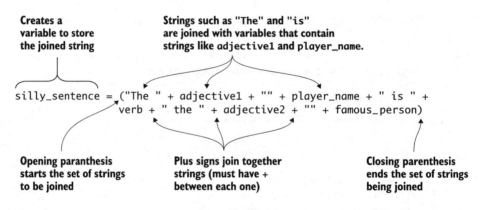

Figure 3.10 silly-sentence is created by joining a set of strings. The strings are a combination of strings you enter with quotation marks around them and strings collected from the game player that are stored in variables. The parentheses are needed because the code is too long to fit on a single line.

On the right side of the equals sign, the parentheses enclose the strings that are being joined to create a sentence. They're joined (or *concatenated*) using the + operator. Because the line is so long, you can use a set of parentheses to break it over two lines. Python recommends limiting all lines to no longer than 79 characters so the code can be easily read. Looking at the left side of the equals sign, you'll see that the resulting string is stored in a variable named silly_sentence.

What's especially awesome is that this code will create a different sentence each time a user enters different words. Because you used variables and the variables are storing the input from the user, it's truly a Silly Sentence Generator!

Troubleshooting

When typing code, it's easy to make mistakes, called *bugs*. Boo to bugs. To track them down and fix them, you *debug* your code. Yay for debugging. You may forget to close a set of quotation marks, you may leave out a parenthesis, or you may misspell a word. Let's look at some common errors you might make and how to fix them.

In the last section, you used the + to join strings and variables that were storing strings. Look at this code, which has an error:

```
silly_sentence = ("The   + adjective1 + " " + player_name + " is " +
                  verb + " the " + adjective2 + " " + famous_person)
```

Do you see the problem? The first string ("The) is missing the closing quotation mark ("The   "). If you were to run this program, Python would output an error (see figure 3.11). Add the closing quotation

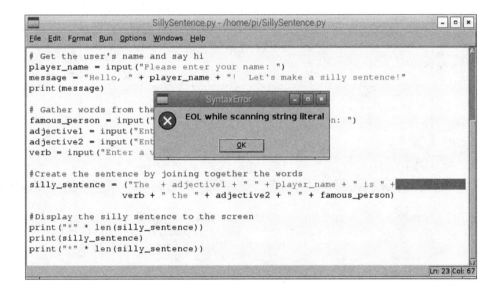

Figure 3.11 If you forget to close a set of quotation marks around a string, you'll receive an error from Python when you try to run your program. Python will highlight in red the line with the error. Check each of the strings to find and fix the error.

mark to the string that is missing it, and then save your program and run it again.

Another common error you might make is to misspell the name of a variable or use different capitalization. Here's the same line of code, but this time there is a misspelled variable and one variable with incorrect capitalization. Can you spot them?

```
silly_sentence = ("The " + adjectve1 + " " + player_name + " is " +
            verb + " the " + adjective2 + " " + Famous_person)
```

The first one is adjectve1, which should be adjective1 (the i is missing). The second error is Famous_person, which should be famous_person (the F should be lowercase). The error you'll see if you run this program is shown in figure 3.12.

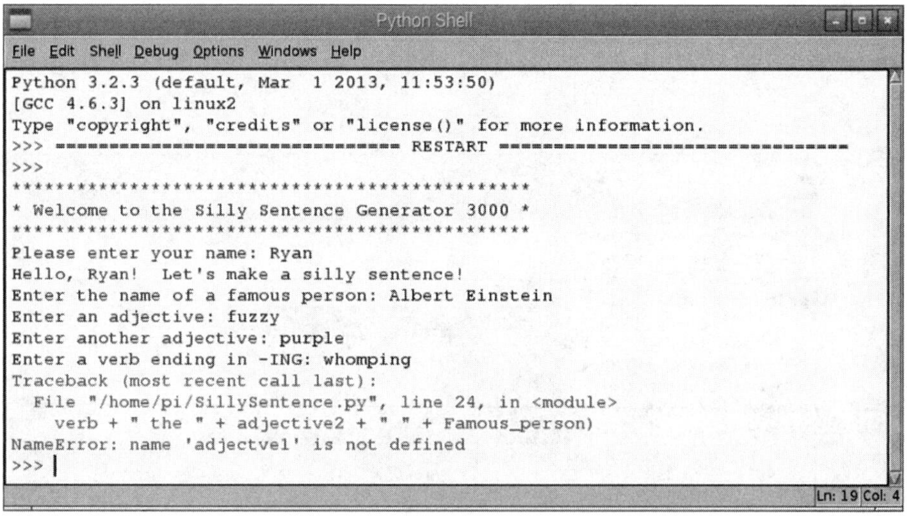

```
Python Shell
File  Edit  Shell  Debug  Options  Windows  Help
Python 3.2.3 (default, Mar  1 2013, 11:53:50)
[GCC 4.6.3] on linux2
Type "copyright", "credits" or "license()" for more information.
>>> ================================ RESTART ================================
>>>
****************************************************
* Welcome to the Silly Sentence Generator 3000 *
****************************************************
Please enter your name: Ryan
Hello, Ryan!  Let's make a silly sentence!
Enter the name of a famous person: Albert Einstein
Enter an adjective: fuzzy
Enter another adjective: purple
Enter a verb ending in -ING: whomping
Traceback (most recent call last):
  File "/home/pi/SillySentence.py", line 24, in <module>
    verb + " the " + adjective2 + " " + Famous_person)
NameError: name 'adjectve1' is not defined
>>> |
                                                          Ln: 19 Col: 4
```

Figure 3.12 A common mistake in programming is to misspell the name of a variable or use incorrect capitalization. The error displayed says there is a problem on line 25 of the program. The type of error is NameError: name 'adjectve1 ' is not defined.

TIP   The spelling and capitalization of a variable must always be the same. If you call a variable `my_number` and then later type `my_nomber` or `My_number`, Python will give you an error.

Correct the error by fixing the spelling of `adjectve1` so it's `adjective1`. After fixing it, you'll still receive an error, but this time because of the capitalization of `Famous_person` (`NameError: name 'Famous_person' is not defined`). Change the capitalization of `Famous_person` to `famous_person`. Once you've made the corrections, save the program and run it again.

You've debugged your program. Superb job!

Completing the program: displaying the silly sentence

You've made your silly sentence, and you want Python to show it to the player. Use the `print` statement to print it out, but like your welcome message, let's add some pizzazz to it!

```
print("*" * 48)
print(silly_sentence)
print("*" * 48)
```

Guess what it does? It prints a row of * characters (asterisks) across the screen 48 times. Then it displays the sentence and prints another row of * symbols 48 times. Try other characters or patterns of characters to see what looks good to you!

It looks pretty good, but you can do a bit better. Test your program by running it, and you'll notice the number of symbols doesn't match the length of the sentence. You've programmed it to display exactly 48 asterisks—no more, no less. Instead, let's update those lines to repeat the symbol to match the length of the silly sentence. You'll use another built-in Python function called `len`, which calculates the length of a string and returns a number telling you the number of characters:

```
print("*" * len(silly_sentence))
print(silly_sentence)
print("*" * len(silly_sentence))
```

```
┌─────────────────────────────────────────────────────────────────────┐
│                  SillySentence.py - /home/pi/SillySentence.py    _ □ x│
├─────────────────────────────────────────────────────────────────────┤
│ File  Edit  Format  Run  Options  Windows  Help                       │
├─────────────────────────────────────────────────────────────────────┤
│ # Title: The Silly Sentence Generator 3000                            │
│ # Author: Ryan Heitz                                                  │
│ # This is an interactive game that creates funny sentences            │
│ # based on input from the user                                        │
│                                                                       │
│ # Display a welcome message                                           │
│ print("*" * 48)                                                       │
│ print("* Welcome to the Silly Sentence Generator 3000 *")             │
│ print("*" * 48)                                                       │
│                                                                       │
│ # Get the user's name and say hi                                      │
│ player_name = input("Please enter your name: ")                       │
│ message = "Hello, " + player_name + "!  Let's make a silly sentence!" │
│ print(message)                                                        │
│                                                                       │
│ # Gather words from the player for our sentences                      │
│ famous_person = input("Enter the name of a famous person: ")          │
│ adjective1 = input("Enter an adjective: ")                            │
│ adjective2 = input("Enter another adjective: ")                       │
│ verb = input("Enter a verb ending in -ING: ")                         │
│                                                                       │
│ #Create the sentence by joining together the words                    │
│ silly_sentence = ("The " + adjective1 + " " + player_name + " is " +  │
│                   verb + " the " + adjective2 + " " + famous_person)  │
│                                                                       │
│ #Display the silly sentence to the screen                             │
│ print("*" * len(silly_sentence))                                      │
│ print(silly_sentence)                                                 │
│ print("*" * len(silly_sentence))                                      │
│                                                                       │
│                                                      Ln: 30 Col: 0    │
└─────────────────────────────────────────────────────────────────────┘
```

Figure 3.13 Silly Sentence Generator 3000 is a fun program that shows how programs can collect information from users, interact with them, and provide a more personal feel.

That's better! Let's look at the code all together (see figure 3.13).

You've completed your program. Let's do some final testing to see what it can do! See figure 3.14 for an example of the game's output.

Fantastic! Feel free to update the code to add more adjectives, verbs, or nouns. You've learned how to get input from a computer user and interact with them by displaying a message to the screen.

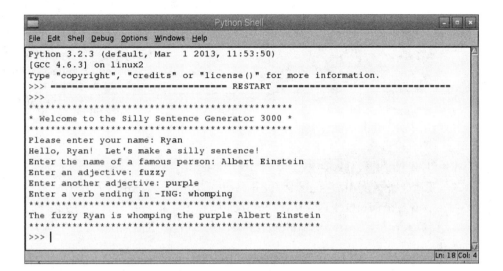

Figure 3.14 The Silly Sentence Generator 3000 makes some absurd sentences based on words you enter.

Fruit Picker Extra: Minecraft Pi

In this Fruit Picker Extra, you'll explore another unique feature of the Pi: it has its own version of Minecraft. Thanks to a collaboration between Mojang, the makers of Minecraft, and the Raspberry Pi Foundation, a free, slimmed-down version of Minecraft is available on the Raspberry Pi. Since September 2014, this version, called Minecraft Pi, is automatically installed with the Raspbian operating system.

What's Minecraft?

Minecraft is a game that takes place in a 3D virtual world made of blocks. At the most basic level, you run around mining (digging blocks by hitting them) and crafting things (combining items in the game to make new items). You can also build things in this virtual world using different types of blocks.

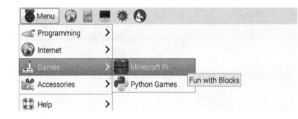

Figure 3.15 Minecraft Pi is a slimmed-down, free version of Minecraft that's based on Minecraft Pocket Edition. It's limited compared to the full version but still oodles of fun!

Launching Minecraft Pi

Look for a Minecraft Pi icon under Menu > Games (see figure 3.15). If you got your Pi before September 2014, see the chapter 6 sidebar "Updating your Pi" to learn how to update Raspbian.

Click the Minecraft Pi icon to open the game. A Minecraft window will open (see figure 3.16). It's a little quirky—you'll see a black window behind the Minecraft window—but this is normal.

Click Start Game to begin to play. Next, click Create New to create a new world. After it's done loading, you'll find yourself in a blocky

Figure 3.16 The Minecraft Pi main screen allows you to start a single-player game or join a multiplayer game. The multiplayer option lets you connect to someone else's world, but you'll need to be on the same network.

Figure 3.17 Each Minecraft world is made of blocks but is different. You might find yourself in a forest or in a desert. The bottom of the screen shows you the items in your inventory. Use the mouse scroll wheel to select different items, or press the numbers 1–9 on your keyboard.

world (see figure 3.17). Each world is different, so you may see trees, water, dirt, or any number of environments.

In Minecraft, you're a player who can walk around using the following controls:

- *W—*Move forward.
- *A—*Move left.
- *S—*Move backward.
- *D—*Move right.
- *Spacebar—*Jump.
- *Mouse movement—*Look around or turn.
- *Escape—*Exit the game.

In addition to the basics, here are some other moves you may need:

- *Double spacebar—*Fly up in the air (double-tap the space bar and then hold it down to fly up). Press the left Shift key to move down. If you're flying, double-tap the spacebar to fall back to the ground.
- *E—*Show the game inventory of blocks and items you can use (it's limited compared to the full version of the game). Drag items you

want to the small squares at the bottom of the screen. Press Escape to hide the inventory screen.

◉ *Scroll wheel or the number 1–9 keys*—Select something from one of your player inventory spots at the bottom of the screen. The item selected is in your hand for you to use.

Once you get the hang of moving around, use the mouse left click to dig or break blocks. Use the mouse right click to place a block or use the tool in your hand. When you're ready to leave, press Escape to exit the game.

> TIP   To exit Minecraft Pi, press Escape > Quit to Title, and then click the X in the corner to close the window.

Python programming interface to Minecraft Pi

Minecraft Pi has a fun inventory of materials and tools—even a sword! What's even better is that there is a Python programming interface for Minecraft Pi. Head over to the Raspberry Pi Foundation website to learn more about how to use Python to interact with Minecraft Pi.

Explore the world, dig an underground base, or build a tree house. What will you do?

Challenges

Try these challenges to see if you can use the input function and strings to create something fun and interactive.

Knight's Tale Creator 3000

In this challenge, try to use what you've learned about input (gathering text) and output (displaying text) to create a Knight's Tale Generator. Here is a story template for you to use:

> *There was a brave knight, [player_name], who was sent on a quest to vanquish the [adjective] evildoer, [famous_person]. Riding on his/her trusty [animal], the brave [player_name] traveled to the faraway land*

of [vacation_place]. [player_name] battled valiantly against [famous_person]'s army using his [sharp_thing] until he defeated them. Emerging victorious, [player_name] exclaimed, "[exclamation]!!!" I claim the land of [vacation_place] in the name of Python.

The words in brackets are meant to be variables that you'll create in your program; you'll need to have the player input those words. Remember to use + to join the strings to create a unique knight's tale, and then print the tale to the screen. Good luck!

Subliminal messages

A *subliminal message* is a hidden message that tries to get people to think of something you want them to think about. Often used in TV commercials, it's a great technique to try with friends and parents to get something you want.[3] In this challenge, try to create a message that is hidden in a large display of characters. The message should be

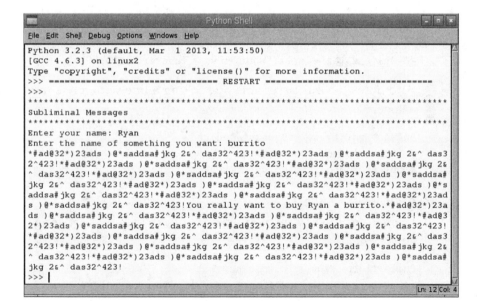

Figure 3.18 The subliminal-message challenge is about hiding a secret message in a bunch of characters on the screen. Can you see the hidden message?

---

[3] Use subliminal messaging at your own risk (send Ryan pizza!). If people know you're trying to manipulate their minds, they may retaliate with subliminal messaging of their own.

constructed by asking for the person's name, the name of something they want, and a pattern of letters, numbers, and symbols. In your program, you should create a message that says, "You really want to buy [player_name] a [thing]", and hide it within a pattern of characters. Figure 3.18 shows an example.

In this example, the hidden message is, "You really want to buy Ryan a burrito." Be sneaky, and see if you can find a way to create and hide a subliminal message!

Summary

In this chapter, you learned how to write interactive programs that get information from a person and provide entertaining responses:

◦ Use the input function to collect text input from a person. Use it with a variable and an equals sign to store the information that a person types in. Here's an example of asking the user to tell you their favorite color and saving it to a variable called favorite_color:

```
favorite_color = input("What is your favorite color?")
```

◦ Add notes to your programs by starting a line with a hashtag (#) and a space:

```
# A comment tells you about the code
# They help you read the code,
# but they are ignored by Python
```

◦ Join strings using +.

◦ Use parentheses when you need to join strings that are longer than a single line:

```
name = input("What is your name?")
favorite_color = input("What is your favorite color?")
message = ("Your name is: " + name + " and your "+
           "favorite color is: " + favorite_color)
```

The game you created uses the same ideas to collect information from users and interact with them in the same way they see every day on websites, mobile apps, and games.

4

Norwegian Blue parrot game: adding logic to programs

In this chapter, you'll learn how to create Python programs that

- *Display an introduction*
- *Collect input from the user*
- *Use* if *statements to respond to users in different ways*
- *Use* while *loops to repeat things over and over*
- *Use Python code libraries to generate random numbers*

Open a popular game, such as Minecraft, or think about a robot, like the Mars rover. Both are computer programs. What do they have in common? They both have the ability to take input and do something with it. What they do depends on the input they're given. In a game, if you press Forward and fall off a ledge, your character falls and dies. If it's your only life, then you're taken to the Game Over screen. Similarly, the Mars rover might be instructed to go to a certain location, but if it detects a large rock in its way, it will stop or attempt to drive around the obstacle.

The logic of how games work or how the rover moves is programmed into them. But how do you create that logic in your programs? You'll learn how by making a simple guessing game about a special parrot, the Norwegian Blue.

Displaying the game introduction

The Norwegian Blue parrot is a fictitious parrot that is the subject of one of the most famous comedy sketches from Monty Python.[1] Your game is about pretending you're visiting a pet shop that has a Norwegian Blue parrot for sale. The shop owner challenges you to guess the age of the parrot (see figure 4.1). If you guess correctly, then you get to take home the parrot for free.

CAN YOU GUESS MY AGE? SQUAWK!

Figure 4.1 The Norwegian Blue parrot has beautiful plumage and makes a great subject for a guessing game.

Each time the game is played, the program selects a different random number between 1 and 20 as the age of the parrot. The game player gets five chances to guess the parrot's age. If the player guesses correctly, the game displays a funny message congratulating them on winning their new parrot. If the player makes a wrong guess, then the program

---

[1] If you haven't seen it, check out this Wikipedia page, which has an audio recording of the comedy sketch: http://en.wikipedia.org/wiki/Dead_Parrot_sketch.

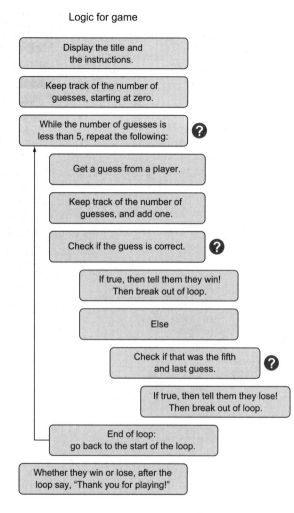

Figure 4.2 The game logic can be expressed in words. The question marks symbolize when the game needs logic to make a decision. This diagram also shows what code needs to be repeated because the player gets five guesses. Each decision has a simple True/False or Yes/No answer.

displays a good-hearted insult, as if it were offended by the player's guess. If the player doesn't guess within five tries, they lose, and the pet shop owner lets them know the parrot's true age (see figure 4.2).

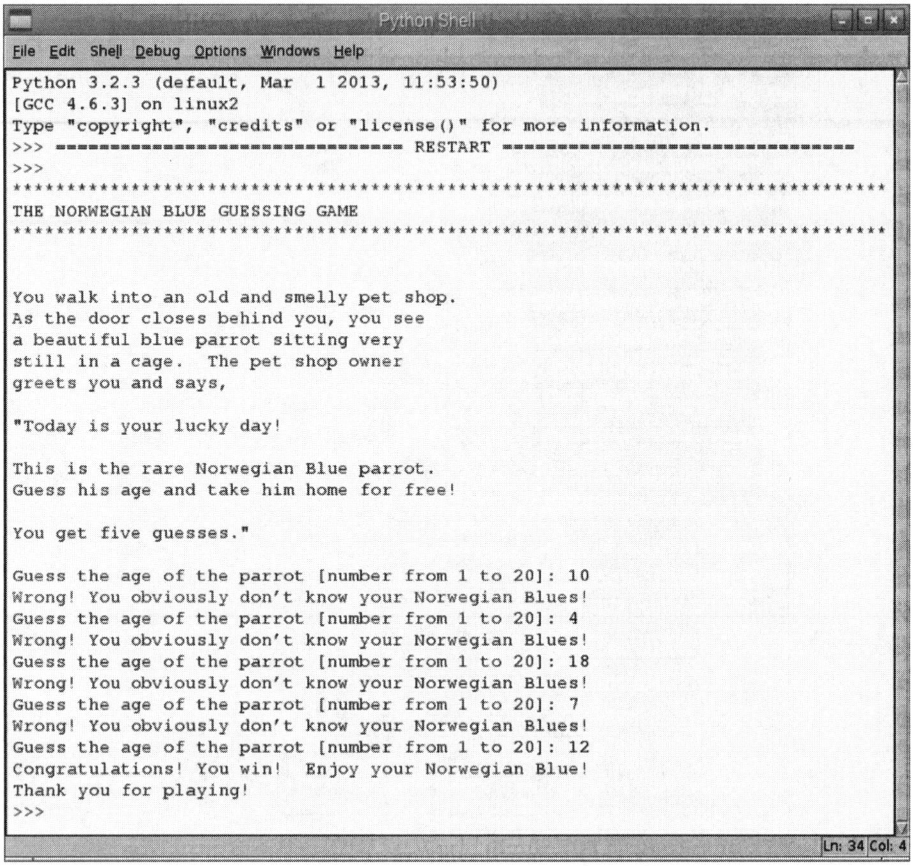

```
Python Shell                                                    _ □ x

File  Edit  Shell  Debug  Options  Windows  Help

Python 3.2.3 (default, Mar  1 2013, 11:53:50)
[GCC 4.6.3] on linux2
Type "copyright", "credits" or "license()" for more information.
>>> ============================== RESTART ==============================
>>>
**********************************************************************
THE NORWEGIAN BLUE GUESSING GAME
**********************************************************************


You walk into an old and smelly pet shop.
As the door closes behind you, you see
a beautiful blue parrot sitting very
still in a cage.  The pet shop owner
greets you and says,

"Today is your lucky day!

This is the rare Norwegian Blue parrot.
Guess his age and take him home for free!

You get five guesses."

Guess the age of the parrot [number from 1 to 20]: 10
Wrong! You obviously don't know your Norwegian Blues!
Guess the age of the parrot [number from 1 to 20]: 4
Wrong! You obviously don't know your Norwegian Blues!
Guess the age of the parrot [number from 1 to 20]: 18
Wrong! You obviously don't know your Norwegian Blues!
Guess the age of the parrot [number from 1 to 20]: 7
Wrong! You obviously don't know your Norwegian Blues!
Guess the age of the parrot [number from 1 to 20]: 12
Congratulations! You win!  Enjoy your Norwegian Blue!
Thank you for playing!
>>>
                                                          Ln: 34 Col: 4
```

Figure 4.3 The Norwegian Blue Guessing Game is about trying to guess the age of a bird in a pet shop.

When this game is completed, you'll be able to play it. The output will look like figure 4.3. In the example, the player guessed four times incorrectly; but on their fifth try, they guessed correctly. They won, and the shop owner gave them the parrot.

Creating the game welcome message and instructions

Let's start by opening IDLE for Python 3 and creating a new program. Open IDLE by clicking the Python 3 icon under Menu > Programming on your Raspberry Pi desktop (see figure 4.4).

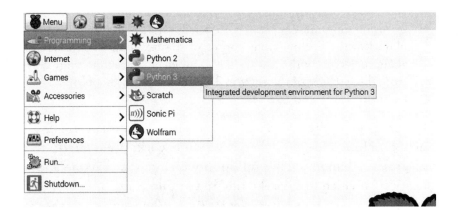

Figure 4.4 Click the Python 3 icon to open IDLE's Python 3 Shell on your Raspberry Pi.

Give your Raspberry Pi a few seconds to open IDLE. You'll see the Python Shell. Press Ctrl-N or File > New Window to open the IDLE text editor. You'll see a blank window, ready for you to start typing in the program.

Let's type in a few comments at the top of the program in the text editor. Start each line with a hash tag (#) and a space.

Listing 4.1   Creating comments at the top of your new program

```
# Title: The Norwegian Blue Parrot Guessing Game
# Author: Ryan Heitz
# The goal of the game is guess the age of a parrot.
# The program generates a random age between 1 and 20.
# The player gets 5 guesses to guess the age correctly.
# If they're correct, they win the parrot!
```

Change the words to whatever you'd like. Comments are notes for you and whoever you might share your program with, so make them read the way you want. Remember to avoid going off the screen with your comments—keep each line pretty short. No more than 79 characters per line is good style; this ensures that your beautiful Python programs fit in the window and don't require the user to scroll or resize the window.

TIP   You can keep track of which line and column your cursor is on by using the cursor-location information (see figure 4.5). It's displayed in the bottom-right corner of the text editor. The letters *Col* stand for column: this shows the number of characters your cursor is from the left side of the screen. The left side is 0, the middle is 40, the right side is 80, and so forth.

The program in the IDLE text editor now contains several lines of comments. Before you go further, save your work: press Ctrl-S to save the program. A window will pop up in which you can name and choose a location in which to save the file. In the File Name text box, type in the name of the file: name it `NorwegianBlue`. When you click the Save button, the file will be saved as NorwegianBlue.py (the .py extension is automatically added by IDLE), and it will be stored on your Pi's SD memory card in the /home/pi folder.[2] Once the program is saved, the text editor displays the location of the file and the filename along the top of the window (see figure 4.5).

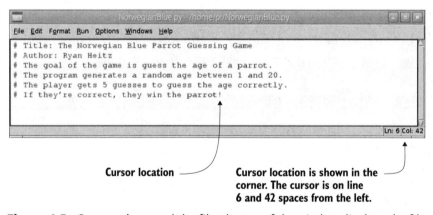

Cursor location ——

Cursor location is shown in the corner. The cursor is on line 6 and 42 spaces from the left.

Figure 4.5 Once you've saved the file, the top of the window displays the filename and the location where the file is stored on your Raspberry Pi (/home/pi/ NorwegianBlue.py). The cursor location is always shown at the bottom right of the window.

---

[2] You can create a new folder in which to store your Python program. You create a folder by opening the Raspbian File Manager application and selecting File > Create New > Folder. Like your shoes, you'll want to remember where you stored your programs so you don't have to spend a lot of time looking for them.

Next you need to let the user know the name of your game and the instructions for playing it. Use Python's built-in print function to write a few lines of code that display a title on the screen.

Listing 4.2 Making the title display on the screen

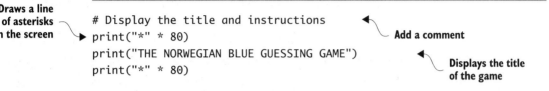

Draws a line of asterisks on the screen

```
# Display the title and instructions
print("*" * 80)
print("THE NORWEGIAN BLUE GUESSING GAME")
print("*" * 80)
```

Add a comment

Displays the title of the game

After they see the title, your game players need to know what to do. You should set the scene for the game and give them instructions. Let's create a variable called instructions and store in it the sentences describing how to play the game. As in Silly Sentence Generator 3000 from chapter 3, this variable will contain a string of characters a few sentences long.

Rather than enter a super-long string all on one line, you want to use a neater way to keep the string on the screen and limit it to not more than 79 characters across (remember, good Python style is to keep text on the screen). In Python, you can use string literals to do this.

> **DEFINITION** *String literals* are strings that can hold multiple lines of text and that appear exactly as you typed them in the text editor when they're displayed on the screen. String literals keep the spaces between lines and characters. To make one, start and end a string with triple double quotes (""") or triple single quotes (''').

Let's add instructions to your program after the program's comments. You'll use a string literal for the instructions and then print it to the display.

Listing 4.3 String literals that hold multiple lines of text

```
instructions = """
You walk into an old and smelly pet shop.
As the door closes behind you, you see
a beautiful blue parrot sitting very
still in a cage. The pet shop owner
```

Start a string literal with """ or '''.

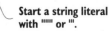

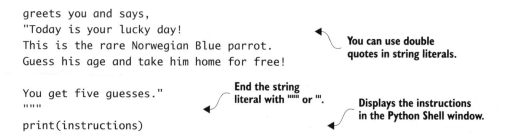

```
greets you and says,
"Today is your lucky day!
This is the rare Norwegian Blue parrot.
Guess his age and take him home for free!

You get five guesses."
"""
print(instructions)
```

You can use double quotes in string literals.

End the string literal with """ or '''.

Displays the instructions in the Python Shell window.

String literals give you the ability to display a string exactly as you type it in the text editor. Think of it as a "what you see is what you get" way of creating strings.

Getting expressive with ASCII art

Before desktop operating systems (OSs) and games had high-end graphics, computers had limited display capabilities. Computer users and programmers invented a new type of art called *ASCII art* that uses text characters to make images.

ASCII is a way of storing characters as binary numbers. For example, the letter *A* is represented as 1000001. Later encodings had many more characters to support more languages, but the name *ASCII art* stuck. ASCII art uses the set of 95 ASCII characters (letters, numbers, and symbols) in cleverly designed patterns to represent images.

Here is an example of ASCII art for your game title that is made by creating a string literal and printing it to the screen. Craft your own ASCII art using a bit of imagination and trial and error:

```
bird_art = """
```

```
###################################################################
                ____
             /  0  \            NORWEGIAN
             |       >
             |UUU) |            BLUE
             |UUU) |
            //UUU) |            GUESSING
            //UUU)  /
           //UU)   /            GAME
          //U)    /
         // -|--|/
       ==// ==W==W====
        //
        /
###################################################################
"""

print(bird_art)
```

Sometimes it helps to blur your eyes a bit to see if the image looks like what you want. Get creative, and think how you can use uppercase and lowercase letters to create effects, like using a *U* to represent feathers on the parrot's wing or *W* for the parrot's claws.

Try these ASCII art sites for fun:

- *www.chris.com/ascii*—A huge collection of ASCII art, sorted by topics
- *http://patorjk.com/software/taag*—A text-to-ASCII art generator (TAAG). You type in words, and it automatically creates ASCII art for you.
- *http://picascii.com*—A tool that converts pictures to ASCII art

See if you can make some ASCII art for the title screen of your game that's even better than this. Have fun with it!

It's always a good idea to test your programs often to catch any mistakes. Test your program now, and see what you get. The title and instructions should display nicely on the screen.

A common mistake you might make when typing in this code would be to forget some of the quotation marks at the beginning or end of the

The closing quotation mark is missing. It should be print ("*" * 80)

Highlighting shows where there is an error in the program.

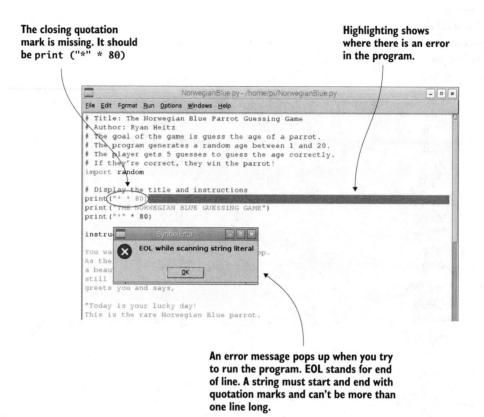

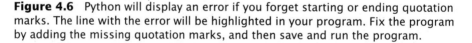

An error message pops up when you try to run the program. EOL stands for end of line. A string must start and end with quotation marks and can't be more than one line long.

Figure 4.6 Python will display an error if you forget starting or ending quotation marks. The line with the error will be highlighted in your program. Fix the program by adding the missing quotation marks, and then save and run the program.

strings. If you do, figure 4.6 shows an example of the error you'll receive in Python.

A similar mistake you might make is forgetting to start your string literals with a triple quotation mark. In this case, Python will give you a syntax error message (see figure 4.7).

It's easy to fix this error by making sure there are triple quotation marks at the beginning and end of the string literal. Use the highlighting shown in the IDLE text editor to figure out which line is causing the problem.

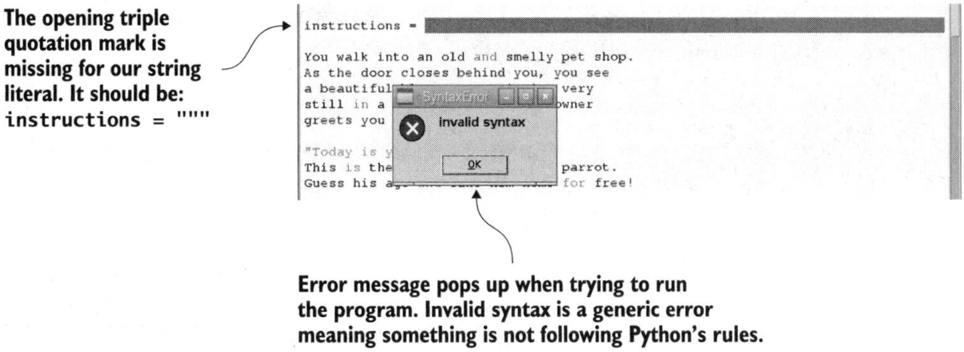

The opening triple quotation mark is missing for our string literal. It should be: instructions = """

instructions =
You walk into an old and smelly pet shop.
As the door closes behind you, you see
a beautiful   very
still in a   owner
greets you

"Today is y
This is the   parrot.
Guess his a   for free!

SyntaxError
invalid syntax
OK

Error message pops up when trying to run the program. Invalid syntax is a generic error meaning something is not following Python's rules.

Figure 4.7   A string literal must start and end with a set of triple quotation marks. If you forget, Python will tell you that you have a syntax error. Add the missing triple quotes to fix the error.

Collecting input from the player

Your game has a proper introduction; now let's start interacting with the player. Games, websites, and apps are all about causing interactions, whether it's to create some fun or help you buy something online. Contrast that with the last movie you watched. Movies don't have any interaction—they're always the same.

A computer program's ability to accept input and respond to that input is special. In text-based games like the one you're creating, this interaction occurs through the keyboard. Players type in answers or make choices, and the game responds.

For this game, you want to ask the game player to guess the age of the parrot. The program knows the parrot's age and checks whether each of the player's guesses matches it. To make this work, you have to give the program the age of the parrot (it's stored in a variable). This gives you something akin to god-like powers as the programmer—as the game's maker, you can decide what the value is. Let's create a variable and set it to a value that you pick. One great thing about being a computer programmer is that only you know the parrot's true age.[3]

---

[3] And anyone else who is reading this book! Later you'll make the game use a random number so even you don't know the parrot's age.

Let's make the parrot old. Create a variable named parrot_age, and assign it a value of 19.

Listing 4.4   Creating an age for the parrot

```
# Making up the parrot's age
# TODO: Make this automatically pick a random number between 1 and 20
parrot_age = 19
```
◄ **Create a variable and store the number 19 in it.**

Notice that in the comments you include a TODO note: this tells you that you have an item to do later.

> **TIP**   Use TODOs in your comments as reminders of areas of your program that are left unfinished or need further improvement. Comments are your friend, and they're there to help you. Use them however you need them!

Next let's get the user's first guess. Use Python's input function (like you did in chapter 2) to collect input from the user and store it in a variable named guess. Give the input function a message that clearly prompts the game player to enter an appropriate value. You don't want them typing in 50 when you're expecting a number between 1 and 20. In this case, you want them to guess a number from 1 to 20.

Listing 4.5   Getting a guess and storing it in a variable

```
# Get a guess from the user
# TODO: Need to make this repeat to give them five guesses
guess =input("Guess the age of the parrot
➥ [Pick a number from 1 to 20]: ")
guess = int(guess)
```

Leave a note to yourself to make this program allow the user to guess five times.

Change the value stored in guess from a string to an integer.

Display a prompt to the user and store whatever they type into a variable called guess.

After gathering input from the user, you need to convert the value from a string (for example, "5") into an integer (simply the integer 5). By default, anything input by the game player is stored as a string (even if what they type in is a number). Figure 4.8 shows this graphically:

```
guess = input("Guess the age of the parrot [Pick a number from 1 to 20]: ")
```

The input function gathers text typed in by the user. It always returns a string, even if you type in a number, like 5.

Creates a new variable (or memory storage box) and names it guess. The string "5" is placed inside it.

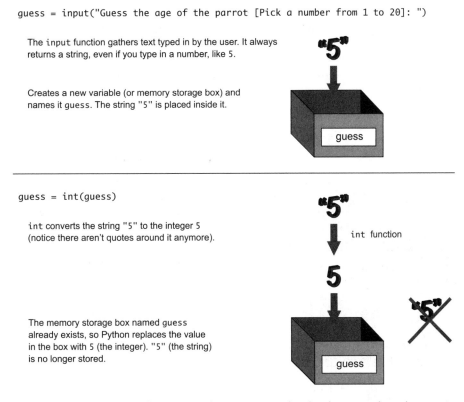

```
guess = int(guess)
```

int converts the string "5" to the integer 5 (notice there aren't quotes around it anymore).

int function

The memory storage box named guess already exists, so Python replaces the value in the box with 5 (the integer). "5" (the string) is no longer stored.

Figure 4.8 The input function gathers text typed in by the user; then the text is stored in a variable as a string data type. You take the value of the variable ("5"), convert it to an integer (5), and store it as the variable.

you're gathering input from the user and then converting it to an integer. The int function takes the value in the guess variable, converts it to an integer, and then stores it back in the guess variable.

One of the perils of working with people is they can type in whatever they want. If someone typed in "one" instead of "1", you'd see an error like this:

```
Traceback (most recent call last):
  File "<pyshell#C>", line 1, in <module>
    int(guess)
ValueError: invalid literal for int() with base 10: 'one'
```

This error is saying you haven't given the int function a valid string that is a number it can convert to an integer.

If you compare the logic you want to create in your code with the program so far, you can see that you've checked off a couple of parts (see figure 4.9).

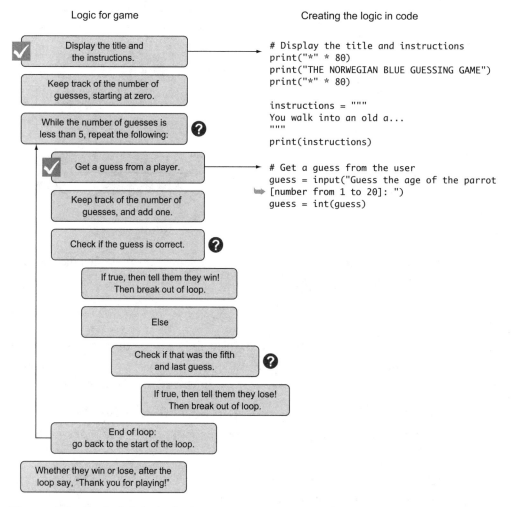

Figure 4.9 On the left is the logic you want to create. On the right is your code. So far, you've welcomed the user and given them the game instructions. You've also added code to collect their guess.

Fabulous! Test the program again to make sure it's working. It'll now ask you to enter a guess. In the next section, you'll see how to test whether the guess is correct.

Using if statements to respond to users in different ways

When you wake up for breakfast, you might walk into the kitchen and look around to see what there is to eat. You use logic to pick your breakfast. If your favorite food is in the kitchen, you'll eat it. For example, if your favorite food is chocolate chip muffins, and there are some in the kitchen, then you'll eat them. If there aren't, you might have a bowl of cereal. In this example, you apply simple logic—you use reasoning to make a decision.

Computer programs use similar logic to interact with users and the world around them. The interactions are based on a set of rules that you (the programmer) write. One of the ways we as programmers can create this logic is with something called the `if` statement.

In your game, you want to test whether the player's guess matches (is equal to) the parrot's age. The logic you want to create in your code is as follows:

- If the player's guess is equal to the parrot's age, congratulate them and give them the Norwegian Blue to take home. End the game.
- Else (if the player's guess isn't equal to the parrot's age) display a mildly insulting message that they're wrong. If it's not their last guess, let them guess again. If it's their last guess, end the game.

Let's use an `if` statement in the program to create the logic you need.

Listing 4.6   Adding logic to the game with an `if` statement

```
# Checking to see if the guess is correct          Check if guess and
if guess == parrot_age:                            parrot_age are equal.
    print("Congratulations! You win!  Enjoy your Norwegian Blue!")
else:
    print("Wrong! You obviously don't know your Norwegian Blues!")
```

If True, this message displays on the screen.

If False, display a different message.

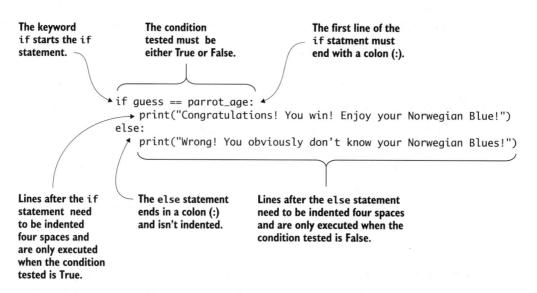

The keyword
if starts the if
statement.

The condition
tested must be
either True or False.

The first line of the
if statment must
end with a colon (:).

```
if guess == parrot_age:
    print("Congratulations! You win! Enjoy your Norwegian Blue!")
else:
    print("Wrong! You obviously don't know your Norwegian Blues!")
```

Lines after the if
statement need
to be indented
four spaces and
are only executed
when the condition
tested is True.

The else statement
ends in a colon (:)
and isn't indented.

Lines after the else statement
need to be indented four spaces
and are only executed when the
condition tested is False.

Figure 4.10 The if statement can control the flow of your programs. This example shows how an if statement can be used to display one message if guess is equal to the parrot's age or a different message if they aren't equal.

Let's take a close look at how the if statement works and how it gives you a way to create logic in your programs (see figure 4.10).

The keyword if is followed by guess == parrot_age, and the line ends with a colon (:). guess == parrot_age is the condition that is being tested. The double equals sign (==) is a special operator that checks the equality of guess and parrot_age.

> TIP   Make sure you don't use a single equals sign when testing equality. Single equals signs are used to assign (or store) values into variables.

If they're equals, the if condition is evaluated as True, and Python will execute the indented commands after it. In this case, you're printing a message:

```
Congratulations! You win!  Enjoy your Norwegian Blue!
```

If the guess is wrong (guess == parrot_age is False), then Python will do the else part. The statements to be executed for the else part are indented four spaces. In this case, if the guess is wrong, the program displays this on the screen:

```
Wrong! You obviously don't know your Norwegian Blues!
```

If you examine the code and think back to the logic you want to create, you can see how the if statement lets you check whether the guess is correct (see figure 4.11).

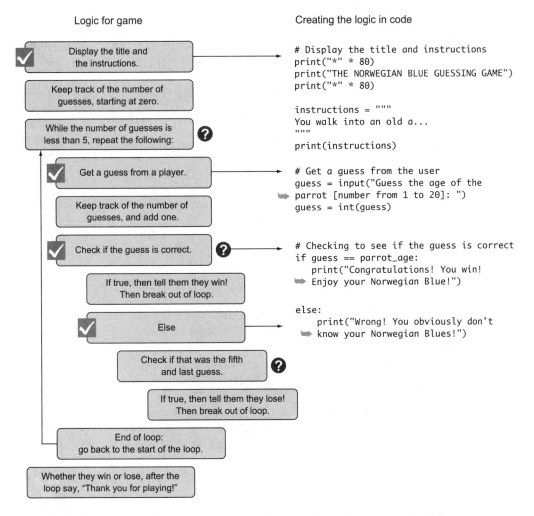

Figure 4.11 The logic you want to create is shown in the code. You use the if statement to check whether the player's guess is correct.

You've seen how the if statement can make a program make a decision. It's an easy way to control programs by checking whether something is True or False.

There is no "Ummm... maybe"

The if statement uses something called *Boolean logic*. In Boolean logic, the answer must always be True or False. There is no "Ummmm... maybe." It's always either True or False.

Boolean logic has its own set of operations for comparisons. These comparisons should be familiar from math class, such as less than (<) and greater than (>). Here is a table of some of the common comparisons you may need to use with your if statements:

Comparison operation	Definition
==	Equal
!=	Not equal
<	Less than
<=	Less than or equal
>	Greater than
>=	Greater than or equal

For this game, you're using the equality comparison to check whether two values are equal to each other.

If you need to reverse the logic in a comparison, you can use the not operator. The not operator changes a True to False or a False to True. If x is True, then not x is False.

Keep these comparison operators in mind. No matter which one you use, Python analyzes the comparison and returns either a True or False answer.

Practicing if statements

Trying more examples of if statements will help you get used to the logic and how to write them. Let's do an example that checks to see whether a secret password is correct. If it is, the code should grant the person access; otherwise it should deny them access.

Listing 4.7 Using an if statement to check a password

```python
password = "cheese"
user_password = input("Enter the password: ")
if user_password == password:
    print("Access granted!")
else:
    print("Access denied!")
```

The equal-to comparison checks if the passwords are equal.

The else part executes if the passwords don't match.

Python's if statements are a powerful tool for creating programs that respond the way you want them to. You now have the ability to make logic so your programs react and respond based on interacting with a user. This is the first step in adding a bit of artificial intelligence to your programs. Fabulous job!

One of the most common mistakes when working with if statements is forgetting to put the colon (:) at the end. Figure 4.12 is an example of an if statement missing the colon.

Errors are common when writing programs. Try to remember to add a colon at the end of your if statements. If Python throws a syntax error box and highlights a space at the end of an if statement, you know what you've done.

A colon (:) is missing at the end of the if statement.

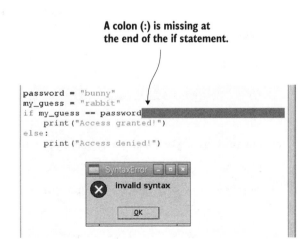

Figure 4.12 A missing colon at the end of an if statement will create a syntax error. Python highlights where the error is located. Add a colon at the end of the line to fix the problem.

Using while loops to repeat things

You have input from the user, but you need a way to let the user repeatedly guess the parrot's age. You might get bored repeating something over and over again, but computers will happily repeat something as many times as you want. The repeating parts of programs are called *loops*.

In the case of your guessing game, you're giving the game player five tries to guess the parrot's age. Python has several types of loops: you'll use the while loop. A while loop repeats over and over until a certain condition or circumstance is no longer true. What it repeats is for you to decide. Each time through the loop, before the program repeats the instructions you gave it, it checks that condition.

Let's look at how you can use a while loop with your if statement to give the user only five guesses. To help, you'll create a variable named number_of_guesses to keep track of the guesses.

Listing 4.8   Using a while loop to repeat instructions

```
number_of_guesses = 0
# While loop will repeat until the number_of_guesses is five
while number_of_guesses < 5:
    # Get a guess from the user
    guess = input("Guess the age of the parrot [number from 1 to 20]: ")
    guess = int(guess)

    # Add one to our guess counter
    number_of_guesses = number_of_guesses + 1

    # Checking to see if the guess is correct
    if guess == parrot_age:
        print("Congratulations! You win!  Enjoy your Norwegian Blue!")
        break
    else:
        print("Wrong! You obviously don't know your Norwegian Blues!")

    # Check to see if this is the fifth guess
    # If True, tell them they lost and reveal the parrot's age
    if number_of_guesses == 5:
        print("You lose!")
        print("The Norwegian Blue is " + str(parrot_age))
```

Start the while loop.

Increase the guess counter by one.

Exit the while loop when the answer is correct.

Check if it's the fifth guess and display the end message if it is.

```
# Stop Indenting (This marks the end of while loop)

print("Thank you for playing!")
```

Notice how you have to rearrange the code in the program a bit. First you start the `while` loop, and then you ask the user to input their guess. Also notice that the code to repeat in the `while` loop is indented (shifted over four spaces). Let's take a closer look at the key elements of the `while` loop (see figure 4.13).

Figure 4.13 Think of the logic you're trying to create, and then translate it into your code. When you need to repeat something, you can use a `while` loop. When you need to check whether something is True or False, you can use an `if` statement.

There is a special thing about a while loop: you must indent all the code that you want the loop to repeat (like you did for if statements). Each line should be indented four spaces from the left (you measure this from where you type the *w* in while). Similarly, you stop indenting code when you want the while loop to end. Code that isn't indented is outside the while loop and is only run after the while loop finishes.

> TIP   The IDLE text editor automatically indents the loop text for you. Indentation is used in Python to group code together.

Notice that you create a variable named number_of_guesses that helps keep track of how many guesses have been made. It starts with a value of 0; after each guess, the value increases by one. When it reaches a value of 5, if the last guess is incorrect, the game should end. As long as the number of guesses is less than five, the program will check the guess entered by the player to see if it's correct. If a guess is correct, the game should congratulate the player, break out of the loop, and end.

A closer look at while loops

while loops run a set of instructions or code repeatedly, but only *while* the condition of the while loop is True. This is useful when you want to have something repeat but need a switch that signifies when it should stop. A very common use of while loops is in games. A loop makes it so the user can play the game again and again until they say they don't want to play anymore.

The while loop in figure 4.14 counts from 0 to 99. Let's look more closely at its parts.

Like an if statement, a while loop has an expression that must be either True or False. The example in figure 4.14 uses count < 100. The line ends with a colon (:), and subsequent lines that belong with the loop should be indented four spaces. In a while loop, you can use any other commands you would normally use in Python. To signify the end of the loop, stop indenting statements. Notice that the print("I finished counting!") isn't indented, so it's only printed once, after the counting is

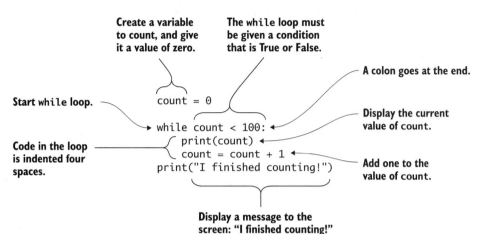

Figure 4.14 You can use a while loop to repeatedly perform a task. Code that is part of the loop is indented four spaces. In this case, this while loop displays the numbers from 0 to 99; when completed, it prints the message, "I finished counting!" Typically, the condition should be such that code in the loop can make it False and thus end the loop.

complete. Python reads the indentation to know when you want your loop to start and end.

> TIP   You can use if statements in while loops. In your game, you use an if statement in a while loop. Sounds fancy, but you want to check whether the player's guess is correct, and you need to do this repeatedly to give them their five guesses.

Using loops can save you from writing a lot of code. They let you order a computer to repeat a series of commands many times. The commands only need to be written once in the loop.

Breaking out of a while loop

Sometimes you need to take a break to eat some food or grab a drink. Python has a break command that lets you break out of a while loop early. In this example, you want your loop to repeat if the player's last guess was incorrect. If the player guesses the parrot's age correctly, then you want to break out of the loop—even though you haven't reached the fifth guess, you want to stop looping because the player got the answer right.

Let's modify the previous example of counting to 99 so it breaks out of the loop when it reaches the number 77. You'll use an `if` statement to do this.

Listing 4.9 *Breaking out of a loop*

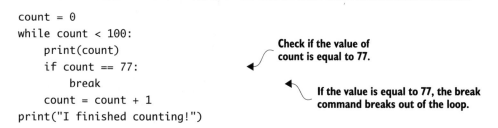

```
count = 0
while count < 100:
    print(count)
    if count == 77:
        break
    count = count + 1
print("I finished counting!")
```

Check if the value of count is equal to 77.

If the value is equal to 77, the break command breaks out of the loop.

Practicing while loops

Let's try another example of using a `while` loop to get the hang of how to write them: a `while` loop that asks your favorite color. See if you can figure out what this program does.

Listing 4.10 *Favorite colors*

```
favorite_color = input("What is your favorite color? ")

while favorite_color != "blue":
    print("Nope, you got it wrong!")
    favorite_color = input("Try again: What is your favorite color? ")

print("Me too! What a coincidence!")
```

This example asks you for your favorite color; if you type in blue, it says, "Me too! What a coincidence!" and ends. If you don't input blue, the program will keep asking you for your favorite color over and over again (until you say it's blue).

Suppose your loop doesn't produce the output you expect. Maybe the guessing game gives you six guesses instead of five. This is when you try to find the problem and fix it—a process also called *troubleshooting*. Fixing errors in `while` loops can be tricky because there may be many commands in the loop. The commands execute quickly, so it can be hard to see what is happening. One troubleshooting technique you can use is to add a `print` function in the loop and use it to print out the value of a variable such as the counter each time through the loop.

In this example, you might add this line in your loop:

```
print(number_of_guesses)
```

This prints out the value stored in the `number_of_guesses` variable each time the code goes through the loop. You can see whether the counter is incrementing as you expect and whether it's starting with the right number.

Using Python code libraries to generate random numbers

You program should be working great. The player gets five guesses, and if they guess the age of the parrot correctly, they win! One exciting part about games is their unpredictability—you never know when you might win or lose. Your next task is to have the program pick a random number for the Norwegian Blue's age. This will make it more thrilling because even you won't know the answer!

If you've ever tried to fix a broken bike, toaster, or car, you probably needed some tools. Bare hands are good for many things, but they probably weren't enough for the job. Similarly, in Python, the standard tools (your bare hands) aren't enough. Sometimes you need to get a toolbox and take out a big hammer, soldering iron, or screwdriver.

Python has toolboxes as well. These toolboxes are also called *modules*. Each toolbox (module) contains different sets of tools (methods) that are useful for specific jobs. Here are some examples of common Python modules:

- `datetime` provides useful tools for getting the current time and date and formatting them nicely.
- `random` gives you the ability to create random numbers.
- `math` supports a larger set of mathematical functions.
- `fileinput` supports reading information from files.

Before you can use these toolboxes, you must first carry them into the room, like you might grab a toolbox of bike tools to fix a bike. To bring in a toolbox, you use the import command:

```
import random
```

You can add this line anywhere in a program before you need to use it to create a random number. Add it right after the comments at the beginning of your game program. This brings in the toolbox at the beginning of the program and makes it easier for other people who read your code to see what toolboxes (or modules) you're using. What the line is actually doing is loading the toolbox into Python's memory so you can use the tools in your program.

Now that you've added the toolbox, you can use a tool called randint to generate a random number between 1 and 20. This code replaces the line parrot_age = 19:

```
parrot_age = random.randint(1,20)
```

Notice that you enter the name of the toolbox, put a period or dot (.), and then put the name of the tool you want to use. This particular tool, randint, needs you to give it two numbers: the lower and upper numbers that the random integer should be between. If you wanted a number between 1 and 100, you'd write

```
parrot_age = random.randint(1,100)
```

With these two lines of code added, the complete code listing should match the code in figure 4.15.

Outstanding! You've made a Norwegian Blue Guessing Game and learned how to create logic in your programs using both if statements and while loops.

Creating the logic in code

Logic for game

```
# Title: The Norwegian Blue Parrot Guessing Game
# Author: Ryan Heitz
# The goal of the game is guess the age of a parrot.
# The program generates a random age between 1 and 20.
# The player gets 5 guesses to guess the age correctly.
# If they're correct, they win the parrot!
import random

# Display the title and instructions
print("*" * 80)
print("THE NORWEGIAN BLUE GUESSING GAME")
print("*" * 80)

instructions = """
You walk into an old and smelly pet shop.
As the door closes behind you, you see
a beautiful blue parrot sitting very
still in a cage.  The pet shop owner
greets you and says,

"Today is your lucky day!
This is the rare Norwegian Blue parrot.
Guess his age and take him home for free!

You get five guesses."
"""

print(instructions)

# Making up the parrot's age
# Automatically picks a random number between 1 and 20
parrot_age = random.randint(1,20)

number_of_guesses = 0

# While loop will repeat until the number_of_guesses is five
while number_of_guesses < 5:

    # Get a guess from the user
    guess = input("Guess the age of the parrot
[number from 1 to 20]: ")
    guess = int(guess)

    # Add one to our guess counter
    number_of_guesses = number_of_guesses + 1

    # Checking to see if the guess is correct
    if guess == parrot_age:
        print("Congratulations! You win!
Enjoy your Norwegian Blue!")
        break
    else:
        print("Wrong! You obviously don't
know your Norwegian Blues!")

    # Check to see if this is the fifth guess
    # If True, tell them they lost and reveal the parrot's age
    if number_of_guesses == 5:
        print("You lose!")
        print("The Norwegian Blue is " + str(parrot_age))
#Stop Indenting (This marks the end of while loop)

print("Thank you for playing!")
```

Logic for game steps:
- ☑ Display the title and the instructions.
- ☑ Keep track of the number of guesses, starting at zero.
- ☑ While the number of guesses is less than 5, repeat the following: ❓
  - ☑ Get a guess from a player.
  - ☑ Keep track of the number of guesses, and add one.
  - ☑ Check if the guess is correct. ❓
    - ☑ If true, then tell them they win! Then break out of loop.
    - ☑ Else
      - ☑ Check if that was the fifth and last guess. ❓
      - ☑ If true, then tell them they lose! Then break out of loop.
  - ☑ End of loop: go back to the start of the loop.
- ☑ Whether they win or lose, after the loop say, "Thank you for playing!"

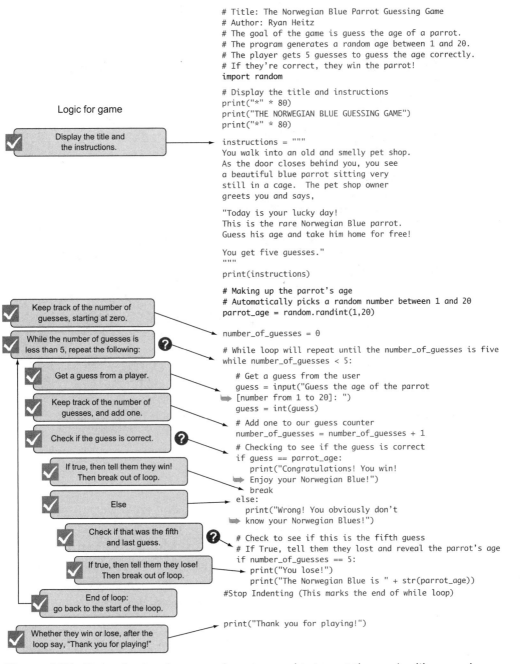

Figure 4.15   To randomly select a number, you need to import the random library and use the randint function to select a random integer between 1 and 20.

Click categories to get different blocks.

Access help documentation.

Each sprite has three tabs for writing programs, loading costumes, and loading sounds.

Cat sprite

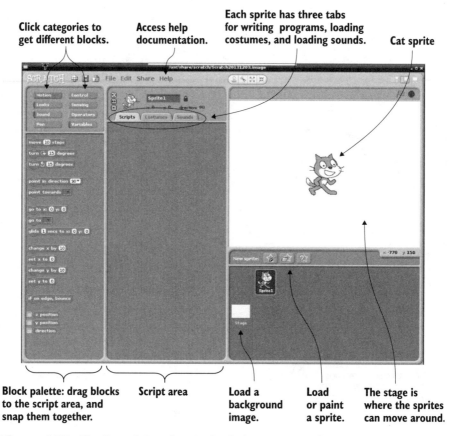

Block palette: drag blocks to the script area, and snap them together.

Script area

Load a background image.

Load or paint a sprite.

The stage is where the sprites can move around.

Figure 4.16 The Scratch interface is divided into an area for sprites to move around and a script area. You can create programs for your sprite by dragging blocks and connecting them in the script area.

Fruit Picker Extra: Scratch

Have you been wondering why your Pi has an icon that is a picture of a cat head? That is the icon for Scratch. Developed by the Massachusetts Institute of Technology (MIT) to help teach programming, Scratch is a simple program you can use to create animations and games on your Raspberry Pi. Scratch is also its own easy-to-use programming language that is based on dragging and dropping program blocks.

Open Scratch by clicking Menu > Programming > Scratch on your Raspbian desktop. When Scratch opens, you'll see a cat in a white square. Figure 4.16 shows an overview of the Scratch interface.

Scratch can do many things, and we won't explain them all. You can learn more about how to create projects with Scratch by clicking Help > Help Pages. The help tells you how to use each block and provides some tutorials.

Do you have an idea for a project? As in Python, you can make programs that ask for input, display messages, generate random numbers, and use if statements and loops. You might add a dog sprite and make it sing like a human when you click it. Or try creating a Scratch version of your favorite classic videogame.

Challenges

Let's play Rock, Paper, Scissors! For this challenge, try to create the classic game.

Rock, Paper, Scissors is played with your hands. Each person simultaneously makes one of three shapes with their hand: the shape of a rock, a piece of paper, or a pair of scissors. If two people make the same shape, it's a tie. The three game shapes interact with each other like this:

- Rock beats scissors.
- Paper beats rock.
- Scissors beats paper.

Let's plan how to attack this challenge. Here are some of the key elements:

- Use a while loop to repeatedly ask the player to choose rock, paper, or scissors.
- Create a list of choices:

    ```
    choices = ["Rock","Paper","Scissors"]
    ```

- Use the random library to have the computer randomly choose among the three choices ("Rock", "Paper", and "Scissors").

○ Remember, randint selects a random integer. You can select and store the random choice in a variable:

```
computer_choice = choices[random.randint(0,2)]
```

○ You can select different items in the list by using a number representing where the item is in the list. This number is called a *list index*. In this case, there are three items in the list. The first item has an index of 0, the second item has an index of 1, and the third item has an index of 2. To display the second item in the list, you write print(choices[1]); the code displays "Paper" on the screen.

○ Use an if statement to compare the player's choice to the computer's choice and let the player know who won.

○ Ask the player if they want to play again. If so, the loop should repeat; if not, the game should end.

See if you can come up with a program! See appendix C for solutions.

Summary

In this chapter, you've learned some new techniques for working with text in Python and a few foundational elements for creating logic in your programs:

○ You can make Python print things just how you want them. String literals allow you to create text that spans multiple lines. Use them to make text appear the same way you typed it in your programs.

○ You can write intelligent code that can make decisions. if statements add logic to programs by responding only if a certain condition is True. You can combine if with else statements to make a program do something different if the condition is False.

○ You don't have to type things repeatedly—you can make Python repeat them for you. while loops can be used to repeat things over and over, as long as a certain condition is True. The break command lets you exit a while loop if you need to.

○ You can use modules (toolboxes) to access more powerful tools to use in your programs. The random module has a tool that generates random integers.

5

Raspi's Cave Adventure

In this chapter, you'll create a game to learn new programming techniques:

- *Drawing flow diagrams to map out complex programs*

- *Using Boolean operators to check input from users*

- *Making code for multiple choices using* if, elif, *and* else *statements*

- *Creating and using your own functions to organize code and avoid repeating code*

- *Nesting* if/else *statements to create games with complex logic*

Like a great book, a game can create an entire imaginary world in your mind. One of the most exciting aspects of games is when you feel like you're inside the game. This doesn't require virtual-reality goggles or high-definition graphics. You can create this immersive feeling even in a completely text-based game by connecting with the player's imagination and creating a world where they can make decisions and determine their own fate. To create games with imaginary worlds, you often have to generate a sense of depth by having the user move from room to room or scene to scene. The game should allow the user to choose their own path and introduce elements of surprise. Finally, you should also have some great descriptions that make the player feel like they're in the room.

In this chapter, you'll create just such a game, based on exploring an underground cavern. Along the way, the player will have to make choices, and if they make a wrong decision, the game is over. If they make the right decision, they'll find untold treasures of gold, rubies, and diamonds!

Project introduction: Raspi's Cave Adventure

The game is set in medieval days: a time of stone castles, knights with swords, and (some say) mythical beasts that breathe fire. Your main character is a young boy named Raspi.[1] One day Raspi is out gathering firewood and gets lost in the forest. He stumbles upon the entrance to a cave. He peers in the entrance and finds that the cave splits into a left tunnel and a right tunnel. He remembers a folk tale his grandmother used to tell of a mysterious cave in this very forest that holds enormous treasures. It's said the treasure is guarded by a ferocious fire-breathing dragon. Raspi can't resist the temptation to explore the cave; although he knows he should turn back, he walks slowly into the dark cavern. This is the start of your next project: Raspi's Cave Adventure.

The game can have many different outcomes, depending on the path the player chooses for Raspi. A short sample of the program's output is shown in figure 5.1.

Figure 5.1 Raspi's Cave Adventure requires the player to make decisions about which way to go. Based on their choices, the player will meet different fates.

---

[1] Because this is your game, feel free to make Raspi a girl or a boy.

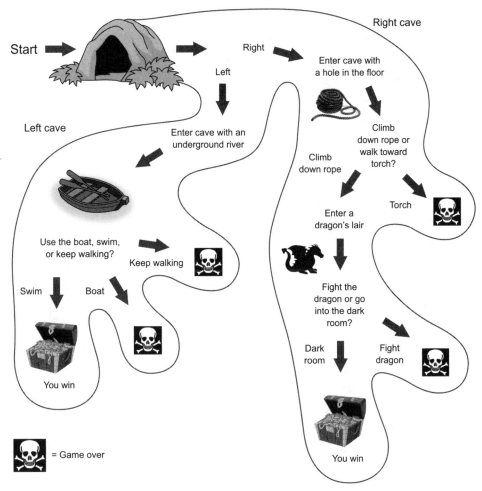

Figure 5.2   This map of the cave system shows that Raspi will need to make many choices. If he makes the wrong ones, it's game over! But if he makes the correct choices, he'll find the legendary treasure!

Let's look at a map of the cave to see where the treasure is and also where the dragon lives! Because you're the game designer and developer, you'll use this as a guide to write the code creating the game logic (see figure 5.2).

Let's examine the different paths and choices Raspi has in the cave and his possible fates. After Raspi enters the entrance to the cave, he can choose to go left or right.

Left cave

If Raspi goes into the left cave, he'll find himself near an underground river. He'll need to decide whether to take a boat down the river, swim down the river, or walk along the side of the river. If Raspi decides to take the boat, he'll soon learn that it has a hole in it, and he'll sink (game over). Should Raspi choose to avoid the river and walk along its edge, he'll quickly become distracted by his thoughts, trip on a rock, and hit his head (game over). If Raspi is adventurous and decides to swim in the river, he'll make it to the other side and find a hidden treasure room filled with riches!

Right cave

If Raspi decides to go into the right cave, he'll need to decide whether to climb down into a hole using a rope or walk toward what appears to be a torch. After walking toward the torch, Raspi will enter a cave full of crystals. The crystal cave sounds promising, but unfortunately a crystal will fall from the ceiling, ending Raspi's life (game over). Alternatively, if Raspi uses the rope and goes down the hole, he'll find himself in the dragon's lair with a final choice: whether to fight the dragon or go into a dark room. If Raspi fights the dragon, the dragon will eat him; but if Raspi heads toward the dark room, he'll discover that it's filled with thousands of gold coins, rubies, and diamonds. Raspi is rich and very much alive!

Hey wait, you need a plan (flow diagrams)

Your goal is to create a program that allows the player to make multiple decisions. You have a map of the cave; now you need to make that map into a diagram that can guide you as you write the code for the game. Much as you did in chapter 2, you'll lay out the logic of the game and then write the code to create that logic.

You can make a map that also functions as a flow diagram. You can visualize the set of decisions and the outcome of each decision. Figure 5.3 shows the map of the cave as a flow diagram.

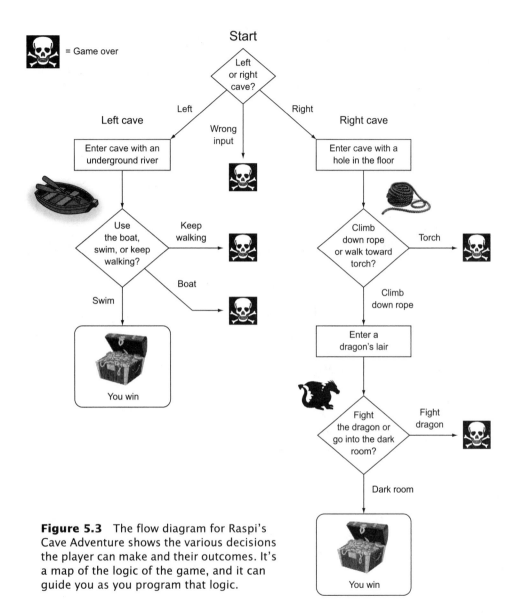

Figure 5.3 The flow diagram for Raspi's Cave Adventure shows the various decisions the player can make and their outcomes. It's a map of the logic of the game, and it can guide you as you program that logic.

Each decision in the diagram is represented by a diamond shape. Inside the diamond is the question at hand. Outside the diamond are arrows representing the possible choices available and the result of each choice. Sometimes choices lead to other choices (other diamonds). Other times, a choice leads to winning the game or game over!

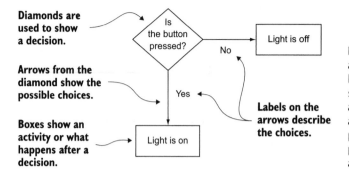

Diamonds are used to show a decision.

Arrows from the diamond show the possible choices.

Boxes show an activity or what happens after a decision.

Labels on the arrows describe the choices.

Figure 5.4 Flow diagrams are ways to visually show the logic of a program. They represent decisions, choices, and activities using diamonds, arrows, and boxes. This example shows a flow diagram for a program that turns on a light if a button is pressed.

Flow diagrams follow a few simple rules (see figure 5.4). You can construct one for any set of decisions, including those used by games, robots, and apps.

A flow diagram is a great way to organize your thoughts and break down complex problems into a series of simple steps. Remember the Python way: simple is better than complex.

Which way should Raspi go? (checking input)

With your diagram in hand, the first bit of logic is the user choosing whether to go left or right. Let's display text to tell the player what they see in the cave, and then prompt them to enter a choice. You prompt the user and collect information with the input function.

Listing 5.1   Choosing the left or right cave

The input function asks the user to enter a choice and stores it in a variable cave_choice.

If False, display text about walking into the right cave.

```
# 1st Choice: Left or Right Cave?
print("You see the cave split into a left and right tunnel")
print("Do you choose to go left or right?")
cave_choice = input("Enter L for left or R for right: ")
if cave_choice == "L":
    # Left cave
    print("You walk into the left cave.")
else:
    # Right cave
    print("You walk into the right cave. The cave starts sloping downward.")
```

Display descriptive text to the screen.

Check if cave_choice is equal to L.

If True, display text about walking into the left cave.

This example uses the input function and then an if/else statement to create the logic you want. The code asks the user to make a choice by typing L or R. The if statement checks whether the user's choice equals "L". If True, then the code displays a message that the player entered the left cave. If their choice isn't equal to L (if that condition is False), then the program moves to the else statement and displays a message that the player entered the right cave.

Handling unexpected input

Users often do unexpected things. As a programmer, one thing you have to be thinking about is what happens if the user does something you don't expect. The person playing your game can type in whatever they want. Let's examine some different possibilities and see what would happen:

- What if the user types in l (lowercase L)?

  If the user types in l, the program checks (evaluates) whether "l" is equal to "L". Because these two strings are different, this condition is False. The program will execute the else statement and display a message that the user entered the right cave.

- What if the user types in left?

  If the user types in left, the program evaluates whether "left" is equal to "L". Because these two strings are different, this condition is False. The program will execute the else statement and display a message that the user entered the right cave.

- What if the user types in something like 44992 or banana just to be silly?

  The program checks whether "44992" or "banana" is equal to "L". Because neither of these equals "L", this condition is False. The program will execute the else statement and display a message that the user entered the right cave.

- What if the user enters anything except L?

  You guessed it; they will see a message that they entered the right cave.

This isn't ideal. Let's improve the code as follows:

1 Permit the user to enter L or l as well as Left or left to enter the left cave.

2 Permit the user to enter R or r as well as Right or right to enter the right cave.

3 Take care of anything else by having the game scold the user for entering the wrong thing and end the game in a humorous way. Maybe a stalactite could fall from the ceiling or a cave spider could bite them!

To create this behavior, you need to introduce the Boolean or operator. You also need to convert the input information to all uppercase letters using Python's upper() method. Finally, to handle all three possible outcomes, you'll use a new if/elif/else statement (see listing 5.2).

Methods

Methods are functions that only work on specific types of Python things, which programmers call *objects*. In this example, .upper() is only able to work on strings, so it's called a *string method*. Methods are called differently than other functions. Methods use *dot notation*, which means you type the name of the thing (object) and then put a dot (.) and the method.

Here are some examples:

- "Left".upper() produces "LEFT".
- "riGHt".lower() makes "right".

Here's the updated code to apply these new ways to avoid errors in user input.

Listing 5.2 Improving the code for the player's choice

The or operator checks if either condition is True.

Gather input from the user. The upper() method converts the user's input to all uppercase.

elif checks if another condition is True.

else handles the case where all if or elif statements are False.

```python
# 1st Choice: Left or Right Cave?
print("You see the cave split into a left and right tunnel")
print("Do you choose to go left or right?")
cave_choice = input("Enter L for left or R for right: ").upper()
if cave_choice == "L" or cave_choice == "LEFT":
    # Left cave
    print("You walk into the left cave.")
elif cave_choice ==  "R" or cave_choice == "RIGHT":
    # Right cave
    print("You walk into the right cave. The cave starts sloping
 downward.")
else:
    # Wrong answer
    print("You seem to have trouble making good decisions!")
```

```
print("Suddenly a stalactite falls from the ceiling and bonks you
⇒ on the head.")
print("Game Over!!!")
```

The upper() method converts the input text to all uppercase. If the user enters LEFT, LeFt, left, or Left, the string is converted to "LEFT".

THE BOOLEAN OR OPERATOR: CHECKING WHETHER EITHER ONE IS TRUE

The or operator checks whether one condition or another condition is True. This gives your code more flexibility—it's able to accept more than one input and still proceed. If either one is True, the if statement is True, and Python does whatever is indented under the if statement.

ELIF IS SHORT FOR ELSE IF

The elif statement is short for else if. It checks whether another condition is True. Think of it like a multiple-choice question. If the user doesn't enter L or Left, the program moves on to the next option. If the user doesn't enter R or r, the program moves to the else statement and drops a stalactite on their head. Game over! Take a closer look at the if/elif/else statement in figure 5.5 to see how to make one.

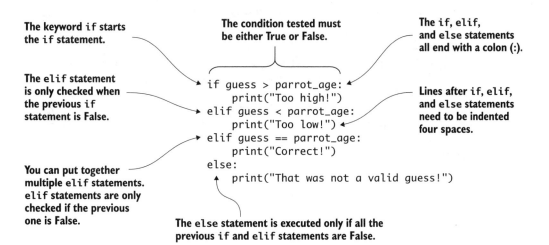

Figure 5.5   The if statement can come in many flavors. This is an if statement with two elifs and an else. It creates logic in the code that can do many different things depending on the user's input. In this case, you're having a player guess the age of a parrot. The program will tell them if their guess is too low, too high, correct, or invalid.

Notice that you can have more than one `elif` statement. In fact, you can have as many as you want. With the `if`/`elif` statement, you can create the logic needed for your cave.

Boolean logic operators: and, or, and not

Python has a complete set of Boolean operators that you can use to make expressions:

- or is used when you want the expression to be True if either of the operands is True.
- and is used when you want the expression to be True only if both operands are True.
- not is used to change an operand from True to False or False to True.

Let's look at a few examples using these operators.

and OPERATOR

Pretend you want to create a program giving you access to the system only if your name *and* password are *both* correct. You could write this using the and operator:

```
if name == "Ryan" and password == "PiTaster":
    print("The name and password are correct!")
    print("Access granted! Welcome!")
else:
    print("Access denied!")
```

Only if both name and password are correct will the program grant you access. Try creating one yourself!

or OPERATOR

Next let's imagine you want to create a program giving someone a free pizza if their age is under 20 *or* they have a coupon. Let's assume you have a variable age that is the age of the person and another variable coupon that already holds a value of True or False. Using the or operator, you create this logic like so:

```
if age < 20 or coupon == True:
    print("You get 1 FREE PIZZA")
else:
    print("No free pizza for you!")
```

If *either* is True, the user gets a pizza. If *both* are True, they get a pizza. If *neither* is True, then no free pizza!

not OPERATOR

Finally, let's say you have a variable `is_absent` that is equal to True or False. `is_absent` tells you whether a student is present or absent. To print a "Welcome to school!" message if a student is *not* absent, you can use the not operator:

```
if not is_absent:
    print("Welcome to school!")
else:
    print("Please return to school as soon as possible. School misses
        you!")
```

The not operator changes a variable or statement that is True to False and a False one to True. It helps you create conditional statements (`if` statements) that make more sense when you read the code. As you can see, the Boolean operators give you many different options for creating logical expressions.

Time to go spelunking (a fancy word for exploring caves) with your new knowledge of `if`/`elif`/`else` and Boolean operators!

Turning flow diagrams into code

For now, let's concentrate on building a program for the left cave. The player has entered the left cave and needs to make their next choice. Looking at the map and the flow diagram, the next thing your player encounters is an underground stream. The player sees a boat and must choose among three options:

- Keep walking along the side of the river.
- Climb into the boat.
- Swim in the river.

Each of these will be an `if` or `elif` statement in your code. But wait! There's a fourth possible outcome—that they don't enter one of the

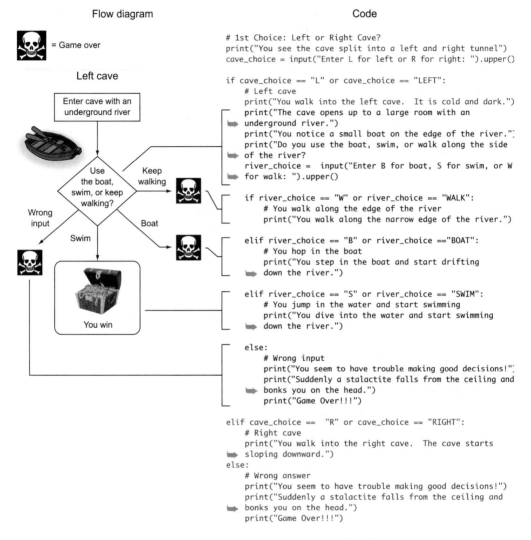

Flow diagram

Code

```python
# 1st Choice: Left or Right Cave?
print("You see the cave split into a left and right tunnel")
cave_choice = input("Enter L for left or R for right: ").upper()

if cave_choice == "L" or cave_choice == "LEFT":
    # Left cave
    print("You walk into the left cave.  It is cold and dark.")
    print("The cave opens up to a large room with an
    underground river.")
    print("You notice a small boat on the edge of the river.")
    print("Do you use the boat, swim, or walk along the side
    of the river?
    river_choice =  input("Enter B for boat, S for swim, or W
    for walk: ").upper()

    if river_choice == "W" or river_choice == "WALK":
        # You walk along the edge of the river
        print("You walk along the narrow edge of the river.")

    elif river_choice == "B" or river_choice =="BOAT":
        # You hop in the boat
        print("You step in the boat and start drifting
        down the river.")

    elif river_choice == "S" or river_choice == "SWIM":
        # You jump in the water and start swimming
        print("You dive into the water and start swimming
        down the river.")

    else:
        # Wrong input
        print("You seem to have trouble making good decisions!")
        print("Suddenly a stalactite falls from the ceiling and
        bonks you on the head.")
        print("Game Over!!!")

elif cave_choice ==  "R" or cave_choice == "RIGHT":
    # Right cave
    print("You walk into the right cave.  The cave starts
    sloping downward.")
else:
    # Wrong answer
    print("You seem to have trouble making good decisions!")
    print("Suddenly a stalactite falls from the ceiling and
    bonks you on the head.")
    print("Game Over!!!")
```

Figure 5.6 The left cave has a stream inside it, and the user has three choices of what to do next. In the code, you create an `if` statement followed by two `elif` statements to cover each of the options. The `else` statement is used to control what happens if the user inputs something other than one of the three choices.

three choices. You'll make this the `else` statement. Figure 5.6 shows the left cave flow diagram and the code that creates the logic you need.

You display a few words about what Raspi sees inside the left cave. You ask the user to choose what to do next. Then, once you've gathered this input, you evaluate that information and respond accordingly. Notice that each of the possible choices appears in an `if` or `elif` statement and is indented under the left cave `if` statement. The user has to choose whether to keep walking (W), use the boat (B), or swim (S). For each case, the program should display information as you designed it in your flow diagram.

This isn't only for caves

Boolean operators and if/elif/else statements are great for when your program needs multiple options or choices. Let's see if you can create a program that has four possible options: A, B, C, and none of the above. The following snippet shows an example of using `elif` statements to create these four possible outcomes. In this example, you're pretending that a person is on a game show and picking a door with a prize behind it:

```
print("Welcome to the Pi Game Show!")
print("There are three doors with prizes behind them: A, B, and C.")
door = input("Select a door by typing A, B, or C").upper()

#Logic for door selection
if door == "A":
    print("You've won a new car!")
elif door == "B":
    print("You've won a new boat!")
elif door == "C":
    print("You've won a trip around the world!")
else:
    print("Uh oh! You didn't follow directions!")
    print("Game Over!!!")

print("Thank you for playing.")
```

Creating programs with choices based on logic is a powerful programming skill. By combining simple choices, you can create complex programs.

Excellent work! You've created the left cave logic for Raspi's Cave Adventure. Let's add more decisions.

Simplify! Making your own functions

Yikes! The code for the left cave is starting to look long (and kind of ugly and hard to read), and you still have the right cave to go. How can you simplify your program?

The answer is *functions*. This time you aren't going to call a built-in Python function—you'll make your own!

Functions are like mini programs that you can create to organize or simplify your code. When you have long programs, you can take logical chunks of code (code that all goes together) and put them in a function. Once you've created (or defined) a function, you can call (or use) the function in your code.

> NOTE   Functions should always be defined at the top of a program. The definition of a function must come before it's called (or used).

Let's see how this works by making (or defining) two functions for the left cave.

Listing 5.3   Creating functions for the left cave

```
# Displays a description of the left cave and their choices
def left_cave():
    print("You walk into the left cave. It is cold and dark.")
    print("The cave opens up to a large room with an underground
➥ river.")
    print("You notice a small boat on the edge of the river.")
    print("Do you use the boat, swim, or walk along the side of the
➥ river?")
    river_choice =  input("Enter B for boat, S for swim, or W for walk:
➥ ").upper()
    return river_choice
```

def defines a function. After def is the name of the function and a colon.

The function's instructions (what it does) must be indented four spaces under the def statement.

Gather input from the user and store it in a variable river_choice.

Send information to the program when the function is called.

```
# Displays text describing the player's demise and a game over message
def wrong_answer():
    print("You seem to have trouble making good decisions!")
    print("Suddenly a stalactite falls from the ceiling and bonks you
➥ on the head.")
    print("Game Over!!!")
```

Display text for ending the game if the wrong input is given.

Before moving on, let's look more closely at how you can make your own functions (see figure 5.7). You've created two functions: left_cave and wrong_answer. Let's rewrite the cave program to use (or call) those

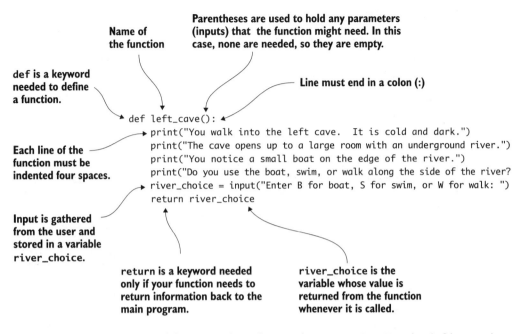

Name of the function

Parentheses are used to hold any parameters (inputs) that the function might need. In this case, none are needed, so they are empty.

def is a keyword needed to define a function.

Line must end in a colon (:)

```
def left_cave():
    print("You walk into the left cave.  It is cold and dark.")
    print("The cave opens up to a large room with an underground river.")
    print("You notice a small boat on the edge of the river.")
    print("Do you use the boat, swim, or walk along the side of the river?")
    river_choice = input("Enter B for boat, S for swim, or W for walk: ")
    return river_choice
```

Each line of the function must be indented four spaces.

Input is gathered from the user and stored in a variable river_choice.

return is a keyword needed only if your function needs to return information back to the main program.

river_choice is the variable whose value is returned from the function whenever it is called.

Figure 5.7 Functions simplify your code and can reduce repetition. Use the def keyword to create a new function, and indent the function code under it. If you need a function to return a value, include a return statement in the function.

functions. Whenever you call a function, it's as if the code is all in that spot, but you've hidden it.

Some functions need to return something; others don't. You might have a function that prints something to the screen or plays a sound; those types of functions don't need to return anything. In the example code, the wrong_answer() function is a good example. You call the function like this:

```
wrong_answer()
```

Alternatively, when a function returns something and you want to store that information, you write it like this:

```
choice = left_cave()
```

This takes whatever information is returned by calling the `left_cave()` function and stores it in a variable named choice. Listing 5.4 shows how you can simplify the program by calling the `left_cave()` and `wrong_answer()` functions.

Listing 5.4   Using the new functions to simplify your code

```
# 1st Choice: Left or Right Cave?
print("You see the cave split into a left and right tunnel")
cave_choice = input("Enter L for left or R for right: ").upper()
if cave_choice == "L" or cave_choice == "LEFT":
    # Left cave
    choice = left_cave()                        ← left_cave() calls your
                                                  function. The information
                                                  returned by the function is
                                                  stored in the variable choice.
    if choice == "W" or choice == "WALK":
        # You walk along the edge of the river
        print("You walk along the narrow edge of the river.")
    elif choice == "B" or choice == "BOAT":
        # You hop in the boat
        print("You step in the boat and start drifting down the
        ➥ river.")
    elif river_choice == "S" or river_choice == "SWIM":
        # You jump in the water and start swimming
        print("You dive into the water and start swimming down the
        ➥ river.")
    else:                                       The statements that displayed game-
        # Wrong answer                          over information are replaced by
        wrong_answer()                          calling the wrong_answer() function.
    elif cave_choice == "R" or cave_choice == "RIGHT":
    # Right cave
    print("You walk into the right cave. The cave starts sloping
    ➥ downward.")
    print("You come to a room with a large hole in the floor.")
else:
    # Wrong answer                              wrong_answer() can be called
    wrong_answer()                              as many times as needed.
```

Amazing! The resulting code is easier to read, and you avoid repeating code. Notice that you call the `wrong_answer()` function twice. This saves you from having to write those lines of code twice. Also, if you ever want to change the ending for a wrong answer, you only have to change it in one place (in the function). In addition to helping you organize your code, the ability to reuse functions is one of their key features. You haven't changed the functionality of your program, but by using functions, you've made it easier to read and simplified it.

> DEFINITION   *Refactoring* is a programming technique that focuses on reorganizing and simplifying code in a program. Refactoring makes the code easier to read and less complex.

Passing parameters: functions with inputs

You've looked at two different functions so far: one that doesn't return anything and one that does. Functions have another feature in addition to their ability to return something—they can also receive information. Think of it as input to a function. In programming speak, you say that the function has a *parameter* or *parameters*. Let's see how this works with an example. Suppose you have a guessing game, and you want to create a function that prints a message to the screen telling the player if their guess is too high, too low, or spot on:

```
def check_guess(guess, answer):
    # Compare the guess to the answer
    if guess == answer:
        print("You're correct!")
        is_correct = True
    elif guess < answer:
        print("Too low!")
        is_correct = False
    elif guess > answer:
        print("Too high!")
        is_correct = False
    else:
        print("Invalid guess")
        is_correct = False
    # Return True or False depending upon if the guess is correct
    return is_correct
```

In this case, the def statement has the name of your function (check_guess). Inside the parentheses are two parameters separated by a comma: these are inputs to the function. The first input or parameter is guess. This is a guess the user has made. The second is answer, which is the number the user is trying to guess. The function then compares guess and answer and tells the user whether they were right or guessed too low or too high. The great thing about this function is that it can work with any numeric guess and answer (1 to 10, 1 to 1,000,000). By using parameters, you make the code more flexible.

The best way to learn about functions is by doing. Here are some functions dos:

- Use a simple name that describes the function.
- Put comments about your function inside the function.
- Return values when you want to use them in a program.

And here are some functions don'ts:

- Use complex names.
- Create functions with only one line of code.
- Forget to put a colon at the end of the `def` statement.
- Forget to call the function in your main program.

Fantastic programming! You're achieving the Zen of Python by simplifying your code with functions.

Finishing the left cave

To complete the left cave, you need to add code for Raspi's choices: walking along the river's edge, taking the boat, or swimming (the winning ending). You'll make each of these choices its own function to help organize your code and keep it uncluttered. You can call the functions in the main program, shown in the next listing.

Listing 5.5   Calling functions for each of the left cave choices

```
# Main Program
# 1st Choice: Left or Right Cave?
    choice = left_or_right()
    if choice == "L" or choice == "LEFT":
        # You walk into the Left cave
        choice = left_cave()
        if choice == "W" or choice == "WALK":
            # You walk along the edge of the river... game over
            walk()
        elif choice == "B" or choice == "BOAT":
            # You get in the boat... game over
            boat()
```

Call a function called walk() that displays messages about Raspi's fate. See the source code for examples of the functions.

Call a function named boat() that tells you what happens if Raspi gets in the boat.

```
    elif choice == "S" or choice == "SWIM":
        # You jump in the water and start swimming... Raspi wins
        swim()
    else:
        # Wrong answer
        wrong_answer()
elif choice == "R" or choice == "RIGHT":
    # You walk in the right cave
else:
    # Wrong answer
    wrong_answer()
```

You guessed it: call the swim() function that contains the code for Raspi swimming.

See the source code for chapter 5 for examples of each of these functions (walk(), boat(), and swim()). They follow a structure similar to the left_cave() and wrong_answer() functions. Feel free to make up your own descriptions of what happens to Raspi or change the outcomes to how you would like them.

Exploring the right cave

In this game, Raspi has two initial cave choices: left or right. Programming the right cave is similar to the left cave. Once again, you'll use the map and flow diagram as your guides. Let's add the logic for the right cave, which starts with the user finding a hole in the ground (see figure 5.8).

The right cave uses logic similar to that of the left cave. You'll use if, elif, and else statements to handle all the possible choices. As with the left cave, notice that you indent the if/elif/else statements under the other if statements to create the logic you desire. *Nesting* is the name given to indenting one set of if statements inside another. The technique of nesting if statements is useful when you have logic that you want executed only if a prior condition is True. In this case, you only want to give the user the choice of fighting the dragon if they have already decided to climb down into the hole using the rope. The logic now matches the flow diagram for the game.

Let's take another look at nesting using a different example. Imagine that you want to write a program that displays a secret message after you

Flow diagram

Code

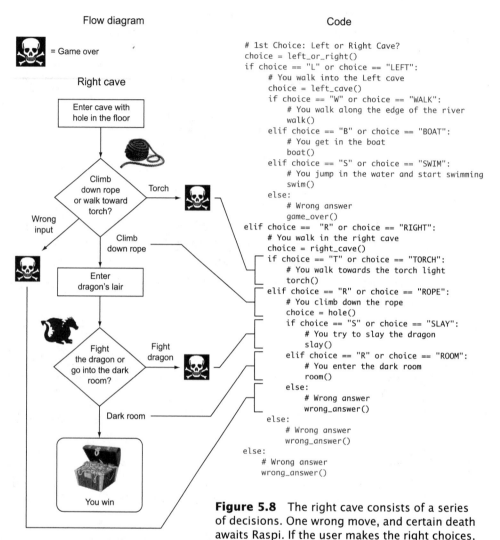

```
# 1st Choice: Left or Right Cave?
choice = left_or_right()
if choice == "L" or choice == "LEFT":
    # You walk into the Left cave
    choice = left_cave()
    if choice == "W" or choice == "WALK":
        # You walk along the edge of the river
        walk()
    elif choice == "B" or choice == "BOAT":
        # You get in the boat
        boat()
    elif choice == "S" or choice == "SWIM":
        # You jump in the water and start swimming
        swim()
    else:
        # Wrong answer
        game_over()
elif choice ==  "R" or choice == "RIGHT":
    # You walk in the right cave
    choice = right_cave()
    if choice == "T" or choice == "TORCH":
        # You walk towards the torch light
        torch()
    elif choice == "R" or choice == "ROPE":
        # You climb down the rope
        choice = hole()
        if choice == "S" or choice == "SLAY":
            # You try to slay the dragon
            slay()
        elif choice == "R" or choice == "ROOM":
            # You enter the dark room
            room()
        else:
            # Wrong answer
            wrong_answer()
    else:
        # Wrong answer
        wrong_answer()
else:
    # Wrong answer
    wrong_answer()
```

Figure 5.8 The right cave consists of a series of decisions. One wrong move, and certain death awaits Raspi. If the user makes the right choices, Raspi will find the treasure. The code uses if/elif/else statements and functions. See the code files for chapter 5 for examples of the functions.

enter the correct secret name ("Tim") and correct secret password ("raspberrypi"). If the secret name is guessed correctly, then the user has to guess the secret password (see figure 5.9) to see the secret message.

If the password is correct, the user has to enter their favorite color. If the color is red, the program will display the secret message (see figure 5.9).

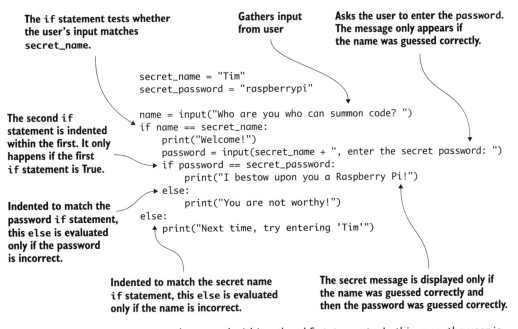

The `if` statement tests whether the user's input matches `secret_name`.

Gathers input from user

Asks the user to enter the `password`. The message only appears if the name was guessed correctly.

The second `if` statement is indented within the first. It only happens if the first `if` statement is True.

Indented to match the password `if` statement, this `else` is evaluated only if the password is incorrect.

```
secret_name = "Tim"
secret_password = "raspberrypi"

name = input("Who are you who can summon code? ")
if name == secret_name:
    print("Welcome!")
    password = input(secret_name + ", enter the secret password: ")
    if password == secret_password:
        print("I bestow upon you a Raspberry Pi!")
    else:
        print("You are not worthy!")
else:
    print("Next time, try entering 'Tim'")
```

Indented to match the secret name `if` statement, this `else` is evaluated only if the name is incorrect.

The secret message is displayed only if the name was guessed correctly and then the password was guessed correctly.

Figure 5.9 `if` statements can be nested within other `if` statements. In this case, the user is only prompted to guess the password if they first guess the secret name correctly. Python uses indentation to figure out what statements belong together and which `if` statements are nested within other ones.

Troubleshooting

A common error when creating `if`/`elif`/`else` statements is forgetting to include the colon at the end of the `if` statement. In this case, when you run the program, you'll see a message pop up in IDLE saying "invalid syntax", and the Python text editor will highlight the end of the line in red (see figure 5.10). You can fix this error by adding a colon at the end of the `if` statement.

Another error is forgetting to put a colon at the end of the `def` statement when creating your own function. In this case, you'll see the same

```
# 1st choice: Left or Right Cave?
choice = left_or_right()
if choice == "L" or choice == "LEFT"
    # You walk into the Left cave
    choice = left_cave()
```

Figure 5.10 Highlighting by IDLE when there is invalid syntax due to a missing colon (:) at the end of an `if` statement

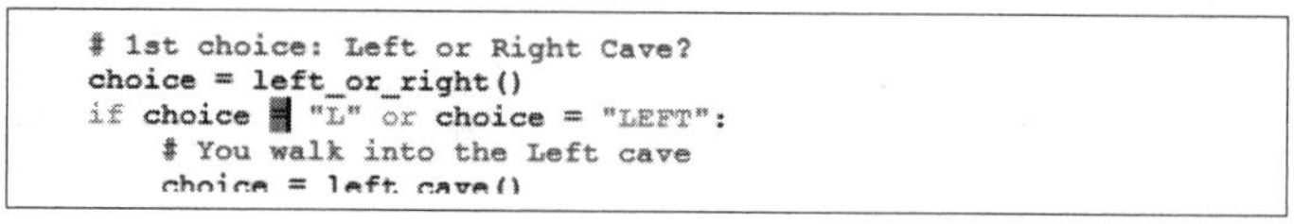

```
# 1st choice: Left or Right Cave?
choice = left_or_right()
if choice █ "L" or choice = "LEFT":
    # You walk into the Left cave
    choice = left_cave()
```

Figure 5.11 Highlighting by IDLE when there is only one equals sign

message ("invalid syntax") and red highlighting at the end of the line missing the colon.

Finally, a third common error is using a single equals sign (=) when comparing two values in an `if` statement. Python will highlight the offending equals sign as shown in figure 5.11. Remember, you need to use a double equals sign (==) to test the equality of two values. This returns True (if the values are equal) or False (if they're not). The single equals sign (=) is used to assign a value to a variable, like x = 7.

Fix this error by replacing the single equals sign (=) with double equals signs (==). As you can see, small problems can cause programs to have errors. If you get really stuck, ask a friend to look at your code, or post your code to a forum and ask for help. You'd be surprised by how helpful other programmers are!

Fruit Picker Extra: playing video

In addition to displaying text, as in the cave adventure game, the Raspberry Pi can output sound, show images, and play videos. Let's see how you can play a video on your Raspberry Pi. See appendix A to learn how to set up your Raspberry Pi's Wi-Fi adapter. There are many different video player apps you can use on your Pi, but a great one is OMXPlayer. It was created specifically for the Raspberry Pi and comes preinstalled with Raspbian. We'll explore the audio (or sound) playback capabilities of OMXPlayer in chapter 8.

To show off your Pi's capability, let's play a high-definition demo video from a movie called *Big Buck Bunny*.[2] It's about 10 seconds long and has no sound. Open LXTerminal, and at the prompt enter

```
omxplayer /opt/vc/src/hello_pi/hello_video/test.h264
```

---

[2] This is a video developed to test video playback and display.

You should see a silent video play for about 10 seconds. Enjoy it! If you know of a video file on the web (.mp4 or H.264 format), OMX-Player can play it as long as you have a good internet connection. For example, to watch the trailer for another video called *Sintel*, make sure you're connected to the internet and type in

```
omxplayer https://download.blender.org/durian/trailer/sintel_trailer-
720p.mp4
```

Why not open movies in a web browser? Because OMXPlayer can play them much more easily—it was designed to use the Pi's graphics processing unit (GPU) for playing videos. This means most of your Pi's resources are available to do other things.

Live streaming: exploring from your Pi

You've been pretending to explore a cave. Now let's see if you can use your Pi to explore the ocean or space by live-streaming videos from web cameras. You can turn your Pi into a way to see the sharks and sea turtles by connecting to a live stream coming from the Monterey Bay Aquarium in California. Or maybe you want to see what the Earth looks like from the International Space Station right now.

With a few steps, you can configure your Pi to play live-streaming videos. First you need a small utility called Livestreamer that can take live video streams and output them for OMXPlayer to play, just like your test video. Let's make sure you have the Python package installer. Make sure you have a working internet connection, and then open the Raspbian command line using the Linux Terminal (select Menu-->Accessories-->Terminal), and install the software:

```
sudo apt-get install python-pip
```

After it finishes, install Livestreamer:

```
sudo pip install livestreamer
```

Now you need a link to a live stream of video. Livestreamer will work with many of the most popular live-streaming sites. For this example, you'll use Ustream, but you could also use YouTube Live and many others. If you go to the Ustream website,[3] you can find links to live-stream videos. Here are few different ones found on the site:

- Watch sharks and turtles at the Monterey Bay Aquarium: www.ustream.tv/channel/9600798.

- Check out the sea life living in the kelp beds at the Monterey Bay Aquarium: www.ustream.tv/channel/9948292.

- See the view from the International Space Station (it may appear dark if the Space Station is in the shadow of the Earth): www.ustream.tv/channel/9408562.

> NOTE These links may change over time. You can get the latest links by searching the Ustream website.

You'll need an internet connection for the next couple steps. You need to figure out the video resolutions available. For the Monterey Bay Aquarium live stream, enter

```
livestreamer http://www.ustream.tv/channel/9600798
```

A few messages appear, and at the bottom are the supported stream resolution(s). For this live stream, you should see a response that says

```
Available streams: mobile_240p (worst, best)
```

This means `mobile_240p` is the only available resolution for the video stream. This is a low-resolution stream, but it's still fun to watch. Tell Livestreamer to send the video to OMXPlayer with this command:

```
livestreamer http://www.ustream.tv/channel/9600798 mobile_240p --
➥ player omxplayer --fifo
```

Great! You should see a video open after a few seconds. It will be low resolution, but sit back and watch the amazing live view of fish, including sharks (see figure 5.12)!

> NOTE Notice that you have to type in `mobile_240p`. You'll type in one of the supported resolutions from the previous step.

---

[3] Explore the UStream live-streaming videos at www.ustream.tv/explore/all.

Figure 5.12 The Pi's monitor is a live stream from an aquarium. Check out that shark! By using Livestreamer and OMXPlayer, you can stream live video from exotic places, like water holes in Africa and the International Space Station.

Press Ctrl-C to stop Livestreamer and OMXPlayer. Enjoy exploring the world from your Pi!

Challenges

These challenges focus on making improvements to the Raspi's Cave Adventure game. If you get stuck, check appendix C for hints and solutions.

Introducing dramatic pauses

This first challenge is to include some drama in the game by adding two-second pauses between the print and input statements throughout Raspi's Cave Adventure. This will create anticipation about what will happen next and give the player more time to read the messages before responding.

Here are some clues for how to accomplish this. First, Python has a built-in `time` module that provides some useful functions for working with time. At the top of the program, you need to add an `import` statement to use this built-in Python toolbox:

```
import time
```

Once you've imported the `time` module, you can call the `sleep` function in the program:

```
time.sleep(1)
```

This example code makes the program pause for 1 second. It takes the form `time.sleep(seconds)`, where `seconds` is the number of seconds you want the program to pause. For example, if you wanted to display a message, wait 3 seconds, and then display another message, you'd write

```
print("It was a dark, dark cave...")
time.sleep(3)
print("Suddenly, a dragon appears out of the shadows.")
```

Go ahead and try to create some drama. If you get stuck, check appendix C or review the code files.

Random demise

Games are always more interesting when they have an element of unpredictability. Try to add some surprises to your game by improving the `wrong_answer` function to randomly display a message from a set of possible ways your player could meet their demise. Here are a couple of examples to get you started:

- Raspi sees a rock on the ground and picks it up. He feels a sharp pinch and drops the rock. He realizes it wasn't a rock but a poisonous spider as he collapses to the ground.

- Standing in the cave, Raspi sees a small rabbit approach. Raspi gets a bad feeling about this rabbit. Suddenly the rabbit attacks him, biting his neck.

Hint: Create if/elif/else statements with different endings, and then use the random module to select from the possible endings.

Play again?

Modify the game so that no matter how it ends, the user is always given the option to play again. Hint: Create a variable play_again that is initially set to "Y". You'll also need to add a while loop to your game that will make the game repeat as long as play_again is equal to "Y".

Scream!

If you have a set of headphones or your Pi is connected to a TV with built-in speakers via an HDMI cable, you should be able to play sounds and hear them. Let's look at a simple program to play a sound on your Pi:

```
import os
scream_file_path =
➡ "/usr/share/scratch/Media/Sounds/Human/Scream-male2.mp3"
os.system("omxplayer " + scream_file_path)
```

Test the program, and you should hear a scream. Now see how you can integrate the scream or other sounds into Raspi's Cave Adventure. You can find more sounds on your Pi in the Scratch folder: /usr/share/scratch/Media/Sounds/.

> NOTE OMXPlayer works best with sound files ending in .mp3. Only some files ending in .wav will work. We'll talk more about sound files and the OMXPlayer in chapter 8.

See appendix C if you need help solving these! Good luck!

Summary

You can create engaging programs by putting logic and instructions together into more complex programs:

- Use flow diagrams to map out complex programs before you begin.
- Create flexible programs that can handle unexpected input through the use of Boolean operators.

- Build programs with multiple choices and outcomes using `if`, `elif`, and `else` statements. Chain together multiple `elif` statements to create as many choices as you need.

- When you have logic embedded within logic, nest `if` statements to create decisions that depend on prior choices or conditions.

- Organize your code and cut down on repetition by defining your own functions and then calling them in your program.

## Part 3

Pi and Python projects

L et's face it. Pressing buttons, playing sounds, and lighting up cool colored lights is fun! Now you get to use your Pi to make those things happen. You're going to create interactive projects that use your Pi's input and output pins. This makes your Pi a special type of computer that doesn't just show images on the screen, but that can control and sense the world around it. This realm is called *physical computing*. Robotics is physical computing, but think about all the creative possibilities such as making interactive art, creating smart rooms that sense your presence and turn on a light or play music, or producing something that can alert you if it's about to start raining or your pet is drinking water.

In part 3, you'll build projects that can interact with the world using Python and your Raspberry Pi. The projects will require some additional parts that you can purchase individually or as part of a kit, such as the CanaKit Ultimate Kit, Adafruit Starter Kit, or MCM Electronics Starter Kit:

- Raspberry Pi 2 Model B including SD card, power supply, cables, keyboard, and monitor
- Breadboard
- GPIO ribbon cable for the Model B+ (40 pin)
- GPIO breakout board
- 1 dozen jumper wires, male to male

- 1 red LED (light-emitting diode)
- 1 green LED
- 1 blue LED
- 3 push buttons
- 3 resistors, 10K ohm
- 3 resistors, 180 ohm (or between 100 and 300 ohms)
- Headphones or powered computer speakers

You start in chapter 6 by setting up your Pi with an electronics bread-board, building a simple circuit, and controlling an LED (light) using Python. You'll learn how to communicate through your Pi's output pins to make something happen. In this case, you'll make an LED light up. Chapter 7 dives into creating an interactive guessing game that uses lights to respond to a player's input, letting them know with differ-ent colors whether their answer is right or wrong. In chapter 8, you'll learn how to listen to your Pi's input pins by wiring up a push button on your breadboard and then responding when it's pushed; and you'll complete a project that combines buttons and sounds to make your own DJ Raspi sound mixer. By the end, the goal is for you to have the knowledge, skills, and confidence to think up and create your own Pi and Python projects.

6

Blinky Pi

In this chapter, you'll be learning about

- *Giving your Pi the ability to talk to the outside world through connectors to anything*

- *Programming the world outside your Pi with simple electric/electronic circuits*

- *Programming the connectors using your previous Python knowledge to make light patterns*

Setting robots in motion, creating smart homes with sensors, and designing an interactive electronic art exhibit sound like vastly different topics, but they're all things you can do with your Raspberry Pi. In each case, the Pi can act as the brain and interact with the world by doing things like

- Checking a robot's sensors and controlling its motors

- Sensing a room's occupants and adjusting the thermostat or lights

- Controlling sound, motion, and light as part of an art display

In this chapter, you'll set up your Pi to control small light bulbs called *light-emitting diodes (LEDs)*. You'll make the LEDs blink using Python. To do this, you'll need to learn a bit about how to build electrical circuits on breadboards. If you've never heard of a breadboard, don't worry! It's a small board with lots of holes in it to make it easier to build electrical circuits. You'll also be using short wires (called *jumper wires*) to connect certain holes. You'll even learn how to add resistors that keep your LEDs from burning out. See figure 6.1 for a list of parts and what they look like; gather the parts, and let's get started!

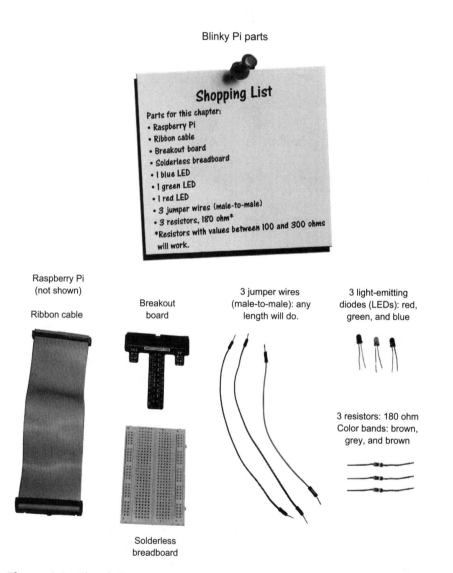

Blinky Pi parts

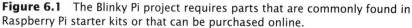

Figure 6.1 The Blinky Pi project requires parts that are commonly found in Raspberry Pi starter kits or that can be purchased online.

Setting up your Pi for physical computing

Your Pi is unique compared to most computers because of its input and output pins, called *GPIO* pins. Let's learn how to work with those pins.

> **DEFINITION** GPIO stands for *general purpose input and output*. These are the pins on your Raspberry Pi that allow it to sense and control things around it.

GPIO pins

The Raspberry Pi 2 Model B and Raspberry Pi 1 Model B+ have 40 pins located on the edge of the board, arranged in 2 rows of 20 pins each (see figure 6.2). Most of the pins on a Pi are used for input and output, so they're often referred to as the Pi's GPIO pins.

> **WARNING** This project is written for Raspberry Pi 2 Model B. Earlier models of the Raspberry Pi have only 26 pins. See appendix B for information about the differences from the more modern Pi boards. To complete this project with a Raspberry Pi 1 Model B, you may select different pins to light up your LEDs.

Side view

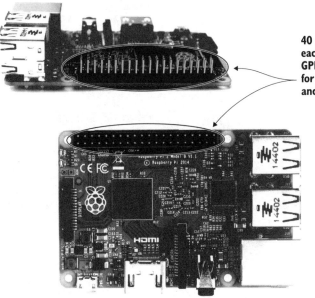

40 pins in 2 rows of 20 pins each. 26 of the pins are called GPIO pins because they're used for general purpose input and output.

Top view

Figure 6.2 The Raspberry Pi 2 Model B has a set of pins arranged along the edge and corner of the Pi board.

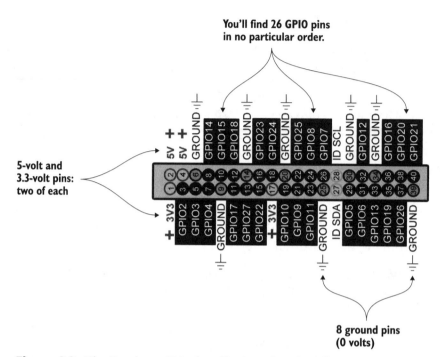

Figure 6.3 The Raspberry Pi B+ has 40 pins. They do different things: some provide 5 volts or 3.3 volts, some are ground pins (0 volts), and many of them are input and output pins that you can program.

Because all the pins look identical, you need a key or diagram to tell you what each one does. Figure 6.3 shows the pins labeled.

Physical pins vs. GPIO pin numbers

In this book, we'll always refer to the GPIO pin numbers, *not* the physical pin locations. The physical pins are numbered from 1 to 40 (shown in the circles in figure 6.3). The GPIO pin numbers go from 1 to 26, and those numbers don't match the physical pin numbers. For example, GPIO 24 corresponds to physical pin 18. By always using the GPIO numbering, it will be easier to wire your circuits and create programs.

Wow, that's a lot of pins! Some pins are for power and are labeled either 3V3 or 5V. These produce 3.3 volts or 5 volts, respectively.

There are also 8 ground pins and 26 GPIO pins[1] — 26 pins, just like there are 26 letters in the alphabet.

The GPIO pins support sending out electrical signals (output) or listening for electrical signals from sensors (input). In your body, your brain can send signals to your hand to smack yourself on the forehead (try it!) — this is just like the output from a Pi. Signals are sent out of your Pi to make something happen in the world.

The opposite of output is input. When someone pokes you, your body can detect that poke using nerves in your body. An electrical signal (input) is sent to your brain so you know you've been poked. This is like the way your Pi can be used to detect input or actions in the world.

You'll learn how to output signals in this chapter and chapter 7. Chapter 8 will cover detecting input from the world, such as detecting when a button has been pressed.

Let's get ready to connect some wires! But wait: connecting an LED directly to the GPIO pins on the board of your Raspberry Pi isn't feasible, because the pins are so close together. What can you do? You need more space to build circuits.

Breaking out the GPIO pins to a breadboard

To give you room, you'll move the GPIO pins over to a breadboard. This is called *breaking them out*. To do this, you need a ribbon cable, breakout board, and solderless breadboard (see figure 6.4).

Breadboards make it simple to prototype circuits. Like a park might provide large, open fields that make it easy to play sports, think of a breadboard as a nice, open electrical playing field where you can play with electrical parts. The breadboard allows you to plug wires and components into small holes. You can build and rebuild circuits on a breadboard with little effort.

---

[1] Oddly, you'll notice that the GPIO pins are numbered from 2 to 27. Pins 0 and 1 are used for communicating with other computer chips using a super-special protocol called I2C. These are labeled ID SDA and ID SCL in figure 6.3.

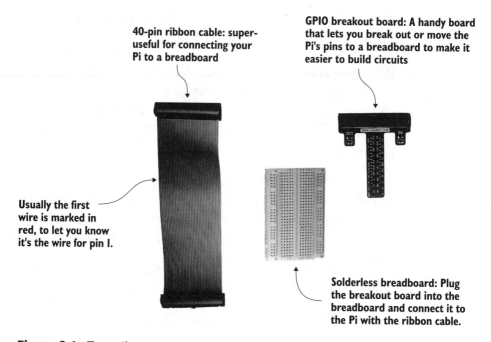

40-pin ribbon cable: super-useful for connecting your Pi to a breadboard

GPIO breakout board: A handy board that lets you break out or move the Pi's pins to a breadboard to make it easier to build circuits

Usually the first wire is marked in red, to let you know it's the wire for pin I.

Solderless breadboard: Plug the breakout board into the breadboard and connect it to the Pi with the ribbon cable.

Figure 6.4   To easily create projects using your Pi's GPIO pins, you can connect the Pi to a breadboard using a ribbon cable and breakout board. The parts shown are examples of the ones commonly found in many Raspberry Pi kits.

Find your breakout board, and insert it into the top of the breadboard. Line up the pins before you push it down *hard* (see figure 6.5). Your particular breakout board may look a little different, but they all act the same. With the breakout board in place, it'll be easier to build circuits with your GPIO pins.

Connect one end of the ribbon cable to the Pi's GPIO pins; line it up carefully before you push it down. Then connect the other end of the cable to the breakout board on your breadboard (see figure 6.6). A breakout board has a notch in it so the ribbon cable will only fit one way.

WARNING   Ribbon cables usually have a stripe that marks the first wire. White or grey ribbon cables often use a red stripe. Black ribbon cables often have a white stripe. These mark the first wire on the cable. Make sure this first wire is connected toward the edge of your Pi's board and away from the USB ports.

Breadboards usually have numbers along the side to label each row. Columns are labeled with letters (a–j).

Insert the breakout board into the breadboard. Make sure to line it up carefully.

The holes allow you to connect components so you can build circuits easily.

Insert it along the top edge of your breadboard. Not sure which way is up? Look at the numbering on the board.

There are two groups of letters. On the left are letters a–e, and on the right are letters f–j.

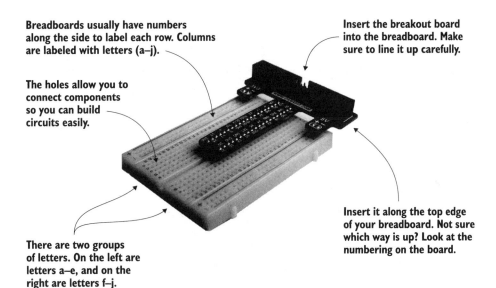

Figure 6.5 Carefully line up the breakout board, and then press it firmly into the breadboard. The two rows of pins on the breakout board should straddle the center gap.

⚠ Caution: Be careful not to bend any pins. Line up the connector and pins before pressing them together.

Connect the ribbon cable to the breakout board.

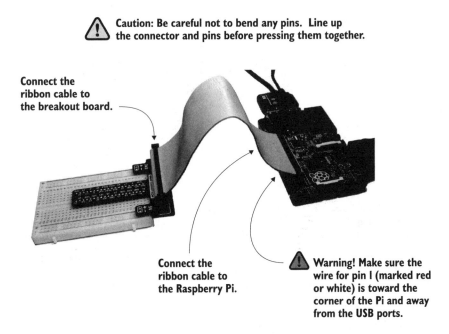

Connect the ribbon cable to the Raspberry Pi.

⚠ Warning! Make sure the wire for pin I (marked red or white) is toward the corner of the Pi and away from the USB ports.

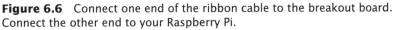

Figure 6.6 Connect one end of the ribbon cable to the breakout board. Connect the other end to your Raspberry Pi.

Breadboard basics

A breadboard[2] has a set of internal connections that you can't see. But if you had X-ray vision, you'd see that certain holes are connected. Let's look at the connections in your breadboard (see figure 6.7).

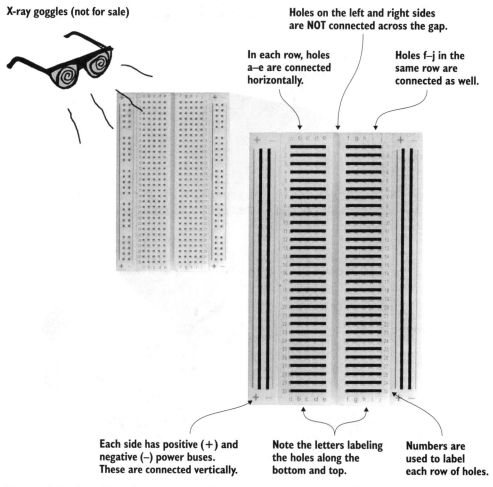

X-ray goggles (not for sale)

Holes on the left and right sides are NOT connected across the gap.

In each row, holes a–e are connected horizontally.

Holes f–j in the same row are connected as well.

Each side has positive (+) and negative (−) power buses. These are connected vertically.

Note the letters labeling the holes along the bottom and top.

Numbers are used to label each row of holes.

Figure 6.7 Breadboards have internal connections. You need to know about them in order to build circuits. Rows of pins are connected horizontally, but not across the gap in the middle. Long rails called *power buses* run vertically along the sides of the board.

---

[2] Prior to the development of the kind of breadboards we're using, people built circuits on pieces of wood that were used to cut bread on (hence the name). They needed a quick way to connect circuits, and by drilling holes and using nails and wires, they could use bread boards to try different circuits.

On this breadboard, rows are labeled with numbers (1–30), and the columns have letters (a–e on the left side and f–j on the right side). You can refer to a specific hole in the breadboard by saying its row number and letter. For example, if you wanted to refer to the hole located in row 25, column c, you could say 25c (see figure 6.8). Just as you might find your seat at a stadium by walking along the aisle to find the correct row, and then moving along the row to find the right seat, you'll use the letters and numbers to guide you in building your circuits.

BREADBOARD (BB) HOLES

We'll refer to the row and column, but we'll prepend the letters *BB* so you know it's the breadboard location we're talking about. Figure 6.8 shows the location of BB25c. If we're talking about a GPIO pin or connection, we'll add *GP* before the number (GPIO pin 21 is GP21).

Try to keep in mind what is connected in a breadboard and what isn't. If you forget, you can always look back at figure 6.7. For example, notice that BB25 a, b, c, d, and e are all connected. Similarly, BB30 f, g,

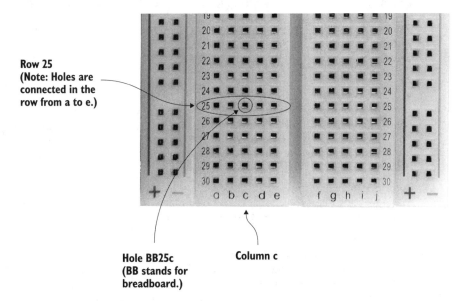

Figure 6.8 To find a specific hole on a breadboard, use the row and column labels. This is a close-up of a breadboard, showing how you can find the location of hole 25c (we'll refer to the hole as BB25c, where *BB* stands for *breadboard*).

h, i, and j are connected. But the left side of the board isn't connected to the right. For example, BB25e isn't connected to BB25f. To connect them, you'd put a jumper from BB25e to BB25f.

You can see vertical columns of holes along the sides of the breadboard. These are the *power buses* and provide easy ways to connect electrical components to power (positive) and ground (negative).

Circuits 101

Let's learn about electricity and circuits. At the simplest level, a *circuit* is a loop or path where the electrical power starts at a source (the positive side of a power source), goes through one or more electrical components (such as a light or motor), and then completes the loop (or path) by connecting back to the negative side of the source.

WHAT IS ELECTRICITY?

Electricity is the flow of charge. Typically, it is the flow of electrons, which have a negative charge. To get electrons to flow, you need to have a difference in charges. Just as the north pole of a magnet is attracted to its opposite—the south pole of another magnet—positive and negative electric charges are attracted to one another. If the charge is free to move, it will move. We generally think of circuits as having electricity flowing from the positive (+) side of the source to the negative (-) side of the source. For your Pi, the power is coming from the power supply (Micro USB plug). The Pi as a power source can provide either +3.3 volts or +5 V (volts). It provides this power through the physical pins 1, 2, and 4, but can also send +3.3 V out any of the 26 GPIO pins (you'll program it to do that soon).

VOLTAGE (VOLTS)

Voltage is a measure of the difference in electrical charge between the positive and negative source. When you have two different charges, they're attracted to one another (positive and negative attract). The greater the difference in charge, the greater the force (or electrical pressure) wanting to move charges through the circuit from the positive side to the negative side.

Voltage is measured in volts (V), named after Alessandro Volta, who is credited with inventing the first battery. A 9 volt (or 9 V) battery has a greater electric force for moving charge than a AA battery, which only has a voltage of 1.5 V.

CURRENT (AMPERES)

The *current* in a circuit is the amount of charge flowing. So whereas voltage is a measure of how badly charges *want* to flow, the current is a measure of how much charge is *actually* flowing.

Imagine that you could be inside a wire and see the charge flowing through it. A large current would mean a lot of charge (usually electrons) bumping along and through the wire over some period of time. A small current in that same wire would mean a lot less charge flowing over that same time period. Current is measured in amperes (A), named after André-Marie Ampère. A current of 1 ampere (or 1 A) is equivalent to the amount of charge of 6.241×10^{18} electrons flowing through a wire per second! That is a lot of charge flowing. You can decrease the current in a circuit by increasing the resistance of the circuit to the flow of electric charge.

RESISTANCE (OHMS)

The *resistance* in a circuit is a measure of how much it opposes the flow of charge (current). A light bulb, a motor, and your body all have resistance. The opposite of resistance is *conductance*. Substances such as metal (copper, silver, and gold) are all good conductors, and this is why we build circuits with metal wires for the electricity to flow through.

Sometimes you need to control the current (the flow of charge). Resistors are used to do this; they're made of materials that slow down the flow of charge. The most common ones are made out of carbon (you'll be using these in your projects). The resistance of a circuit is measured in ohms, named after Georg Ohm, and is represented using the Greek symbol omega (Ω).

PI CIRCUITS

You can think of your Pi as providing 3.3 V from the positive side of the Pi or, later, coming out of one of the GPIO pins. This +3.3 V is a force that is trying to push electric charge to the negative (-) side of your source. The negative side is sometimes called the *ground*—think of it as a big sink or reservoir to which electricity wants to flow if there is a path to get there. During the next few chapters, you'll build circuits with LEDs and resistors. You use a resistor with an LED to decrease the flow of electric charge (the current) so it won't be too large and burn out your LED. Burning an LED smells bad!

On your breadboard, think of all the GPIO pins as potential sources of voltage (positive). Circuits from the GPIO pins should end back at any one of the many ground (negative) connections.

Building the LED circuit

Your first project is to light up a red LED. You'll control the LED using GPIO pin 21 (GPIO21). You need these parts:

- Raspberry Pi, ribbon cable, and breakout board connected to your breadboard
- 1 red LED (5 mm)
- 1 180 ohm resistor
- 1 jumper wire (male-to-male)

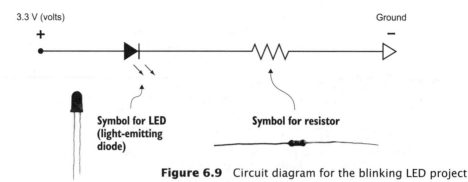

3.3 V (volts)   Ground

**Symbol for LED
(light-emitting
diode)**   **Symbol for resistor**

Figure 6.9 Circuit diagram for the blinking LED project

You'll build the LED circuit on your breadboard and then program it to light up. Figure 6.9 shows the circuit diagram. To light the LED, you'll have electricity (+3.3 V) flow from your Pi's GPIO pin 21 through the LED, through the resistor, and then to ground (0 V).

Figure 6.10 shows the LED circuit built on the breadboard. Note that there are many different ways to create this circuit—this is just one way. Let's walk through the steps to build the circuit.

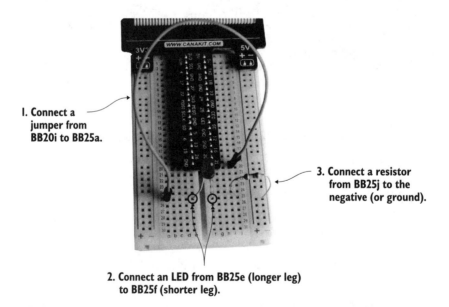

**1. Connect a
jumper from
BB20i to BB25a.**

**3. Connect a resistor
from BB25j to the
negative (or ground).**

**2. Connect an LED from BB25e (longer leg)
to BB25f (shorter leg).**

Figure 6.10 LED circuit built on the breadboard. You're using GPIO pin 21 as the power source. The light won't turn on until you program the voltage to come out of the pin.

NOTE   You may have a different breadboard than the one used in this book. If so, the numbering on your breadboard may be different than what is shown here. In that case, you'll need to create the circuit following the same principles, but with different numbered holes.

Step 1. Connect the jumper from GPIO pin 21

Raspberry Pi GPIO pins can output 3.3 V. You could pick any pin, but this project uses GPIO pin 21.

Connect a short piece of wire from GPIO21 on your breadboard to an empty row on the breadboard. Use row 25. Firmly push the wire into the hole. The metal tip of the wire should go down into the hole, not sit on top.

The breakout board pins are connected to rows on the breadboard. We'll refer to the holes on the breadboard (see figure 6.11). Insert one end of the jumper into BB20i and the other end into BB25a.

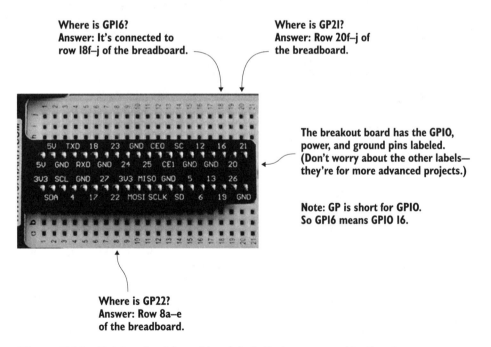

Where is GPI6?
Answer: It's connected to row 18f–j of the breadboard.

Where is GP2I?
Answer: Row 20f–j of the breadboard.

The breakout board has the GPIO, power, and ground pins labeled. (Don't worry about the other labels—they're for more advanced projects.)

Note: GP is short for GPIO. So GPI6 means GPIO 16.

Where is GP22?
Answer: Row 8a–e of the breadboard.

Figure 6.11   The breakout board has labels that correspond to the pins on your Pi. To connect a wire to GP16, you plug it into the breadboard in the hole labelled BB18f or BB18j.

Step 2. Add the red LED

It's time to connect the red LED. LEDs only let electricity flow through them one way, so it's important to put them in the right way. LEDs have two wires or *legs*. The longer leg is called the *anode* and connects to the positive side of the circuit (see figure 6.12). The shorter leg, called the *cathode*, connects to the negative or ground side of the circuit.

With the red LED, connect the longer leg to BB25e and the shorter leg to BB25f. You may need to bend the legs and push them a bit to get them into the holes.

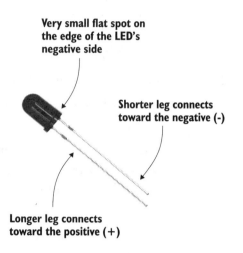

Very small flat spot on the edge of the LED's negative side

Shorter leg connects toward the negative (-)

Longer leg connects toward the positive (+)

Figure 6.12 LEDs have two legs (wires) coming out of them. The longer leg is called the anode and connects to the positive side of the circuit. The shorter one is called the cathode and connects to the negative side of a circuit.

Step 3. Connect a resistor

Grab your 180 ohm resistor.[3] You can identify a resistor by its color-coded bands. A 180 ohm resistor has colored bands of brown, grey, and brown (see figure 6.13). They are followed by a fourth band that

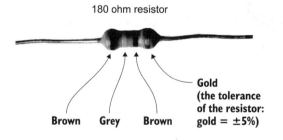

180 ohm resistor

Brown   Grey   Brown

Gold (the tolerance of the resistor: gold = ±5%)

Figure 6.13 The value of a resistor is determined by its colored bands. See the sidebar "Resistor color codes" for a chart; there are also many online color-code charts.

---

[3] If you don't have a 180 ohm resistor, you can use a resistor with a value between 100 and 330 ohms. If you use a resistor with a value that is too large, the LED may not light up or will be dim. Try experimenting with different resistors to adjust the brightness.

indicates the tolerance or quality of the resistor. Common colors for the fourth band are gold (±5% tolerance) and silver (±10% tolerance).

The resistor prevents too much electric current[4] from passing through your LED and burning it out. Insert one end of the 180 ohm resistor into BB25j and the other end into the negative (-) power bus (or ground).

Electricity will flow either way through a resistor, so which way you connect it doesn't matter. Remember that the negative power bus or ground rail is running vertically along the right side of the breadboard. Most boards have a blue stripe next to it.

Resistor color codes

Resistors have color codes that tell their value and tolerance. This chart shows you how to read the resistor color bands.

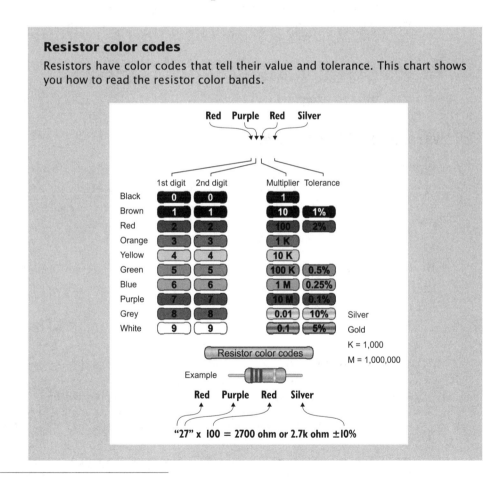

---

4 Current is a measure of the flow of electric charges per second. If the current through an LED is too high, the LED will burn out.

> *(continued)*
>
> For example, consider a resistor with red, purple, red, and silver bands. Follow these steps to use the chart:
>
> ○ Look up the digit for the first band and the digit for the second band, and put them together. In this case, the digits are 2 and 7: put them together, and you get 27. Note that you don't add the numbers; you treat them as the first and second digits of the resistor value.
> ○ Find the multiplier by looking up the color for the third band. In this case, it's 100 ohms (red).
> ○ Put it all together: 27 × 100 ohms is 2,700 ohms or 2.7K ohms (K = 1,000).
> ○ The fourth band (silver) tells you the resistor has a tolerance of ±10%.
>
> A red, purple, red, and silver resistor is a 2.7K ohm resistor with a ±10% tolerance. Use this handy chart any time you need to look up the value of a resistor.

That's it! You have a completed LED circuit built on your breadboard. Now it's time to program it!

Software: blinkLED program

Open IDLE by choosing Python 3 under Menu > Programming. This opens IDLE to the Python 3.x Shell. In the Python Shell, let's check to see if your Pi has the GPIO libraries you need already installed:

```
>>>  import RPi.GPIO as GPIO
```

If you don't see an error, you're ready to go. If you see an error saying there is no module named RPi.GPIO, please refer to the sidebar "Updating your Pi."

> **Updating your Pi**
>
> Before programming, you need to check that your Pi is up to date. Make sure your Pi is connected to the internet. Open the Terminal program by going to Menu --> Accessories --> Terminal, and run the following commands to update your Raspberry Pi and be certain you have the Raspberry Pi GPIO packages you need.
>
> First, let's update the apt-get database. The apt-get program handles installing and removing software from your Pi. In Terminal, enter this command:
>
> ```
> pi@raspberrypi ~ $ sudo apt-get update
> ```

You'll need to wait while a bunch of files are downloaded and installed. You'll see lots of messages displayed in Terminal. When the command completes, you'll see the Terminal $ prompt again. Next, to get the latest Pi software, enter

```
pi@raspberrypi ~ $ sudo apt-get upgrade
```

Once again, files will be downloaded and installed. After a series of messages, you'll see a warning about the upgrade using additional disk space, and this prompt: "Do you want to continue [Y/n]?" Enter Y and press Enter to continue the upgrade.

This is a great time to grab a sandwich and soda. It can take 15 minutes or more for the update to complete. When it's finished, you'll have the latest Raspberry Pi software and Python libraries, including the ones you need to communicate with and control the GPIO pins.

You're going to write a program that blinks an LED. It'll send a voltage (+3.3 V) out of a GPIO pin to light the LED, then turn it off, and repeat that over and over. Begin by creating the following new program in IDLE. In the Python Shell, start a new program by pressing Ctrl-N or selecting File > New Window.

Listing 6.1   Blinking LED program

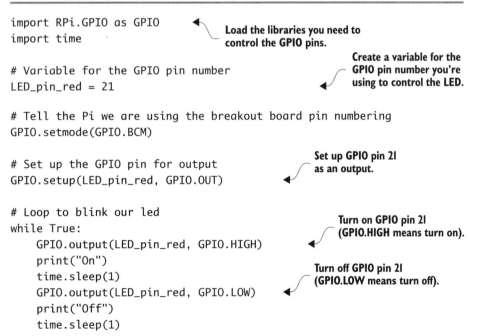

```python
import RPi.GPIO as GPIO
import time
```
Load the libraries you need to control the GPIO pins.

```python
# Variable for the GPIO pin number
LED_pin_red = 21
```
Create a variable for the GPIO pin number you're using to control the LED.

```python
# Tell the Pi we are using the breakout board pin numbering
GPIO.setmode(GPIO.BCM)
```

```python
# Set up the GPIO pin for output
GPIO.setup(LED_pin_red, GPIO.OUT)
```
Set up GPIO pin 21 as an output.

```python
# Loop to blink our led
while True:
    GPIO.output(LED_pin_red, GPIO.HIGH)
    print("On")
    time.sleep(1)
    GPIO.output(LED_pin_red, GPIO.LOW)
    print("Off")
    time.sleep(1)
```
Turn on GPIO pin 21 (GPIO.HIGH means turn on).

Turn off GPIO pin 21 (GPIO.LOW means turn off).

Save the program as blinkLED.py in your home folder. The program can't be run the same ways you've run programs before using IDLE.

Running the program

Select Run > Run Module (or press F5) from the IDLE text editor to run your program. With older versions of Raspbian, programs using GPIO pins must be run from the Raspbian command prompt as the superuser (or root)[5]. If you run the program at the Python Shell in IDLE, you'll get an error:

```
RuntimeError: No access to /dev/mem. Try running as root!
```

In this case, you use the sudo command to do this. To run the blink-LED.py program, open LXTerminal and enter the following command:

```
pi@raspberrypi ~ $ sudo python3 blinkLED.py
```

Behold the blinking LED! Try making the light blink faster by adjusting the value in the sleep function. Use a smaller number of seconds, such as 0.5 or 0.1.[6] To stop the program, press Ctrl-C.

> NOTE   Stopping the program with Ctrl-C may result in the light being left on (depending on when you press it). Also, the next time you run the program, you may see a runtime error, but the program still works. We don't cover it here, but look online for the Python commands try/except/finally and the GPIO.cleanup() command. It's a fancy way to make sure all the GPIO pins are reset when you exit the program.

TROUBLESHOOTING

If the light isn't blinking, here are some things you can check:

- Are the on and off messages displaying on the screen? If so, it's probably not your code that has a problem. Check the circuit on the breadboard. Make sure the ribbon cable is connected properly, with

---

[5] In October 2015, the Raspberry Pi Foundation released Raspbian version "Jessie," which allows you to run programs using the GPIO pins directly from IDLE. With "Jessie" you don't need to open the command prompt. Simply press F5 or select Run > Run Module from the IDLE text editor menu to run your programs.

[6] Too small a number may cause the light to appear to stay on, but more dimly. This is because your eyes can only perceive blinking that is greater than about 1/25th of a second, or 0.04 of a second.

the first wire connected toward the edge of your Pi, away from the USB ports. Double-check that the jumper, LED, and resistor are connected to the correct holes.

- Could your LED be inserted the wrong way? Make sure the shorter leg is toward the negative or ground side. Try turning it around.
- Double-check the size of the resistor you used in the circuit. If the resistor is too large, the LED won't light up. A resistor that is between 100 and 300 ohms should work.
- Look through your Python program for errors. Check that you have set `LED_pin_red` equal to 21 and that you're setting it `HIGH` and then `LOW`.

blinkLED: how it works

Let's take a closer look at how the blinkLED.py code works.

LOADING LIBRARIES

The `import` commands load the libraries or toolboxes you want to use in your program:

```
import RPi.GPIO as GPIO
import time
```

These commands load the Python libraries for controlling the Pi's GPIO pins. They also load the `time` library so you can use the `sleep` function to control the rate of blinking.

Importing libraries with the as keyword

Notice the `as` keyword in `import RPi.GPIO as GPIO`. Why can't you just type `import RPi.GPIO`?

The `as` keyword tells Python to load the library to a certain name you specify. It's kind of like giving the whole library a nickname. In this case, it's so you can refer to `RPi.GPIO` as simply `GPIO`.

An example will make it clearer. Once you've imported the `RPi.GPIO` library as `GPIO`, you can type `GPIO.setmode(GPIO.BCM)`. Without it, you would have to type `RPi.GPIO.setmode(RPi.GPIO.BCM)`. You can see how using `as GPIO` saves you some typing!

Once the libraries are loaded, you can set up your GPIO pins.

SETTING UP A GPIO PIN FOR OUTPUT

To set up a GPIO pin, you first need to tell Python on your Pi that you'll be referring to pins by the standard breakout numbering scheme. These are the numbers printed on the breakout board. You use the set-mode function:

```
GPIO.setmode(GPIO.BCM)
```

BCM stands for Broadcom—the maker of the computer chip that the Pi uses. Next you tell your Raspberry Pi that you'll be using LED_pin_red (GP21) for output, meaning you're planning to send some electricity out of it:

```
LED_pin_red = 21
```

```
GPIO.setup(LED_pin_red, GPIO.OUT)
```

GPIO.OUT prepares GP21 to send out +3.3 V of electricity.

LOOPING AND BLINKING

Finally, you create an infinite while loop and turn the LED on (set GPIO.HIGH) and off (set GPIO.LOW). You also add a delay using the sleep method found in Python's time library. Notice how the sleep function takes a parameter that is the number of seconds to sleep or pause. In this case, you use 1 second:

```
while True:
    GPIO.output(LED_pin_red, GPIO.HIGH)
    print("On")
    time.sleep(1)
    GPIO.output(LED_pin_red, GPIO.LOW)
    print("Off")
    time.sleep(1)
```

The print commands display messages to the screen. Although they aren't necessary to blink the LED, they can help debug your program. If you do use them, the screen could quickly fill with messages. Set a longer delay time to prevent this. If you see the messages on the screen but your LED isn't lighting up, then you probably have an error in your circuit and not in your program. Check your wiring, try turning around the LED, or try a different LED in case that one is defective.

Adding more LEDs

One LED is fun, so three LEDs must be lots of fun. Let's try adding green and blue LEDs and modify the program to control them. Here are the parts you need:

- Raspberry Pi and circuit from before
- 1 green LED
- 1 blue LED
- 2 180 ohm resistors
- 2 jumper wires (male-to-male)

Building the circuit

You'll follow the same process as before to add the green and blue LEDs. Figure 6.14 shows what the circuit diagram looks like now, and figure 6.15 shows the circuit on a breadboard.

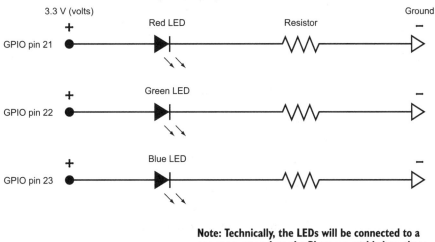

Note: Technically, the LEDs will be connected to a common ground on the Pi, so we could show these wires all connected together to one ground.

Figure 6.14 Circuit diagram for three LEDs: red, green, and blue. You'll use 180 ohm resistors like before. They will all be controlled by different GPIO pins. Red will use 21, green will use 22, and blue will be connected to pin 23. You could use any of the 26 different GPIO pins.

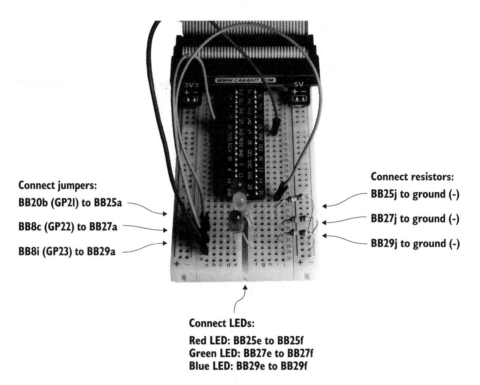

Connect jumpers:

BB20b (GP21) to BB25a

BB8c (GP22) to BB27a

BB8i (GP23) to BB29a

Connect resistors:

BB25j to ground (-)

BB27j to ground (-)

BB29j to ground (-)

Connect LEDs:

Red LED: BB25e to BB25f
Green LED: BB27e to BB27f
Blue LED: BB29e to BB29f

Figure 6.15   The three-LED circuit is built on the breadboard. Each LED and its corresponding resistor are placed in a row together. This example uses rows 25, 27, and 29.

To add the green LED, follow these steps:

1 GP22 is located on the *left side of the breakout board in row 8* on the breadboard. Connect it to *row 27*: insert one end of the jumper into BB8c and the other end into BB27a.

2 Connect the long leg of the green LED to BB27e and the shorter leg to BB27f. Bend the legs if needed.

3 Connect a 180 ohm resistor (brown, grey, and brown) from BB27j to the closest hole in the negative power bus.

Here are the steps to add the blue LED:

1 GPIO23 is located on the *right side of the breakout board in row 8* on the breadboard. Connect it to *row 29*: insert one end of the jumper into BB8i and the other end into BB29a.

2 Connect the long leg of the blue LED to BB29e and the shorter leg to BB29f. Bend the legs if needed.

3 Grab a 180 ohm resistor. You guessed it! It's color-coded brown, grey, and brown. Connect it from BB29j to the closest hole in the negative power bus.

Multiple LEDs: program it!

You need to make a few changes to the program to add more LEDs and get them all blinking at the same time. The following listing shows the updated code.

Listing 6.2   Three blinking LEDs

```python
import RPi.GPIO as GPIO
import time

# Variable for the GPIO pin number
LED_pin_red = 21
LED_pin_green = 22
LED_pin_blue = 23
```

Create variables for the GPIO pins you're using for the green and blue LEDs.

```python
# Tell the Pi we are using the breakout board pin numbering
GPIO.setmode(GPIO.BCM)

# Set up the GPIO pins for output
GPIO.setup(LED_pin_red, GPIO.OUT)
GPIO.setup(LED_pin_green, GPIO.OUT)
GPIO.setup(LED_pin_blue, GPIO.OUT)
```

Set up GPIO pins 22 and 23 as outputs.

```python
# Loop to blink our LEDs
while True:
    GPIO.output(LED_pin_red, GPIO.HIGH)
    GPIO.output(LED_pin_green, GPIO.HIGH)
    GPIO.output(LED_pin_blue, GPIO.HIGH)
    print("On")
    time.sleep(1)
    GPIO.output(LED_pin_red, GPIO.LOW)
    GPIO.output(LED_pin_green, GPIO.LOW)
    GPIO.output(LED_pin_blue, GPIO.LOW)
    print("Off")
    time.sleep(1)
```

Turn on the GPIO pins.

Turn off the GPIO pins.

Save the code as blinkLED3.py, and try running it. Open LXTerminal, and enter the following command:

```
pi@raspberrypi ~ $ sudo python3 blinkLED3.py
```

Fantastic! You have your own light show going on!

Challenges

Try these challenges to practice controlling your Raspberry Pi's GPIO pins. Each one provides a unique problem to solve.

Wave pattern

Change the program to make each LED turn on, one at a time, until they're all on. Then, turn each LED off, one at a time. Hint: play with where you put the time.sleep(1) command. Can you make the LEDs light up and turn off in a wave pattern?

Simon Says

Write a function that blinks the LEDs and that can take five parameters representing a pattern of colorful blinks. Each parameter is a string representing a color: red, blue, or green. The function should blink the lights in the appropriate pattern. Here is a series of Simon Says patterns you should try to make your function produce:

Red, green, red, red, blue

Blue, green, blue, green, red

Green, blue, blue, red, green

Random blinking

Create a program that generates random durations for how long the lights stay on and off. The durations should be random floating-point numbers between 0 and 3 seconds. Hint: you can use the random method to generate a random floating-point number between 0 and 1.0. Here is an example:

```
off_random_time = random.random() * 3
```

To scale this number so that it's between 0 and 3, you can multiply off_random_time by 3. If you get stuck on the challenge, check appendix C and the chapter source code for hints and solutions.

Summary

In this chapter, you learned the following things:

- A Pi is capable of interacting with the world around it. With a few extra parts, you can set it up for physical computing projects.
- A Pi can send out electrical signals! You can send output through the GPIO pins, and this can be used to light up LEDs or control many other electronic components (motors, buzzers, relays, and so on).
- Breadboards are like playgrounds for electronics. They make it easy to create circuits for your Pi because you can easily build and take apart circuits for use with the Pi.
- The RPi.GPIO library has built-in functions to set up and control output (voltage) to GPIO pins with Python.

Just imagine the possibilities of controlling pretty much any electrical device using your Raspberry Pi. Even better, imagine making the device work based on sensors (inputs) so you can create smart devices programmed by you!

7

Light Up Guessing Game

In this chapter, you'll be learning about

- *Simplifying and improving your code with more thoughtful design and use of functions*
- *Building a circuit to control a special LED (light bulb) that can make and combine red, green, and blue light*
- *Adding together colors of light to create new colors*
- *Making your Pi come alive by having it respond using different colored light*

Your Raspberry Pi has a unique ability to interact with the world around it. In the last chapter, you made lights blink based on a programmed pattern. Nice, but that isn't truly interactive, because the Pi always blinks a pattern that you program it to do. In this chapter, let's see if you can create an interactive project that *responds* to you through its GPIO pins. You'll draw on what you've learned about conditional logic (if/elif/else) to have your Pi make decisions and respond. As you did in earlier chapters, you'll need to gather input, use loops, and apply a few other programming techniques to get it done.

You're making a Light Up Guessing Game, but not just any one: this game will illuminate a small light called an *RGB* (stands for red, green, blue) *LED*, which can make any color. You'll use your Pi, breadboard, and electrical parts, along with a program you're going to write. Your Pi will let the player know if they're correct by flashing the RGB in different colors if their guess is too high or too low.

Figure 7.1 shows the parts you need. You'll notice that some of them are the same as in chapter 6, but you'll also need an RGB LED. Let's get started!

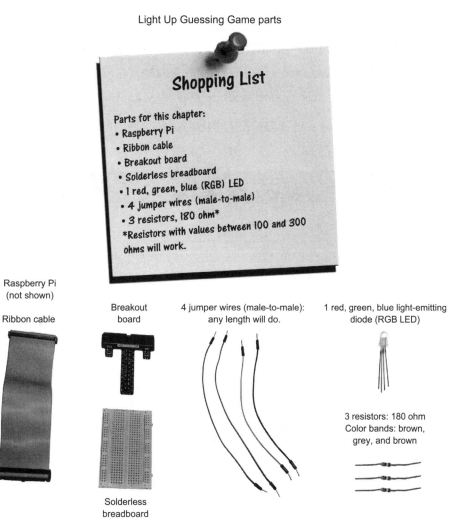

Figure 7.1 The Light Up Guessing Game uses a red, green, blue (RGB) LED. An RGB LED can produce many different colors because it has three LEDs (colored red, green, and blue) packed inside it.

Guessing Game design

The object of the game is to guess a magic number. This time, the Pi will give feedback to the user by lighting up the RGB LED in different colors. Here are some game details:

- The magic number is a randomly generated number between 1 and 20.
- The player is given five tries to guess the number correctly.
- If they guess correctly, the RGB LED flashes green.
- If the guess is too high, the RGB LED flashes red.
- If the guess is too low, the RGB LED flashes blue.
- The player is given the choice to play again.

Figure 7.2 shows a sample of the game's output.

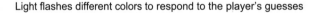

```
File Edit Tabs Help
pi@raspberrypi ~ $ sudo python3 LEDGuessingGame.py

********************************************************************************
                            Light Up Guessing Game
********************************************************************************

Game Play:
I'm thinking of a number between 1 and 20. You have five guesses to guess it.
After each guess, my light will blink.

    Red ---> Your guess is too high!
    Green ---> Your guess is correct!
    Blue --> Your guess is too low

Guess 1 - What is your guess?: 9
Guess 2 - What is your guess?: 14
Guess 3 - What is your guess?: 12
Guess 4 - What is your guess?: 11
Guess 5 - What is your guess?: 10
You lost!
Better luck next time!
Would you like to play again [Y/N]? █
```

Light flashes different colors to respond to the player's guesses

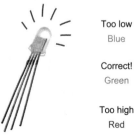

Too low
Blue

Correct!
Green

Too high
Red

Figure 7.2   The Light Up Guessing Game responds to the user after each guess. Lights on the breadboard light up to let the player know if their guess is too high or too low.

You'll approach this project in two parts. The first part is to build the circuit (the hardware), and the second part is writing the program (the software).

Hardware: building the circuit

Let's get building! You're building a circuit on your breadboard to control a new type of LED that can make any color you want. You'll start by connecting your Pi's GPIO pins to the breadboard using the ribbon cable and GPIO breakout board. Refer back to chapter 6 (section 6.1) if you need a reminder about how to set this up. Your Pi and breadboard should look like figure 7.3.

Numbers, numbers, numbers!

As first explained in chapter 6, you need a way to find a particular hole on your breadboard, and to do that you'll use the numbers and letters. Remember, this is much like the way you might find your seat at a stadium for a concert or sporting event.

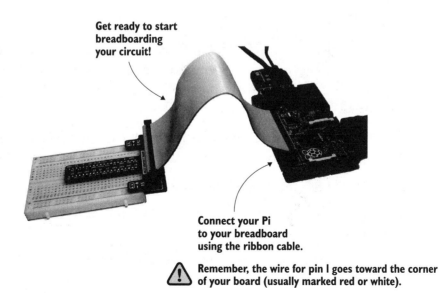

Get ready to start breadboarding your circuit!

Connect your Pi to your breadboard using the ribbon cable.

⚠ Remember, the wire for pin I goes toward the corner of your board (usually marked red or white).

Figure 7.3 The Pi, breakout board, and breadboard setup. And you thought your desk was messy before!

To refer to a specific hole on the breadboard, we'll refer to the row and column, but we'll add the letters *BB* to stand for *breadboard*. Not too hard, right? Finding breadboard holes involves searching for the row and then the column. When referring to a GPIO pin, we'll add the letters *GP* in front. For example, GPIO pin 12 is referred to as GP12.

Wiring an RGB LED

You're wiring up a new type of LED, called an RGB LED.

> **DEFINITION**   An RGB LED is a light bulb that consists of three LEDs: one red (R), one green (G), and one blue (B), all in a single plastic LED bulb casing.

The RGB LED can produce pretty much any color you want, using the three tiny LEDs inside it. By powering these in varying amounts, you can mix light to make colors.

The RGB LED has four *legs* (or wires) coming out of it, so you'll need to figure out how to wire it up. It's a bit different than the single-color LEDs you wired up in chapter 6, but it's pretty easy to use.

Circuit sketch

The circuit diagram for the Light Up Guessing Game is shown in Figure 7.4. To light the RGB LED, you'll have electricity (+3.3 V) flow from your Pi's GPIO pins 12, 16, and 21; through each resistor; through the LED; and then to ground (0 V).

You'll build the RGB LED circuit on the breadboard and then program it to light up. Wire it up in this order:

1 Put the RGB LED into the breadboard.

2 Connect the three jumper wires, which will connect the GPIO pins to the LED (one for each color).

3 Add the three resistors to connect the jumpers to the LED's red, green, and blue legs.

4 Add the final jumper wire to connect the ground leg of the LED to the negative (ground) power bus.

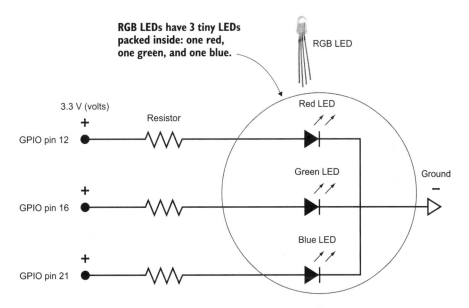

RGB LEDs have 3 tiny LEDs packed inside: one red, one green, and one blue.

RGB LED

3.3 V (volts)

Resistor

Red LED

GPIO pin 12

Green LED

Ground

GPIO pin 16

Blue LED

GPIO pin 21

Figure 7.4   Circuit diagram for the Light Up Guessing Game project

When it's done, the circuit will look like what you see in figure 7.5. Let's walk through the steps to build this circuit.

Figure 7.5   The RGB LED circuit you're building on the breadboard uses GPIO pins 12, 16, and 21 to power the LEDs. The light won't turn on until you program the voltage to come out of the pins.

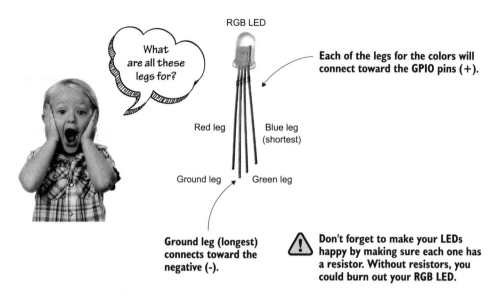

Figure 7.6 The RGB LED has lots of legs! The longest leg is the ground. The other ones are for red, green, and blue. This applies to what is called a *common cathode* RGB LED, which is what comes in Pi kits and what you'll find most commonly at electronics suppliers.

STEP 1. ADD THE RGB LED

Before you can add it to the breadboard, let's look a bit closer at the RGB LED. Remember that there are three tiny LEDs (red, green, and blue) inside it. You need to be able to figure out which leg is which color and which one is ground. Figure 7.6 is a handy reference.

> NOTE You'll need to bend the RGB LED's legs quite a bit to get them into the holes on the breadboard. Try to bend them to line up with the holes, and slowly push the legs in all at once.

Grab your RGB LED, and let's insert it into the breadboard. You're going to put it in rows 22, 24, 26, and 28 along column h on the breadboard. Here's where to connect the legs:

- Red leg into hole BB22h
- Ground leg (longest leg) into hole BB24h
- Green leg into hole BB26h
- Blue leg (shortest) into hole BB28h

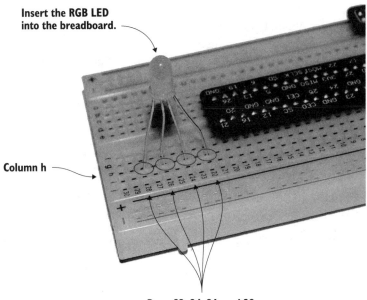

Insert the RGB LED into the breadboard.

Column h

Rows 22, 24, 26, and 28

Figure 7.7 Bend the legs of the RGB LED, and insert it into the breadboard at BB22h, BB24h, BB26h, and BB28h. The longest leg goes into hole BB24h.

When it's inserted, it will look like Figure 7.7. Double-check that it's pushed down into the breadboard so all the legs will make a good connection.

Good job! You just completed the trickiest part.

STEP 2. CONNECT THE GPIO JUMPER WIRES

The breakout board has numbers on it that refer to the Raspberry Pi's GPIO numbering system. Remember that we refer to GPIO pins by adding *GPIO* before the number of the pin. So if we're talking about GPIO pin 12, it's GPIO12.

Question: What hole on your breadboard is next to *GPIO12* (GPIO pin 12)?

Answer: Look closely, and you'll see that the holes next to it are *BB16i* and *BB16j*.

NOTE   The color of the jumper wires doesn't matter, but it's sometimes helpful to pick ones that match the colors of the LED legs. When you're troubleshooting problems, that can help you easily remember which GPIO pin is controlling each color of light coming out of the RGB LED.

Now that you've located the holes near the GPIO pins, you can start connecting jumper wires as follows:

- Jumper wire from BB16j to BB22a (connects GP12 to the red leg of the RGB LED)

- Jumper wire from BB18j to BB26a (connects GP16 to the green leg of the RGB LED)

- Jumper wire from BB20j to BB28a (connects GP21 to the blue leg of the RGB LED)

When you've added the wires, the circuit will look like figure 7.8.

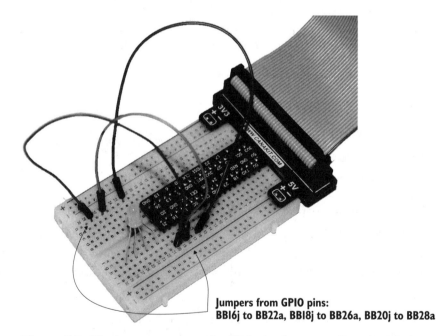

Jumpers from GPIO pins:
BB16j to BB22a, BB18j to BB26a, BB20j to BB28a

Figure 7.8 The jumpers connect the GPIO pins from your Pi to the RGB LED. If you have an earlier model Pi, you can use other GPIO pins. Just remember which ones you're using, and use these numbers when you program the Pi to turn the GPIO pins on and off.

STEP 3. ADD THE THREE RESISTORS

It's time to connect your 180 ohm resistors![1] They should have bands of brown, grey, and brown, followed by a fourth gold or silver band. Remember that electricity will flow either way through a resistor, so the way you connect it doesn't matter. Figure 7.9 is a handy diagram that reminds you how you can figure out the value of a resistor by using the colored bands.

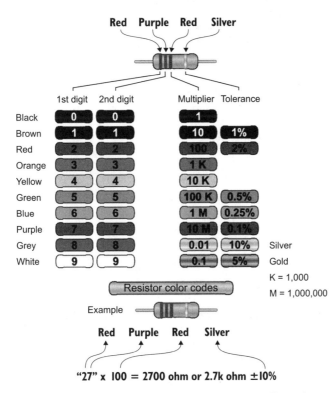

	1st digit	2nd digit	Multiplier	Tolerance	
Black	0	0	1		
Brown	1	1	10	1%	
Red	2	2	100	2%	
Orange	3	3	1 K		
Yellow	4	4	10 K		
Green	5	5	100 K	0.5%	
Blue	6	6	1 M	0.25%	
Purple	7	7	10 M	0.1%	
Grey	8	8	0.01	10%	Silver
White	9	9	0.1	5%	Gold

Resistor color codes

K = 1,000
M = 1,000,000

Example

Red   Purple   Red   Silver

"27" x 100 = 2700 ohm or 2.7k ohm ±10%

Figure 7.9   The colored bands on a resistor tell you how much resistance the resistor has. For this project, you want a brown (1), grey (8), brown (×10) resistor, or 18 × 10 = 180 ohm resistor. Don't have one? Any resistor between about 100 and 300 ohms should work well.

---

[1] This is a safe value that won't risk damage to your Pi and will keep things simple. For those of you who are into precision, technically you might want to use slightly different resistors for each color LED (red, green, and blue), because each one requires a different amount of electrical current (amps) to make it shine. Check out some of the online resistor calculators and Pi forums on RGB LEDs if you're interested.

Add resistors:
BB22c to BB22f, BB26c to BB26f, BB28c to BB28f

Remember: Resistors can be placed either way. It doesn't matter.

Figure 7.10 Add your resistors! Make sure you push them down into the breadboard holes. If you don't like them sticking up so high, you can trim the ends using wire cutters.

Connect the resistors as follows:

- Insert one end of the first resistor into BB22c and the other end into BB22f.
- Insert one end of the second resistor into BB26c and the other end into BB26f.
- Insert one end of the third resistor into BB28c and the other end into BB28f.

Once they're added, you'll have something that looks like figure 7.10. Now you're ready for the final step!

STEP 4. ADD THE JUMPER TO GROUND

Remember that a ground rail runs vertically along the right side of the breadboard, with a blue stripe next to it. Add a jumper from BB24j to

The jumper completes the circuit, but don't
expect the RGB LED to light up just yet! You
need to tell your Pi to send it some electricity
from the GPIO pins (12, 16, and 21).

Add a jumper from
BB24j to ground(-).

Figure 7.11   The jumper is added to connect the ground of the RGB LED to the
ground of the Raspberry Pi. The jumper can connect anywhere along the ground
rail (it usually has a blue stripe running next to it).

the negative (-) power bus or ground rail (any hole next to the blue
stripe will do). Figure 7.11 shows how it looks.

Wahoo! You've completed the RGB circuit on the breadboard. With
the circuit complete, it's time to write your program so you can test it.

Color mixing with an RGB LED

You can program your RGB LED to light up red, green, or blue by turning on or
off GPIO pins 12, 16, and 21. But RGB LEDs can make more colors by mixing
different amounts of red, green, and blue light. For example, you can combine
equal amounts of red and blue light to make a nice magenta color. Or to make
your LED yellow, you can combine equal amounts of green and red. Televisions
work on the same principle. This concept, called *additive color*, means mixing
varying amounts of different colors of light to make new colors.

(continued)

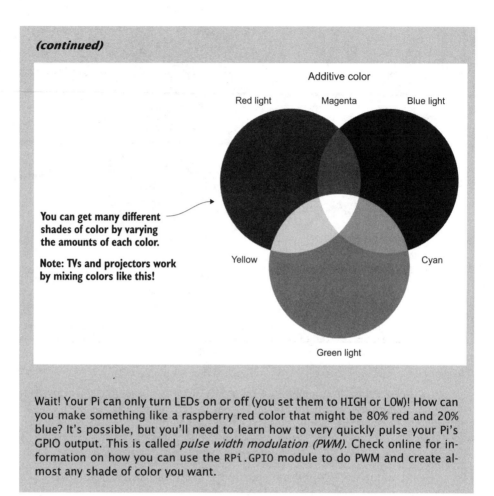

Additive color

Red light   Magenta   Blue light

You can get many different shades of color by varying the amounts of each color.

Note: TVs and projectors work by mixing colors like this!

Yellow   Cyan

Green light

Wait! Your Pi can only turn LEDs on or off (you set them to HIGH or LOW)! How can you make something like a raspberry red color that might be 80% red and 20% blue? It's possible, but you'll need to learn how to very quickly pulse your Pi's GPIO output. This is called *pulse width modulation (PWM)*. Check online for information on how you can use the `RPi.GPIO` module to do PWM and create almost any shade of color you want.

Software: LEDGuessingGame program

You're creating a game to guess a magic number. As mentioned at the start of the chapter, you'll design the game play based on these simple rules (feel free to change them to your liking):

- The magic number is a randomly generated number between 1 and 20.
- The player is given five tries to guess the number correctly.
- If they guess correctly, the RGB LED flashes green.
- If they guess too high, the RGB LED flashes red.
- If they guess too low, the RGB LED flashes blue.

- After five guesses, the game is over.
- The player is given the choice to play again.

As you've seen in earlier chapters, programming is often about breaking down complex problems into smaller ones and then solving them. Let's start by laying out a quick diagram outlining what the program should do (see figure 7.12).

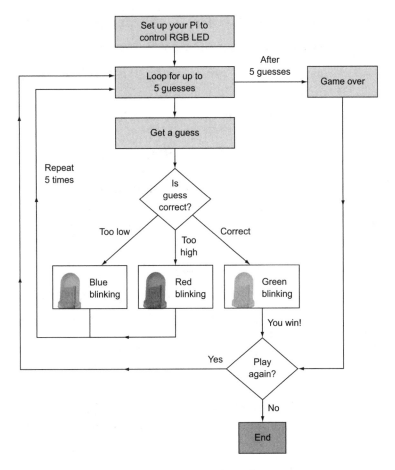

Figure 7.12 Flow diagram showing how the guessing game should work. Notice how you're blinking LEDs if the guess is too low, too high, or correct. You also give the player the choice of whether they'd like to play again.

As you approach this program, let's see if you can simplify the code by organizing it into *functions*, especially when you have chunks of code that can be easily separated. Remember that you can use functions to organize your code and simplify it. You'll create three functions to handle each of the flashing lights, to simplify the main part of your program:

- `flash_red`—Flashes the RGB LED red
- `flash_blue`—Flashes the RGB LED blue
- `flash_green`—Flashes the RGB LED green

You'll also create a function to display a message when the game is over.

Now that you have a plan, let's code it in this order:

1 Import libraries, create the flashing and game-over functions, and set up the GPIO pins for RGB LED output.

2 Display the title and introduction, create a loop, and get and check up to five guesses.

3 Add logic to allow the user to decide if they want to play again.

Let's begin! Open IDLE by choosing Python 3 under Menu > Programming. This opens IDLE to the Python 3.x Shell. In the Python Shell, start a new program by pressing Ctrl-N or selecting File > New Window.

Setting up the GPIO pins for the RGB LED

In the IDLE 3 text editor, you'll first load the Python libraries you need, create functions, and prepare your Pi to send electricity to the RGB LED (see figure 7.13).

SETTING UP YOUR PI'S GPIO PINS

You need to get your Pi ready for output to the GPIO pins and tell the Pi which pins you plan to use (see listing 7.1). If you recall from the earlier wiring, you're using these pins to control the three LEDs that are inside the RGB LED:

- GP12 for the red LED
- GP16 for the green LED
- GP21 for the blue LED

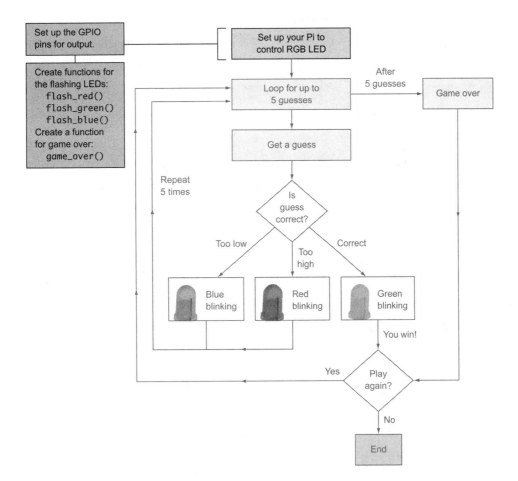

Figure 7.13 The program starts by importing the Python libraries you'll need to use, setting up your Pi's GPIO pins for lighting up the LEDs, and defining the functions you'll need.

Later, you'll write the code to control those pins. Let's start by importing the GPIO library for the Raspberry Pi and setting up the GPIO pins so they can output a voltage to control the RGB LED.

Listing 7.1   Setting up the Pi's GPIO pins

```
# Light Up Guessing Game
# Ryan Heitz
```

```
# importing the libraries we need
import RPi.GPIO as GPIO
import time
import random
```

Import several libraries you'll need later.

```
#Tell the Pi we want to use a breakout board
GPIO.setmode(GPIO.BCM)

# Create variables for the pins used for LEDs
LED_pin_red = 12
LED_pin_green = 16
LED_pin_blue = 21
```

Pick which GPIO pins you'll use to light the LEDs.

```
# Blink speed in seconds
blink_time = 0.25
```

Create a variable to store how long the light should blink on and off.

```
# Tell the Pi which Pins we will use
# Set them up as OUT pins (send electricity out)
GPIO.setup(LED_pin_red,GPIO.OUT)
GPIO.setup(LED_pin_green,GPIO.OUT)
GPIO.setup(LED_pin_blue,GPIO.OUT)
```

Tell your Pi to set up three GPIO pins for output.

Great! You've started by importing the time and random libraries, because you'll need them to flash the LED and help you generate a random number when the game starts. You define variables for the pins you're using and even add a variable, BlinkTime, that says how much time you'll blink the light on and off. Finally, you tell your Pi that you want to use three pins as output. Now let's write the functions.

CREATING FUNCTIONS TO SIMPLIFY THE CODE

You need three functions to flash the three LEDs inside the RGB LED and one for game over. Name the flashing functions flash_red, flash_blue, and flash_green, as shown in the following listing.

Listing 7.2   Functions that flash LEDs different colors

Use a for loop to flash the LED five times.

```
# Blinks an LED.
def flash_red():
    for i in range(1,6): #Blink on and off 5 times
        # Turning on LEDs
```

Define the name of the flashing function.

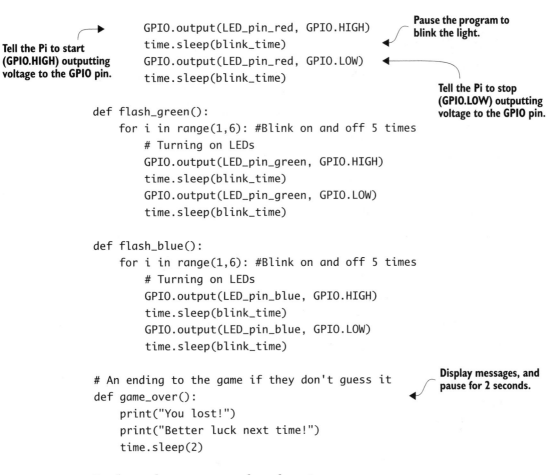

Tell the Pi to start (GPIO.HIGH) outputting voltage to the GPIO pin.

```
            GPIO.output(LED_pin_red, GPIO.HIGH)
            time.sleep(blink_time)
            GPIO.output(LED_pin_red, GPIO.LOW)
            time.sleep(blink_time)
```

Pause the program to blink the light.

Tell the Pi to stop (GPIO.LOW) outputting voltage to the GPIO pin.

```
def flash_green():
    for i in range(1,6): #Blink on and off 5 times
        # Turning on LEDs
        GPIO.output(LED_pin_green, GPIO.HIGH)
        time.sleep(blink_time)
        GPIO.output(LED_pin_green, GPIO.LOW)
        time.sleep(blink_time)

def flash_blue():
    for i in range(1,6): #Blink on and off 5 times
        # Turning on LEDs
        GPIO.output(LED_pin_blue, GPIO.HIGH)
        time.sleep(blink_time)
        GPIO.output(LED_pin_blue, GPIO.LOW)
        time.sleep(blink_time)

# An ending to the game if they don't guess it
def game_over():
    print("You lost!")
    print("Better luck next time!")
    time.sleep(2)
```

Display messages, and pause for 2 seconds.

In the code, you create four functions:

- flash_red()
- flash_green()
- flash_blue()
- game_over()

The three flashing functions blink a different color LED in the RGB LED. The blinking is created by using a for loop and the sleep function while you switch the output from the GPIO pin from HIGH (on) to LOW (off). Think of this as being like standing at a light switch and flipping it on and then off, five times.

Before you go any farther, save the program as LEDGuessingGame.py in your home folder.

When to use functions

Believe it or not, we don't always know when to create a function. The ability to figure that out is a skill that comes with experience in writing programs and seeing patterns. Here are some tips for deciding what to make a function:

⊙ Is there a group of instructions that you'll need to use over and over again, with little variation?

⊙ Do you have large blocks of code that make your programs hard to read?

Functions can simplify your code and make it easier to update.

REFACTORING YOUR FUNCTIONS

Did you notice that the functions for flashing the LEDs are very similar? Most of the code in each function is the same except for the GPIO pin, so let's see if you can improve this code to make it simpler. This process of simplifying code is called *refactoring*.

What if you rewrote the three functions as a single function, as shown in listing 7.3? This new function takes one parameter, LED_pin, that represents the number of the GPIO pin you want to control. It can be any one of the GPIO pins you're using for the colors of the RGB LED. For example, if LED_pin is 16, this corresponds to GPIO pin 16, which should blink the green light.

Listing 7.3   **Refactoring the three flashing functions to a single function**

```
# Blinks an LED.
def flash(LED_pin):
    for i in range(1,6): #Blink on and off 5 times    ◄── The function takes one parameter as input (the GPIO pin number).
        # Turning on LEDs
        GPIO.output(LED_pin, GPIO.HIGH)
        time.sleep(blink_time)                         ◄── Turn the signal to the LED on and off.
        GPIO.output(LED_pin, GPIO.LOW)
        time.sleep(blink_time)
```

In this case, you're refactoring a set of functions that are very similar to a single function that takes a parameter (LED_pin). This parameter makes the function more flexible or dynamic so it can take the place of the three separate functions.

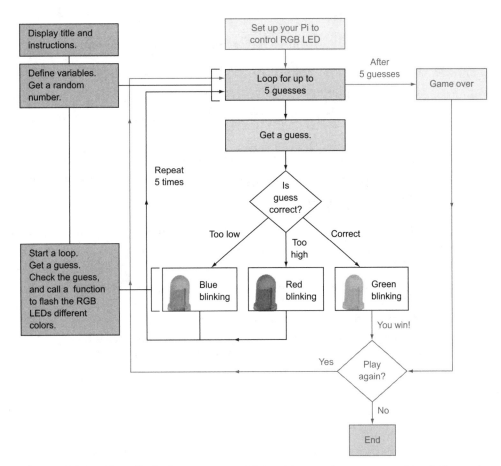

Figure 7.14 After displaying the game title and instructions, you need to define variables to store important game information, including a random number the player is trying to guess. The main loop in the game is repeated to allow the user to make five guesses; it also blinks the lights.

Main game loop and logic

The next part of the program creates the main game loop (see figure 7.14). You'll do the following:

⦾ Set up the game.

⦾ Display the title and instructions for the person playing.

⦾ Create some variables, and get a random number.

⦾ Create the loop and guessing logic.

GAME SETUP

Let's look at some of the variables you'll need for the game:

- `number_in_my_head` holds a random number (an integer between 1 and 20) that the player is trying to guess.
- `count_guesses` helps you count and keep track of how many guesses the player has made.
- `play_again` tracks the status of whether the player wants to play again. You'll use a Boolean type for this, because it should always be True (yes, let's play again) or False (no, let's not play again).

The next listing adds these three variables and sets them up. You also create and display the title and game instructions.

Listing 7.4   Creating variables and displaying the game title and instructions

```
# A random number for our game
number_in_my_head = random.randint(1,20)
count_guesses = 1  # Counter for the number of guesses

# Used to keep track of whether they want to play again
play_again = True

title = """
********************************************************************
                      Light Up Guessing Game
********************************************************************
"""

print(title)

intro = """
Game Play:
I'm thinking of a number between 1 and 20. You have five guesses to
   guess it.
After each guess, my light will blink.

  Red ---> Your guess is too high!
  Green ---> Your guess is correct!
  Blue --> Your guess is too low
"""
```

Fantastic! The variables set the stage for the guessing-game logic. It's a lot like the foundation of a house—you need it in order to build the rest.

Guessing Game Loop and logic

The code features two loops, one inside the other. The outer loop gives the user the option of playing again—we'll call this the Play Again Loop. Within that loop is another that gives the player five guesses— we'll call this the Guessing Game Loop.

The main game loop involves getting a guess, checking the guess, blinking the RGB LED the appropriate color, and then repeating until the player guesses right or has used all five guesses. The next listing shows the program for the Guessing Game Loop and the logic for checking guesses.

Listing 7.5   *Guessing Game Loop*

Start the game loop that gives the player 5 chances to guess correctly.

Call the flash function and tell it to flash the RGB LED a certain color.

Display a prompt for a user to enter their guess.

Exit (break out of) the game loop if the player guesses correctly.

Call after the player has guessed 5 times.

```python
while count_guesses < 6:
    guess = input("Guess " + str(count_guesses) + ": ")
    guess = int(guess)  # Convert the input string to an integer
    count_guesses += 1  # Add one to the number of guesses
      to keep track
    if guess == number_in_my_head: # Guessed it correctly
        flash(LED_pin_green)
        print("You won!")
        break # Breaks out of loop
    elif guess > number_in_my_head: # Guess too high
        flash(LED_pin_red)
    elif guess < number_in_my_head: # Guess too low
        flash(LED_pin_blue)
else: # For the while loop, it happens when the while condition
  isn't True
    game_over()
# End of game
```

The Guessing Game Loop contains the logic to

- Keep track of the number of guesses.
- Get a guess.
- Check to see if a guess is correct, too high, or too low.

Where is the logic for responding to the player? It's in the loop. Each time you get a guess, a series of if/elif statements checks whether the guess is correct, too high, or too low. Based on which of those cases is True, the flash() function is called to flash the appropriately colored LED on and off. If the user guesses the number correctly, the RGB LED will flash green, and then the break command will exit the while loop.

Notice that you add an else statement to the while loop. When the number of guesses has been exceeded (count_guesses is greater than 5), the else statement is triggered and the game_over function is called. The else block only happens when the while condition is checked and is False (in this case, when the number of guesses has exceeded 5).

In the next section, you'll see how to give the player the option of playing again.

Adding the Play Again Loop and logic

You want to add a feature to the game that lets the user choose whether they want to play again. To do this, you need another loop that goes around the Guessing Game Loop (see figure 7.15). The Play Again Loop needs to repeat the Guessing Game Loop as long as the user answers that they want to play again.

Listing 7.6   Play Again Loop

```
while play_again:
    print(intro)                                   Start the Play Again Loop that repeats
                                                   as long as play_again is True.
    # Guessing Game Loop
    while count_guesses < 6:
        # Loop code hidden
    else
        game_over()
    # End of Guessing Game Loop
    answer = input("Would you like to play again [Y/N]? ")
    if answer.upper() ==  "Y":
        # Starting over. Get a new random number and reset the counter

        number_in_my_head = random.randint(1,20)
        count_guesses = 1                          Reset the number
                                                   of guesses to I.
```

Print instructions.

Ask the user if they want to play again.

Get a new random number.

```
    else:
        play_again = False
print("Good bye!")
GPIO.cleanup()
```

Set play_again to False, which causes the Play Again Loop to end.

Reset the GPIO pins used in this program (set them back to input).

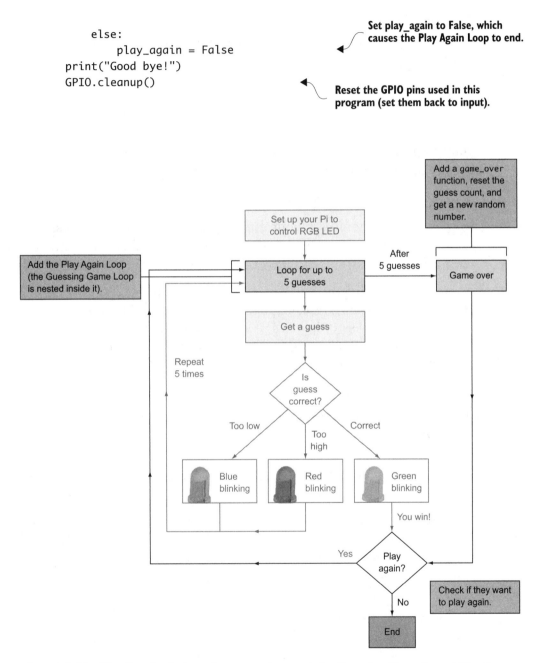

Figure 7.15 The Play Again Loop is wrapped around the Guessing Game Loop. After the player has exhausted their guesses or guessed the number correctly, they're asked if they want to play again. Depending on their answer, the game will either start over or end.

Awesome job! You have put together a circuit to control an RGB LED and written the Python code to make a game interact with it. Now, let's test it.

Playing the game

Save the code as LEDGuessingGame.py, and try running it. Select Run > Run Module (or press F5) from the IDLE text editor to run your program. If you have an older version of Raspbian (prior to October 2015), open Terminal and enter the following command:

```
pi@raspberrypi ~ $ sudo python3 LEDGuessingGame.py
```

Excellent! You should see your guessing game start up. Let's test it to see if it works. Try seeing if you can guess the number. Try getting it wrong, just to make sure the game_over function works.

> NOTE Remember that any programs that use GPIO pins must be run from the Raspbian command prompt as the superuser (or root). The sudo command lets you do this. If you try running the program at the Python Shell in IDLE, then you'll get the error that ends "RuntimeError: No access to /dev/mem. Try running as root!"

Troubleshooting

If the lights aren't blinking after each guess is made, here are some things you can check:

- Check the circuit on the breadboard. Is the ribbon cable connected properly, with the first wire connected toward the edge of the Pi, away from the USB ports?
- Double-check that the jumper, RGB LED, and resistors are connected to the correct holes on the breadboard. Could your RGB LED be inserted the wrong way (the shorter legs go toward the negative or ground side)? Try turning it around if you aren't sure.
- Look through your Python program for errors. If necessary, edit the program to add some print statements so you can see which parts are working. For example, in the inner loop that handles the five guesses, you can use the print function to display the value of count_guesses:

```
print(count_guesses)
```

⚙ Try adding a `print` message in the `flash` function so you're sure it's being called. For example, you could add

```
print("Blinking the LED")
```

If you've enjoyed playing your game, try some additional challenges to increase the fun factor!

Challenges

These challenges use the RGB LED that you've already wired up. If you can't figure them out, check appendix C for hints and solutions.

Game winner

Write a function in the game that creates a flashing animation whenever the user correctly guesses the number. For example, you could try quickly flashing the RGB LED different colors.

Easter egg

Was the last one too easy? Well, try this: create an Easter egg in your game. Create logic so that if someone types in a certain word (maybe *Spam*), the program displays a secret message and flashes the light in a crazy way.

Warmer and colder

Expand the logic of your program to make the speed of the blinking indicate whether the player's guess is close to or far away from the correct answer. As a hint, think about the blinking speed you've set. Let's say a guess is off by 10 (the player guesses 15, and the magic number is 5). You want the light to blink slowly. You can take the difference (ignore any negative signs) and divide it by 10. This will make the blinking speed one-tenth of the difference, or once every second if you're off by 10 (pretty slow). If the player's guess is off by 2, the light will blink every two-tenths of a second (pretty fast). This way, the blinking speed tells the player if their guess is close or far away.

Darth Vader surprise

Let's see if you can get an image of Darth Vader to pop up if the player doesn't correctly guess the number. Here's a hint to get you started. Install the Linux image-viewing software called fim,[2] a program that allows you to open images from the Raspbian command line. To install fim, make sure your Pi is connected to the internet, and then open Terminal and use the following command:

```
pi@raspberrypi ~ $ sudo apt-get -y install fim
```

Next, download an image of Darth Vader and have the game display it on the screen. Let's say you've downloaded an image called Darth_Vader.jpg. You can display it with these commands in Python:

```
import os
os.system("fim Darth_Vader.jpg")
```

Good luck! May the Force be with you!

Summary

In this chapter, you learned that

- Pis can respond in rich and exciting ways by interacting through the GPIO pins in your programs.

- Functions, loops, and conditional statements can be combined with your Pi's output capabilities to create programs that react to people and the environment.

- RGB LEDs are very cool because they can make different colors and are actually three LEDs packed into one small package.

- A while loop can have an else statement that allows you to control what happens when the loop condition is no longer true.

---

[2] fim is the improved version of fbi, image-viewing software for Linux that can be run from the command line.

- A play again loop can be wrapped around a main game loop to allow users to play the game over and over again.

- *Refactoring* is a fancy word that just means simplifying or shortening your code by looking for ways to make it more efficient. Be careful, though—you don't want to simplify something so much that it becomes too hard to understand (remember the Zen of Python)!

8

DJ Raspi

In this chapter, you'll be

- *Giving your Pi the ability to respond to input signals by making it interact with you in response to button presses*

- *Learning about electronic buttons and how to build circuits on a breadboard with them*

- *Running Raspbian operating system commands so your programs can play music, show videos, and more*

- *Using Python to store sets of information called lists*

- *Exploring how you can play sounds on your Pi and make your Pi into a music machine*

We don't think about our five senses (taste, smell, touch, hearing, and sight), but without them we wouldn't be able to feel, know, and interact with the world around us. Think of your Pi as a person who, until now, has had a limited set of senses. So far, your Pi has only been able to respond to keyboard keys being pressed and mouse clicks.

Like a mad scientist bringing something to life, in this chapter you're going to embark on a project to wire up a new sense of touch for your Pi.

Okay, maybe it won't be as crazy as creating a bionic creature, but a button gives your Pi a sense of touch. You'll wire a couple buttons to the Pi's GPIO pins (recall that GPIO stands for general-purpose input/output, so this is how your Pi can sense and affect the environment). Then you'll program your Pi to react to button presses. Exciting times are ahead!

This project is a small glimpse of all the different senses you could possibly give your Pi. Electronic components that can detect the environment around them are called *sensors*. A button is one of the simplest sensors, because it can detect touch. What other sensors could you add? How about some of these ideas:

- A camera that can track a ball or face using special software called *computer vision* that can recognize objects (this is similar to how a Microsoft Kinect works)
- Super-human capabilities like a proximity sensor to detect when someone is walking nearby (like the ones used to trigger the doors to open at the grocery store)
- A microphone so it can hear

All this is possible with a Pi, some determination to figure it out, and a bit of fearlessness about trying new things.

Project overview

In this chapter, you'll turn your Pi into DJ Raspi—a musical computer that plays different sounds when you press buttons. You'll wire up two mini pushbuttons on your breadboard and figure out how to write the code to make the buttons play sounds. Later, if you want, you can add other sensors to your Pi and program them. This project will give you an example of how to work with input from sensors. Figure 8.1 shows the parts you'll need.

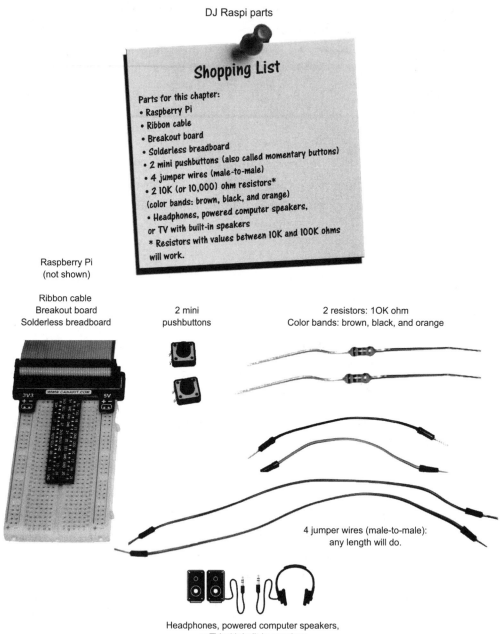

DJ Raspi parts

Shopping List

Parts for this chapter:
- Raspberry Pi
- Ribbon cable
- Breakout board
- Solderless breadboard
- 2 mini pushbuttons (also called momentary buttons)
- 4 jumper wires (male-to-male)
- 2 10K (or 10,000) ohm resistors*
(color bands: brown, black, and orange)
- Headphones, powered computer speakers,
or TV with built-in speakers
* Resistors with values between 10K and 100K ohms
will work.

Raspberry Pi
(not shown)

Ribbon cable
Breakout board
Solderless breadboard

2 mini
pushbuttons

2 resistors: 10K ohm
Color bands: brown, black, and orange

4 jumper wires (male-to-male):
any length will do.

Headphones, powered computer speakers,
or TV with built-in speakers

Figure 8.1 The DJ Raspi project requires several different parts to turn your Pi into a music player. The length and color of the jumper wires don't matter.

Gather the parts and get ready for some fun. You'll notice that some of them are the same as in chapters 6 and 7, but you'll also need a few new items. Most of these are included in Raspberry Pi starter kits, but you can find them at online electronics retailers as well. You'll approach this project in two parts: building the circuit (the hardware) and writing the program (the software). Let's go!

Setting up your Pi to play sounds

To start, let's get your Pi ready to play sounds. A Pi can output sounds through the headphone jack (also called the *3.5 mm audio port*) or through HDMI. Before you start, plug in your headphones, powered computer speakers, or, alternatively, a TV with built-in speakers connected via an HDMI cable.

All sounds aren't the same: audio formats

If you wanted to leave a secret message for someone, you could choose several different ways to make the message into a secret code. You could use different symbols to represent words, or you might substitute letters or shift letters around. There are many different ways to encode something.

Similarly, people have come up with many different ways to store sounds (or audio files). These ways (called *formats*) are different ways of compressing or encoding the information in a sound to make it easy to store on a computer or music player. Sometimes sounds are encoded so they will only work on certain music players.

Here are some common formats:

- *MP3*—The most common audio file format used in most audio players. The files end in .mp3.
- *WAV or WAVE*—Stands for Waveform Audio File Format. It's used on many Windows computers. These files end in .wav.
- *Ogg*—An open format that was developed for streaming applications. The files end in .ogg.

Each format uses a different method to compress or shrink a sound and make it smaller to store. The Pi has many different software applications for playing audio. Each one can play different formats. Check the Raspberry Pi forums if you want to learn more about the different players and what they're best for.

You'll be focusing on playing MP3s from your Pi, because that is a common audio file format. What can you use to play them?

OMXPlayer and MP3s

When you watch movies or listen to music on a computer, you may use iTunes or Windows Media Player. Raspbian has its own equivalent called OMXPlayer that can play sounds or videos. Lucky for you, it's capable of playing MP3 files (or MP3s)—one of the most common audio formats.

> DEFINITION   OMXPlayer is a video and audio player that was created for Raspberry Pi.

If you don't have an MP3, you can test OMXPlayer using one of the sounds already on your Pi. There are quite a few MP3s in the folders included with the Scratch software. Open File Manager, and go to this folder to see some of them: /usr/share/scratch/Media/Sounds/Vocals/. In the folder, you'll see both MP3 and WAV format files (see figure 8.2).

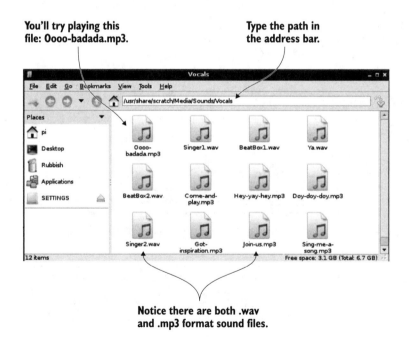

You'll try playing this file: Oooo-badada.mp3.

Type the path in the address bar.

Notice there are both .wav and .mp3 format sound files.

Figure 8.2   When you install Raspbian on your Pi, it comes with Scratch, which has a number of sound files including vocals, sound effects, animal sounds, and drum beats.

To play an MP3 using OMXPlayer, open Terminal, and enter

```
pi@raspberrypi ~ $ omxplayer /usr/share/scratch/Media/Sounds/Vocals/
➥ Oooo-badada.mp3
```

You should hear a short music clip of a woman singing. Enjoy the song!

> **NOTE** In Terminal, pressing the up and down arrows cycles through previous commands. Press the up arrow once and then press Enter to run the last command again.

Fantastic! Your Pi can speak to you now.

Troubleshooting

What if you have speakers or headphones plugged in but don't hear anything? OMXPlayer should automatically detect whether to output the sound to the 3.5 mm audio output or HDMI. If it doesn't, try this command for the headphone jack (3.5 mm audio output):

```
pi@raspberrypi ~ $ omxplayer -o local /usr/share/scratch/Media/Sounds/
➥ Vocals/Oooo-badada.mp3
```

-o is a special switch or *flag* that lets OMXPlayer know that you want to tell it something. In this case, -o stands for *output*, and it tells OMXPlayer where you want to output the sound. In this case, you set it to -o local, which outputs sound to the 3.5 mm (headphone jack) output.

Switches (flags)

Switches, such as -o for output, act like options or special controls for a program. They're common when using the command-line interface. You can usually get a list of what switches a program has by making the command print out its help information. Most programs that you can run at the command line will give you a list of all switches or flags when you type the name of the program and then -h. The -h switch- stands for *help*. Try it with OMXPlayer:

```
pi@raspberrypi ~ $ omxplayer -h
```

You'll see a long list of options you can use to control how video and audio files are played. Try -h with other command-line programs to see what results you get.

If you need to specify sending the sound to speakers in your monitor, then use the -o switch and specify hdmi for output to the HDMI port:

```
pi@raspberrypi ~ $ omxplayer -o hdmi /usr/share/scratch/Media/Sounds/
➥ Vocals /Oooo-badada.mp3
```

Now that you know you can play music, let's build the circuit and write some code to create your DJ Raspi!

Hardware: building the circuit

Building time! You're building a circuit on your breadboard to detect or listen to buttons. When a button is pressed, your circuit will send electricity flowing to a GPIO pin on your Pi. You'll start by connecting the Pi's GPIO pins to the breadboard using the ribbon cable and GPIO breakout board. Refer back to chapter 6 (section 6.1) if you need to recall how to set this up.

A reminder about numbers

Like finding a seat in a stadium, we'll refer to the holes on a breadboard using the prefix *BB*. So the hole located in row 25, column a, is *BB25a*. Similarly, we'll refer to the Pi's GPIO pins using the prefix *GP* and then the pin number. So GPIO pin 24 is called *GP24* for short.

Wiring a button

Let's get busy wiring the buttons. There are many different types of buttons, but you'll be using a mini pushbutton (see figure 8.3). These buttons commonly come in Raspberry Pi kits along with jumper wires, resistors, and LEDs. If you need to purchase them, you can find them at many online electronics retailers in packs of 10 or 20 for less than the cost of a cheeseburger. With the parts gathered, let's assemble the circuit.

Figure 8.3 The mini push-button makes a nice clicking sound when you press the black button in the middle. Pressing it acts like closing a switch to complete a circuit.

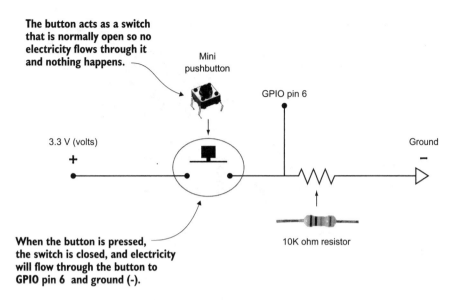

The button acts as a switch that is normally open so no electricity flows through it and nothing happens.

Mini pushbutton

GPIO pin 6

3.3 V (volts)

+

Ground

−

When the button is pressed, the switch is closed, and electricity will flow through the button to GPIO pin 6 and ground (-).

10K ohm resistor

Figure 8.4   The circuit diagram for the first button in the DJ Raspi project shows how electricity will flow through the circuit. The button is a switch that allows electricity to flow to GP06 and ground (-) when it's pressed or closed.

Circuit sketch

The circuit diagram for the DJ Raspi is shown in figure 8.4. To listen to whether a button is being pressed, you'll have electricity (+3.3 V) flow from your Pi to the button. When the button is pressed, the electricity will flow through the button and then split. A small amount of electricity will flow to GPIO pin 6 (GP06) and the rest will flow through the 10K ohm resistor and then to ground (0 V). Let's put it together on the breadboard.

Let's build the button circuit on the breadboard and program your Pi to know when the button is being pressed. You'll give your Pi the ability to feel the button being pressed, by wiring up the button in this order:

1 Add the mini pushbutton to the breadboard.

2 Connect a jumper wire from 3.3 volts to the button. You'll use the positive power bus (+) that runs along the side of the breadboard.

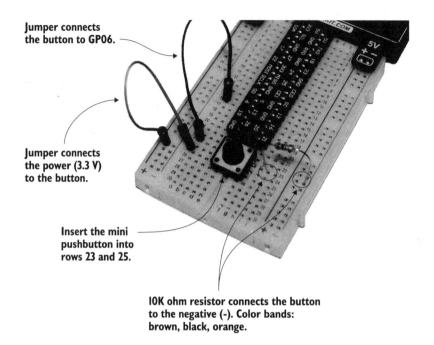

Jumper connects
the button to GP06.

Jumper connects
the power (3.3 V)
to the button.

Insert the mini
pushbutton into
rows 23 and 25.

10K ohm resistor connects the button
to the negative (-). Color bands:
brown, black, orange.

Figure 8.5 The mini pushbutton will have 3.3 volts connected to it
from the positive power rail. When the button is pressed, power flows
through the button and splits. Some electrical current goes to GP06
(GPIO pin 6), and the rest goes through the resistor and then to the
negative power bus (-).

3 Add the resistor from the button to the negative power bus (-), also
  called ground.

4 Connect the second jumper wire from the button to GP06 (GPIO pin 6).

The completed circuit for one button will look like what you see in figure 8.5.

Don't forget, nothing will happen when you press the button. You
have to program your Pi to react to this new-found sense of touch.
Let's go through the steps to build the circuit:

STEP 1. ADD THE MINI PUSHBUTTON.

Let's look at how pushbuttons work before we go on. If you had X-ray
goggles, you would see that the left and right legs at the top of the

button are connected. Similarly, the left and right legs along the bottom of the button are connected. The top and the bottom of the button aren't connected.

But when you press the button, figure 8.6 shows what happens. Pressing the button pushes down a small metal bar so that the top and bottom are connected. We say the switch is *closed*. When you let go of the button, the spring in the button pushes the metal bar back up, and the

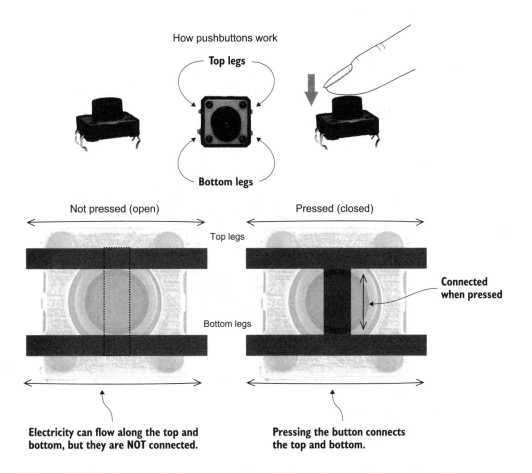

Figure 8.6 In a button, the legs are connected along the top and are separately connected along the bottom. When the button is pressed, the top and bottom are connected by a small metal bar.

switch is open again. Grab your mini pushbutton, and let's insert it into the breadboard.

> **NOTE** You'll need to push the button into the breadboard very firmly. If the button legs aren't lined up with the breadboard holes, you may accidentally bend some of the button legs. Don't worry—you can bend them back and try again. If a leg breaks off, use a new button.

You're going to put the button in rows 23 and 25 along columns d and g on the breadboard. Connect the legs:

* Top legs: *BB23d* and *BB23g*
* Bottom legs: *BB25d* and *BB25g*

When the button is inserted, it will look like figure 8.7. Double-check that it's pushed down into the breadboard so that all the legs will make a good connection. Good job—you just completed the trickiest part!

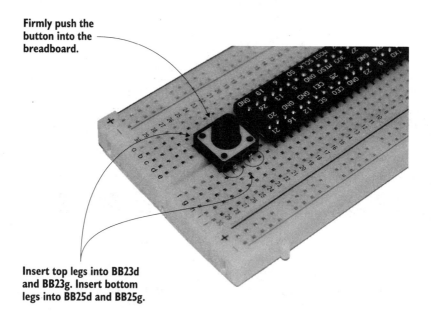

Firmly push the button into the breadboard.

Insert top legs into BB23d and BB23g. Insert bottom legs into BB25d and BB25g.

Figure 8.7 Align the pushbutton with the breadboard holes, and then press it down into the breadboard. Make sure you press it so the button legs are down into the breadboard holes and make a good connection. If you accidentally bend the legs, don't worry! Just bend them back and try again.

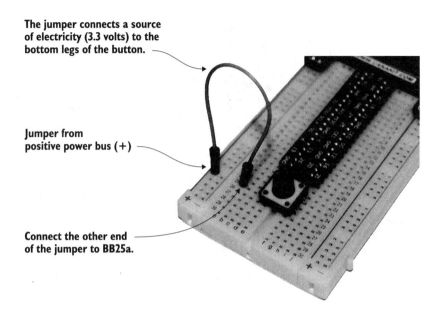

The jumper connects a source of electricity (3.3 volts) to the bottom legs of the button.

Jumper from positive power bus (+)

Connect the other end of the jumper to BB25a.

Figure 8.8   The jumper connects power (3.3 volts) to the bottom of the button.

STEP 2. CONNECT A JUMPER WIRE FROM 3.3 VOLTS TO THE BUTTON.

You need to connect the button to a source of electrical current. You'll use the positive power rail along the edge of the breadboard as the source of power (you could also directly connect the jumper to the 3V3 pin on the breakout board).

Connect the jumper wire from the *positive power bus* (+) to *BB25a*. Remember, you can connect the jumper to any hole along the power rail (it has a red line next to it). When you've added the wire, it will look like figure 8.8.

Fantastic! Now you have electricity reaching the bottom legs of the button.

STEP 3. ADD THE 10K OHM RESISTOR.

Time to connect your 10K ohm resistor. It has bands of brown, black, and orange followed by a fourth gold or silver band. *Remember that*

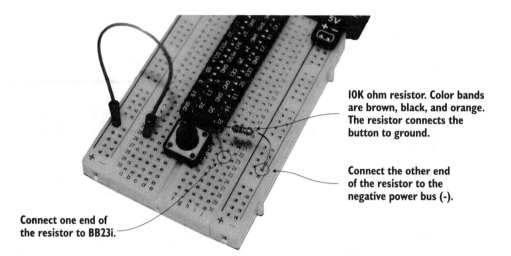

IOK ohm resistor. Color bands are brown, black, and orange. The resistor connects the button to ground.

Connect the other end of the resistor to the negative power bus (-).

Connect one end of the resistor to BB23i.

Figure 8.9 Add the resistor. Make sure its ends are pushed down into the bread-board holes.

electricity will flow either way through a resistor, so it doesn't matter which way you place it.

You're connecting the resistor from the top of the button to the negative power bus (-). This is the set of holes with a blue stripe next to it running along the edge of the breadboard.

Insert one end of the resistor into *BB23i* and the other end into the *negative power bus (-)*. You can choose any hole along the blue line. Once the resistor is added, you'll have something that looks like figure 8.9. Now you're ready for the final step.

STEP 4. ADD THE JUMPER TO A GPIO PIN.

A small amount of electricity needs to reach a GPIO pin (you'll use GP06), so you need a jumper wire from the top of the button to a hole next to the GPIO pin. To make this connection, add a jumper from *BB23a* to *BB16a*. Figure 8.10 shows how it looks.

When the button is pressed, a small amount of electricity will flow to GP06 and through the resistor to ground. Nothing happens yet, but next you'll write a Python program to detect that electricity and play some sounds.

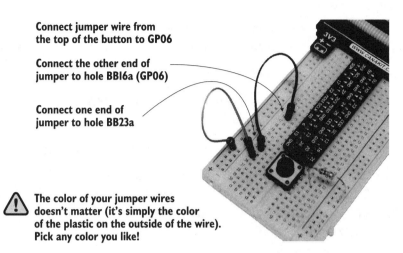

Connect jumper wire from the top of the button to GP06

Connect the other end of jumper to hole BB16a (GP06)

Connect one end of jumper to hole BB23a

⚠ **The color of your jumper wires doesn't matter (it's simply the color of the plastic on the outside of the wire). Pick any color you like!**

Figure 8.10 The jumper connects the top of the button to GP06. Later, you'll set your Pi to listen for electrical input on this GPIO pin.

Adding the second button

Let's add a second button to the board. Figure 8.11 shows what it will look like when it's done.

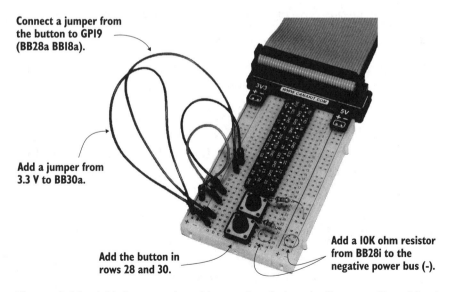

Connect a jumper from the button to GP19 (BB28a BB18a).

Add a jumper from 3.3 V to BB30a.

Add the button in rows 28 and 30.

Add a 10K ohm resistor from BB28i to the negative power bus (-).

Figure 8.11 Add the second pushbutton just below the first one. The wiring is the same, but you'll connect it to GP19 (GPIO pin 19). Any available GPIO pin will work, but remember that your code will have to reflect the GPIO pins you select.

To add another button, you'll create the same circuit but place the button in rows 28 and 30 on your breadboards. You'll wire the button to GP19.

STEP 1. ADD THE MINI PUSHBUTTON.

Insert the button so that the top legs are in *BB28d* and *BB28g* and the bottom legs are in *BB30d* and *BB30g*.

STEP 2. CONNECT A JUMPER WIRE FROM 3.3 VOLTS TO THE BUTTON.

You need to connect power from the positive power bus to the bottom of the button. The power rail is the line of holes with a red line running next to it. Insert a jumper from anywhere along the *positive power bus (+)* to *BB30a*.

STEP 3. ADD THE 10K OHM RESISTOR.

To prevent too much electricity from flowing when the button is pressed, you need to add a resistor. As before, you'll add a 10K ohm resistor (color bands are brown, black, and orange) to connect the top of the button to the negative power bus (-).

Insert one end of the resistor into *BB28i* and the other end into the *negative power bus (-)*. Any hole along the blue line will work.

STEP 4. ADD THE JUMPER TO A GPIO PIN.

Finally, when the button is pressed, you need electricity to flow to a GPIO pin. For the second button, you're using GP19. Connect a jumper wire from *BB28a* to *BB18a* (GP19).

Terrific! The second button is connected, and you've completed the button circuit. Let's call the first button Button 1. It's wired to GP06. The second button, Button 2, is wired to GP19. Now that everything is wired up, let's write code for it!

Software: the DJ Raspi program

Your project is to turn your Pi into an awesome music player that is controlled by buttons. Here's how it will work:

- Pressing Button 1 makes the Pi play random music clips.
- Pressing Button 2 makes the Pi play random vocal (singing) sounds.

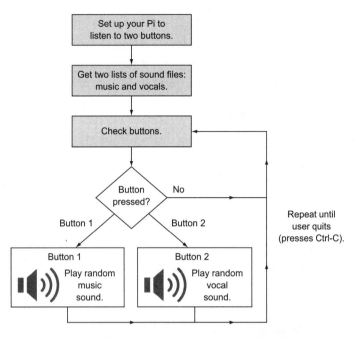

Figure 8.12   A flow diagram showing how the DJ Raspi program should work. The program must gather a list of sounds at the beginning and then check whether the buttons are pressed. The buttons will be checked over and over again.

You'll need one of the following to hear the sounds:

⊙ Headphones

⊙ Powered computer speakers

⊙ Your Pi connected via HDMI to a TV with built-in speakers

Let's think through how this program will work. Figure 8.12 shows a quick diagram of the logic.

Let's write the code in this order:

1 Set up your Pi to listen to input coming from the buttons.

2 Gather a list of music and vocal sounds.

3 Program a loop to check the buttons. If they're pressed, then play random sounds.

You'll try to use functions along the way to simplify your code.

Let's begin! Open IDLE by choosing Python 3 under Menu > Programming. In the Python Shell, start a new program by pressing Ctrl-N or selecting File > New Window.

Setting up the Pi: initializing the buttons

In the IDLE text editor, you'll start by loading the Python libraries you'll need to use. You'll also set up a couple of the Pi's GPIO ports to listen for electrical signals coming in from the buttons being pressed. In the flow diagram, this is the first step of initializing the buttons (see figure 8.13).

When you set up the GPIO ports, you use GPIO.IN to tell the Pi that you plan to use that port as an input. To prepare your Pi for input to the

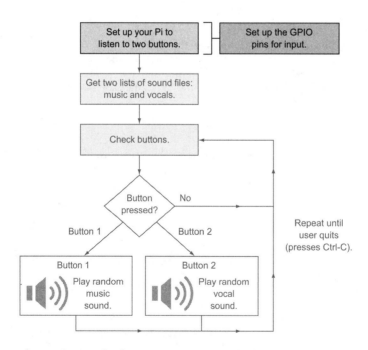

Figure 8.13 The first step is to set up the buttons as inputs. This will mean your Pi is ready to check whether it's detecting any voltage coming in, which will happen when a button is pressed.

GPIO pins, you need to tell it which pins you plan to use. Based on the circuit, you're using these pins as inputs:

- GP06 for Button 1
- GP19 for Button 2

The following listing shows how you can use the GPIO.setup command to set a GPIO pin to input.

Listing 8.1   Setting up GPIO pins for input

```
# DJ Raspi
# Ryan Heitz

# importing the libraries you need
import RPi.GPIO as GPIO
import time
import random
import os

# Variables for the button GPIO input pins
button_pin1 = 6
button_pin2 = 19

#Tell the Pi we want to use a breakout board
GPIO.setmode(GPIO.BCM)

# Set up GPIO pins as input pins (detect electrical signals coming in)
GPIO.setup(button_pin1,GPIO.IN)
GPIO.setup(button_pin2,GPIO.IN)
```

Import the os library that lets you execute a Raspbian command.

Store the value of the GPIO pins.

Set up the pins for input (notice you use GPIO.IN).

You may notice that you import a new os module. We'll talk about why you need that in the next section when you gather your lists of sound files.

Getting a list of sounds

Lists are everywhere around you. You make lists of things you need to do, gifts to buy, places you want to visit, and favorite things, such as your top-10 movies or books.

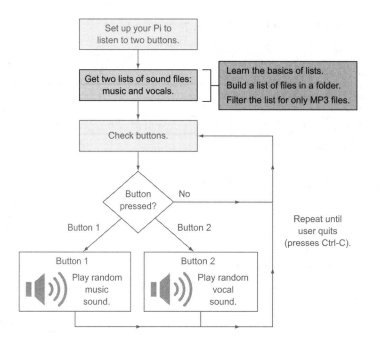

Figure 8.14 The next step of the DJ Raspi program gets a list of sound files. Later, you'll add the part that uses the button to trigger playing random sounds from the lists.

Your DJ Raspi needs a *list* of sound files: one for music clips (or loops) and one for vocals. Based on the design, you need to get a list of files from a folder on your Pi, and then you need to select a random sound file from the list and play it (see figure 8.14).

In Python, you can create lists or groups of things easily. Let's look at some examples.

Let's create a list of basketball player names. Open IDLE to the Python 3.x Shell by choosing Python 3 under Menu > Programming. In the Python Shell, make a list:

```
>>> basketball_players = ["Kevin Durant", "LeBron James", "Chris Paul",
➥ "John Wall"]
```

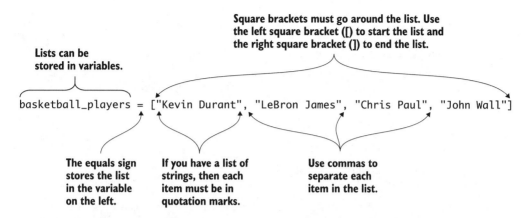

Figure 8.15 You make lists by using square brackets to enclose a set of things. Each thing in the list should be separated with a comma. Python will even let you make lists that combine different types of data, like strings and integers.

Print out the list like this, and you'll see what's inside:

```
>>> print(basketball_players)
['Kevin Durant', 'LeBron James', 'Chris Paul', 'John Wall']
```

To make a list of the items, put them in a set of square brackets ([]) and separate each item with a comma (see figure 8.15). For lists of strings, each item in the list has to have quotation marks around it. Pretty simple! That's the Python way.

Try creating a list called favorite_numbers, like so:

```
>>> favorite_numbers = [22, 27, 49, 121, 2, 25]
```

Display the contents of the list using print:

```
>>> print(favorite_numbers)
[22, 27, 49, 121, 2, 25]
```

NOTE   When making a list of numbers, you don't use any quotation marks.

Enjoy making lists of some of your favorite things!

More things you can do with lists

There are lots of things you can do with lists! Let's try a few.

You make a list longer by adding more items to it. To do this, use the append method. Let's add the name Stephen Curry to the list of basketball_players. Here is how you can use append to do that:

```
>>> basketball_players.append("Stephen Curry")
```

Use print to see the result:

```
>>> print(basketball_players)
['Kevin Durant', 'LeBron James', 'Chris Paul', 'John Wall', 'Stephen Curry']
```

Excellent! To remove an item from a list you can use the remove method. If you wanted to take John Wall out of the list, write

```
>>> basketball_players.remove("John Wall")
```

Print the list again to see if it worked:

```
>>> print(basketball_players)
['Kevin Durant', 'LeBron James', 'Chris Paul', 'Stephen Curry']
```

Wonderful! If you need to put a list in order alphabetically or from lowest to highest, you can use the sort method like so:

```
>>> favorite_numbers.sort()
```

Check that it worked by printing the list to the screen:

```
>>> print(favorite_numbers)
[2, 22, 25, 27, 49, 121]
```

The numbers are all sorted! This works on lists made of strings as well. If you sort the list of basketball_players, it puts them in alphabetical order based on the first letter of each string. Python has many built-in methods for lists.

Check the online Python documentation[a] for more things you can do with lists. Then sit back and enjoy thinking about all you can do with them in your future programs.

---

[a] Go to the Python website for more information on things you can do with lists: https://docs.python.org/3.4/tutorial/datastructures.html.

For your DJ Raspi, let's see how to

- Get the value of an item stored in a list.
- Get the length of a list.

Getting a value of an item stored in a list

Let's start with a fresh list of basketball players:

```
basketball_players = ["Kevin Durant", "LeBron James", "Chris Paul",
➡ "Stephen Curry"]
```

As you've seen, lists store information. What you might not know is that each spot in a list is given a number called the *index*. The index of the first item in the list is zero (0). The second item has an index of 1. The third item's index is 2, and so on. To get the third item in the basketball_players list, you'd type

```
>>> print(basketball_players[2])
Chris Paul
```

If you want to search a list and have Python tell you the index of where an item first appears in the list, you use the index method:

```
>>> basketball_players.index("Kevin Durant")
0
>>> basketball_players.index("Stephen Curry")
3
```

If the item isn't in the list, Python will give you an error saying so:

```
>>> basketball_players.index("Me")
Traceback (most recent call last):
  File "<pyshell#40>", line 1, in <module>
    basketball_players.index("Me")
ValueError: 'Me' is not in list
```

> NOTE Remember that the index for lists starts counting at 0, not 1! For example, basketball_players[1] gives you "Lebron James", the second item in the list.

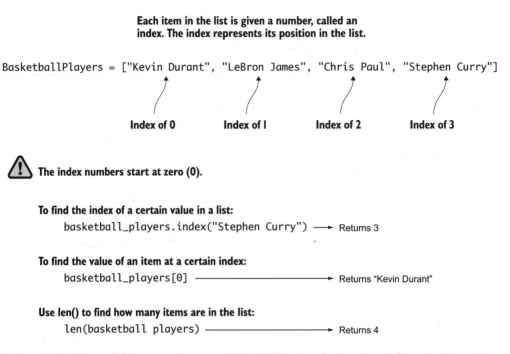

Each item in the list is given a number, called an index. The index represents its position in the list.

BasketballPlayers = ["Kevin Durant", "LeBron James", "Chris Paul", "Stephen Curry"]

Index of 0   **Index of I**   **Index of 2**   **Index of 3**

⚠️ **The index numbers start at zero (0).**

To find the index of a certain value in a list:
basketball_players.index("Stephen Curry") ⟶ Returns 3

To find the value of an item at a certain index:
basketball_players[0] ⟶ Returns "Kevin Durant"

Use len() to find how many items are in the list:
len(basketball players) ⟶ Returns 4

Figure 8.16 Sets of things can be stored in lists. You can retrieve items from the list using the index, which represents the position of an item in the list. The index of a list starts at 0.

Figure 8.16 shows examples of the indexes for a list and how you can get a specific item in a list.

Getting the length of a list

Finally, there are times when you've loaded information into a list and you need a way to check how long the list is. Use the len() function to do that:

```
>>> yummy_snacks = ["chips", "popcorn", "donuts", "cheese",
   "pretzels", "spam"]
>>> print(len(yummy_snacks))
6
```

Great job—you know the basics of lists. Now let's see how you can create lists of MP3s.

Building a list of sound files with the os library

To make the DJ Raspi project work, you need to

1 Grab two lists of sound files from folders on your Pi.
2 Make OMXPlayer play sound files from Python as part of the DJ Raspi program.

Let's learn how.

The Pi has both these abilities through a Python module called the os module (OS stands for *operating system*). With it, you can run operating system commands (things you can type in the Terminal window) from your Python programs. This is fantastic, because it means you can get lists of files and also call OMXPlayer to play a certain file—exactly what you need!

GETTING A LIST OF FILES FROM A FOLDER: USING LISTDIR()

Your Pi has some sound files on it already, as you saw in section 8.1. You'll use the files in these two folders:

- ◉ /usr/share/scratch/Media/Sounds/Music Loops/
- ◉ /usr/share/scratch/Media/Sounds/Vocals/

The os library provides a built-in function, os.listdir(some_path), to get a list of files at some_path. To get a list of Scratch music loops and vocals, use these commands:

```
# Folders with sound files
path_music = "/usr/share/scratch/Media/Sounds/Music Loops/"
path_vocals = "/usr/share/scratch/Media/Sounds/Vocals/"

# Creating two lists with the files in the folders
sounds_music = os.listdir(path_music)
sounds_vocals = os.listdir(path_vocals)
```

If you print the lists, you'll have something that looks like this:

```
print(sounds_music)
['Cave.mp3', 'Techno.mp3', 'HipHop.mp3', 'Triumph.mp3', 'Medieval2.mp3',
➥ 'HumanBeatbox2.mp3', 'DripDrop.mp3', 'Xylo3.mp3', 'GuitarChords1.mp3',
```

```
➡ 'DrumSet2.mp3', 'Xylo2.mp3', 'DrumSet1.mp3', 'Garden.mp3',
➡ 'GuitarChords2.mp3', 'Jungle.mp3', 'Xylo1.mp3', 'Eggs.mp3',
➡ HumanBeatbox1.mp3', 'Drum.mp3', 'DrumMachine.mp3', 'Techno2.mp3',
➡ 'Medieval1.mp3', 'xylo4.mp3']
```

```
print(sounds_vocals)
['Oooo-badada.mp3', 'Singer1.wav', 'BeatBox1.wav', 'Ya.wav',
➡ 'BeatBox2.wav', 'Come-and-play.mp3', 'Hey-yay-hey.mp3',
➡ 'Doy-doy-doy.mp3', 'Singer2.wav', 'Got-inspiration.mp3',
➡ 'Join-you.mp3', 'Sing-me-a-song.mp3']
```

Wow—you have nice-looking lists! But wait: it looks like `sounds_vocals` has WAV (.wav) files and MP3s. Let's filter out the WAVs so you only have MP3s.

FILTERING FOR ONLY MP3S

To filter a list, you can use Python's *list-comprehension* feature. List comprehension is a quick way of creating lists. When you use it, you can include certain conditions or operations that are applied to the items in the list, such as making sure all the files in the list end with .mp3. Let's look at how you can use list comprehension to create a new list from your old list, but only keep the files in the list that end with .mp3:

```
sounds_music = [sound for sound in sounds_music if
    sound.endswith('.mp3')]
sounds_vocals = [sound for sound in sounds_vocals if sound.endswith
➡ ('.mp3')]
```

The list comprehension has a `for` loop inside it. In this case, Python is looping through the list of sound files in your original list of sounds. For each item in the list, Python only adds it to the new sounds list if it matches the condition of being a file ending with .mp3.

Playing a sound when a button is pressed

Next in your plan is to write the code that will play a random sound from your lists when a button is pressed. You'll need this to be in a loop

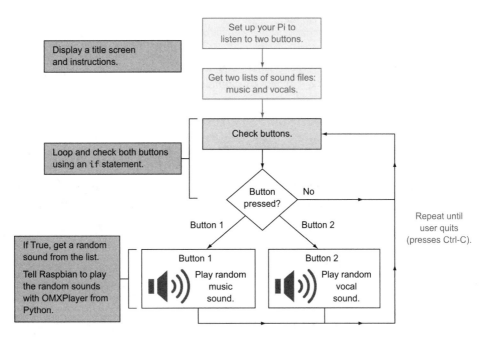

Figure 8.17 The main part of the DJ Raspi program is the loop to check the buttons. You'll use a while loop to check the buttons over and over again. If one of them is pressed, you'll tell Raspbian to play a random sound using OMXPlayer.

so the buttons are repeatedly checked to see whether they're being pressed (see figure 8.17). Let's start by creating the game's title and creating the main game loop.

LOOP TO CHECK THE BUTTONS

First let's add some code to display a title screen and the DJ Raspi instructions. Feel free to make the title screen fancier!

Listing 8.2   DJ Raspi title screen

```
# Clear the screen
os.system("clear")
```

◄ **The clear command makes the Terminal a blank, black window.**

```
#Display a title screen
title = """
    DJ RASPI!!!
    Press Button 1 for Music Sounds
    Press Button 2 for Vocal Sounds
    Press Ctrl + C to exit
"""
print(title)
```

 Use triple quotation marks (""") to create a string literal for the title.

Now let's write the code to loop over and over again to check whether either button is being pressed. When a button is pressed, the GPIO pin will give you a response of True, and you can then call a function to play a random MP3.

Listing 8.3   DJ Raspi game loop

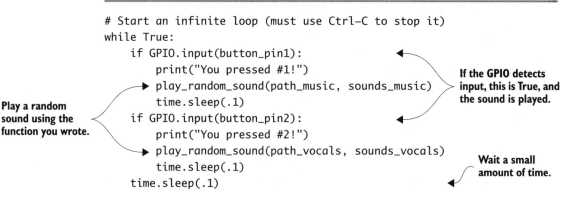

```
# Start an infinite loop (must use Ctrl-C to stop it)
while True:
    if GPIO.input(button_pin1):
        print("You pressed #1!")
        play_random_sound(path_music, sounds_music)
        time.sleep(.1)
    if GPIO.input(button_pin2):
        print("You pressed #2!")
        play_random_sound(path_vocals, sounds_vocals)
        time.sleep(.1)
    time.sleep(.1)
```

Play a random sound using the function you wrote.

If the GPIO detects input, this is True, and the sound is played.

Wait a small amount of time.

The code repeatedly checks whether Button 1 or Button 2 is pressed. If Button 1 is pressed, the code plays a random music sound. If Button 2 is pressed, the code plays a random vocals (singing) sound. If neither is pressed, the code loops around and checks them again. The loop never ends, so you'll need to press Ctrl-C to exit the program.

PLAYING SOUNDS: USING OPERATING SYSTEM COMMANDS FROM PYTHON

You're ready to play your sounds! The os module will let you run operating system commands (ones you normally run using Terminal). To play the first sound in the sounds_music list, you could write

```
os.system("omxplayer -o local '" + path_music + sounds_music[0] + " &")
```

Later in this chapter, we'll explain why the end of that command has an ampersand (&). The result of this command would be the same as typing this at the Raspbian command line:

```
omxplayer -o local "/usr/share/scratch/Media/Sounds/Music Loops/
    Cave.mp3"
```

> **NOTE**   Remember, if you're outputting the sound to HDMI (if your TV has speakers), you need to change -o local to -o hdmi.

Excellent! Let's review what you've learned so far:

- Your Pi can play sounds that are in MP3 format using OMXPlayer.
- Python can store sets of things as lists.
- The Python os library has a function called listdir(path) that can give you a list of sounds in a folder.
- Python's os library has an os.system(command) function that can run operating system commands from Python, such as playing sounds with OMXPlayer.

Functions!

Let's think about how you can write the functions for DJ Raspi. You'll want to create two functions:

- get_MP3_sounds — This function will get a list of sounds ending in .mp3 from a specified folder. You'll tell the function (pass it a parameter) the name of the folder where you want to get the MP3 sound files. The function will return a list of sounds.
- play_random_sound — This function will take a list of sounds, pick a random number, and then use os.system to tell Raspbian to play the sound with OMXPlayer.

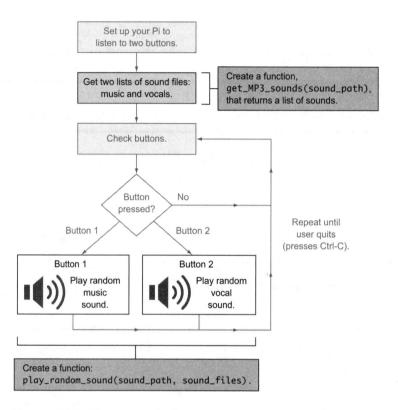

Figure 8.18   There are two places where you can create functions so you can reuse code. One function creates a list of sound files, and the other function plays a random sound when a button is pressed.

Figure 8.18 shows where these functions fit into the flow diagram.

Why not make this a single function? One reason is that you only need to load a list of sound files once, near the beginning of the program. You play the sound files every time a button is pressed. Listing 8.4 shows the code for the get_MP3_sounds and play_random_sound functions.

> **NOTE**   Remember to put these functions near the beginning of the program. They must be added before they're used for the first time.

At the end of this listing, you use (or call) get_MP3_sounds twice to get your lists of music and vocal sound files.

Listing 8.4   Functions for loading and playing sound files

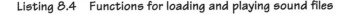

Use the listdir function to get a list of files in a folder on your Pi.

Comprehension filters the list to only keep files ending in .mp3.

```
# Returns a list of mp3 sound files for the path given
def get_MP3_sounds(sound_path):
    sound_filesound_files = os.listdir(sound_path)
    sound_filesound_files = [sound_file for sound_file in
  sound_filesound_files
                    if sound_file.endswith('.mp3')]
    return sound_filesound_files

# Plays a random sound from a list of mp3s for the path given
def play_random_sound(sound_path, sound_filesound_files):
    random_sound_index = random.randint(0,len(sound_filesound_files)-1)
    os.system("omxplayer -o local '" + sound_path +
            "/" + sound_filesound_files[random_sound_index] + "' &")

# Get the list of music loops and vocals (mp3s only)
sounds_music = get_MP3_sounds(path_music)
sounds_vocals = get_MP3_sounds(path_vocals)
```

Use the randint and len functions to get a random sound number.

Play the sound with os.system.

You may have noticed that a few extra things are added to this line:

```
os.system("omxplayer -o local '" + sound_path +
        "/" + sound_filesound_files[random_sound_index] + "' &")
```

This line joins the command to run OMXPlayer with the path to your sound files (`sound_path`) and the random sound file you want to play (`sound_filesound_files[random_sound_index]`). At the end, you add an ampersand (`&`). The ampersand tells Raspbian to run the command in the background. This is so you can quickly press one button and then the other.

Doing multiple things at once: meet the ampersand (&)

When you play sounds, you want to be able to press the buttons quickly, like a DJ, and have the sounds overlap to create interesting music. Normally, your Pi would play one sound, and, when it was finished playing, let you play another. Not what you want. Here is an example of playing two sounds. You can't run the second command until the first one is finished:

```
omxplayer /usr/share/scratch/Media/Sounds/Vocals/Oooo-badada.mp3
omxplayer /usr/share/scratch/Media/Sounds/Vocals/Hey-yay-hey.mp3
```

(continued)

Luckily, your Pi can do a few things at once. You might have several different windows open at the same time. Each window is connected to some underlying code or set of instructions running on your Pi. These underlying sets of code are called *processes* or *threads*. Raspbian, like other modern operating systems, manages these processes and assigns each one its own unique ID number. An ampersand (&) placed at the end of a command tells your Pi to run the command as another process in the background alongside any other processes.

Try these two commands again, but this time with ampersands:

```
omxplayer /usr/share/scratch/Media/Sounds/Vocals/Oooo-badada.mp3 &
omxplayer /usr/share/scratch/Media/Sounds/Vocals/Hey-yay-hey.mp3 &
```

Notice the ampersand (&) at the end of each command. In this way, the Pi will play your sound, but the code won't make your Pi wait for the sound to finish before doing something else. Adding an ampersand at the end of the OMXPlayer command makes the button play each sound in the background. Remove the ampersand to play one sound at a time. Because this is a feature of the OS, the concept of using ampersands to execute commands as their own unique processes applies to other Linux commands that you know already or will learn.

Great! You're ready to test your project!

Testing: your first gig as DJ Raspi

Save the code as DJRaspi.py, and try running it. Select Run > Run Module (or press F5) from the IDLE text editor to run your program. If you have an older version of Raspbian (prior to October 2015), programs that use the GPIO pins must be run from the Raspbian command prompt as the superuser (or root). Open Terminal, and enter the following command:

```
pi@raspberrypi ~ $ sudo python3 DJRaspi.py
```

You should see the title screen display. Test it by pressing the buttons to see if they work.

> NOTE   Remember that any program that uses GPIO pins must be run from the Raspbian command prompt as the superuser (or root).

Believe it or not, it's rare for a program to work perfectly the first time. If it doesn't, read through the following "Troubleshooting" section and review your circuit and program to try to figure out how to get it working.

Troubleshooting

If sounds aren't playing when you press the buttons, here are some things you can check:

- Check the circuit on the breadboard. Is the ribbon cable connected properly, with the first wire connected toward the edge of your Pi, away from the USB ports?
- Double-check that the jumpers, buttons, and resistors are in the right holes and pressed all the way into the breadboard.
- Does your program print "You pressed #1!" and "You pressed #2!"? If it does, you know your circuit is working, and either it's an issue with the code to load the sound files or your speakers or headphones aren't working. Try running one of the following commands from Terminal to check whether the speakers are working.

  For headphones or speakers plugged into the 3.5 mm audio output:

  ```
  omxplayer -o local /usr/share/scratch/Media/Sounds/Vocals/
  ➥ Oooo-badada.mp3
  ```

  For TV speakers connected by HDMI:

  ```
  omxplayer -o hdmi /usr/share/scratch/Media/Sounds/Vocals/
  ➥ Oooo-badada.mp3
  ```

- Look through your Python program for errors. Try adding some print statements to your functions to make sure they're getting the list of MP3 files properly.

If you've enjoyed creating DJ Raspi, check out the button challenges.

Challenges

Try some of these button activities for extra fun!

Double button press surprise

Give your program a surprise button combination. See if you can make pressing both buttons at once play a new set of sound effects.

Hint: When you want something to happen only if both conditions are True, you can use the ampersand (&). The `if` statement will only be True if both the first *and* second conditions are True. It looks like this:

```
if GPIO.input(button_pin1) & GPIO.input(button_pin2):
    print("Both buttons are pressed!")
```

Here is the path to some Scratch sound effects on your Pi:

```
path_effects = "/usr/share/scratch/Media/Sounds/Effects/"
```

Yoda Magic 8 Ball

There is a great classic toy called the Magic 8 Ball. It's a ball that displays an answer to a question when you shake it. Ask it a question, and you'll get some truly magical advice. The Magic 8 Ball has 20 different answers, ranging from "It is certain" to "My sources say no."

> NOTE I don't recommend using the Magic 8 Ball to advise you on major life matters!

Your challenge is to make a Magic 8 Ball program:

⊙ Ask a question aloud, and then press a button.

⊙ Pressing the button makes your Pi select a random Yoda clip from a folder and play it.

To get started, find some short sound files of Yoda sayings. One place to find them is on soundboard.com. Search for "yoda" to see if you can locate some good clips (you'll need to create an account to download them for your personal use).

Bonus: Try to give your Pi a handy button that plays Monty Python sound clips whenever you press it.

Continuing to explore

Now that you've given you Pi a new sense of touch, you'll only need to change a few lines of code to make many other projects, such as these:

- An interactive display that shows different digital photographs each time a button is pressed
- Your own Raspberry Pi movie player that plays clips or movies at the press of a button
- An MP3 music player that shuffles through your favorite songs

You can also expand past buttons to sensors, such as passive infrared (PIR) sensors or cameras. For example, PIR sensors detect motion near the sensor. These are great for creating a Pi security system or something that scares people when they come to your door. Maybe you want to trigger a movie to make a frightening zombie head appear or generate a blood-curdling scream. Your only limit is your imagination and mischievous thoughts.

Summary

In this chapter, you learned that

- A Pi can sense the environment around it using the input capability of the GPIO pins. This creates incredible possibilities to make the Pi have human or even superhuman senses.
- Python lists make it easy to store and retrieve sets of things like numbers, sound files, images, and videos.
- Buttons act as simple switches that send a small amount of electricity to your Pi's GPIO pins, which it can detect. You have nothing to fear in wiring up buttons or other sensors!
- Python programs can run Raspbian commands using the os library. This opens lots of possibilities for your programs, from playing

music to showing or taking videos, displaying or taking pictures, and accessing information from websites.

You've completed a great adventure in learning Python programming and how to use your Raspberry Pi. But there is much more excitement ahead of you. Check out appendix D for even more ideas of projects you can do with your Pi. With your Raspberry Pi, knowledge of Python, and a bit of fearlessness, the possibilities are endless!

Appendix A

Raspberry Pi troubleshooting

In this appendix, you'll learn how to solve common issues when setting up a Raspberry Pi. We'll cover common Pi startup (or boot) issues, including how to fix an issue with an SD card for your Pi or set up a new SD card.

Making sure your Pi has power

Sometimes a Pi won't start up. Before you try something drastic like creating a new SD card for your Pi, check the Pi's power:

- When you plug in your Pi, does the Pi's red power light come on?

  Look for a small, red light (LED) on your Pi board. All Pis have them, but you may need to take off your case if you can't see the Pi board. The red power light tells you that your Pi is receiving power. It should come on when you plug in your Pi and stay on the whole time you're using it. If it doesn't come on, that means your Pi isn't receiving power. Check that the power supply is plugged in. If you're using a power strip, check that it's turned on. Sadly, some power supplies are poorly made. Get a new power supply if it's a power issue.

- Next to the red light, does the green activity light (LED) flash a lot when you plug in your Pi?

The flashing is a sign that your Pi is doing some work. The green activity light should turn on and off, flashing quickly at times, as your Pi boots up. When it's done starting up, the green light will turn off and only come on when your Pi is actively doing something like opening a game or Python. If the green light comes on and stays on, but nothing is displayed to the screen, it's likely an issue with your SD card. Jump ahead to section A.4 to learn how to create a new SD card.

If you suspect a power issue, purchase a new power supply and try it out. Providing sufficient electrical power (2 amps) at the correct voltage (5 volts) is important for a Pi to work correctly.

Checking the connection to your TV or monitor

If the red light is staying on and the green light turns on and off after you plug in your Pi, but you don't see any image on your TV or monitor, it's time to check the connection to your screen. Here are a few things to investigate, depending on the type of TV or monitor you're using.

If you're connecting an HDMI cable from your Pi to your TV or monitor, try these things:

○ Check that the TV or monitor is turned on.

○ Check that the TV or monitor is set to the correct input. They typically have multiple inputs, and you must press an input button to select the proper one. Otherwise, the screen will display nothing or a message saying no input is detected.

○ If you have an extra HDMI cable, try using it to see if it's an issue with the cable.

If your setup requires that you use an adapter to connect your Pi to your TV or monitor, then you may need to make sure your adapter works or is the correct type. There are two common types of adapters:

○ *HDMI-to-DVI adapter*—This adapter is used to connect the Raspberry Pi's HDMI cable to a monitor with a digital visual interface (DVI) port. Sometimes you might purchase a bad adapter that doesn't work. If you can, try connecting your Pi to another TV or monitor that uses HDMI to check whether it's an issue with the adapter. Again, if the red light comes on and the green light flashes, but you don't see anything on your screen, it's likely an issue with the monitor connection.

- *HDMI-to-VGA adapter*—Older monitors don't have HDMI or DVI ports and may only have a video graphics array (VGA) port. Your only option may be to buy an HDMI-to-VGA adapter to connect your Pi to the monitor. Not all HDMI-to-VGA adapters work. Your best bet is to buy one that is advertised to work with the Pi from a store that sells Raspberry Pis. If you aren't sure, try hooking up your Pi to another TV or monitor using only the HDMI cable to test whether that is your issue.

If, after all those steps, you don't see a picture, it's likely an issue with your SD card.

Pi starts booting up but then stops

Another issue you may see is that your Raspberry Pi starts booting up, you see a series of messages displayed on the screen, and then the messages stop but the Pi doesn't reach the Raspbian desktop or command line. If this is the case, it's likely that the SD card has been damaged. But another reason is that there could be something wrong with one of your GPIO pins.

If you're building circuits on a breadboard connected to your Pi (see the examples in chapters 6–8), the Pi may fail to boot all the way up if a wire is improperly connected. To see whether this is the issue, disconnect the ribbon cable and breadboard from your Pi and try powering it up again. If the problem persists, it's likely an issue with the SD card.

Making your Pi a new SD card

Still not starting up? An issue with an SD card is a common reason. The SD card may stop working if the Pi is turned off when information is being stored (or written) on the card, or it may fail with age.

> NOTE   When an SD card fails, you'll need to start over, and you'll lose any data or new applications installed on the card. In the future, you can create a backup of your SD card. Check out online forums to learn how to do this.

You have a couple options if you think this is the problem:

1 Clean and reset your SD card with the Raspberry Pi New Out of the Box Software (NOOBS).

2 Purchase a new card from one of the many online stores that sell Raspberry Pis. They cost around $10.

Let's go over how to clean and set up your SD card with NOOBS. To perform these steps, you need another computer, such as a Windows PC or a Mac.

Reformatting your SD card

Formatting is the process of setting up the memory storage so that information can be put on it. To reformat your SD card and set it up with a fresh version of NOOBS, do the following:

1 Using your other computer, download and install the SDFormatter software from the SD Association website: https://www.sdcard.org. On the website, look under Downloads, and download the appropriate version of SDFormatter for either Windows or Mac. Follow the install instructions to load the software on your computer.

2 Insert your SD card into the computer. Take note of which drive letter is assigned to the SD card after it's inserted: it may be E:, F:, or similar.

> NOTE   For the Raspberry Pi Model 2 and B+, the SD card is a microSD card, so you'll need a microSD-to-SD card adapter in order for it to insert into the SD card slot on your computer. You can purchase such an adapter online.

3 Open SDFormatter, select the correct drive letter for your SD card, and then click Format (see figure A.1). It'll ask if you want to continue. Accept the warnings to reformat the SD card.

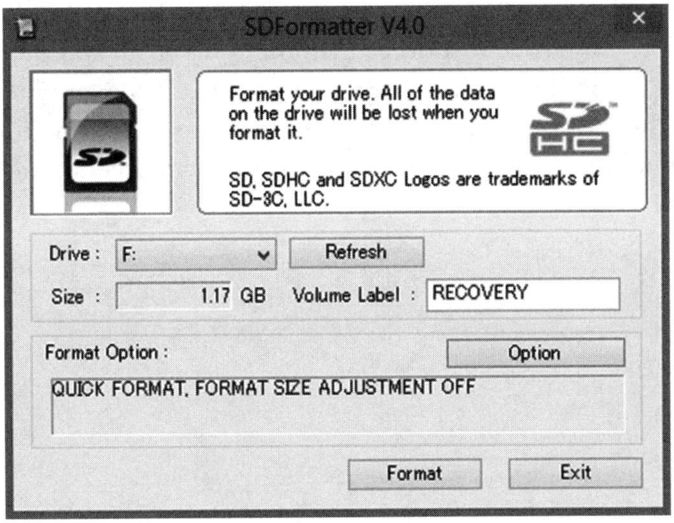

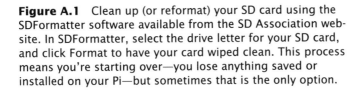

Figure A.1   Clean up (or reformat) your SD card using the SDFormatter software available from the SD Association website. In SDFormatter, select the drive letter for your SD card, and click Format to have your card wiped clean. This process means you're starting over—you lose anything saved or installed on your Pi—but sometimes that is the only option.

4 Go to the Raspberry Pi website at https://www.raspberrypi.org/downloads, and click the link to download the NOOBS zip file. It's a large file, so grab a snack while you're waiting for the download.

5 Extract the NOOBS zip file, and drag all the extracted files onto your SD card.

6 Once the files have been copied, take the SD card out of the computer and put it into your Raspberry Pi. With your keyboard, mouse, and monitor connected, plug in the Pi to see if it boots up. If it doesn't, it's probably time to purchase a new NOOBS SD card for your Pi from a local or online store that sells Raspberry Pis.

Problems not covered here

Not everything can be covered here, so get online! A large amount of troubleshooting information is posted on the Raspberry Pi forums. If you're stuck, search the internet for "Raspberry Pi troubleshooting," and you'll find numerous resources. Although we're all special, it's rare to have an issue with the Pi that no one else has discovered. Chances are, many other people have had the same issue, so read the forums to benefit from all the knowledge that comes from the diverse community of Raspberry Pi users!

Appendix B

Raspberry Pi ports and legacy boards

In this appendix, you'll find information about some of the Raspberry Pi ports and connections that we didn't discuss in chapter 1. Our focus is on the Raspberry Pi 2 Model B. The connections and ports that we'll cover in more detail include the following:

- Wireless internet connections using a USB Wi-Fi adapter
- 3.5 mm audio/video port
- Camera Serial Interface (CSI) port
- Ethernet port
- TV or monitor connection options

In section B.2 of this appendix, we'll review key differences between the legacy Raspberry Pi 1 models as compared to the Raspberry Pi 2 Model B. We'll look more at these popular, but older models:

- Raspberry Pi 1 Model B rev 2 (released September 2012)
- Raspberry Pi 1 Model B+ (released July 2014)

Let's take a closer look at ports and connections.

Raspberry Pi ports

The Raspberry Pi has many different ports, and you can connect many different things to it. In chapter 1, we covered most of the common ones you'll use, but we'll talk about a few of the other ports here. For reference, figure B.1 shows the ports and their typical uses for the Raspberry Pi 2 Model B.

Now let's look in a little more detail at some of the ports and connections we didn't cover in chapter 1 or in later chapters.

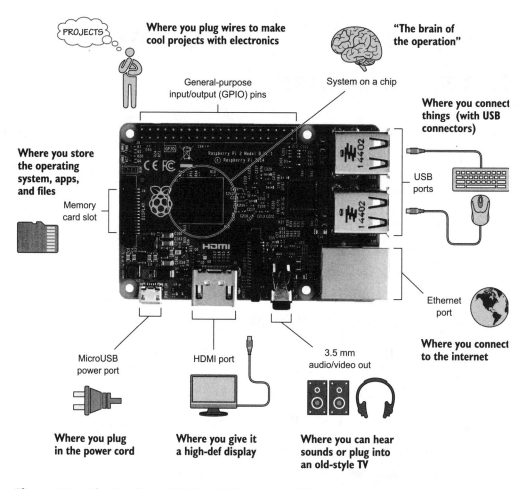

Figure B.1   The Raspberry Pi 2 Model B has many different input and output ports that allow you to connect a keyboard or mouse, monitor, and even high-definition cameras.

Connecting to a wireless network

A preferred way to connect to the internet is using a USB Wi-Fi adapter. Once connected, you can surf the web, download applications from the Pi Store, or remotely log in to your Pi from another computer. Most of us don't have our Pi set up near an Ethernet cable, so connecting wirelessly is the best and only option. Let's look at how you do it.

PLUGGING IN YOUR USB WI-FI ADAPTER

With your Raspberry Pi turned off, plug your USB Wi-Fi adapter into one of the USB ports. There are many different USB Wi-Fi adapters that will work for the Pi. Most kits come with one, but if you need to buy one, refer to the Raspberry Pi forums (see https://www.raspberrypi.org/forums/) to research those that are known to work. Stores that sell Raspberry Pis also tend to sell compatible USB Wi-Fi adapters.

CONFIGURING YOUR WI-FI CONNECTION

To connect to a Wi-Fi network for the first time, follow these steps:

In the top-right corner, click the network icon (looks like two small computers connected). You'll see a list of available Wi-Fi networks (see figure B-2).

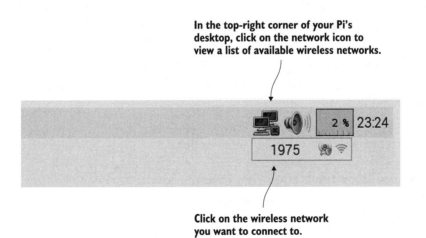

In the top-right corner of your Pi's desktop, click on the network icon to view a list of available wireless networks.

Click on the wireless network you want to connect to.

Figure B.2 The network connection icon is located near the top-right corner of the Raspbian desktop. Clicking on it allows you to view nearby wireless networks.

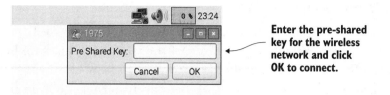

Figure B.3   Enter the pre-shared key for the network and click OK to connect to it.

Click on the Wi-Fi network name that you want to connect to.

Clicking on a Wi-Fi network name will make a small box appear. Enter the pre-shared key (also called the Wi-Fi password) and click OK to connect (see figure B.3). The network icon will change into a Wi-Fi icon showing the strength of the Wi-Fi signal.

Fantastic! Open a web browser, such as your Raspberry Pi's Epiphany web browser, and go to one of your favorite websites to enjoy your new Wi-Fi connection.

TROUBLESHOOTING

If you weren't able to connect, check that your pre-shared key was entered correctly. If it's correct and your web browser shows an error message saying "cannot resolve hostname," then your Pi may need to renew its IP address. The IP address is a unique series of numbers that a wireless router assigns to your Pi and other devices on the network. To renew your Pi's IP address, open the Terminal and enter these two commands:

```
pi@raspberrypi ~ $ sudo dhclient –v –r eth0
pi@raspberrypi ~ $ sudo dhclient –v eth0
```

If you still are unable to connect to the internet, check with the person who set up or manages the network to get help.

3.5 mm audio/video port

Whether it's Beethoven, Lady Gaga, or the creeper explosions in Minecraft, you'll want to listen to sounds on your Pi. Meet the 3.5 mm

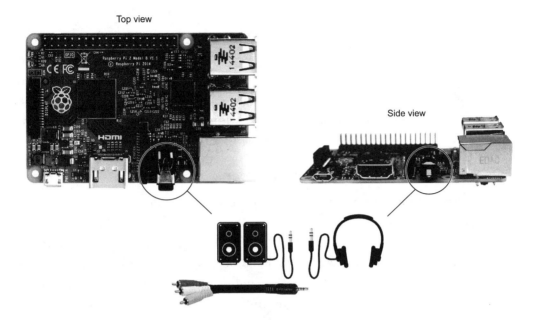

Figure B.4   The Raspberry Pi's 3.5 mm audio/video port is used to connect headphones or speakers for playing sounds. It can also function as a low-quality video output, if you purchase a 3.5 mm-to-RCA composite video adapter.

audio/video port (see figure B.4). This port is a black connector[1] with a round hole. It gets its name from the fact that the hole is 3.5 mm in diameter. Connect either headphones or a set of powered-computer speakers to listen to sounds from your Raspberry Pi.

> TIP   If you connect computer speakers, use powered speakers, such as the type used with a desktop computer or iPod. The sounds that come out of the Raspberry Pi 3.5 mm audio/video port are only loud enough for a set of earphones or headphones. If you would like a roomful of people to hear your music, connect a set of powered speakers, which contain a built-in amplifier to boost the sound.

Starting with the Raspberry Pi 1 Model B+ and the Raspberry Pi 2 Model B, this port can also be used to output a video signal. The video

---

[1]   In older versions of the Raspberry Pi, the port may be blue rather than black.

signal isn't high resolution like the HDMI port, but in a pinch, it's an option. The output video signal is composite or single-channel video, meaning all the video signal comes out in a single wire. It's what many of the older DVD players and video game consoles used at one time. You can purchase a cable that plugs into the port and at the other end has RCA connectors for plugging your Pi into an older TV.

Camera Serial Interface: connecting a camera

If you'd like to try time-lapse photography or set up a camera to take pictures of wild animals or your pet, you'll want to add a camera to your Pi. The best way to add a high-def digital camera to your Raspberry Pi is with the Raspberry Pi camera module. Created by the Raspberry Pi Foundation, it doesn't usually come with Pi kits, so you'll have to buy it separately. The module contains a 5 megapixel camera mounted on a circuit board and comes with a short ribbon cable (see figure B.5).

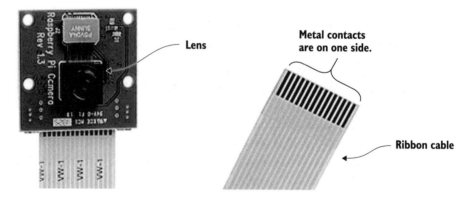

Figure B.5 The Raspberry Pi camera module was created by the Raspberry Pi Foundation to take high-def digital photographs and video. The camera attaches to the Pi using a ribbon cable that connects to the Camera Serial Interface port. The camera module can be programmed using Python and used for nature photography or creating your own home-surveillance system.

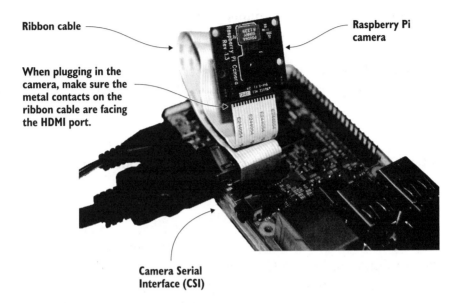

Ribbon cable

Raspberry Pi camera

When plugging in the camera, make sure the metal contacts on the ribbon cable are facing the HDMI port.

Camera Serial Interface (CSI)

Figure B.6 The Raspberry Pi camera can connect to the CSI port, which is located between the HDMI port and the 3.5 mm audio/video port. To connect a camera, you need to lift up the black connector, insert the ribbon cable (metal contact toward the HDMI port), and push down on the black connector again.

The camera connects to your Pi's Camera Serial Interface (CSI) port (see figure B.6) and can take still photographs or high-def video. The module is able to connect easily to the Pi and record high-def video while consuming less processing power than using a USB camera with your Pi.

To connect the camera module, follow these steps:

1 Open the CSI connector on your Pi by lifting up on the top portion of the black plastic connector.

2 Insert the end of the ribbon cable into the CSI connector. The shiny metal contacts on the ribbon cable should face away from the Ethernet port and toward the HDMI port (see figure B.6).

3 Push the black plastic connector back down to close it, clamping the ribbon cable into the connector.

> **TIP** The Pi camera board comes with a short ribbon cable. If you need a longer one, you can find extension cables at online stores such as Adafruit.

Once the camera module is connected, you need to enable it. Open Terminal to enter Raspbian command-line mode. Enter the command to open the Raspberry Pi configuration menu:

```
pi@raspberrypi ~ $ sudo raspi-config
```

When the blue screen and Raspberry Pi configuration menu appear, select option 5: Enable Camera. Select Enable, and then select Finish on the main configuration menu. Your Pi will ask if you would like to reboot now; select Yes. When your Pi has rebooted, test out your camera by opening Terminal and typing

```
pi@raspberrypi ~ $ raspistill -t 3000 -o PiPhoto.jpg
```

This will turn on the camera and take a picture after 3 seconds. The -t 3000 part tells the raspistill program the time to wait—in this case, it's set it to 3,000 milliseconds or 3 seconds. The image is saved to a file called PiPhoto.jpg. You can view the file by opening File Manager and looking in your pi\home folder. Check out online resources for more that you can do with your camera, including using PiCamera, a Python library for controlling the camera.

If you're thinking about taking videos or photos at night, there is an alternate version of the Pi camera module called the Pi NoIR (for near infrared) camera module. It uses the same CSI port and connects the same way. One difference is that you'll need to shine an infrared light source at the target you're filming. With the Pi NoIR, you're armed for some great new possibilities for nighttime mischief with your Pi.

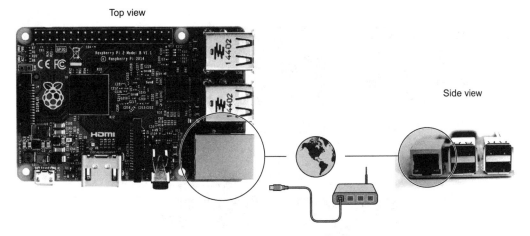

Figure B.7 The Ethernet port on the Raspberry Pi supports connecting a Pi to a home network. Connect an Ethernet cable from your Pi to your router or modem to access the internet. With your Pi connected to a network, you can remotely connect to the Pi from another computer using special programs such as SSH and VNC Server.

Ethernet port

Having a connection to the internet lets you use your Pi to surf the web and download software; you can even control your Pi from another computer. Your Raspberry Pi's Ethernet port is located next to the USB ports (see figure B.7). Using the Ethernet port is an easy way to connect a Raspberry Pi to the internet. The only trouble is that you'll need to have your Pi where an Ethernet cable connection can reach it.

TV or monitor connection options

It's easiest to connect your Pi to a TV or monitor if it has an HDMI port or DVI port; this is covered in chapter 1. But what if you don't have one of those ports? There are other ways to connect your Pi. Let's first identify a couple different types of ports you might see on the back of your TV or monitor and then learn how to connect your Pi to them.

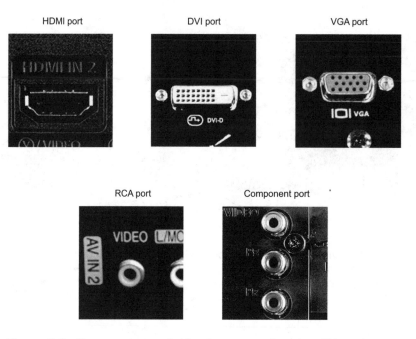

Figure B.8 Common types of video input ports found on TVs and monitors. A Raspberry Pi can connect to any one of these ports. Some ports
(DVI, VGA, RCA [or composite], and component) require using
special adapters or converters with a Pi.

IDENTIFYING PORTS AND MAKING THE CONNECTION

Take time to study the connections on your TV or monitor. Try to identify the video ports, comparing them to the pictures of connectors in
figure B.8.

For certain ports, you may need to buy an adapter that converts one
type of port to another. We'll cover VGA, RCA, and component ports.
See chapter 1 for the HDMI and DVI port connections.

RCA PORT

This type of port is a yellow, round connector. It's usually found next to
red-and-white RCA audio connectors.

You'll need to purchase a special cable that is a 3.5 mm four-pole plug
at one end and an RCA composite video and audio cable at the other

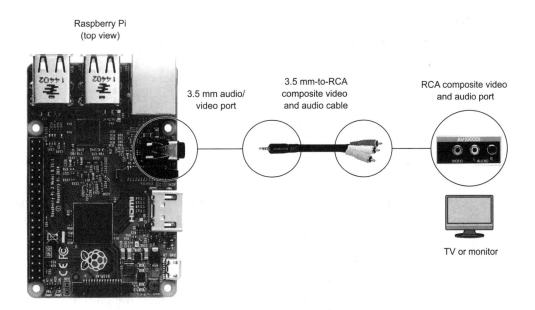

Raspberry Pi
(top view)

3.5 mm audio/
video port

3.5 mm-to-RCA
composite video
and audio cable

RCA composite video
and audio port

TV or monitor

Figure B.9 The Raspberry Pi can be connected to a TV or monitor using an RCA video cable. The cable connects from the Pi's 3.5 mm audio/video port to the RCA video input port on the TV or monitor. Using the RCA connection produces a low-quality picture but can be a good option if you don't have a TV or monitor that supports HDMI.

end. Plug the cable into the 3.5 mm audio/video port, and plug the other end into your screen's composite video input. Typically, the screen will have red-and-white audio-input connectors next to the video input. Connect the red-and-white RCA audio connectors if you want to have sound as well (see figure B.9).

VGA PORT

A VGA port has a flat top and bottom with sides that slant inward. The port has three rows of five round pin holes. Connecting a Pi to a TV or monitor with a VGA port isn't recommended because you'll need to purchase an adapter and may run into potential issues with configuring your Pi to detect your monitor. If you decide to try this option, you'll need an HDMI-to-VGA adapter. You'll also need to update the configuration settings on your Raspberry Pi. This isn't covered in this book, but the Raspberry Pi forums can provide you with more information on altering the configuration settings to use an HDMI-to-VGA adapter.

COMPONENT VIDEO INPUT

A component video port on a TV has a set of three round connectors that are green, blue, and red. Using this port isn't recommended because of the additional cost of a converter and because you may have to do additional configuration of your Pi to successfully connect to your monitor. If you decide to use this option, you'll need a component-to-HDMI converter. Such a converter should come with its own power supply. Avoid ones that don't, because they won't work with your Pi. The converter will cost you around $50, so if you have other options, save your money—try using a different TV or monitor, or put that money toward a new or used LCD or LED monitor for your Pi.

With the ports covered, let's examine the differences between the Raspberry Pi 2 Model B and older model boards.

Legacy boards

The Raspberry Pi is made by the Raspberry Pi Foundation, and several versions and models have been released over the last several years. We'll show and discuss the major differences between the boards.

Raspberry Pi 1 Model B

The Raspberry Pi 1 Model B was the version of the Pi that many came to love. The Pi was originally conceived to help develop a new generation of programmers and hackers, but it was unexpectedly popular with many hobbyists and entrepreneurs because of all the great things they could do and make with it. The board looks a bit different from the Raspberry Pi 2 Model B (see figure B.10)

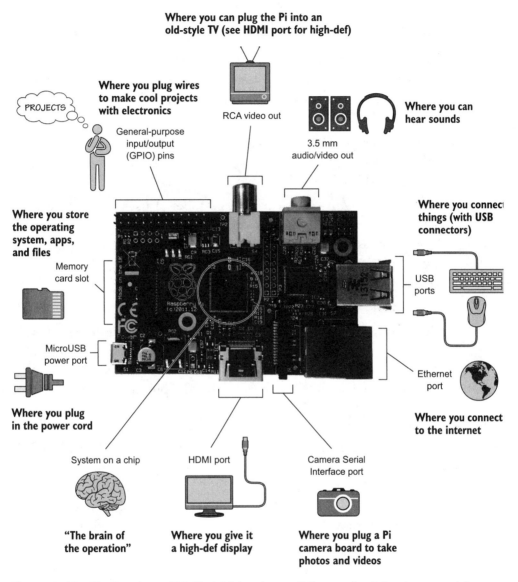

Where you can plug the Pi into an
old-style TV (see HDMI port for high-def)

Where you plug wires
to make cool projects
with electronics

PROJECTS

RCA video out

General-purpose
input/output
(GPIO) pins

Where you can
hear sounds

3.5 mm
audio/video out

Where you store
the operating
system, apps,
and files

Where you connect
things (with USB
connectors)

Memory
card slot

USB
ports

MicroUSB
power port

Where you plug
in the power cord

Ethernet
port

Where you connect
to the internet

System on a chip

HDMI port

Camera Serial
Interface port

"The brain of
the operation"

Where you give it
a high-def display

Where you plug a Pi
camera board to take
photos and videos

Figure B.10 The Raspberry Pi 1 Model B has been wildly popular. It has been used for a
spectrum of applications from scientific research to art and education.

Here are a few key differences between the Raspberry Pi 1 Model B and the Raspberry Pi 2 Model B:

- *USB ports*—The Pi 1 Model B has only two USB ports. This makes it challenging to connect a keyboard, a mouse, and a USB Wi-Fi adapter. A great workaround is to use a powered USB hub to connect more USB devices.

- *RCA (or composite) video out*—The Pi 1 Model B has a dedicated RCA connector to connect it to old-style TVs. The Pi 2 Model B has integrated this into the 3.5 mm audio/video port.

- *System on a chip*—The earlier Pi Model B uses a single-core 700 MHz processor, whereas the Pi 2 Model B uses a quad-core 900 MHz processor. Thus the newer model is about four times faster.

- *Memory card slot*—The Pi 1 Model B used a standard size SD card. The Pi 2 Model B uses a mini-SD card slot that has a spring mechanism to hold the card in securely.

- *GPIO pins*—The number of pins and how they're numbered is different on the earlier Model B. There are only 20 pins on the older model; the newer model has 40 pins. If you're working with a Pi 1 Model B, refer to online references for the pin numbering.

Raspberry Pi 1 Model B+

After the Raspberry Pi 1 Model B came the Raspberry Pi 1 Model B+. The boards look very different. In contrast, if you compare the Raspberry Pi 1 Model B+ to the later Raspberry Pi 2 Model B, they're nearly identical—in terms of available ports and the location of those ports, they're exactly the same. Figure B.11 shows the Raspberry Pi 1 Model B+.

The key differences from the Raspberry Pi 2 Model B are as follows:

- *System on a chip*—The B+ has a single-core, 700 MHz processor, whereas the Pi 2 Model B has a quad-core, 900 MHz processor.

- *Working memory (RAM)*—The Model B+ has 512 MB compared to the Pi 2 Model B's 1 GB.

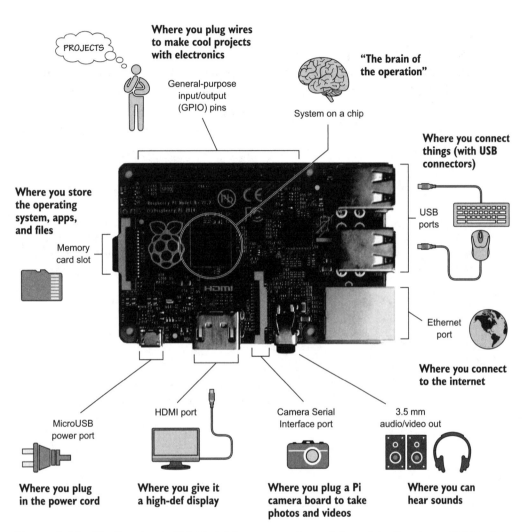

PROJECTS

Where you plug wires to make cool projects with electronics

General-purpose input/output (GPIO) pins

"The brain of the operation"

System on a chip

Where you connect things (with USB connectors)

USB ports

Where you store the operating system, apps, and files

Memory card slot

Ethernet port

Where you connect to the internet

MicroUSB power port

HDMI port

Camera Serial Interface port

3.5 mm audio/video out

Where you plug in the power cord

Where you give it a high-def display

Where you plug a Pi camera board to take photos and videos

Where you can hear sounds

Figure B.11 The Raspberry Pi 1 Model B+ was a major revision of the Raspberry Pi 1 Model B. It increased the number of USB ports from two to four, added more pins for GPIO, and changed to a microSD memory card slot. The ports on the Raspberry Pi 1 Model B+ are the same as those on the Raspberry Pi 2 Model B.

Other boards

We aren't covering the Raspberry Pi Model A or A+, but many of the ports are the same. The main difference is that the Model A and A+ have only one USB port, no Ethernet port, and less working memory (RAM)—256 MB. The Model A and A+ are useful when you have a project that needs a smaller computer that requires less power than the Model B or B+.

Appendix C

Solutions to chapter challenges

In this appendix, you'll find answers to the challenges presented at the end of each chapter. For challenges that require more lines of code than will fit on a page, I provide hints and snippets of code. The complete programs for the solutions are found in the code download that goes with this book. Comments are included in the code to help you understand the design and function of the programs. The solutions to the challenges are organized by chapter. Let's begin!

Chapter 1

At the end of the first chapter, you go on a scavenger hunt:

- *Squirrel*—To find the squirrel game, choose Menu > Games > Python Games. After you select how you would like sound (audio) to be output, you'll see a list of Python games. The squirrel game is near the middle of the list. Win the game, and achieve Omega Squirrel.

- *Calculator*—Select Menu > Accessories > Calculator. 89 × 34 is 3,026.

- *Shutdown*—Shut down or restart your Raspberry Pi by choosing Menu > Shutdown. The shutdown menu lets you choose to shut down, reboot, or log out.

To keep the cat from flipping upside down when it points in a new direction, click this button so that the cat will only face left and right.

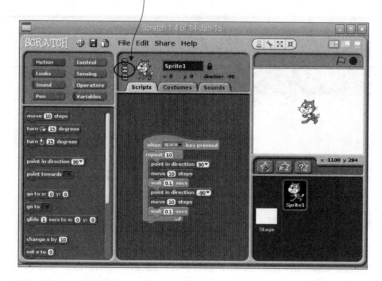

Figure C.1 Make the cat dance in Scratch by dragging program blocks into the script area.

- *Black desktop*—To change the desktop background to black, right-click anywhere on the desktop and select Desktop Preferences. In the Desktop Preferences window, look in the middle of the screen for a Background Color label. Click the white box to select a new background color. Click OK to select the color, and then click Close to close the Desktop Preferences window.

- *Scratch bonus*—To open Scratch, select Menu > Programming > Scratch. When Scratch opens, construct a program by dragging blocks into the script area for your cat sprite. Figure C.1 shows an example of a dancing cat program that makes the cat dance back and forth 10 times when the space bar is pressed.

Chapter 2

The challenges in this chapter are about displaying characters to the screen and doing some mathematics.

The Matrix

Create a screen full of 1s and 0s by using the `print` function and the multiplication operator like this:

```
matrix = "010010110100110010011000101100101111 0000010101"
print(matrix * 100)
```

Building a brick wall

To solve this one, create a variable named `brick` and give it a string of characters like this:

```
brick = "|__"
print(brick * 1000)
```

To make the bricks look like raspberries, you could try

```
brick = "|_o88{_"
print(brick*300)
```

Use your imagination to visualize that this is a sideways raspberry brick. The bracket is the leaf on top of the raspberry.

Pi electrons

You're trying to figure out how many electrons per second it takes to equal 1 amp flowing into your Raspberry Pi. The calculation using Python looks like this:

```
>>> electron_charge = 1.60 * 10**-19
>>> electrons_flowing = 1 / electron_charge
>>> print(electrons_flowing)
6.249999999999999e+18
```

The answer is 6,250,000,000,000,000,000. That's a lot of electrons!

Chapter 3

These challenges are about gathering input, joining together strings, and displaying text to the screen.

Knight's Tale Creator 3000

To make this program, you want to first print a title and then gather a series of words from the player:

```
title = "Knight's Tale Creator 3000"
print("*" * 80)
```

```
print(title)
print("*" * 80)
```

Gather input from the player
and store it in variables.

```
player_name = input("Enter your name: ")
adjective = input("Enter an adjective: ")
famous_person = input("Enter the name of a famous person: ")
animal = input("Enter the name of an animal: ")
vacation_place = input("Enter a place you would go on vacation: ")
sharp_thing = input("Enter the name of something sharp: ")
exclamation = input("Enter something you might exclaim aloud: ")
```

Next, you join the input words with the story. You can do this sentence by sentence to make the code a bit easier to follow:

```
sentence1 = "There was a brave knight, " + player_name + ", who was
➡ sent on a quest to vanquish the " + adjective + " evildoer,
➡ " + famous_person + ". "
sentence2 = "Riding on his/her trusty " + animal + ", the brave " +
➡ player_name + " traveled to the faraway land of " + vacation_place
➡ + ". "
sentence3 = player_name + " battled valiantly against " + famous_person +
➡ "'s army using his " + sharp_thing + " until he defeated them. "
sentence4 = "Emerging victorious, " + player_name + " exclaimed, '" +
➡ exclamation + "!!!' I claim the land of " + vacation_place + " in the
➡ name of Python."
```

Finally, let's join the sentences and display the tale to the screen:

```
tale = sentence1 + sentence2 + sentence3 + sentence4
print(tale)
```

Subliminal messages

You're trying to create a message that's hidden in a large display of characters. You start by asking for the person's name and something they would like:

```
title = "Subliminal Messages"
print("*" * 80)
print(title)
print("*" * 80)

player_name = input("Enter your name: ")
thing = input("Enter the name of something you want: ")
```

Gather input from
the player.

Next, create a pattern of letters, numbers, and symbols in which you'll hide the message:

```
weird_characters = "*#ad@32*)23 )@*sad# 2&^ 32^423!"
```

Finally, you create the full message by making it read "You really want to buy [player_name] a [thing]", but hide it by printing out on the screen the pattern of characters before and after the message:

Create the message.

```
message = "You really want to buy " + player_name + " a " + thing + "."
print(weird_characters * 10 + message + weird_characters * 10)
```

Hide it between the weird characters.

Chapter 4

This chapter's challenge is about using some of your new skills, like if/then (or conditional) statements, as well as toolboxes like the random module.

Rock, Paper, Scissors!

For this challenge, you start by importing the random module, creating a title, and defining any variables you're going to need:

```
import random

play_again = "Yes"
choices = ["Rock","Paper","Scissors"]
```

Next, you want to display the title and then start a while loop that will gather the player's choice and get a random computer choice:

```
title = "Rock, Paper, Scissors!"
print("*" * 80)
print(title)
print("*" * 80)
```

Get a random computer choice.

```
while play_again == "Yes":
    print("Choose Rock, Paper, or Scissors:")
    player_choice = input("Enter your choice: ")
    computer_choice = choices[random.randint(0,2)]
```

Get the player's choice.

You then want to display the two choices and use an if statement to test whether the player and computer choices are the same. If not, you want to check whether you have one of the following Player versus Computer combinations:

- Rock (Player) beats scissors (Computer)
- Scissors (Player) beats paper (Computer)
- Paper (Player) beats rock (Computer)

You program all this inside the `while` loop because you want it to be repeated as long as the player wants to play. At the end of the loop, the player is asked if they want to play again:

Display the two choices.

```
print("You choice is " + player_choice + ".")
print("The computer's choice is " + computer_choice + ".")
if player_choice == computer_choice:
    print("It's a tie")
else:
    if ((player_choice == "Rock" and computer_choice == "Scissors") or
        (player_choice == "Scissors" and computer_choice == "Paper") or
        (player_choice == "Paper" and computer_choice == "Rock")):
        print("!" * 80)
        print("You win!")
        print("!" * 80)
    else:
        print(":(" * 40)
        print("You lose!")
        print(":(" * 40)
play_again = input("Do you want to play again [Yes/No]? ")
```

You create a large `if` statement that tests whether `player_choice` and `computer_choice` form one of the winning combinations. Each of the combinations is wrapped in parentheses, and you use or between them. This ensures that if any one of the combinations is correct, the winning message will be displayed.

Chapter 5

Introducing dramatic pauses

You were given some good hints about how to do this in chapter 5. Rather than display too much code here, I suggest that you head over to the code download to see what this looks like.

Random demise

In this challenge, you're creating a more random and exciting end for your adventurer, Raspi. For this, you need to import the random module at the top of your program, define some new variables for the different endings, and create a list of the endings. This will allow you to have the computer pick a number:

```
import time
import random

demise1 = """Raspi sees a rock on the ground and picks it up. He feels a
➡ sharp pinch and drops the rock. Just then he realizes it wasn't a rock
➡ but a poisonous spider as he collapses to the ground."""
demise2 = """Standing in the cave, Raspi sees a small rabbit approach
➡ him. Raspi gets a bad feeling about this rabbit. Suddenly, the
➡ rabbit attacks him, biting his neck."""
demise3 = """Whoa, is that a piece of gold? As Raspi walks over to it,
➡ he doesn't see a hole in the floor. Suddenly, he falls down the hole,
➡ never to be heard from again."""
endings = [demise1, demise2, demise3]
```

You use triple quotation marks, called *string literals*, to make strings that span multiple lines. You also store the three different endings in a list called endings.

Finally, to solve this challenge, change the wrong_answer function to get a random number, select an ending, and then display it to the screen:

```
def wrong_answer():
    print("You seem to have trouble making good decisions!")
    time.sleep(2)
    random_ending = endings[random.randint(0,2)]     ← Select a random ending
    print(random_ending)                                from the list of endings.
    time.sleep(2)
    print("Game Over!!!")
```

Check the code download to see how it all works together.

Play again?

To add a play-again option, add a new variable at the top of your program and set it equal to "Y" to start:

```
play_again = "Y"
```

Next, put all of your cave-selection logic in a `while` loop. The `while` loop will depend on the value of `play_again`, but you'll use the string function `upper()` to make the `play_again` value all uppercase. This helps if the user accidentally enters y instead of Y:

```
while play_again.upper() == "Y":
```

At the end of the `while` loop, you also need to ask the user if they want to play again. Store their response in the `play_again` variable:

```
print("Do you want to play again?")
play_again = input("Enter Y for yes or N for no: ")
```

Another part of this challenge is adding a scream sound (or any other sound you want). First, make sure you import the os module and set up a variable with a sound file:

```
import os
scream_file_path =
➥ "/usr/share/scratch/Media/Sounds/Human/Scream-male2.mp3"
```

Add a new line to the `wrong_answer` function that calls OMXPlayer and tells it to play the scream sound:

```
os.system("omxplayer " + scream_file_path)
```

Run the program to test it out! Add it to all the other game-over endings in the game to make it even more fun!

> NOTE   Make sure you have speakers or headphones connected, or you won't hear anything.

Chapter 6

Wave pattern

Let's turn on each LED one by one. Then, when they're all on, you'll turn them off one by one. Each light is turned on or off by setting its state to HIGH (on) or LOW (off). You create the sequence by adding a time delay between each command:

```
while True:
    GPIO.output(LED_pin_red, GPIO.HIGH)
    time.sleep(1)
```

Turn on the LEDs one by one.

Loop to blink the LEDs in a wave pattern.

```
GPIO.output(LED_pin_green, GPIO.HIGH)
time.sleep(1)
GPIO.output(LED_pin_blue, GPIO.HIGH)
time.sleep(1)
GPIO.output(LED_pin_red, GPIO.LOW)
time.sleep(1)
GPIO.output(LED_pin_green, GPIO.LOW)
time.sleep(1)
GPIO.output(LED_pin_blue, GPIO.LOW)
time.sleep(1)
```

◄ **Turn off the LEDs one by one.**

You can adjust the sleep time to get a faster or slower animation.

Simon says

In this challenge, you're creating a program that blinks lights in a pattern like the classic game *Simon*. As before, the program requires that the GPIO and time modules be imported and the GPIO pins be set up properly. See the code download for the full code listing. Start by defining the simon_says function:

```
def simon_says(color1, color2, color3, color4, color5):
    colors = [color1, color2, color3, color4, color5]
    for i in range(0,5):
        color = colors[i]
        if color == "red":
            GPIO.output(LED_pin_red, GPIO.HIGH)
            time.sleep(1)
            GPIO.output(LED_pin_red, GPIO.LOW)
        elif color == "green":
            GPIO.output(LED_pin_green, GPIO.HIGH)
            time.sleep(1)
            GPIO.output(LED_pin_green, GPIO.LOW)
        elif color == "blue":
            GPIO.output(LED_pin_blue, GPIO.HIGH)
            time.sleep(1)
            GPIO.output(LED_pin_blue, GPIO.LOW)
        time.sleep(1)
```

Create a list with the five colors.

Loop through the five colors.

◄ **Grab the name of a single color and turn the color on and off.**

This creates a list with all the colors and loops through them one by one. For each one, the function checks its value and turns on and off the LED of that color. To use the function, you call it and give it the pattern you want to create, along with some helpful messages:

```
print("Ready for #1!")
time.sleep(1)
print("Simon Says: red, green, red, red, blue")
time.sleep(1)
print("Watch my lights!")
time.sleep(1)
simon_says("red", "green", "red", "red", "blue")

print("Ready for #2!")
time.sleep(1)
print("Simon Says: blue, green, blue, green, red")
time.sleep(1)
print("Watch my lights!")
time.sleep(1)
simon_says("blue", "green", "blue", "green", "red")

print("Ready for #3!")
time.sleep(1)
print("Simon Says: green, blue, blue, red, green")
time.sleep(1)
print("Watch my lights!")
time.sleep(1)
simon_says("green", "blue", "blue", "red", "green")
time.sleep(1)
print("Thank you for playing!!!")
```

Call the simon_says function to play the pattern.

Go, Simon, go!

Random blinking

This challenge is about blinking LEDs on and off for random amounts of time between 0 and 3 seconds. Let's see how to do it. I won't show the top part of the program with the typical setup of the GPIO pins; refer to the code download for the full code listing. At the top of your program, don't forget to import the random module so you can use it to generate random numbers:

```
import random
```

To accomplish this challenge, you need to create two variables and store in them a random number between 0 and 3. These variables are the amount of time the lights should stay on and off:

```
on_random_time = random.random() * 3
off_random_time = random.random() * 3
```

Next, you can use the random time with the sleep function to make the light blink. Put this inside a loop, making sure that each time through the loop, new random on and off times are created:

Loop to blink the LED.

```
while True:
    on_random_time = random.random() * 3
    off_random_time = random.random() * 3
```

Get a random number.

Turn the lights on for a random amount of time.

```
    GPIO.output(LED_pin_red, GPIO.HIGH)
    GPIO.output(LED_pin_green, GPIO.HIGH)
    GPIO.output(LED_pin_blue, GPIO.HIGH)
    time.sleep(on_random_time)
```

```
    GPIO.output(LED_pin_red, GPIO.LOW)
    GPIO.output(LED_pin_green, GPIO.LOW)
    GPIO.output(LED_pin_blue, GPIO.LOW)
    time.sleep(off_random_time)
```

Turn the lights off for a random amount of time.

The off and on times change each time through the loop. Enjoy some fun blinking!

Chapter 7

The chapter challenges involve using your Guessing Game and controlling the RGB LED.

Game winner

Let's write a function to quickly flash the RGB LED three different colors. Define a new function called winning_flash:

Flash three different colors 20 times.

```
def winning_flash():
    for i in range(0,20):
        GPIO.output(LED_pin_red, GPIO.HIGH)
        time.sleep(0.05)
        GPIO.output(LED_pin_red, GPIO.LOW)
        time.sleep(0.05)

        GPIO.output(LED_pin_green, GPIO.HIGH)
        time.sleep(0.05)
        GPIO.output(LED_pin_green, GPIO.LOW)
        time.sleep(0.05)
```

Function to create a winning flash sequence.

Flash the red LED.

Flash the green LED.

```
GPIO.output(LED_pin_blue, GPIO.HIGH)
time.sleep(0.05)
GPIO.output(LED_pin_blue, GPIO.LOW)
time.sleep(0.05)
```
◀   **Flash the blue LED.**

If you need help figuring out where to add this function and call it in your code, check the code download for more answers. You add it to the `if` statement when `guess` is equal to `number_in_my_head` so you get a wonderful flashing celebration when you win.

Easter egg

To make an Easter egg in your program, you need to have the code check to see whether the player entered a certain value instead of the usual number guess. Edit the main portion of the logic for the LED Guessing Game program to first check whether the secret word was entered. If it wasn't, the program continues to convert the input text into an integer and check whether the guess was correct, too high, or too low. If the player enters the word *Spam*, you call an `easter_egg` function:

```
while count_guesses < 6:
        guess = input("guess " + str(count_guesses) + " – What is your
        ⮡ guess?: ")
        if guess == "Spam":
            easter_egg()
        else:
            guess = int(guess)
            count_guesses += 1
            if guess == number_in_my_head:
                flash(LED_pin_green)
                print("You won!  No doom for you!")
                break
            elif guess > number_in_my_head:
                flash(LED_pin_red)
            elif guess < number_in_my_head:
                flash(LED_pin_blue)
    else:
        game_over()
```

Check to see if "Spam" was entered. →

◀ **Call the easter_egg function.**

As a special bonus, you can create an `easter_egg` function that displays a Spam song or whatever message you'd like.

```
def easter_egg():
    crazy_flash()                          ◄⟍   Define a special
    print("Easter Egg!!!")                       Spam Easter egg.
    time.sleep(1)
    print("""
            Spam spam spam spam.
            Lovely spam!
            Wonderful spam!
            Spam spa-a-a-a-am spam spa-a-a-a-am spam.
            Lovely spam!
            Lovely spam!
            Lovely spam!
            Lovely spam!
            Lovely spam!
            Spam spam spam spam!
            """)
```

In the easter_egg function, you call a crazy_flash function. The one shown here makes the RGB LED quickly flash purple and green. It's similar to how you created the winning_flash function:

Function to create a crazy flash sequence.

Flash different colors 20 times.

```
def crazy_flash():
    for i in range(0,20):
        GPIO.output(LED_pin_red, GPIO.HIGH)       Flash the red and
        GPIO.output(LED_pin_blue, GPIO.HIGH)      blue LED together.
        time.sleep(0.05)
        GPIO.output(LED_pin_red, GPIO.LOW)
        GPIO.output(LED_pin_blue, GPIO.LOW)
        time.sleep(0.05)

        GPIO.output(LED_pin_green, GPIO.HIGH)
        time.sleep(0.05)                          Flash the green LED.
        GPIO.output(LED_pin_green, GPIO.LOW)
        time.sleep(0.05)
```

Create your own easter_egg and crazy_flash functions, or see the code download for example ones that you can modify.

Warmer and colder

Let's alter the guessing game to flash slower if you're colder or further from the correct answer, and flash faster if you're warmer or closer to the correct answer. Add some calculations so that `blink_time` is determined by the difference between the guess and the correct answer:

Calculate the difference between the guess and the actual number and divide by 10.

```
elif guess > number_in_my_head:
    blink_time = abs(guess - number_in_my_head)/10
    flash(LED_pin_red)
elif guess < number_in_my_head:
    blink_time = abs(guess - number_in_my_head)/10
    flash(LED_pin_blue)
```

The `abs` function gets the absolute value—the distance a number is from zero. You need to do this because you can't tell your Pi to sleep for a negative amount of time. That would be silly! You make this addition for both cases: when the player's guess is higher and lower than the actual number. You divide the numbers by 10 to speed up `blink_time` and make sure your light isn't blinking too slowly.

Finally, a nice touch is to add extra information to the game instructions so the player knows the blinking speed gives them a hint about how close or far they are. See the code download for an example.

Darth Vader surprise

Using what you learned in chapter 7 and a couple of new things, let's see if you can make a Darth Vader image pop up on the screen when you lose the game. You'll need an internet connection for the next few steps. Download a good Darth Vader image from the web, and make sure to save it to the home\pi folder where your Python programs are located. Take special note of the filename.

After downloading the image, install the `fim` image-viewing software on your Raspberry Pi:

```
pi@raspberrypi ~ $ sudo apt-get -y install fim
```

> **NOTE**   Make sure you include a line at the top of the program to import the os module.

When it's done, test that `fim` works from Terminal:

```
pi@raspberrypi ~ $ fim Darth_Vader.jpg
```

NOTE   When `fim` is running, you need to press Esc (escape) to exit.

When you exit `fim`, the screen will display remnants of the image. It's a funny issue, which you can fix by grabbing one of your windows by the title bar and swiping it around the screen to erase the image remnants and return it to the normal Raspbian desktop appearance.

In the Guessing Game, because you need to call `fim` from your Python program, add a line to import the os module at the top of the program:

```
import os
```

Next, edit the `game_over` function to display the image. The `game_over` function is called only when the player guesses incorrectly five times:

```
def game_over():
    print("You lost!")
    print("Better luck next time!")
    time.sleep(2)
    os.system("fim -a Darth_Vader.jpg")
```

Notice that you use `fim` with the `-a` option to display Darth Vader. This option automatically scales the image to fill the full screen. Here are some commands you can use to rotate or resize the image when it's displayed on the screen:

Option	Result
+/–	Zoom in/out
A	Automatically scale
F	Flip
M	Mirror
R/r	Rotate 10 degrees clockwise / counterclockwise
Esc/q	Quit

Test it to see if it works!

Chapter 8

Let's see what fun things you can do with buttons.

Double button press surprise

This challenge involves taking the project from the chapter and making something new and different happen when both buttons are pressed at the same time. In this case, you'll make your Pi play a percussion sound to go with your vocals and music. You don't need to change any of the wiring because you already have the two buttons.

First let's add some code at the top of the program to create a path to where the sound effects are stored:

```
path_effects = "/usr/share/scratch/Media/Sounds/Effects/"
```

Next get a list of effects from the folder and store the list in a variable, sounds_effects. Put this next to where you load the other lists:

```
sounds_effects = get_MP3_sounds(path_effects)
```

Finally, you need to tell your program to check whether button 1 and button 2 are pressed. You're going to modify the main game loop to first check if both are being pressed. You use the if/elif statement for this. Use the Boolean "and" operator—the ampersand (&)—to make this if statement true only if both button 1 and button 2 are pressed. If they aren't, the statement will next check button 1, and finally it will check button 2:

Start an infinite loop (must use Ctrl-C to stop it).

```
while True:
    if GPIO.input(button_pin1) & GPIO.input(button_pin2):
        #print("You pressed both #1 and #2!")
        play_random_sound(path_effects, sounds_effects)
        time.sleep(.1)
    elif GPIO.input(button_pin1):
        #print("You pressed #1!")
        play_random_sound(path_music, sounds_music)
        time.sleep(.1)
    elif GPIO.input(button_pin2):
        #print("You pressed #2!")
        play_random_sound(path_vocals, sounds_music)
        time.sleep(.1)
    time.sleep(.1)
```

Pause slightly before checking the button for input again.

Let's test to see if it works! Check out the code download if you need further details on the program.

Yoda Magic 8 Ball

Before you dive into the programming for this challenge, you need to work on the hardware. Because this challenge needs only one button, remove button 2 from the breadboard, along with its jumper wires and resistor. Your breadboard should have one button now, connected to GPIO 6.

Next, gather a set of Yoda sounds. You can download sounds from Soundboard once you create a free account. For this example solution, you'll use five sound files, but feel free to use any ones you want. Make sure they're MP3 sound files so they'll work with OMXPlayer. The Yoda sound files in this example solution are as follows:

- Fear in You.mp3
- I am strong.mp3
- No.mp3
- Patience.mp3
- Use the Force.mp3

Much like the classic Magic 8 Ball game, the answers are sometimes clear and other times strange or unclear.

As in the DJ Raspi project, you need to import several modules for this project, set up your Pi's GPIO pin for input (detecting electrical signals), and create some variables. Most notably, you need to create a variable for the folder with your Yoda sound files:

```
import RPi.GPIO as GPIO
import time
import random
import os

button_pin = 6
play_again = "Y"

GPIO.setmode(GPIO.BCM)
GPIO.setup(button_pin,GPIO.IN)

path_yoda = "/home/pi/yoda/"
```

Import the libraries you need.

Variable for the GPIO pin used by the button.

Set the path to the Yoda sound files.

Use the same `get_MP3_sounds` and `play_random_sound` functions from your DJ Raspi project. One slight improvement you can make to the `play_random_sound` function is to hide the messages that OMXPlayer displays on the screen (they make it harder to read what the game is telling you to do). Change this one line to divert all the output messages to an empty or null location:

```
def play_random_sound(sound_path, sound_files):
    random_sound_index = random.randint(0,len(sound_files)-1)
    # print("Playing: " + sound_files[random_sound_index])
    os.system("omxplayer -o local '" + sound_path +
                "/" + sound_files[random_sound_index] + "' >/dev/null")
```

This is a great example of being able to reuse code! Next, you'll gather the list of MP3 Yoda sounds from the folder.

```
sounds_yoda = get_MP3_sounds(path_yoda)
```

After printing out a nice title, you then show instructions to the player and enter the main loop that checks whether the button was pressed. In this loop, you call the `play_random_sound` function so the Raspberry Pi responds with an answer to the player's question:

```
print("*" * 80)
print("Ask aloud a Yes or No question, then press the button: ")
print("*" * 80)
```

```
while play_again.upper() == "Y":
    if GPIO.input(button_pin):          ◄──  Check if the button
                                             has been pressed.
        print("Yoda is considering your question...")
        time.sleep(1)
        print("Listen to Yoda's answer:")
        time.sleep(.5)
        play_random_sound(path_yoda, sounds_yoda)
        print("*" * 80)
        print("Ask aloud a Yes or No question, then press the button: ")
        print("*" * 80)
else:
    print("Thank you for consulting Yoda!")
```

Enjoy making your future decisions with the help of Yoda!

Appendix D

Raspberry Pi projects

In this appendix, you'll find short discussions and descriptions of projects you can do with your Raspberry Pi. The goal is to launch you on your way. This isn't a detailed set of instructions, but rather hints and basic steps for how you can make some of these projects.

Halloween heads

Halloween can be an inspiring time to use your Raspberry Pi to create a fun or scary display for your home. Let's face it—it's fun to scare people on Halloween. This project is about building a system for surprising trick-or-treaters who come to your door. When they approach, their movement will trigger a motion sensor that will display a video of a face talking or singing. The video is projected onto a Styrofoam head that is placed next to the door.

Here is what you'll need for this project:

- Raspberry Pi with a breadboard, a breakout board, and a ribbon cable
- Passive infrared (PIR) motion sensor
- Projector
- Powered computer speakers
- Styrofoam heads (one or more)

- Small tables: one for the Pi and projector, and another for the Styrofoam head

- Extension cord and power strip

- Video of a singing or talking head

To construct this project, here are the steps:

1 Connect your Raspberry Pi to the breadboard, and add the PIR sensor. This is similar to how you added the mini pushbutton in chapter 8.

2 Download a video with a talking or singing head, or record your own. Write a Python program to play the video when the PIR sensor is triggered. This is similar to the DJ Raspi program, which plays a sound when the button is pressed.

3 Test your program with the sensor and video working together.

4 Set up a small table about 10 feet from your front door. On the table, set up your Raspberry Pi, breadboard with PIR sensor, speakers, and projector. Place the PIR sensor so that it will detect motion as someone approaches the door. Use an extension cord to provide the electrical power needed. (Only set this up if no rain is predicted!)

5 Set up another small table or box next to your door. Place the Styrofoam head on it. Position the head so that the projector's video displays the face on the head. Test and adjust the projector and the positioning of the head so that everything is aligned. When the video plays, the head will appear to come alive!

Here are a couple of key resources that may help you with this project:

- Visit the SparkFun website at www.sparkfun.com and search for PIR sensors. This company has lots of great components that can help you make almost any electronics project you can imagine.

- You can make the whole screen blank (all black) by using OMX-Player with the blank option like so:

```
pi@raspberrypi ~ $ omxplayer -b singheads.mp4
```

Time-lapse photography

You can easily connect a high-definition camera to your Raspberry Pi that is capable of taking digital photographs or videos (see appendix B for more information). In this project, you explore how you can set up your Pi to take time-lapse photographs.

Time-lapse photography typically involves taking a series of photographs and then stitching them together into a video. The individual photographs may be taken seconds, minutes, hours, or days apart. This technique is commonly used to show an accelerated view of something happening. Here are some examples of time-lapse scenes:

- A glacier slowly retreating over the course of a year
- The sun rising and setting, and the moon rising and setting
- A plant growing

Here are some simple steps to get started with a time-lapse photography project:

1 Set up your Raspberry Pi with the Pi camera kit, and test that it's working.

2 The subject of your time lapse determines how you need to mount the Pi camera. The camera doesn't come with a case or any way to hold it up, so you'll need to engineer a mount of some kind. Cardboard, hot glue, craft sticks, and duct tape are all great materials for fabricating something to hold up the camera. LEGO blocks can also be a useful material.

If you're going to leave the camera outside for a long time, consider whether you'll need to waterproof your Raspberry Pi. Plastic containers left over from takeout food can make a great case; you'll just need to make holes in the container for wires and seal any gaps with hot glue.

3 Plan how to get electrical power to your Pi. That may determine where you set up the Pi and camera.

4 Program your Raspberry Pi to take the photographs and store them in a folder. Open LXTerminal, and install the `picamera` module for Python 3.X:

```
pi@raspberrypi ~ $ sudo apt-get install python3-picamera
```

To get you started, you can use a program like this to capture a series of photographs. This example takes a photograph every 3 minutes:

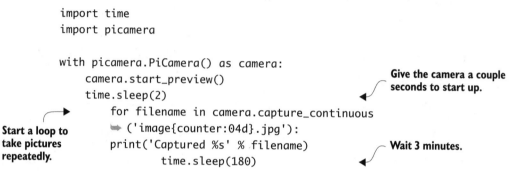

```
import time
import picamera


with picamera.PiCamera() as camera:
    camera.start_preview()                          Give the camera a couple
    time.sleep(2)                                    seconds to start up.
        for filename in camera.capture_continuous
        ('image{counter:04d}.jpg'):
            print('Captured %s' % filename)          Wait 3 minutes.
                time.sleep(180)
```

Start a loop to take pictures repeatedly.

When the camera has finished taking images, you can press Ctrl-C to end the program.

> **NOTE** This program saves the images in the folder where the program is being run. You should make a folder for your time-lapse project and run the program from that folder.

Next you'll need to combine the images into a video. You can use an application called `mencoder` to turn images into a movie. Install it like this:

```
pi@raspberrypi ~ $ sudo apt-get install mencoder
```

Then you'll create a simple text file that contains all the names of the images you want to combine. You can use the list command (`ls`), select all the files ending in .jpg, and output the list to a text file:

```
pi@raspberrypi ~ $ ls image*.jpg > list.txt
```

Next use `mencoder` to combine all the individual images into a time-lapse movie. This example makes a movie called TimeLapseMovie.avi:

```
pi@raspberrypi ~ $ mencoder -nosound -ovc lavc -lavcopts
 vcodec=mpeg4:aspect=16/9:vbitrate=8000000 -vf scale=1920:1080 -o
 TimeLapseMovie.avi -mf type=jpeg:fps=24 mf://@list.txt
```

When it's done, you can watch the movie using OMXPlayer:

```
pi@raspberrypi ~ $ omxplayer TimeLapseMovie.avi
```

You can read more online about the mencoder options available.

Raspberry Pi robot

The Raspberry Pi can readily be turned into a robot by adding servomotors and sensors using the Pi's GPIO capabilities. The Pi can be programmed in Python to make decisions, gather input from sensors, and control servomotors to interact with the world.

Although you could assemble you own robot from scratch, there are some Raspberry Pi robot kits that can make it a lot easier. For this project, we'll discuss using the GoPiGo kit from Dexter Industries. It's an affordable, well-engineered kit that within a few hours will let you have your Pi moving around under your control. You can add an ultrasonic sensor (detects objects in front of it) and write a Python program to make your Pi GoPiGo robot navigate the room autonomously (on its own) using the same if/else statements you learned earlier.

We'll cover the basic steps for building the GoPiGo (you can read the full set of instructions online at www.dexterindustries.com/GoPiGo):

1 Build your GoPiGo robot following the online instructions. Connect your Raspberry Pi to the robot: it fits upside down on top of the GoPiGo board. The Pi communicates to the GoPiGo board through the GPIO pins.

2 Insert the GoPiGo SD card into your Pi. The SD card contains a custom distribution of Raspbian. Connect your Pi to a keyboard, mouse, USB Wi-Fi adapter, and TV or monitor. Later you'll be able to connect to your GoPiGo remotely from another computer. Power it up using the provided battery pack. Boot up your Pi, and connect the GoPiGo to your wireless network.

3 Set up your computer to remotely access your Pi from another computer. This means you'll be able to see your Raspbian desktop from another Windows or Mac computer in your home. To do so, you use software called VNC. You need to install VNC Server on your

Raspberry Pi and then install VNC Client on your computer. There are some great tutorials on how to do this, such as the one on the Adafruit website. Go to https://learn.adafruit.com, and search for "installing VNC."

4 Using VNC, connect to your Raspberry Pi from your home Windows or Mac computer. Once you're sure VNC Server and Client are working properly, you can disconnect your Pi from the monitor, keyboard, and mouse, leaving only the USB Wi-Fi adapter plugged in. Your GoPiGo is ready to move!

5 From the VNC Client on your Windows or Mac, open LXTerminal on your Pi. Change directories to the GoPiGo Python folder on the desktop using the cd command:

```
cd Desktop/GoPiGo/Software/Python/
```

Run the GoPiGo test controller Python program:

```
sudo python basic_test_all.py
```

After the program starts, you can use these keys to move your GoPiGo around the room:

w	Move forward
a	Turn left
s	Move back
d	Turn right
x	Stop
t	Increase speed
g	Decrease speed

Excellent! You've made your Raspberry Pi into a robot. Add sensors and make programs to navigate around a room, or attach a Pi camera and stream video to another computer so you can see what your Raspberry Pi sees.

Index

MORE TITLES FROM MANNING

Hello World!
Second Edition

by Warren Sande and Carter Sande

ISBN: 9781617290923
464 pages
$39.99
December 2013

Hello App Inventor!

by Paula Beer and Carl Simmons

ISBN: 9781617291432
360 pages
$39.99
October 2014

Hello! iOS Development

by Lou Franco and Eitan Mendelowitz

ISBN: 9781935182986
344 pages
$29.99
July 2013

For ordering information go to www.manning.com